SWIMMING FASTER

SWIMMING

A Comprehensive Guide

ERNEST W. MAGLISCHO

F A S T E R

to the Science of Swimming

California State University, Chico

M A Y F I E L D   P U B L I S H I N G   C O M P A N Y

To my coaches—Bob Wherry, Bob Bartels,
and Sam Cooper—and to all the swimmers I've coached.
Thank you for all you've taught me.

Library of Congress Catalog Card Number: 81-81278
International Standard Book Number: 0-87484-548-3

Manufactured in the United States of America
Mayfield Publishing Company
285 Hamilton Avenue
Palo Alto, California 94301

Sponsoring editor: C. Lansing Hays
Manuscript editor: Kate Fuller
Designer: Al Burkhardt
Illustrator: Mary Burkhardt
Technical consultant: Christopher Zawojski
Photographer: T. R. Santos
Cover designer: Al Burkhardt
Production manager: Cathy Willkie/Michelle Hogan
Compositor: Computer Typesetting Services, Inc.
Printer and binder: The Book Press

Figure 9.1 "The effect of training progression on
blood lactate," from H. T. Edwards, L. Brouha, and R.
T. Johnson, "Effets de l'entraînement sur le taux de
l'acide lactique sanguin au cours du travail
musculaire," *Le Travail Humain*, vol. 8, no. 1 (1940), is
used by permission of *Le Travail Humain*.

Some of the stroke patterns in this text are based on
stroke plots appearing in R. M. Brown and J. E.
Counsilman, "The Role of Lift in Propelling the
Swimmer," *Biomechanics*, ed. J. M. Cooper (North
Palm Beach, Fla.: Athletic Institute, 1971), pp. 184–
185. Adapted by permission of The Athletic Institute.

Contents

v

PART **Two**

Physiology Applied to Training Swimmers

PART **Three**

Other Aspects of Training

Preface

Coaches and swimmers can learn a great deal from scientific data about the principles and techniques of swimming. Thus it is unfortunate that so many researchers present their findings in terminology that is comprehensible only to other researchers and seldom recommend ways in which their findings can enhance athletic performance. *Swimming Faster* is an attempt to bridge the gap between research and application in the sport of competitive swimming.

I have written this book with coaches, athletes, and students of competitive swimming in mind. I have tried to present the pertinent research of others in language understood by the swimming community and to suggest how results of this research can be applied to competitive swimming. These applications are not presented as scientific fact, however. Rather, they are presented as educated guesses based on analysis of the scientific literature and my practical experience as a coach.

The book is divided into three parts. Part One, "Stroke Mechanics," covers the hydrodynamic principles involved in efficient swimming. The lift principle is discussed in detail in the first chapter, and the point is made that the majority of world-class swimmers use their limbs like propellers (rather than like paddles) to move through the water. In chapters 2, 3, 4, and 5, the four competitive strokes—the front crawl stroke, the butterfly stroke, the breaststroke, and the back crawl stroke—are described. These descriptions differ considerably from traditional accounts: I try to show that most of the propulsion in swimming is generated by downward, upward, inward, and outward sweeps of the limbs rather than by backward pulls and pushes. The strokes are described very thoroughly, and illustrations show each stroke from several different views to help readers visualize the mechanics three-dimensionally. This has been done to provide readers with a complete understanding of the propulsive aspects of each stroke. A chapter on the techniques of starting, turning, and finishing races completes Part One.

Part Two, "Physiology Applied to Training Swimmers," is devoted to the training process. It begins with Chapter 7, on energy metabolism as it relates to swimming performance. The important metabolic processes are described, and research on the causes of fatigue and methods for delaying fatigue is presented. Additional physiological aspects of training are examined in Chapter 8. Particular attention is given to research concerning fast twitch and slow twitch muscle fibers and the anaerobic threshold concept—two topics currently of concern to coaches and athletes. In Chapter 9, I apply information from the two preceding chapters to the conditioning process. The approach to training that is recommended relies heavily on the *specificity of training* principle but not on the usual *swimming at race pace* interpretation of that principle. In the final chapter in Part Two, I discuss the construction of daily, weekly, and yearly training programs.

Part Three, "Other Aspects of Training," focuses on such important aspects of competitive swimming as pacing, strategy, warming up, improving muscular strength and joint flexibility, and nutrition and body composition.

I am indebted to many talented and generous people who assisted in the preparation of this book. The comments and suggestions of the swimming coaches who reviewed the original manuscript were invaluable. Those reviewers were Nort Thornton of the University of California at Berkeley; Jim Gaughran, formerly of Stanford University; and George Haines of Stanford University.

I wish to commend the staff of Mayfield Publishing Company—particularly Nancy Sears, art director, and Pat Herbst, managing editor—for their professionalism and care. Very special thanks go to Al Burkhardt and Mary Burkhardt. The clarity of the interior design, the well-ordered layout of hundreds of photographs, reflects Al's skill and patience. Mary's drawings are, in my opinion, the most lifelike to appear in a textbook on competitive swimming. I'm most appreciative of the Burkhardts' dedication to this project. I also want to acknowledge the efforts of my typists—Eleanor Johnson, Marjorie Roberts, Jane Bentham, and Pat Bower.

I want to express my appreciation to my wife Cheryl. This book could not have been published without her help in reviewing and typing portions of the manuscript during a hectic editing process. I also want to thank my son Scott, whose artwork served as the prototype for the illustrations.

Finally, I want to thank everyone who participated in the filming sessions. I am particularly grateful to my photographer, T. R. Santos, for his assistance and steady good humor. Swimmers who gave unselfishly of their time were Per Arvidsson, Brian Brink, Kim Carlisle, Chris Cavanaugh, Rick Cozad, Marsha Dahlgren, Mark Doyle, Jackie Heeney, Tracy Huth, Jim Johnson, Tanya Kawazu, Todd Lincoln, Tim Murphy, Kryston Peterson, Peter Rocca, Kim Rohm, David Santos, Jill Symons, David Tittle, Mark Vagle, and Lori Vendl. I am indebted to each of you.

E.W.M.

Foreword

I believe that *Swimming Faster* is one of the most comprehensive and scientific books on competitive swimming ever written. Ernie Maglischo has covered every phase of each stroke as well as every competitive aspect of the strokes and the events in a way that is practical for everyone to understand.

In my opinion this is an outstanding textbook to be used in the college classroom. Dr. Maglischo's most important contribution to swimming is his ability to present scientific data graphically to help the young coach starting out in our sport. *Swimming Faster* may easily become a bible to coaches and swimmers alike.

Competitive swimming is a unique sport because it often holds the interest of entire families for many years. Since parents become so involved in this sport, it is important that they understand what happens to their son or daughter as he or she progresses and develops from being a very young age-group swimmer, through high school and college, to the senior level. Not only swimmers and present and future coaches will benefit from *Swimming Faster*. Every parent with children in swimming programs should read this book, for it will improve understanding of strokes, training, and the reasons some athletes perform better than others.

Ernie Maglischo has performed at the top of his chosen field as a college coach. At Oakland University in Rochester, Michigan, his team won the NCAA Division II championship. At Chico State in California, his teams have won three Division II championships and one Division III championship. Dr. Maglischo's swimmers always perform with great stroke technique and efficiency and have always attacked their races with outstanding conditioning and an organized plan.

I commend Ernie Maglischo for writing a book so complete in every way. Swimming will be better off as a result.

George Haines
Stanford University

Introduction: Historical Perspective

Until the late 1960s, attempts to describe the stroke mechanics of competitive swimmers were based on empirical judgments. That changed when J. E. Counsilman (1968) and C. E. Silvia (1970), in two separate publications, applied scientific laws to develop new theories of hydrodynamic propulsion. Newton's third law of motion—for every action there is an equal and opposite reaction—was the most prominent of the physical laws employed by the two men. They reasoned that pushing water backward (the action) would cause swimmers to be propelled forward (the reaction). This effect has been called **drag propulsion.** In drag propulsion, forward motion results from the resistance of water (drag) to the backward movements of swimmers' limbs.

Counsilman's and Silvia's theories were widely accepted and influenced the teaching of stroke mechanics throughout the world. As a result, swimmers' hands and feet were likened to paddles for pushing water backward. The most nearly perfect stroke mechanics were believed to be those that allowed swimmers to push water directly backward under the midline of their bodies for the longest possible distance.

The theory that pushing water directly backward was the most effective method of propulsion was later modified when analysis of high-speed underwater motion pictures showed that swimmers' hands and feet followed a weaving rather than a straight, backward path during the competitive strokes. The explanation for this observation was that the weaving path allowed swimmers to find slowly moving or still water to push against and thus gain more resistance than they would by pushing against water that had already been accel-

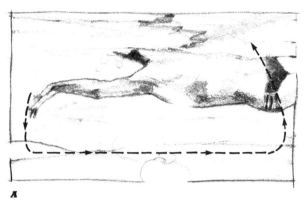

A

Figure I.1. Two theories of drag propulsion. The front and back crawl swimmers in ***A*** illustrate the stroke patterns that were believed to be most efficient when the "push directly backward to go forward" theory was popular.

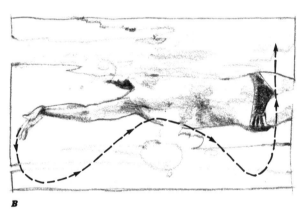

B

Swimmers in ***B*** are pushing backward in a weaving path that supposedly allows them to push against "still" water and thus gain greater propulsion.

erated backward. The differences in stroke patterns dictated by the two theories of propulsion are shown in Figure I.1.

While the members of the competitive swimming community were teaching stroke mechanics according to his previous theories, Counsilman continued his investigation of hydrodynamics. In 1971, with Ronald Brown, he proposed that hydrodynamic **lift** rather than drag was the method of propulsion preferred by world-class swimmers. Counsilman and Brown filmed swimmers wearing flashing lights on their hands in a darkened pool. The stroboscopic effect of light flashes appearing on the developed film indicated the true patterns of hand and foot movements relative to a fixed point in the pool rather than to the swimmers' bodies. The results showed that the lines of motion were predominantly lateral and vertical. This study was a milestone in swimming research and is a credit to the authors, particulary "Doc" Counsilman, who has been the major contributor to our knowledge of competitive swimming.

Since then, several other researchers have provided evidence that lift is the preferred source of propulsion (Barthels and Adrian 1974, Plagenhoff 1977, Schleihauf 1974, Schleihauf 1977). Examples of the stroke patterns of the four competitive strokes, drawn from light tracings, are shown in Figure I.2. They show the hands traveling in predominantly lateral and vertical directions with minimal backward motion. Each swimmer's hands finish their underwater stroking movements at very nearly the same spot in the pool where they began, indicating clearly that the swimmers did not push their hands backward past their bodies as much as their bodies traveled forward past their hands.

Figure I.2. Stroke patterns of the four competitive strokes drawn from light tracings. (Adapted from Brown and Counsilman 1971, Schleihauf 1974, and Schleihauf 1976.)

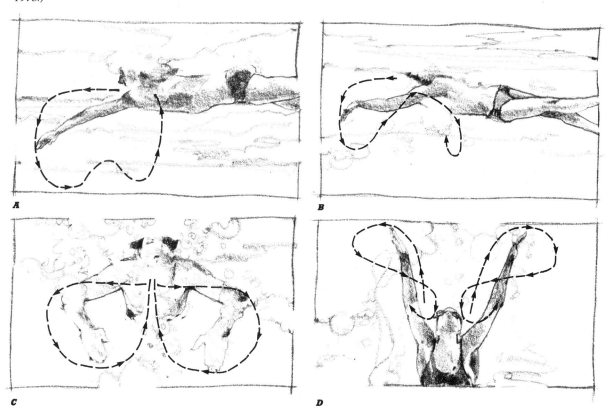

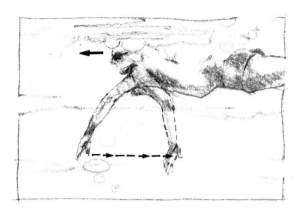

Figure I.3. A theoretical stroke pattern for drag propulsion. If pushing backward against the water were the sole means of propulsion, a swimmer's hand would push backward against the water with such force that the resistance behind his hand would push his body forward much faster than his hand was traveling backward. The result would be that his hand would travel backward only a short distance in a nearly horizontal path. But, in fact, humans are not powerful enough to exert enough force on the water to "anchor" the hand. That is why propulsion is probably lift dominated, with the actual stroking movements circular, like those in Figure I.2.

If pushing backward were the preferred means of propulsion, we would expect to see a stroke pattern like that in Figure I.3. Swimmers would create so much resistance with their hands as they pushed backward that their bodies would be accelerated forward more rapidly than their hands would move backward. The small amount of hand motion that did occur would most likely be in a predominantly backward direction rather than in lateral and vertical directions. However, since the stroke patterns of world-class swimmers are in predominantly lateral and vertical directions, some force other than drag must be the preferred source of propulsion. That force is presumed to be *lift*.

At the time of this writing, competitive swimming communities throughout the world seem to be separated into two camps as far as theories of propulsion are concerned: traditionalists and lift theorists. Traditionalists continue to believe that the greatest amount of propulsive force is achieved by pushing the hands and feet in a predominantly backward direction. Lift theorists, while conceding that some drag force is used for swimming propulsion, believe that lift provides the greatest amount of propulsive force.

The sequence of photographs in Figures I.4 and I.5 support the lift theory of propulsion. The swimmer in Figure I.4, a national-level butterflyer and world-class individual medley swimmer, was filmed as he passed a grid, marked in 6-inch squares, that had been painted on the side of the pool. The grid made it possible to determine the direction and distance his limbs and trunk moved in relation to fixed points in the pool.

Notice that his hands entered the water at grid line 8 while his hips were on line 22 (see fig. I.4A). When his hands reached the end of what is commonly referred to as the pull, they had moved downward over 18 inches but had not moved backward at all (see fig. I.4B). During that same period, his hips traveled forward more than 36 inches, beyond grid line 16. His forward propulsion was undoubtedly the result of the downward (and inward) sweep of his hands.

In the next phase of the stroke, pictured in frame C, his hands pushed backward nearly 24 inches and upward nearly 18 inches while his hips traveled forward approximately 30 inches. Propulsion was probably drag-dominated through this phase of the stroke.

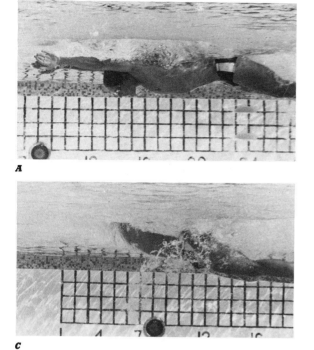

A

B

C

Figure I.4. A butterfly swimmer using a combination of lift and drag force for propulsion.

An even more striking example of a swimmer using lift for propulsion is shown in the sequence of photographs in Figure I.5. Nearly all of this national-level breaststroke swimmer's propulsive force is lift dominated. He begins the propulsive phase of his armstroke when his hands are on grid line 7 and his hips are between lines 15 and 16 (see fig. I.5A). When he is midway through the armstroke, his hands have, like the butterflyer's, traveled downward nearly 18 inches (see frame B). They are still on grid line 7, having not moved backward at all. Nevertheless, his body was propelled forward, as evidenced by the fact that his hips moved forward almost 24 inches during this time, from grid line 15 in frame A nearly to line 11 in frame B.

The propulsive force of the swimmer's kick is also lift dominated. The directions of his feet during the kick are shown in frames C, D, and E of Figure I.5. Contrary to popular opinion, he does not push his feet backward very much. Notice that his feet are on grid line 11 when he begins the propulsive phase of the kick (see fig. I.5C) and that they are on line 12 when he completes the kick (see frame E). They were swept downward (and outward and inward) over 18 inches while traveling backward only 6 inches, from line 11 in frame C to line 12 in frame E. This motion of his feet caused his body to travel forward over 12 inches, as can be seen from the fact that his hips moved from grid line 8 to line 6 during the kick.

Figures I.4 and I.5 indicate that swimming propulsion is, as lift theorists contend, a result of both lift and drag forces, with lift force predominating.

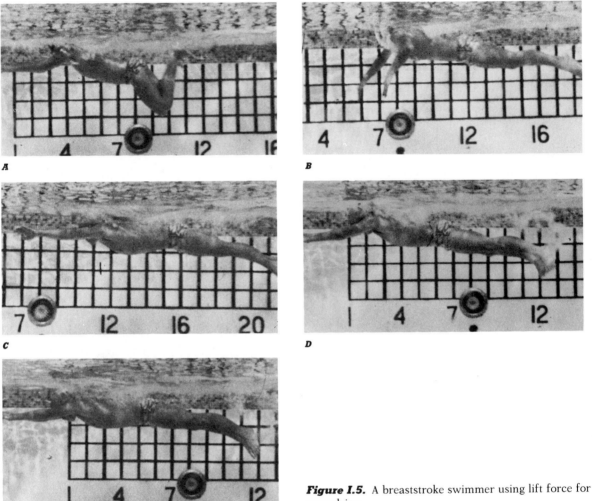

Figure I.5. A breaststroke swimmer using lift force for propulsion.

When swimmers were filmed swimming the front crawl and backstroke in front of a grid, the propulsive movements of their hands and feet were also in predominantly lateral (and vertical) directions with minimal backward motion. Apparently, swimmers get most of their propulsion from lift-producing upward, downward, inward, and outward movements of their hands and feet.

The theoretical basis for the lift theory of propulsion will be described in detail in Chapter 1. An attempt will be made to identify some propulsive movements of the hands and feet that have been overlooked in many previous descriptions of stroke mechanics.

REFERENCES

Barthels, K., and Adrian, M. J. 1974. "Three Dimensional Spatial Hand Patterns of Skilled Butterfly Swimmers." *Swimming II*, ed. J. P. Clarys and L. Lewillie, pp. 154–160. Baltimore: University Park Press.

Brown, R. M., and Counsilman, J. E. 1971. "The Role of Lift in Propelling the Swimmer." *Biomechanics*, ed. J. M. Cooper, pp. 179–188. Chicago: Athletic Institute.

Counsilman, J. E. 1968. *Science of Swimming*. Englewood Cliffs, N.J.: Prentice-Hall.

Plagenhoff, S. 1971. *Patterns of Human Motion*. Englewood Cliffs, N.J.: Prentice-Hall.

Schleihauf, R. E., Jr. 1974. "A Biomechanical Analysis of Freestyle." *Swimming Technique* 11:89–96.

———. 1976. "A Hydrodynamic Analysis of Breaststroke Pulling Efficiency." *Swimming Technique* 12:100–105.

Silvia, C. E. 1970. *Manual and Lesson Plans for Basic Swimming, Water Stunts, Lifesaving, Springboard Diving, Skin and Scuba Diving*. Published by the author.

PART One

Stroke Mechanics

CHAPTER *1*

The Hydrodynamics of Competitive Swimming Strokes

The success of world-class competitive swimmers can be attributed primarily to their ability to generate propulsive force while reducing their resistance to forward motion. Some methods for increasing propulsive force and reducing resistance to foward motion will be discussed in this chapter.

Lift

Recent research indicates that the use of hydrodynamic lift may be the most effective method for increasing propulsive force. Lift is most easily described in terms of aerodynamic function. Once this is done, the role of this phenomenon in swimming can be more easily explained.

Aerodynamic Lift Theory

The relationship of aerodynamic lift to flight is illustrated in Figure 1.1. The airplane in this illustration moves forward in a horizontal direction. The airstream immediately in front of the plane exerts a pressure that opposes the plane's forward motion. This pressure is termed **drag**. *Drag force always acts opposite to the direction in which an object is moving.*

As the airplane travels forward, the airstream immediately in front is diverted over and underneath the wing surfaces. Notice that the surface of the wing is curved on top and flat underneath. The distance air must travel to get from the leading edge to the trailing edge is greater over the larger curved surface. According to Bernoulli's theorem the air passing over the top of the wing will be accelerated so that it reaches the trailing edge at the same time as the air flowing underneath (Aviation Research Associates 1943). This accelera-

11

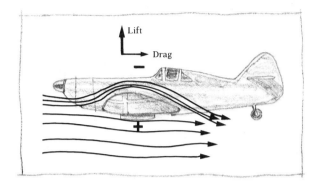

Figure 1.1. The relationship of aerodynamic lift to flight.

tion is indicated by compression of the airstream lines passing over the upper surface of the wing (see fig. 1.1). Bernoulli's theorem further states that the pressure of the air passing over the top of the wing will decrease as its rate of flow increases (Barna 1969). In contrast, the pressure of the slower moving air underneath the wing remains the same or increases slightly. The result is a pressure differential between the two surfaces with the pressure beneath the wing being higher, as indicated in Figure 1.1 by the plus sign.

Since fluids (air is technically a fluid) tend to move from areas of higher pressure toward areas of lower pressure, an upward force is exerted against the undersurface of the wing. This force, which causes the plane to rise into the air and remain aloft, is termed **lift.**

The amount of lift force is proportional to the difference in pressure between the two wing surfaces which is, in turn, dependent upon the shape of the wing surfaces and the forward speed of the airplane. As the speed of the plane becomes greater, the difference in pressure on the wing surfaces increases until the lift is sufficient to raise the airplane from the ground. It is important to remember that *lift force is always exerted in a direction that is perpendicular to the direction of drag force* (see fig. 1.2).

The pressure differential between the top and the underside of the wing may be increased by adjusting the **angle of attack** of the wing. The angle of attack is the angle formed by the inclination of the wing to its direction of motion. The effect of the angle of attack on lift is illustrated in Figure 1.3.

When the angle of attack is very slight, as shown in Figure 1.3*A*, the amounts of lift and drag are relatively small because little disruption in the direction of flow occurs as the airstreams pass the wing. In Figure 1.3*B*, the wing is pitched upward at an angle of 25 degrees, causing an increase in lift force. This occurs because the air passing under the wing is deflected downward. In accordance with Newton's third law of motion, for every action there is an equal and opposite reaction, the deflection of air downward causes a counterforce to be exerted on the wing in an upward direction. This counterforce causes a further increase in the pressure differential between the upper and lower surfaces of the wing and there is a corresponding increase in lift force.

Slightly increasing the angle of attack will increase lift; too great an angle

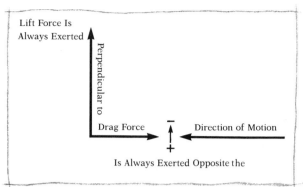

Figure 1.2. Drag and lift force. This diagram depicts the relationship between drag, lift, and the direction of movement. Swimmers' movements through the water will be resisted by the water immediately in front of and around their body parts. That water resistance is termed *drag*. Drag force always acts in a direction that is opposite the direction of motion. This opposition creates a *lift* force. Lift force always acts perpendicular to drag.

Figure 1.3. Effect of the angle of attack on lift force.

A. Both drag and lift forces are minimal because the angle of attack is so slight that the direction of the flow of the oncoming air is not disturbed sufficiently to create a significant pressure differential between the two surfaces of the airfoil.

B. The angle of attack is sufficient to cause the air flowing over and under the wing to be deflected downward. This increases the pressure differential so that a large lift force is exerted.

C. The angle of attack is too great and the air cannot pass around the wing. Instead it bounces backward off

the flat undersurface of the airfoil and becomes turbulent. The air passing over the upper surface cannot change directions rapidly enough to follow the curved contour of the upper surface of the airfoil, and a low pressure area of turbulent eddy currents is formed. This turbulence creates a pressure differential opposite the direction the wing is moving in and will cause the plane to stall and lose altitude. Little if any lift force occurs at such obtuse angles of attack.

D. The angle of attack is below the horizontal. The lift force will act in a downward direction and the plane will lose altitude.

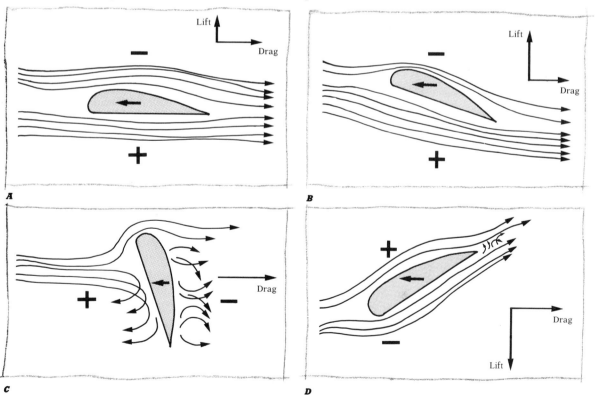

will decrease or even eliminate it. This is shown in Figure 1.3*C*. The angle of attack is so great that airstreams cannot pass around the wing. Instead, the molecules rebound off the flat undersurface and become turbulent, creating a high pressure area. The airstream passing over the upper surface cannot change directions rapidly enough to follow the curved contour and breaks away from the boundary layer, leaving a lower pressure of eddy currents behind the airfoil. This creates a rather large pressure differential opposite the direction of motion, which causes considerable resistance. Since the pressure differential is exerted opposite rather than perpendicular to the direction of motion, there is little if any lift force associated with such obtuse angles of attack. Airplanes usually stall and lose altitude when their wings are pitched in this manner.

Angles of attack that are below the horizontal have an even more devastating effect on flight. This is illustrated in Figure 1.3*D*. The air passing over the wing is actually deflected upward, exerting a counterforce in a downward direction. This reverses the direction in which the pressure differential is acting and the plane will lose altitude.

Swimmers probably use the principles of aerodynamic lift by shaping their hands like wings and moving them rapidly to create lift force. By carefully regulating the pitch of their hands and feet throughout the propulsive phases of each stroke, swimmers can achieve the most effective angle of attack, thereby increasing lift.

The Application of Aerodynamic Lift Theory to Swimming Propulsion

If you hold this book so that the wing in Figure 1.3*B* appears to be moving toward the floor, you will notice that lift force appears to be exerted in a "forward" rather than in an "upward" direction. If you are having trouble visualizing lift occurring in this situation, remember that the direction of lift is always perpendicular to drag. It is unfortunate that the term *lift* was given to this force because it suggests movement in an upward direction. In reality, lift force can be exerted in any direction that is perpendicular to the direction in which drag force is occurring (see fig. 1.2).

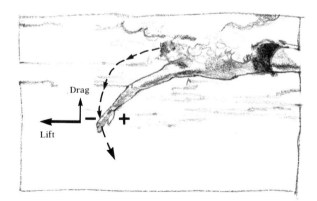

Figure 1.4. Lift force and propulsion while swimming the front crawl stroke.

The swimmer in Figure 1.4 illustrates how the hand, and possibly the arm, of a front crawl stroke swimmer could produce a propulsive lift force while it is moving downward. Shortly after entry, the hand and arm move downward (and somewhat outward). This motion is opposed by water drag in the opposite direction. Notice that the swimmer's hand is shaped like an airplane wing with the upper surface (knuckle side) more rounded and thus longer than the underside (palm surface). Notice also that the hand and arm are pitched downward and backward.

The direction and speed of arm motion, the shape of the hand, and the angle of attack cause the water passing over the knuckle side to be accelerated while water passing underneath is deflected backward. This creates a pressure differential between the two surfaces. Pressure over the knuckle side is reduced while pressure under the palm side is increased, generating lift force in a forward direction.

So far, this discussion has centered on how lift force can be exerted on the hand and arm of a swimmer. At this point, a logical question would be, how can a force acting to "lift" the hand and arm in a forward direction propel a swimmer's body? The answer is that the tendency of the hand and arm to be "lifted" in a forward direction is resisted by their downward movement and by stabilization at the shoulder joint. Since the hand and arm are not free to move forward, the lift force is transferred to the swimmer's body, which is freely suspended in the water, propelling it forward past the arm. The stabilizing activity at the shoulder joint requires some backward pressure on the water, which undoubtedly gives swimmers the false impression they are pushing their hand backward while in reality the hand is moving, in this case, downward through the water.

Propeller Theory and Swimming Propulsion

In the previous section, the forces on a swimmer's hand and arm were compared to those on an airplane wing because the comparison makes it easier to understand how swimmers could use lift force for propulsion. In reality, swimmers use their hands and feet as propellers rather than as wings. Since propellers are nothing more than rotating wings (airfoils), they can produce lift in essentially the same way airfoils do.

The illustration in Figure 1.5*A* shows how forward motion can be caused by a rotating propeller. The leading edge of each blade "bites" into the undisturbed water, causing it to flow toward the trailing edge. The curved upper surfaces of the blades and their angles of attack generate lift by causing the pressure to be reduced over the anterior surface while the posterior surface deflects water in a backward direction. As a result, any object that is connected to this propeller will move in a forward direction.

In a similar manner, a swimmer's hands and feet can act as a set of propeller blades by changing direction and pitch throughout the stroke. Frames *B*, *C*, and *D* of Figure 1.5 illustrate this activity. In the front crawl stroke the hand and arm move downward shortly after entering the water (see fig. 1.5*B*). This is followed by an inward and upward sweep (see fig. 1.5*C*) and then by an outward and upward sweep (see fig. 1.5*D*).

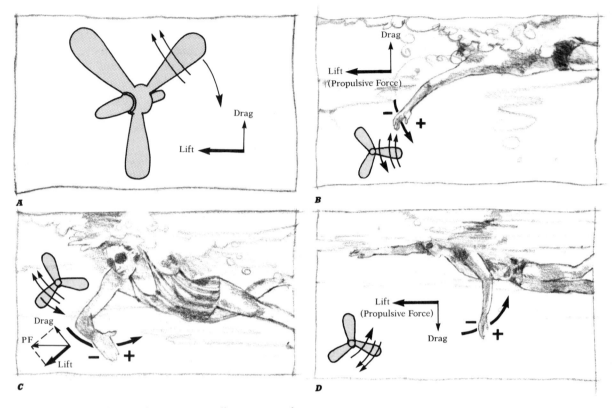

Figure 1.5. Similarities between propeller action and the underwater armstroke of the front crawl.

In Figure 1.5*B*, the fingertips are the leading edge of the blade during this downward and outward sweep. The hand is pitched downward, outward, and backward in order to achieve an angle of attack that will cause water to be deflected backward as it passes under the palm. The flow of water upward, inward, and backward past the hand creates a drag force. The resulting pressure differential between palm side (+) and knuckle side (−) causes a lift force to be created in a perpendicular direction. This lift force propels the swimmer forward. The inward sweep causes water to travel outward past the hand from the thumb side to the little finger side (fig. 1.5*C*). The drag force causes a pressure differential between the palm side (+) and the knuckle side (−) that exerts a resultant force which propels the swimmer forward.

The wrist edge of the hand is the leading edge as it sweeps upward at the end of the underwater stroke (see fig. 1.5*D*). Water drag occurs in a downward direction, with the pressure differential between the palm side (+) and the knuckle side (−) exerting a lift force in a perpendicular or forward direction. This force will propel the swimmer forward.

Analyses of underwater motion pictures of world-class swimmers reveal that the hands (and feet) change directions several times during the propulsive phases of each competitive stroke. Every time the hands and feet change directions, the direction of water flowing across the hands and feet changes too, so that they act as new blades rotating into undisturbed water where additional lift force can be generated as the force from the preceding movement is dissipating. The pitch of the hands and feet changes with each change of direction so that the most effective angle of attack is always being used. Thus, by changing direction and pitch, swimmers can use their hands and feet as a propeller with three (or more) blades.

The Physics of Analyzing Swimming Strokes for Their Propulsive Capability

Up to this point, the nature of swimming propulsion has been oversimplified. For one thing, lift has been presented as the propulsive force, when in reality the most efficient propulsion occurs when the forces of lift and drag are combined to form a third **resultant** force. This resultant force, because it is a combination of lift and drag, is larger and usually more propulsive than either of its constituents. The following information on vector analysis may clarify the true nature of swimming propulsion. Hopefully it will substantiate the premise that swimming propulsion is lift dominated and will provide a basis for identifying limb motions that are most propulsive.

The Combination of Forces When the perpendicular forces of lift and drag act about a common point, they produce a resultant force of greater magnitude than either of the two original forces. The resultant force will be exerted in a direction that is somewhere between the original forces. When the directions and magnitude of the lift and drag forces are known, the direction and magnitude of the resultant force can be determined by vector analysis. The procedure for this analysis is shown in Figure 1.6. The forces of lift and drag are represented by arrows (vectors). The direction of each arrow indicates the direction in which the force is acting; the length of each arrow represents the magnitude of the force it represents. The resultant force is determined by joining the vectors of the perpendicular forces

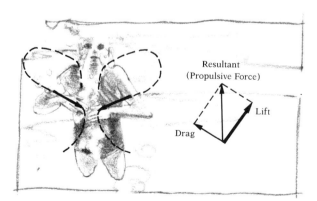

Figure 1.6. A procedure for determining the direction and magnitude of propulsive force through vector analysis. The diagonal (resultant) drawn between the lift and drag vectors represents the composite effect of the two forces and indicates both the direction and magnitude of body motion.

of lift and drag to form a rectangle. The diagonal dividing the rectangle into two right triangles accurately depicts the direction and magnitude of the resultant force.

When the resultant force is exerted in a horizontal direction, as it is in Figure 1.6, it can propel the swimmer forward. In this case the magnitude of propulsive force should be greater than it would be if lift had been used. It would seem, therefore, that, where possible, the resultant force should be used for propulsion in preference to either lift or drag. Several examples of ways in which limb direction can be altered so that resultant forces are used for propulsion will be described later in chapters on the four competitive strokes.

Determining the Direction of Propulsive Force

When neither the lift nor the resultant force is acting in a forward direction, the magnitude of propulsive force can be determined in the manner shown in Figure 1.7. Once the direction and magnitude of the resultant force (line *AB*) has been established, a horizontal line (*AC*) is extended from the point of intersection of the lift and drag forces. This line represents the forward propulsive component of the resultant force. The magnitude of propulsion can be determined by dropping a perpendicular line (*BC*) from the end of the resultant force until it intersects the forward component. The length of line *AC* represents the amount of propulsive force exerted.

The accuracy of this representation depends, of course, on the accuracy with which the direction and magnitude of the lift and drag forces have been represented by their respective vectors. If one knew the actual magnitude of a resultant force in pounds, the magnitude of the propulsive force could be calculated by multiplying the resultant force by the cosine of the angle that is formed by the resultant and thrust vectors (angle *A*).

Force Magnitude and Propulsion

There are occasions when a resultant force of considerable magnitude that is acting in some direction other than forward can produce greater propulsive force than one of less magnitude that is exerted in a forward direction. This phenomenon is illustrated in Figure 1.8. In this case a greater amount of muscular force, as indicated by the greater length of the drag vector in Figure 1.8*A*,

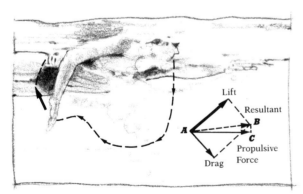

Figure 1.7. Resolving for propulsive force when neither the lift nor resultant forces act in a forward directon. In this example, the lift and resultant forces are acting in forward and upward directions,. The forward component of the resultant force is propulsive and can be determined by drawing a horizontal line (*AC*) in a forward direction from the point of intersection of the lift and drag forces. A perpendicular line (*BC*) is then extended from the resultant force until it intersects this horizontal line at point C. The length of line AC represents the magnitude and direction of propulsive force during this portion of the underwater armstroke.

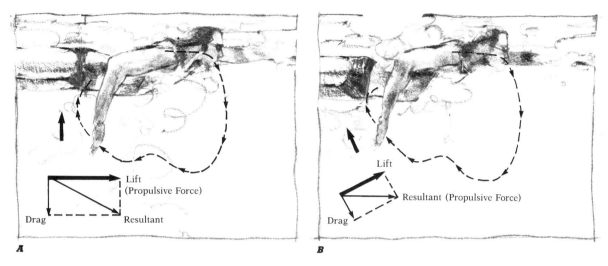

Figure 1.8. The relationship of the magnitude of vector forces to the magnitude of propulsive force.

compared to that in Figure 1.8*B*, generates more propulsive force even though the swimmer in 1.8*B* is utilizing the resultant force for propulsion. This fact notwithstanding, a stroke will usually be more propulsive when the resultant force is acting in a forward direction. This is because less muscular force will be required to obtain the same amount of propulsion. The two diagrams in Figure 1.8*C* illustrate this point. In this case the same amount of muscular effort, indicated by the drag vectors, produces more propulsive force when the resultant rather than lift force is the propelling force.

The Importance of Limb Direction, Pitch, and Velocity to Efficient Swimming

Athletes can either swim faster or use less muscular effort at submaximal speeds when their limbs are moving in the right directions, at an optimal velocity, with their hands and feet inclined or pitched at the proper angle of attack.

Limb Direction Downward, upward, inward, and outward sweeps of the limbs are most effective because they generate lift-dominated propulsion. It should be pointed out that swimmers can also propel their bodies forward by pulling and pushing their hands backward against the water. Research indicates, however, that the most successful swimmers use lift-dominated propulsion (Brown and Counsilman 1971, Barthels and Adrian 1974, Schleihauf 1974, Schleihauf 1978a, Schleihauf 1978b). Although most of the swimmers in these studies were taught to push water backward, their superior *feel* for propulsion has apparently caused them, unconsciously, to substitute lift-dominated lateral and verti-

Table 1.1   *A Comparison of Drag-Dominated and Lift-Dominated Propulsion*

Form of propulsion	Direction of limb movement	Results		Maximum propulsive force that can be generated
		Drag force	Lift force	
Drag-dominated	Horizontally backward	Considerable	Little	Less
Lift-dominated	Vertical, lateral, and backward	Less	Considerable	More

cal propeller-like movements for drag-producing paddling actions in many parts of the various stroke cycles.

There are several reasons why lift-dominated propulsion may be superior to drag propulsion. The use of downward, outward, inward, upward, and backward limb motions probably increases foward acceleration and the total distance over which propulsive force can be generated during each stroke cycle. As a result, swimmers using lift-producing movements should achieve more distance per stroke. The combination of a slower turnover rate and more acceleration per stroke should reduce the energy required to swim races. Characteristics of lift-dominated and drag-dominated propulsion are summarized in Table 1.1.

Although lateral and vertical limb motions are usually more propulsive than backward motions, there are portions of the various competitive strokes where the magnitude of propulsive force, although lift-dominated, can be increased by the addition of some backward limb movement. The upward sweep of the arm in the backstroke is a good example of this phenomenon. Notice in Figure 1.9A, that when the swimmer's hand travels directly upward, the magnitude of propulsive force is less than when some backward motion is also included, as in Figure 1.9B. This is because sweeping the hand diagonally upward causes the larger resultant force to act in a forward direction.

Last, it should be mentioned that there are phases of each stroke where propulsion should be drag-dominated. Swimmers use their hands and feet as paddles during distinct changes in limb direction so that propulsive force can be maintained until the hands and feet have established sufficient pitch and velocity in the new direction for propulsion, once again, to become lift-dominated. The manner in which these transitions are accomplished will be described in the chapters on each competitive stroke.

Pitch   The **pitch,** or direction of inclination, of the hands and feet is as important to efficient propulsion as moving the limbs in the proper directions. Errors in either pitch or direction prevent swimmers from achieving peak performances.

	Results		
Relative muscular effort	Relative distance per stroke	Energy expended	Relative efficency
More force required for same amount of propulsion	Less distance per stroke	More energy expended because of faster turnover	Less efficient
Less force required for same amount of propulsion	More distance per stroke	Less energy expended because fewer strokes required	More efficient

It is important to make a clear distinction between *pitch* and *angle of attack. Pitch* refers to the direction in which the hands and feet are inclined. *Angle of attack* refers to the number of degrees they are inclined in a given direction.

Swimmers' limbs will be pitched in one or more of the following directions during various phases of the strokes:

Figure 1.9. The effect of upward diagonal stroking on propulsive force.

A. This swimmer is stroking almost directly upward (and inward) in the backstroke. The force diagram shows that lift force will propel the swimmer forward while a resultant force of greater magnitude is exerted in a downward and forward direction. This force will tend to pull the swimmer's shoulder downward, increas-

ing drag and, in the process, reducing forward speed.

B. This swimmer is stroking diagonally upward. In this case, he will be propelled forward by the resultant force. The swimmer should achieve greater forward speed during this phase of the stroke provided, of course, that the angle of attack is correct and the amount of muscular force exerted by the swimmer in **B** is the same as that exerted by the swimmer in **A**.

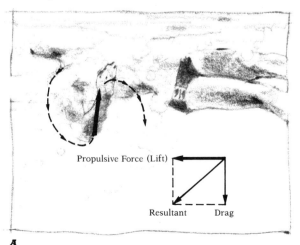

A

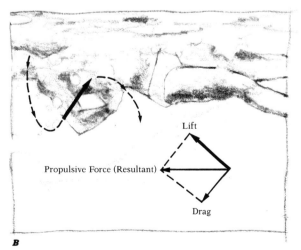

B

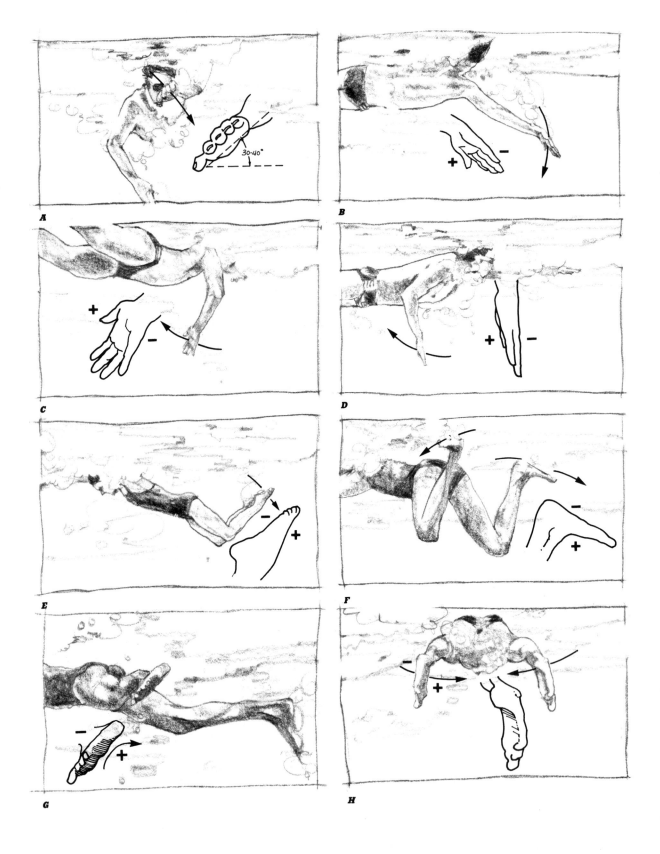

A

B

C

D

E

F

G

H

- inward—palms of the hands or soles of the feet facing slightly toward the middle of the body
- outward—palms and soles facing away from the body
- downward—palms and soles facing away from the body toward the bottom of the pool
- upward—palms and soles facing somewhat upward toward the body
- backward—palms or soles facing toward the rear of the body

These pitches are illustrated in Figure 1.10.

The pitch of swimmers' hands and feet is easily seen with the naked eye. The angles of attack are not so easily discerned because refraction makes accurate measurement difficult. However, the most effective angles can be estimated from aerodynamic principles. The drawings in Figure 1.3 illustrate that angles near zero and 90 degrees are ineffective and that the most effective angles of attack are probably between 20 and 50 degrees. The drawings in Figure 1.11 illustrate these facts with respect to hand pitch in swimming.

The drawings in Figure 1.11 are side views showing the various pitches that a front crawl stroke swimmer might use during the final portion of the underwater armstroke. The hand is moving upward in the direction of the arrow. In Figure 1.11*A* the angle of attack is nearly zero. The swimmer's hand is

---

Figure 1.10. Hand and foot pitch in competitive swimming. The pitch of swimmers' hands and feet will be referred to throughout this book as they are described here. Hand pitch is determined by the direction the palm is facing in relation to the body, and foot pitch is determined by the direction the sole is facing.

A. Outward hand pitch. The palm is rotated outward and backward slightly, away from the body. The hand is usually flexed slightly at the wrist and "cupped" somewhat. This probably increases the magnitude of lift force.

B. Downward hand pitch. The hand is flexed at the wrist somewhat so that the palm faces downward and backward. The hand is also cupped slightly with the palm pitched outward.

C. Inward hand pitch. The palm is facing inward somewhat, toward the body. It is also pitched upward slightly.

D. Backward hand pitch. The hand is extended at the wrist so it faces backward. This is accomplished by relaxing the wrist and allowing the water pressure behind the palm to push the hand into an extended position. The term *backward* may not be the most accurate way to describe the hand pitch shown here. As can be seen in **C**, the hand is actually pitched backward and upward in relation to the direction it is moving.

The term *backward* was used because swimmers comprehend the hand position better when it is referred to in this way.

E. Upward foot pitch. The feet are plantar flexed at the ankles. This is accomplished by relaxing the ankles and allowing upward water pressure to point the toes upward as the feet begin to kick down. Water pressure also causes the feet to be pitched inward during this phase.

F. Outward foot pitch. Outward foot pitch is used in the first propulsive phase of the breaststroke kick. The soles of the feet face outward away from the body. This is accomplished by dorsiflexion and eversion at the ankle joints. The range of motion is limited in these directions and special flexibility exercises should be used to increase this range if an effective breaststroke kick is desired. The soles of the feet usually face upward as well as outward.

G. The feet face down away from the body. They remain dorsiflexed but are somewhat inverted when pitched in this direction.

H. Inward foot pitch. The soles of the feet face inward toward the body. They are inverted at the ankles and dorsiflexed in the breaststroke kick, as shown here. They are plantar flexed and pitched inward during the flutter and dolphin kicks.

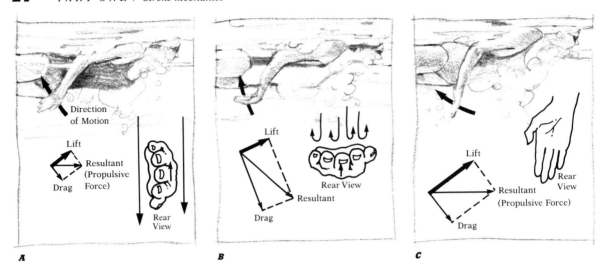

Figure 1.11. The effect of three angles of attack on propulsive force.

on its edge. In this case, both drag and lift forces are minimal. The water passing underneath the palm is not deflected backward enough to cause a significant counterforce, and the pressure differential between the two surfaces of the hand is not great enough to cause an adequate lift force. (This position is used for lifting the hand from the water in the front crawl and butterfly strokes because it offers minimal resistance to motion.)

In Figure 1.11*B* the swimmer's hand is at an angle of attack of 90 degrees with respect to its upward motion. That is, the palm is facing directly upward, pushing water toward the surface. In this case, the drag component is considerable while lift is minimal and the resultant force has a greater downward than forward component. Pushing upward against the water with a flat palm disturbs the flow of water molecules and causes them to become turbulent. This turbulence causes a pressure differential between the palm and knuckle side that creates more downward than forward force, and the swimmer's body will be pulled downward.

In Figure 1.11*C*, the swimmer's hand is pitched upward at an angle of attack of 35 degrees with respect to the upward direction in which it is moving. This angle allows the water molecules passing over the hand to be deflected backward gradually and with minimal turbulence. This increases the pressure differential between the palm and knuckle sides, producing a horizontal resultant force that propels the swimmer's body forward.

The most effective angles of attack for propulsion are probably between 20 and 50 degrees. At smaller angles the drag may not be sufficient to cause an adequate pressure differential and lift will be diminished. With larger angles, the drag component of force may be so great that turbulence occurs, in which case the pressure differential is lessened or caused to act in a direction that retards rather than increases propulsive force.

There is research that partially verifies these observations. Schleihauf (1978a) has reported swimmers using angles of attack as slight as 15 degrees and as great as 73 degrees during various phases of the four competitive strokes. In a separate study, Schleihauf (1978b) measured drag and lift forces on plaster casts of human hands in an open water channel. The most effective angles of attack for producing lift varied between 15 and 55 degrees, depending on the direction of water flow across the hand.

Wood and Holt (1978) used a wind tunnel to measure the lift and drag forces on plaster models of swimmers' hands. They also found angles of attack between 15 and 55 degrees most effective for producing lift.

Although the research procedures were excellent in both studies, these data should be applied only in a general sense. Accurate measurement of hand pitch is a monumental task. The problems of measuring an angle in three dimensions from data that are filmed in two-dimensions are further complicated by the fact that swimmers are constantly changing the direction and pitch of their limbs throughout the entire stroke cycle. Each change in direction probably requires a somewhat different angle of attack in order to maintain the greatest lift force throughout the stroke.

Great swimmers of the past have probably used that nebulous phenomenon we call *feel for the water* to find the proper angles of attack (and directions of movement) during each phase of the competitive strokes. Present swimmers will need to do the same until further research is available.

In the meantime, swimmers can learn a great deal about the best angles of attack and stroke patterns by studying motion pictures of world-class swimmers. Look for the following:

1. the directions of pitch during each phase of the stroke
2. the manner in which pitch changes as the swimmer passes from one phase of the stroke to another
3. the general directions of motion during each phase of the stroke

With this information as a guide, and with the knowledge that the most productive angles of attack are somewhere between 20 and 50 degrees, swimmers can determine their own optimum directions of movement and angles of attack through practice and experimentation.

The effects of paddling on propulsion. The most common mistake swimmers make when first attempting to master the use of lift for propulsion is to push water inward, outward, downward, or upward with the palms of their hands pitched at an angle that is nearly perpendicular to their direction of motion. The results of these mistakes are illustrated in Figure 1.12. When swimmers push water inward or outward with the palms of their hands pitched like paddles rather than like propellers, drag force dominates and the body moves laterally more than forward. Pushing upward or downward will cause equally serious reductions of forward velocity by causing the body to move vertically. This is because the water cannot pass smoothly over the flat surface. Instead, the molecules rebound in all directions, increasing turbulence and drag. Little

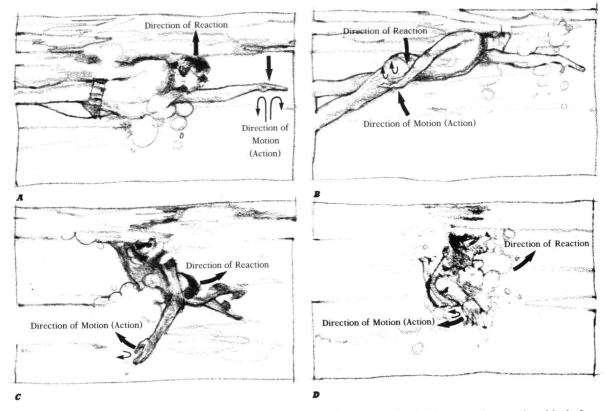

Figure 1.12. The effect of paddling on body movement and propulsion.

In **A** the swimmer is pushing downward with the palm of his hand pitched perpendicular to its direction of motion. This causes the body to be pushed upward more than it is propelled forward. In **B** the swimmer is pushing upward. His hips are submerged and little forward propulsion is generated. The effects of paddling inward and outward are shown in **C** and **D**. In both cases the body is pushed out of alignment in a direction that is opposite to that in which the hand is moving.

or no lift force is present because the pressure differential between palm and knuckle side acts opposite rather than perpendicular to the direction of motion.

Swimmers must use the edges of their hands (and feet) as propeller blades, pitching them at the correct angle of attack and moving them in such a way that water is deflected backward gradually as it passes from leading to trailing edges. Although it is true that the palm of the hand may be used like a paddle to push water backward during certain transition points in the underwater stroke, it must never be used to push water in other directions.

The significance of air bubbles behind the hands and feet. Finding the correct stroke patterns and angles of attack can be aided by observing the air bubbles behind the arms and legs of swimmers. Many coaches have noticed that world-class swimmers have fewer air bubbles than swimmers of lesser achievement. This is probably because the better swimmers are using more effective angles of attack. Air bubbles indicate turbulence, and such turbulence is increased when the swimmers push air and water downward and inward from the surface with the palms of their hands. This action will, as indicated in Figure 1.12*A*, push the body upward and sideward, increasing drag and reducing forward velocity. The disappearance of air bubbles shortly after the hand enters the water is an indication that the angles of attack are more suitable for producing lift-dominated propulsion.

Velocity In theory, increases in limb speed produce corresponding increases in propulsive force. Thus, increasing limb speed should increase forward velocity. However, if the angle of attack is near zero, it is possible to slip your limbs through the water quite rapidly. In that case, the limbs encounter minimal drag and little or no lift force is produced.

An accurate statement of this general principle is, *When limbs are pitched correctly and moving in the proper directions, increases in limb speed produce corresponding increases in propulsive force.* This suggests that an optimum speed of limb motion will produce the greatest forward velocity. This is because the increase in drag force makes it impossible to move your limbs through the water at maximum speed when they are pitched at angles greater than zero. Thus, the optimum speed of limb motion is the maximum speed that can be attained when the limbs are moving in the proper direction and when they are pitched at the correct angle of attack.

The optimum speed of limb movement is dependent on such factors as mechanical efficiency, muscular power, and joint flexibility. Thus, it probably varies with every swimmer and with every competitive style. Unfortunately, research is not available to help us in designating any optimum range of limb velocities. There are, however, data available on the hand velocity of one world-

Figure 1.13. Velocity curves of Mark Spitz's freestyle. (Adapted from Schleihauf 1974.)

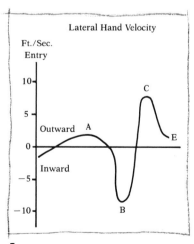

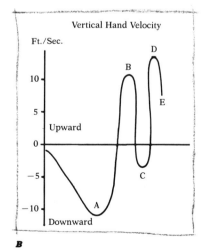

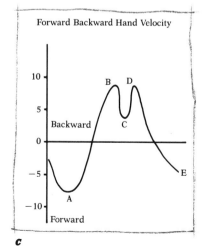

class swimmer, Mark Spitz. Velocity curves of Spitz's freestyle were first presented by Schleihauf in 1974. They are shown in Figure 1.13 with some adaptations to aid in interpretation.

The first curve indicates lateral hand velocity. There is a gradual acceleration outward after entry (A) followed by a rapid acceleration inward under his body (B). His hand is accelerated outward, once again, (C) through what is commonly known as the **push phase of the armstroke.** Outward acceleration diminishes as his hand releases the water prior to beginning the recovery (E).

Vertical hand velocities are illustrated in the second curve. Acceleration takes place in a downward direction after entry (A) followed by an upward acceleration (B) as his hand is brought under his body. This is followed by a slight acceleration in a downward direction (C), after which there is a rapid acceleration upward (D) to the end of the underwater armstroke (E).

The third curve indicates forward and backward hand velocities. His hand moves forward and then downward after entering the water (A). There is then an acceleration in backward speed (B) as his hand moves under his body. That is followed by a deceleration in backward speed as it moves outward (C). That is then followed by acceleration in a backward direction to the finish of the underwater stroke (D). The propulsive phase of the stroke ends as his hand nears the surface and begins to move forward (E).

These velocity curves provide further proof that although both lift and drag forces are used for propulsion, lift force predominates. It is obvious that both the magnitude and the velocity of the vertical and lateral hand movements are greater than the backward movements during most phases of the underwater armstroke. Since we know that lift forces result from vertical and lateral limb movements, we have convincing evidence that lift forces dominate swimming propulsion (Schleihauf 1974).

Applying Lift Theory to Competitive Swimming Strokes

Once the principles of using lift to generate propulsion are understood, coaches and swimmers can apply them to improve the stroke mechanics of competitive swimmers. The first step in this process is to identify the components of swimming strokes. From the extensive study of motion pictures of world-class competitive swimmers, four basic arm actions and four kicking movements have been identified from which all strokes are constructed. The true nature of these movements cannot be adequately conveyed by the commonly used terms *pull* and *push;* therefore, a change in stroke terminology is needed before these basic stroking motions are described.

Stroke Terminology In references to underwater stroking mechanics in this book, the term **sweep** will replace the popular terms *pull* and *push.* This is because *sweep* is descriptive of the lift-producing, propeller-like vertical and lateral motions of the limbs, while *pull* and *push* suggest using the hands and feet as paddles. Since each stroke is composed of several sweeps in different directions, a prefix will be attached to each. The prefix indicates the predominant direction of the

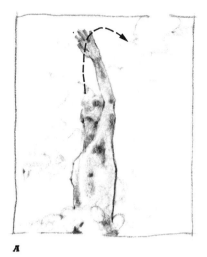

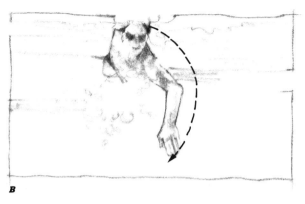

A

B

Figure 1.14. Determining the predominant direction of motion during a sweep. The swimmer's hand moves both outward (**A**) and downward (**B**) after entering the water. The downward motion is of greatest magnitude, therefore, this movement is called a downsweep.

movement being described. A swimmer's limbs actually travel in three directions at once during each phase of the various competitive strokes. The predominant direction is the one of greatest magnitude. For example, the swimmer in Figure 1.14 is midway through the initial underwater movement in the front crawl stroke. The arm is moving downward and outward, as indicated by the underneath (A) and front (B) views. The downward motion predominates. Therefore, although it would be more precise to refer to this movement as a down and out sweep, in the interest of simplicity the movement has been termed a *downsweep.*

The Four Sweeping Motions of the Competitive Strokes

The four sweeping motions from which all competitive armstrokes are constructed are the **outsweep**, the **downsweep**, the **insweep** and the **upsweep**.

Outsweep. The outsweep is the initial underwater movement in the breaststroke and butterfly (see fig. 1.15). It is more noticeable in the breaststroke, however, because the wide arm entry of the butterfly minimizes the outward motion.

In the outsweep, your hands move outward in a curvilinear path. The palms of your hands should be pitched outward and backward. The amount of outward pitch is greater here than in any of the other sweeps. It is nearly 90 degrees from the horizontal. Your hands should be almost completely on their sides with the little fingers above the thumbs. The backward pitch should be sufficient to allow your fingertips to be the leading edge, with the water being deflected backward over the palms from fingertips to wrists. Your hands should also be cupped slightly to improve their airfoil shape. The outsweep ends when your hands have traveled a short distance outside the width of your shoulders (see fig. 1.15).

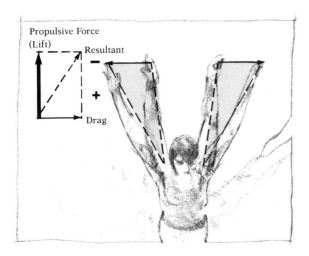

Figure 1.15. The outsweep. The hands move outward with the palms pitched out and back. A high pressure area on the palm side, relative to an area of lower pressure on the knuckle side, creates a pressure differential which causes a lift force that propels the swimmer forward. The distance over which the outsweep is generally used is illustrated by the arrows in the stroke plot.

The outsweep begins slowly, with outward limb velocity accelerating until the end of the movement. Propulsion from the outsweep is small as compared to that of other stroking motions. It is used primarily to feel for a "catch" in the water. Most swimmers report that the outsweep feels like a gentle stretch rather than a forceful propulsive movement.

The way propulsion is generated during the outsweep is illustrated in Figure 1.15. Drag created by the outward direction of motion and the outward and backward pitch of the hands causes the water passing over the longer knuckle side to be accelerated while the water passing under the palm side travels more slowly and is deflected backward. This creates a pressure differential between the two sides which exerts a lift force that propels the swimmer forward (Bernoulli's theorem). The tendency of the hands and arms to be moved (lifted) in a forward direction is resisted by stabilizing muscular action in the shoulders, and the lift force is transferred to the swimmer's body, causing it to be thrust forward over the arms. This gives the sensation of pushing backward against the water, although the hands are actually moving outward. The resultant component of force, which is acting in an inward and forward direction, is cancelled by an equal and opposite force that is created by the other hand so that lateral body alignment is not disturbed. Schleihauf's data (1978a) indicate that swimmers in the butterfly and breaststroke use angles of attack between 38 and 62 degrees relative to the outward direction of motion during the outsweep. These angles are illustrated in Figure 1.16. Although present knowledge does not permit an exact determination of the most effective angle within this range, the lesser angles (38 to 50 degrees) are recommended. Lift force should be greater at these angles because the hands act more like propellers than like paddles. At angles greater than 50 degrees the palm tends to push water sideward rather than causing it to be deflected backward as it passes from fingertips to wrists. Pushing sideward will increase the lateral component of force (drag) while reducing the forward component (lift).

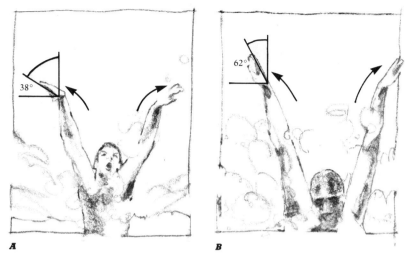

Figure 1.16. Angles of attack used in the outsweep. Angles of attack between 38 and 62 degrees have been reported among world-class swimmers during this phase of the butterfly and breaststroke armstrokes.

Some swimmers appear to separate their fingers somewhat during the outsweep. The characteristic pattern is to have the first finger slightly anterior to the others. Their thumbs also tend to be separated from the fingers. This position of the fingers is illustrated in the photographs of a butterflyer and a breaststroker in Figure 1.17.

Swimmers may unknowingly use these finger positions because they enhance the lift effect. Schleihauf (1978b) and Wood and Holt (1978) have reported increases in lift associated with this position of the fingers and thumb

Figure 1.17. Hand position during the outsweep of the breaststroke (**A**) and butterfly (**B**). Notice that the swimmers keep their thumbs separated from their fingers and that their index fingers are slightly behind the others. This position of the fingers and thumb is characteristic of many world-class swimmers during the outsweep of these two strokes. It may improve the airfoil shape of the hands and therefore increase lift force.

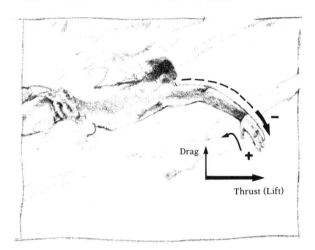

Figure 1.18. The downsweep. Once a catch is made, the hand moves downward and outward with the palm pitched out, down, and back. Water flows upward and inward being accelerated over the knuckle side, while the water passing under the palm is deflected backward. The difference in pressure between the two surfaces exerts a lift force that propels the swimmer forward. The arrows indicate the usual distance over which the downsweep is used.

when lift and drag forces were measured on plaster models of the hands suspended in an open water channel (Schleihauf) and in a wind tunnel (Wood and Holt).

Downsweep. Front and back crawl swimmers use the downsweep to begin their underwater armstrokes. It is also used in a somewhat different form during the early stages of the breaststroke and butterfly armstrokes. The drawing in Figure 1.18 illustrates the downsweep as it is used in the front crawl stroke.

After making a catch, your hand should be directed downward and

Figure 1.19. The downward and outward angles of attack during the downsweep. Angles of attack between 32 and 49 degrees have been reported among world-class swimmers with respect to the downward direction of hand motion. These angles are illustrated in the side views (**A**). It appears from motion picture films that swimmers pitch their hands outward 30 to 40 degrees during the downsweep. These angles are illustrated in the underneath view (**B**).

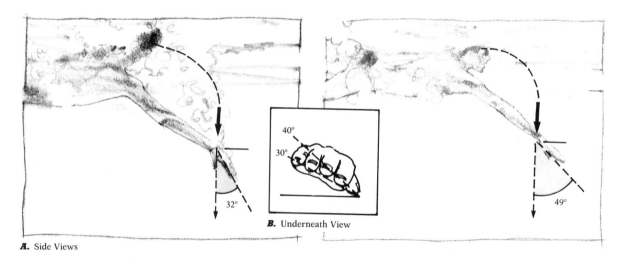

B. Underneath View

A. Side Views

slightly outward in a curvilinear path. Your hand should be pitched downward, outward, and backward. The water should sweep diagonally upward and inward past your hand from the fingertips on the little finger side toward the wrist on the thumb side. The downsweep ends as the hand reaches its deepest position in the stroke. After that the motion becomes an insweep (upsweep in backstroke). Downward limb speed accelerates from the beginning to the end of the downsweep.

The downsweep can propel swimmers in the following manner: the downward and outward hand motion, together with the hand pitched downward, outward, and backward, causes the water passing over the longer, curved, upper surface to be accelerated upward, inward, and backward while the water passing under the palm is slowed and deflected backward. This creates a pressure differential between the palm and knuckle sides of the hand that exerts a lift force in a forward direction. When resisted by muscular effort, the lift force is transferred to the body and propels it forward.

Schleihauf's data (1978a) indicate the angles of attack relative to the downward direction of hand movement vary between 32 and 49 degrees among the crawl stroke swimmers he evaluated. These angles are shown in Figure 1.19A. Once again the lesser angles are recommended because they should provide propulsion that is lift rather than drag dominated. At angles greater than 50 degrees, swimmers could tend to push water downward with their palms rather than deflect it backward.

So far, we have no exact measurements for the outward angles of attack. In motion pictures the hands appear to be pitched outward at angles of attack between 30 and 40 degrees relative to the outward direction of movement. The drawings in Figure 1.19B (simulated underneath view) illustrate this range of angles.

Many swimmers appear to be cupping their hands during the downsweep. They probably do this to improve the airfoil shape, thereby increasing propulsive force.

Insweep. The insweep plays an important role in the underwater armstroke of all competitive strokes, except the backstroke. In that stroke the corresponding movement is termed an *upsweep* because the supine body position dictates motion that is predominantly upward rather than inward. Nevertheless, the mechanics are nearly identical in all respects except direction.

The insweep is shown in Figure 1.20. It begins as the downsweep ends. The direction is inward, upward, and backward. The insweep ends as the swimmer's hand approaches the midline of the body. The hand is accelerated inward, upward, and backward from beginning to end of the motion.

The palm of your hand should be pitched inward, upward, and backward during the insweep. The hand usually remains "cupped" somewhat, perhaps to maximize lift force.

Propulsion is generated in the following manner. Since your hand is traveling inward, upward, and backward, water will flow downward, outward, and forward across the hand, creating a pressure differential between the knuckle

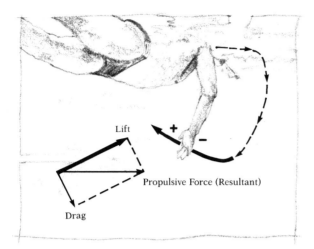

Figure 1.20. The insweep. The hand follows a circular path, downward, inward, and upward under the body. The direction and pitch of the hand cause water to be deflected backward, increasing the pressure differential between palm (+) and knuckle (−) sides of the hand that propels the swimmer forward.

side, where water flow is accelerated, and the palm side, where it is slowed and deflected backward. This pressure differential exerts a lift force in upward, outward, and forward directions which, when combined with the drag force, creates a resultant force that acts in a horizontal direction to propel the swimmer forward. The manner in which propulsion is generated during the upsweep of the backstroke armstroke will be described in the chapter on that stroke.

Schleihauf's data (1978a) on world- and national-class swimmers indicate that angles of attack relative to the inward direction of motion range from 30 to 60 degrees during the insweep. These angles are illustrated in Figure 1.21B.

Figure 1.21. Angles of attack used in the insweep. Angles of attack between 30 and 60 degrees have been reported relative to the inward hand movements. The angles of attack relative to the upward portion range from 25 to 80 degrees.

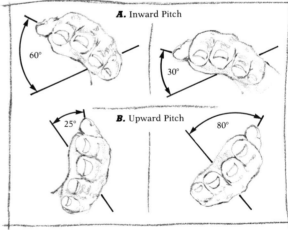

The angles of attack relative to the upward direction of motion were between 30 and 80 degrees. These angles are also illustrated in Figure 1.21*B*.

Although the data are too meager to make a definitive judgment, there are indications that swimmers who push backward more than inward during the insweep choose the smaller angles of attack. This permits the hand to be used more like a paddle to generate drag-dominated propulsion, whereas propulsive force is probably lift dominated among swimmers who use the larger angles. Although some world-class swimmers apparently use drag-dominated propulsion during this sweep, swimmers who use angles of attack between 30 and 50 degrees with respect to both the inward and the upward directions of hand motion should attain greater forward velocities with less effort because propulsion will be lift dominated.

How far should your hand sweep under your body during the insweep? This question has been a subject of controversy for several years. Some world-class swimmers bring their hands across the midline of their bodies toward the opposite hip. Others sweep their hands inward only to the midline, and some do not sweep their hands inside the body line at all. These three styles are shown in Figure 1.22.

There are two explanations for the dissimilar insweep distances among world-class swimmers. The first explanation may be that some swimmers can generate more propulsive force by sweeping their hands inward. Therefore, those who can use the insweep effectively probably sweep their hands inward to a greater extent. Other swimmers, perhaps because they were taught to push

Figure 1.22. Three insweep styles.

A. A minimal insweep. The swimmer's hand was wide of the shoulder during the downsweep and travels inward only to the near border of the body.

B. The most commonly used insweep style. The hand is brought inward to the midline. Swimmers who begin the insweep with the hand in line with their shoulder generally use this style.

C. The crossover style. The hand is swept inward past the midline. Swimmers who begin the insweep with the hand to the inside of their shoulder seem to prefer this style.

A   *B*   *C*

water backward early in their careers, may use a reduced inward sweep and push backward for propulsion because they generate more force that way.

A second explanation is that swimmers who begin the insweep with their hands in a wider position do not need to sweep them under their bodies very much to get optimum propulsion from this motion. Conversely, swimmers who begin the insweep with their hands inside their shoulder may need to sweep inward beyond the midline in order to utilize the full propulsive potential of this motion.

A recent report indicates that neither of these explanations may be accurate. Crist (1979) found that butterfly swimmers traveled 13.56 centimeters further with each stroke when they allowed their hand to sweep inward beyond the midline during the insweep. The crossover and regular strokes were also compared for forward speed during the entire armstroke. An average increase in speed of 5.61 centimeters per second was found in favor of the crossover stroke. Crist estimated these swimmers would have been, on the average, 1.78 seconds faster for 100 meters using the crossover stroke than using their regular strokes. We cannot be certain such improvement would have occurred, however.

The 100 meter times of these subjects were estimated from the velocity achieved during one stroke. The effect of fatigue must also be evaluated. A

Figure 1.23. The upsweep. The hand moves outward, upward, and backward from underneath the body to the thigh. The upsweep has two parts, illustrated in frames **A** and **B**.

A. The outward portion of the upsweep. The hand pitch is outward and backward. Hand movement and pitch cause drag force to be exerted in an inward direction and a lift force to be exerted in a perpendicular direction. They combine to create a resultant force that propels the swimmer forward.

B. The upward portion of the upsweep. The hand is pitched backward and outward, and travels upward, backward, and outward. The hand movement and pitch cause drag in a downward, inward, and forward direction and lift in a forward and outward direction. The combination of these two forces creates a resultant force that propels the swimmer's body forward.

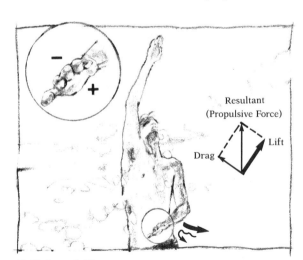

A. Underneath View

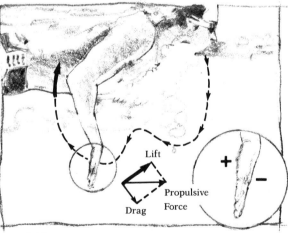

B. Side View

longer insweep requires greater effort and for this reason may be more fatiguing. Therefore, this style cannot be recommended at this time although it does appear to be worthy of further investigation.

Upsweep. The upsweep follows the insweep in the front crawl and butterfly strokes. It is illustrated in Figure 1.23. The corresponding movement in the back crawl is called a *downsweep* and is described in the chapter on the back crawl.

The upsweep consists of two distinct motions: an initial outward and backward movement followed by an upward, outward, and backward sweep. The outward and backward movement acts as a transition, allowing a smooth change of direction from the previous insweep. These two motions should be thought of as one sweep because swimmers seem to learn them more rapidly when they are presented in that form.

During the first portion of the upsweep, the pitch of your hand is changed from inward and upward to outward and backward, and hand speed is accelerated outward and backward. Swimmers relax their wrists during this motion, allowing water pressure to push their hands into an extended position, giving the false impression that they are pushing downward instead of backward. This can be seen in the point marked A in the side view of the stroke plot in Figure 1.23*B*. Since stroke plots are drawn by tracing the path of the middle finger, the extension of a relaxed hand would cause the position of this finger to drop deeper in the water and the hand would appear to be moving downward for a short time.

The second portion of the upsweep occurs as your hand passes outside the border of your body. Upward motion increases although the hand continues to travel outward and backward as well. Your hand remains pitched outward and backward with the pitch also becoming somewhat upward as the movement continues.

The upsweep ends as your hand passes the anterior portion of your thigh. At that point, pressure on the water is released and momentum carries the hand upward and forward out of the water into the recovery.

Propulsive force is generated during the upsweep as shown in the two sections of Figure 1.23. When the hand sweeps outward and backward, water flows inward and forward and is accelerated over the knuckle side while being deflected backward over the palm. This creates a pressure differential between palm and knuckle side that causes a propulsive (resultant) force to be exerted in a forward direction (see the underwater view in fig. 1.23). This force propels the swimmer forward.

During the upward portion, the direction of motion is upward, outward, and backward; and water flows downward, inward, and forward past the hand. The upward pitch of the hand causes the water passing over the palm side to be deflected backward, while the water molecules passing over the knuckle side are accelerated. This causes a pressure differential that exerts a lift force on the hand. This force when combined with the drag force exerts a resultant force that propels the swimmer's body forward. Swimmers report that the upsweep feels like the most powerful portion of the underwater stroke.

It is important that upward hand velocity exceed the speed of backward motion during this phase. Otherwise propulsion will be drag rather than lift dominated. Because the elbow is extending during the upsweep, many people have thought that propulsion is drag dominated during this phase. It is evident from the stroke plot in the side view of Figure 1.23 that upward motion exceeds backward motion during this sweep. In addition, the velocity curves in Figure 1.13 show that upward hand speed is greater than backward speed during the upsweep. Although the arm is extending somewhat at the elbow, the hand travels faster upward than backward, and the extension is not completed underwater. Films show that the arms of most world-class swimmers leave the water flexed at the elbow in the butterfly and freestyle strokes. The major amount of elbow extension takes place after the arms leave the water. Notice in Figure 1.24 that the swimmers' elbows were flexed as their arms left the water. Notice also that their arms were not completely extended after their hands left the water. The preponderance of upward rather than backward hand motion during the upsweep provides further evidence that lift is the preferred source of propulsive force in this phase of the underwater armstroke.

Figure 1.24. Upward versus backward hand motion during the upsweep. The photographs show a butterfly (frames **A** and **B**) and a freestyle swimmer (frames **C** and **D**) as their arms leave the water with elbows flexed. Contrary to traditional teaching, they do not push the water backward until their arms are completely extended.

A

B

C

D

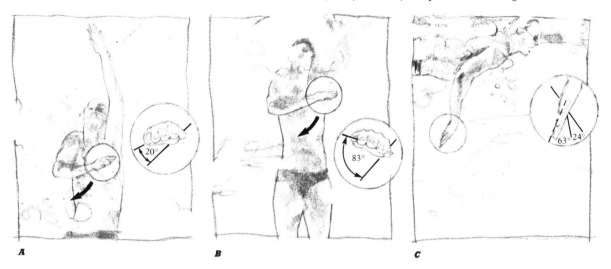

Figure 1.25. Angles of attack in outward and upward directions during the upsweep.

A–B. Angles of attack of between 20 and 83 degrees have been reported during the outward and backward portion of the upsweep. These angles are shown here from underneath.

C. The upward pitch is between 24 and 63 degrees during the upward portion of the upsweep, as shown here from the side.

Schleihauf's data (1978a) show that the angle of attack relative to the outward and backward portion of the upsweep varies from 20 to 83 degrees. These angles are illustrated in the underneath view shown in Figure 1.25. Swimmers who push backward more than outward seem to use the larger angles of attack, indicating they are using drag-dominated propulsion. Those swimmers who use lift-dominated propulsion sweep their hand(s) outward more than backward and use angles of attack between 30 and 40 degrees. Butterfly swimmers seem to prefer drag-dominated propulsion through this phase as evidenced by the fact that the subjects in Schleihauf's study used angles of attack between 59 and 73 degrees when swimming this stroke. On the other hand, most crawl stroke swimmers exhibited angles of attack between 20 and 40 degrees. This difference is probably due to the fact that swimmers can roll their bodies to the side when swimming the crawl stroke. This allows them to sweep the hand outward and upward more, whereas butterfly swimmers must sweep their hands backward to a greater extent in order to get them outside their hips where they can sweep upward. Since lift-dominated propulsion is believed superior to propulsion that is drag dominated, it is recommended that crawl stroke swimmers sweep their hands outward more and use angles of attack between 30 and 40 degrees. However, butterfly swimmers may need to push

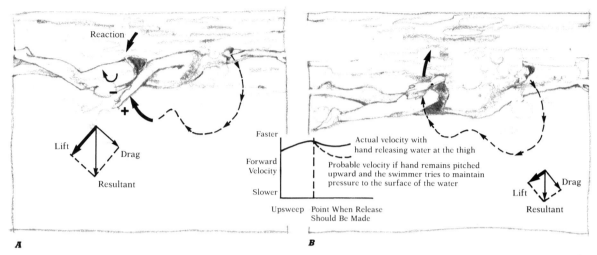

A *B*

Figure 1.26. The effect of applying force with the hand until it reaches the surface of the water. The force diagram accompanying this illustration demonstrates that swimmers should not attempt to maintain pressure on the water after their hands pass their thighs when swimming the freestyle and butterfly strokes. This is because the hand will be moving forward and upward at that time (see the stroke pattern). The elbow, which left the water before the hand, is moving forward into the recovery and pulls the hand with it. If the swimmer continues to push against the water, a considerable amount of drag force will be exerted in a downward and backward direction (see the force diagram in **A**). This will create a resultant force that is also directed downward and backward. This force will pull the hips downward and decelerate forward speed. If, however, pressure is released and the hand is turned on its side as it passes the thigh, the reduction in surface area and upward force will reduce the magnitude of drag force and also the retarding effect on forward propulsion that it creates (see the force diagram in **B**).

their hands backward through this phase. Therefore, they should use angles of attack that are between 60 and 80 degrees.

According to Schleihauf's data, the angles of attack relative to the upward direction of hand movement vary between 24 to 63 degrees. These angles are illustrated in the side view of Figure 1.25. The smaller angles of attack are recommended because of their superiority in producing lift-dominated propulsive force. Larger angles increase drag force, pulling the hips downward and reducing forward speed (see Figure 1.12*B*). No differences were noted between butterfly and crawl stroke swimmers with regard to the angles of attack used through the upward phase of the upsweep. The most skilled swimmers in both strokes used angles of attack between 30 and 40 degrees.

Many swimmers are mistakenly taught to maintain pressure on the water until their hands reach the surface during the upsweep. Actually, no propulsive force can be generated after your hand passes your thigh. It will be moving forward into the recovery at this time, and as can be seen in Figure 1.26, most of the force will be acting in a downward direction. This will cause a reaction (counterforce) that tends to submerge your hips, decelerating forward speed in the process. Swimmers usually relax pressure on the water as their hands pass their thighs, and they turn their palms inward so they can leave the water on edge with minimal drag.

The Importance of Conservation of Momentum

You may have noticed that all of the sweeps discussed in the previous section are circular or angular in nature. That is because angular movements provide the most efficient stroke patterns. Stroking in a curvilinear path allows change of direction from one sweep to the next with minimal muscular effort and no loss of propulsive force.

According to Newton's first law of motion, the inertia of a moving object must be overcome by a force before its direction can be changed. Linear motions of an arm or leg require abrupt changes of direction, whereas circular motions allow a gradual change during the transition from one sweep to the next. Since linear motions have linear momentum (momentum is a measure of the force required to stop, start, or change the direction of an object), a great deal of muscular effort is required to "brake" the momentum of a limb in a previous direction and to then accelerate it in a new direction. In addition, the muscular force that causes this change of direction will be accompanied by an equal and opposite force (Newton's third law of motion) that will be transferred to the body, "throwing" it out of alignment in the opposite direction, increasing body drag, and decelerating forward speed.

Circular stroke patterns conserve momentum. That is, the angular limb movements allow for gradual changes of direction. These changes begin before motion in the previous direction has been completed so that the muscular force required to overcome the inertia of the previous movement is reduced, leaving

Figure 1.27. A comparison of the effect of angular and linear stroking motions on propulsive force and body alignment. The swimmer in **A** is moving his hand in a circular path as he makes the transition from downsweep to upsweep in the back crawl stroke. This circular movement conserves angular momentum, reducing the muscular effort required to make the change of direction while also reducing the magnitude of reactive force that would disrupt body alignment. The swimmer in **B** is stroking in a linear path and must make an abrupt change of direction to begin the upsweep. The muscular effort required to stop the downward motion and then to start the hand moving upward is considerably increased from that in **A**. In addition, the reactive force causes his trunk to be submerged, increasing drag and reducing forward velocity.

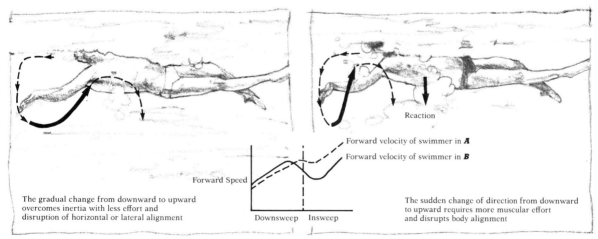

The gradual change from downward to upward overcomes inertia with less effort and disruption of horizontal or lateral alignment

The sudden change of direction from downward to upward requires more muscular effort and disrupts body alignment

Forward velocity of swimmer in **A**
Forward velocity of swimmer in **B**

Reaction

Forward Speed

Downsweep   Insweep

A   **B**

more force available for propulsive purposes. Drag is also reduced because with less force required to change direction there is less possibility of disrupting body alignment. The effect of angular and linear changes of direction is compared in Figure 1.27. The swimmer in Figure 1.27A sweeps the hand down, out, in, and up in a circular path as he makes the transition from downsweep to upsweep in the back crawl stroke. The circular motion of the arm conserves angular movement, reducing the muscular effort required to make the change of direction and reducing the magnitude of reactive force that would disrupt body alignment.

Compare this with the linear stroke pattern illustrated in Figure 1.27B. In this case the downsweep had no outward component. As a result the downward motion of the arm had to be stopped at the end of the downsweep before the arm could change direction and begin moving upward. The amount of muscular force required, to stop and then accelerate the hand in a new direction is considerably greater than that required when changes of direction are made in a circular manner. In addition, the counterforce will push the swimmer's hips downward.

The Dropped Elbow   Many people consider the "dropped elbow" the most serious mechanical fault in competitive swimming. This is because coaches have observed that the fastest swimmers keep their elbows above their hands during the downsweeps and insweeps of the various underwater armstrokes, while slower swimmers allow their elbows to drop lower in the water and travel backward in advance of their hands. The dropped elbow is illustrated in Figure 1.28. The dropped elbow position is not very propulsive because the flat undersurface of the forearm and palm push downward on the water causing a rather large drag force that acts in an upward as well as forward direction. This wastes force that could have been used for propulsion while also disrupting horizontal alignment and increasing resistance to forward motion. There is little, if any, propulsion produced with a dropped elbow stroking position.

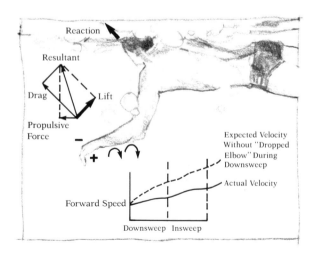

Figure 1.28. The dropped elbow. The dropped elbow occurs during the downsweeps and insweeps of the various strokes. It is caused by trying to push water directly backward. The dropped elbow causes most of the force to be directed upward, reducing propulsion while also disrupting horizontal alignment and increasing resistance to forward motion.

For years swimmers have been told to keep their elbows up and push water backward at the same time. This is difficult, if not impossible, to do. One need only simulate stroking motions on land against resistance to understand this difficulty. You are able to apply more force when your elbows are below your hands and moving in advance of them because the biceps contribute to the total force produced and because the posterior deltoid and latissimus dorsi muscles work at more effective angles of pull. Thus it is quite natural for swimmers who have been taught to push water backward to seek the stronger (elbow down) position as they push their hands backward through the water. However, as shown in Figure 1.28, they exert force in directions that reduce rather than increase propulsive force. The dropped elbow is not evident when swimmers use lift for propulsion. The fastest swimmers do not drop their elbows because they are not pushing their hands backward through the water. Although they may not realize they are doing so, they are sweeping their hands in primarily downward and inward directions during the first half of the underwater armstroke. It is natural for the elbow to remain above the hand when the hand is moving downward and outward or inward and upward. The use of sweeping, rather than paddling, motion eliminates the problem of a dropped elbow.

Chronic Shoulder Pain

There seems to be less incidence of chronic shoulder pain when swimmers use lift-dominated rather than drag-dominated propulsion. This may be because strain on the tendons and ligaments of the shoulder joint is reduced when the elbow remains above the hand as a natural result of downward and inward motion, rather than straining against the tendency to drop it while pushing the hands backward through the water.

Chronic shoulder pain is believed to be caused by friction that develops as the proximal head of the humerus "rubs" across the supraspinatus tendon, the biceps tendon, and the coracoacromial ligament (Kennedy 1978). Medial rotation, that is, trying to keep your elbow up while pushing your hand backward, increases this friction because it causes the humerus to be thrust forward in closer contact with the ligamentous structure of the shoulder joint (see fig. 1.29). Medial rotation should be less intense when your hand is moving downward. Therefore, the friction between the humerus and the tendons and ligaments of the shoulder joint should be reduced. Many swimmers with a history of severe tendonitis have experienced little or no shoulder pain when they substituted sweeping for paddling motions.

The Role of the Legs in Hydrodynamic Propulsion

For years there has been controversy as to whether the flutter kick of the front and back crawl and the dolphin kick of the butterfly were propulsive. The principal argument against their propulsive capability was that the feet cannot be placed in an effective position to push water backward during each kick cycle. This argument does not apply to lift-dominated propulsion because the feet

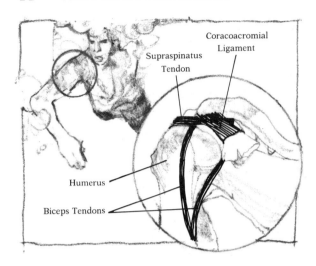

Figure 1.29. Anatomy of the shoulder joint. Chronic shoulder pain is believed to be caused by friction that develops when the head of the humerus rotates past the supraspinatus tendon, the biceps tendon, and the coracoacromial ligament. Rotating the upper arm in a medial direction, as swimmers do when they attempt to push water backward while maintaining a "high" elbow, will thrust the humerus forward and should therefore increase this friction. Sweeping the hand down and out, rather than pushing it backward, allows the elbow to remain above the hand without thrusting the humerus forward. This should reduce friction and the likelihood of developing chronic shoulder pain.

need not face backward in order to propel the swimmer forward. When lift is used, propulsion can be generated during the flutter and dolphin kicks in much the same manner that a dolphin is propelled by the vertical movements of its tail. The propulsive actions of a dolphin's tail are illustrated in Figure 1.30. The downward motion of the tail creates a pressure differential that exerts a lift force in a forward direction and propels the animal forward.

There appear to be five leg sweeps used in the competitive strokes. The dolphin and flutter kicks of the butterfly, front crawl, and back crawl contain a downbeat and upbeat. In the breaststroke the leg movements are best described as an outsweep, downsweep, and insweep. These leg sweeps and their propulsive capabilities will be described in detail in later chapters on the competitive strokes.

Teaching Swimmers to Use Lift for Propulsion

Some swimmers find it difficult to grasp the concept of using their hands as propeller blades after so many years of being instructed to use them as paddles.

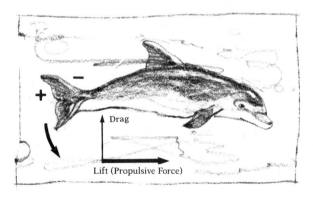

Figure 1.30. A dolphin's propulsive tail action. The way in which a dolphin propels its body with its tail is shown. Downward motion of the tail causes drag in an upward direction. Since lift occurs perpendicular to drag, it acts in a forward direction and propels the dolphin forward.

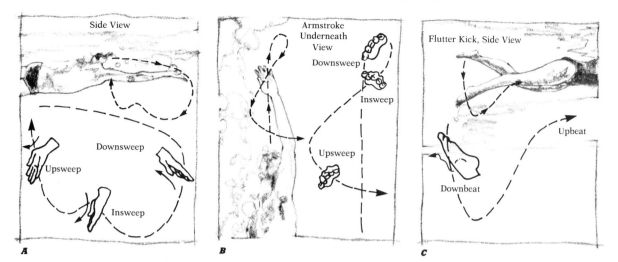

Figure 1.31. The effect of hand and foot pitch on deflecting water backward. Perhaps the easiest way to teach swimmers to use the proper angles of attack is to show how the pitch of the hands and feet can cause water to be deflected backward as it passes over them. Side and underneath views (**A** and **B**) of the crawl stroke armstroke are used to illustrate this point. The various outward and inward hand pitches and the way they deflect water backward are shown in the enlarged stroke patterns.

The downbeat of the flutter kick is used to illustrate the concept of water being deflected backward by the feet (**C**). This concept will be discussed further in the chapters on the four competitive strokes.

They can learn to move their limbs in lateral and vertical rather than backward directions easily enough. However, achieving the proper pitch seems to be difficult. Swimmers who have been taught to push water backward tend to pitch their hands almost perpendicular to the direction of motion, using them like paddles to push water downward, inward, upward, and backward. This is worse than no pitch at all because, as was illustrated in Figure 1.12, there is little if any lift force produced, and the drag force is exerted opposite the direction of limb motion, disrupting body alignment and decelerating forward speed.

Swimmers seem to "find" the correct angles of attack more quickly when they are taught to visualize water being deflected backward by their hands and feet as they travel in lateral and vertical directions. Swimmers find the concept of deflecting water backward easier to understand than a detailed academic discussion of vector forces, which may be beyond their comprehension and interest. They also find it easier to accept because the concept of deflecting water backward resembles the idea of pushing water backward that they had previously accepted.

The drawings in Figure 1.31 illustrate how the proper pitch can cause water to be deflected backward during each of the four basic sweeping motions of the arms that were described earlier in this chapter. They are presented to assist readers in grasping the concept of deflecting water backward with limb motions that are primarily in lateral and vertical directions. In most cases, the pitch of the hands is illustrated at an angle of attack that is somewhat greater than it should actually be. This was done to show clearly how the various hand pitches can cause water molecules to be deflected backward. Presenting hand and foot pitches in this manner will not cause swimmers to pitch their hands at too great an angle. Their "feel" for the water will help them "find" the proper angle of attack once their hands are pitched in the correct direction.

The Downsweep of the Armstroke

As can be seen in Figure 1.31*A*, pitching the hands out, back (underneath view), and down (side view) as they travel outward and downward causes water passing under the palm to be deflected backward from the fingertips to the wrist. This, of course, increases the pressure differential between the knuckle and palm sides of the hands so that more lift is produced and forward propulsion is greater.

The Insweep of the Armstroke

During the insweep, the hand is moving inward, backward (underneath view), and upward (side view). It is pitched inward and upward so that the water is deflected backward as it passes under the palm from the thumb to the little finger side (see fig. 1.31*A*).

The Upsweep of the Armstroke

The hand travels outward, backward (underneath view), and upward (side view) during the upsweep. Therefore, the direction of water flow will be downward, forward, and inward. With the hand pitched out and up, water will be deflected backward as it passes over the palm from the wrist toward the fingers.

The Downbeat of the Kick

In the flutter and dolphin kicks, the feet travel downward (and outward) during the downbeat, deflecting water backward as they do so (see fig. 1.31*B*). The feet are pitched upward so that the direction of the water that passes over them is changed from upward to backward.

Reducing Water Resistance to Forward Motion

Efficient propulsive force will not in itself ensure peak performances. The water resistance that retards the forward motion of a swimmer's body must also be reduced. This resistance is termed **drag.** Don't be confused by the fact that this term was used in the description of propulsive stroking movements. The drag force that resists the vertical, lateral, and backward movement of a swimmer's limbs is used to generate propulsion; the drag force that retards forward motion of the body reduces velocity without contributing to propulsive force in any way. Reducing the drag that retards forward motion of the body is just as important to efficient swimming as increasing propulsive force.

Laminar Versus Turbulent Flow

Reducing drag is a matter of streamlining your body so there is minimal disturbance to the flow of water molecules that pass by it. Water molecules will flow

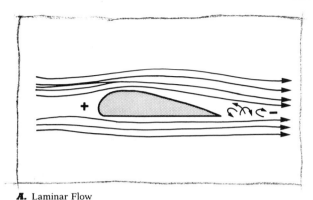

A. Laminar Flow

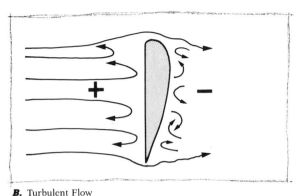

B. Turbulent Flow

Figure 1.32. Laminar versus turbulent flow. Laminar flow is shown in **A**, and turbulent flow is shown in **B**.

in a steady, smooth course past a streamlined object that does not obstruct that flow. This undisturbed motion of fluids is termed **laminar flow.** Laminar flow is illustrated in Figure 1.32*A*.

Laminar flow involves little resistance because the water molecules slip past the object with little change in direction or loss of speed (see fig. 1.32*A*). However, if the molecules are caused to flow around an object that presents an obstruction to their direction of motion, they are diverted from their path and become **turbulent.** They rebound in random directions intruding upon adjacent laminar streams, colliding with the molecules in those streams and causing them to become turbulent. This disturbance extends to the laminar flow of other streams in an ever widening circumference (see fig. 1.32*B*), creating a high-pressure area in front of the object that retards its forward motion. This is because the sudden and violent changes of direction of the water molecules slow their forward speed and in some cases reverse their direction (Hay 1973). The molecules that do travel around the object cannot change direction quickly enough to follow its contour. Therefore they also become turbulent, forming a low-pressure area behind the object. A characteristic of such a low-pressure area is the formation of whirling currents called **eddy currents.** These currents create a suction effect that retards forward progress. Thus, turbulent flow creates a high-pressure area in front that holds a swimmer back, and a low-pressure area behind that tends to pull the swimmer back.

Turbulent flow is increased in relation to the shape of the objects that obstruct laminar streams. As illustrated in Figure 1.33, flat objects (see fig. 1.33*A*) cause abrupt changes in water direction that increase turbulence. This is because a large number of flow streams are disturbed as the water molecules travel a greater distance to pass around the objects. On the other hand, tapered or streamlined objects create less turbulence because the water molecules can change directions gradually as they pass around them (see fig. 1.33*B*).

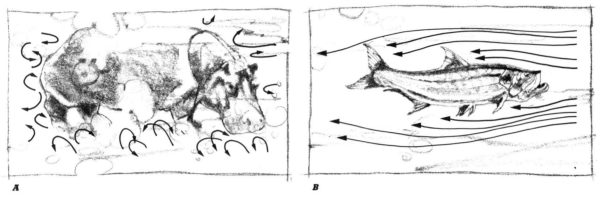

Figure 1.33. The effects of shape on laminar flow. **A** shows a flat surface, and **B** shows a tapered surface.

The ideal form for creating minimal drag is that of a fish (see fig. 1.33*B*). Fish have gently curving forms that cause minimal disturbances of the laminar flow of water as they pass through it. The tapered leading edge reduces turbulence in front because the streams of water molecules can change direction gradually as they flow around the fish's body. The tapered trailing edge reduces eddy currents behind the fish because the water molecules unite and re-establish laminar flow almost immediately after flowing past the fish's tail.

Unfortunately, the human body is larger and has flatter surfaces than those of a fish. Therefore, some drag is unavoidable. However, certain body positions

Figure 1.34. Good and poor horizontal alignment during the front crawl stroke. Swimmer **A** is in an inclined position. The hips are deep and the kick is unnecessarily wide and deep. As a result, this swimmer's body takes up more space in the water than it needs to and thus disrupts the flow of a large number of water streams.

Swimmer **B** is in a streamlined position. The entire body is nearly horizontal with the surface and the kick is not excessively deep. This position minimizes turbulence and form drag because fewer streams of water are disrupted.

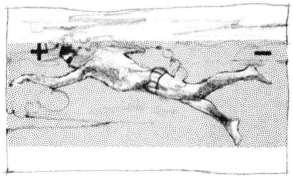

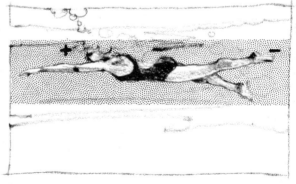

can permit swimmers to present more streamlined shapes to the oncoming water. These body positions will be discussed later in this chapter.

Types of Drag   Experts have defined three categories of drag that act on bodies that are suspended in a fluid. They are **form drag, wave drag,** and **frictional drag.**

Form drag. Body positions that are less than horizontal take up more space and thus increase resistance to forward motion. Excessive vertical and lateral movements of the body do the same because they also cause the body to take up more space and thus disrupt the laminar flow. The increased resistance caused by poor horizontal and lateral alignment is termed *form drag* because it is caused by the forms swimmers' bodies take as they move through the water.

In order to reduce form drag, swimmers should maintain their bodies near the surface with minimal inclination from head to feet. (There are exceptions to this statement where butterfly and breaststroke swimming are concerned. They will be described in the chapters concerning those strokes.) A contrast between good and poor horizontal body alignment is shown in Figure 1.34. The swimmer in Figure 1.34*A* carries the head and shoulders too high in the water. The back is arched in an attempt to hydroplane while swimming the front crawl. This position of the upper body forces the hips downward and the kick is deeper than that of the streamlined swimmer in Figure 1.34*B*. The inclined body of the swimmer in Figure 1.34*A* takes up more space in the water, encountering and disrupting the laminar flow of a greater number of water molecules. These molecules change directions more abruptly and intrude on adjacent streams, disrupting their laminar flow as well. The turbulence in front and the eddy currents behind create a large pressure differential that will retard forward velocity.

An increase in form drag also occurs when there is excessive lateral motion of the swimmer's body. The effect of excessive lateral body motion on form drag is illustrated in Figure 1.35*A*. Front and back crawl swimmers sometimes use improper recovery and stroking actions that cause their hips to swing outward in one direction while their feet swing outward in the other direction. This increases the number of water molecules that become turbulent, resulting in an increase in form drag.

Excessive up and down motions of the body increase form drag in much the same manner (see fig. 1.36). The butterfly swimmer in Figure 1.36*A* is undulating excessively. This causes the swimmer to disturb the laminar flow of a greater number of water molecules than are disrupted by the swimmer in Figure 1.36*B*. The increased turbulence in front and the eddy currents behind create a large pressure differential that acts opposite the swimmer's forward direction of motion, reducing forward velocity. In addition, such motions also increase wave drag, which will be discussed next.

Wave drag. Wave drag is caused by turbulence at the surface of the water. When a swimmer's movements increase the size of waves, the increased tur-

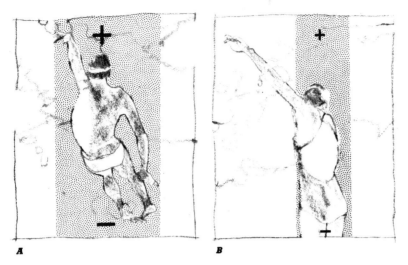

Figure 1.35. The effect of excessive lateral motion on drag. Backstroke swimmer **A** suffers the effects of excessive lateral body motion on form drag. Recovering the right arm in a lateral manner causes the hips and legs to swing outward in opposite directions. This increases turbulence because the laminar flow of a greater number of water molecules is disrupted. The turbulence increases the high pressure area in front and the low pressure area behind, reducing forward speed.

Swimmer **B** has recovered the arm in a more linear fashion. The swimmer's body remains in good lateral alignment and thus causes less form drag.

Figure 1.36. The effect of excessive vertical motion on drag. The butterfly swimmer in **A** is undulating excessively, disturbing the laminar flow of a large number of water molecules. The increased turbulence in front and the eddy currents behind create a large pressure differential opposite the swimmer's direction of motion, reducing forward velocity. The swimmer in **B** is undulating the proper amount. This swimmer disrupts a minimum number of laminar streams, and form drag is minimized.

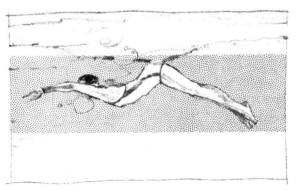

bulence creates a high-pressure area in front of the swimmer, literally a "wall of water," that retards forward motion. Waves exert such a powerful retarding effect that they increase drag in proportion to the cube of the velocity. That is, when swimmers double their speed through waves, drag is increased by a factor of eight (Northrip, Logan, and McKinney 1974). In most other fluid motion, drag increases in proportion to the square of the velocity.

The most common causes of wave drag, other than poor pool design and inadequate racing lanes, are smashing arm entries and excessive lateral and vertical body movements.

The speed of a swimmer who smashes his hand into the water will be reduced by 30 percent within 1/16 of a second after the entry takes place. It then requires nearly half an arm stroke to regain the original velocity. Thus, the average velocity is reduced for the entire stroke cycle. This reduction in forward speed, when multiplied by several strokes per pool length, can be devastating. Smashing arm entries and excessive lateral and vertical body movements should be minimized whenever possible.

Frictional drag. The friction between a swimmer's body and the water molecules that come in contact with it causes the laminar flow of those molecules to be interrupted. As a result, they collide with other molecules behind and adjacent to them, increasing drag and retarding forward motion.

The major factor in frictional drag is surface smoothness. Smooth surfaces cause less friction. For this reason, swimmers have adopted the practice of shaving the hair from their bodies before important races. In addition, they wear suits that fit smoothly over the skin with no gaps or wrinkles to "catch" water. Some swimmers also cover their bodies with oil and other substances that are supposed to reduce friction between the skin and the water.

Experience seems to indicate that these procedures have a beneficial effect on performance. However, Clarys (1978) has stated that frictional drag is negligible on the moving swimmer's body. His research indicates that swimmers, even in the most streamlined position, create so much wave and form drag that the laminar flow of water around their bodies cannot possibly be maintained. In other words, the turbulence from wave and form drag is already so great that any increase in drag due to skin friction would be negligible.

Why then do we see nearly universal reductions in time when swimmers "shave down" and wear the new friction-reducing bathing suits? There are several possible explanations for this contradiction. The most obvious is that frictional drag does exert a significant retarding effect on forward velocity. It is also possible that shaving down and wearing skin suits have become "big meet" rituals that accompany and, therefore, are mistakenly believed to be related to improvements in performance. A third explanation is that shaving down increases swimmers' kinesthetic sensitivity and, in so doing, improves their stroke efficiency and thus their performances. Results indicate it would be wise to continue shaving down and wearing skin suits until we know the effect of frictional drag on swimming speed.

The Effect of Speed on Drag   Drag increases as an algebraic function of increased speed. The effect is so potent that when forward velocity is doubled, drag is quadrupled. This information may seem academic since it would be foolish for competitors to swim slowly and lose races for the sake of reducing drag. However, it indicates the wisdom of pacing the early portions of most races. An athlete who swims the first half of a race at a slower speed than an opponent will not be required to expend as much energy to overcome drag. If the swimmer's pace is sufficient to remain in contention, and if the athletes are nearly equal in ability, the swimmer who paces him- or herself should be able to win the race by finishing faster than a more fatigued competitor.

REFERENCES

Aviation Research Associates. 1943. *How Planes Fly.* New York: Harper and Row.

Barna, P. S. 1969. *Fluid Mechanics for Engineers.* New York: Plenum Press.

Barthels, K., and Adrian, M. J. 1974. "Three Dimensional Spatial Hand Patterns of Skilled Butterfly Swimmers." *Swimming II*, ed. J. P. Clarys and L. Lewillie, pp. 154–160. Baltimore: University Park Press.

Brown, R. M., and Counsilman, J. E. 1971. "The Role of Lift in Propelling Swimmers." *Biomechanics*, ed. J. M. Cooper, pp. 179–188. Chicago: Athletic Institute.

Clarys, J. P. 1978. "Human Morphology and Hydrodynamics." Paper presented at the International Congress of Sports Sciences, July 25–29, University of Alberta, Edmonton, Canada.

Crist, J. M. 1979. "An Analytical Comparison Between Two Types of Butterfly Pull Patterns: The Crossover and the Keyhole." *Swimming Technique* 15 (4):110–117.

Firby, H. 1975. *Howard Firby on Swimming.* London: Pelham.

Hay, J. G. 1973. *The Biomechanics of Sports Techniques.* Englewood Cliffs, N.J.: Prentice-Hall.

Kennedy, J. C. 1978. "Orthopaedic Manifestations." *Swimming Medicine IV*, ed. B. Eriksson and B. Forberg, pp. 94–97. Baltimore: University Park Press.

Northrip, J. W., Logan, G. A., and McKinney, W. C. 1974. *Introduction to Biomechanic Analysis of Sport.* Dubuque, Iowa: Wm. C. Brown.

Schleihauf, R. E., Jr. 1974. "A Biomechanical Analysis of Freestyle." *Swimming Technique* 11:89–96.

———. 1978a. "Swimming Propulsion: A Hydrodynamic Analysis." *American Swimming Coaches Association 1977 World Clinic Yearbook*, ed. B. Ousley, pp. 49–86. Fort Lauderdale, Fla.: American Swimming Coaches Association.

———. 1978b. "The Coefficient of Lift and Drag for Human Hand Models as Measured in an Open Water Channel." Paper presented at the International Congress of Sports Sciences, July 25–29, University of Alberta, Edmonton, Canada.

Wood, T. C., and Holt, L. 1978. "Fluid Dynamic Analysis of the Propulsive Potential of the Hand and Forearm in Swimming." Paper presented at the International Congress of Sports Sciences, July 25–29, University of Alberta, Edmonton, Canada.

CHAPTER 2

The Front Crawl Stroke

The front crawl stroke, or freestyle, has evolved into the fastest of the competitive strokes. The mechanics of this stroke involve (1) the armstroke, (2) the kick, (3) the timing of arms and legs, (4) the body position, and (5) the breathing.

The Armstroke

The underwater armstroke consists of a downsweep, insweep, and upsweep. These were described in general terms in chapter 1. In this chapter they will be discussed as they relate to the specific parts of the front crawl armstroke: the entry, catch, stretch, and recovery.

Entry   The entry should be made forward of your head, between the middle of your head and the tip of your shoulder. Your arm should be flexed slightly, with your elbow above your hand so that your fingertips are the first part of your arm to enter the water. Your hand should enter 8 to 10 inches behind a point that could be reached by your completely extended arm. It should be slipped into the water on its side with the palm facing outward 30 to 40 degrees from a prone position (see frame *E* of fig. 2.12). This allows the fingertips to slice into the water with minimal drag. It is a good teaching technique to have swimmers attempt to move their wrists, elbows, and shoulders through the same "hole" in the water that was made by their hands at entry. This is not actually possible; however, an attempt to do so will encourage an entry with the proper reach and minimal turbulence. The swimmers in Figure 2.1 are entering their arms correctly.

A

B

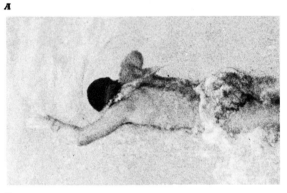

C

Figure 2.1. Arm entry during the front crawl stroke, side (*A* and *B*) and top (*C*) views.

Common errors on entry. Many swimmers enter their hands in a prone position, as shown in Figure 2.2. This will increase drag because the flat surface of the back of their hand pushes forward against the water. Swimmers who insist on entering their hands in a prone position can reduce drag if wrist flexion is minimal. In this position the back of the hand is not presented to the oncoming flow.

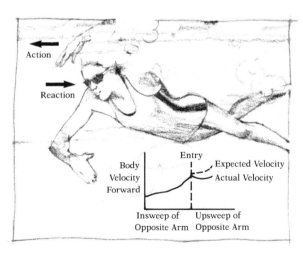

Figure 2.2. Incorrect hand entry, pushing water forward at entry. The swimmer in this illustration has placed her hand in the water with her wrist flexed. This causes the flat surface of the back of her hand to be pushed forward against the water (action) creating drag (reaction) that decelerates her forward speed.

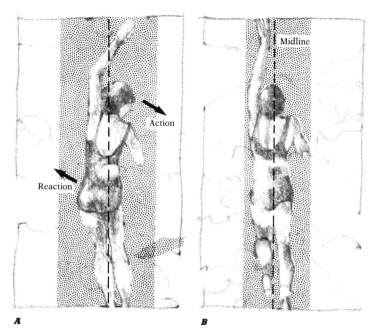

Figure 2.3. The effect of overreaching on the entry. Swimmer **A** is overreaching on the entry. Reaching across the midline causes her hips to be pulled outward, which increases form and wave drag. Swimmer **B** is entering properly. Her body remains aligned and drag is reduced.

Overreaching is another common error. The effect of this mistake is illustrated in Figure 2.3*A*. Your hips and legs can be pulled out of alignment as a reaction to the action of reaching across your head. Drag will be increased accordingly.

Underreaching, entering your arm into the water too close to your head, can also be detrimental to forward speed. It increases the possibility of pushing your arm forward through the water for a longer distance, exerting a counterforce that reduces forward velocity. The effect of this error is illustrated in Figure 2.4.

Smashing your hand downward into the water should also be avoided. It causes unnecessary vertical body motions and increases surface turbulence and wave drag (see fig. 2.5).

Stretch   After entry the swimmer's arm is extended forward under the surface. This phase of the armstroke is called a **stretch** rather than a **glide** because the arm does not stop moving forward. However, the swimmer does not begin the propulsive phase of the stroke immediately. It would be inefficient to begin stroking immediately after entry because the other arm is midway through its propulsive phase. It would also be inefficient to stop moving the arm forward because,

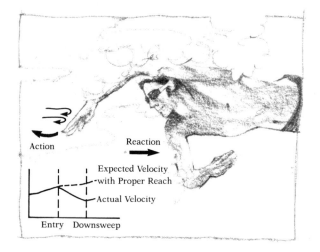

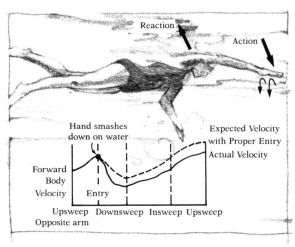

Figure 2.4. The effect on propulsion of underreaching on the entry. When swimmers place their hands into the water too early, as the swimmer in this illustration is doing, they tend to extend their arm downward, then upward in a curvilinear path that exerts unnecessary force against the oncoming flow of water. As a result, a counterforce reduces forward velocity.

Figure 2.5. The effect on propulsion of smashing the hand into the water. The swimmer in this illustration is smashing her hand downward into the water. This causes unnecessary upward motions of the trunk and head and also increases the turbulence in front of the swimmer, creating waves that retard her forward speed.

according to the law of inertia, additional muscular force would be required to restart the arm motion when it is time to begin applying propulsive force. The stretch is illustrated in frames *C* to *F* of Figure 2.6. These photos show Chris Cavanaugh's freestyle. Side and underneath views of his stroke are shown in Figures 2.7 and 2.8 respectively. Be careful to slide your hand and arm forward in a gentle manner so that drag against the stretching arm is not so great that it reduces the propulsive force generated by the stroking arm. Your arm should not be directed upward or downward because either motion in either direction would present the broad surface of your hand and arm to the oncoming flow. The effect of this error is illustrated in Figure 2.4.

Figure 2.6. A front view of the freestyle. The swimmer is Chris Cavanaugh. Chris has won several national championships in the freestyle and individual medley events. Most recently he won the 100-meter freestyle and the high point trophy at the 1981 USS Long Course Championships.

A-C. The downsweep of his right arm.

C-D. The insweep of his right arm and entry of his left.

E-F. The upsweep of his right arm, the stretch of his left.

G. The release of his right arm. Notice that his palm is facing inward so his hand can leave the water with minimal drag.

H-I. The downsweep of his left arm.

J. The insweep of his left arm.

K-L. The upsweep of his left arm.

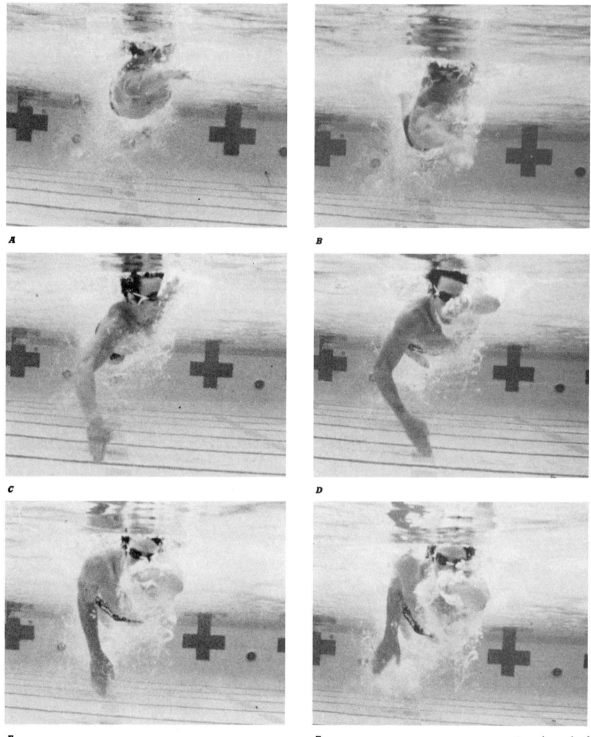

A

B

C

D

E

F

continued overleaf

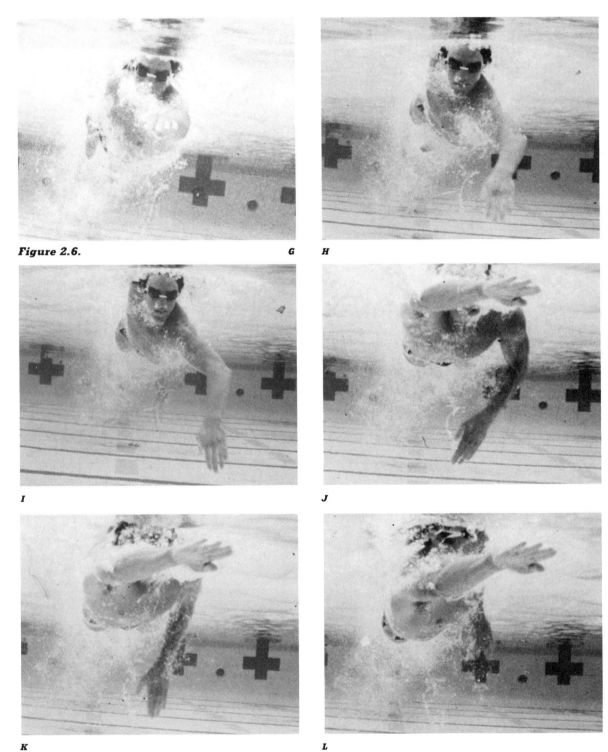

Figure 2.6.

G

H

I

J

K

L

During the stretch your wrist should remain in a natural position midway between flexion and extension. Your hand may be rotated to a prone (palm downward) position as it slices forward. The stretch should be timed so the stretching arm is nearing complete extension as the other arm finishes its underwater stroke. At that point, the catch is made.

Figure 2.7. Chris Cavanaugh's freestyle, viewed from the side.

A-B. The downsweep of his right arm.

C. The insweep of his right arm.

D-E. The upsweep of his right arm.

F-G. The downsweep of his left arm.

H. The insweep of his left arm.

I-J. The upsweep of his left arm.

A

B

C

D

continued overleaf

Figure 2.7.

E   F

G   H

I   J

Figure 2.8. Chris Cavanaugh's freestyle, viewed from underneath.

A-C. The downsweep of his left arm.

D-E. The insweep of his left arm.

F-H. The upsweep of his left arm.

I. The downsweep of his right arm.

J-K. The insweep of his right arm.

L-M. The transition from the insweep to the upsweep. He uses his hand like a paddle to push water backward.

N-O. The upsweep of his right arm.

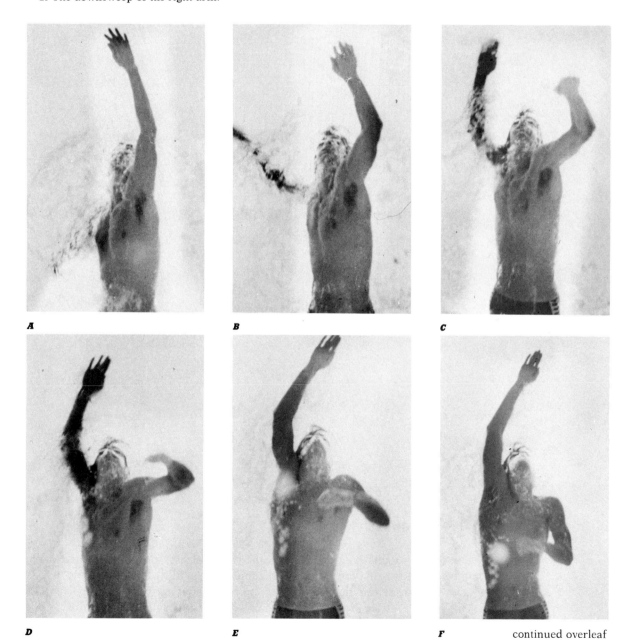

A

B

C

D

E

F continued overleaf

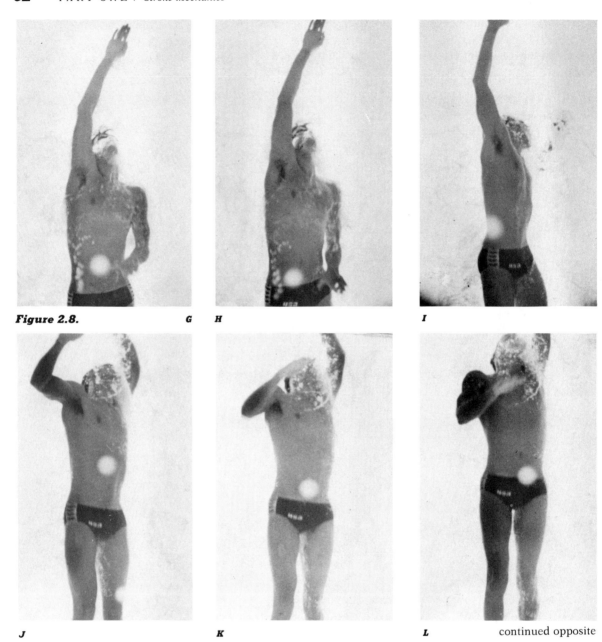

Figure 2.8.   G   H   I

J   K   L   continued opposite

Catch   The catch is made precisely as the other arm releases pressure on the water. The swimmer is making a catch in frame *A* of Figure 2.9. The wrist is flexed downward approximately 40 degrees and rotated outward as it was upon entry. This pitch creates a lift force on the hand. The elbow begins to flex at this point, in order to stabilize the hand. The force is transferred to the body so that the

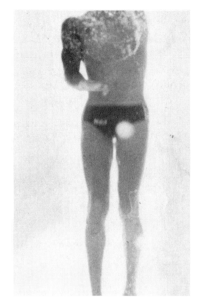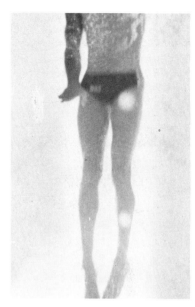

Figure 2.8.   M   N   O

head and shoulders surge forward over the arm. Elbow flexion is the signal that the most propulsive phases of the underwater armstroke have begun.

It is very important that swimmers make a strong catch. The hand should be moving slowly during the stretch and they should "feel" for the catch before accelerating hand speed downward and outward in the first propulsive phase of the armstroke, the downsweep.

Downsweep The downsweep is pictured in frames *A* and *B* Figure 2.9. Stroke plots showing the direction of hand motion from front, side and underneath views are shown in Figure 2.10. The downsweep occurs between letters C and D in Figure 2.10.

Your hand should sweep downward and outward in a curvilinear path. You should not consciously emphasize the outward motion. It occurs naturally. As your shoulder rolls into the stroke, following your arm downward, your hand will automatically slide outward.

Your elbow is gradually flexed during the downsweep to keep your hand traveling in a downward direction. No attempt should be made to pull your arm backward under your body.

The downward velocity of your hand gradually increases from beginning to end of the downsweep. Downward velocity must exceed backward velocity for propulsion to be lift dominated. (The way in which this sweep provides propulsion was described in Chapter 1.)

Your palm should be pitched downward, outward and backward during the downsweep, causing water to be deflected backward as it passes under the palm from fingertips to wrist. The effect of this hand pitch on the deflection of water backward is shown in the stroke plots of Figure 2.10. Your hand should

Figure 2.9. A diagonal view of the front crawl stroke. The swimmer is Todd Lincoln, high school All-American in the 200-yard and 500-yard freestyles. He is using a 6-beat kick.

A–B. The downsweep of the right arm. His right hand has entered the water, and it sweeps down and out with his palm pitched out and back.

C. The insweep of the right arm and entry of the left. After the downsweep, he sweeps his hand inward, upward, and backward until it is under his head and near the midline of his body.

D–G. The upsweep of the right arm, stretch of the left. As his hand passes under the midline of his body, he begins to sweep it backward, outward, then upward un-

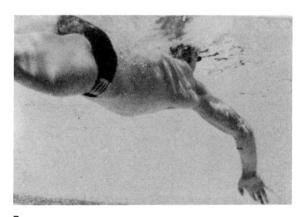

A

B

C

D

E

F

til it reaches the front of his thigh. His palm is pitched outward, upward, and backward.

H. The release of the right arm and the beginning of the downsweep of the left arm. When his hand approaches his thigh, he releases pressure on the water and turns his palm inward so his hand can leave the water on its side with minimal resistance.

I. The downsweep of the left arm.

J–L. The inseep of the left arm, entry of the right. Notice the inward and upward pitch of his left hand.

G

H

I

J

K

L

continued overleaf

Figure 2.9.   **M**   **N**

O

Figure 2.9. continued

M-N. The upsweep of the left arm, stretch of the right. Notice the upward, outward, and backward pitch of his left hand.

O. The release of the left arm and beginning of the downsweep of the right arm.

be cupped somewhat to improve its airfoil shape. Angles of attack of 30 to 40 degrees are recommended relative to both the downward and outward directions of movement.

As your hand approaches its deepest point, the downsweep is "rounded-off" into an insweep. The downsweep appears to be the least propulsive phase of the underwater armstroke. Swimmers use less effort in this phase than in later sweeps. However, it is important to execute the downsweep correctly so that the arm will be in position for an effective insweep.

Common errors in the downsweep. Some swimmers have been taught to turn the palm inward immediately upon entry on the mistaken theory that this quickly places the hand in position to pull water backward. This would be a good teaching technique if drag were the major source of propulsion. Since it is not, turning the palm inward immediately after entry reduces propulsion during the downsweep and also places the hand in a poor position to execute the insweep that follows. This error is illustrated in Figure 2.11. The inward force of the palm against the water creates a counterforce that produces unwanted lateral movements of the body. These movements increase drag and reduce forward velocity.

Many swimmers who have been taught to pull inward immediately after entry, begin their underwater stroke in this manner but manage, perhaps because of their "feel" for propulsion, to get their hand pitched outward and moving downward and outward during the downsweep. This "self-correction,"

Figure 2.10. Stroke plots of the front crawl stroke viewed from the front, side, and underneath. These stroke plots show how the combination of proper hand pitch and direction of movement can cause water to be deflected backward so that the swimmer's body is accelerated forward. Diagrams such as these help swimmers visualize how forward motion can be achieved by propeller-like sweeps of the hands.

A. Front View **B.** Side View **C.** Underneath View

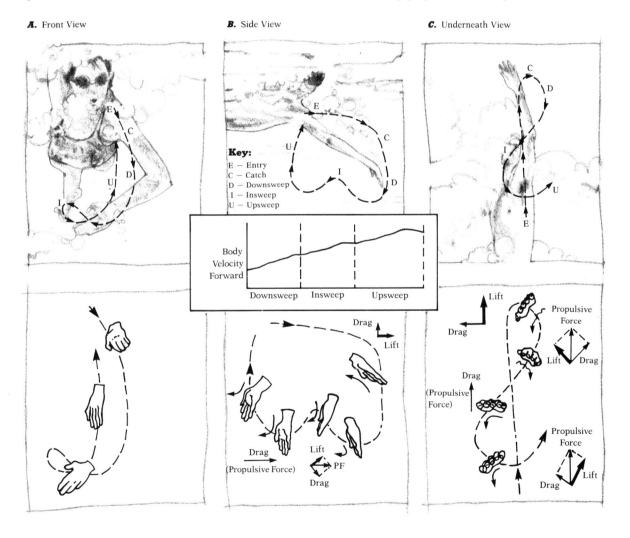

Key:
E — Entry
C — Catch
D — Downsweep
I — Insweep
U — Upsweep

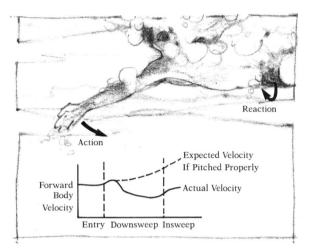

Figure 2.11. The effect of pitching the hand inward immediately after entry. The swimmer in this illustration is shown making the mistake of pitching the hand inward almost immediately after entry. This reduces forward velocity during the downsweep and subsequent insweep and may cause drag-increasing sideward body motion as well.

which can be seen in the films of several world-class freestylers, is further evidence that the downsweep should be performed as described.

Pushing down on the water with the palm is another common mistake that is made during the downsweep. (This error was discussed in Chapter 1.) The angle of attack of the palm is too obtuse; drag force pushes your body upward and horizontal alignment is disrupted. To correct this error, flex your wrist and cup your hand slightly during the downsweep so that water is deflected backward gradually from fingertips to wrist. In this way lift rather than drag force will predominate, form drag will be reduced, and propulsive force will be increased.

A third problem is the dropped elbow. (This error was also discussed in Chapter 1.) If the elbow drops below the hand during the downsweep, it is because you are trying to push your hand backward through the water rather than sweeping it downward. The dropped elbow rarely, if ever, occurs if you direct your hand downward during this phase of the stroke.

Insweep The insweep is illustrated in frames *I* and *J* Figure 2.9. The distance over which it is employed is marked by the letters D and I in the stroke plots in Figure 2.10.

The insweep begins as your hand approaches the deepest point of the downsweep. The direction of hand motion is "rounded-off" from downward and outward, becoming inward, upward, and backward as your hand sweeps under your body from a position outside the shoulder to one near or beyond the midline. The hand is accelerated inward, upward, and backward reaching a peak as your hand approaches the midline of your body. The pitch of your hand is rotated from an outward, downward, and backward facing position to an inward, upward, and backward pitch during the insweep. This causes water to be deflected backward as it passes across the palm from thumb to little finger side (see fig. 2.10). Angles of attack of 20 to 40 degrees are recommended with respect to both the inward and upward directions of hand movement (Schleihauf 1978).

It is very important to make the transition from downsweep to insweep in the proper manner. Propulsion should be drag dominated during this and other transition phases in order to maintain forward speed until the hands have changed pitch and lift can, once again, become the predominant propulsive force. This is achieved by pushing backward against the water during the time the hand is facing backward while changing from an outward to inward pitch. Notice, in the stroke plots in Figure 2.10, that hand motion is almost directly backward and that the palm is facing almost directly backward during this and other transition points in the stroke. The transitions between sweeps are also drag dominated in the other competitive strokes.

Some swimmers sweep the hand inward beyond the midline of the body; others complete the insweep somewhere between the outer border and the midline. The reasons for this discrepancy were discussed in chapter 1. The distance the hand travels under the body probably depends on the swimmer's ability to attain an inward and upward pitch early in the insweep. If the swimmer is slow to change pitch, the hand will have to sweep under the body a greater distance to gain adequate propulsion. If the pitch is changed effectively, the hand will sweep inward to approximately the midline before making the transition to the next propulsive phase, the upsweep.

Swimmers usually sweep the arm opposite their breathing side inward over a longer distance. This is because most swimmers roll more to the breathing side and a larger insweep is needed to rotate their bodies back to a prone position.

Common errors in the insweep. Some swimmers make the mistake of pitching the hand inward before it passes inside the shoulder line. This reduces propulsion from the downsweep and causes the insweep to be terminated early because, when the hand is pitched inward too soon, it will rotate past the optimum angle of attack before the insweep is completed. An opposite, but nonetheless common problem is failing to pitch the hand inward and upward during the insweep. Many swimmers "slip" their hand inward with little or no inward pitch, reducing the lift force and lessening the propulsive force that could have been exerted.

Upsweep   The upsweep is best viewed in frames *D* to *G* of Figure 2.9. The distance covered during this sweep is marked by the letters I and U on the stroke plot in Figure 2.10.

The transition from insweep to upsweep can be seen clearly in frames *D* and *E* of Figure 2.9. Propulsion is drag dominated during this phase. You should be pushing backward as the direction of hand motion and pitch are changing from inward toward outward. The transition takes place as your hand passes under your head. Push almost directly backward from chest to waist, as indicated by the stroke plots and hand positions in the side and underneath views in Figure 2.10. The transition is completed as your hand passes your hips. From there, hand motion accelerates outward as well as upward and backward until your hand approaches the anterior portion of your thigh. *Do not try to "push" water to the surface.* Pressure is released as your hand approaches your thigh, and your palm is rotated inward so it can slide out of the water on edge with minimal drag.

Your hand should be pitched outward and upward during the upsweep (see fig. 2.10). This pitch is attained by relaxing your wrist and allowing the water to "push" your hand into the proper position. The downward, forward, and inward pressure of the water will cause your hand to be extended and rotated outward at the wrist. The hand will appear to be facing backward; however, as can be seen in the side view stroke plots in Figure 2.10, it is actually pitched upward with respect to its direction of motion. The outward and upward angles of attack should be between 30 and 40 degrees to their respective directions of motion. This causes water to be deflected gradually backward as it passes downward and inward from wrist to fingertips (see fig. 2.10).

Although swimmers appear to be pushing water backward during the upsweep, the side view stroke plot in Figure 2.10 shows clearly that the hand is moving almost directly upward once it passes outside the hips. Also, the surface photographs of the recovery in Figure 2.12 show that the swimmer's elbow is somewhat flexed when his hand leaves the water. Actually, the elbow should remain flexed until late in the upsweep. At that time, extending it somewhat will prevent your hand from traveling forward when your elbow leaves the water and starts forward in the recovery. In this way, propulsion can be maintained until your hand approaches your thigh. After that, however, your hand should follow your elbow because further extension would only interfere with the smooth transition from upsweep to recovery.

Hand speed is accelerated outward and then upward during the upsweep (see fig. 1.13). This is the most propulsive phase of the stroke and swimmers apply force accordingly.

Common errors in the upsweep. The most common mistake made during the upsweep occurs when swimmers think of this motion as a push backward. When a swimmer is trying to push the hand backward, the upsweep is initiated with a rapid extension of the elbow that causes the backward speed of the hand to exceed its outward and upward speed. Because of this, propulsion becomes drag dominated and thus less efficient. Less distance is traveled with each stroke and a more rapid turnover is used to compensate.

Another mistake swimmers often make is to push water upward with the palm. This occurs when they are instructed to push backward to the surface. They mistakenly believe they are pushing backward, when in reality they are pushing water upward. (This error is illustrated in fig. 1.26.) The drag force on the palm acts in a downward direction that tends to submerge the hips and decelerate forward speed. Pressure on the water should be released as the hand approaches the thigh, and it should pass the thighs on its side with the palm facing inward (see frame *H* of fig. 2.9).

Recovery   The purpose of the recovery is to place the arm in position for another stroke. Most front crawl swimmers prefer a high-elbow recovery because it serves this purpose without wasting effort or disturbing body alignment.

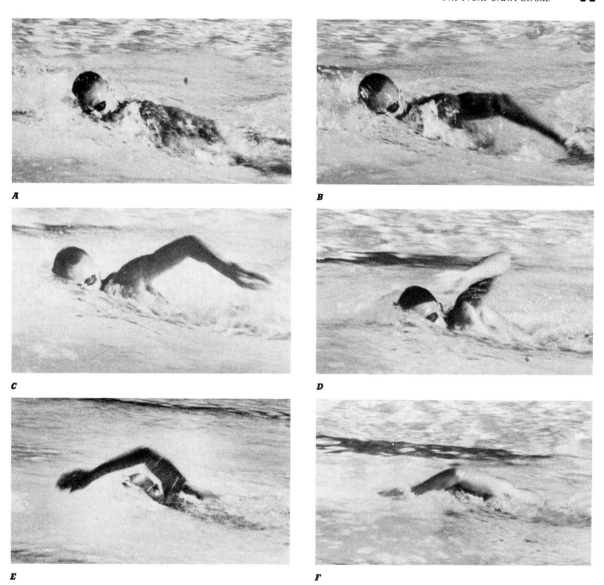

Figure 2.12. The high-elbow recovery. The swimmer is David Tittle, NCAA Division II national record holder in the 200-yard freestyle.

The high-elbow recovery. The sequence of photographs in Figure 2.12 shows a side view of a swimmer executing a high-elbow recovery. When executing the high-elbow recovery, your elbow will break through the surface, moving forward while your hand is completing the upsweep (see frame *A* of fig. 2.12). It will be flexed slightly at this time. Your elbow travels upward and forward after leaving the water with your forearm and hand following. Your palm is rotated inward as it leaves the water so that your hand can slide out, little finger first, with minimal drag (see frame *B* of fig. 2.12). Your arm should travel upward, outward, and forward during the first half of the recovery, with motion becoming forward, inward, and downward as you reach for the entry.

You should begin reaching forward for the entry as your hand passes your shoulder (see frame *D* of fig. 2.12). At that time, your arm begins extending. It continues to extend until it enters the water in front of your shoulder. The entry is made as described earlier in this chapter. The overlap between the end of the upsweep and the beginning of the recovery conserves angular momentum, reducing the muscular effort required to overcome the upward inertia of the arm and start it moving forward.

Once underway, the recovery should be as linear as possible to reduce lateral and vertical forces that would disrupt body alignment. Outward rotation of the shoulder and continued elbow flexion during the first half of the recovery will accomplish this by reducing lateral and upward motions of the hand. Your arm should be relaxed as much as possible during the recovery in order to give your muscles a rest between strokes.

The hand-swing recovery. Another recovery style that has been used by many world-class swimmers is shown in the sequence of photographs in Figure 2.13. This style has been termed the hand-swing recovery because the hand, rather than the elbow, leads the arm movement over the water.

As in the high-elbow recovery, your elbow comes through the surface before your hand. However, your arm is nearly extended after your hand leaves the water. Your hand swings out of the water and is carried above, rather than below your elbow, as it (the hand) travels upward, outward, and forward over the water. Continue this action through the first half of the recovery, with the emphasis on swinging your hand high overhead rather than low and laterally.

When your hand approaches a position above your shoulder, flex your elbow to bring your hand downward and inward. This allows the reach and entry to be made in the same manner described for the high-elbow recovery; that is, with the elbow flexed and the palm pitched outward (see frame *C* of fig. 2.13).

The hand-swing recovery seems best suited for athletes who are "hand oriented" in the learning of skills and to those who have limited shoulder flexibility. The former are able to control their recovery better when they lead with the hand rather than the elbow. Such control may be particularly important when the arms are moving at a rapid rate, as in sprinting. This may account for the observation that more sprinters than distance swimmers use the hand-swing style. Swimmers with limited shoulder flexibility may find it less restrictive to swing their hand overhead because the shoulder can be rotated outward. Greater flexibility is required to swing the arm over the water when the shoulder is rotated inward than when it is rotated outward. When the hand is carried below the elbow it is impossible to rotate the shoulder outward until the second half of the recovery, when the reach for the entry is made.

A

B

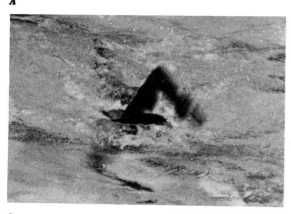

C

Figure 2.13. The hand-swing recovery. Swimmers who use this recovery style roll on their side and swing their hand high overhead in the first half of the recovery. They then flex their elbow, so the entry can be made with a high elbow.

It is interesting that many swimmers use the hand-swing recovery on their breathing side and a lateral recovery with the opposite arm. This is probably because they roll more to the breathing side and can rotate their shoulder outward so that their hand can be carried over the water high and linearly. Because they rotate less to the other side, the shoulder cannot be rotated outward sufficiently and they must recover that arm in a low and lateral manner.

Common errors in the recovery. The most common errors swimmers make during the recovery are (1) "rushing" the arm over the water, and (2) recovering in a low lateral manner. The first wastes energy. The second disrupts lateral alignment.

Rushing the recovery is not easy to correct. A swimmer's natural reaction is to hurry the arm forward in the mistaken notion that it can begin applying force immediately after it enters the water. This does not happen, however. Since your arm travels a shorter distance over the water than underneath, the recovering arm will arrive for the entry when the other arm is only midway through the underwater portion of the armstroke. Thus, it will have to glide in

Figure 2.14. Dropping the elbow on the recovery. The swimmer in this illustration is shown committing the error of dropping her elbow during the reach. This causes her elbow to "drag" forward through the water (**A**) and places it below her hand at entry (**B**), where it will be difficult to attain a good position for an effective downsweep.

front until the stroking arm has completed the upsweep. It is obvious that nothing is gained by rushing the recovery. In reality, more energy is expended and the force of the rapidly moving recovery arm may disrupt lateral body alignment. The recovery should be relaxed and effortless with the arms synchronized so the recovering arm does not arrive early for the entry.

Swinging the arm low and laterally over the water tends to pull the hips outward and disrupts lateral alignment. The recovery must be as linear as possible. In the high-elbow style, this is accomplished by flexing the elbow and carrying the hand close to the body. In the hand-swing recovery, a linear motion is achieved by swinging the hand overhead more than outward.

A less common but nonetheless serious fault is failure to maintain a high elbow during the reach for the entry. This error is illustrated in Figure 2.14. The swimmer makes the mistake of reaching forward for the entry before the hand passes the shoulder. The early reach causes the elbow to drop below the hand and push forward through the water before the hand enters. This increases drag. In addition, it will require more time and effort to get the hand below the arm for an effective downsweep. Swimmers should be cautioned to wait until the hand passes the shoulder before reaching forward.

Timing of the Arms

During the first half of the twentieth century it was common to use catch-up timing. One arm would glide (rest) in front after entry and would not begin the underwater stroke until the other arm had entered the water and nearly "caught-up" with it. The swimmer in Figure 2.15 is using a catch-up stroke.

The theory behind this timing was that muscles were given a rest during the glide. Counsilman (1968) has argued convincingly against this theory. He stressed that the catch-up stroke was less effective because, between the time

Figure 2.15. The catch-up stroke. This swimmer is using a catch-up stroke. He delays beginning the downsweep of the left arm until his right arm enters the water. This delay in applying propulsive force with the left arm causes him to decelerate while he is recovering his right arm.

when the recovering arm leaves the water and the gliding arm begins to stroke, there is an interval when neither arm is supplying propulsive force. This causes a deceleration of forward velocity that far outweighs any rest afforded the muscles.

Today, most world-class swimmers use a more continuous timing. This does not mean, as some instructors have taught, that one arm enters the water as the other leaves. There must be some overlap to the armstroke. One arm should enter the water before the other completes the underwater stroke. In this way, the arm entering the water can be stretched forward and placed in an effective position to apply force while the other arm finishes the upsweep. If the recovering arm did not enter the water until the other had left, there would be a deceleration phase between the upsweep of one armstroke and the downsweep of the other, which would also reduce forward velocity.

There has been considerable controversy concerning the amount of overlap that should occur in the front crawl stroke. Some swimmers feel that the stroking arm should be under the chest when the recovering arm enters the water while others believe the stroking arm should be beneath the waist when the other enters.

This conflict over timing tends to ignore the real relationship of the arms during the stroke. When the armstroke is thought of as three sweeps rather than as a pull and push, the correct timing of the arms is obvious. Among the majority of swimmers, the recovering arm enters the water as the other arm begins the upsweep. The recovering arm then stretches forward until the other arm completes the upsweep, before beginning its propulsive phase. The swimmer in Figure 2.9 is using this timing (see frame C).

Another timing that has been observed among world-class swimmers, particularly 6-beat kickers, has the recovering arm entering the water as the other arm begins the insweep. This is illustrated in Figure 2.6, frame C.

The observation that some swimmers have the stroking hand under the chest while others have it under the waist when the recovering arm enters the water has to do with whether the swimmer enters the recovering arm during the insweep or the upsweep of the stroking arm. If the recovering arm enters during the insweep the amount of overlap appears to be greater. Since both methods are used by world-class freestylers, it is impossible at this time to determine which style is superior.

Instructions for Teaching the Sweeps of the Front Crawl Stroke to College, High School, and Older Age-Group Swimmers

The preceding description of the front crawl armstroke was much too involved to be used for instructing swimmers. For teaching purposes, some simplified instructions for these techniques follow.

a. Entry. Enter your arm into the water directly in front of the shoulder with your elbow slightly flexed and your palm facing outward.

b. Stretch. After entry, stretch your arm forward while the other arm completes its underwater stroke.

c. Catch. When that stroke is completed, press down and out and back on the water until you feel a solid catch. Your wrist should be flexed and your palm should be pitched outward somewhat.

d. Downsweep and insweep. Once the catch is made, sweep your hand downward and then inward toward the midline of your body. Slowly rotate your palm inward and upward as you do so.

e. Upsweep. When your hand passes your head, push the water out, up, and back toward your thigh. Rotate your palm outward and flatten your hand as you do so.

f. Release. Release pressure on the water as your hand approaches your thigh. Then, turn your palm inward so that your hand leaves the water on its side, little finger first.

Instructions for Teaching the Sweeps of the Front Crawl Stroke to Younger Age-Group Swimmers

These instructions are even less complicated.

a. Put your hand in the water in front of your shoulder with your palm facing out.

b. Press down and back (keep your palm facing out as you do).

c. Then sweep your hand in and up under your head (with your palm facing in and up).

d. As your hand passes your head, push the water out, up and back to your thigh (with your palm facing out and back).

e. Bring your hand out of the water little finger first.

The Flutter Kick

The flutter kick consists of two distinct movements, a downbeat and an upbeat. The swimmer's legs are also moving laterally during these movements. The significance of the lateral kicks will be discussed later in this section. For now, the kick will be described as though it takes place in up and down directions only.

Figure 2.16. The flutter kick.

A–D. The upbeat of the right leg, the downbeat of the left. After completing its downbeat, the right leg sweeps upward and inward in an extended position. The swimmer's right foot is maintained in a natural position by water pressure. In the meantime, his left leg begins its downbeat. Notice that his left foot is pitched inward and upward by the pressure of the water underneath it. The left leg sweeps down and out until it is completely extended at the knee. His foot does not kick downward more than 12 or 14 inches.

E–F. The downbeat of the right leg, the upbeat of the left. After completing its downbeat, the left leg sweeps upward and inward while the right leg sweeps downward and outward.

A

B

C

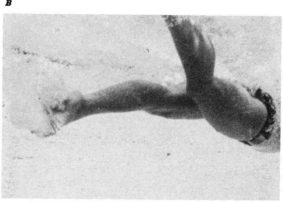

D

E

F

Downbeat   In order to conserve angular momentum, the downbeat begins before the leg has finished its preceding upbeat. The action is as follows: When your heel nears the surface, flexion at the hip joint begins, causing your thigh to start downward while your lower leg flexes at the knee and continues upward (see frames *C* and *D* of fig. 2.16). This action overcomes the inertia of the upbeat, changing the direction of motion to downward without using excessive muscular effort.

Hip flexion results from contraction of the iliopsoas, rectus femoris, sartorius, and gracilis muscles. Knee flexion is passive, being caused by the upward force of water on your relaxed lower leg. Water pressure also forces your foot and ankle, if properly relaxed, into plantar flexion and inversion; that is, your toes are pointed up with the soles pitched inward (see frame *A* of fig. 2.16).

Your thigh continues moving downward until your knee reaches a depth of 8 to 10 inches (the same depth as your chest). (See fig. 2.16, frame *E*.) At that point, a forceful extension at the knee joint starts the lower leg moving downward.

Your lower leg continues sweeping downward (and in some cases forward) until your leg is completely extended at the knee (see frame *D* of fig. 2.16). Your feet should be pitched upward and inward as much as possible during the downbeat. The proper amount of knee flexion (approximately 30 to 40 degrees) and inward rotation at the hip joint helps in attaining the proper pitch. Ankle flexibility exercises that develop plantar flexing and inverting ability are also beneficial.

Your foot should be 12 to 14 inches deep at the end of the downbeat (see frame *D* of fig. 2.16). Another way to judge the proper depth of the kick is that your foot should be only slightly deeper than your chest at the end of the downbeat. To kick any deeper would only increase drag while not contributing any significant propulsive or stabilizing forces.

Upbeat   The upbeat overlaps with the downbeat so that the downward inertia of the leg can be overcome as the direction of motion changes from downward to upward. This is accomplished by simultaneously extending your hip and knee joints so that your thigh begins moving upward while your lower leg is completing its downward sweep (see frames *D* and *E* of fig. 2.16).

Once the change of direction is effected, your leg sweeps upward and forward in a curvilinear path. Your lower leg and ankle are relaxed and the downward force of water on the posterior portion of your leg and the sole of your foot keeps your leg extended and your ankle in a natural position, midway between plantar flexion and dorsiflexion, throughout the upward motion (see frames *A* and *B* of fig. 2.16). The upbeat ends when your foot nears the surface of the water. At that time, your hip is flexed and the downbeat begins.

Lateral Leg Motion   As mentioned earlier, your legs move in lateral as well as vertical directions during the flutter kick. The lateral motions serve to stabilize your body as it is rolled from side to side. Lateral alignment can be preserved if your legs kick in the same direction your hips are moving as you roll from side to side. The proper sequence is illustrated in Figure 2.9.

During the downsweep of the right arm, the swimmer's right leg kicks down and in as he rolls his right shoulder and hip down and in (see frames *A* and *B*, fig. 2.9). The left leg kicks up and in to coincide with the upward movements of his left shoulder and hip as his left arm is recovering over the water.

During the insweep of the right arm the swimmer kicks down and in with his left foot and up and in with his right, facilitating the rotation of his left shoulder and hip downward as his left arm reaches forward for the entry (see frames *C* and *D*, fig. 2.9). During the upsweep, his right foot kicks down and out and his left foot up and out as the swimmer continues to roll his left shoulder and hip downward (see frames *E* to *H*, fig. 2.9). A similar sequence occurs during the right armstroke.

The kick is usually practiced with a board. This seems to be a reasonable procedure for improving endurance and for improving the mechanics of the vertical leg actions. However, kicking with a board inhibits lateral kicks. Therefore it may also be advisable to practice kicking without a board in order to improve the lateral leg motions.

> The following drill is used by many coaches to practice lateral kicking. Swimmers kick down the pool on their sides with the lower arm extended overhead and the other arm extended backward, resting against the thigh. After kicking four, six, eight, or some other designated number of times, they roll to the opposite side, reverse the positions of their arms, and repeat the sequence.

Timing of the Arms and Legs

The number of kicks per stroke cycle (two armstrokes) has been a matter of controversy throughout the history of competitive swimming. Two-, four-, and six-beat kicks have received the most publicity. Of these, the six-beat kick has emerged as most popular. Other styles are not without advocates, however. Many distance swimmers and their coaches prefer a two-beat kick, while the four-beat kick has been used by a smaller but significant number of world-class swimmers.

The Six-Beat Kick

When one thinks of the underwater armstroke as three sweeping motions rather than as a pull and push, it becomes apparent why the six-beat rhythm is the most popular style. There is a symmetry of one kick per arm sweep.[1] The sequence of photographs in Figure 2.17*A* shows this symmetry.

1. Actually there are two kicks per arm sweep because one leg is kicking upward as the other is kicking downward. However, it has become common practice to refer to leg rhythms according to the number of downbeats, and on that basis there are three kicks per armstroke.

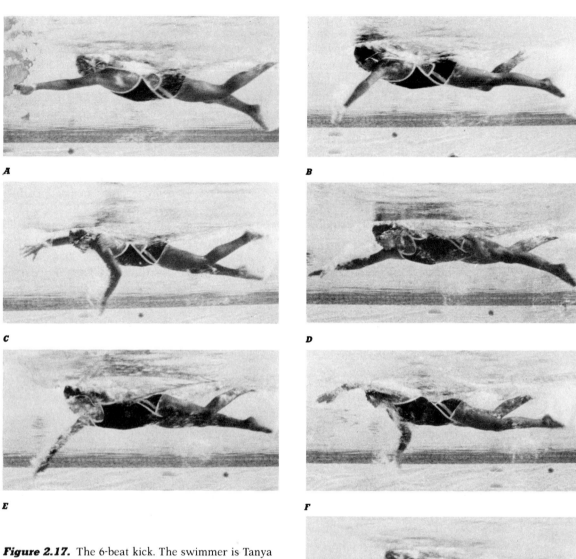

Figure 2.17. The 6-beat kick. The swimmer is Tanya Kawazu, a 10-year-old AAA swimmer in the freestyle events. She exhibits the typical timing of arms and legs observed with 6-beat freestylers. She executes 3 down-beats during each armstroke.

A-B. She kicks down with her left leg during the downsweep of her left arm.

C. She kicks down with her right leg during the in-sweep of her left arm.

D. She kicks downward with her left leg once again, as she executes the upsweep with her left arm.

E. She kicks down with her right leg during the downsweep of her right arm.

F. She kicks down with her left leg during the in-sweep of her right arm.

G. She kicks down with her right leg once again, as she executes the upsweep with her right arm.

The downsweep of the left arm occurs simultaneously with the downbeat of the left leg (see frames *A* and *B* of fig. 2.17). The insweep of the left armstroke is coordinated with the downbeat of the opposite leg (see frame *C*), and the upsweep of the left arm is combined with another downbeat of the leg on the left side (see frame *D*). The identical sequence occurs during the right armstroke (see fig. 2.17, frames *E* to *G*). This timing is so precise that the beginning and end of each downbeat of the kick coincide with the beginning and end of the corresponding arm sweep. Large sweeps require large kicks, while the kicks are smaller when a particular sweep is used over a short distance. This probably explains why many swimmers have what appear to be major and minor kicks during each stroke cycle.

This coordination of arm and leg actions has been observed among all the world- and national-class 6-beat crawl strokers that are available for viewing on film. Such precision undoubtedly helps to maintain lateral and horizontal body alignment. It is also possible that simultaneous applications of force by the arms and legs may increase the total propulsive force of the armstroke in some phases of the stroke cycle. The propulsive capacity of the kick will be discussed later.

It is tempting to recommend the 6-beat kick as the best possible style. The precise coordination of one kick to each arm sweep should encourage more effective use of each of the three sweeps in the armstroke. Also, the manner in which the kick aids body roll and counterbalances those forces from the armstroke that are potentially disruptive suggests a combination of arm and leg motions that is ideal. These observations notwithstanding, the fact that many world-class swimmers use other rhythms makes such a recommendation unwise at this time.

The Two-Beat Kick

The rhythm of the 2-beat kick is illustrated in Figure 2.18. There are two kicks per arm cycle; or, more accurately, one downbeat per armstroke. Each downbeat begins during the insweep of the arm on that side. The downbeat is completed simultaneously with the finish of the upsweep of that arm. The legs drag during the recovery and downsweep of the next arm stroke.

A 2-beat kick should reduce the energy required to swim a given distance because the leg muscles are not working as vigorously as they would in a 6-beat rhythm. Female swimmers seem to prefer the 2-beat kick, while males tend to use more vigorous rhythms. Perhaps the average female, because of greater buoyancy, can kick less frequently and yet maintain her legs near the surface. On the other hand, males who tend to be less buoyant, may require a more vigorous kicking rhythm to prevent their legs from "sinking." Two rhythms that are frequently used by swimmers who prefer a deemphasized kick to a 6-beat style are the 2-beat crossover and the 4-beat kicks.

The Two-Beat Crossover Kick

The 2-beat crossover kick appears to be a compromise between the energy saving 2-beat kick, which may not be vigorous enough to maintain horizontal and lateral alignment, and a 6-beat rhythm that requires more energy than a particular swimmer may want to expend. The 2-beat crossover kick is also popular

Figure 2.18. The 2-beat kick. The swimmer in these photographs exhibits the timing of one leg beat to each armstroke that is typical of this rhythm.

A–B. Her legs "drag" during the downsweep of the left arm.

C–D. She then kicks downward with her left leg during the insweep and upsweep of that armstroke.

E. The same timing is evident on the right armstroke with her legs "dragging" during the downsweep.

F–G. She then kicks downward with her right leg during the insweep and upsweep of the right arm.

A

B

C

D

E

F

G

among swimmers who tend toward a lateral arm recovery. Crossing the legs counteracts the lateral arm swings and maintains the alignment of the hips.

The swimmer in Figure 2.19 is using a 2-beat crossover kick. You will notice that there are really four rather than two kicks per arm cycle; two major beats and two minor crossover beats. Each of the two major kicks is executed during the insweep and upsweep of the armstroke in the identical coordination described for the 2-beat kick. The two crossover beats take place during the downsweeps of the arms. Notice in frames *A* and *B* of Figure 2.19 that the downbeat of the swimmer's left leg and the upsweep of the left arm are completed simultaneously. However, the swimmer's legs do not drag after completing that kick. Instead, the left leg kicks up and in, while the right is brought down and in. These kicks are not completed. The legs cross and hit together midway through their respective motions (see fig. 2.19, frame *C*). The legs are then uncrossed in time for the right leg to kick downward as the right arm sweeps in and up (see fig. 2.19, frames *D* to *F*). After that, another partial kick is executed, this time with the left leg crossing over the right (see frames *F* and *G* of fig. 2.19), and the cycle begins again.

Figure 2.19. The 2-beat crossover kick in the freestyle. This series of photographs, taken from a rear view, shows the timing of arms and legs in the 2-beat crossover kick.

A-B. The left leg completes a downbeat during the insweep and upsweep of the left arm.

C. The right leg crosses over the left during the downsweep of the right arm.

A

B

C

continued overleaf

Figure 2.19.   **D**   **E**

F   **G**

Figure 2.19. continued

D-F. The legs uncross and the right leg completes a downbeat during the insweep and upsweep of the right arm.

G. The left leg crosses over the right during the downsweep of the left arm.

The Four-Beat Kick   The rhythm of the 4-beat kick also seems to be a compromise timing. It is used primarily but not exclusively by male swimmers to save energy while maintaining lateral and horizontal alignment. There are at least two styles of the 4-beat kick in common use. One is a "hybrid." That is, it is a combination of the 6-beat and 2-beat styles. The other, while being thought of as a 4-beat kick, is really a 6-beat rhythm with two beats deemphasized. The hybrid style is illustrated in Figure 2.20.

The swimmer uses a 2-beat rhythm during the right armstroke, kicking down during the insweep and upsweep of that armstroke (see fig. 2.20, frames A to D). He uses a 6-beat rhythm during the left armstroke and executes three downbeats in the same precise coordination described for the 6-beat kick. That

Figure 2.20. The 4-beat style: a combination of 6-beat and 2-beat timing. These photographs of Chris Cavanaugh, taken from underneath, show the typical timing of arms and legs when a swimmer uses a 4-beat kick that is a combination of 2-beat and 6-beat timing.

A–D. Chris uses 2-beat timing during his right armstroke. Notice that he kicks down only once, with his right leg, during the insweep and upsweep of the right armstroke.

E–F. He uses a 6-beat rhythm during the left armstroke. The downbeat of his left leg occurs during the downsweep of his left arm.

A

B

C

D

E

F

continued overleaf

Figure 2.20.   **G**   **H**

I   **J**

Figure 2.20. continued

G-H. He kicks down with his right leg during the insweep of his left arm.

I-J. The downbeat of the third kick is executed with the left leg once again. It occurs during the upsweep of his left arm.

is, the right leg kicks down in combination with the downsweep and upsweep of the armstroke while the left leg kicks down during the insweep (see fig. 2.20, frames *E* to *J*).

Contrary to the photos in Figure 2.20, the two-beat rhythm is frequently used in conjunction with the armstroke on the breathing side, possibly for the following reasons:

1. Kicking is accompanied by contraction of the rectus abdominus muscles. Contraction of these muscles could interfere with breathing, inhibiting descent of the diaphragm during inspiration. Therefore, kicking only once on the breathing side may prevent such interference by reducing the number of contractions.

2. Swimmers will generally roll more toward the breathing side and a longer insweep of the opposite arm is required to rotate the body back toward a prone position. Longer sweeps probably require more frequent kicks for counterbalancing.

The second 4-beat rhythm is, in reality, a modified 6-beat kick. Close examination of swimmers who use this style reveals that 2-beats have been deemphasized to the point of being barely noticeable. These deemphasized kicks usually correspond to arm sweeps that have also been abbreviated. The swimmer in Figure 2.21 is using a modified 6-beat rhythm. The two kicks that accompany the insweep of the right and the left arms are abbreviated to the point of being barely noticeable.

Is the Flutter Kick Propulsive?

This question has been debated for several years. Some people believe that the kick acts only as a stabilizer, while others are convinced that it also adds to the total propulsive force of the stroke. Still others believe the kick is both propulsive and stabilizing in the sprint events but only serves a stabilizing function in distance races.

There seems to be no disagreement concerning the stabilizing nature of the flutter kick. The sequence of photographs in Figure 2.6 provides visual evidence that the flutter kick balances the armstroke. Two questions need to be considered concerning the propulsive capabilities of the flutter kick: Does it contribute to total propulsive force when combined with the armstroke? Assuming the flutter kick is propulsive, would it be advisable to use it for that purpose?

In regard to the first question, look at Figure 2.22. These drawings show plots of the flutter kick during various phases of one arm stroke. They were drawn from motion pictures of a swimmer passing in front of a grid painted on the side of the pool. In this way the direction of his foot movements could be determined in relation to a fixed point. The swimmer is using a 6-beat kick. Notice the legs are moving downward and forward (see fig. 2.22, frames *B* and *C*) and upward and forward (see fig. 2.22*D*) during two of the three kicks per armstroke. This is because his arms are accelerating his body forward at a faster rate than his legs can sweep downward or upward. The force diagram in

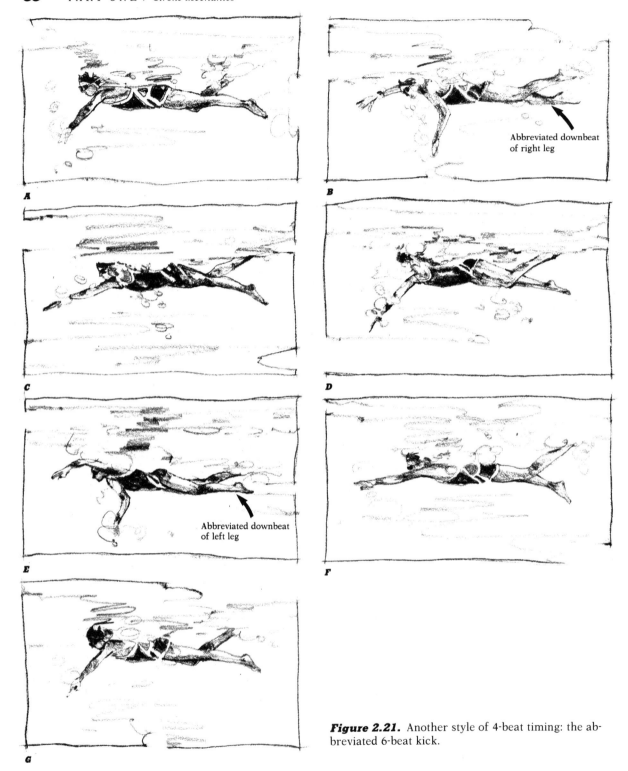

Figure 2.21. Another style of 4-beat timing: the abbreviated 6-beat kick.

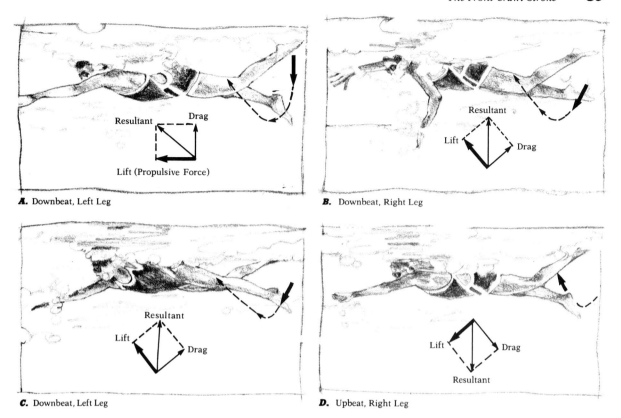

A. Downbeat, Left Leg

B. Downbeat, Right Leg

C. Downbeat, Left Leg

D. Upbeat, Right Leg

Figure 2.22. Kick plots and force diagrams of the flutter kick in the front crawl stroke.

Figure 2.22*B* shows that downward and forward motion of the right foot should provide little lift force during the insweep of the left arm. The major function of this downbeat is probably to aid the insweeping arm in rotating the body toward a prone position. The downbeat accompanying the upsweep of the left armstroke is probably not propulsive either, because the left foot travels down and forward (see fig. 2.22*C*). This kick probably prevents the swimmer's hips from being pulled downward by the force of the upsweeping arm.

Swimmers' feet travel upward and forward during the upbeats that accompany all phases of the armstroke. Movement in this direction exerts force downward and is probably not propulsive (see the force diagram in fig. 2.22*D*). The upbeat that accompanies the downsweep of the armstroke probably prevents the hips from being elevated by the downward force of the arm. The upbeat accompanying the insweep of the armstroke probably aids rotation of the body toward a prone position because it travels inward as well as upward and forward. The upbeat that accompanies the upsweep of the armstroke also aids rotation by traveling outward as well as upward and forward.

The only kicks that may be propulsive are the two downbeats that accompany the downsweep of each arm. Forward velocity is at its lowest point during these sweeps and the leg travels almost directly downward for a short time. The force diagram in Figure 2.22A shows that some lift force can be generated by this motion.

The downward movement and the pitch of the foot causes water to be deflected backward from ankle to toes. This creates a pressure differential between the instep ($+$) and the sole ($-$) sides that exerts a lift force in a forward direction. This force may contribute to forward propulsion. The first portion of the downbeat should be most effective where propulsion is concerned because the direction is almost entirely downward at this time. Consequently, the lift force acts in a horizontal direction. After that, the foot movement becomes increasingly forward as the downsweep accelerates the body forward faster than the feet are moving downward. Thus, regarding the first question, the kicks accompanying the downsweep of each arm may contribute to propulsion, although it is obvious that the amount of propulsion that could be generated by the kick is small in comparison to that of the armstroke.

Adrian, Singh, and Karpovich (1966) have provided information concerning the second question, the advisability of using the kick for propulsion. They measured the oxygen consumption of twelve competitive swimmers while they were kicking only, pulling only, and when swimming the full stroke. Kicking used four times more oxygen than pulling. When kicking at a speed of 3.5 feet per second the oxygen requirement was 24.5 liters compared to a requirement of only 7 liters when pulling at the same speed. These results are supported by the work of other researchers (Holmer 1974, Charbonnier et al. 1975, Astrand 1978) all of whom have found that kicking causes a considerable increase in the energy cost of swimming.

These data present a persuasive argument that it would be wise, at least in middle-distance and distance races, to sacrifice any additional propulsion that might be generated by the kick in favor of conserving energy and delaying fatigue so that a faster pace can be maintained later in the race.

Although saving energy may be the reason distance and middle-distance swimmers use a deemphasized kick, it is not readily understandable why some sprinters use abbreviated kick rhythms. Success in sprinting depends more on attaining maximum speed than on conserving energy. If the flutter kick is propulsive sprinters could be sacrificing speed by using a deemphasized rhythm. American female swimmers have used 2-beat kicks for several years. Contemporary male sprinters are increasingly using these and other deemphasized rhythms. Jonty Skinner and Jack Babashoff are two notable examples. We can only conjecture as to whether they might be faster using a 6-beat kick. Controlled research is needed to determine whether these deemphasized rhythms are more efficient for some sprinters or whether the 6-beat kick is the superior style for all.

Variations in Style

All swimmers use the three arm sweeps described in this chapter when swimming the front crawl stroke. However, many swimmers emphasize some of these sweeps and deemphasize others. There may be any number of reasons for these variations. Swimmers may be shortening their least effective sweep and putting more time and effort into one that is more propulsive. Such factors as body build, sex, and lack of flexibility or power may necessitate individual modifications. They may be the result of having been taught to push water straight backward at an early age (this would explain the tendency toward an abbreviated insweep that is seen with many swimmers). High mileage training at an early age may have developed a deemphasized kicking rhythm, which in turn caused certain arm sweeps to become abbreviated.

The most common variation is to deemphasize the insweep and exaggerate the upsweep. The kicks that would normally be coordinated with the insweep are either eliminated or abbreviated. Another variation is to abbreviate the downsweep and begin the insweep almost immediately after entry. Swimmers who use this style almost invariably use a 2-beat or 2-beat crossover kicking rhythm. Perhaps the abbreviated downsweep causes them to eliminate the kicks that would normally accompany this phase of the armstroke. The 2-beat kickers also adjust the timing of their arms so that the entry of one arm occurs when the opposite arm is in its upsweep, rather than insweep phase (see fig. 2.18). If they did not do this the entering arm would begin applying propulsive force before the other had completed its underwater stroke.

Body Position

As indicated in the previous chapter, swimmers encounter less drag when the body is in a streamlined position that allows water molecules to change directions gradually as they pass around it. To be streamlined the body must be in good horizontal and lateral alignment.

Horizontal alignment is best evaluated from a side view where the depth and inclination of the body are readily observable. Proper lateral alignment is best evaluated from above. Body roll is also an important factor in maintaining alignment. Body roll is best evaluated from a front view.

Horizontal Alignment

The great swimmer Johnny Weissmuller and his coach Bill Bachrach advised hydroplaning while swimming the front crawl stroke (Bachrach 1924). For many years this advice influenced swimmers to arch their backs and carry their heads and shoulders high in the water. This body position, illustrated in Figure 2.23*A*, is not efficient for swimming. Energy is wasted overcoming form drag caused by the inclined body position and the deep kicks that are required to hold the head and trunk high in the water. Swimmers also waste energy by pushing down on the water with their hands in order to maintain their shoulders and head high in the water. This energy could have been put to better use increasing propulsive force.

Sprinters ride higher in the water because their speed increases the drag force under their bodies, which in turn "lifts" them higher in the water in much the same way that a boat hydroplanes as its speed is increased. No attempt should be made to augment this natural "hydroplane" by arching your

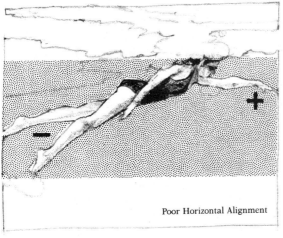

Poor Horizontal Alignment

Streamlined Body Position

A

B

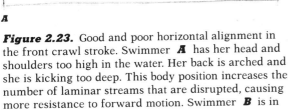

Figure 2.23. Good and poor horizontal alignment in the front crawl stroke. Swimmer **A** has her head and shoulders too high in the water. Her back is arched and she is kicking too deep. This body position increases the number of laminar streams that are disrupted, causing more resistance to forward motion. Swimmer **B** is in a streamlined position and takes up less space in the water. By not presenting a large flat surface to the oncoming flow (as swimmer **A** does), drag is reduced and less propulsive force is needed to attain the same speed.

back and pushing down on the water. Your body should remain in good horizontal alignment.

A horizontal body position is illustrated in frame *B* of Figure 2.23. Drag is reduced as compared to the swimmer in frame *A*, because this swimmer's body takes up less space in the water. As a result, fewer streams of water molecules are diverted from laminar to turbulent flow. The pressure in front as well as the eddy currents behind are reduced, with resistance to forward motion decreased accordingly.

If you are aligned horizontally, your face will be in the water with the water line somewhere between your hairline and the middle of the top of your head. You should make no attempt to hold your head unnaturally high, nor should you push it downward excessively; Clarys (1978) has reported that lifting the head can increase total drag 20 to 35 percent. Your back should not be arched. Your eyes should be focused forward and downward to maintain a forward orientation.

Lack of buoyancy is not a significant hindrance to good horizontal alignment. Many great swimmers have been nonfloaters. When you move through the water the drag beneath your body increases your buoyancy; therefore, it is possible for even nonfloaters to maintain good horizontal alignment without using muscular force to hold their bodies at the surface.

The depth of your kick is an important factor in horizontal alignment. A kick that is too deep, like that of the swimmer in Figure 2.23*A*, causes an increase in form drag without contributing to propulsive force. The proper depth of the kick is best judged in relation to your body. You should kick only slightly lower than an imaginary line extending backward from the deepest part of your trunk (your chest), as illustrated in Figure 2.23*B*.

Although kicking too deep is the more prevalent error, it is also possible for the kick to be too narrow. Alley (1952) has demonstrated that a normal kick, one with a leg spread of approximately 12 inches, is superior to a shorter kick where the leg spread is approximately 6 inches. Although there should be less form drag with a narrow kick, it is probably less effective because some stabilizing and perhaps some propulsive force is lost. A kick that is acceptable in both width and depth is shown in Figure 2.18.

Lateral Alignment The swimmer in Figure 2.24*A* shows excellent lateral alignment. The swimmer's shoulders, hips, and legs move as a unit, rolling in time with the movements of the arms. This keeps the hips and legs inside the width of the body and the swimmer takes up very little space in the water. As a result, the flow of only a small number of water molecules is diverted, and form drag is minimized.

Figure 2.24. Good and poor lateral alignment in the front crawl stroke. Swimmer **A** is in good alignment. He has recovered in a linear manner, reducing the angular momentum of his recovering arm so that the counterforce on his trunk is not sufficient to pull his body out of alignment. Swimmer **B** has recovered in a lateral manner with enough force to exert a counterforce that causes her hips to swing outward.

A   **B**

On the other hand, the lateral recovery of the swimmer in Figure 2.24*B* has caused the swimmer's hips and legs to swing out of alignment. Their lateral motions increase form drag and wave drag because the laminar flow of a greater number of water molecules is disrupted when the swimmer's hips and legs swing outside the width of the body.

There are several ways swimmers can disrupt their lateral alignment. Some of the more common errors are recovering in a low lateral manner, over-reaching on the entry, and pulling the head backward when breathing.

The effect of a lateral recovery and overreaching were discussed earlier in this chapter. Pulling the head backward while breathing is illustrated in Figure 2.3*A*. The swimmer pulls the head backward toward the right shoulder while rotating it to the right for a breath. This causes the hips to move outward toward the left while the legs react by swinging outward toward the right. The swimmer in Figure 2.3*B* shows good breathing mechanics. This swimmer's head is rotated to the side, but maintained in alignment with the spine.

The Importance of Body Roll

Crawl stroke swimmers are continually rotating their bodies around the longitudinal axis. In fact, they spend more time on their sides than they spend in a flat position. Rolling is an indispensable aid to maintaining lateral body alignment and reducing drag. Although it is possible to roll too much, most swimmers roll too little. Crawl stroke swimmers should roll at least 45 degrees to each side (from a prone position). Most swimmers roll more than 45 degrees toward their breathing side. The proper amount of roll is shown in Figures 2.6 and 2.9.

Disruptions in lateral alignment occur when swimmers try to maintain a flat body position. They try to "hold" their trunk in a prone position when their arms are sweeping downward and upward. This is impossible to do. The vertical movements of your shoulders exert a counter-force on your hips and legs that will cause them to move laterally if your trunk is not allowed to "roll" in the directions the arms are moving. Thus, your shoulders should follow your arms, your hips should follow your shoulders, and your legs should kick in lateral directions that facilitate these "rolling" motions.

Perhaps the most common error where body roll is concerned is failing to rotate enough to bring the shoulders out of the water where the recovery can be executed correctly. When the shoulders are in the water, the recovery must, of necessity, be more lateral, causing the hips and feet to be pulled out of alignment. During the recovery you should roll your body enough that your shoulder is clear of the water until your hand entry is made (see fig. 2.12).

Breathing

The act of turning your head for a breath should be coordinated with the roll of your body. This reduces the potentially disruptive effect that turning the head to the side can have on lateral alignment. The correct sequence of breathing actions is shown in Figure 2.6. Your face should turn sideward as your body rolls toward the breathing side. The breath should be taken when you are rolled maximally toward the breathing side, and your head should be returned as you roll toward the opposite side.

The most opportune time to begin rotating your face out of the water is when the arm on the opposite side is entering the water (see fig. 2.6, frames *J* to *L*). This is because the downward sweep of that arm will cause you to roll toward the breathing side. Turning your head in time with the roll of your body allows your mouth to clear the water for a breath without the necessity of lifting your head from the water. Your mouth may not appear to be above the surface because you will be breathing below a bow wave that was created by your forward motion (see frame *C* of fig. 2.12).

After the breath is taken, your face is returned to the water. The return should also be coordinated with your body roll. That is, your face is returned to the water as the arm on the breathing side reaches forward for the entry and your body begins to roll toward the opposite side (see fig. 2.6, frames *C* and *D*).

Do not hold your breath as you return your face to the water. Exhalation should begin immediately after the breath is taken. It should, however, be slow and controlled so all of your air is not expelled before you are ready to take your next breath.

Common Errors in Breathing

Turning the head too early is a frequent mistake in breathing. The effect of this error is illustrated in Figure 2.25*A*. Some swimmers have been taught from an early age to breathe as they stroke with the arm on the breathing side. The

Figure 2.25. An error in breathing: turning the head too soon. Swimmer **A** is turning her head before her left arm enters the water. Since her body is rolled to the left at this time, she will have to "rush" her right arm through the recovery to get her body rolled to the right so her face can clear the water for a breath. This should reduce propulsion from the stroking arm, while the increased recovery force of the recovering arm will waste energy and disrupt lateral alignment. Swimmer **B** is breathing correctly. He waits until his left arm enters the water, and he is rolling to the right before he turns his head for a breath.

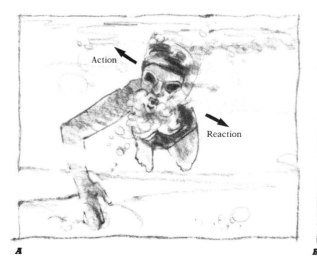

A

B

swimmer in Figure 2.25A will be rolled away from the breathing side at that time. This will make it very difficult to get her mouth clear of the water. She will probably rush her right arm through its underwater stroke, "slipping" water as she does, in an attempt to get her body rolled toward the breathing side in time to catch up with her rotating head. She will also "rush" the other arm through the recovery for the same reason. The result of these actions will be a loss of propulsion from the stroking arm while the force of the vigorously swinging recovery arm will exert a counterforce on the body that will disrupt lateral alignment.

Another mistake, pulling the head backward as it is rotated, was discussed earlier in this chapter in the section on lateral alignment.

A third error occasionally seen among novice competitive swimmers is lifting the face from the water when breathing. These swimmers usually try to swim with a "flat" body position and must be taught to use body roll to help the mouth clear the water without lifting the head.

Alternate Breathing

Alternate breathing has been used by many world-class swimmers, particularly females. Coaches use alternate breathing as a stroke balancer because it encourages swimmers to roll their bodies equally to both sides. The increased rotation encourages more propulsive strokes and a high-elbow recovery on each side so that the possibility of disrupting lateral alignment is reduced.

Although the practice of alternate breathing seems to be gaining in popularity, it is not recommended. Alternate breathers inhale twice during every three stroke cycles, whereas conventional breathers inhale during every stroke cycle. The loss of one breath out of every three probably reduces oxygen consumption, and as a consequence, fatigue may occur earlier in the race.

The stroke-balancing effect of alternate breathing is limited. Although the stroke may become more symmetrical when the swimmer uses alternate breathing, there is no permanent improvement in mechanics that carries over to conventional breathing. That is, when swimmers return to breathing during every stroke cycle, the unbalanced stroke returns. Apparently, alternate breathing balances your stroke only when you are breathing alternately.

It has been argued that alternate breathing increases pulmonary diffusing capacity to a greater extent than does conventional breathing. It is believed that restricting breathing causes extra oxygen to be consumed with every breath which compensates for the fewer breaths taken. Even if this were true, and there is no evidence that it is, it would be wiser to breathe conventionally in races and breathe alternately in practice sessions. Because the supply of oxygen is always less than needed during competition, it would be wise to further increase an already increased oxygen supply by breathing more frequently.

These criticisms notwithstanding, there is a circumstance in which alternate breathing would be recommended. When all other attempts have failed, it may be used as a "last resort" for balancing a stroke. Of course, in this case alternate breathing should be used in competition as well as training. Experiment before doing so, however, to find out whether the improvement in stroke efficiency offsets the loss of oxygen.

Breathing Frequency in Freestyle Competition Most coaches recommend restricted breathing patterns (breathing every second or third arm cycle) for short races such as the 50 and 100 freestyles because propulsive force is believed to be reduced when the head is rotated to the side. However, holding your breath reduces the oxygen supply and may cause fatigue earlier in the race. The dilemma facing a swimmer is that breathing too often may reduce speed, whereas breathing too little may cause fatigue. Thus, it is necessary to decide whether speed is reduced by breathing, and if so, whether increasing speed or reducing fatigue is more important to success in these races.

25 and 50 races. The 25 and 50 races are too short for fatigue, in terms of oxygen deprivation, to be a limiting factor. It takes all-out efforts in excess of 30 seconds for the effects of oxygen deprivation to reduce speed. Thus the 25-yard distance is usually swum without a breath. Some athletes also swim the 50 without breathing, although most take one to three breaths during the race. These breaths, rather than supplying oxygen to the muscles, probably expel carbon dioxide and reduce the distress caused by a buildup of that substance (carbon dioxide buildup causes a compelling need to breathe before the effects of oxygen deprivation are felt).

When using a three-breath pattern, the first breath is taken approximately five to seven yards before the turn. The second breath is taken on the final length, one-third of the way back, and the third breath is taken two-thirds of the way back.

Swimmers who prefer a two-breath pattern use two different methods when swimming the 50. In the first method, the initial breath is taken five to seven yards from the turn and the second is taken at the half-way point of the second length. In the second method, the first length is swum without a breath and two breaths are taken during the second length. The first of those breaths is taken one-third of the way back and the second is taken two-thirds of the way to the finish.

There are also two methods used by swimmers who prefer a one-breath pattern in the 50. In the first, the breath is taken five to seven yards before the turn. In the second method, the breath is taken on the final length about one-third of the way back. This last pattern appears to be the most effective way to swim a 50 and is suggested for high school and college sprinters. Swimming the first length without breathing improves the likelihood of completing that distance at a faster speed and also increases the probability of turning more efficiently. Those swimmers who cannot use this pattern without "tieing up" in the final 5 or 10 yards/meters should settle for a two- or three-breath pattern.

Similar breathing patterns are also appropriate for 50-meter races. The one-breath pattern is recommended for experienced senior swimmers. That breath should be taken two-thirds of the way through the race. In the two-breath pattern, the first breath is taken just before the half-way point and the second at the three-quarters mark. In the three-breath pattern, the first breath is taken before the halfway point and the final two breaths are taken in the second half length as needed (but not within 5 meters of the finish).

Age-group swimmers may find all of these patterns too difficult to use. Younger swimmers require several additional seconds to complete a 50 race and, with increasing time, there is a greater possibility of fatigue being increased by oxygen deprivation. In such cases the breathing patterns described for 100-yard races are recommended.

Most age-group swimmers, even six-year-olds, can be trained to swim 25 yards with one breath. Older age-groupers seem to have more success swimming the distance without a breath.

100 races. The 100-yard and 100-meter events present a complex problem where breathing patterns are concerned. Many coaches and swimmers believe a compromise between increasing speed and delaying fatigue must be struck in these races. Therefore, they recommend restricted breathing patterns.

A popular pattern is to take one breath on the first 25, two on the second, and then to breathe every second arm cycle for the remainder of the race. Some swimmers restrict their breathing even more, breathing only three times during each of the last two lengths (or six times during the final 50 meters if swimming a long course).

Most athletes might swim these events faster if they took more breaths during the first half of the race. Since it requires several seconds for oxygen to get from your lungs to your muscles, it is very likely the air you inhale in the first half of the race will be supplying oxygen to your muscles during the second half. Breathing early in the race should reduce the rate at which an oxygen deficit accumulates and allow you to complete the second half of the race faster. The small amount of time that may be sacrificed by breathing early in the race should be more than compensated for by your increased speed in later portions.

The following breathing pattern is recommended for the 100 distances. Take the first breath early in the race, perhaps after the first five seconds (12 to 15 yards/meters). After that, breathe on a regular basis, once every arm cycle or every other arm cycle, until the final 5 or 10 yards/meters. At that point, delaying fatigue is no longer a consideration and you should hold your breath and sprint for the finish.

Some time should be spent early in the season helping each swimmer find the breathing pattern that is most effective for him or her. The following drill is recommended for that purpose.

Swim a series of six to eight 50s at the end of a particularly strenuous practice session. (Do the drill at the end of a practice so the swimmers will be as fatigued as they would be in the second half of a 100 race.) Swim the repeats at 100 speed starting each with a turn to simulate the second half of a 100 race. Alternate in a random manner the various breathing patterns that might be used during a 100 race. Caution the swimmers to maintain the same effort per repeat. Check for this by counting heart rates immediately after each swim. Keep a record of the times and breathing patterns used. The pattern that consistently produces the fastest times should be the one used in competition. If two or more patterns produce identical times, the one that allows for more frequent breathing should be used because that pattern will provide a greater oxygen supply.

Longer races. In races of 200 yards and longer, it is generally agreed that swimmers should breathe during every stroke cycle after the first 10 yards/meters. Any increase in drag or decrease in propulsive force occasioned by frequent turning of the head is more than compensated for by the increased oxygen supply.

REFERENCES

Adrian, M., Singh, M., and Karpovich, P. 1966. "Energy Cost of the Leg Kick, Arm Stroke and Whole Stroke." *J. App. Phys.* 21:1763–1766.

Alley, L. E. 1952. "An Analysis of Water Resistance and Propulsion in Swimming the Crawl Stroke." *Research Quarterly* 23:253–270.

Astrand, P. 1978. "Aerobic Power in Swimming." *Swimming Medicine IV*, ed. B. Eriksson and B. Forberg, pp. 127–131. Baltimore: University Park Press.

Bachrach, W. 1924. *The Outline of Swimming*. Chicago: Bradwell.

Charbonnier, J. P., Lacour, J. P., Riffal, J., and Flandrois, R. 1975. "Experimental Study of the Performance of Competitive Swimmers." *J. App. Phys.* 34:157–167.

Clarys, J. P. 1978. "Human Morphology and Hydrodynamics." Paper presented at the International Congress of Sports Sciences, July 25–29, University of Alberta, Edmonton, Canada.

Counsilman, J. E. 1968. *The Science of Swimming*. Englewood Cliffs, N.J.: Prentice-Hall.

Holmer, I. 1974. "Energy Cost of the Arm Stroke, Leg Kick, and the Whole Stroke in Competitive Swimming Style." *J. App. Phys.* 33:105–118.

Schleihauf, R. E., Jr. 1978. "Swimming Propulsion: A Hydrodynamic Analysis." *American Swimming Coaches Association 1977 World Clinic Yearbook*, ed. B. Ousley, pp. 49–86. Fort Lauderdale, Fla.: American Swimming Coaches Association.

CHAPTER 3

The Butterfly Stroke

The butterfly stroke involves (1) the armstroke, (2) the dolphin kick, (3) timing of arms and legs, (4) body position, and (5) breathing.

The Armstroke

The underwater armstroke consists of an outsweep, catch, downsweep, insweep, and upsweep. The entry and recovery will also be described. The underwater armstroke is illustrated in Figures 3.1, 3.2, 3.3, 3.4, and 3.5.

Stroke plots of the underwater armstroke viewed from the side, the front, and from underneath are shown in Figure 3.6. The recovery is pictured in Figure 3.7.

Figure 3.1. Underwater armstroke of the butterfly, viewed diagonally. The swimmer is David Santos, a national-level butterfly swimmer and a world-class individual medley swimmer.

A. The entry. His hands are on their sides. His head is down.

B. The outsweep. His hands sweep outward. They are pitched out and back.

C. The catch and downsweep. As his hands pass outside shoulder width, he begins to sweep them downward. His palms are pitched down slightly as well as out and back. His elbows begin to flex.

D-E. The insweep. His hands sweep down and in and up, until they are under his head. His palms are pitched in and up.

F. The transition from insweep to upsweep. The swimmer pushes back as he changes the pitch of his hands from in to out.

G. The upsweep. His hands sweep up and out with his palms pitched out and back.

H. The release. As his hands approach his thighs, he releases the water by turning his palms inward and allowing them to leave the water on their sides.

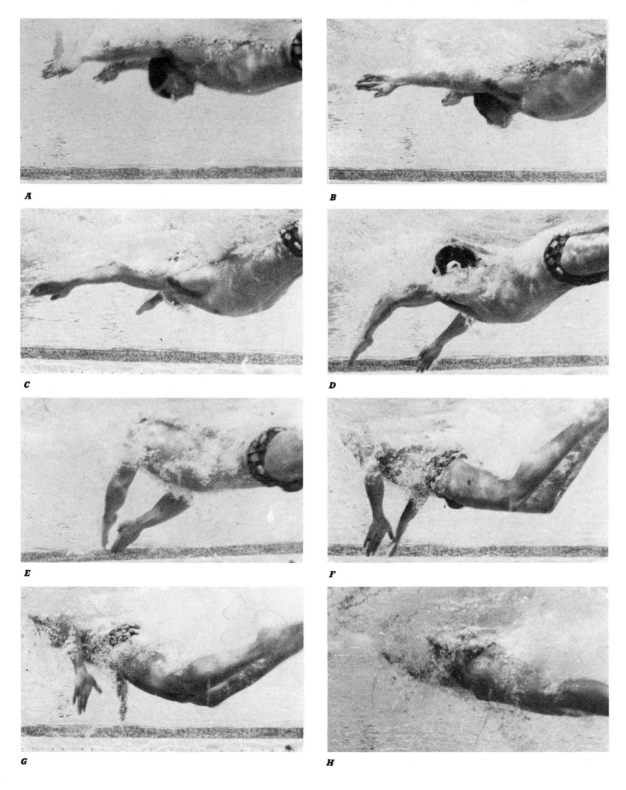

A

B

C

D

E

F

G

H

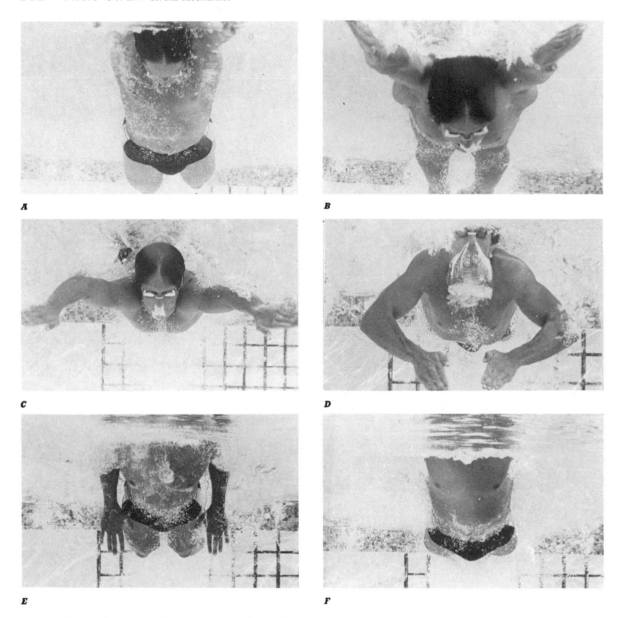

Figure 3.2. A front view of David Santos's butterfly.

    A. Entry.

    B. Outsweep and completion of first kick.

    C. Downsweep.

    D. Insweep.

    E. Upsweep.

    F. Recovery and completion of the second kick.

A

B

C

D

E

F

continued overleaf

Figure 3.3. A side view of the butterfly. The swimmer is Jill Symons, a world-class butterflyer and individual medley performer. She was the fourth-place finisher in the 100-meter butterfly at the 1975 World Swimming Championships.

A-B. The entry and completion of the downbeat of the first kick.

C. The outsweep of the arms.

D-F. The insweep of the arms and upbeat of the legs.

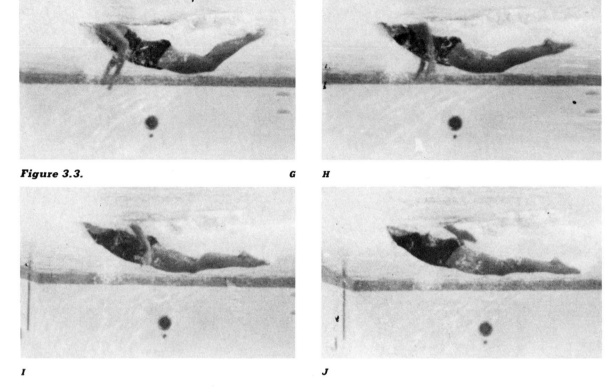

Figure 3.3.   **G**   **H**

                                                          I   **J**

Figure 3.3. continued

G-I. The upsweep of the arms and completion of the second kick. She breathes during this phase.

J. The release of the arms.

Entry   Your hands should enter the water in line with or slightly outside your shoulders. Your palms should be pitched outward approximately 45 degrees from the surface of the water. In this way the edges of your hands slice into the water with minimal drag. The swimmer in Figure 3.1*A* is entering his hands into the water correctly.

Most world-class butterflyers have their elbows flexed upon entry. This is preferable to a completely extended position. With your elbows flexed at entry, extending your elbows immediately after entry will start your hands moving outward even while your upper arms are traveling inward. This action overcomes the inward inertia your hands developed during the recovery and effects a smooth change of direction into the outsweep. If your arms were completely extended at entry, you would have to stop their inward motion before you could accelerate them outward. The energy cost would increase considerably and the counterforces exerted by this stop-start action would decrease forward velocity.

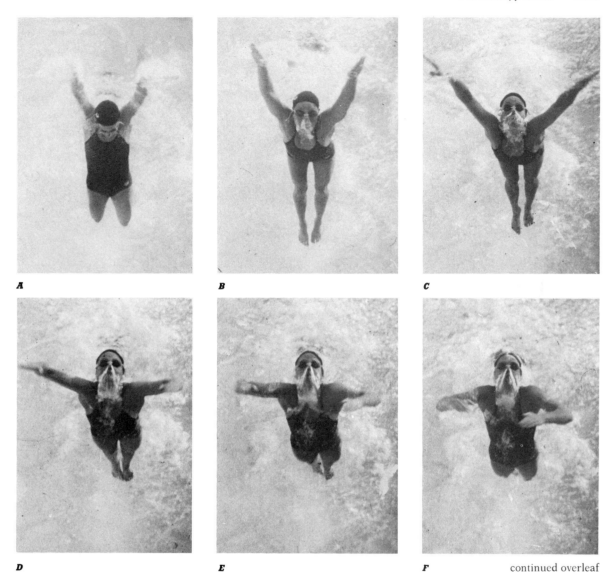

A

B

C

D

E

F   continued overleaf

Figure 3.4. The butterfly stroke viewed from underneath. The swimmer is Jill Symons.

A. The entry. Notice that her elbows are flexed slightly, so that extending her arms after they enter the water will overcome their inward inertia and they can begin sweeping outward with minimal muscular effort.

B–C. The outsweep of the arms and completion of the first kick. Notice the outward pitch of her hands.

D–G. The insweep of the arms and upbeat of the legs. Notice the inward pitch of her hands in **G**.

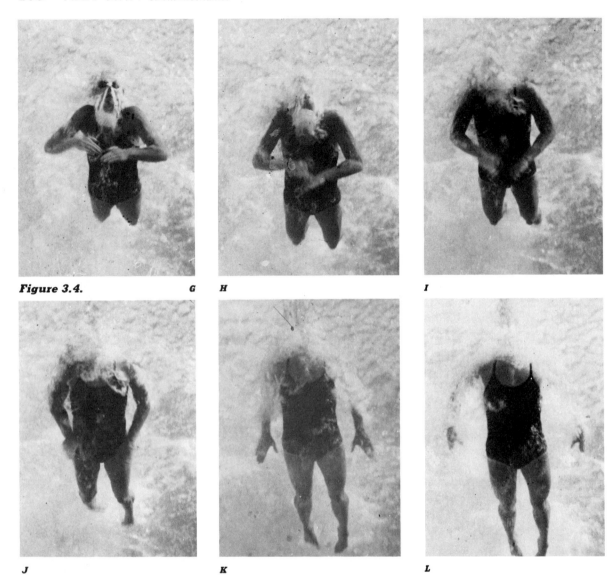

Figure 3.4.   **G**   **H**   **I**

J   **K**   **L**

Figure 3.4. continued

H-J. The upsweep of the arms and downbeat of the second kick. She breathes during this phase of the stroke. Notice the outward pitch of her hands in photos **I** and **J.**

K-L. The release. Notice that her hands leave the water on their sides with palms facing inward.

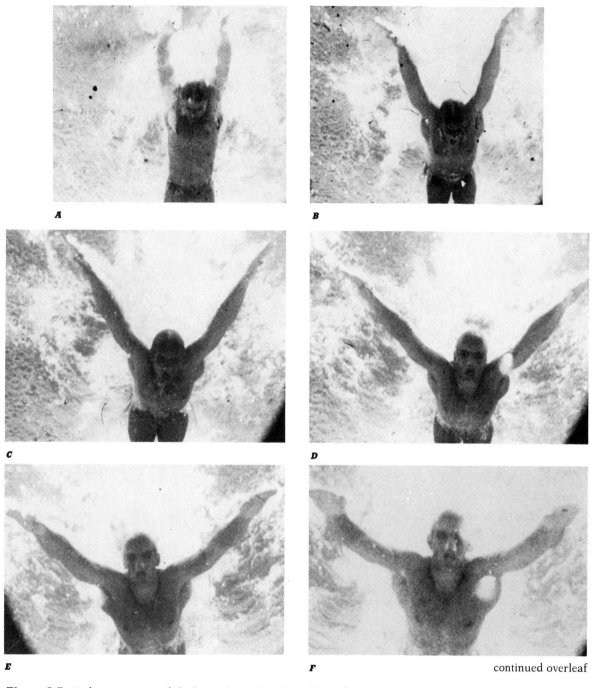

continued overleaf

Figure 3.5. Underwater view of the butterfly stroke of Per Arvidsson, 1980 Olympic champion and several times NCAA champion in the butterfly.

A. The entry.

B-C. The outsweep.

D-E. The catch and downsweep.

F-H. The insweep.

Figure 3.5.   **G**   **H**

I   **J**   continued opposite

Figure 3.5. continued

I-J. The transition from insweep to upsweep.

K-L. The upsweep.

Common errors on entry. One of the most common mistakes at entry is to push the backs of your hands inward and forward against the water. This action substantially increases drag as the forward force of your hands causes a counterforce that reduces forward velocity. The effect of this error is illustrated in Figure 3.7. Your hands should be at their narrowest width as they enter the water and should begin moving outward immediately thereafter.

Outsweep   The outsweep can be seen clearly in frames *B* and *C* of Figure 3.4. The stroke plots in Figure 3.6 show the outsweep between points E and O. It begins imme-

Figure 3.5.   **K**   **L**

M   **N**

Figure 3.5. continued

M-N. The release.

diately after entry. As indicated in the previous section, extension of the elbows starts the hands moving outward almost immediately as they enter the water. Your hands continue outward in a curvilinear path until they pass shoulder width, where the catch is made.

Your fingertips lead the motion with the palms of your hand pitched outward and backward. The hands are pitched outward nearly 90 degrees from the prone position and are pitched backward from 40 to 50 degrees relative to the forward direction in which the swimmer is moving. Your hands should be slightly "cupped," resembling an airfoil (see fig. 3.4C).

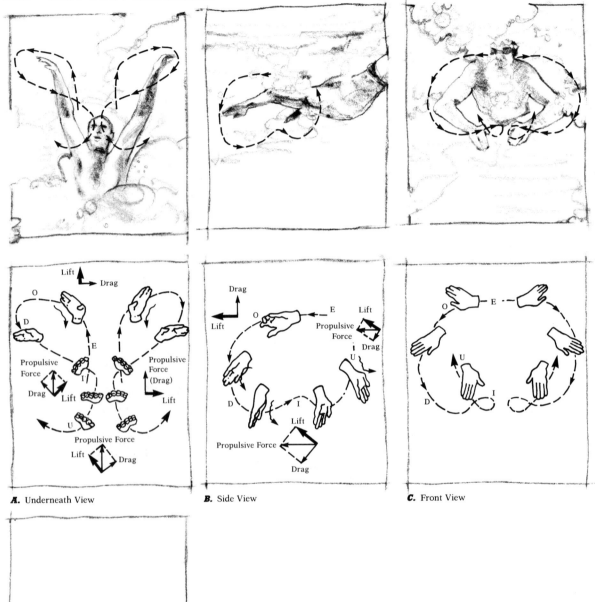

A. Underneath View

B. Side View

C. Front View

Figure 3.6. Stroke patterns of the butterfly armstroke viewed from underneath (**A**), from the side (**B**), and from the front (**C**). These stroke patterns were drawn from underwater films of national-level butterflyers. The force diagrams indicate how propulsion can be generated by the propeller-like sweeps of the hands. The way proper hand pitch causes water to be deflected backward is also shown.

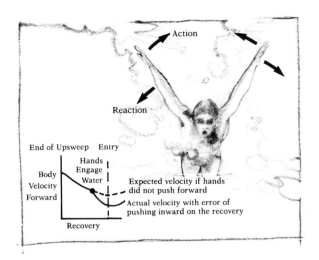

Figure 3.7. The effect of pushing your hands forward and inward during the butterfly entry. This swimmer has recovered his arms too low over the water. Therefore, his arms and then his hands hit the water before reaching the desired entry position. They are then pushed forward and inward, exerting a reactive force that operates counter to his forward direction of motion. Biomechanical analyses of swimmers committing this error indicate that forward velocity is reduced 50 percent as the arms and hands push forward. This is indicated by the solid line on the graph. The dotted line indicates that there would have been a smaller loss of velocity if the hands had begun moving outward immediately upon entering the water.

The outsweep is quite short and may not be significantly propulsive. Most swimmers say that the outsweep feels like a stretching action that is preparatory to making the catch and starting the propulsive phases of the armstroke. More than likely it is a reaction to the downbeat of the dolphin kick. That kick causes your hips to rise, which in turn submerges your shoulders somewhat and pushes your hands outward. Therefore, much of the acceleration in forward speed at this time is probably caused by the kick.

Common errors in the outsweep. Many swimmers make the mistake of turning the palms in and pulling the hands under the body immediately after entry. If you do this, your hands will not sweep outward far enough to place them in position for an effective downsweep and insweep. This will cause you to lose the propulsive force from a large portion of these sweeps and will inhibit the downbeat of your kick and the propulsive force that would have resulted from that action. You should feel that you are stretching forward after entry and you should not try to apply force with your hands until the downbeat of the kick has been completed. By that time your hips will have risen to the surface and your hands will have traveled outward sufficiently to make a powerful downsweep and insweep.

Catch   The catch is made as your hands pass outside shoulder width. It coincides with completion of the downbeat of the first kick. The pitch of your hands is changed from outward and backward to outward, *downward*, and backward. This causes your elbows to flex because the lift force created by the pitch of your hands causes your body to be thrust forward over them. The catch position can be seen clearly in frame *C* of Figure 3.1.

Downsweep   The downsweep is shown between points O and D in the stroke plots of Figure 3.6. After the catch is made, your hands sweep down and out in a circular path.

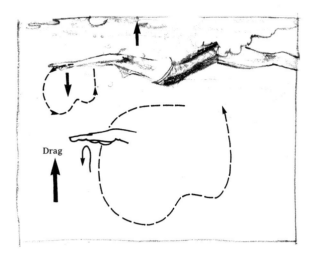

Figure 3.8. The error of pushing down during the downsweep. This swimmer is pushing down on the water with the hands during the downsweep. The flat, almost perpendicular pitch creates a large drag force that tends to lift the swimmer's head and trunk toward the surface. This pitch generates very little propulsive force; therefore, the swimmer travels upward more than forward. Swimmers should be taught to keep their hands pitched outward and to sweep them outward during this phase.

This causes the water that is flowing upward and inward to be deflected backward from thumb to little finger side as it passes under your palm. The downsweep ends as your hands approach the deepest point in the stroke (see fig. 3.3*D*). At that time the transition from downsweep to the next phase of the armstroke, the insweep, occurs. Downward hand speed accelerates from catch to completion of the downsweep.

Common errors in the downsweep. The most common error is to use the wrong angle of attack. Many swimmers pitch their palms entirely downward rather than outward and downward. They then push almost directly downward with the palms of their hands exerting a large drag force that pushes the head and trunk upward more than forward. The effect of this error is shown in Figure 3.8. Attempting to push the hands downward during the downsweep usually causes dropped elbows and a loss of propulsion. This problem will not occur if you emphasize maintaining an outward pitch of the hands as they sweep down and out.

There seem to be two reasons why swimmers push down excessively during the downsweep. The first is that they may have been taught to turn their hands inward immediately after entry so they will be in a better position to push water backward. Therefore, they flatten their palms immediately after the catch is made in an attempt to begin pushing water back under their body.

The second reason for this error is that some swimmers undulate their bodies too much. They tend to drive the head downward excessively at the catch and must then push down on the water to bring the head back to the surface. This "climbing action" wastes effort that could have been used to propel their bodies forward.

Insweep   The insweep begins as your hands pass under your elbows. It can be seen most clearly in frames *D* to *G* of Figure 3.4. It is marked by the letters D to I in the stroke plots in Figure 3.6.

During the insweep your hands sweep inward, upward, and backward in a circular path until they are under your head and near the middle of your body. This is accomplished by flexion of the elbows. Throughout the insweep and the downsweep that preceded it, your elbows act as shafts with your hands rotating around them like propellers. The backward motion in this sweep increases propulsive force by causing the resultant force rather than the lift force to be exerted in a forward direction (see the force diagrams in the side and underneath views of Figure 3.6). Your hands should be pitched inward, upward, and backward during the insweep. This will cause the water to be deflected backward as it passes over your palms from the thumb to little finger sides.

Many swimmers sweep their hands inward within a fraction of an inch of one another. Others sweep only slightly inside the confines of their trunk. The probable reasons why some swimmers sweep inward more than others were discussed in Chapter 1. Since world-class butterflyers have used both styles, the best method cannot be identified at this time. The width of the hands at the end of the outsweep is probably the factor that determines how far the hands are swept under the body. Swimmers who sweep outward a longer distance naturally start their insweeps with their hands further apart. Therefore, they may be able to utilize the propulsive potential of the insweep without bringing their hands very close together under their bodies. On the other hand, swimmers who begin the insweep with their hands closer together may need to sweep them to midline or beyond in order to maximize propulsion during this phase of the stroke.

The insweep is a powerful propulsive movement with swimmers exerting force accordingly. Hand speed is accelerated inward, upward, and backward from the beginning to the end of the insweep.

Common errors in the insweep. The most common mistake swimmers make during the insweep is to pitch the hands inward too early. When your hands are

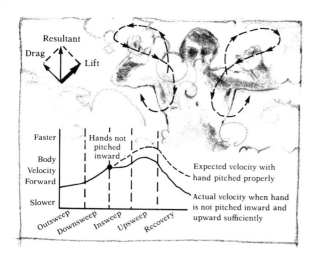

Figure 3.9. The effect on propulsion of failing to pitch the hands inward during the insweep. The swimmer in this illustration does not pitch her hands inward during the insweep. As a result, the angle of attack is so slight that water passes under her palm with little backward deflection taking place. This produces very little lift force and, therefore, very little propulsive force.

pitched inward before they pass under your elbows, they will continue to rotate inward, passing the optimal angle of attack before the insweep is completed. Thus, some propulsive force is lost from the last portion of the insweep.

Another common error is failing to pitch the hands inward during the insweep. In this case, the angle of attack is less than needed for optimal lift and the hands "slice" inward with little propulsion occurring. The stroke plot in Figure 3.9 shows the effect of this error.

Upsweep   The action of the arms during the upsweep can be seen clearly from different perspectives in Figures 3.1, 3.3, and 3.4. It is indicated by the letters I to U in the stroke plots in Figure 3.6. As with all other stroke movements, the beginning of the upsweep overlaps with the end of the insweep. This is done so inward inertia can be overcome with less muscular effort. The technique for executing the upsweep is as follows:

When your hands approach the midline of your body, their direction of motion is gradually changed from inward, upward, and backward to backward, outward, and upward (see frames *H* to *J* in fig. 3.4). Once the change of direction has been completed, your hands continue sweeping back, out, and up until they approach the anterior portions of your thighs, where the release is made. The pitch of your hands is gradually changed from inward and upward to outward and backward during the transition from insweep to upsweep. This is accomplished by relaxing your wrists and allowing water pressure to push your hands into an extended and outwardly rotated position.

The outward, upward, and backward motion of your hands together with their outward and backward pitch causes water to be deflected backward gradually as it passes over your palms from wrist to fingers. (Actually the hands are pitched upward somewhat with respect to the direction of motion after the transition is made. However, as indicated in Chapter 1, swimmers achieve the proper hand pitch position more easily when they try to flatten their palms through this phase.)

During the transition phase, the outward pitch should provide an angle of attack that is between 60 and 70 degrees to the outward direction of hand movement. This rather large angle of attack is used because propulsion is drag dominated during this phase. The stroke plots in Figure 3.6 show that backward hand motion is greater here than in any other part of the stroke.

When your hands pass outside your hips the motion becomes more upward until the sweep is completed. The upward angle of attack of the hands should be between 30 and 40 degrees relative to the upward direction of motion (see fig. 3.1*G*).

The upsweep is a powerful motion, perhaps the most powerful phase of the armstroke. Hand speed should be accelerated in outward and upward directions from the beginning to the end of the movement.

Common errors in the upsweep. The most frequent error swimmers make during the upsweep is to push water almost directly upward. This forces your hips down while contributing little, if any, propulsive force. The effect of this

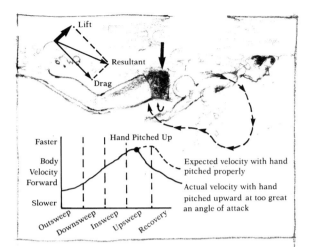

Figure 3.10. The effect of pushing water upward during the upsweep. The swimmer's hands are pitched upward at too great an angle during the upsweep. This is a "stall" angle that creates little propulsive force and a large amount of drag force. This drag force will pull the swimmer's body downward, decelerating forward velocity in the process.

mistake is illustrated in Figure 3.10. It is usually made by swimmers who try to push water backward to the surface of the water. The upsweep should end as your hands approach your thighs. No useful purpose can be served by continuing your stroking efforts beyond this point because swimmers cannot maintain an effective angle of attack after their hands reach their thighs. Swimmers should be cautioned to turn their palms inward as they pass their legs so their hands will leave the water on their sides with less upward force being exerted.

Recovery   Side views of the recovery are shown in Figure 3.11 for both the breathing (frames *A* to *E*) and the nonbreathing (frames *F* to *I*) strokes. Your elbows will break through the surface while your hands are still completing the upsweep. When the upsweep ends, relax your pressure on the water, turn your palms inward, and allow your hands to follow your arms up and outward over the water. Your arms continue traveling upward and outward (more out than up) until they pass your shoulders, at which time the motion becomes inward and forward until the entry is made. Contrary to popular opinion, your arms will not be completely extended as they leave the water (see frame *A* of fig. 3.11). Extension takes place after they leave the water and are traveling upward and outward over the surface.

Butterflyers, unlike freestylers and backstrokers, can recover their arms over the water in a low, lateral manner without disturbing lateral alignment. The simultaneous sideward motions of both arms counteracts the lateral force of each so that no lateral motion of the body takes place.

Your arms should be relaxed during the recovery. Your hands should leave the water in a thumbs-down position and remain in that position throughout the recovery (see frames *B* to *D* of fig. 3.11). Your elbows should be flexed slightly as you reach forward for the entry so that the inward motion of your arms can be changed to outward with less effort as the entry is made.

Although the recovery is low and lateral, your arms should be carried high

A   B

C   D

E   F   continued opposite

Figure 3.11. David Santos's butterfly recovery. These photos show the breathing and nonbreathing strokes.

enough to remain clear of the water until the entry is made. Butterflyers have traditionally been taught to keep their shoulders in the water during the recovery, which makes it difficult to keep the arms from "dragging" forward through the water as they reach for the entry position. When your shoulders are out of the water during the recovery, it is easier to keep your arms free of

Figure 3.11.

I

the water until your hands are near the correct entry position. Notice that the shoulders of the swimmer in Figure 3.11 are out of the water during most of the recovery.

This technique is usually not recommended because upward motion of the shoulders is thought to increase form drag. Supposedly, the hips and legs drop deeper in the water to compensate for the raised shoulders. This does not necessarily occur, however. Analysis of motion pictures of world-class butterfly swimmers who use this technique do not show their hips and legs dropping when their shoulders are raised for a breath. *If your body is moving forward faster than it is traveling upward,* your hips and legs will be pulled in the same direction your trunk is moving. When the trunk travels forward and upward, your legs should also be pulled forward and upward, reducing, rather than increasing, form drag. In addition, the shoulders will be traveling downward and forward as the entry is made which will continue to pull the hips and legs upward and forward over the top of the parabolic path that is characteristic of the undulating nature of this stroke.

Swimmers who have experimented with both styles feel that recovering with their shoulders out of the water is easier than maintaining them in a submerged or even partially submerged position. Their recoveries are completed with less effort, they take fewer strokes per length, and they swim faster times.

Another advantage of recovering with your shoulders out of the water is that your shoulders will not be pushed forward through the water on the recovery. It is accepted that freestylers and backstrokers can reduce form and wave drag by recovering with their shoulders out of the water. There is a trend for breaststrokers to do likewise. It seems reasonable, therefore, that butterflyers should also use this technique. Of course, the shoulder lift can be overdone. If the upward movement of the shoulders exceeds their forward motion the hips and legs will be submerged. To prevent this occurring, caution swimmers to keep both head and shoulders moving forward as well as upward during the recovery.

The final advantage of this recovery technique was mentioned earlier in connection with the entry. Swimmers can keep their arms from "dragging" forward through the water until late in the recovery if their shoulders are out of the water.

Common errors in the recovery. The most common mistake during the recovery has already been mentioned. That is, dragging the arms forward through the water. This should be avoided at all costs. Another common error is to recover the arms with too much upward motion. There is no advantage in lifting your arms higher than is necessary to keep them clear of the water throughout most of the recovery.

Instructions for Teaching the Butterfly Armstroke to College, High School, and Older Age-Group Swimmers

a. Entry: Your hands should enter the water slightly outside shoulder width with palms facing outward.

b. Outsweep: Reach out with your fingertips and press outward with your hands as you finish the downbeat of the first kick.

c. Downsweep: After completing the first kick, sweep your hands down and out, keeping your palms pitched outward while you do.

d. Insweep: As your hands pass their deepest point, begin sweeping them inward underneath your head. Gradually change the pitch of your hands from outward to inward as you sweep them inward.

e. Upsweep: As your hands pass under your head, begin pushing the water backward, outward, and upward toward the surface. Your palms should be pitched out and back.

f. Release: Release pressure on the water as your hands approach your thighs. Turn your palms inward as they pass your legs and allow the momentum of the upsweep to carry your hands up and out of the water. They should leave the water on their sides, little fingers first, to minimize drag.

Instructions for Teaching the Butterfly Armstroke to Younger Age-Group Swimmers

a. Your hands should enter the water outside your shoulders.

b. Don't begin stroking immediately. Reach out with your hands while you kick down.

c. After you complete the first kick, sweep your hands in a circle down, out and in and up until they are nearly together under your head.

d. After that, push the water out, up, and back toward the surface.

e. Let go of the water as your hands pass your legs.

f. Bring your hands out of the water little finger first.

The Dolphin Kick

The dolphin kick consists of a downbeat and upbeat. These are shown in Figure 3.12. There are two complete kicks (two downbeats and two upbeats) during every armstroke. The downbeat of the first kick occurs during the outsweep of the armstroke. The second downbeat accompanies the upsweep of the armstroke.

Upbeat
The upbeat is illustrated in frames *A* to *C* of Figure 3.12. It begins as your knees near full extension in the downbeat of the preceding kick. At this time, hip extension starts your thighs moving upward while your lower legs are extending at the knee joints. This rebound-like action of the thighs reduces the muscular effort required to overcome the downward inertia of the legs and start them moving upward.

Once the downbeat is completed, your legs sweep upward and forward until they are in line with your trunk. At this time your hips begin to flex as the downbeat of the next kick begins.

Your legs should be in an extended position and your feet should be in a natural position midway between plantar flexion and dorsiflexion as they travel upward. If your knees and ankles are relaxed, the downward pressure of the water will place them in this position, with no muscular effort required. The upward motion of the legs is accomplished by the hip extensors, the gluteus maximus, and the hamstring muscles.

Downbeat
The downbeat is initiated by flexing at the hip joints as your feet pass above the level of your body. Your thighs begin moving downward as water pressure beneath your legs causes your relaxed lower legs to flex at the knees. This action overcomes the upward inertia of the legs so they can change directions with the least amount of effort.

As hip flexion nears maximum, approximately 70 to 80 degrees, your knees begin extending and your lower legs accelerate downward. The downbeat ends when your legs are completely extended (see frames *D* to *G* of fig. 3.12).

Your feet should be pitched upward and inward as much as possible during the downbeat. The upward pitch should be 70 to 85 degrees relative to the downward direction of motion. This angle of attack is shown in Figure 3.12*D*.

Most world-class butterflyers spread their knees at the beginning of the downbeat and then bring them together during the sweep (see frames *A* to *C* of fig. 3.4). This is accomplished by abduction and outward rotation at the hip joints. There are probably two purposes served by separating the legs in this manner: (1) it is easier to pitch your feet inward and upward when your knees

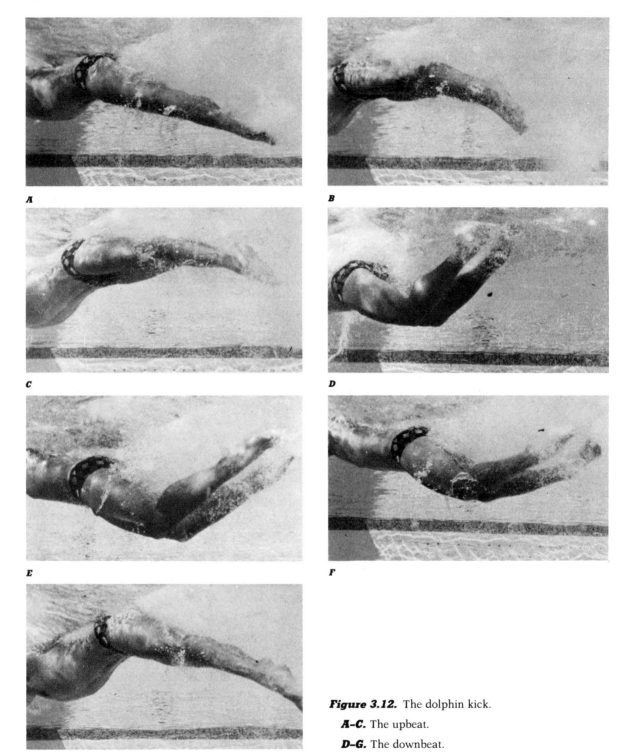

Figure 3.12. The dolphin kick.

A–C. The upbeat.

D–G. The downbeat.

are apart, and (2) your feet should remain pitched in and up longer if your thighs can be rotated inward as your knees are extending.

A good dolphin kick also depends on excellent flexibility of the ankle joints and feet. The ability to plantar flex the ankles and invert the feet allows swimmers to keep their feet pitched upward and inward for a longer period of time, which will increase propulsion.

Is the Dolphin Kick Propulsive?   Some believe that the dolphin kick functions only to maintain a swimmer's hips near the surface of the water; others believe that it is propulsive as well. Force diagrams of the dolphin kick indicate that the downbeat of the first kick may both elevate the hips and propel the body forward while the downbeat of the second is useful only for elevating the hips (see fig. 3.13). The force diagrams also indicate that neither upbeat is propulsive.

The legs are moving in a primarily downward direction during the downbeat of the first kick. This is because that beat takes place during the arm recovery. Forward velocity is at its lowest point then and the legs can sweep downward faster than the swimmer is moving forward. The force diagram indicates that this could create a lift force that would be propulsive. If the feet are pitched upward and inward, the flow of water molecules will be slowed and deflected backward as they pass from ankles to toes, over the curved instep surfaces. This will create a pressure differential between the two sides of the feet that will exert a lift force in a forward direction.

The body's forward velocity is so great during the downbeat of the second kick and the upbeat of both kicks that the legs are being pulled forward faster than they can sweep upward and downward. In these cases, most of the force is exerted in vertical directions and there should be little, if any, propulsion from these kicks.

While the downbeat of the first kick is probably propulsive, it also elevates the hips to reduce form drag. The upbeat that follows probably helps to lower the hips so the body is horizontally aligned during the underwater armstroke. The downbeat of the second kick probably keeps the hips from being submerged by the upward force of the arms as they complete the upsweep. The upbeat following the second kick is probably nothing more than a recovery motion that puts your legs in position for the next downbeat.

Although the dolphin kick does cause some elevation and submersion of the hips, these actions should not be excessive. When the kick is properly executed, the hips should rise just above the surface during the downbeat of the first kick and fall just below the surface on the subsequent upbeat. The downbeat and upbeat of the second kick should merely cancel other forces and prevent the hips from moving vertically. Excessive up and down hip motion increases form and wave drag and, therefore, reduces forward velocity.

Some swimmers who are learning the dolphin kick push their hips up and down to get the proper amount of undulation. This practice should be discouraged. Executing the kick in this manner usually leads to excessive vertical motions of the body. It is better to allow the vertical motions of the hips to occur as a natural reaction to the proper leg movements. The rise and fall of the hips

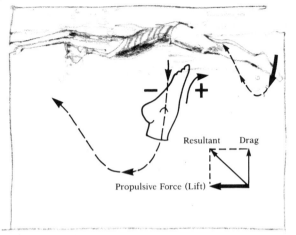

A. Downbeat of First Kick

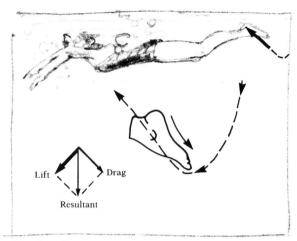

B. Upbeat of First Kick

C. Upbeat of Second Kick

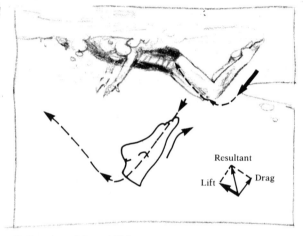

D. Downbeat of Second Kick

Figure 3.13. Kick plots of the dolphin kick. These patterns were drawn from films of world- and national-level butterflyers. The downbeat of the first kick (**A**), the one accompanying the recovery and arm entry, is directed primarily downward because the forward velocity of the body is at its lowest point at this time. As indicated by force diagram **A**, forward propulsion can be generated from this motion (providing, of course, that the feet are pitched properly). Therefore, the first kick is probably propulsive.

The feet travel upward and forward during the upbeat of the first kick (**B**), because the arms are pulling the body forward faster than the legs are moving upward. There is likely to be very little, if any, propulsion associated with this movement. Force diagram **B** shows that most of the force is directed downward and forward. Therefore, the major function of this upbeat is

probably to bring the hips down in line with the body from the elevated position they attained during the preceding downbeat.

In a like manner, the upbeat of the second kick (**C**) is probably not propulsive, because the feet also sweep upward and forward during this phase (see force diagram **C**).

The downbeat of the second kick (**D**) is probably not propulsive either, because the direction of motion is downward and forward. That beat occurs during the most propulsive phase of the armstroke, the upsweep, and the body is traveling forward faster than the feet are traveling downward. As a result, most of the force is directed upward rather than forward (see force diagram **D**). The primary function of this kick is probably to counteract the force of the swimmer's upsweeping arms so the hips are not pulled too far under water.

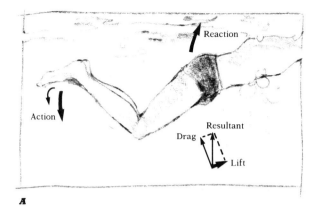

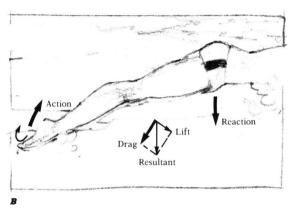

Figure 3.14. The effect on propulsion of pitching the feet improperly during the dolphin kick.

Swimmer **A** has his feet pitched downward during the downbeat of the dolphin kick. As a result, the force is directed downward, exerting a resultant force that pushes the hips upward.

Swimmer **B** has his feet pitched upward during the upbeat. Most of the force is in a downward direction, causing the hips to be pulled downward, disrupting horizontal alignment, increasing form drag, and reducing forward velocity.

should be an effect, not the cause, of a good kick. When the legs are used properly, the hip movements will not be excessive and the kicks will be more effective in their propulsive and stabilizing functions.

Common errors in the dolphin kick. The most common error swimmers make when executing the dolphin kick is failing to pitch their feet properly. The effect of this error is shown in Figure 3.14. If they lack sufficient plantar-flexion ability, their feet will be pitched downward on the downbeat (see fig. 3.14). This increases the upward component of force and the hips will be elevated but will not be pushed forward to any great extent.

If the feet are pitched up during the upbeat, the effect will be to increase downward force and the hips will be pushed downward excessively (see fig. 3.14).

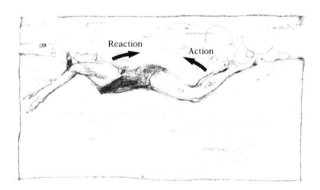

Figure 3.15. The effect on propulsion of bending the knees during the upbeat. This swimmer is making the all-too-common error of bending her knees on the upbeat of the dolphin kick. The forward force of her legs causes a counterforce in the opposite direction that will reduce her forward velocity. Butterfly swimmers should kick up from the hip, being sure to keep their lower legs relaxed so the water pressure above their legs will keep them in an extended position as they execute the upbeat.

Another common mistake is to bend your knees on the upbeat and sweep only your lower legs upward. This causes your thighs to remain deep in the water increasing form drag. The lower legs will also push forward against the water as they sweep upward and a counterforce will be produced that will reduce forward speed. The effect of this error is illustrated in Figure 3.15.

Timing of the Armstroke and Kicks

It was mentioned in the previous section that there are two kicks to each armstroke. The usual way to teach correct timing to novice butterfly swimmers is to indicate that the downbeat of one kick occurs as the hands enter the water while the second downbeat takes place as they leave the water. This explanation, although correct, is an oversimplification of the complex timing between the arm and leg movements in this stroke.

The downbeat of the first kick is executed during the entry and outsweep of the armstroke. It is completed as the catch is made (see frames *A* to *C* of fig. 3.3), and the following upbeat takes place during the down and insweeps of the arms (see frames *D* to *F* of fig. 3.3). The downbeat of the second kick is synchronized with the upsweep of the armstroke (see frames *G* to *J* of fig. 3.3), and the subsequent upbeat accompanies the arm recovery. Each leg beat should be synchronized with the corresponding arm motion so perfectly that they each begin and end at the same time. Propulsion suffers when these precise relationships are disturbed. One example of incorrect timing is the one-kick butterfly, which is discussed in a later section.

Asymmetry of the Two Dolphin Kicks The dolphin kicks are somewhat different in each phase of the stroke cycle. The downbeat of the first kick appears to be longer than the second downbeat. The upbeat that follows also appears to be longer than the corresponding upbeat that follows the second kick. These differences have led some experts to consider the first kick as more powerful than the second. It is often described as major while the second kick is considered a minor beat. Although the first kick is probably more propulsive than the second, there is a risk in thinking of it as a more powerful movement. It causes some swimmers to put more effort into the first kick and to reduce their effort during the second kick. Occasionally, the second kick is reduced so much that it does not generate enough force to keep the hips near the surface during the upsweep of the armstroke.

Actually, the effort put into both kicks should be equal or nearly so. Differences in body position, not effort, cause the first kick to appear more powerful. When the swimmer's head is down during the first downbeat, the hips can travel up and forward for a longer distance which in turn, permits the legs to kick downward for a greater length of time. The head and shoulders remain down during the first two sweeps of the armstroke, which allows time for a longer and higher upbeat. Conversely, the swimmer's head and shoulders are elevated during the second kick, which inhibits the hip rise and the downward motion of the legs during the downbeat and their upward movement during the subsequent upbeat. It is probably best to teach swimmers to put equal effort into both kicks and to realize that the changing body position will cause the first kick to be longer and more propulsive than the second.

One-Kick Butterfly

Many butterfly swimmers, particularly novices, are unable to complete the downbeat of their second kick. This makes it difficult to maintain their hips near the surface and an increase in form drag results. The 1-kick butterfly is difficult to correct because the solution is not as obvious as it seems. That is, telling swimmers to kick twice during each stroke cycle will not correct the problem. An error in the armstroke, not the kick makes it impossible for them to finish the second kick. That error is usually an abbreviated down and in sweep of the arms. A short down and in sweep sets in motion a chain of events that cause the underwater armstroke to be completed before two kicks can be executed.

The upbeat of the legs that follows the downbeat of the first kick takes place during the downsweep and insweep of the armstroke. Your knees should be flexed, ready to execute the downbeat of the second kick when these sweeps are completed. If the downsweep and/or insweep are abbreviated your legs will not have time to finish their upward motion before the insweep of the arms is completed. Therefore, the downbeat of the second kick will not begin until the upsweep of the armstroke is well underway. This leaves time for only a partial kick down before your hands leave the water. Apparently, swimmers must terminate that kick prematurely in order to get their legs up and in position for the first downbeat as they recover their arms.

One-kick butterflyers should be instructed to use a longer downsweep to correct this problem. This will allow them time to get their legs in position for the second kick before the upsweep begins which will, in turn, permit them to complete that kick before their hands leave the water.

Body Position

It is useless to talk of one body position when describing the butterfly. There are three positions that the body assumes during each stroke cycle. Each plays an important role in reducing drag.

1. Your body should be as level as possible during the most propulsive phases of the armstroke; the downsweep, the insweep, and the upsweep (see frames *D* to *J* of fig. 3.3).
2. Your hips should travel upward and forward through the surface during the first kick and the outsweep of the armstroke. If this does not occur, the kick has not been propulsive (see fig. 3.3*C*).
3. The force of the second kick should not be so great that it pushes the hips above the surface (see fig. 3.3*J*). It is used only to keep them from being pushed downward as your arms sweep upward.

Common Errors in Body Position

Problems occur when swimmers undulate too little or too much. Too little undulation reduces propulsion and your hips and legs sink when the leg "drive" is not sufficient to keep them elevated. Since the legs are deeper, more laminar streams are disrupted and drag increases accordingly.

Failure to undulate sufficiently is usually caused by one or both of the following:

1. Pulling your hands in under your body immediately after entry. The effect of this error was described in the section on the outsweep of the armstroke.
2. Failure to drop your head underwater as the arms enter. This retards the upward motion of the hips.

Swimmers who undulate excessively are kicking too deep in an effort to raise their hips above the surface. This increases form drag during the time the legs are below the body. In addition, raising the hips excessively results in a compensatory drop that places them deeper than necessary. This increases both form drag and wave drag (see fig. 1.36).

Breathing

Proper breathing is illustrated in Figures 3.3 and 3.4. Your face should break through the surface of the water at completion of the insweep and you should breathe during the upsweep and the first half of the recovery. Your head drops back into the water as your arms reach forward for the entry. Your head moves in advance of your arms, dropping under water an instant before your hands enter (see frame *A* of fig. 3.4).

Your entire head should be submerged at entry. However, it should be only slightly beneath the surface. Many swimmers dive downward in order to elevate their hips. This technique is not recommended as it may lead to excessive downward movements of the head and body that will increase drag. It is more efficient to elevate the hips by kicking downward correctly.

Breathing Sequence and Frequency

It is an oversimplification to describe breathing only in terms of when the breath is taken. Some important aspects of the breathing cycle are overlooked. The proper sequence of head movements must begin early in the stroke cycle if you are to have your face out of the water at the proper time. Your head should begin moving upward precisely as the catch is made (see fig. 3.4C). It continues traveling upward during the down and in sweeps of the armstroke, reaching the surface at the end of the insweep. As described previously, the breath is taken during the upsweep and the first half of the recovery and your head is returned to the water as your hands reach forward for the entry. Swimmers generally thrust their chins forward as their faces break through the surface. This encourages forward motion of their bodies while they take a breath.

Butterflyers are usually advised to breathe once during every two armstrokes. It is important, however, that their shoulders rise almost as high out of the water on the nonbreathing stroke as they do on the breathing stroke so that their arms can remain clear of the water during most of the recovery. This prevents their shoulders from "plowing" forward through the water. The correct positions of the head and shoulders on the nonbreathing stroke are shown in frames *F* to *I* of Figure 3.11.

Common errors in breathing. Swimmers often make the mistake of lifting their heads up and back to take a breath. The backward force will reduce forward velocity. You should practice thrusting your head and shoulders forward as you breathe.

Another problem is breathing too late in the armstroke. If your head remains down during the catch and downsweep, there will not be time for your mouth to reach the surface and for you to inhale before the underwater portion of the armstroke is completed. This will cause you to delay bringing your arms out of the water until you have taken a breath and there will be a noticeable "hitch" in your stroke.

Breathing Frequency During Butterfly Races

Lifting the head to breathe is believed to increase drag because the hips sink to compensate for the weight being held above the water. Therefore, butterflyers are usually advised to breathe once every two armstrokes to compromise between the need to consume oxygen and the desire to maintain a horizontal body position.

While this breathing pattern is used by most swimmers in 100-yards/meters races, some find it too difficult to maintain for the 200 distances. For this reason, they use breathing patterns where two or three breaths are taken in succession before a nonbreathing stroke is completed. These breathing patterns are referred to as 2-and-1 and 3-and-1 cycles. The extra breathing strokes increase oxygen consumption while the periodic nonbreathing strokes are used to regain horizontal alignment.

Although these patterns are almost universally recommended, many butterflyers disregard them and breathe during every stroke cycle in races. This pattern is seen most frequently in 200 races although some swimmers also breathe during every stroke in the 100 events. This may not be a mistake but, rather, another example of the "wisdom of the body" superseding traditional teaching. Some butterflyers do not lose horizontal alignment when breathing. It might not be essential or even wise for them to use a restricted breathing pattern if drag were not reduced by doing so. Each butterfly swimmer should determine his or her most effective breathing pattern by using a drill similar to the one that was recommended for this purpose in the previous chapter on the front crawl stroke.

At the end of a hard workout, *when you are somewhat fatigued*, swim a set of eight to twelve 50 or 100 butterflys. Alternate breathing patterns, using 3-and-1, 2-and-1, 1-and-1, and "every armstroke" styles. Repeat this drill over several days, discarding the patterns that are obviously less effective until you find the one that is consistently faster. Use that pattern in races. If there is no difference in speed between certain patterns, use the one that provides the greatest oxygen supply.

Figure 3.16. Breathing to the side in the butterfly. This photograph shows that swimmers must raise their shoulders out of the water just as high or higher when breathing to the side. This technique is not recommended.

Breathing to the Side

Some butterfly swimmers breathe to the side. They believe this decreases the distance they must lift their head and shoulders out of the water to take a breath and therefore lessens the possibility of losing good horizontal alignment when breathing. They reason that since freestylers are more efficient when they breathe to the side, butterflyers should be also. This reasoning overlooks an important difference in the two strokes. Freestylers can roll their bodies to bring their face above the surface and only minimal head lift is required to get their mouths clear of the water for a breath. Butterflyers must remain in a prone position. Therefore, they must lift the head and shoulders out of the water for a breath whether they breathe to the side or to the front. In fact, they have to lift their heads and shoulders just as high or higher out of the water when breathing to the side as when breathing to the front. A swimmer is shown breathing to the side in Figure 3.16. Although recovering with the shoulders above the surface is recommended, the swimmer's shoulders should not be unnecessarily high. Therefore, breathing to the side is not recommended.

CHAPTER *4*

The Breaststroke

Propellerlike arm and leg sweeps are more noticeable in the breaststroke than in any of the other competitive styles. The breaststroke involves body position and breathing, the armstroke, the kick, and the timing of the armstroke and kick.

Body Position and Breathing

The traditional style used by American swimmers when swimming the breaststroke is characterized by a "flat" body position, with the swimmer's hips remaining at or near the surface and the shoulders staying in the water throughout the entire stroke cycle. Breathing is accomplished by lifting and lowering the head so that the flat position of the trunk and legs is not disturbed. This style is illustrated in Figure 4.1.

Today there is a trend toward a dolphinlike breaststroke in which the hips are lowered and the shoulders are brought upward and forward out of the water when breathing. This style is shown in Figure 4.2. Eastern Europeans have used it for years. Some Western swimmers, the most notable being David Wilkie and Tracy Caulkins, have also had considerable success with the dolphin-style breaststroke.

The dolphin style, or what Howard Firby has named the natural style breaststroke (Firby 1975), involves bringing the face out of the water by lifting the shoulders upward and forward as the insweep of the armstroke is executed (see frames *A* and *B*). A breath is taken during the final portion of the insweep and the first part of the recovery. The head is then returned to the water as the arms are extended forward in the recovery (see frames *E* and *F*).

129

A *B*

C *D*

Figure 4.1. The flat body position in the breaststroke.

There are several reasons why the dolphin style should be superior to the flat style for increasing propulsive force and reducing drag:

1. There is a propulsive downsweep of the arms and legs in the dolphin style that, when executed correctly, causes the head and shoulders to surge upward and forward. Breaststrokers will not be nearly so effective if they reduce this downsweep in order to keep their shoulders low in the water.

2. There is a possibility that, as in the butterfly, carrying your shoulders upward and forward over the water during the leg and arm recoveries will cause less drag than pushing them forward through the water.

3. Lowering your hips as you breathe may actually reduce rather than increase form drag because your legs can be recovered with less flexion at the hips. If your hips are on the surface of the water, it is necessary to push your thighs downward and forward during the leg recovery in order to keep your feet underwater as they are brought up to your buttocks. This downward and forward motion of the thighs increases drag so much that many "flat" breaststrokers actually stop moving for a short period of time near the end of the leg recovery.

A comparison of the drag created by the two styles of leg recovery is shown in Figure 4.3. The important difference is that there is less forward movement of the thighs when the legs are recovered by lowering the hips. Notice, by comparing Figure 4.1*C* and Figure 4.2*D* that the hips are flexed much less when the recovery is completed by lowering the hips in the dolphin style. They present a gradually sloping surface to the water and drag should be reduced because the water molecules can pass around the thighs with less tur-

Figure 4.2. The dolphin-style breaststroke.

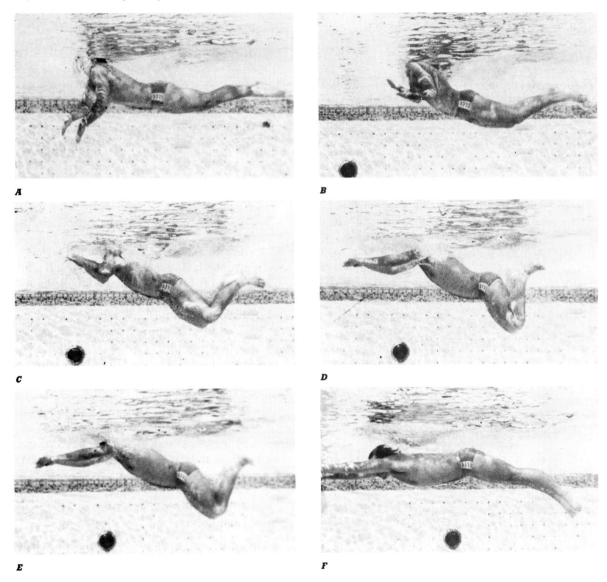

A

B

C

D

E

F

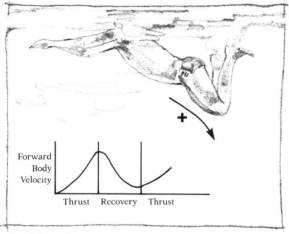

A. Dolphin Style

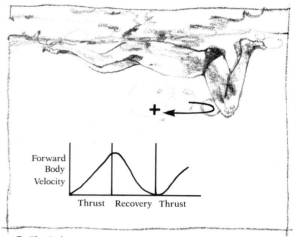

B. Flat Style

Figure 4.3. The effect of hip flexion on forward motion in the breaststroke recovery. The dolphin-style swimmer is recovering his legs by dropping his thighs toward the bottom of the pool and bringing his heels toward his buttocks. He flexes his hips only enough to keep his feet beneath the surface during the recovery and to make a powerful thrust when the propulsive phase of the kick begins. Since hip flexion is slight, the water can change directions gradually as it passes around his thighs, and drag should be minimal.

The swimmer using the flat-style breaststroke keeps his hips near the surface and, therefore, must flex them more during the leg recovery in order to keep his feet from coming out of the water as he brings them toward his buttocks. This causes him to push his thighs downward and *forward* against the water, increasing form drag and decelerating his forward speed.

bulence occurring. When the hips are kept at the surface in the flat style, the thighs must be flexed more at the hip so the feet can remain underneath while the legs are recovered. With the hips flexed the thighs present a much "flatter" surface to the oncoming flow of water molecules which should increase drag and reduce forward velocity. The thighs are also pushed forward against the water more when the hips are flexed. This forward movement of the thighs will create a counterforce that tends to hold the swimmer back.

The previous discussion might lead one to think that hip flexion should be avoided during the leg recovery. That is not true. Swimmers must flex their hips somewhat. Regardless of whether they use the flat- or dolphin-style breaststroke, there must be a certain amount of hip flexion so that the propulsive phase of the kick can be executed with optimum force. The dolphin style is superior because (1) swimmers spend less time with their hips flexed during the recovery and (2) they do not flex their hips as much as they do in the flat style.

Body Position   As with the butterfly stroke, it is useless to talk of *one* body position for the dolphin breaststroke, yet there are two important points to keep in mind:

1. Your body should be as streamlined as possible during the propulsive

phases of the armstroke. Your hips should be near the surface with your legs in line with your body. Your legs should be held close together in an extended position with toes pointed and there should be minimal incline from head to feet.

2. Your face and your trunk should be in the water and perfectly flat during as much of the propulsive phases of the kick as possible. Your arms should be nearly extended when the kick begins and completely extended as it nears completion.

Figure 4.4. Surface view of the breaststroke showing late breathing. The swimmer in these photographs is Lori Vendl, a national-level breaststroke swimmer and age-group record holder.

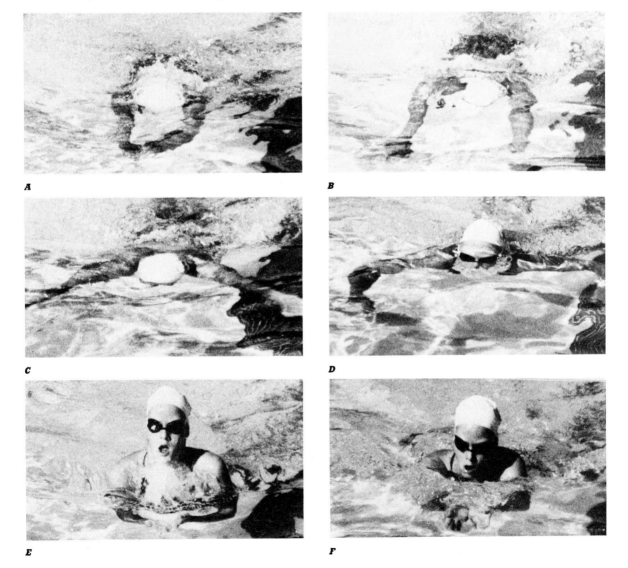

A

B

C

D

E

F

Breathing

The proper breathing sequence is illustrated in Figure 4.4. Your head should be brought upward and forward out of the water during the downsweep of your arms. This allows you to use the downward force of that portion of the armstroke to lift your head. Take your breath during the insweep of the armstroke and return your face to the water before the kick begins.

Common Errors in Body Position and Breathing

It should be noted that the dolphin motions of the body can be overdone in the breaststroke. Swimmers should not raise their shoulders out of the water any higher than is necessary to recover their legs with minimum hip flexion. The shoulders should be clear of the water but the chest should not be clearly visible. Swimmers should lift their shoulders up and forward rather than up and back as they breathe. As in the butterfly, when the forward motion of the trunk exceeds its upward speed the hips and legs will be pulled upward and forward as well. If the upward motion is excessive, or worse, if the head and shoulders are lifted backward, there will be a significant deceleration of forward speed.

The Armstroke

The breaststroke armstroke consists of an outsweep, catch, downsweep, insweep, and a recovery. Front, side, and underneath views are shown in Figures 4.5, 4.6, and 4.7 respectively. Stroke plots made from front, side, and underneath views are shown in Figure 4.8.

Figure 4.5. The breaststroke viewed from the front. The swimmer is David Santos, a national-level breaststroker and world-class individual medley swimmer.

A. The insweep of the legs is completed as the outsweep of the arms begins.

B-C. The outsweep of the arms. The arms sweep directly outward beyond shoulder width. Notice that the palms of his hands are pitched out and back. This phase of his stroke would be better if the palms were curved so that the hands assumed a more effective airfoil shape.

D. The catch and downsweep. The catch is made by pitching the palms downward slightly and changing the direction of the hands from outward to downward. The elbows begin to flex (frame **D**), and he sweeps out and down (frame **E**). The legs are held in a streamlined, gliding position during the outsweep and downsweep. The downward motion of the hands lifts the head and shoulders upward and forward for the breath.

E-G. The insweep. The hands continue circling, with the direction changing from downward and outward to downward and inward and finally to inward

and upward (see frame **G**). As the hands pass under the elbows, their pitch is changed from outward to inward (see **E** and **F**) and finally to upward (**G**). The upward motion of the hands lowers the hips, and the knees begin to flex, initiating the leg recovery.

H-I. The recovery of the arms and legs. The swimmer releases pressure on the water as the hands are coming together, and the momentum of their upward and inward action causes a "follow-through" that carries them up near the surface. Some swimmers cross their hands during this phase, and the "follow-through" causes many to turn their palms upward. The breath is taken. The head and shoulders are at their highest point during this phase, making it easy to do so. The legs are recovering during this phase.

As the hands come together, the elbows are squeezed downward and forward, changing the direction the hands are moving in from upward to forward to initiate the recovery. The swimmer turns the palms down and reaches forward. The head and shoulders are returning to the surface of the water.

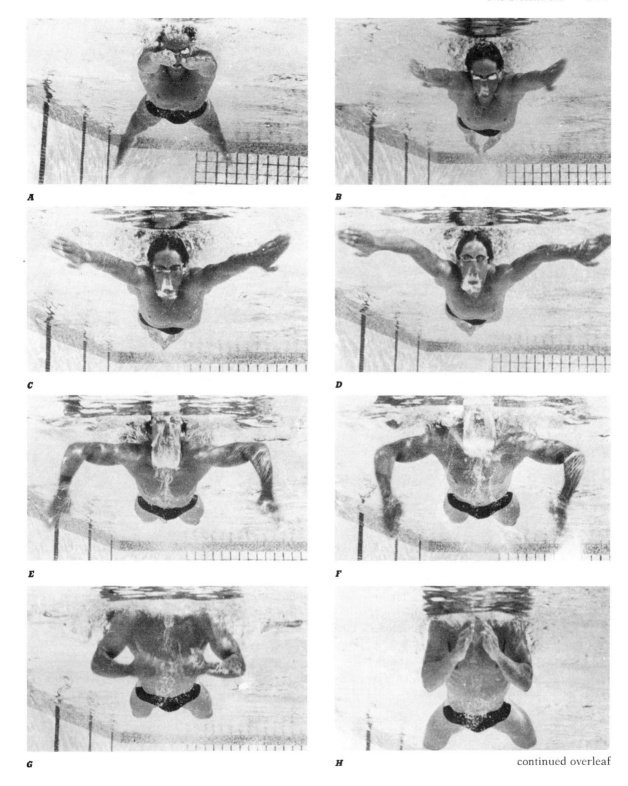

A

B

C

D

E

F

G

H

continued overleaf

Figure 4.5. continued

J–K. The recovery of the arms; outsweep and down-sweep of the legs. The legs begin sweeping outward as the arms reach forward. They continue their motion, circling downward as the arms near complete exten-sion. The head and shoulders have returned to a flat position in the water.

L. The outsweep of the arms begins as the legs are sweeping inward.

Figure 4.5.   **I**

J

K

L

Outsweep   The outsweep is best seen in frames *B* to *D* of Figure 4.7. It is marked by the letters O and C in the stroke plots in Figure 4.8. It is a gentle stretching motion that may provide only a small amount of propulsive force, if any, to the armstroke. The purpose of the outsweep is probably to put your arms in position for an effective insweep. To serve this purpose, it should be wider than many traditionalists have recommended.

Figure 4.6. Side view of the breaststroke armstroke. The swimmer is Jim Johnson, a national-level breast-stroke swimmer.

A. The recovery.

B. The outsweep.

C. The catch.

D–F. The insweep.

G–H. The recovery.

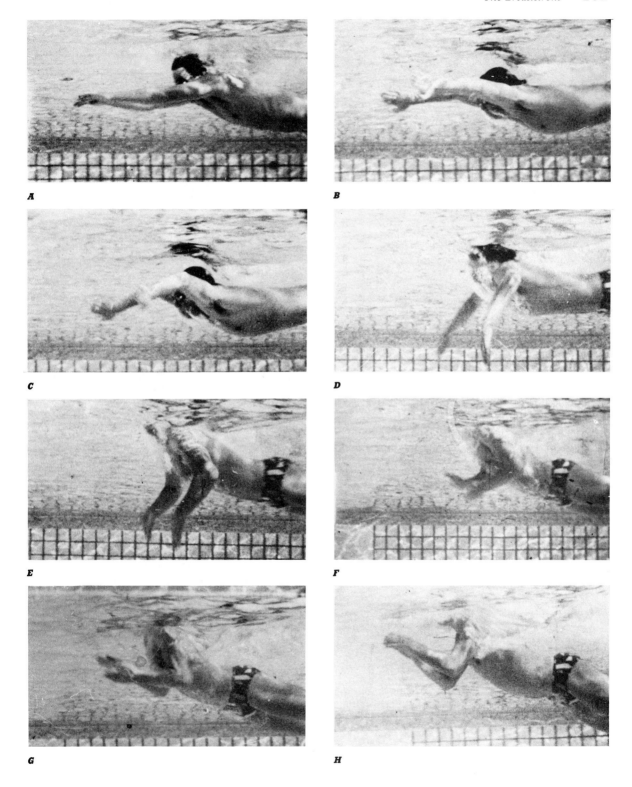

A

B

C

D

E

F

G

H

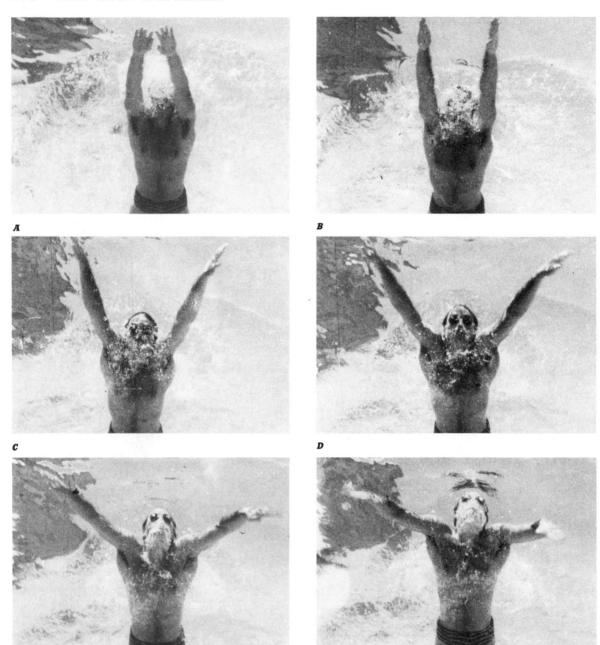

Figure 4.7. Jim Johnson's breaststroke armstroke viewed from underneath.

A. Completion of the arm recovery.

B-C. The outsweep. Notice the outward pitch of the hands.

D. Catch.

E. The downsweep.

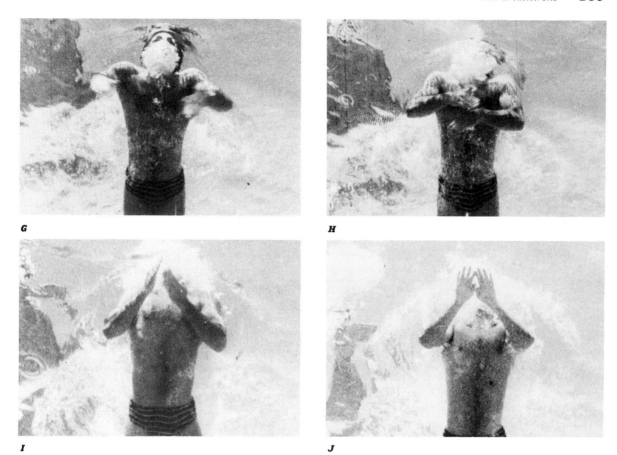

G

H

I

J

Figure 4.7. continued

F-H. The insweep.

I-J. The recovery.

There is no glide in the competitive breaststroke. The beginning of the outsweep and the end of the arm recovery overlap so that the forward inertia of the arms can be overcome with less effort. The hands start moving outward until they pass shoulder width where the catch is made. Your arms should remain extended throughout the outsweep. Elbow flexion begins at the catch.

Your hands should be pitched out and back, with your fingertips acting as the leading edge of the "propeller blade." Your hands should be pitched outward nearly 90 degrees from a prone position. The backward pitch should present an angle of attack of between 30 and 40 degrees relative to the outward direction the hands are moving. The hands should be cupped slightly to improve the airfoil shape (see fig. 4.7*D*).

Common errors in the outsweep. Perhaps the most common mistake swimmers make during the outsweep is to use a narrow stroke with the hands (and

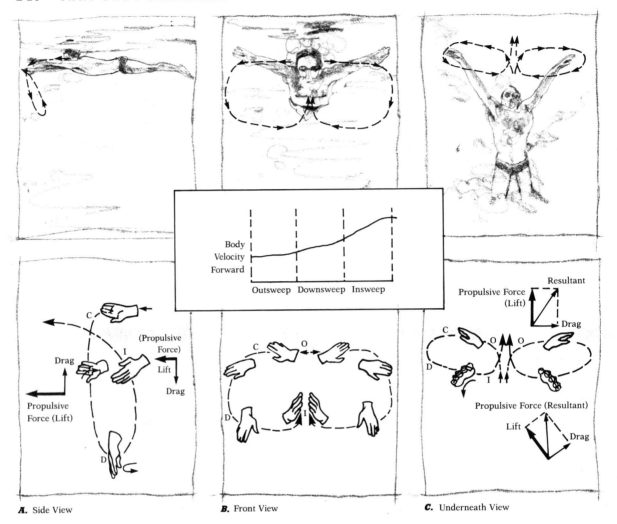

A. Side View **B.** Front View **C.** Underneath View

Figure 4.8. Stroke plots of the breaststroke armstroke. These drawings show the armstroke patterns from the side, front, and underneath. The manner in which propulsion can be generated is indicated by the force diagrams. The hand pitches that will deflect water backward during each phase of the armstroke are also shown.

arms) directed backward and downward more than outward. The narrow stroke has been popular with traditionalists who believe swimmers should begin pushing water backward immediately. Schleihauf (1977) has shown that a wider sweep is more propulsive. Propulsive force was increased approximately 5 pounds when one of his subjects used a wider outsweep. The effect on the subsequent phases of the armstroke was even more striking. There was an increase in force of nearly 10 pounds during the insweep because the swimmer started the insweep from a wider position and thus was able to apply force over a longer distance.

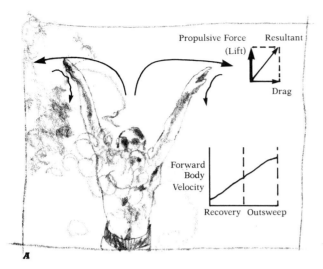

Figure 4.9. The effect of "paddling" outward on propulsion. Swimmer **A** is shown with the hands pitched so that water is deflected backward from fingertips to wrist as the swimmer sweeps outward. In this case a lift force is exerted and forward acceleration can be achieved. Swimmer **B** is shown using the hands as pad-dles to push water outward. This creates a rather large drag force in inward directions. Body alignment is not disrupted because the inward force of one arm is counteracted by that of the other; however, there is less propulsive force associated with this hand pitch.

This information notwithstanding, an outsweep that is too wide can be just as serious a problem as a stroke that is too narrow. An excessively wide outsweep, in which the arms sweep well beyond shoulder width, will cause a delay in starting the more propulsive phases of the armstroke. The catch should be made as your hands pass outside shoulder width.

Using the hands as paddles rather than as propellers is another common error. This causes swimmers to push water outward with the flat surfaces of their palms rather than cupping their hands and allowing water to be deflected backward from fingertips to wrist, as shown in Figure 4.9A. When water is pushed outward, the major force produced is a drag force that is directed inward. Any propulsion that might be achieved during the outsweep will probably be minimized by pushing water outward.

Catch   The catch is made as your hands pass outside shoulder width. Your hands change pitch from outward and backward to outward, downward, and backward. The lift force generated by this pitch causes your head and shoulders to surge forward over your arms. The catch position can be seen clearly in Figure 4.5D. It is indicated by the letter C in the stroke plots in Figure 4.8.

Downsweep   Once the catch is made, your hands sweep downward and outward in a circular path until they approach their deepest point. Your elbows continue to flex acting like a shaft with your hand rotating around them in a propellerlike manner. The downward and outward speed of your hands should be accelerated from the beginning to the end of the downsweep. Your hands should remain pitched outward and downward throughout the downsweep. The outward and downward angles of attack should be between 30 and 40 degrees to their respective directions of motion. The manner in which propulsive force is generated during the downsweep is described in Chapter 1. It is illustrated by the force diagrams in Figure 4.8. The manner in which this pitch of the hands can cause water to be deflected backward is also shown.

Common errors in the downsweep. The most common mistake swimmers make during the downsweep is to sweep their hands inward rather than downward. This reduces the length of the propulsive phase of the armstroke. It also makes it more difficult to get the head and shoulders out of the water for a breath.

Insweep   An excellent insweep is shown in frames *E* to *H* of Figure 4.7. The insweep is marked by points D and I in the stroke plots of Figure 4.8. It begins as your hands approach their deepest point in the downsweep. The transition from downsweep to insweep is made in a circular manner with the hands sweeping first downward and inward and then inward, upward, and backward. The insweep ends as your hands approach the level of your elbows in their upward sweep. You should accelerate the movement of your hands, inward and upward, throughout the insweep.

The pitch of your hands should change gradually from outward and downward to inward and upward throughout the insweep. The change to an inward pitch should not take place until your hands have passed under your elbows, however, or they will rotate past the optimum angle of attack early in the insweep and some propulsion will be lost. According to Schleihauf's data, the angle of attack should be 30 to 40 degrees relative to the inward direction the hands are moving (Schleihauf 1977). The angle of attack relative to their upward direction of motion is not known but appears, from analysis of underwater motion pictures, to be between 30 and 40 degrees. The manner in which propulsive force can be generated during the insweep is shown in the stroke plots in Figure 4.8C. Notice how the inward and upward pitch of the hands causes water to be deflected backward over the palms as it passes downward from the thumb side to the little finger sides.

Your elbows should follow your hands down, in, and up during the insweep, and you should "squeeze" them in under your ribs as the insweep is completed (see frames *F* and *G* of Figure 4.6). This elbow squeeze increases the upward inertia of the hands causing them to change directions from upward to forward as the recovery begins. This explanation of the elbow squeeze should be enlarged upon because it is controversial.

Some people believe that bringing the elbows downward toward the ribs reduces propulsive force. This is true only if the elbows are collapsed backward and inward *ahead* of the hands. When they *follow* the hands downward and inward, they quite naturally pass by the ribs, conserving angular momentum in the process.

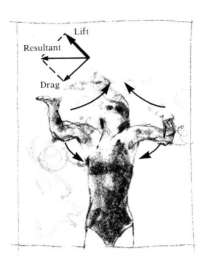

Figure 4.10. The effect of "collapsing" the elbows during the insweep. The illustration shows an underwater view of a swimmer committing the error of collapsing the elbows inward ahead of the hands during the insweep. This causes the insweep to be terminated early because the direction the hands are moving in is changed from inward and backward to inward and forward by the action of the swimmer's elbows. When this happens, the resultant force of the armstroke will be exerted outward and downward. The only way this swimmer can prevent a considerable deceleration of forward speed is to release pressure on the water and pitch the hands at a small angle of attack so that very little force is exerted in any direction. This is what most swimmers do. Unfortunately, their forward velocity is also reduced, because they have terminated their propulsive efforts early. If they had swept the hands inward ahead of the elbows, they could continue to generate propulsive force until the arms are under the chest.

The effect of collapsing the elbows is shown in Figure 4.10. This action reduces propulsion in the same way a dropped elbow causes a loss of propulsive force in other strokes. When the elbows move downward and inward ahead of the hands, the pitch of the forearms and hands becomes downward. They push down in the water and most of their force is exerted upward rather than forward. The only way the swimmer can prevent this force from retarding forward velocity is to release pressure on the water and begin moving his hands forward into the recovery. This is what most swimmers who commit this error do. Unfortunately, this action also results in a loss of propulsion because it causes the insweep, the most propulsive phase of the breaststroke, to be terminated early. If the hands are swept inward ahead of the elbows, they can continue generating propulsive force for a longer time.

You will notice that the swimmer in Figure 4.7*l*. has turned his palms upward at the end of the insweep. This motion is superfluous where propulsion is concerned, yet it is common among world-class breaststrokers. It is probably nothing more than a follow-through action. After the rapidly moving hands (which were changing pitch from inward to upward) release pressure on the water, they will continue their upward motion for a short time, in this case until the palms turn upward.

Common errors in the insweep. The most common mistake swimmers make during the insweep has been described already. It is to start the hands forward before the propulsive phase of the insweep is completed. The effect of this error on propulsion is illustrated in Figure 4.10. Propulsive force can be generated for a longer period of time if your hands are kept moving in an inward direction until they are almost together under your chest.

Another error swimmers make in the insweep is to pitch their hands inward before they pass under their elbows. If you do this, your hands will rotate past the optimal inward and upward angles of attack before the insweep is completed and propulsion will be reduced during what should be the most powerful phase of the armstroke.

Recovery

The recovery is best seen in frames *F* to *H* Figure 4.6. It begins when your hands are nearly together under your chin. Your hands release pressure on the water and the inward and forward motion of your elbows starts the hands forward in the recovery. The pitch of your hands is quickly changed from upward to downward as the hands move forward. Your hands should be together and your fingertips should slip forward quickly and gently in a straight line, approximately 8 to 10 inches underwater. Your wrists should be neither flexed nor hyperextended. The slightest amount of either will cause the palm or knuckle side of your hands to push forward against the water.

Common errors in the recovery. The most common error swimmers make during the recovery is to push their hands forward with too much force. This causes a counterforce that decreases velocity. The hands should be slipped forward gently.

Another problem is lack of streamlining. The importance of extending the arms in an almost straight, forward direction with the wrists in a natural position midway between flexion and extension has already been mentioned. It goes without saying that your hands should be kept together. If they are apart, more surface area is presented to the water and drag is increased.

The Downsweep: An Alternate Way to Begin the Armstroke

The downsweep can be an alternate way to start the armstroke. The swimmer in Figure 4.11 is using this style. Notice that her hands move outward and downward rather than directly outward in frames *A* and *B*.

Swimmers who prefer this style use their hands the same way they would in the downsweep of the front crawl stroke. The hands are pitched down and out as they sweep down and out. The arms remain straight until the hands pass shoulder width (see fig. 4.11*A*). At that time the elbows begin to flex and the propulsive phase of the downsweep begins.

In spite of the fact that several world-class swimmers have successfully used the downsweep to begin the armstroke, this style is not recommended. Propulsion should be greater if the stroke begins with an outsweep because the subsequent downsweep and insweep will be longer.

Instructions for Teaching the Armstroke to College, High School, and Older Age-Group Swimmers

a. Outsweep: With your palms pitched out and back, sweep your hands outward until water pressure causes your elbows to begin flexing.

b. Downsweep and Insweep: As your hands pass outside your shoulders, begin pressing down and out and then in, up, and back in a wide propellerlike sweep that is completed as your hands come together under your shoulders. Keep your hands pitched out until they pass under your elbows. Then pitch them in and up during the remainder of the sweep.

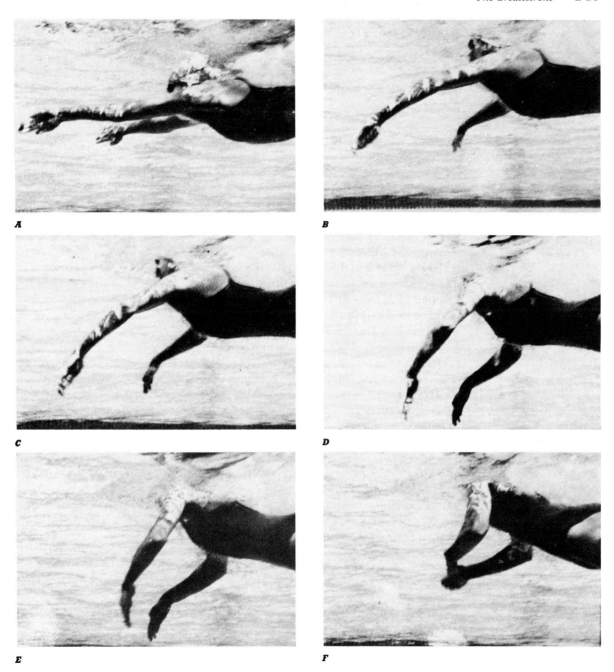

A

B

C

D

E

F

Figure 4.11. The downsweep; an alternate way to start the breaststroke armstroke. The swimmer is Janet Heeney, a national-level breaststroker. She sweeps her hands down and out, rather than out, before making the catch. Once the catch is made, the insweep is executed as shown in frames **C** to **F**.

c. When your hands come together, squeeze your elbows in and reach forward for the next stroke. Rotate your palms downward as you reach forward.

Instructions for Teaching the Armstroke to Younger Age-Group Swimmers

Sweep your hand out, down, in, and up under your shoulders. Then reach forward for the next stroke.

The Kick

Prior to 1960 the breaststroke kick was taught as a "wedge" action. Swimmers extended their legs in an inverted V-shape and then attempted to compress a wedge of water backward as they squeezed their legs together. Counsilman demonstrated the fallacy of this "compression theory" by showing that colored water dropped into the V between the swimmer's legs was simply washed over and under them, rather than propelled backward, as the legs were squeezed together (Counsilman 1968). Counsilman and Chet Jastremski then revolutionized the breaststroke kick with a narrow whip-style leg action that is used by most breaststrokers today.

Initially, it was believed that the narrow kick was superior because water could be pushed backward with the soles of the feet. It is now believed that the superiority of the whip kick lies in the ability to use your feet as propeller blades rather than paddles.

Firby (1975) demonstrated the propellerlike capabilities of the feet in a unique way. He fashioned two plaster models of feet and joined them end to end to form a propeller with two blades (see Figure 4.12). This "foot propeller" was attached to a toy boat with a model airplane rubber band. When wound and released the rotating feet propelled the toy boat forward in the same way

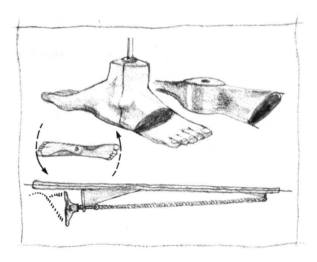

Figure 4.12. The feet as propeller blades. (Reprinted from H. Firby, *Howard Firby on Swimming* [London: Pelham Books, 1975], p. 75, by permission of Pelham Books Ltd.)

A

B

C

D

Figure 4.13. A diagonal view of Janet Heeney's breaststroke kick.

A. Janet Heeney demonstrates excellent mechanics in the breaststroke kick. The upward sweep of her arms causes her hips to be lowered; her knees begin to flex, initiating the leg recovery.

B-C. The recovery. The feet are brought upward and forward by continued flexion at the knees and minimal flexion at the hips. Notice that the toes are pointed and that the feet are inside the width of the hips to reduce drag.

D-E. The outsweep. As the feet near the buttocks, the swimmer dorsiflexes and everts the feet as much as possible and begins sweeping them outward and backward. The feet are pitched up and out and back during this phase of the kick. The arms should be nearly extended and the trunk flat at the surface during this and subsequent propulsive phases of the kick.

E

continued overleaf

Figure 4.13.   **F**

G

H

I

Figure 4.13. continued

F. The downsweep. As her legs approach their widest point, the swimmer pitches her feet down slightly and sweeps her legs downward and outward and then downward and inward in a circular path.

G–H. The insweep. As her legs reach a completely extended position, the swimmer inverts her feet and

sweeps them inward until they come together. Notice the excellent position of her feet.

I. The follow-through and glide. The feet follow through during the final portion of the kick, causing them to travel upward until they are together. They are then held close together with legs extended in a streamlined position in line with the trunk, until the most propulsive phases of the armstroke are completed.

the propeller of an outboard motor would drive a real boat. Breaststrokers use their feet as propellers, rotating them outward, downward, and inward in a circular path. Although some backward motion occurs, the feet do not push directly backward against the water. The breaststroke kick consists of an outsweep, a downsweep, an insweep, a glide, and a recovery. Diagonal and underneath views are shown in Figures 4.13 and 4.14 respectively. Kick plots made from back, side and underneath views are shown in Figure 4.15. They show the directions the feet should move, the pitch they should have, and how a combination of these two factors exerts propulsive force.

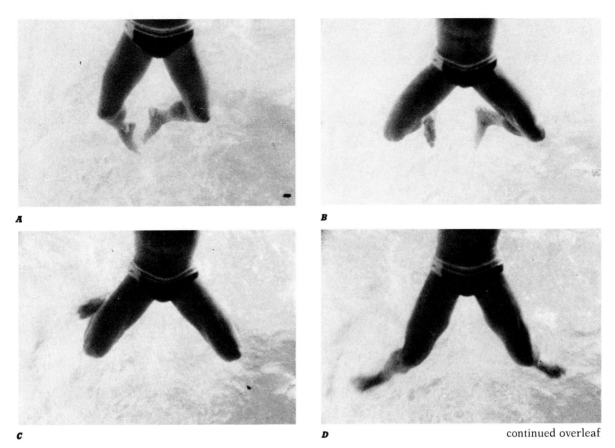

A

B

C

D   continued overleaf

Figure 4.14. David Santos's breaststroke kick, viewed from underneath.

A–B. The recovery. Notice that the feet are inside the width of the knees.

C–D. The outsweep.

Outsweep The outsweep is marked by the letters O and *D* in the kick plots of Figure 4.16. It can be seen clearly in Figures 4.13 and 4.14. The outsweep begins as your legs near the end of the recovery. Your hips and knees should be flexed and your heels should be above your buttocks. Your feet are inside your shoulders and your knees are approximately shoulder width apart. There is no hesitation between the end of the recovery and the beginning of the outsweep. As your feet near your buttocks, they are circled outward and backward until a catch is made. The outsweep ends when your legs are nearly extended.

The soles of your feet should be facing backward, upward, and outward

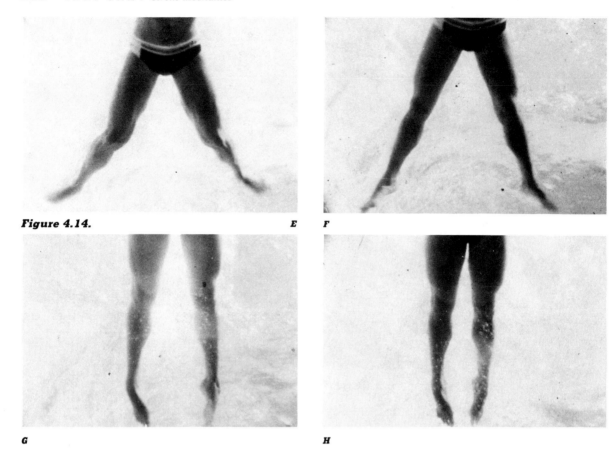

Figure 4.14.   E   F

G   H

Figure 4.14. continued

E–F. The downsweep.

G. The insweep.

H. The glide.

during the outsweep. The proper pitch is achieved by inward rotation at the hip, dorsiflexion at the ankle joints and eversion of the feet. Your toes are the leading edge of the propeller blade with water passing inward and forward over the surfaces of your feet from toes to heels. The water molecules are accelerated past the more rounded instep surfaces of the feet while being deflected backward over the surfaces of the soles. This causes a pressure differential between the two surfaces that exerts propulsive force in a forward direction.

The ability to dorsiflex the ankles and evert the feet is undoubtedly related to the amount of propulsive force that can be generated during the outsweep. For this reason, all breaststrokers and individual medley swimmers should practice stretching exercises to improve their range of motion in these directions.

Contrary to popular belief, you should not stop your legs and set your feet at the end of the recovery because additional effort will be required to get them moving again. When the beginning of the outsweep and the end of the recovery overlap the forward inertia of the feet can be overcome with less muscular effort as they change directions from forward to outward. Most swimmers indicate the outsweep is a gentle motion which gradually builds in force as the feet approach the next phase, the downsweep.

Common errors in the outsweep. The most common mistake swimmers make during the outsweep is pitching the feet improperly. Some swimmers do not possess the dorsiflexing and everting flexibility to pitch their feet upward and outward sufficiently to cause water to be deflected backward over the soles as their feet circle out and back.

Another error in pitch and direction occurs when they attempt to push water straight backward with the soles of their feet. The feet will travel backward more than outward. Propulsion will be drag dominated and, therefore, less effective.

Downsweep As your legs near extension they begin sweeping *downward* as well as outward and backward. Your feet should be pitched out and down so the water is deflected backward as it flows upward over the soles from the big toe side to the little toe side. This pitch is achieved by inverting the feet and rotating outward at the hip. Your feet remain dorsiflexed at the ankles. The downward and outward movement of your feet, together with their downward and outward angles of attack, causes water molecules to be accelerated backward past the soles, creating a pressure differential that exerts a lift force that will propel you forward. Your feet should continue sweeping out and down until your legs are completely extended (see frames *E* and *F* of fig. 4.13). The pitch of the feet and the way propulsive force can be exerted during the downsweep are shown in the kick plots and force diagram drawn from a side view in Figure 4.15.

Although your legs are extending at the knees during the downsweep, the kick plots in Figure 4.15 that are drawn from a side view, show clearly that the feet are moving downward faster than they are moving backward. This is because the downsweep of the kick is accelerating the swimmer's body forward at a faster speed than his legs are extending backward. Swimmers should emphasize the downward rather than the backward movements of their feet. This will increase propulsive force during the downsweep. This downward motion of the legs will cause a swimmer's hips to be elevated slightly in a dolphinlike action that is noticeable in many world-class breaststrokers.

Common errors in the downsweep. The most common mistake swimmers make during the downsweep is to push their feet backward faster than they are sweeping downward. This causes propulsion to be drag dominated and forward velocity will be reduced.

Insweep When your legs are nearly extended, your feet gradually change directions from downward to inward. They then sweep inward across the water until

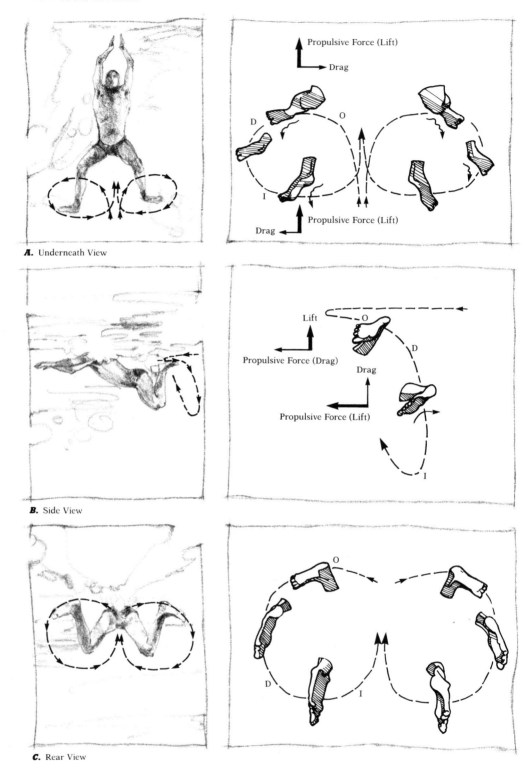

A. Underneath View

B. Side View

C. Rear View

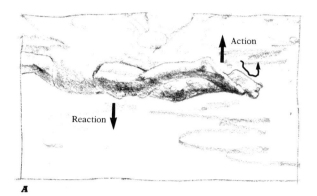

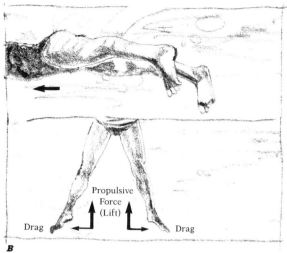

Figure 4.16. The effect on propulsion of pointing the toes during the insweep of the breaststroke kick. Swimmer **A** is shown pointing the toes and sweeping the feet up and in during the insweep. This pitch of the feet provides an angle of attack that exerts a drag force in a downward direction and tends to pull the body downward while reducing forward speed. Swimmer **B** is shown completing the insweep by sweeping across the water with ankles dorsiflexed and feet inverted. This angle of attack is more effective, because it should create a large lift force in a forward direction.

they come together. Your feet should be pitched inward as much as possible during this phase. This is accomplished by continued inversion of the feet and outward rotation at the hips. Your feet remain dorsiflexed at the ankles (see frames *G* to *I* of fig. 4.13).

The direction of motion, the pitch, and the way that propulsion is generated during the insweep are shown in the kick plots and force diagrams in Figure 4.15 that are drawn from an underneath view. The inward pitch of the feet together with their inward movement causes water to be deflected backward from the inner to outer borders of the feet. It is accelerated over the longer airfoil-shaped instep surfaces causing the pressure on the sole side to exceed that on the instep side until a pressure differential is created that propels the swimmer forward.

The insweep is completed when your feet are nearly together. At that time, pressure is released and your feet continue inward and upward until they are on the same level as your hips. This puts your legs in line with your trunk so that form drag will be minimal during the subsequent armstroke.

Common errors in the insweep. The most common error swimmers make is to plantar flex their ankles (point their toes backward and upward) early in the insweep. The effect of this error is illustrated in Figure 4.16*A*. It causes the

Figure 4.15. Kick plots of the breaststroke kick, viewed from underneath, side, and rear. These drawings illustrate how propulsion is generated by the breaststroke kick. The force diagrams accompanying the underneath and side views show how the outward, backward, downward, and inward motions of the feet can propel swimmers forward. Also shown is the manner in which the proper foot pitch will deflect water backward.

propulsive phase of the insweep to be terminated early because the feet are no longer in a position to generate very much force in a forward direction. Instead, most of the force is directed upward, exerting a downward force on the swimmer's body that will decrease forward velocity. This mistake is a result of incorrect teaching at an early age. Swimmers are commonly taught to finish the breaststroke kick by pointing their toes. They should not point their toes until the propulsive phase of the insweep is completed and the leg glide has begun.

Leg Glide While limb motion is continuous in most strokes, there is a definite glide of the legs after the insweep of the breaststroke kick is completed (see frames *B* to *G* of fig. 4.5). This is so the legs will be in horizontal alignment with the trunk while the armstroke is executed. In this way, the effect of form drag on the propulsive force of the armstroke will be reduced. If a swimmer were to recover the legs during the armstroke, the forward motion of the legs would increase drag and reduce forward velocity. Additionally, any incline of the legs from hips to feet will increase form drag.

Recovery The leg recovery begins as your arms complete the insweep (see fig. 4.2 *B*). The upward force of your arms causes your hips to be lowered. Your legs are then relaxed at both the hip and knee joints and your knees drop toward the bottom of the pool. Once the insweep of the armstroke is completed your heels are brought rapidly but gently upward and forward toward your buttocks by flexing at the knees and some flexion and outward rotation at the hip joints. Your ankles should be plantar flexed and your feet inverted and held close together to minimize drag as they travel upward and forward. The recovery ends as your feet approach your buttocks (see fig. 4.2*D*). Near the end of the recovery your feet begin moving out into the outsweep portion of the kick.

Common errors in the recovery. The most common mistake swimmers make during the recovery is to push their thighs downward and forward. The effect of this error was discussed earlier in this chapter. It causes the legs to be flexed excessively at the hip joints and the swimmer's forward velocity decelerates.

Another mistake is to recover the legs during the propulsive phase of the armstroke—that is, during the insweep. When this happens the legs act as brakes, reducing the forward propulsion that is being generated by the armstroke.

A third mistake is to recover with the knees too wide, in the fashion of the wedge kick. Although the knees should be somewhat wider than the hips during the leg recovery, recovering them at any greater width increases form drag unnecessarily.

The "hands back" drill is excellent for teaching the proper leg recovery. It is performed without a kickboard. Swimmers extend their arms backward beside their hips and attempt to touch their feet to their hands as they finish the

> leg recovery and begin the propulsive phase of the kick. With the arms in this position the swimmers will be forced to recover their legs by submerging their hips.

The Dolphin Kick: A Recent Innovation in the Breaststroke

Some swimmers kick their legs upward after they complete the insweep of the breaststroke kick. This upkick is similar to the upbeat of the dolphin kick. It is believed to provide additional propulsion during the breaststroke kick. There is some doubt about this however. The kick plot in Figure 4.17 shows that the feet move upward and forward during this upkick because the armstroke is "pulling" the legs forward faster than they are moving upward. The force diagram indicates that little if any propulsion would be generated by this motion. Most of the force is exerted downward and backward and could reduce forward velocity. The legs should be brought upward in line with the body after the insweep is completed. This motion should be gentle rather than rapid and powerful, however.

Sore Knees

Coaches and breaststroke swimmers know what a serious problem sore knees can be. They are generally caused by chronic inflammation of the medial collateral ligaments and the medial menisci. These structures can be seen in the illustration of the knee joint in Figure 4.18.

The knee joint permits little outward rotation of the lower leg. When swimmers attempt to sweep their feet outward the medial collateral ligaments can be stretched and the medial menisci which attach to these ligaments can be injured. The swimmer in Figure 4.18 is shown stretching these tissues during the outsweep of the breaststroke kick. Some breaststrokers reduce this stretching effect by pushing their feet *backward* as well as outward during the outsweep. This causes less stress on the ligaments and menisci. Although sweeping

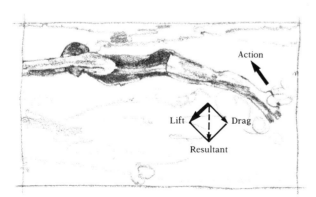

Figure 4.17. The dolphin kick in the breaststroke. This breaststroker is executing an upkick with her legs after completing the insweep of the kick. Analysis of underwater motion pictures of breaststroke swimmers show that the legs travel forward as well as upward during this upkick. It is doubtful that propulsive force could be generated by this action. The force diagram shows that most of the force would be exerted in a downward direction.

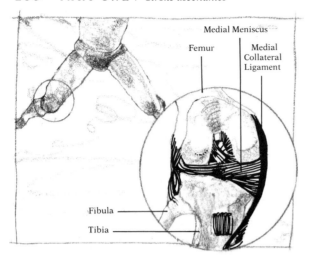

Medial Meniscus

Femur

Medial Collateral Ligament

Fibula

Tibia

Figure 4.18. The knee joint.

outward in this manner will reduce the "stretch" on the soft tissues of the knee joints, it is less propulsive than a sweep that is directed in a more outward direction. This is because pushing back with the feet causes propulsion to be drag dominated rather than lift dominated.

It may be possible to prevent sore knees and yet use a lift-dominated outsweep by recovering your legs with your feet inside your knees. In this way your feet can be directed outward for a longer distance during the outsweep before they pass outside the knees where outward rotation would place stress on the medial collateral ligaments and medial menisci. This should generate more propulsive force during the outsweep and will also reduce the backward movement of the legs.

Instructions for Teaching the Breaststroke Kick to College, High School, and Older Age-Group Swimmers

a. Recovery: Recover your legs by lowering your hips and gently pulling your feet up to your buttocks. Do not push your thighs forward against the water. Your feet should be held close together and your knees should be turned out slightly.

b. Outsweep: Begin circling your feet outward when they approach your buttocks. Turn your feet outward as much as possible while you sweep them outward.

c. Downsweep: As your feet pass outside your shoulders, begin pushing down on the water with them.

d. Insweep: Continue circling your feet downward and inward until they come together. Turn the soles of your feet inward as they sweep inward across the water and try to touch the soles of your feet together. *Do not point your toes at the end of the kick.* If you kick correctly, the downward and inward force of your feet will cause your hips to rise slightly in a dolphinlike action.

  e. When the insweep is completed, bring your legs up in line with your body and hold them in a streamlined position during the armstroke.

Instructions for Teaching the Breaststroke Kick to Younger Age-Group Swimmers

  a. Bring your feet up toward your buttocks by lowering your hips and your knees.
  b. When your legs are close to your buttocks, turn your toes out and circle your feet out, down, and in until they come together.
  c. Hold your legs straight while you do the armstroke.

Timing of the Armstroke and Kick

There are three styles of breaststroke timing in use today: continuous, glide, and overlap. When continuous timing is used, the armstroke begins simultaneously with completion of the propulsive phase of the kick. In glide timing there is a short interval between the completion of the kick and the beginning of the armstroke. In overlap timing the armstroke begins during the insweep of the legs.

Most coaches agree that glide timing is ineffective because swimmers decelerate from the time the propulsive phase of their kick ends until their armstroke begins. Therefore, many experts advocate "continuous" timing. The theory behind continuous timing is that there will be no "gap" in the application of force if the armstroke begins just as the kick ends. That is not true, however. The fallacy in this theory is that some degree of overlap is required to produce truly continuous timing. The arms do not supply much propulsive force until late in the outsweep. Therefore, to prevent deceleration between the time the propulsive phase of the kick ends, and propulsive force from the arms begins, the swimmer must use an "overlap" timing in which the outsweep of the arms is initiated before the insweep of the kick is completed. Analysis of underwater motion pictures indicates that most world-class breaststrokers use an overlap style of timing.

"Poor" kickers seem to have the greatest amount of overlap. This is undoubtedly so their arms will dominate the stroke. Although the increased turnover is more fatiguing, it is probably faster to swim this way than to take fewer armstrokes and depend on a weak kick for propulsion.

When you use overlap timing, your arms should begin sweeping out as your legs sweep inward (see fig. 4.5, frames *A* and *B*). If the catch of the armstroke is made simultaneously with completion of the propulsive phase of the kick, there will be a continuous application of propulsive force. Breaststroke swimmers with strong kicks will make the catch when their legs come together. Those with weak kicks will make the catch earlier.

Breathing Frequency During Breaststroke Races

Breaststrokers should breathe once every stroke cycle in all races regardless of distance. Breathing is such an integral part of the timing of this stroke that it aids rather than interferes with propulsion. For example, elevating the upper body for a breath encourages a more effective downsweep of the arms and makes it possible to recover the legs with less hip flexion. Breathing also seems to encourage the proper timing between kick and armstroke. When swimmers keep their faces in the water during a stroke cycle they tend to rush through the armstroke and upset their rhythm.

The Underwater Armstroke

Prior to the 1960s breaststroke races were swum underwater with the swimmer surfacing for a breath only once or twice per length. This style was outlawed because of the potential danger of prolonged breathholding. Today,

Figure 4.19. The underwater armstroke of David Santos, viewed from underneath.

A. The glide. The swimmer pushes off the wall at a downward angle. Notice the excellent streamlined position, with the arms extended and one hand on top of the other.

B. The outsweep. As the speed from his push-off be-

gins to subside, he sweeps the hands directly outward and backward beyond shoulder width. The hands should be pitched out and back.

C-D. The catch and downsweep. As the hands approach their widest position, he changes their pitch toward downward and begins sweeping his hands downward in a circular path.

A

B

C

D

Figure 4.19. continued

E–G. The insweep. The hands continue circling downward, then inward and upward, until they are together under the chest (some swimmers cross their hands during the insweep). The hands are pitched inward as they pass under the elbows (frame ***E***).

H–J. The upsweep. As the hands come together, the swimmer begins pushing them backward, outward, and upward, until the arms are completely extended at the posterior portion of the thighs. The pitch of the hands is changed slowly from inward to outward and upward during this phase.

E

F

G

H

I

J

continued overleaf

Figure 4.19.   **K**   **L**

M   **N**

Figure 4.19. continued

K-N. The recovery of the arms and legs. The swimmer glides in a streamlined position until the
momentum from his pullout begins to subside, and
then he recovers the arms gently along the body and
flexes the legs in preparation for the kick to the
surface.

the rules permit breaststroke swimmers to take only one underwater stroke per
length, immediately after the start of the race and after each turn. After completing that stroke, they must kick to the surface so that some part of the body,
usually the head, is above the surface of the water before the next armstroke
begins.

Since the underwater armstroke is more propulsive than the surface armstroke, swimmers should practice until they can execute it as well as possible. Many races are lost because of poor underwater pullouts.

The underwater pullout is similar to an exaggerated butterfly armstroke. It consists of an outsweep, catch, downsweep, insweep, and upsweep. The underwater armstroke is illustrated from an underneath view in Figure 4.19, from a side view in Figure 4.20, and from a front view in Figure 4.21. It begins with a glide.

Figure 4.20. David Santos's underwater armstroke, viewed from the side.

    A. The glide position.

    B. The outsweep.

    C. The downsweep.

    D-G. The insweep.

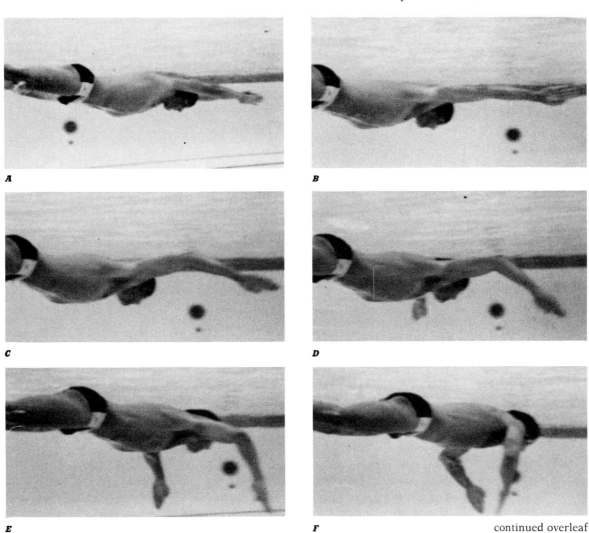

A

B

C

D

E

F

continued overleaf

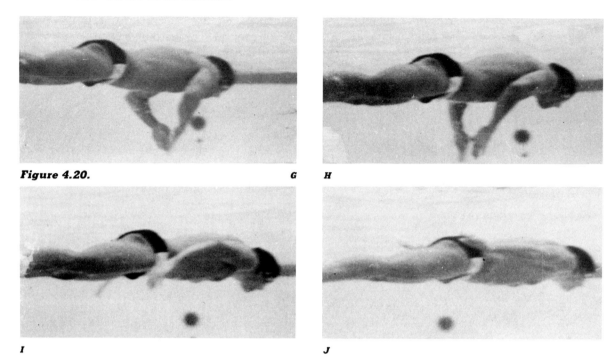

Figure 4.20.   G   H

Figure 4.20. continued

H–J. The upsweep.

Initial Glide   After the push-off or dive, hold a streamlined position until you begin to lose your speed. Your arms should be together and stretched tightly overhead during the glide. Placing one hand over the other helps in maintaining this position. Your head should be between your arms and your body should not sag nor pike at the waist. Your legs should be together with your toes pointed (see fig. 4.19*A*).

Outsweep   As you approach race speed, begin sweeping your hands outward until they are outside your shoulders where the catch is made. Your arms should be extended and your palms should be rotated outward nearly 90 degrees from the prone position. They should also be pitched backward (see fig. 4.19*B*). As in all outsweeping motions of the arms, your hands should be cupped slightly so that the water flows inward and backward past the palms from the fingertips toward the wrists. *Do not push water sideward with the palms of your hands.* The stroke plot in Figure 4.22 drawn from an underneath view shows how propulsive force can be generated during the outsweep. The outsweep is probably the least propulsive phase of the underwater armstroke. It is primarily a stretching motion of the arms that places the hands in position to make an effective catch.

Catch As your hands pass outside shoulder width, they are pitched downward as well as outward and the catch is made (see fig. 4.19*C*). As in other strokes, the beginning of the major propulsive phases of the armstroke is signaled by flexion at the elbows as the change in hand pitch and direction causes an increase in lift force that propels the head and shoulders forward over the arms.

Figure 4.21. David Santos's breaststroke pullout, a front view.

A. The initial glide.

B–C. The outsweep.

D–E. The downsweep. Notice the excellent downward pitch of the hands.

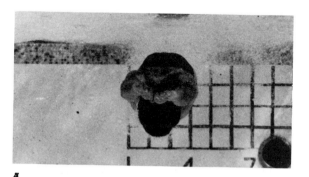

A

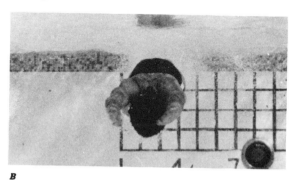

B

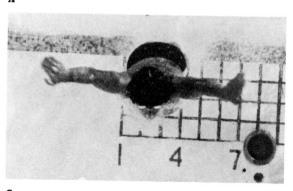

C

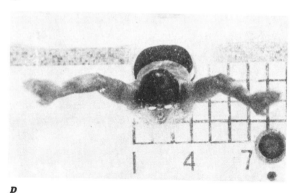

D

E

F

continued overleaf

Figure 4.21. G   H

I   J

Figure 4.21. continued

  F-G. The insweep.

  H-I. The transition from insweep to upsweep.

  J-K. The upsweep. Notice the excellent position of the hands in **J**.

K

Downsweep   Once the catch is made, continued flexion at the elbows allows the swimmer's hands to sweep out and down in a circular path. The hands remain pitched out and down throughout this motion so that the water molecules that are flowing upward are deflected backward underneath the palms from thumb to little finger sides. Downward hand velocity increases from beginning to end of the

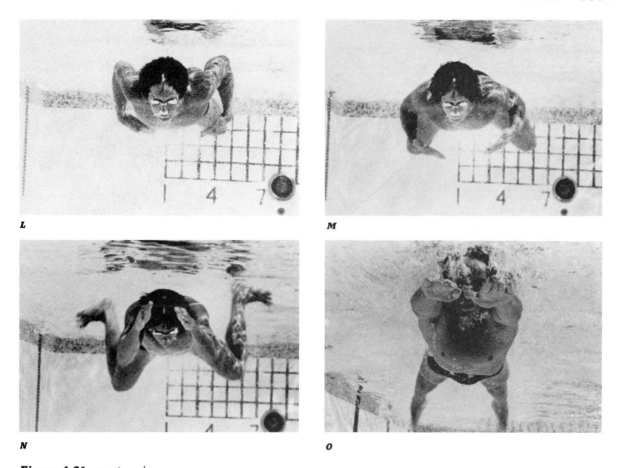

L

M

N

O

Figure 4.21. continued

L–O. The arm recovery and kick to the surface.

downsweep. (The downsweep is best seen in frames *D* and *E* of Figure 4.21.) The way propulsive force is generated during this phase of the armstroke is illustrated by the force diagram in Figure 4.22, which accompanies the side view.

Insweep   As your hands approach a position directly below your elbows, they gradually change directions from outward and downward to inward, upward, and backward as the insweep begins. Your hands continue moving inward, upward and backward until they are nearly together under your head at the midline of your body. Some swimmers cross their hands during the insweep.

   The palms of your hands should gradually rotate from an outward and downward to an inward and upward pitch during the insweep (see frames *E* to *G* of Figure 4.20). The way that propulsion is generated by the insweep is

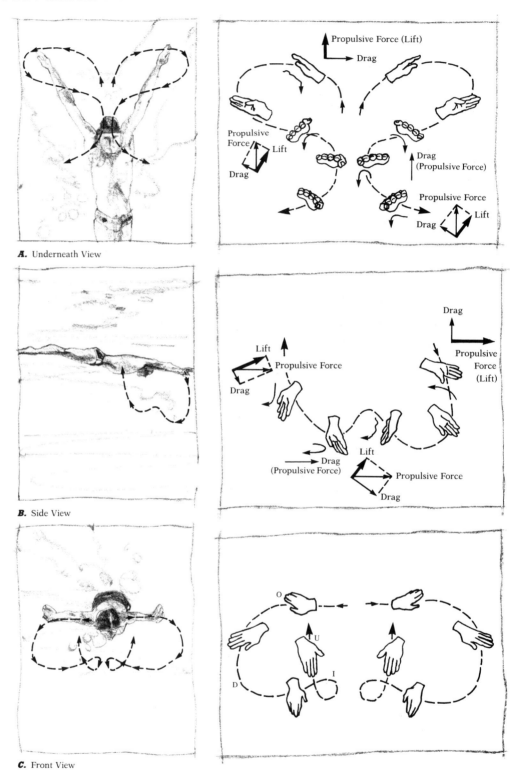

A. Underneath View

B. Side View

C. Front View

shown by the force diagrams accompanying the underneath and side views in Figure 4.22. The hand pitch that will deflect water backward under the palms is illustrated in the stroke plots of this same figure.

Upsweep   The upsweep begins as your hands approach the end of the insweep. The inward inertia of your hands is overcome by pushing them backward and then sweeping them outward, upward, and backward until your arms are completely extended. The upsweep is best seen in frames *H* to *K* of Figure 4.21.

Hand pitch should change from inward and upward to outward and backward during the upsweep. This pitch is achieved by relaxing your wrists and allowing the downward and inward pressure of the water to position your hands properly. Your elbows will be extending throughout this final portion of the upsweep; however, your body will be accelerating forward with such speed that the upward motion of your hands will exceed their backward speed.

The upsweep is completed by pushing water upward and outward with the palms of your hands as your arms are nearing complete extension. Your hands should be beside your thighs at the end of the upsweep and your palms should be facing outward (see fig 4.19*J*). The palms are then turned inward and your hands are held in contact with your thighs to improve streamlining during the glide. This final push upward is not for propulsive purposes but, rather, is used to keep your body submerged during the glide that follows. The way that propulsive force is generated during the upsweep is shown by the force diagrams drawn from underneath and side views in Figure 4.22.

The Second Glide   Since the underwater armstroke accelerates your body beyond speeds that can be attained at the surface, you should glide until you decelerate to race speed before kicking to the surface. Maintain your body in a streamlined position during the glide, with your arms held close to your sides, your legs straight and together and your toes pointed. Your head should be in line with your body and there should be no arch nor pike to your trunk.

Kick-up to   As you approach race speed, begin reaching for the surface by sliding your
the Surface   arms forward along the anterior portions of your body (see frames *K* and *L* of Figure 4.19). Make these movements gently, being careful to keep your arms close to your body to reduce the surface area and forward force of the arms so that drag is minimized. Your arms should move forward by means of elbow flexion until they pass your face. At that point, begin reaching forward and upward for the surface by extending your arms at the elbow joints (see frames *M* and *N* of Figure 4.19).

Your legs should be recovered as your arms are reaching forward. The leg recovery should also be as gentle as possible in order to reduce drag. For the same reason, the legs should be recovered with as little hip flexion as needed

Figure 4.22. Stroke plots of the underwater armstroke. These drawings show the directions of motion and angles of attack used in the underwater armstroke. Underneath, side, and front views are shown.

for an effective kick. The outsweep of the kick is timed to coincide with the final extension of your arms (see frames *N* and *O* of Figure 4.21). If timed properly, your head should break through the surface as your arms near complete extension. In this way the first surface armstroke can begin without delay.

Do not make the mistake of taking a breath before you begin the first surface armstroke. To do so will cause you to decelerate because the surface armstroke will be delayed while you inhale. That armstroke should begin when your head breaks the surface and your first breath should not be taken until the usual time, when you are into the insweep. A word of caution concerning this technique: although stroking into the first breath saves time, there is an ever-present danger of being disqualified for beginning the first surface stroke before your head is above the water. You must learn to feel your head break the surface before you begin that stroke.

REFERENCES

Bergen, P. 1978. "Breaststroke." Talk presented at the 1978 World Swim Coaches Clinic, September 13–16, 1978, Chicago, Illinois.

Counsilman, J. E. 1968. *Science of Swimming.* Englewood Cliffs, N.J.: Prentice-Hall.

Firby, H. 1975. *Howard Firby on Swimming.* London: Pelham Books.

Schleihauf, R. E., Jr. 1977. "A Hydrodynamic Analysis of Breaststroke Pulling Efficiency." *Competitive Swimming Manual for Coaches and Swimmers,* ed. J. E. Counsilman, pp. 241–247. Bloomington, Ind.: Counsilman.

CHAPTER 5

The Back Crawl Stroke

In the early days of competitive swimming the back crawl stroke was believed to be an "upside down" version of the front crawl. That impression abated during the period when the drag theory of propulsion was in vogue. The belief that the back crawl is really an inverted version of the front crawl is strengthened when lift theory is applied to the mechanics of this stroke. The similarities between the two strokes are remarkable. Those similarities will be discussed in this chapter in terms of the components of the back crawl stroke: the armstroke, the kick, timing of the arms and legs, body position, and breathing.

The Armstroke

The underwater armstroke is pictured in Figures 5.1, 5.2, and 5.3. It consists of three sweeps: a downsweep, an upsweep, and another downsweep.

The three sweeps of the armstroke are labeled in the stroke plots shown in Figure 5.4. The plots, made from side, underneath, and front views, describe the movement of the index finger of the right hand in relation to a fixed point in the pool. The three distinct changes of direction observed in these plots lend support to the theory that the stroke consists of three sweeping movements rather than a pull and push. The three sweeps plus the entry, catch, and recovery will be described in the following sections.

Entry   In the backstroke, your arm should enter the water forward of your head and in line with your shoulders. Your arm should be fully extended. Your hand should enter the water little finger first with the palm facing outward (see fig. 5.3*A*). In this way it can slice into the water with a minimum of turbulence.

169

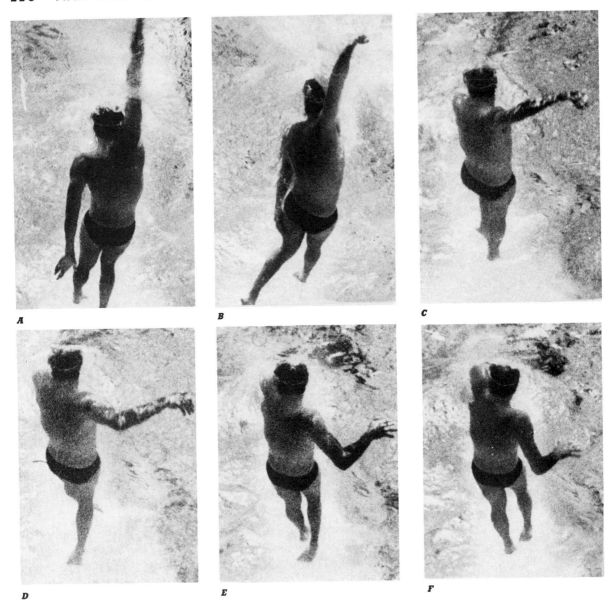

Figure 5.1. The back crawl stroke viewed from underneath. The swimmer is Peter Rocca, silver medalist in the backstroke events at the 1976 Olympic Games and several times AAU and NCAA champion.

A. The entry of the right arm, recovery of the left.

B-C. The initial downsweep of the right arm, upbeat of the first kick. Notice the rotation of the body toward the right. This brings the body into alignment during the propulsive phases of the armstroke.

D-F. The upsweep of the right arm, upbeat of second kick.

G-I. The final downsweep of the right arm, entry of the left arm, and upbeat of the third kick.

J-K. The initial downsweep of the left arm, upbeat of the fourth kick, recovery of the right arm.

L-N. The upsweep of the left arm, upbeat of the fifth kick.

Figure 5.1. G H I

J K L continued overleaf

An excellent teaching technique is to ask swimmers to imagine that each of them is lying supine on the face of a clock with their heads pointing at twelve o'clock and their feet pointing at six o'clock. Then the entry position can be communicated by telling the swimmers to enter their hands into the water at 11 o'clock on the right side and at 1 o'clock on the left side. The proper entry position is shown in Figure 5.1A.

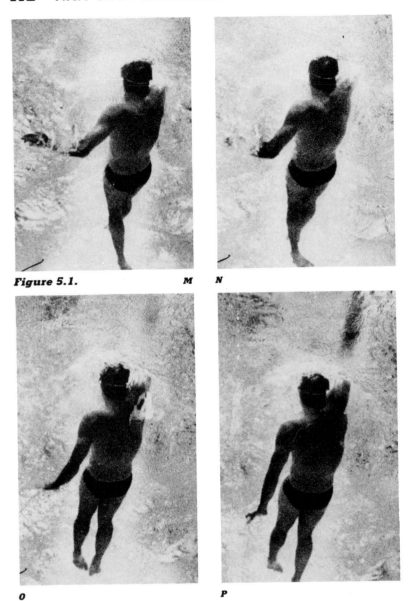

Figure 5.1.   **M**   **N**

Figure 5.1. continued

O-P. The final downsweep of the left arm and upbeat of the sixth kick.

Common errors on entry. Some of the most common mistakes swimmers
make on the entry are overreaching, underreaching, and smashing the hand
into the water.

Overreaching will occur if you reach across the 12 o'clock position toward
the opposite shoulder. Your hips will be pulled outward by this motion and lat-

Figure 5.2. A diagonal view of the back crawl stroke. The swimmer is Todd Lincoln, a national-level backstroker.

A. The entry. The left hand enters the water in front of the shoulder, with arm extended and palm facing sideward.

B. The initial downsweep. The swimmer sweeps the hand down and out, turning the palm toward the bottom as he does so. During most of the downsweep, the arm should be pitched out and back.

C-D. The upsweep. As the hand nears its deepest point, the swimmer begins sweeping it upward, in-ward, and backward in a circular path. He slowly changes the pitch of the palm to upward and inward as he does so. (The hand is pitched upward too much in frame **D**.)

E-I. The final downsweep. As the hand nears the surface, the swimmer begins sweeping it backward and then downward in a circular path. The pitch of the hand is gradually changed to downward during this phase. The downsweep ends when the arm is completely extended and well below the thigh. This swimmer has an excellent final downsweep, as indicated by the positions of the hand in frames **F** through **I**.

A

B

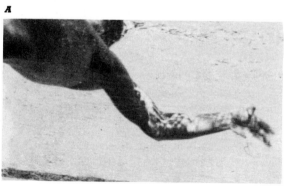

C

D

E

F

continued overleaf

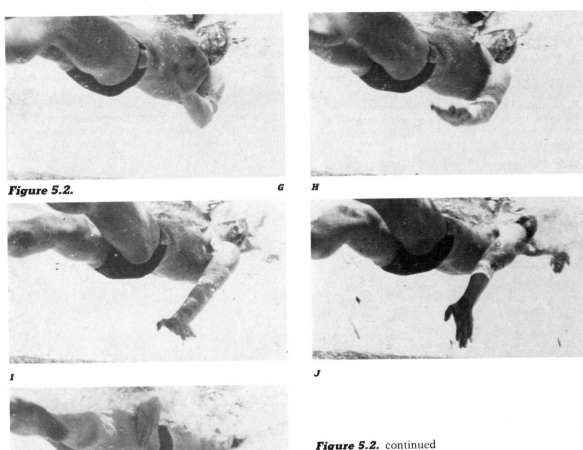

Figure 5.2.   **G**   **H**

I   **J**

Figure 5.2. continued

J–K. The release and recovery. When the arm is completely extended, the swimmer releases the water and turns the palm inward so it can be brought out of the water on its side with minimal resistance. The swimmer recovers by lifting the shoulder (not the hand) upward in order to bring the arm out of the water.

K

eral alignment will be disrupted. Overreaching is illustrated in Figure 5.5.

Underreaching will occur if your hand enters the water before reaching the 1 o'clock or 11 o'clock positions. A portion of the propulsive phase of the first part of the underwater armstroke will be lost. This will reduce the length of time over which propulsion can be generated during the armstroke.

Smashing your hand and arm into the water will increase wave drag. Swimmers who commit this error usually smash the back of the hand into the water rather than slicing it in on its side. The effect of this error is illustrated in Figure 5.6. Smashing entries can reduce forward velocity by 50 percent immediately after entry.

Catch After entry your hand will travel forward, downward, and outward while your palm is rotated to a downward pitch (see fig. 5.2*B*). When that pitch is attained, the lift force exerted by your hand will cause your elbow to flex and the propulsive phase of the armstroke will begin.

Figure 5.3. Todd Lincoln's backstroke, viewed from the front.

A. The entry.

B-C. The initial downsweep. Notice the body roll and the lateral movements of the legs. He kicks up and out with the left leg and down and out with the right.

D-E. The upsweep. He kicks up and in with the right leg and down and in with the right.

A

B

C

D

E

continued overleaf

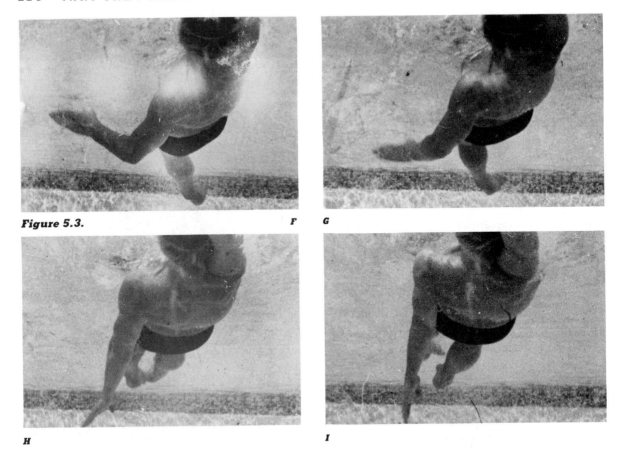

Figure 5.3.   **F**   **G**

H   **I**

Figure 5.3. continued

F–I. The final downsweep. He kicks up with the left leg and down with the right.

Common errors at the catch. The most frequent error swimmers commit when making the catch is to drop their elbows. This happens when they attempt to push water backward with their hand rather than sweeping it downward and outward after entry. The effect of this error is illustrated in Figure 5.7. In her hurried attempt to push backward, the swimmer in this illustration flexes her elbow before the catch is made and pushes her hand backward through the water with her elbow traveling in advance of her hand. In this position, the arm pushes forward and downward against the water exerting a considerable amount of drag opposite the direction of movement. In addition, the resultant force, which is exerted upward and forward, will tend to disrupt horizontal alignment. The effect of these factors will, of course, be a reduction in forward velocity. When swimmers learn to sweep the hand down and out after entry, the dropped elbow will no longer be a problem.

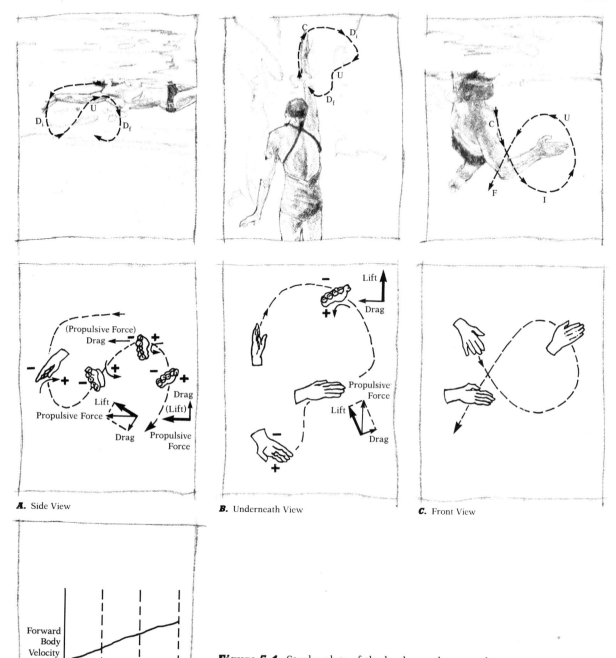

A. Side View

B. Underneath View

C. Front View

Figure 5.4. Stroke plots of the back crawl armstroke. The stroke patterns are illustrated from side, front, and underneath views. The diagrams indicate how propulsive force is generated by the combination of hand direction and angle of attack. The manner in which the proper hand pitch causes water to be deflected backward during each phase of the stroke is also shown.

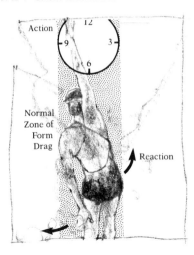

Figure 5.5. The effect of overreaching on lateral alignment. This swimmer is overreaching. She recovered laterally, swinging her right hand behind her head and causing it to enter beyond the 12 o'clock position. This action exerts a counterforce on the hips. They are pulled outward, which in turn causes a reaction in the legs. They swing outward in the other direction. The result of these unnecessary swinging movements of the trunk and legs is that turbulence is created, and both form drag and wave drag are increased.

Initial Downsweep   The initial downsweep is best seen in frames *B* and *C* and *I* and *J* of Figure 5.1. The directions of hand motion during the initial downsweep are shown between points C and D$_i$ on the stroke plots in Figure 5.4. After the catch is made, your hand should sweep down and out in a circular path until it is approximately 18 to 24 inches deep. Your shoulder and hips should rotate toward the downsweeping arm. Downward and outward hand speed accelerate throughout the downsweep.

Your hand should be pitched downward, outward, and backward. Most swimmers cup their hands slightly to improve their airfoil shape and increase the lift force they produce. Both the outward and downward angles of attack should probably be between 30 and 40 degrees. These angles and the way they cause water to be deflected backward are also shown in Figure 5.4, *A* and *B*.

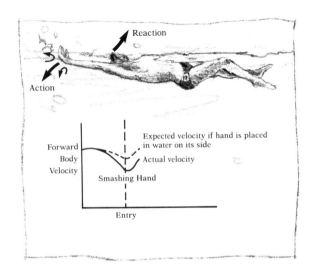

Figure 5.6. The effect of smashing the hand into the water. This swimmer is smashing the back of his hand into the water. Pushing the flat surface of the back of the hand downward and forward into the water will impart an upward and backward force to the head and shoulders that will disrupt horizontal alignment and reduce forward velocity.

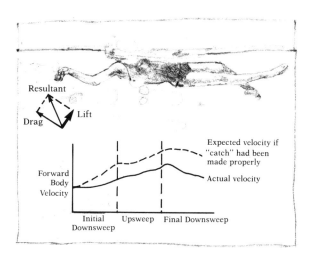

Figure 5.7. The error of pushing back during the downsweep. This swimmer is "dropping" her elbow and pushing back during the downsweep. This exerts a considerable drag force opposite the forward direction her body is moving. The resultant force also disrupts horizontal alignment by causing her head and shoulder to "bounce" upward. The result is that velocity is reduced during the downsweep and all later phases of the armstroke. This loss of speed is indicated on the velocity graph.

The manner in which propulsive force can be generated during the initial downsweep is illustrated in Figure 5.4A. The downward and outward movement of the hand causes water to flow upward and inward from fingertips to wrist. The water flowing over the knuckle side is accelerated, creating a low pressure area on that side relative to an area of higher pressure on the palm side. The resulting pressure differential accelerates the swimmer forward.

The downsweep of the back crawl is really very much like the downsweep of the front crawl stroke. Both are downward and outward movements with the palm pitched downward, outward, and backward.

Common errors in the downsweep. Perhaps the most common error made during the downsweep is pushing backward against the water (see fig. 5.7). Propulsion becomes drag rather than lift dominated and some forward velocity is probably lost when this occurs.

Another mistake swimmers make when first learning to use lift for propulsion is to sweep the hand either downward or outward, rather than down and out. Incorporating both outward and downward motion into the downsweep causes the larger resultant force instead of the lift force to be exerted in a forward direction and propulsion should be increased. You will notice that lift appears to be the propulsive force of the initial downsweep. This is because of the two-dimensional nature of the stroke plots in Figure 5.4. The initial downsweep (and the sweeps of every stroke) must be visualized in three dimensions to understand the true nature of propulsion.

Upsweep   The photos of Peter Rocca in Figure 5.1 show him using an excellent upsweeping motion with his right arm (see frames *C* to *E*). The directions of hand motion during the upsweep are indicated by the lines between points D and U on the stroke plots in Figure 5.4.

You should make the transition from downsweep to insweep by increasing the outward motion of your hand as it nears the end of the downsweep. This allows you to change the direction your hand is moving from downward to upward with minimal muscular effort and no disruption of lateral alignment.

After the transition is made, your hand should continue upward and backward and inward toward the surface until it is approximately 6 to 8 inches underwater. Your elbow should be flexed more than 90 degrees as the upsweep phase of the armstroke is completed. Your fingertips should be pointing upward and outward toward the surface (see fig. 5.3*E*).

Hand pitch should be changed to upward and inward during the upsweep. According to the data presented by Schleihauf (1978) the upward angle of attack is somewhere between 30 and 40 degrees. The inward angle is not known although it is probably between 30 and 40 degrees relative to the inward direction of motion. These angles of attack are shown in stroke plots in Figure 5.4.

The force diagrams in Figure 5.4, drawn from side and underneath views, show how propulsion is produced during the upsweep. The upward, backward, and inward motion of the hand causes drag in a downward, forward, and outward direction. A lift force is exerted perpendicular to the drag force and the two combine to exert a resultant force that propels the swimmer forward. The magnitude of that resultant force is increased by the upward and inward hand pitch which, by deflecting water backward as it passes over the palm from thumb to little finger side, creates a greater pressure differential between the palm (+) and knuckle (−) sides of the hand.

Motion pictures show that backstrokers close their fingers and cup their hands slightly during the upsweep. They also carry their thumbs somewhat separated from their fingers. The significance of these positions is not known, although it is possible that they increase the pressure differential between the palm and knuckle sides of the hands. Upward hand velocity accelerates throughout the upsweep, reaching maximum as the transition to the next sweep is made.

If you can picture a backstroke swimmer in a face-down rather than a face-up position, you will see that the upsweep of the back crawl is very similar to the insweep of the front crawl. Both are the middle sweeps of their respective armstrokes and both are directed upward and inward, although backstrokers cannot sweep their hands under their bodies for obvious reasons.

Common errors in the upsweep. The most common mistake swimmers make in this phase of the armstroke is to sweep the hand upward without changing the backward and downward pitch used in the preceding downsweep. Swimmers taught to push water backward usually commit this error. The effect of this error on propulsion is shown in Figure 5.8. The swimmer in Figure 5.8*A* keeps his hand facing backward and downward as he slices it upward through the water. The angle of attack is so slight that water is not deflected backward over the palm and the pressure differential between the palm and knuckle sides is not sufficient to create any significant amount of propulsion. The stroke plot in Figure 5.8*B* shows the proper hand pitch during this phase of the armstroke. The hand should be pitched upward between 30 and 40 degrees so that water is deflected backward as it passes over the palm. This

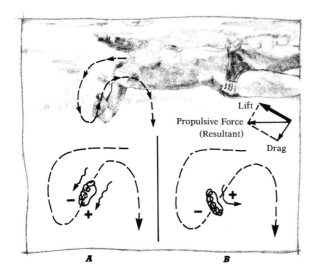

Figure 5.8. The effect on propulsion of using backward hand pitch during the upsweep. Stroke plot **A** shows why "slicing" the hand upward through the water with a very slight angle of attack is not very propulsive. Water can pass around the hand without being deflected backward, and the pressure differential between the palm and knuckle side will not be sufficient to cause any significant amount of propulsion. Stroke plot **B** shows the proper hand pitch during this phase of the armstroke. The hand is pitched upward approximately 40 degrees so that water is deflected backward. This increases the pressure differential between the palm and knuckle side of the hand, and the swimmer should be propelled forward at a faster speed.

increases the pressure differential between palm ($+$) and knuckle ($-$) side and the swimmer should be propelled forward at a faster speed.

When swimmers first attempt to pitch their hands upward during the upsweep, they sometimes pitch them at too great an angle of attack to the oncoming flow of water. The effect of this error is shown in Figure 5.9. The perpendicular angle of attack prevents water from passing around the hand and the water becomes turbulent. The force is directed downward and will pull the swimmer's shoulder down, and retard forward speed.

Another mistake swimmers make when learning to use lift for propulsion is to sweep the hand straight up rather than diagonally upward. The effect of this error is discussed in Chapter 1. Propulsion is generated by the lift force

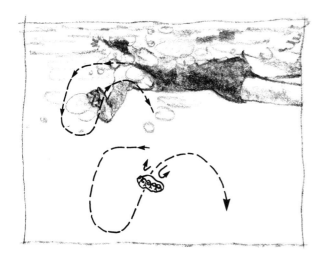

Figure 5.9. The effect on propulsion of pitching the hand upward too much during the upsweep. If the hand is pitched upward at too great an angle, water cannot pass around it without becoming turbulent. Therefore, most of the force will be exerted upward, pulling the shoulder down and decelerating forward speed.

while the resultant force is exerted downward and forward. This prevents the swimmer from achieving the maximum possible forward speed.

Final Downsweep An excellent view of the final downsweep is shown in frames *F* to *I* of Figure 5.2. The stroke plots in Figure 5.4 depict the direction of motion and hand pitch during this sweep. The final downsweep is designated by the letters U and D_f.

It begins as you are completing the preceding upsweep. The transition is made by pushing water backward with the palm of your hand as it passes over the highest point in the S-shaped stroke pattern (see fig. 5.2*F*). This allows you to maintain propulsive force while hand direction is changed from upward to downward. After the transition your hand should sweep downward and inward until your arm is completely extended below your thigh.

The pitch of your hand is gradually changed from inward and upward to downward and outward during the transition from upsweep to downsweep. It remains pitched in this direction until the final downsweep is completed.

The downward angle of attack varied from 47 to 63 degrees among the backstroke swimmers in Schleihauf's study (1978). Angles near 40 degrees are recommended because of their greater effectiveness for producing lift-dominated propulsion. The outward angle of attack should probably be between 30 and 40 degrees.

The manner in which propulsion is generated by the final downsweep is illustrated in Figure 5.4*A*. The downward motion of the hand causes water to be accelerated upward over the knuckle side while the downward and outward pitch causes the molecules passing under the palm to be deflected backward. The resulting pressure differential exerts a resultant force in a nearly horizontal direction.[1] The final downsweep is probably the most propulsive phase of the armstroke. It corresponds to the upsweep of the front crawl, except, of course, that the movements are in opposite directions.

It should be noted that the majority of world-class backstroke swimmers keep their fingers pointing sideward during the final downsweep, as the swimmer in Figure 5.2 is doing. This is so the hand can be pitched downward and outward at the most effective angle of attack. Backstroke swimmers have traditionally been taught to keep their fingers pointing at the surface through this phase. The theory behind this technique was that the hand could be kept perpendicular to the oncoming flow of water, making it a more effective paddle for pushing water backward. However, a sideward position of the fingers is more propulsive where lift-dominated propulsion is concerned (see fig. 5.10). This explains why the most successful backstrokers position their hands in this manner during this phase of the armstroke.

Backstrokers complete the final downsweep at various distances below their thighs. The optimal distance the hand should sweep downward is not known. Until such time as it has been determined swimmers should attempt to

---

1. Lift is shown as the propulsive force in the side view in Figure 5.4. This is because of the limitation of depicting a three-dimensional movement in two dimensions. If it could be diagrammed in three dimensions the combination of downward and inward hand motion would be shown to create a resultant, rather than lift, force in a forward direction.

keep propulsion lift dominated by sweeping the hand well below the thigh. It is likely that backstrokers who do not finish the final downsweep below their thigh are pushing backward more than downward and in the process are sacrificing some propulsive force.

Common errors in the final downsweep. The most common mistake swimmers make during the final downsweep has already been mentioned—that is, to push back with the palm of their hand. When they push backward, swimmers can utilize drag-dominated propulsion only until the hand reaches the thigh; whereas lift force can be generated until the hand is well below the thigh when they sweep it downward. The effects of a backward push and a downward sweep on propulsion are compared in Figure 5.10.

Recovery   The photographs in Figures 5.11 and 5.12 show a swimmer executing the recovery correctly from both side and top views. His hand is lifted from the water by rolling his shoulder upward as he completes the final downsweep (see fig. 5.12*E*). The entry of his opposite arm and the subsequent roll of his body toward the entering arm also help to bring the shoulder of his recovering arm out of the water. All of these actions help to overcome the downward inertia his arm developed during the downsweep so it can be "pulled" upward into the recovery with less muscular effort and no disruption in horizontal alignment.

Once the downsweep is completed, your hand should be rotated inward until your palm faces your thigh so it can leave the water on its side with mini-

Figure 5.10. A comparison of pushing backward and sweeping downward on propulsion during the final downsweep. Stroke plot **A** shows a swimmer pushing back during the final downsweep. His palm is facing backward and is being used as a paddle. This causes propulsion to be drag dominated, which should lessen both the magnitude of propulsive force and the length of time over which it can be applied. Stroke plot **B** illustrates that a downward direction of motion should generate a larger propulsive force over a longer period of time.

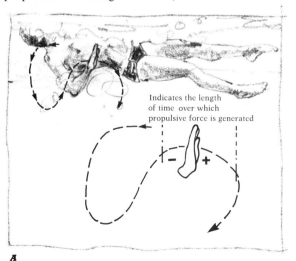

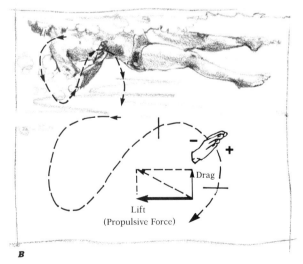

A

B

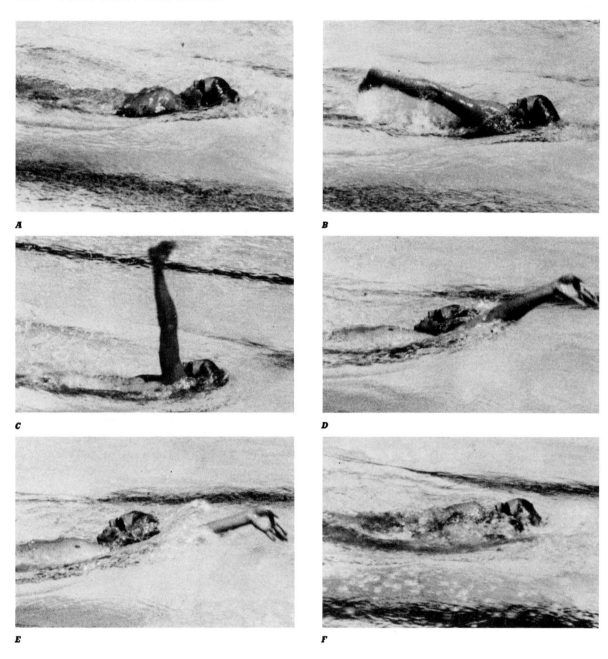

Figure 5.11. The arm recovery of the back crawl stroke, a side view. The swimmer is Todd Lincoln.

A. The recovery of the left arm is executed by lifting the left shoulder.

B. The hand comes out of the water with palm facing inward. This position can be seen more clearly in frame **G** .

C. The palm is rotated outward as it passes overhead.

D-E. The arm enters the water, in a fully extended position, directly ahead of the shoulder, with the palm facing outward.

Figure 5.11. continued

F–J. The recovery of the right arm. Notice the relaxed position of the hand and arm in frame **G.** (The hand should be rotated outward more in **I** and **J.**)

mal resistance (see fig. 5.2*K*). Some people have advocated removing the hand from the water little finger first. That method would cause your arm to be rotated inward at the shoulder during the recovery. This position is more restrictive, therefore more effort is required to swing your arm upward. Less effort is required when your shoulder is rotated outward as it would be when your hand leaves the water thumb first.

After leaving the water, your arm travels upward and then forward and downward to the entry position. Your palm will be facing inward during the first half of the recovery. As your hand passes overhead it is rotated outward so the entry can be made little finger first (see frames *G* and *H* of Figure 5.11). Your hand and arm should be as relaxed as possible during the recovery so that your muscles receive some rest between underwater armstrokes.

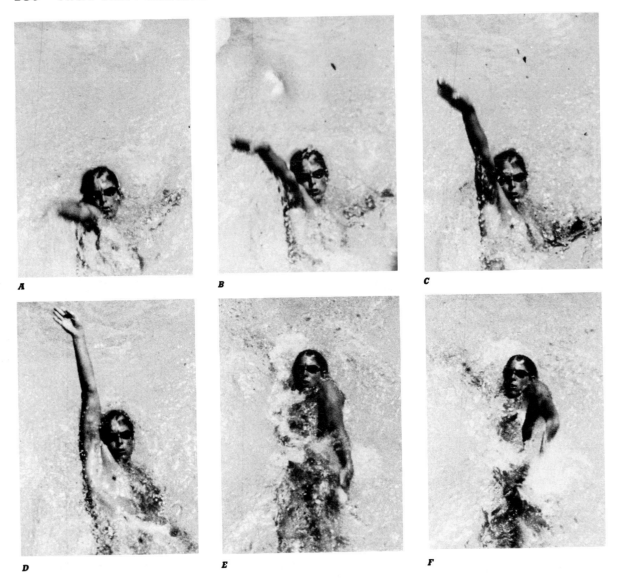

Figure 5.12. Todd Lincoln's arm recovery, viewed
from the top.

Common errors in the recovery. At one time it was believed that the recovery should be made low and laterally over the water. Later, it was learned that backstrokers who recover their arms laterally may pull their hips and legs out of alignment. The sideward force of the arm causes the hips to be pulled outward in the same direction, which in turn causes a counterforce on the legs, causing them to swing outside the body in the opposite direction. The effect of a lateral recovery on body alignment is described in Chapter 1.

Perhaps the most frequent mistake swimmers make is to initiate the recov-

Figure 5.12.   G   H

I   J

ery by lifting the hand rather than the shoulder from the water. Lifting your hand causes your shoulder to submerge. As a result, the recovery is made with your shoulder underwater and drag is increased as your shoulder and later your upper arm are pushed forward through the water.

Timing of the Arms   The hand of the recovering arm should enter the water as the stroking arm completes its downsweep (see frames *I* and *J* of Figure 5.2). In this way one arm can begin applying propulsive force almost immediately after the other releases pressure below the thigh. An additional benefit of this timing is that the downsweep of one arm causes body roll that initiates the recovery of the opposite arm.

Another important factor in timing the armstroke is that one arm should reach its highest point in the recovery as the other arm is beginning the final downsweep. Your body will have returned to a prone position at that time and will be free to rotate toward the recovering side as the arm travels downward for the entry. Should the recovering arm pass overhead before you have rotated back to a prone position, the downward force of the recovery arm and the upward force of the stroking arm will oppose one another with the force being transferred to your trunk and limbs, pushing them out of alignment.

Instructions for Teaching the Backstroke Armstroke to College, High School, and Older Age-Group Swimmers

a. Place your hand in the water directly in front of your shoulder with your palm facing out.

b. After it enters, make a strong catch by turning your hand down and out and pushing down on the water.

c. Initial downsweep: Once the catch is made, sweep your hand down and out, turning your palm toward the bottom as you do. Roll your shoulders, hips, and legs toward the downsweeping arm.

d. Upsweep: When your hand passes its deepest point turn your palm upward and sweep it upward, inward, and backward in a diagonal path until your arm is flexed nearly 90 degrees.

e. Final downsweep: As your hand approaches the surface, sweep it backward and downward past your thigh. Pitch your palm downward and outward as you do.

f. Recovery: When your arm is extended at the end of the downsweep, lift your shoulder out of the water to initiate the recovery. Your arm will follow your shoulder. Your hand should leave the water on its side with palm facing inward. Recover your arm directly overhead, rotating your palm outward as it passes overhead.

Instructions for Teaching the Backstroke Armstroke to Younger Age-Group Swimmers

a. Place your hand in the water directly in front of your shoulder with your palm facing away from your body.

b. After your hand enters the water, press it down and out.

c. Then sweep your hand in and up toward the surface, gradually bending your arm.

d. When your hand comes near the surface, push the water down below your leg by extending your arm.

e. Recover your hand straight overhead.

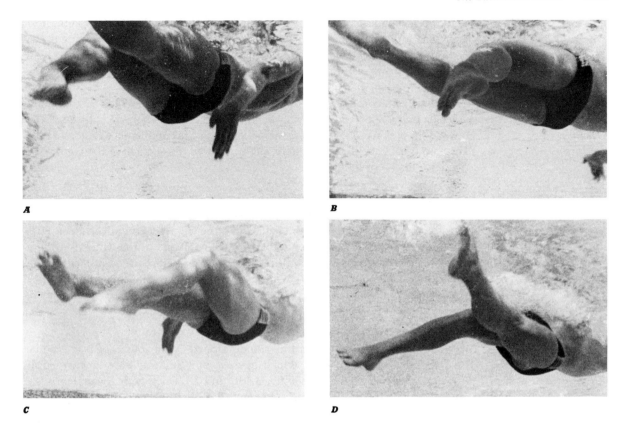

A

B

C

D

Figure 5.13. The backstroke kick.

A-B. The upbeat of the right leg, the downbeat of the left.

C-D. The upbeat of the left leg, the downbeat of the right.

The Kick

The kick consists of an alternating upbeat and downbeat. The mechanics are much like the flutter kick of the front crawl, except that because the swimmer is in a supine position the downbeat of the back crawl kick corresponds to the upbeat of the front crawl and vice versa.

The major difference between the flutter kicks of the two strokes is that a backstroke swimmer's leg will be flexed more when the upbeat begins, whereas the leg of the front crawl swimmer is somewhat straighter as he begins the corresponding downbeat. The kick is pictured in the series of photographs in Figure 5.13.

Upbeat

The upbeat begins as your foot passes below your buttocks. At that point, flexion at the hip starts the thigh traveling upward while the water pressing down on your relaxed lower leg pushes it into a flexed position. Water pressure will also push the ankle and foot into a plantar flexed and inverted position (see fig. 5.13*B*).

Hip flexion continues until your thigh approaches the surface. At that point your leg is extended vigorously at the knee accelerating your lower leg and foot toward the surface. The upbeat ends when the leg is completely extended at the knee. Your toes should be just at or slightly below the surface of the water (see frames *C* and *D* of fig. 5.13).

Common errors in the upbeat. One of the most common mistakes backstrokers make during the upbeat is to use a bicycling motion. They flex their hips too much and do not completely extend the leg at the knee. This mistake is easily spotted because the knee and thigh will come out of the water. Bicycling increases drag because the thigh pushes upward against the water exerting a force that acts counter to the swimmer's forward direction of motion. It is a good teaching technique to instruct swimmers to straighten the leg completely on the upbeat and to keep the knee underneath the water.

Downbeat

As the upbeat ends, the upward inertia developed by the lower leg is overcome by extension at the hip joint, which causes your thigh to start downward as your lower leg is extended (see fig. 5.13*C* and *D*). Once your lower leg is extended, it will follow your thigh downward and the downbeat is underway.

The upward pressure of the water beneath your leg maintains it in an extended position during the downbeat. Water pressure also pushes your foot into a natural position where it is neither plantar flexed nor dorsiflexed (see fig. 5.13*C*). Your leg should be relaxed at the knee and ankle joints so your leg and foot can be positioned correctly by the water.

The downbeat ends when your foot passes below your buttocks. At that point your hip is flexed and the upbeat begins. Don't push your thigh downward excessively. The downward force will push your hips up and disrupt horizontal alignment.

Common errors in the downbeat. Kicking too deep is probably the major problem most swimmers have with the backstroke kick. This mistake is illustrated in Figure 5.14. When the kick is excessively deep, form drag increases because of the additional laminar streams that become disrupted. In addition, the excessive downward force of the lower leg exerts an upward and backward force on your body that will decelerate your forward velocity. The proper depth of the kick is between 15 and 18 inches.

Timing of the Legs

One leg should reach the top of the upbeat as the other leg reaches its deepest position (see fig. 5.13*D*). The slight overlap between the two beats (the thigh of one leg will start upward before the other leg is completely extended) probably

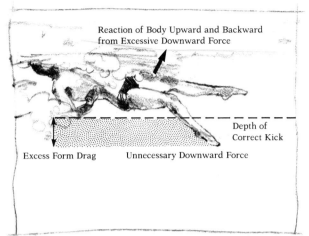

Figure 5.14. The effect on form drag of kicking too deep. This swimmer is kicking downward excessively. This causes the leg to disrupt the laminar flow of water streams that would otherwise have passed below the body with no interruption. As a result, form drag is increased and forward velocity will be slowed. In addition, the excessive downward force of the kick exerts a counterforce on the hips and trunk that tends to push them upward, disrupting horizontal alignment and further increasing drag.

allows time for the knee of the lower leg to be flexed so it can begin extending immediately as the other completes its upbeat.

Timing of the Arms and Legs

World-class backstrokers, almost without exception, use 6-beat timing. The sequence of photographs in Figure 5.15 shows this timing. There are three upbeats to each armstroke, one accompanying each sweep. The correct sequence is as follows:

1. The right leg kicks up during the initial downsweep of the right arm (see frames *A* to *C* of Figure 5.15).
2. The left leg kicks up during the upsweep of the right armstroke (see frames *D* to *F*).
3. The right leg kicks up, once again, during the final downsweep of the right armstroke (see frames *G* to *I*).

The sequence is repeated during the left armstroke. That is, the left leg kicks up during the initial downsweep of the left arm, the right leg kicks up during the upsweep and the left leg kicks up during the final downsweep.

The similarity between the timing of this stroke and the 6-beat timing of the front crawl is remarkable. It lends support to the theory that 6-beat timing may be the most efficient method for both strokes, at least for distances of 200 meters and less.

Is the Backstroke Kick Propulsive?

The same doubts have been expressed concerning the propulsiveness of the back crawl kick as were mentioned in relation to the flutter kick of the front crawl stroke.

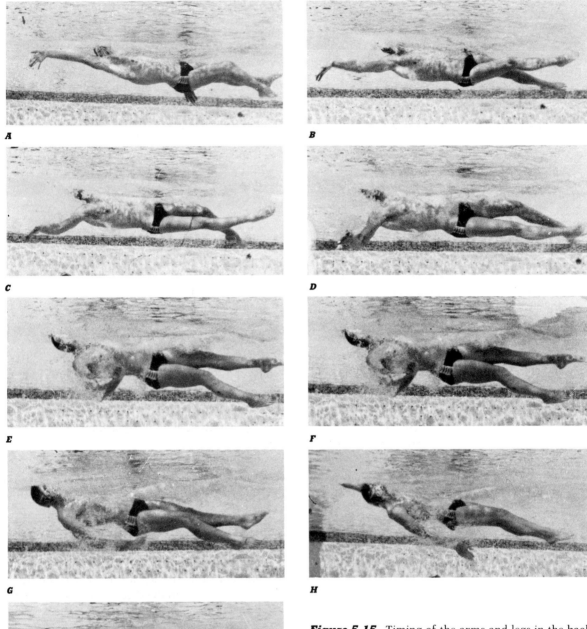

Figure 5.15. Timing of the arms and legs in the backstroke. The swimmer is using a 6-beat kick, 3 kicks to each armstroke. During the initial downsweep of the right arm, he kicks up with the right leg. He then kicks up with the left leg as he completes the upsweep with that arm. The right leg kicks up again as he completes the final downsweep of the armstroke. The same sequence is repeated during the left armstroke.

1. Although the backstroke kick is obviously propulsive by itself, does it contribute to the total propulsive force when combined with the armstroke?
2. If it does, is the expenditure of effort worth the gain in speed?

The first question can be answered theoretically, by means of force diagrams of the kick (see fig. 5.16). The kick plots were drawn from motion pictures of a national-level backstroke swimmer as she swam past a grid painted on the side of the pool. The grid lines make it possible to determine the directions her feet were moving in relation to a fixed point.

The force diagram in Figure 5.16*A* shows that some propulsive force could be generated by the upbeats that accompany the initial downsweep of each armstroke. That kick is directed upward for a significant distance. This is because forward velocity is at its lowest point in the stroke cycle during the initial downsweep. Therefore, the foot travels upward faster than it is "pulled" forward by the armstroke. The upward motion of the swimmer's foot causes the water molecules above it to be deflected backward over the instep surface. This creates a pressure differential between the instep (+) and sole (−) surfaces which exerts a lift force in a forward direction. This lift force could possibly propel the swimmer forward. The most effective portion of this upbeat should be the first half when the direction of motion is upward. After that, forward velocity increases and the foot is pulled forward.

The remaining upbeats, those accompanying the upsweep and final downsweep of each armstroke, probably contribute little, if at all, to the propulsive force of the stroke. The force diagram in Figure 5.16*B* shows that the feet move forward and upward, causing most of the force to be directed downward. This downward force probably serves a stabilizing function by preventing the hips from being lifted out of the water by the armstroke.

The legs travel forward and downward during downbeats accompanying all of the propulsive sweeps of the armstroke. As a result, most of the force they produce is directed upward (see fig. 5.16*C*). These kicks probably serve to return the feet to a position for the next upbeat and possibly also prevent the hips from being submerged during the armstroke.

Since the upbeats that accompany the initial downsweep of each armstroke may be propulsive, the second question, concerning whether the expenditure of effort is worth the propulsive force, must be considered. Unfortunately, there is no research that answers this question. Therefore, judgments must, once again, be made on an empirical basis. There are two observations affirming the wisdom of using these upbeats for propulsion.

1. Unlike crawl swimmers, few successful backstrokers use de-emphasized kick rhythms such as 2-beat or 4-beat patterns.
2. Most successful backstrokers are good kickers. This is in contrast to the crawl stroke where a poor kick has not prevented many swimmers from achieving world-class times.

Since the kick seems to play a more prominent role in this stroke, it is recommended that backstrokers use a 6-beat kick. They should not always kick

A. The Upbeat Accompanying the Initial Downsweep of the Armstroke

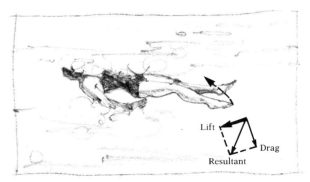

B. Upbeats Accompanying Later Phases of the Armstroke

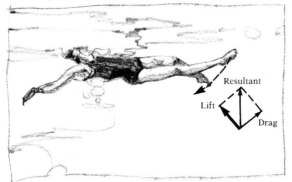

C. All Downbeats of the Kick

Figure 5.16. Kick plots and force diagrams of the backstroke kick. These drawings were made from motion picture films of a backstroke swimmer as she swam past a grid painted on the side of the pool. They show that a significant amount of propulsion is probably generated by the legs during only two upbeats of

every 6-beat cycle. These are the upbeats that accompany the initial downsweep of each armstroke.

A. Forward velocity of the swimmer's body is at its lowest point during that phase of the stroke cycle, enabling the leg to travel almost directly upward. As can be seen in the force diagram, upward foot motion could generate some propulsive force.

B-C. During the remaining four upbeats (**B**) and the six downbeats (**C**) in the stroke cycle, the swimmer's arms are pulling her body forward so fast that her legs travel either upward and forward or downward and forward. In the former case, most of the force is directed downward rather than forward. In the latter case, force is primarily upward. These kicks probably stabilize the hips, preventing them from being pulled out of alignment during the upsweep and final downsweep of the armstroke.

at full force throughout the entire race, however. It may be advisable to kick gently during the first half of 200 races in order to conserve energy for the second half of the race. The full force of the kick should be saved for the final sprint when delaying fatigue is no longer a consideration.

Body Position

Backstrokers have more problems maintaining horizontal and lateral alignment than do swimmers of other strokes. They have a tendency to "sit" in the water, with their hips down and head up, destroying horizontal alignment. They also tend to recover laterally, which pulls their body out of lateral alignment.

Horizontal Alignment A backstroke swimmer's body should be nearly horizontal with the surface of the water. The back of the head should be in the water with the water line passing just under the ears. (The wake will cover a swimmer's ears.) The chin should be slightly tucked with eyes focused backward and upward toward the feet. This head position is shown in Figure 5.12.

The correct position for your head is best described as natural. It should be in line with your body. It should not be held out of the water or forced backward into the water. The former position would cause your hips and legs to sink while the latter position would cause your back to be arched and rigid. Although your body should be straight, it should not be rigid. There should be a slight shoulder slump and a slight inclination from head to feet (see fig. 5.15). This position will allow you to kick more effectively. If your hips are too high your thighs will break through the surface on the upbeat, while low hips will increase form drag. Your trunk and legs should also be in a natural position. There should not be any arch to your back nor any excessive pike at the waist.

The following positions should be checked periodically to insure proper horizontal alignment:

1. The back of your head should be in the water.
2. Your chest should be just above the surface.
3. Your hips should be just below the surface.
4. Your legs should be just beneath the surface when they finish the upbeat of the kick.
5. Your kick should not be deeper than 15 to 18 inches.

Lateral Alignment

The proper lateral alignment is shown in Figures 5.1 and 5.3. Your hips and legs should remain within shoulder width at all times. Rolling your body and kicking laterally aids in maintaining lateral alignment. The swimmers in these photos are almost out of alignment at one point in their strokes (see fig. 5.1*I* and fig. 5.3*A*), but both recover quickly and align their bodies for the propulsive phases of the armstroke.

The Importance of Body Roll

The initial downsweep of the arm requires hyperflexion at the shoulder joint. Since the range of such motion is very limited in this action, swimmers roll their bodies toward the downsweeping arm to prevent their body from being pulled out of lateral and horizontal alignment. If this roll is not timed properly or if the shoulders roll while the hips and legs are maintained in a flat position, the body will be pulled out of alignment.

In addition to the stabilizing effect body roll has on lateral alignment, rolling also makes it possible to downsweep more effectively. Additionally, drag is reduced on the shoulder of the recovering arm because it will be out of the water until late in the recovery. The sequence of photographs in Figures 5.1 and 5.3 shows the amount of body roll used by most successful backstrokers. They roll approximately 45 degrees to each side.

When your hand enters the water and travels downward your trunk and legs should roll toward that side. Your body should continue to roll until the downsweeping arm passes its deepest point and starts upward. At that time you begin rolling toward the other side (see frames *D* and *K* of Figure 5.1). It is very important to roll your entire body. Your shoulders must follow your arm and your hips and legs must follow your shoulders if good lateral alignment is to be maintained.

The Importance of Diagonal Kicking

You will notice in the photographs in Figure 5.3 that the swimmer is not kicking straight up and down. Most of the kicks are directed diagonally upward and downward. These diagonal kicks are essential to good backstroke swimming. They exert a stabilizing effect that aids the swimmer in maintaining horizontal and lateral alignment in spite of the potentially disrupting sweeps of the armstroke.

The pattern of these kicks is as follows. When the left arm makes the initial downsweep, the left leg kicks up and out while the right leg kicks down and out (see frames *A* to *C* of fig. 5.3). In addition to the propulsion supplied, these kicks probably prevent the hips from moving out of horizontal and lateral alignment. When the upsweep of the armstroke is made, the right leg starts upward and inward but finishes this kick traveling straight upward while the body begins rotating to the right (see frames *D* and *E* of Figure 5.3). The left leg starts down and in but finishes the kick traveling straight down. This action probably assists in rotating the body toward the left side. The left leg kicks up and in and the right down and in during the final downsweep (see frames *F* to *I* of Figure 5.3). This action probably maintains the hips in horizontal alignment when the force of the downsweeping arm might cause them to be elevated.

Common Errors in Body Position

The most common mistakes, swimming with the head up and piking at the waist, have already been mentioned. These errors were illustrated in Chapter 1.

Overreaching on the entry, using a lateral rather than vertical recovery, pushing outward with the palm during the initial downsweep, and pushing the hand inward rather than downward during the final downsweep are all actions that can disrupt lateral alignment. They cause backstrokers to move "snake-like" through the water with their hips and legs swinging from side to side. Pushing downward and upward excessively during the initial downsweep and upsweeps respectively can also disrupt horizontal alignment.

Stroke Drills to Improve the Backstroke

There are two excellent drills for learning body roll and diagonal kicking. The first is one-arm swimming. The second is kicking on the side.

One-arm swimming. In this drill, athletes swim repeats stroking with one arm only while the other arm remains at the side. Swimmers should be cautioned to roll until the shoulder opposite the stroking arm "pops" out of the water during every armstroke. This is also a good drill for teaching the armstroke, because swimmers can concentrate on one arm at a time.

Kicking on the side. Kicking with one arm overhead and one arm at the side is an excellent way to improve diagonal kicking. Swimmers should practice this drill with their bodies rotated toward the arm that is stretched overhead. They should be rolled to that side until the opposite shoulder is out of the water. After completing 6, 8, 10 or some other designated number of kicks, they can recover the other arm overhead, bring the arm that was overhead to their side, and continue kicking.

This drill seems to encourage swimmers to use diagonal kicks and body roll, whereas the traditional style of kicking, with both hands overhead, encourages them to kick vertically. Both types of kicking drills should be used in training.

Breathing

Some coaches recommend inhaling on one arm recovery and exhaling on the other when swimming backstroke. This is probably good advice. Trained athletes will take between 40 and 50 breaths per minute during strenuous exercise (Astrand and Rodahl 1977). Since swimmers take between 60 and 80 strokes in a 100 race, inhaling on every other arm recovery would allow them to take 30 to 40 breaths during the time it takes to swim 100 yards/meters. In addition, this breathing pattern encourages a more uniform stroke rhythm.

REFERENCES

Astrand, P. O., and Rodahl, K. 1977. *Textbook of Work Physiology.* San Francisco: McGraw-Hill.

Schleihauf, R. E., Jr. 1978. "Swimming Propulsion: A Hydrodynamic Analysis." *American Swimming Coaches Association 1977 World Clinic Year Book*, ed. R. M. Ousley, pp. 49–85. Ft. Lauderdale, Florida: American Swimming Coaches Association.

CHAPTER **6**

Starts, Turns, and Finishes

In these days of crowded pools and high-mileage training programs, there is little time to perfect the techniques of starting, turning, and finishing. Ideally swimmers should practice these techniques while swimming repeats in practice so that neither time nor yardage is sacrificed. However, circle swimming, which is necessitated by crowded pools, makes it difficult, if not impossible, to perform these techniques correctly.

Circle swimming forces swimmers to cross from one side of the lane to the other while making the turn. They also hesitate going into and coming out of the turn in order to avoid collisions. Unfortunately, these habits become so ingrained that many swimmers hesitate and cross the lane when turning in competition.

Proper finishing is neglected because swimmers tend to finish slowly when their teammates are crowded at the end waiting to start the next repeat. Under these conditions, the incoming swimmer generally relaxes and coasts for the final two or three yards of each repeat. Many swimmers lose races they might have won because, out of habit, they slow up for the last two or three strokes to the wall.

Time should be set aside each week for practicing correct starts, turns, and finishes. The 6,000 to 8,000 yards of training that would be lost each week should not affect the endurance of swimmers who are training well in excess of 60,000 yards per week. On the other hand, perfecting these techniques may make the difference between success and failure in many races.

Data gathered over several years indicate that, on the average, improved starts can reduce race times by at least one-tenth of a second. Improved turns will decrease race time at least 0.2 seconds per length, and improved finishes can reduce time by at least an additional tenth of a second. Thus, just two hours of practice per week could improve a swimmer's 50-yard time by at least 0.4 seconds. It could mean a minimum reduction of 0.8 seconds in a 100-yard race, because there are two additional turns. Improvements in longer races should be even more dramatic. For example, improving turns could reduce your time for a 1,650 by as much as 15 seconds.

The significance of such improvements can be shown by the observation that only 0.38 seconds separated the first and third place finishers in the 100-yard freestyle at the 1980 NCAA Division I Championships. There was 0.40 seconds difference between the sixth and twelfth qualifiers in that same event. A difference of 15 seconds in the 1,650-yard freestyle could have advanced a swimmer *seven* places in the finals. Certainly, practicing starts, turns, and finishes is time well spent.

Standing Starts for Freestyle, Butterfly, and Breaststroke Races

Over the years many starting styles have been used in freestyle, butterfly, and breaststroke events. Initially, swimmers took a starting position with arms extended backward. They soon found that they could start their body moving toward the water more quickly by swinging their arms backward (action-reaction principle). Therefore, they assumed a preparatory position with arms in front. They would swing the arms straight backward, then forward again after the starting signal. This straight backswing start was later replaced by a circular backswing on the theory that a longer armswing would generate additional momentum and increase the distance traveled through the air.

The circular armswing has now been replaced by a faster method, the grab start. The grab start was introduced by Hanauer in the late 1960s and has rapidly gained in popularity since that time (Hanauer 1972). Several research studies have verified that the grab start is faster than other methods (Jorgenson 1971, Roffer and Nelson 1972, Bowers and Cavanaugh 1975, Cavanaugh et al. 1975, Thorsen 1975). The grab start is superior because you can get your body moving toward the water faster by pulling against the starting platform with your hands than by swinging your arms backward. Once you enter the water, there is greater loss of momentum with the grab start because your arms do not generate as much force as would be produced by a circular backswing. However, studies indicate that the ability to get your body quickly in motion with a grab start outweighs any loss of momentum that occurs after entry. When starting speed was timed from a gunshot to the point where the first stroke was taken, the grab start was usually faster. For example, Thorsen (1975) found the horizontal and vertical velocities were greater with the conventional start, yet the grab start was faster by 0.1 seconds to the point of entry.

Cavanaugh et al. (1975) suggest that swimmers leave the block faster with a grab start because they begin applying force before the gunshot. The researchers fitted a starting platform with a strain gauge to measure horizontal and vertical forces created by the hands and legs. They found swimmers anticipated the start by tensing their leg muscles before the gunshot. They were able to avoid a false start because they were gripping the block with their hands.

Although research has verified the grab start as the fastest method for freestylers and butterflyers, there has been some doubt that it is the best starting style for breaststroke races. The deep entry and long underwater glide used with the breaststroke dive allows more time for deceleration. Thus, some coaches and swimmers have reasoned that it might be advisable to sacrifice a quick departure from the starting platform and use a circular armswing to gain more momentum during the glide. Beritzhoff (1974) tested this theory by

Figure 6.1. The grab start.

A. Preparatory position. The swimmer grasps the front of the block. Head is down, knees are flexed slightly, and hips are above the feet so that his center of gravity will be as near the front of the starting platform as possible.

B. The pull. At the starting signal, he exerts a quick pull against the front of the block. This starts his body falling forward.

C. As he falls forward, he lifts his head and flexes his legs in preparation for the drive from the starting platform.

D-E. The leg drive. The swimmer begins extending the legs when the knees are approximately level with the feet and the hips are above the knees. He drives his body upward and outward. In the meantime, he reaches forward, outward, and then downward with

A

B

C

D

Figure 6.1. continued

the arms. Although the head is up during the early part of the leg drive, notice in **E** that the swimmer looks down before his feet leave the block.

F-G. The flight. The flight path is arc-like, with the swimmer piking at the waist as he passes the peak of the arc (see frame **G**).

H-J. The entry. The swimmer attempts to have his entire body pass through the same "hole" in the water. After entering the water, he lifts his hands toward the surface during the glide. As he begins to lose speed from the dive, he should take two kicks and one strong armstroke that will bring him upward and forward through the surface.

E

F

G

H

I

J

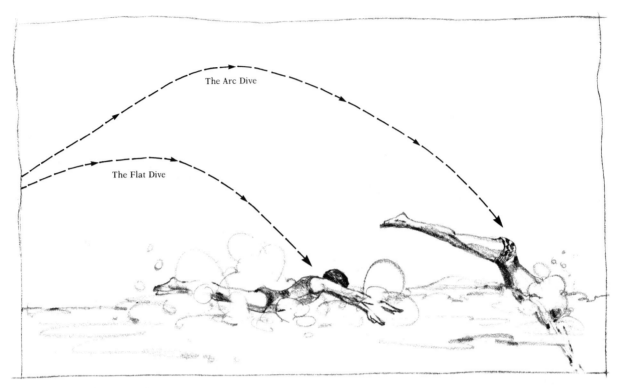

Figure 6.2. The arc and flat dives. The swimmers shown here illustrate the advantages of the arc dive over the flat dive. The arc dive allows the swimmer to travel farther over the water and, upon entry, she will create much less turbulence. This allows a faster underwater glide, and the swimmer reaches the pullout point in a shorter time than would be the case with a flat dive. When using the flat dive, a swimmer will tend to reach the peak of the trajectory sooner and then drop toward the water so rapidly that there is not enough time to incline the body for a "clean" entry. As a result, the swimmer's hands, chest, hips, and feet will hit the water in different spots at almost the same moment. This creates considerable turbulence and causes rapid deceleration during the underwater glide.

comparing the starting speeds of breaststroke swimmers using the grab start and the circular backswing start. The grab start was faster. Breaststroke swimmers reached a point 12-1/2 yards from the starting end of the pool an average of 0.150 seconds faster when they used a grab start. This advantage was noted despite the fact that all but one of the subjects had preferred the circular backswing start in competition prior to taking part in the study.

Mechanics of the Grab Start

The grab start is shown in the series of photographs in Figure 6.1. Notice that the swimmer's body travels in an arc rather than in a flattened path. When using this "arc" dive, your body is driven upward and then downward into the water in a path that permits your head and feet to enter the water in very nearly the same spot. This entry is less turbulent and creates less drag than the flat dive. Therefore, swimmers glide through the water at a faster speed.

The flat dive causes the swimmer's body to hit the water in several different spots at once, as shown in Figure 6.2. In particular, the feet hit the water behind the point where the head and hands have entered. As a result, the swimmer's trunk and legs are dragged forward during the glide, causing turbulence and rapid deceleration. The difference in turbulence created by the arc dive and the flat dive is illustrated in Figure 6.2. The arc dive is a significant improvement over the flat dive and should be taught to all swimmers. It will be described in combination with the grab start.

Preparatory position. After the command "take your marks," you should assume a preparatory position in which your toes grip the front edge of the starting platform. Your feet should be approximately shoulder width apart. This position of the feet permits a stronger leg drive than can be produced if your feet are placed outside your shoulders or positioned close together. Grasp the front edge of the block with the first and second joints of your fingers. Your hands may be either inside or outside your feet. The most effective placement is not known. Both styles have been used by world-class swimmers.

Your knees should be flexed approximately 30 to 40 degrees and your elbows should be flexed slightly. Your head should be down, and you should look at the water just beyond the starting platform (see fig. 6.1*A*). These knee and head positions are different from those that are usually recommended. They offer some advantages, however. A small amount of knee flexion places

Figure 6.3. Two preparatory positions for the grab start. These drawings illustrate the detrimental effect of flexing the knees too much and looking ahead in the preparatory position. The head-up position and excessive knee bend of swimmer ***A*** tends to shift her center of gravity backward. As a result, it must travel forward a greater distance before passing the front edge of the starting platform, where the leg drive can begin. This increases the time required to leave the starting platform. Swimmer ***B*** is using the correct preparatory position. Her hips are above the front edge of the starting platform and need to travel only a short distance before the leg drive can begin. The fact that the knees are not flexed very much will not affect the power of the leg drive. Knee flexion will increase as she falls forward, and the leg drive can be made with maximum force.

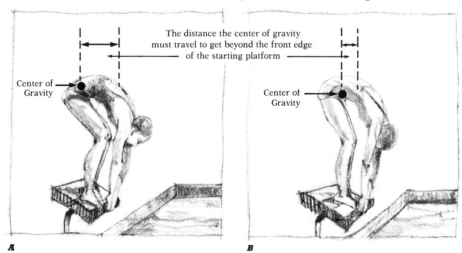

The distance the center of gravity must travel to get beyond the front edge of the starting platform

Center of Gravity

Center of Gravity

A

B

your hips closer to the front edge of the starting platform. This is desirable because the speed with which you leave the block is dependent on how fast you can get your center of gravity, which is located in the hip region, beyond the front edge of the starting platform. A deep crouch would place the center of gravity farther back, and additional time would be required to move it beyond the front edge of the starting block. The position of the center of gravity in preparatory positions that involve a deep crouch and minimum knee bend are compared in Figure 6.3.

The position of the swimmer's head in Figure 6.3B brings her center of gravity nearer the front edge of the starting platform. Looking downward and forward enables her to place her hips over the front edge of the starting platform.

Faster reactions to the starting signal. Once you are in the preparatory position you should focus all your attention on the starting commands. This will allow you to react as quickly as possible when the starting signal sounds. Henry and Rogers (1960) have shown that concentrating on the starting signal rather than the starting movements produces faster reaction times. They believe the brain functions as a computer. The more information that is fed into it in the form of technical instructions, the slower the readout or reaction time will be. This means that if, while waiting on the block, you concentrate on the myriad movements you will execute during the dive, it will take longer to get in motion when the starting signal is sounded. If, instead, you concentrate only on the starting signal, you will react faster. Measurements with several athletes indicate the difference will be in the neighborhood of 0.03 to 0.06 seconds.

A word of caution. If this technique is to be used successfully, you must learn the mechanics of the start so thoroughly that they can be performed correctly without conscious thought. It would do no good to react fast with a poor dive. The time gained in reacting would be lost several times over during the flight through the air and the glide through the water. Thus, you will not be able to use this technique until you learn to dive correctly. In the meantime, you can improve your reaction time by reducing your self-instructions to the absolute minimum needed to perform a good dive. "Readout" time should be reduced by concentrating only on those parts that are incorrect. Meanwhile, however, work toward starting correctly without conscious thought.

The dive. At the sound of the starting signal, you should pull upward against the starting platform (see fig. 6.1B). This will pull your center of gravity forward beyond the front edge of the starting platform and you will begin moving toward the water. There is no need to use a long, powerful arm pull. This will not add speed or force to the dive. Once your hips are moving downward, gravity will determine your speed toward the water and no amount of additional pulling will increase that speed. A quick pull is all that is required to get your hips moving. After that, you should release the block and get your hands forward to lead your body's trajectory from the starting platform.

Once your hands release the block, there should be a rapid increase in knee flexion as your body falls toward the water. The leg drive begins when the angle formed by your upper and lower legs is approximately 90 degrees (see fig. 6.1*D*). At this point, your knees will have fallen forward and downward until they are in front of your feet, and your hips will be directly above your knees. A powerful extension at the hip and knee joints followed by plantar flexion at the ankles will drive your body upward and forward away from the starting platform. The angle of take-off, from feet to hips, should be approximately 40 to 50 degrees from the top edge of the starting platform. That take-off position is illustrated in frame *E* of Figure 6.1.

Your arms should "lead" your body through the proper trajectory. After releasing the starting platform, they are flexed and driven upward while your knees are falling forward. Your hands should be inside your shoulders and approximately level with your knees when the leg drive begins so that the simultaneous extension of both the arms and the legs will maximize take-off power (see frames *D* and *E* of Figure 6.1). After that, your arms extend upward, forward, and then downward in a circular path. They extend faster than your legs so that they are reaching downward for the entry before the leg drive is completed.

The movements of your head are as important as those of your arms in executing a good dive. You should look up as you "fall" forward so that your body remains above your feet where your legs can drive it upward and forward. However, in order to get a good entry, you must begin looking down for the entry before the leg drive is completed.

Lowering your head as your feet leave the block establishes a downward trajectory for your upper body so that it passes the peak of the arc earlier in your flight through the air. This allows time to "pull" your hips and legs over the peak so they can be in line with your trunk as they enter the water. When your head is held up too long during the flight, your body passes the peak of the arc in a horizontal position or, even worse, in a position where your body is inclined upward (see fig. 6.4*A*). Your body will fall toward the water in this position and it will be impossible to get your legs up in line with your trunk for a "clean" entry. You will either hit the water in a flat, rather painful position, or you will pike your body before it hits the water. In either case your trunk and legs will hit the water behind the place where your hands and head entered and will create waves that reduce forward speed during the glide. The effect of this mistake is illustrated in Figure 6.4.

If the proper trajectory has been attained, you may travel through the air in a piked position with your trunk and legs inclined downward. Your legs will come up in line with your trunk as it enters the water. Your arms should be fully extended as they enter the water. Your head should be between your arms and your hands should be together. Your legs should be fully extended and together with toes pointed. The angle of entry should be approximately 30 to 40 degrees from the surface of the water (Beritzhoff 1974). This steep angle of entry will cause you to plunge deep beneath the surface unless some adjustments are made immediately after entry to change the direction your body is moving. A directional change from downward and forward to forward and up-

Figure 6.4. The effect of keeping the head up during the flight through the air. Swimmer **A** is making the mistake of keeping her head up too long during the dive. This causes a delay in getting the upper body inclined downward for the entry. As a result, the legs do not pass over the peak of the trajectory in time to get aligned with the trunk for a "clean" entry. She hits the water in a "piked" position with the legs and feet behind the point where the hands and trunk have entered. This increases drag and decelerates forward speed during the glide.

Swimmer **B** is using the correct head movements. The head is down as she passes the peak of the trajectory, and the trunk starts down immediately. This "pulls" the legs over the top in time to get them aligned for a less turbulent entry and a faster underwater glide.

ward is accomplished by lifting your hands toward the surface and arching your back shortly after you enter the water. The timing of these actions will vary according to how quickly you wish to reach the surface. In shorter races, they will occur before your legs are submerged so that you come to the surface more quickly. In longer races it will occur after your legs enter the water.

After the entry, you should glide in a streamlined position until you approach race speed. Your arms should be extended and together, with your head between them. Your legs should be together and extended at the hip and knee joints, with toes pointed. There should be no arch or pike at the waist. As you begin to lose speed from the dive, start kicking (1 or 2 kicks is sufficient) and pull yourself through the surface. If the first armstroke is timed properly, your head will come through the surface as the armstroke nears completion. Don't lift your head before you begin that stroke or you will disrupt your horizontal alignment and increase drag.

Do not delay in attaining the proper stroke rhythm once you reach the surface. Breathing and looking around are two of the most common causes for such delays. For this reason, it is best to delay breathing for at least two strokes after the start, while you settle into race pace (breaststroke excepted).

Common errors in the grab start. The two most common problems in the grab start are landing flat and entering the water in a piked position. The first of these faults is illustrated in Figure 6.2 (flat entry) and the second in Figure 6.4*A* (pike entry). In both cases, drag causes rapid deceleration during the glide. These poor mechanics can be corrected by reaching downward and forward for the entry position and by looking down before your feet leave the block.

Another problem in the dive is timing the hand lift after entry so the dive is neither too shallow nor exceedingly deep. If you lift your hands too early, your feet will drop in the water behind the point where your arms entered. If you lift them too late, your dive will be too deep and you will decelerate before you can reach the surface and begin stroking.

When the grab start is used in breaststroke races, swimmers should probably use a slightly greater angle of entry so they can glide beneath the surface for a longer period of time.

Relay Starts   In relay races the rules permit the second, third, and fourth swimmers to start their dives before their incoming teammate has finished his or her segment of the race. However, "some part of the body" (the toes) must be in contact with the starting platform when the incoming swimmer touches the wall; otherwise, the team could be disqualified. Because the starting swimmer can be in motion before the incoming swimmer touches the wall, a relay start can be 0.6 to 1.0 seconds faster than a "gun" start. Therefore, a team with good relay starts could swim a time that is 1 to 4 seconds faster than the sum of their best gun start times. This could easily make a difference of two or more places in today's closely contested championship meets and will frequently be the deciding factor in dual meet victories. With two relays in dual meets and a minimum of three in championship meets, practicing relay starts could easily improve a team's total by at least 14 points. For this reason, swimmers should practice relay starts until they can regularly leave the block as early as possible without being disqualified.

The lead-off swimmer is the only member of a relay who should use a grab start. Later swimmers should use a circular backswing start. Since they are permitted to be in motion before the touch is made, the grab start is not needed and the circular backswing will give them additional momentum after they enter the water.

The circular backswing start is illustrated in Figure 6.5 as it would be used in a relay race. Except for the armswing, it is similar to the grab start.

Proper timing of the armswing is critical so that the outgoing swimmer gains the maximum possible advantage without leaving early. The outgoing swimmer must make judgments based on the incoming teammate's speed and distance from the wall. In freestyle relays the usual practice is to "wind up"

A

B

C

D

E

F

G

H

when the incoming swimmer's head crosses the "T" of the lane lines on the bottom of the pool. The outgoing swimmer may have to delay the armswing slightly in medley relays because breaststrokers, butterflyers, and backstrokers require slightly more time to cover the distance from the "T" to the wall.

Another method swimmers use for timing the take-off in relay races is to begin the armswing as the incoming swimmer begins his or her last arm recovery. In this case the armswing should start slowly so it can be checked if it becomes obvious that the incoming swimmer will take an extra stroke before touching the wall. Once you can see when the incoming swimmer's arm(s) will reach the wall, accelerate your armswing and begin to drive off the starting platform.

Be sure to practice relay starts with other relay members. Having your coach or teammates judge your starts will aid you in determining when to start your armswing in relation to a particular swimmer's distance from the wall.

Backstroke Starts

Regarding the backstroke start, NCAA and USS short-course rules differ from USS long-course and FINA rules in a very important way. The long-course rules require that your feet be entirely submerged while you are in the preparatory position, while short-course rules stipulate only that some part of your body must be in the water. This difference in the rules provides a definite advantage to swimmers in short-course competition because they can place their toes over the top edge of the gutter and get a powerful upward drive from the wall that should enable them to get a longer flight through the air. In long-course competition swimmers must push against the flat end wall making it more difficult to drive the body over the water.

Some swimmers have used a standing backstroke start in short-course competition on the theory that it allows even a longer flight than the conventional start. The advantages and disadvantages of the standing start will be discussed later in this chapter. The conventional backstroke start will be described first. The conventional backstroke start is shown in Figure 6.6.

Mechanics of the Conventional Backstroke Start

Preparatory position. For the preparatory position you should be in the water gripping the backstroke bar loosely with your hands. Your feet are in contact with the wall. Upon the command "take your marks," pull yourself into a crouched position. In short-course competition, place your toes and the balls of your feet over the top edge of the gutter; in long-course competition, place them against the flat wall below the gutter.

Figure 6.5. The relay start.

A–B. The wind-up. The waiting swimmer's arms begin circling in a counterclockwise direction as the incoming swimmer starts his last arm recovery.

C–E. The arm swing is accelerated as the outgoing swimmer is certain that the incoming swimmer will touch the wall at completion of that arm recovery.

F. The take-off. The outgoing swimmer's feet are still in contact with the starting platform as the incoming swimmer touches the wall.

G. The flight. The angles of take-off and flight are the same as described for the grab start.

H. The entry.

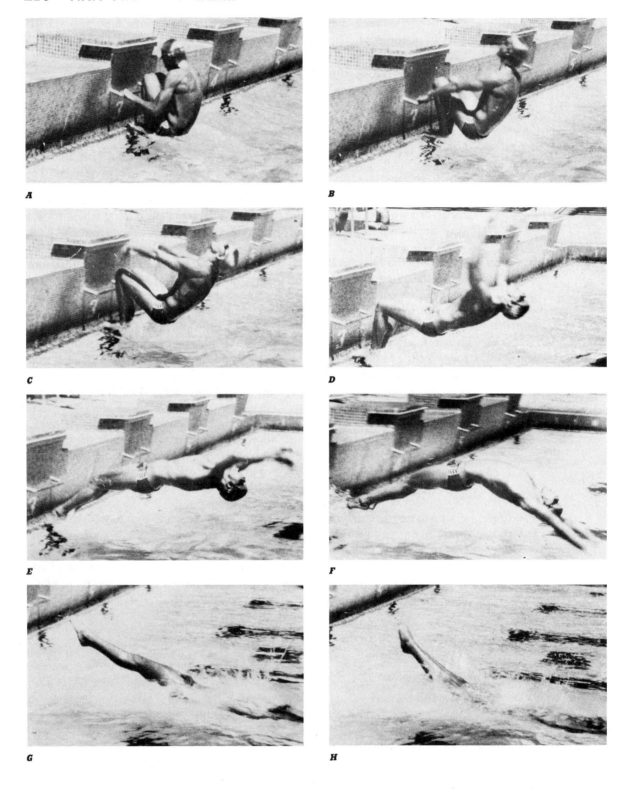

A

B

C

D

E

F

G

H

Your head should be down and you should be looking at the gutter in front of you. Your elbows should be flexed approximately 90 degrees to hold your body in a crouched position. Your hips should be out of the water with your knees flexed tightly (see fig. 6.6*A*).

Drive from the wall. When the starting signal is given, you should throw your head up and back and push your body upward and away from the starting platform by extending your arms (see fig. 6.6*B*). The extension of your arms is followed by a vigorous extension of the legs that drives your hips upward and backward over the water. The drive from the wall is completed with a powerful plantar flexion of the ankles (see frames *C* to *F* of Figure 6.6).

After releasing the bar, your arms continue upward and slightly outward. They should be flexed at the elbows, not straight, as has been traditionally taught (see frames *A* and *B* of Figure 6.7). (The reason for this alteration in technique will be explained later.) Your arms should pass overhead and extend backward and downward for the entry as your legs complete their extension (see frames *C* to *E* of Figure 6.7).

The flight. Your body should travel through the air in an arc; your arms should be extended, your back arched, your legs extended, and your toes pointed. Your entire body should be out of the water during the flight (see fig. 6.6*F*). This is difficult to accomplish in long-course competition; however, with practice you should be able to keep your body clear of the water during the flight in short-course races because you can drive off the top of the gutter. The movements of the head should lead your body during the flight, establishing the proper trajectory for a clean entry with minimal turbulence. Your head should be moving up and back as you begin to drive from the wall, but you should pull it down and back before your feet leave the wall (see frames *C* to *E* of Figure 6.6). The initial upward motion will encourage you to drive upward with your legs. The downward motion makes it possible for your trunk to pass over the peak of the trajectory sooner so that your legs will be pulled up and remain clear of the water for a longer time. The proper head action can be

Figure 6.6. The conventional backstroke start.

A. Preparatory position. The swimmer has his body tucked in a tight ball with elbows and knees flexed and head down.

B. The arm extension. At the starting signal he throws his head back and drives his body from the wall by extending his arms.

C–E. The drive from the wall. When the arm extension is completed, he drives his body upward and outward from the wall by extending his legs. The swimmer should be looking at the other end of the pool before his feet leave the wall.

F. The flight. He travels through the air in an arched position.

G–H. The entry. The swimmer should attempt to have his entire body enter through nearly the same "hole" in the water. This is accomplished by piking at the waist as the upper body enters the water.

After entry, the swimmer lifts his hands toward the surface to bring his body upward during the glide. As he begins to lose speed from the dive, he takes one or two kicks, followed by an armstroke that brings the body upward and forward through the surface.

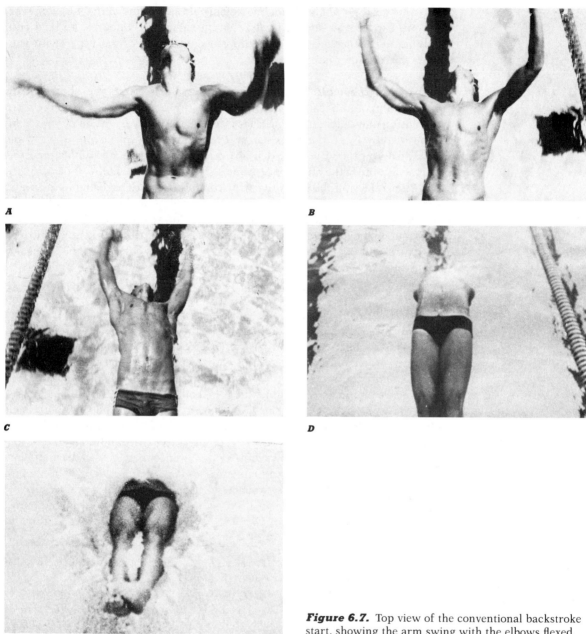

A

B

C

D

E

Figure 6.7. Top view of the conventional backstroke start, showing the arm swing with the elbows flexed.

achieved by throwing your head upward and backward at the starting signal and looking for the other end of the pool as your legs are extending.

The entry. The entry should be made in a streamlined position, with your arms extended and together, your head between your arms, your legs extended and together, and your toes pointed. The angle of entry should be such that your hands enter first, followed by your head, trunk, and legs. It would be ideal for your entire body to enter through the same spot where your hands entered the water. This is difficult if not impossible to accomplish because your body is so near the water during the flight through the air. Your hips will usually enter the water slightly behind the point where your head entered. You can keep your legs from dragging through the water by lifting them during the flight. Lifting your legs by piking at the waist will help them remain clear of the water until they can enter in nearly the same spot as your hips.

The glide. After entry you should lift your hands to change direction from downward and forward to forward and upward. The amount of lift will depend upon the angle of entry and the length of the race. If you have dived too deep or the race is short, lift should be rapid and forceful. If your entry was more shallow or the race is longer, it should be slower and less forceful.

Place the back of one hand in the palm of the other to aid in maintaining the streamlined position you had at entry. Keep your head between your arms and your body straight with no arch to the back and no pike at the waist. Your legs should remain extended and together with your toes pointed. Do not lift your head and disturb this streamlined body position until you have initiated the first armstroke. That armstroke is taken when you begin to lose speed from the dive. At that time take one or two kicks and begin pulling yourself up and forward, "through" the surface and into the proper stroking rhythm for the race.

Arm position during the backstroke start. In the description of the backstroke start, it was recommended that your arms be carried overhead in a flexed position during the drive from the wall (see fig. 6.7). These instructions differ from the armswing that is traditionally taught with the backstroke start. In that method, the arms swing over the water low and laterally with elbows extended. There are at least two advantages to swinging your arms with flexed elbows until they pass your head.

Your arms will get overhead faster when they are carried over the water with elbows flexed. In the same manner that a runner can recover her leg forward faster when it is flexed than when it is extended (Wells and Luttgens 1976), backstrokers' arms will move overhead faster because they are closer to the axis of rotation (the shoulders) and the moment of inertia is less. Also, when your elbows swing around in a flexed position, they can be extended in a forward direction as they pass overhead, adding momentum to the drive from the wall.

Common errors in the conventional backstroke start. Two of the most common problems in backstroke starting are: (1) dragging your legs through the water during the dive and (2) landing flat on your back. There can be several related causes for making these mistakes during the backstroke start: failing to get your head back quickly enough, failing to get your arms back quickly enough, failing to arch your body during the flight, and failing to drive upward from the wall. There is a drill that can help correct these problems.

> Lay a small piece of rope across the lane at the point where your hips should reach the peak of their flight. Dive over the rope without touching it. You will have to push your body up and forward and keep your hips and feet clear of the water to accomplish this.

Many backstrokers make the mistake of kicking their bodies to the surface before they begin the armstroke. Since the kick is less propulsive than the armstroke, delaying the first stroke could cause them to decelerate below race speed while they are waiting to reach the surface. Time and energy will be wasted regaining that lost speed.

Standing Backstroke Start

The standing backstroke start is illustrated in Figure 6.8. In the preparatory position, stand in the gutter and grasp the starting handles. Your knees should be flexed, with your head and shoulders over the block (see fig. 6.8A).

At the starting signal, you simultaneously throw your head upward and backward and push your body upward and backward with your arms (see fig. 6.8B). Then, you throw your arms upward and backward with your elbows flexed, extend your arms as you extend your legs, and drive upward and forward from the wall (see frames *C* and *D* of Figure 6.8). Be sure to look back as your feet leave the wall. The flight through the air is made in an arc. Try to enter your hands, head, hips, and feet through nearly the same "hole" in the water.

In theory, the standing start should be superior to the conventional style. Your additional height in the preparatory position should permit a longer, higher flight and a smoother, less turbulent entry.

Unfortunately, few swimmers are able to perform it well. They tend to lose the height advantage by "sitting down" in the water after the gunshot. Considerable practice is required to master the standing start as compared to the conventional style. Perhaps if more time were spent perfecting the standing start, backstrokers would find it superior to the conventional method.

Turns

Swimmers spend 2 to 3 seconds of each pool length turning and gliding, or put another way, they are turning during at least 10 to 20 percent of the time it takes to swim short-course races. These techniques deserve more attention than they are usually given. Perfecting turns is one of the quickest and easiest ways to improve race times. There are many styles of turning. Each has advocates.

There seem to be two styles of freestyle flip turn in use. The techniques of both are the same except that in one swimmers push off on their sides, while in the other they push off on their backs. The flip turn with a push-off on the back will be described because it is believed to be the faster method.

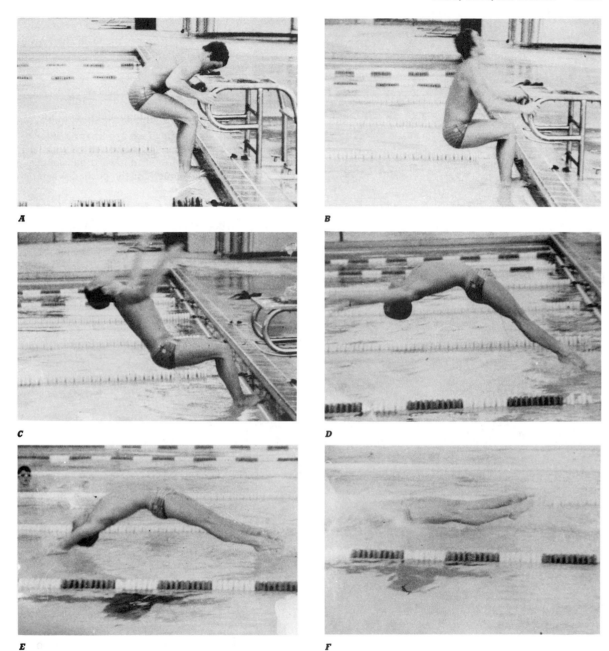

Figure 6.8. The standing backstroke start.

   A. The preparatory position.

   B-C. The drive from the wall.

   D. The flight.

   E-F. The entry.

Figure 6.9. The freestyle flip turn.

A. As the swimmer approaches the wall, she leaves her left hand at her side and propels her body into the turn with her right arm.

B-C. As she completes the armstroke, she executes a short dolphin kick and begins the somersault.

D-E. She completes the somersault, planting her feet on the wall so that they face upward and sideward. Simultaneously, she has pushed down with her hands in order to bring her head toward the surface so that her body will be aligned for the pushoff when her feet reach the wall.

B

C

D

E

There are four styles of backstroke turns. The tumble turn is believed to be inferior to the others and will not be described. Each of the remaining three styles will be described because no one method has proven superior to the others.

There is general agreement concerning the techniques of the butterfly and breaststroke turns. The turn is the same in both events with the exception that breaststrokers angle their push-offs deeper because of the underwater pullout.

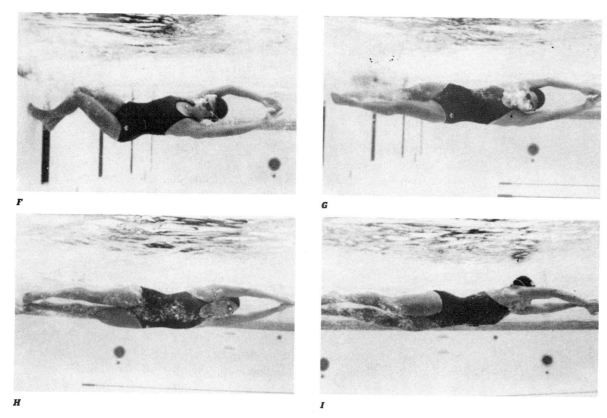

F

G

H

I

Figure 6.9. continued

F-H. She pushes off on her back, rotating to a prone position during the leg extension and glide that follows.

I. As she loses momentum from the pushoff, she takes one or two kicks and begins her armstroke.

Freestyle Flip Turn   The sequence of illustrations in Figure 6.9 shows a swimmer executing the flip turn correctly.

The approach. In the freestyle you should sight the wall as you approach the turn. In this way you can make modifications in the armstroke that will permit you to start the turn at the proper distance from the wall. Do not breathe during the final one or two armstrokes prior to the turn, so you can "sight" the wall and prevent errors in judgment that could cause you to miss the turn (see fig. 6.9*A*).

The turn. The turn begins approximately 3-1/2 to 4 feet from the wall. With one stroke to go, one hand is left at your hip and the other hand (which was in the water in front of you) is swept down, in, and up until your hips pass over it (see frames *A* and *B* of Figure 6.9). Your eyes should be focused on the wall at the beginning of that stroke. However, once the stroke begins, your head is quickly driven downward in order to initiate the somersault.

Your legs should be tucked as your feet travel over the water. Your hands, which were back at your hips, are brought downward toward your head as it moves toward the surface (see frames *D* and *E* of Figure 6.9). Your head should come up between your arms as your feet reach the wall so your body is aligned and ready for the push-off. When properly aligned, your head will be at the same level as your feet. Your hands will be overhead with elbows flexed. Your feet should be "planted" on the wall with toes pointed upward and slightly outward in the same direction you are facing (see fig. 6.9*E*). You should remain in a tucked position throughout the turn. This will help you somersault faster.

Your head should be turned somewhat sideward as it comes up toward the surface to enable you to begin rotating toward a prone position. Your face is usually turned away from the arm with which the last stroke was taken prior to turning (see frames *E* and *F* of Figure 6.9).

The push-off. Your feet should hit the wall at a depth of 12 to 15 inches with knees flexed (see fig. 6.9*E*). Begin extending your legs immediately when you make contact. You will be on your back when the push-off begins and you will rotate toward a sideward position during the leg extension and finally to a prone position during the glide (see frames *G* to *I* of Figure 6.9). Do not waste time turning on your side before beginning the push-off. Twisting to your side will cause you to delay leaving the wall for a precious few hundredths of a second. Rotating your body during the push-off and glide may increase drag somewhat; however, any loss in speed during the glide will be more than compensated for by your increased speed in getting off the wall.

Drive off the wall powerfully, extending your arms and legs simultaneously. Glide with your body in a streamlined position with arms extended overhead and one hand over the other. Keep your head between your arms, your back straight, your legs extended and together, and your toes pointed. Hold this position as you rotate toward a prone position (see Figure 6.9, frames *E* to *H*).

Since you will be traveling faster than race speed when you leave the wall, hold the glide position until you begin to lose speed. The shorter the race, the shorter the glide will be. As you approach race speed, take one or two kicks and begin the first armstroke. That stroke should be taken with the underneath arm, rather than with the top arm as the swimmer in Figure 6.9 is doing. This will provide a more powerful pullout and will aid in completing your rotation to a prone position. The pullout should be timed so your head breaks through the surface when you are midway through that stroke.

Most swimmers make a small dolphin kick with their legs as they begin the somersault (see fig. 6.9*B*). This accelerates their hips and legs out of the water and aids in getting their feet over the water faster. They also turn their palms toward the bottom of the pool and push down with them as their head starts upward to aid in pulling it and their trunk up to the push-off position (see fig. 6.9*D*).

Although many swimmers are taught to keep their legs straight as they are brought over the water, your knees should actually be flexed in excess of 90 degrees. The "tuck" turn is preferable to the "pike" turn for two reasons:

1. Your feet will travel over the water more quickly in a tucked position because they are closer to the axis of rotation (your hips). Because of this, the moment of inertia is reduced and less effort will be required to swing your legs over the water. Advocates of the pike turn mistakenly believe the feet travel into the wall faster when they are further from the axis of rotation. Any diver will tell you they can somersault faster in a tucked, rather than piked, position.

2. When your knees are flexed and your legs come over the water, your feet will be moving almost directly backward as they make contact with the wall. This allows you to drive off the wall immediately when contact is made. With the pike turn, your feet will be coming downward at the moment of impact and there will be a short delay while you overcome their downward inertia before you can push off.

Common errors in the flip turn. Many people mistakenly believe they can increase their turning speed by thrusting their legs over the water. The movements of your head—not your feet—regulate turning speed. Driving your head downward, backward, and then upward as rapidly as possible will bring your feet to the wall at the proper time for the push-off. Thrusting your legs over the water causes them to reach the wall before your head and trunk are aligned for the push-off. This mistake is illustrated in Figure 6.10. You can see that this swimmer is not in position to push off when his feet reach the wall (see fig. 6.10*A*). Therefore, he must waste time aligning his body before the push-off can be executed. A time and motion analysis of this swimmer's turn indicated a delay of 0.406 seconds in aligning his body for the push-off.

Figure 6.10. The error of thrusting the legs over in the flip turn. This swimmer has made the mistake of arching his back and thrusting his legs over the water rather than bringing his head up toward the surface. As a result, his head is too deep and his body is not aligned when his feet reach the wall (***A***). Therefore, he must delay pushing off until his head is brought up in line with his feet (***B***). The delay cost this swimmer 0.406 seconds. Compare this swimmer's body position when his feet have reached the wall with the correct contact position of the swimmer in frame *E* of Figure 6.9.

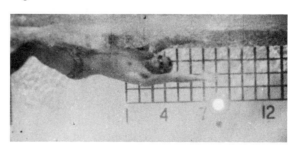

A *B*

Another common mistake is gliding into the turn. This was a common practice several years ago. The rationale was that you could start the turn farther from the wall and, therefore, swim less distance during each length. Although swimmers trained in this style would begin the turn before their opponents, they would usually reach the wall behind them because they were decelerating during the glide. You should always stroke into a turn even if you must take a half stroke to do so. Stroking allows you to accelerate rather than decelerate into the turn. Although you may start the turn somewhat closer to the wall, the small amount of extra effort will be justified by the time saved.

A common mistake in this turn and in the turns of other strokes is to push off in a nonstreamlined position. Swimmers who make this error arch their backs and drop their abdomens; their hands are apart, their heads are up, and their legs are apart. It is easy to see how drag is increased by this body position. With practice, swimmers quickly correct most of these errors in streamlining. They learn to align their bodies and hold their hands and legs together in an extended position. Correcting the head position is another matter, however. This head-up position is nearly a universal error among swimmers because they look forward on the push-off to keep their goggles from filling with water. They may do this literally thousands of times in practice. It is no wonder that it becomes a habit carried into competition even when the goggles are not worn. Time should be spent conditioning swimmers to keep their heads down on the push-off when the most important meets of the season approach. Some swimmers place the head below the arms during the glide. This should also be discouraged because it increases drag.

A final problem associated with turns in this and other strokes is that swimmers frequently lose time by gliding too long or too little after the push-off. In the first case they allow their bodies to decelerate to less than swimming speed. They then require additional time and energy to regain race speed. When they begin the pullout too early, they "spin their wheels." They are traveling so fast that their arms cannot accelerate them further and their stroking movements increase form drag without adding any propulsive force. Begin the pullout when you feel yourself losing speed from the pushoff.

Backstroke Turns   There are at least four styles of backstroke turns in use today: the tumble turn, the spin turn, the roll turn, and the Naber turn. The tumble turn is really a one-half somersault with a 180-degree spin. Only the 180-degree spin is used in the spin turn, which is superior to the tumble turn because it involves fewer changes of direction.

The roll turn involves touching the wall while legally on your back, then rolling onto your stomach, executing a somersault, and pushing off on your back. This turn is difficult to perform legally because the rules for backstroke events do not permit you to turn over beyond the vertical toward a prone position until your hand has touched the wall. There is a tendency with this turn to roll beyond the vertical before touching the wall. The roll turn is not recommended until rule changes reduce the likelihood of disqualification. It will be described, however. The Naber turn is very much like the spin turn, with the exception that your face remains out of the water during the spin. Although there is some controversy concerning the effectiveness of this style, many swimmers prefer it. Therefore, it will also be described.

The spin turn. The spin turn is illustrated in Figure 6.11. The prerequisite to making any good backstroke turn is to learn to judge your distance from the wall with a minimum of "looking around." You should use the backstroke flags to determine when you are approaching the turn, and then count the number of strokes required to reach the wall.

Ideally, it would be best to swim into the turn without looking for the wall beforehand. However, because of varying pool conditions and fatigue-induced changes in stroke efficiency, you cannot always depend upon stroke counting to get into the turn properly. Therefore, it may be advisable to allow swimmers to take one glance at the wall as a precaution against missing the turn. That look should be taken approximately two strokes from the wall. You should look backward and somewhat sideward over the shoulder of your stroking arm. At that time you will be rotating toward the stroking arm and your head can be turned without disrupting lateral alignment.

Once you have determined that your next recovery will bring your hand in contact with the wall, you should submerge your head and recover your arm overhead and across your face toward the wall so you will be spinning around as the touch is made (see frames *A* and *B* of Figure 6.11).

Your hand should make contact with the wall across the midline of your body. Your fingers should be approximately 12 inches beneath the surface, pointing downward and somewhat sideward in the direction of the spin. Your arm should be flexed slightly after the touch is made so you can subsequently push yourself around by extending it (see fig. 6.11*B*).

After the touch is made, extend the "contact" arm and spin around on your back with your head and trunk submerged (see fig. 6.11, frames *C* and *D*). Remain flat on your back throughout the spin. Your legs should be lifted clear of the water and swung around toward your hand as you extend your arm. Your free arm, which was at your side when the spin began, aids the rotation by pushing water toward the top of your head with the palm (see fig. 6.11*D*).

If you touch the wall with your right hand, you should swing your legs to the right and vice versa. This leg swing is accomplished by hip and knee flexion. Your feet will be planted on the wall at almost exactly the same spot where your hand made contact. In the meantime your hand will come away from the wall and begin reaching overhead. Although some swimmers bring that arm over the water, it is faster to flex your elbow and slice your arm through the water.

Your arms, still flexed at the elbows, should be overhead and together with your trunk aligned for the push-off when your feet reach the wall. Your feet should make contact at a depth of approximately 12 to 18 inches, with toes pointing directly upward (see fig. 6.11*E*). Begin the push-off immediately as your feet make contact with the wall by extending your legs and arms vigorously. Finish the leg drive with a powerful plantar flexion of your ankles.

Figure 6.11. The spin turn in the backstroke.

A. The swimmer looks back as he reaches for the wall.

B. He touches the wall with fingers pointing down and inward.

C. He uses his contact arm to continue his spinning motion by pushing against the wall with his hand. His legs are brought out of the water with knees flexed as he pushes his body around to the side with his contact arm.

D. Midway through the rotation he takes his contact arm off the wall so he can get it overhead before his feet reach the wall. He uses his free arm to continue his rotation by pulling his palm inward toward his head.

E. His arms are overhead and his body is aligned as his feet reach the wall so that he can begin to push off without delay.

F. He pushes off straight forward, not upward. His body is streamlined with arms overhead, the back of one hand in the palm of the other. (His head should be between his arms, and he should be looking back at his hands.)

Push off at a depth of 12 to 18 inches so you can glide beneath the surface turbulence. Be sure your head is on the same level as your feet when you push off so that your body will travel straight in a forward direction. Many swimmers push off at an upward angle, which causes them to travel through the surface turbulence. The glide will be longer and faster if the push-off is straight forward. The presence of water beneath your body will bring your body to the surface without the necessity of angling the push-off upward.

Glide in a streamlined position with no excessive arch to your back or pike at the waist. Your arms should be completely extended with your head between them. Your hands should be together with the back of one hand lying in the palm of the other. As you begin to lose speed from the push-off, start kicking and take the first stroke. That stroke should bring you upward and forward through the surface and into your race rhythm.

Many swimmers make the same mistake in the backstroke turn that was mentioned in conjunction with the backstroke start. That is, they glide to the surface before they begin stroking. Make sure you pull yourself "through" the surface.

The Naber turn. John Naber popularized a spin-type turn in which his face was out of the water. It is illustrated in Figure 6.12.

The approach to the wall is made in the same manner described for the spin turn, except that you do not put your face underwater. Your hand should make contact with the wall slightly behind your head so that the spin is initiated a moment before you make contact with the wall. The touch is made approximately 6 to 8 inches beneath the surface with your fingers pointing sideward, in the direction of your spin (see fig. 6.12, frames *A* and *B*). Flex your elbows after making contact to allow your body to glide into the wall. In the meantime, lift your feet from the water and bring them around into the wall with knees and hips flexed (see fig. 6.12, frames *C* and *D*).

Begin extending your contact arm as your feet pass overhead. This will push your head and shoulders away from the wall and bring your feet into it. The turn is executed on your side with your face out of the water (see fig. 6.12, frames *B* to *E*). As your feet are coming into the wall, bring the contact arm out of the water and recover overhead with a flexed elbow, similar to the high-elbow recovery of the front crawl stroke (see fig. 6.12*E*). Your head should follow your arm over the water, and you should grab a breath of air as you go. In the meantime, the palm of your free arm pushes upward against the water to aid in bringing your head under for the push-off. The hand of the contact arm is sliced under water and meets the other arm overhead. Be certain your body drops underwater on your side so that resistance is minimal. Your feet should be planted on the wall with your toes pointed sideward, *not upward*, and the push-off should be made on your side, *not on your back* (see fig. 6.12*E*).

In order to comply with the rules for backstroke turns, be certain your shoulders (USS competition) or hips (NCAA competition) are not beyond the vertical toward a prone position as your feet leave the wall. Rotate to your back during the push-off and glide that follow. Glide in a streamlined position until

A

B

C

D

E

F

Figure 6.12. The Naber backstroke turn.

A–B. The swimmer touches the wall with the right hand. That hand contacts the wall under water with palm flat and fingers pointing to the side.

C–D. He "rides" into the wall by allowing his elbow to flex. At the same time, he flexes his legs and trunk and begins to lift his legs over the water.

E–G. As the legs come over the water, he pushes the body away from the wall by extending the right arm.

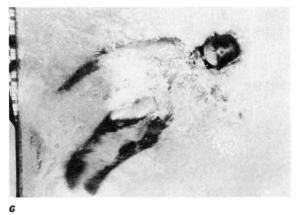

G

H

I

J

Figure 6.12. continued

H-I. As the feet travel into the wall, the right hand is brought over the water. In the meantime he pushes up against the water with the palm of the left hand in order to pull his head and shoulders down under the water for a deep pushoff.

J. The hands should meet overhead as the feet reach the wall so the pushoff can begin without delay.

K. He pushes off on his side, rotating toward his back as he does so. He glides in a streamlined position until he begins to lose speed from the turn, at which time he begins to kick and then pulls his body up through the surface with his first armstroke.

K

you begin to lose speed (see fig. 6.12*K*). Then take one or two kicks and pull your body up and forward through the surface.

The major advantages of the Naber turn are that swimmers get a breath during the turn and with the head up there is greater control coming into the

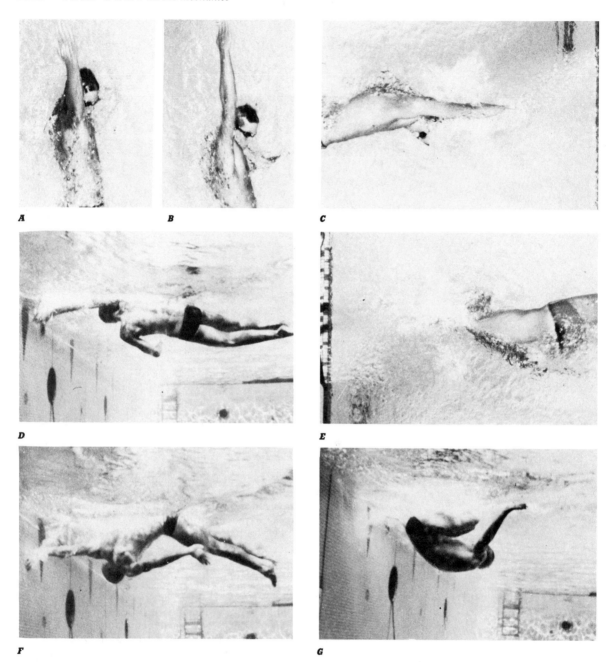

A **B** **C**

D **E**

F **G**

Figure 6.13. The roll turn in the backstroke.

A-B. On the last arm recovery before touching the wall, the swimmer reaches behind his head while rotating toward a prone position. The swimmer in this sequence will touch the wall with the right hand while rotating toward the left.

C-D. He touches the wall before his hips pass a vertical position. The palm is flat with fingers pointing downward.

H

I

J

K

Figure 6.13. continued

E-I. After touching the wall, he completes the rotation to a prone position and somersaults into the wall. As the somersault is being executed (**G** and **H**), he pushes the palm of his left hand downward toward the top of his head to aid the somersault. He quickly brings the right hand over the surface and down to meet the left so that both are together overhead when the feet

reach the wall. In this way his body will be aligned, and the pushoff can begin without delay.

J. He pushes off in a streamlined position.

K. He glides until approaching race speed, at which time he begins to kick and then pulls his body forward and upward through the surface with his first armstroke.

wall. Swimmers who have difficulty "hitting" backstroke turns will usually be faster with this style.

Another advantage of the Naber turn is that it may take less time to swing your feet into the wall when you turn on your side than it takes to spin around on your back. Both your legs and trunk seem to travel a shorter distance to the wall with the Naber turn than with the spin turn. Therefore, they reach the push-off position more quickly. Although your legs drag through the water during the Naber turn, your trunk should encounter less resistance because it is out of the water for a greater portion of the spin.

The major disadvantages of the Naber turn are that there is a delay getting your head and shoulders submerged for the push-off and that swimmers tend to use a shallow push-off. Nevertheless, it is believed to be potentially faster, principally because it allows a more controlled approach to the wall and a faster spin.

The Naber turn can be executed very quickly if swimmers master the technique of turning on their side as their feet travel over the water and into the wall. If they insist on spinning around on their backs with their faces out of the water (a common mistake swimmers make when learning this turn), it will not be faster than the spin turn. The advantages and disadvantages of this turn were described so readers can draw their own conclusions.

It should be mentioned that a variation of the Naber turn can be used quite effectively in individual medley races during the change from the backstroke to breaststroke legs. The turn is exactly the same until the push-off is made. Because they will be swimming breaststroke, swimmers should push-off on their sides and rotate toward a face-down position during the glide so that they can execute a powerful underwater pullout.

The roll turn. The illustrations in Figure 6.13 show a backstroke swimmer executing a roll turn. He is on his side as he reaches for the wall (see frames *A*, *B*, and *C*). To avoid disqualification, you must be careful to touch the wall before your shoulders (USS competition), or your hips (NCAA competition), have passed the vertical when you rotate from a supine to a prone position. The swimmer in Figure 6.13*D* makes the touch at a depth of 12 inches with his fingertips pointing toward the bottom of the pool. His arm is slightly across his head.

Once a safe touch is made, he accelerates the rotation of his shoulders and hips until he is in a prone position. Then he brings his legs over the water, executing a somersault much like the one used in the freestyle flip turn, except that there is no twist. When he completes the somersault, he is directly on his back, looking up at the surface (see fig. 6.13*I*).

Midway through the somersault, his contact hand is released from the wall and slipped through the water until it is overhead. In the meantime, the palm of his free arm pushes down on the water to help bring his head toward the surface. His hands should be overhead and his body aligned for the push-off before his feet contact the wall (see fig. 6.13*I*). Immediately when they make contact, he simultaneously extends his legs and arms in the push-off (see fig. 6.13*J*). His body is held in the same streamlined position during the glide that was described in the section on the spin turn. The kick and first stroke are also executed in the same manner as described for the spin turn.

Butterfly and Breaststroke Turns
The short-course rules for butterfly and breaststroke turns differ from long-course rules in ways that give the swimmer an advantage in the former competitions. While the rules for all competitions require swimmers to touch both hands to the wall simultaneously, long-course rules require that the shoulders remain level until the touch is made, whereas short-course rules allow swimmers to anticipate the turn by lowering one shoulder as they reach for the wall.

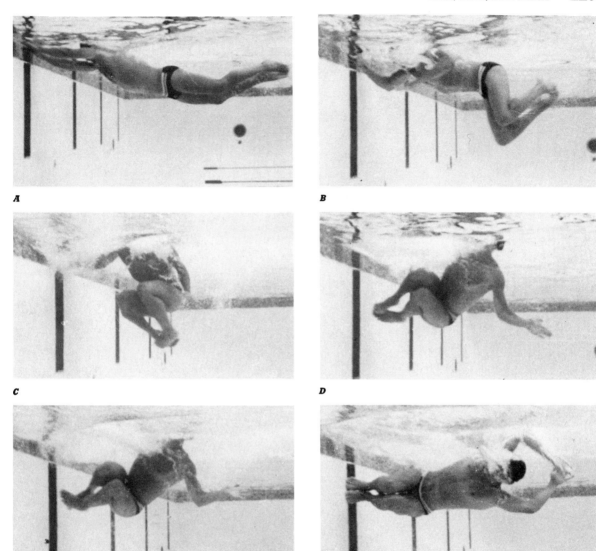

A

B

C

D

E

F   continued overleaf

Figure 6.14. The turn used in butterfly and breast-stroke races.

A. The swimmer reaches for the wall and begins to bend his knees and rotate toward the left in preparation for the turn. Anticipating the turn in this manner is reason for disqualification in long course competition; it is, however, permissible in short course races.

B-C. He tucks his legs tightly and pulls them in to the wall with the right hand. In the meantime, he takes his left hand from the wall and pulls his left elbow into his ribs.

D-E. As his feet pass under his body, he removes his right hand from the wall and brings it over the water. He reaches out with the left arm and pushes upward with it in order to continue moving his feet into the wall and also to bring his head and shoulders under water.

F. The hands meet overhead, and the body is aligned for the pushoff as the feet reach the wall. The feet are planted sideward on the wall.

Figure 6.14.   **G   H**

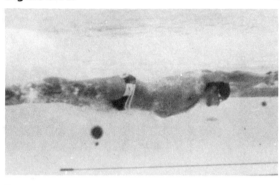

I   **J**

Figure 6.14. continued

G-H. He pushes off on his side, rotating to a prone position as he extends his legs.

I. The glide. Notice the streamlined position of the body.

J. As he begins to lose speed from the pushoff, he executes one or two kicks and begins his armstroke.

The second major advantage in short-course competition is that after the turn, swimmers need not be in a perfectly prone position until they begin their first stroke. For these reasons, you should be able to turn faster in short-course competition.

Turning in short-course competitions. The turn is shown in Figure 6.14. Swimmers should dip one shoulder as they reach for the wall. This will allow them to begin rotating before they touch the wall. The touch is made with both hands on the same level in order to comply with the rules. If there is a gutter, grasp it and pull your hips and legs toward the wall. If the wall is flat, place your palms against it and flex your elbows before extending them to push your body away from the wall.

As you pull your legs toward the wall, flex your hips and knees so that they travel the shortest possible distance into the wall (see frames *B* and *C* of Figure 6.14). Do not swing your legs around to the side as many swimmers do.

Almost immediately as your feet start inward, one hand is removed from the gutter and brought downward into your ribs (see fig. 6.14*C*). From there it is extended, palm up, toward the other end of the pool (see fig. 6.14*D*). Push up with that palm to help pull your trunk down into the water for the push-off (see fig. 6.14, frames *E* and *F*).

In the meantime you should push yourself away from the wall with your other arm. Bring that arm over the surface in the manner of a high-elbow recovery and slice it into the water fingertips first with your palm facing outward (see fig. 6.14, frames *D* to *F*). Your head should follow your arm over the water. Take a breath just before it enters the water. Your head should be submerged with both hands overhead and your body aligned for the push-off as your feet reach the wall (see fig. 6.14*F*). Proper alignment is with your body on its side, your head and feet at nearly the same depth, and your hands together overhead. When your feet reach the wall, there is a vigorous extension of your legs coupled with a strong extension of your arms that drives you away from the wall. A forceful plantar flexion of your ankles completes the push-off (see fig. 6.14, frames *G* and *H*). In butterfly races, the push-off should be made in a straight forward direction, angled neither downward nor upward. (The push-off for breaststroke races will be described later.) You should gradually rotate to a prone position during the final stages of the push-off and the early portion of the glide. In order to comply with the rules, be certain you are in a prone position at the beginning of the first armstroke.

Common errors during the butterfly and breaststroke turns. Many swimmers pull their bodies too high out of the water during the butterfly and breaststroke turns. This is time consuming and requires unnecessary muscular effort. You should keep your head near the surface during the turn. Only one shoulder should come out of the water, and that shoulder should be pulled up only enough to initiate the change of direction.

Another common error is to drop underwater in a prone or nearly prone position. This mistake is illustrated in Figure 6.15. It slows the turn because additional time is spent on the wall while you rotate your body toward a prone position, and because your descent underwater is slowed when your chest pushes downward against the water.

Another mistake swimmers make in these turns is to push-off too near the surface. The increased form and wave drag caused by their body positions and the surface turbulence causes them to decelerate rapidly during the glide. Throwing both arms over the water is the usual cause of this error. The best technique is to get your body underwater and aligned before pushing off. If you don't "hang" on the wall as you pull your legs inward, you will have time to get your body beneath the surface and aligned before your feet reach the wall.

Important differences between the butterfly and breaststroke turns. The turns in these two strokes are similar in every respect except the angle of the

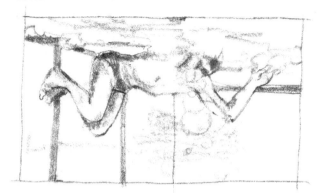

Figure 6.15. The effect of turning toward the prone position before pushing off. The swimmer in this illustration is making the mistake of turning toward a prone position as he drops under water. This causes him to stay on the wall longer and increases resistance during the descent by presenting more surface area to the water.

push-off. Breaststrokers will angle their push-off downward so the glide is deeper and the underwater pullout can be executed more effectively. This position was shown in Figure 4.20.

Breaststrokers are allowed one armstroke and one kick underwater. The underwater stroke is described in Chapter 4. It should begin as you decelerate to race speed. After it is completed, glide until you once again decelerate to race speed and then kick upward through the surface and get into your race rhythm as quickly as possible.

Turning in long-course competitions. In long-course competition swimmers must touch the wall with both hands simultaneously and on the same level. These rules slow the turn but do not change the mechanics a great deal. The only difference is that swimmers must delay rotating their shoulders until after they touch.

Breathing After Turns

Backstroke and breaststroke swimmers should breathe during their first stroke out of the turn. In the backstroke no head movement is required that could possibly increase drag, while in the breaststroke, breathing helps establish stroke rhythm. Whether to breathe immediately after the turn in the butterfly and freestyle is a subject of controversy. Although butterfly and freestyle swimmers are often advised to keep their faces in the water until two (or more) strokes have been taken after the turn, this may not be the best method to use, at least for races in excess of 200 yards/meters. Holding your breath will decrease oxygen consumption and may increase fatigue. If you have approached the wall properly, that is, without taking a breath as you sight the wall, you will have spent nearly five seconds without breathing by the time you complete the turn and take two strokes. Depriving yourself of oxygen for this length of time could cause a more rapid onset of fatigue in longer races. If this is the case, the time saved on turns may be lost because of a reduction in pace later in the race.

Delaying your breath for one or two strokes out of the turn might be justified in 100 and perhaps in 200 races. Oxygen consumption is not as important to success in these races. Therefore, it might be faster to swim through the backwash from the turn before taking your first breath. The fastest method for these races can be determined by timing turns to a distance of 10 yards out from the wall. These times should be taken during repeats when swimmers are somewhat fatigued. If restricting breathing is faster, use that method. However, it is senseless to restrict breathing if no time is saved by doing so.

Finishing Races

Many races have been lost because swimmers glide into the finish. On the other hand, races have also been lost because swimmers took more strokes than needed to reach the wall. The techniques of finishing races should be practiced so that minor stroke adjustments can be made as you approach the wall and you can accelerate to the finish with a minimal glide and no extra strokes.

Finishing Freestyle Races

The advent of electronic timing systems has made obsolete the once popular method of looking up and "splashing" water into the wall at the finish of races. This technique was used to fool judges into believing the touch had been made before the hand had actually made contact with the wall. The turbulence and the head-up position often made it appear that the swimmer had reached the wall before the touch was actually made. Electronic timing has eliminated this deception and swimmers must now touch the timing pads to win races.

The fastest way to accomplish the touch is by "jabbing" your arm straight forward. The swimmer in Figure 6.16 is shown finishing in this manner.

The jab finish is superior to swinging the arm low and laterally over the water because the jab requires a shorter radius of rotation than the roundhouse swing. It is also a natural continuation of the recovery and does not require you to overcome the upward inertia of your arm in order to swing it laterally into the wall.

To execute the jab finish, when you have judged that your next arm recovery will bring your hand to the wall, accelerate your recovery speed, bring your arm rapidly over the water in the normal high-elbow manner, and then jab your hand quickly forward to hit the touchpad. You should lean into the recovery to give added reach to your arm. Make the touch near or at the surface of the water if the pool and timing equipment permit you to do so. Touching near the surface will decrease the distance your hand must travel and the drag it encounters as compared to reaching forward and downward to touch the pad. Touch with your fingertips, not the palm of your hand. A fingertip touch will save valuable hundredths of a second. Your face should remain in the water during the finish because lifting your head will shorten your reach. It should be turned away from the finishing arm to increase your reach.

While reaching with one arm, your other arm should be stroking vigorously to accelerate your body toward the wall. You should also kick vigorously to further increase your speed over the last few inches. Don't stop kicking until the touch is made. Kicking in this manner is especially important if your reach is less than a stroke short. When this happens kicking will get your hand to the wall faster than taking another stroke, even a partial stroke. You should save 0.1 to 0.3 second by stretching and kicking. Of course, this

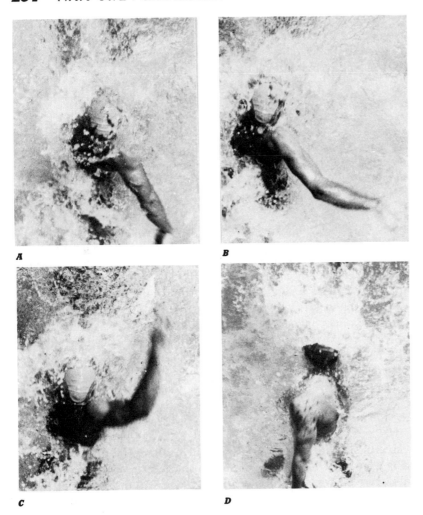

A   B

C   D

Figure 6.16. Finishing freestyle races. With one
stroke to go, the swimmer accelerates his recovery and
brings his arm over the water with the elbow flexed. He
extends it quickly into the wall, leaning toward the arm
to increase his reach. He maintains a powerful kick until he makes contact, in order to prevent deceleration.

advice holds true only when you have misjudged the finish by less than one
stroke. If you are one stroke or more from the wall, it is faster to take the extra
stroke.

Finishing
in the Butterfly,
Breaststroke,
and Backstroke

Butterfly, backstroke, and breaststroke swimmers should also lunge for the wall
without lifting their heads or splashing water. Their arms should be fully extended and they should touch the pad at or near the surface of the water with
their fingertips.

Butterfly. Since a two-hand touch is required in the butterfly, the lunge must be made with both arms simultaneously. The last few armstrokes should be the most powerful of the race and your hands should be accelerated into the wall on the last recovery. Make this recovery with flexed elbows so the moment of inertia is reduced when your hands are jabbed quickly into the wall. The kick is also accelerated as you reach for the wall. Your face should be in the water and you should be stretching every fiber of your body in order to reach the wall as quickly as possible.

If you misjudge the finish and find yourself less than an armstroke from the wall, continue stretching and kicking until you reach it. An additional half stroke will, as in the freestyle, take more time than a stretch.

Breaststroke. In the breaststroke you should also lunge for the finish with both hands simultaneously. Your final few armstrokes and your final recovery should be accelerated so that your arms can be sliced forward as quickly as possible. Your arms should be kept close together to reduce drag. Your face should remain in the water as you stretch for the wall so you have maximum reach. In long-course competition you must be certain that your head is not completely submerged or you can be disqualified. You may drop your head slightly underwater to increase the reach in short-course races.

Kick vigorously as you reach for the wall in order to accelerate your body to the finish. Should your reach be slightly short, stretch for the wall.

Backstroke. In the backstroke you should count the number of strokes you will need to cover the distance from flags to wall. This is usually the same number you'll need to reach the turn. Nevertheless, it is a good idea to practice finishing because the number of strokes may change when you are accelerating toward the wall at the end of a race. The backstroke finish is shown in Figure 6.17.

Figure 6.17. Finishing backstroke races.

A. With one stroke to go, the swimmer accelerates his arm into the wall. He carries it overhead with the elbow flexed to increase hand speed.

B. He should rotate toward the arm to increase his reach as he reaches for the wall. He maintains a powerful kick until contact is made.

A

B

The mechanics of the backstroke finish are as follows: When you determine that one more arm recovery will bring you to the wall, you should accelerate that recovery and jab your hand into the wall by first flexing and then extending your elbow. Rotate your body toward the finishing arm in order to increase the extent of your stretch. Your head should be stretched forward and sideward toward the finishing arm to aid the stretch. You should stroke vigorously with your other arm and kick vigorously to further accelerate your hand into the wall. Contact should be made with your fingertips at or near water level.

If you misjudge the touch, the best strategy would be to continue stretching and kicking until you make contact with the wall. This advice, of course, applies only to finishes that have been misjudged by less than one armstroke.

Breathing While Sprinting to the Finish

Breathing while you sprint to the wall should have no effect on your speed in backstroke races. In the breaststroke, breathing seems to be necessary to stroke rhythm and therefore should not be restricted. However, turning or lifting your head for a breath will slow your speed to the finish in freestyle and butterfly races. Therefore, in these events you should train yourself to swim as much of the final 25 yards/meters as you can tolerate without taking a breath. Since there is no need to save energy during the final sprint, oxygen deprivation can be disregarded in favor of additional speed. However, you should not hold your breath so long that you decelerate before reaching the wall.

With practice, most swimmers can be trained to hold their breath for the final 10 yards with no loss in speed. Certainly all swimmers are capable of restricting breathing for the final four or five strokes (6 to 8 yards). Practice this technique in races and practice repeats until you know how much of the final portion of the race you can sprint without breathing and without losing speed.

REFERENCES

Beritzhoff, S. T. 1974. "The Relative Effectiveness of Two Breaststroke Starting Techniques Among Selected Intercollegiate Swimmers." Master's thesis, California State University, Chico, California.

Bowers, J. E., and Cavanaugh, P. R. 1975. "A Biomechanical Comparison of the Grab and Conventional Sprint Starts in Competitive Swimming." *Swimming II*, ed. J. P. Clarys and L. Lewillie, pp. 225–232. Baltimore: University Park Press.

Cavanaugh, P. R., Palmgren, J. V., and Kerr, B. A. 1975. "A Device to Measure Forces at the Hand During the Grab Start in Swimming." *Swimming II*, ed. J. P. Clarys and L. Lewillie, pp. 43–50. Baltimore: University Park Press.

Hanauer, E. S. 1972. "Grab Start Faster Than Conventional Start." *Swimming World* 13:8–9, 54–55.

Henry, F. M., and Rogers, D. E. 1960. "Increased Response Latency for Complicated Movements and a 'Memory Drum' Theory of Neuromotor Reaction." *Research Quarterly* 31:448–458.

Jorgenson, L. W. 1971. "A Cinematographical and Descriptive Comparison of Three Selected Freestyle Racing Starts in Competitive Swimming." Doctoral dissertation, Louisiana State University.

Roffer, B. J., and Nelson, R. C. 1972. "The Grab Start Is Faster." *Swimming Technique* 8:101–102.

Thorsen, E. A. 1975. "Comparison of the Conventional and Grab Start in Swimming." *Tidsokroft für Legenspuelset* 39:130–138.

Wells, K. F., and Luttgens, K. 1976. *Kinesiology.* Philadelphia: W. B. Saunders Company.

PART Two

Physiology Applied to Training Swimmers

y Metabolism Related to ning Performance

results of training are adaptations of the physiological functions ge both the storage and release of energy for muscular contrac-rocesses by which energy is stored and released are collectively etabolism. When swimmers expend energy and combat fatigue basis in training, the physiological functions that are involved in and release of energy are enhanced in such a way that more is made available at a faster rate. Therefore more work can be performed with less fatigue. The purpose of this chapter is to give swimmers a good understanding of the processes by which energy is metabolized during exercise and to describe some of the training-induced adaptations in these processes that may improve performance.

Energy Metabolism During Swimming Races

Potential energy for muscular activity is stored in the muscles themselves. The energy is stored in the form of bonds that hold compounds of inorganic phosphate and other chemicals together. When nerve impulses stimulate muscle fibers, the chemical bonds are broken and the energy is released in a form that can be used to support the mechanical work of muscular contraction.

Fuels for Muscular Contraction   Where exercise is concerned, the four most important energy containing chemical compounds are adenosine triphosphate (ATP), creatine phosphate (CP), glycogen, and fats. All four substances are stored in muscle cells. Glycogen is also stored in the liver and can be transported to the muscles by the blood. An

241

additional supply of fat is stored in the body as adipose tissue. When it is needed, it can be transported by the blood to muscle cells.

ATP is the only one of these compounds that can supply energy for muscular contraction. That is, only energy released by the breakdown of ATP can be used by muscle fibers. The energy from the other compounds is used to replace energy that was lost from ATP, so that contraction can continue for long periods of time.

ATP is composed of adenosine and three phosphate bonds. Each bond contains a potential source of energy for muscular contraction. The simplified chemical structure of ATP is:

ATP = Adenosine $\sim$ P $\sim$ P $\sim$ P

The symbol $\sim$ indicates high-energy bonds.

When a nerve impulse stimulates a muscle fiber, the protein filaments of that fiber, myosin and actin, combine. This combination activates an enzyme, ATPase, which in turn causes one of the phosphate bonds to be split from the ATP molecule. In the process, the energy in that bond is released and used by the muscle fibers as the source of "power" for contractions. The breakdown of ATP and the release of energy for muscular contraction is shown here:

ATP + ATPase $\rightleftarrows$ ADP + P + Energy
Energy + Actomyosin (Actin + Myosin) = muscular contraction

The substance remaining after the breakdown of ATP is termed *adenosine diphosphate* (ADP), *di* because it now contains only two phosphate bonds. This is the chemical structure of ADP:

ADP = Adenosine $\sim$ P $\sim$ P

Each muscle cell contains only enough ATP to sustain one or two contractions. Thus, if swimmers are to swim more than a few feet after the dive, the ADP must be converted back to ATP so that more energy is available and muscular contraction can continue. This conversion requires replacement of the phosphate and free energy that were lost in the breakdown of ATP.

There are three metabolic processes through which the replacement of phosphate and energy can be accomplished.

1. The breakdown of creatine phosphate (CP), a process known as the ATP-CP reaction.
2. The breakdown of glycogen. This process, known as *glycolysis*, consists of two phases, an anaerobic phase and an aerobic phase, both of which produce ATP.
3. The breakdown of fats. This is known as *lipid metabolism*.

Where exercise is concerned, the major differences among these processes involve the speed with which they can release energy and phosphate for the replacement of ATP.

Although all of these processes begin releasing energy almost immediately with the onset of exercise, CP is the most important source of energy and phosphate when sprinting 25- and 50-yard/meter races. The ATP-CP reaction can replace ATP so rapidly that no reduction in movement speed takes place. This is because only one step, the splitting of phosphate from creatine, is required to release energy. This is the chemical structure of CP:

> Creatine Phosphate = Creatine + Phosphate + Energy

There is only enough CP stored in muscles to "fuel" this reaction for 5 to 10 seconds. After that, glycolysis and lipid metabolism must become the major sources of ATP replacement. When that occurs, sprint speed cannot be maintained because these processes release energy and phosphate more slowly than the ATP-CP reaction.

The anaerobic phase of glycolysis is the most rapid of the glycolytic and lipid metabolic processes. It releases energy and phosphate for ATP replacement in eleven steps, whereas the aerobic phase and lipid metabolism require many more reactions. After the first 5 to 10 seconds of a long sprint (100 yards/meters), ATP is replaced almost exclusively by energy released during the anaerobic phase of glycolysis. This allows swimmers to continue near maximum speed for 40 to 50 seconds before the waste product of anaerobic glycolysis, lactic acid, causes fatigue.

Both the aerobic and anaerobic phases of glycolysis contribute substantially to ATP replacement in longer races. Because the aerobic process is relatively slow, it cannot be the only source of energy in races or the pace would be too slow for swimmers to be competitive. However, training and proper pacing, that is, even or negative splitting, can increase the contribution of aerobic glycolysis and the onset of fatigue can be delayed.

Energy and phosphate are released more slowly through lipid metabolism than through any of the previously mentioned metabolic processes. Lipid metabolism contributes little to the energy supply in even the longest event on the competitive program, the 1,650 yard/1,500 meter freestyle. However, it is a significant contributor of energy during training sessions. The release of energy by lipid metabolism reduces the rate of glycogen breakdown and makes it possible for a swimmer to train several hours a day over a period of several days without becoming so fatigued that it is impossible to swim repeats of reasonable quality. A knowledge of each of these metabolic processes, the ATP-CP reaction, glycolysis, and lipid metabolism, is essential to understanding the training process.

The ATP-CP Reaction

The splitting of CP releases the energy and phosphate required to convert ADP to ATP. It is catalyzed by the enzyme creatine-phosphokinase (CPK). The replacement of ATP by CP (the ATP-CP reaction) is illustrated as follows:

> CP + CPK $\leftrightarrows$ C + P + free energy
> P + free energy + ADP = ATP

As indicated previously, this process extends the ability of muscles to contract at maximal speed by replacing ATP as rapidly as it is being broken down.

The ATP-CP reaction is dependent on the supply of CP in the muscle cells.

After 4 or 5 seconds of maximal effort, the CP supply is reduced to the point where all of the ATP cannot be replaced by this process (diPrampero 1971). After 5 to 10 seconds of maximal effort the CP supply is nearly depleted and the slower glycolytic process becomes the primary source of ATP replacement for muscular contraction (Gollnick and Hermansen 1973, Danforth 1965). This sequence of biochemical reactions explains why the maximal movement speed of humans begins to decline after 4 or 5 seconds, with a more pronounced reduction occurring after 10 to 15 seconds. These time relationships are significant to the training process and will be discussed more fully later.

Glycolysis   The process of glycolysis involves first the conversion of glycogen to glucose. Since glycogen is nothing more than a long chain of glucose molecules, this is a simple procedure. It is catalyzed by the enzyme phosphorylase.

Figure 7.1. Anaerobic phase of glycolysis. The enzymes regulating the process are in parentheses.

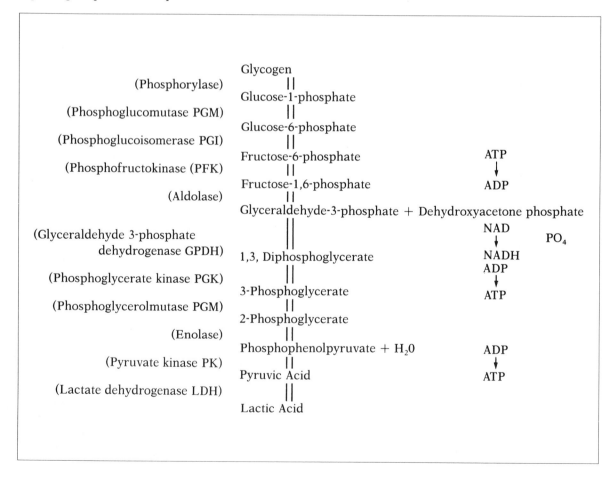

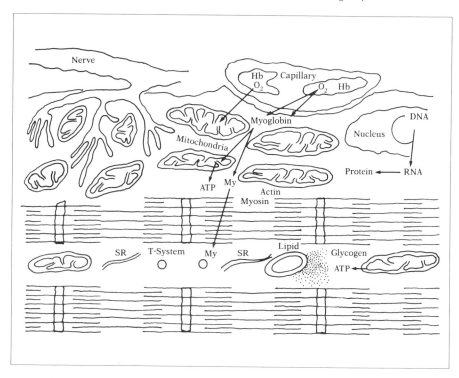

Figure 7.2. A schematic drawing of a muscle fiber showing the path of oxygen diffusion from capillaries to mitochondria. The oxygen is transported in combination with myoglobin. (Adapted from D. W. Edington and V. R. Edgerton, *The Biology of Physical Activity* [Boston: Houghton Mifflin, 1976], p. 16, by permission of the publisher.)

The anaerobic phase of glycolysis. Once glucose has been produced, it is broken down through ten additional steps that, along with the first step, constitute the anaerobic phase of glycolysis. In the process, each molecule of glucose yields two molecules of ATP. This process is illustrated in Figure 7.1.

The first eleven steps of glycolysis take place in the cytoplasm (protoplasm) of the muscle fibers. They are **anaerobic** processes; that is, they do not require the presence of oxygen. If at the end of this phase there is sufficient oxygen available, the pyruvate and NADH which have been produced, will enter the mitochondria of the muscle cells where aerobic metabolism takes place.

The aerobic phase of glycolysis. The mitochondria are rod-shaped bodies found in cells (see fig. 7.2). After the end-products of anaerobic glycolysis, pyruvate and NADH, which contains hydrogen atoms, enter the mitochondria, they are oxidized to carbon dioxide (CO_2) and water (H_2O).This occurs through the citric acid cycle (also known as **Krebs cycle**) and the electron transport chain.

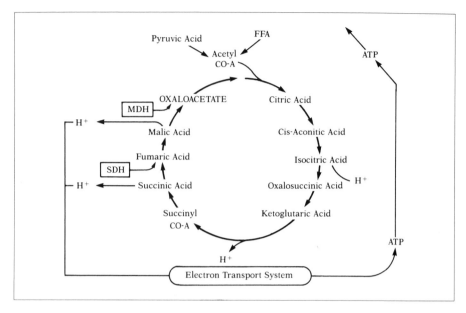

Figure 7.3. The citric acid cycle. (Adapted from D. L. Costill, "Adaptations in Skeletal Muscle During Training for Sprint and Endurance Swimming," *Swimming Medicine IV*, ed. B. Eriksson and B. Furberg [Baltimore: University Park Press, 1978], pp. 233–248, fig. 8, by permission of the author and publisher.)

Oxygen must be present in the mitochondria in order for these metabolic processes to take place. Hence, metabolism occurring in the mitochondria is referred to as **aerobic** (meaning with oxygen). A large number of enzymes located in the mitochondria and collectively known as the **mitochondrial enzymes** or the **aerobic enzymes,** regulate the citric acid cycle and the electron transport chain. These processes are illustrated in Figures 7.3 and 7.4 respectively. The enzymes regulating these processes are designated. The processes themselves are not important to this discussion and will not be described.

Thirty-six molecules of ATP are replaced when pyruvate and hydrogen atoms are oxidized by means of the citric acid cycle and electron transport chain. This is a very efficient process and results in the formation of end products that can easily be eliminated without causing fatigue (CO_2 and H_2O).

The production of lactic acid during anaerobic glycolysis. When sufficient oxygen is not available, some of the pyruvic acid and NADH are prevented from entering the mitochondria. These two substances then react with one another to form lactic acid. When this occurs the muscle tissues become acidic and fatigue occurs. This final step in the anaerobic phase of glycolysis is as follows:

Pyruvic acid + NADH + M-LDH $\rightleftharpoons$ Lactic acid + NAD.

The conversion is catalyzed by the muscle form of the enzyme lactate dehydrogenase.

Deriving energy from anaerobic glycolysis is considered less desirable than deriving energy aerobically, because the aerobic process produces 36 molecules of ATP compared to only 2 molecules produced in the anaerobic phase. Also, the anaerobic phase stops with the formation of lactic acid. However, while

Figure 7.4. The electron transport chain. Carrier 1 is cytochrome b; Carrier 2 is coenzyme Q; Carrier 3 is cytochrome C; Carrier 4 is cytochrome A; and Carrier 5 is cytochrome oxldase. The bold lines in the diagram show the path of electrons. (Adapted from D. R. Lamb, *Physiology of Exercise: Responses and Adaptations* [New York: Macmillan, 1978], fig. 3.5, by permission of Macmillan Publishing Company, Inc. Copyright © 1978 by David R. Lamb.)

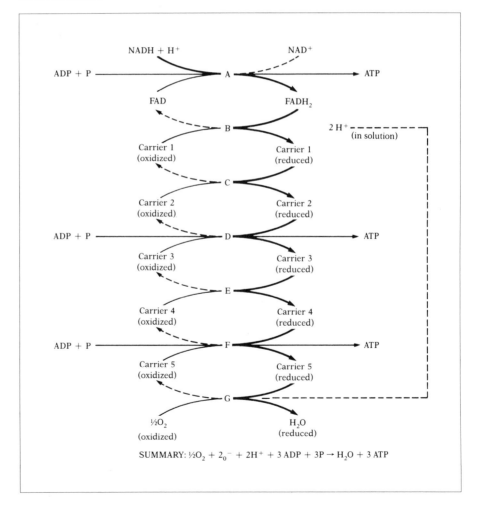

aerobic glycolysis may be more efficient in terms of ATP replacement, it involves so many steps that it proceeds too slowly to supply energy as rapidly as it is needed in swimming races. Thus, in order to maintain an adequate pace, some energy has to be supplied by the quicker but less productive anaerobic phase. There is more dependence on anaerobic glycolysis in shorter races where greater speeds are required. This dependence is reduced in favor of aerobic glycolysis in longer races where the pace is slower.

The interaction of aerobic and anaerobic processes during exercise. The tendency to refer to glycolysis as either aerobic or anaerobic can lead to the false impression that there are two distinct processes occurring. Actually, aerobic and anaerobic glycolysis are two phases of the same process. It has become common practice to refer to the breakdown of glycogen to lactic acid as anaerobic glycolysis and the breakdown of glycogen to CO_2 and H_2O as aerobic glycolysis, even though the second process is merely a continuation of the first one, with the step in which lactic acid is formed having been skipped. Glycolysis is anaerobic until the formation of pyruvate and NADH. At that time, lactic acid will be produced or, in the presence of sufficient oxygen, the pyruvate and NADH will be metabolized to CO_2 and H_2O through the citric acid cycle and the electron transport chain.

Since there is never enough oxygen available to metabolize all of the pyruvate and NADH that are being formed (except at levels of effort that are too slow for swimming races), some of these substances inevitably combine to form lactic acid. Thus, in all swimming events, energy is being replaced by both aerobic and anaerobic glycolysis simultaneously.

Relative Energy Contributions of Different Metabolic Processes

The relative contributions of the ATP-CP reaction, aerobic glycolysis, and anaerobic glycolysis during exercise of different durations are listed in Table 7.1.

Table 7.1 is based on time, not distance, because energy metabolism is dependent on time rather than distance; however, the distances that usually correspond to the durations listed are also shown. The organization of the table allows swimmers of varying abilities to determine the probable contributions of these energy-supplying processes according to the times rather than distances of their races. For example, an athlete who swims 200 yards in 3:40.0 seconds would receive approximately the same contribution from the three processes as an athlete who swims 400 yards in the same time.

This table is meant to be used as a guide; it should not be viewed as completely accurate. In fact, the contribution of anaerobic glycolysis in all events beyond 100 yards is probably greater than indicated in the table. This is because mechanisms within the body remove lactic acid from the working muscles and blood during exercise. The removal of lactic acid has the effect of reducing the total lactate content of the blood during and immediately after exercise; therefore, it can appear that less energy was supplied through anaerobic glycolysis.

The relative contributions of these three energy supplying processes depend to some degree on the following factors:

Table 7.1 *The Estimated Contributions of the ATP-CP Reaction, Anaerobic Glycolysis, and Aerobic Glycolysis During Exercise of Different Durations*

Time	Usual race distance	Percent ATP-CP reaction	Percent anaerobic energy replacement	Percent aerobic energy replacement
10–20 sec.	25–50 yards/meters	78	20	2
40–60 sec.	100 yards/meters	25	65	10
1:30–2 min.	200 yards/meters	10	65	25
2–3 min.	200 yards/meters	10	50	40
3–5 min.	400 meters–500 yards	7	40	53
5–6 min.	400 meters–500 yards	7	38	55
7–10 min.	800 meters–1,000 yards	5	30	65
10–12 min.	1,000 yards	4	25	70
14–18 min.	1,500 meters–1,650 yards	3	20	77
18–22 min.	1,500 meters–1,650 yards	2	18	80

1. The pace. Faster speeds require rapid muscular contractions. In such cases, energy must be supplied quickly. For this reason, the body must rely on the faster ATP-CP and anaerobic glycolysis to supply most of the energy for short events while aerobic glycolysis provides more energy in longer events.

2. The athlete's ability to consume oxygen. A swimmer who consumes more oxygen during a race will be able to oxidize more pyruvate and NADH in the mitochondria and decrease dependence on anaerobic glycolysis. Fatigue will be reduced in the process because less lactic acid is produced.

3. Stroke efficiency. Swimmers with more efficient stroke mechanics can swim a given pace with fewer strokes and/or less effort per stroke. This decreases the total energy requirement as well as the contribution from anaerobic glycolysis. A slower and more efficient stroke should also permit more of the force to come from slow twitch muscle fibers, which are fully discussed later. Slow twitch fibers have a higher capacity for aerobic glycolysis; fast twitch fibers have a higher capacity for anaerobic glycolysis.

Training improves the swimmer's skill, oxygen consumption, and individual muscle fiber use, all of which allow more energy to be supplied aerobically during races. When this effect occurs, fatigue can be delayed considerably. The mechanisms involved in this shift from an anaerobic to aerobic energy supply are discussed later.

Liver Glycogen: A Backup Source of Energy

Under normal dietary conditions, muscle cells contain enough glycogen to replace ATP for well in excess of one hour. In addition, there is a reserve supply of glycogen stored in the liver. During exercise, liver glycogen is converted to glucose, poured into the bloodstream, and transported to the muscles where it is absorbed and used to supplement the muscle's glycogen supply. Glucose will be converted to glucose-6-phosphate, a reaction that is catalyzed by the enzyme hexokinase. The breakdown of glucose-6-phosphate then proceeds through the steps shown in Figures 7.1, 7.3, and 7.4. In distance swims and other forms of endurance training, the use of some liver glycogen can reduce the rate of muscle glycogen depletion so a particular pace can be maintained for a longer period of time.

Lipid Metabolism

Fat stored in muscles and beneath the skin as adipose tissue serves as another source of energy for ATP replacement. Fat stored in the body as triglycerides is converted to free fatty acids (FFA) and glycerol, a process that is catalyzed by the enzyme lipoprotein lipase (LPL). The FFA enters the mitochondria with the aid of another enzyme, carnitine palmytyl transferase (CPT). From there it is converted to acetyl coenzyme A with the help of acetyl Co-A synthetase and is oxidized via the citric acid cycle. In the process, 131 molecules of ATP are formed. Thus the oxidation of fatty acids supplies abundant energy. However, the process of releasing FFA from triglycerides is so slow that swimmers could not sustain an adequate pace in any race if lipid metabolism were the only source, or even the primary source, of energy. Thus, although there is enough adipose tissue on the bodies of most athletes to supply energy for several days, it would not support high-quality or even moderate-quality work. An adequate supply of muscle and liver glycogen must be available to support the rapid rate of energy use through the faster aerobic and anaerobic phases of glycolysis.

Nevertheless, lipid metabolism plays an important role in training, where swimmers are concerned. During endurance exercise, trained athletes burn more fat and less glycogen for energy than untrained people (Saltin and Karlsson 1971a). In one study, trained subjects used 20 percent fewer carbohydrates for the same work than did their untrained counterparts (Saltin 1975).

Increased rates of lipid metabolism have effects similar to those of liver glycogen metabolism. Muscle glycogen is depleted at a slower rate during training so that a particular pace can be maintained over a longer set of repeats with some muscle glycogen left to supply energy anaerobically during quality swims later in the training session. Lipid metabolism is also important in preventing depletion of muscle glycogen from day to day. In this way, swimmers can work twice a day for several days with a greater average intensity.

The Causes of Muscular Fatigue

For purposes of this discussion, fatigue is defined as a loss of speed. The usual definition of fatigue includes sensations of pain and tiredness. Although these sensations accompany reductions in speed in events of 100 yards and longer, they are not always present in sprints even though there is often a noticeable loss of speed in the final 5 yards or so of 25- and 50-yard/meter races.

The effect of lactic acid accumulation on fatigue has been mentioned in the previous section. Although lactate accumulation is probably the primary cause of fatigue in races of 100 to 1,650 yards, it is not the major cause in 25 and 50 sprints. Very little excess lactate was found in the blood of swimmers after a 50-

meter swim (Torma and Székely 1978). Thus, the nature of fatigue in short sprints must be somewhat different than in longer events. It is also interesting to note that although distance runners complain of fatigue, lactate accumulation has not always been maximal at the completion of their races. This indicates that factors other than lactic acid accumulation may cause fatigue in distance events and in training.

Fatigue in 25- and 50-Yard/Meter Sprints

Swimmers experience fatigue, defined as a loss of speed, after the first 4 or 5 seconds of sprints (diPrampero 1971), with a more noticeable reduction in speed after 20 seconds (Danforth 1965, Gollnick and Hermansen 1973). The probable explanation for the loss of speed is that progressive depletion of CP forces greater reliance on glycolysis for replacement of ATP. Since the glycolytic process proceeds more slowly than the ATP-CP reaction, energy cannot be replaced fast enough to support the rapid and powerful muscular contractions needed to maintain maximum speed.

Training can reduce the effects of fatigue that results from CP depletion. The CP content and possibly the ATP content of exercised muscle fibers can be increased by the proper training (Mathews and Fox 1976; Eriksson, Gollnick, and Saltin 1973; MacDougall, Ward, Sale, and Sutton 1975; Karlsson, Nordesjö, Jorfeldt, and Saltin 1972; Karlsson, Diamant, and Saltin 1971; Yakolev 1965). Of even greater importance may be the effects of training on the enzymes that regulate the breakdown of ATP and CP. The activities of these enzymes have also been shown to increase with the proper type of training (Wilkerson and Evonuk 1971; Kendrick-Jones and Perry 1967; Thorstensson, Sjödin, and Karlsson 1975; Costill, Coyle, Fink, Lesmes, and Witzman 1978).

Increases in a muscle's supply of ATP and CP should extend a swimmer's ability to maintain maximum speed for a longer time in the sprints. An increase in the activity of the enzymes regulating the ATP-CP reaction should have a similar effect.

Fatigue in the 100, Middle-Distance, and Distance Events

Lactate accumulation resulting from anaerobic glycolysis is believed to be the cause of fatigue in middle-distance and distance races. As indicated previously, the paces in these events are too fast for aerobic processes to provide all of the energy for ATP replacement. Since a sizable portion must be supplied anaerobically, lactate accumulates and fatigue occurs.

Lactate accumulation is not directly responsible for fatigue; rather, it is the effect of this substance on the pH of body fluids. pH is a measure of the balance between acidity and alkalinity in substances. A pH of 7.0 is considered neutral. Resting skeletal muscle cells are very nearly neutral, and blood pH is slightly alkaline, measuring 7.4 at rest.

During exercise, anaerobic glycolysis causes lactic acid to accumulate. This causes the muscle cells to become acidic. When some of the lactic acid diffuses into the bloodstream, the pH of the blood is reduced and so is the pH of other body compartments served by the circulation. Researchers have reported muscle cell pH as low as 6.40 after strenuous exercise (Bergstrom 1962, Hermansen and Osnes 1972). Such acidity in muscle tissue is a significant cause of fatigue, for the rate of glycolytic metabolism is reduced when muscle pH falls below 7.0. As the rate of glycolytic activity decreases, muscle contractile rate and thus movement speed must also decrease. It has been proposed that glycolytic activity ceases at a pH of 6.3. Hill (1940) showed that the formation of lactic acid stopped when muscle pH dropped to that level. The fact that the rate of glycolysis declines in proportion to decreasing muscle pH belies the frequently expressed opinion that swimming is 90 percent mental and 10 percent physical. The physiological aspects are far more prominent than that.

While it is true that some athletes lack the capacity or the motivation to endure pain and therefore slow down in response to a declining pH, coaches and swimmers should understand that even swimmers who do "push on" in spite of pain must necessarily slow down as their tissues become progressively more acidic. Swimmers who will tolerate the pain of acidosis can swim faster longer. However, tolerance for pain is not in itself sufficient to insure peak efforts and certainly will not account for 90 percent of a swimmer's performance. Proper training and pacing are required to delay the retarding effect of a declining pH on the rate of energy release.

Muscle Glycogen Depletion and Fatigue

When the pace of exercise is reduced enough that severe acidosis does not occur, work can continue as long as there is sufficient glycogen in the muscles to support it. When muscle glycogen is depleted athletes experience "heavy" or "dead" sensations rather than the acute muscle pain accompanying acidosis (Holloszy, Booth, Winder, and Fitts 1975). Repeat times will fall off dramatically and athletes may complain of insufficient energy to complete a workout. Why the depletion of muscle glycogen should cause fatigue when fatty acids are available for energy is a mystery at present. Some researchers are of the opinion that a minimum amount of glycogen is needed in order to metabolize lipids (McArdle, Katch, and Katch 1981).

Fatigue from muscle glycogen depletion is probably a common occurrence when swimmers train twice a day, two to three hours per session, five to six days per week. A chronically low muscle glycogen content may, in part, explain the poor performances of athletes in practice and in meets, prior to tapering.

Muscle glycogen will be particularly low when several high-quality training sessions occur in succession. Quality swimming depletes muscle glycogen more rapidly than quantity repeats. During submaximal work (less than 70 percent effort) liver glycogen may account for 10 to 20 percent of the energy supplied (Hultman and Nilsson 1971) and an additional 30 to 40 percent may come from the oxidation of fats (Carlson, Ekelund, and Fröberg 1971; Keul, Doll, and Keppler 1972). However, during quality swimming there is a greater dependence on glycolysis in order to replace energy rapidly. When this occurs, the contributions of liver glycogen and fats are reduced and muscle glycogen is depleted more rapidly.

A diet that is high in carbohydrates, 70 percent or more, will cause repletion of muscle glycogen within 24 hours (Hultman, Bergström, and Roch-Norlund 1971; MacDougall, Ward, Sale, and Sutton 1975). Thus, it is a good idea for swimmers in hard training to increase their carbohydrate intake over the 45 to

55 percent in the average diet. By so doing, adaptations to training will be improved and overtraining will be less likely because they can train more intensely from day to day with less fatigue.

More will be said in the chapter on nutrition about the effect of muscle glycogen depletion on training. The question to be considered at present is, can muscle glycogen depletion cause fatigue during swimming races? At first, the answer to this question would seem to be an obvious no. The longest event on the competitive program is 14 to 20 minutes in length and biopsies have shown that glycogen remains in the muscles after one hour of strenuous exercise (Saltin and Karlsson 1971a). This appears to indicate that there would be enough muscle glycogen to support the energy requirement for several 1500-meter races. However, this is only true if the rate of energy release via glycolysis is not reduced when muscle glycogen stores become partially depleted. Several researchers have postulated that partial depletion brings on just such a reduction (Hultman and Bergström 1973; Klaussen, Piehl, and Saltin 1975).

It is entirely possible that a reduction in glycolysis could be a metabolic defense to prevent depletion. Most writers who believe fatigue does not occur until muscle glycogen is completely depleted have defined fatigue as cessation of exercise. Where swimming races are concerned, being unable to maintain a given pace must also be considered as fatigue. If partial muscle glycogen reduces the glycolytic rate to the point where this occurs, then such depletion would also have to be considered a cause of fatigue.

In order to determine whether such partial depletion could cause a reduction in pace, we must decide if a muscle's glycogen supply can be depleted enough to reduce the rate of glycolysis in the time required to swim races.

In regard to this question, several studies have demonstrated that 65 to 83 percent of the muscle's glycogen supply can be lost in 6 to 30 minutes of maximal exercise (Gollnick et al. 1973, Edgerton et al. 1975, Hultman 1967b). In one of these studies (Gollnick et al. 1973) muscle glycogen depletion was 67 percent after 6 one-minute efforts with 10 minutes rest between efforts. There is a possibility the reduction may have been even greater had the work been continuous.

Another possibility in this regard is that some muscle fibers may be completely depleted by short periods of work although biopsies may show glycogen remaining in the total muscle. A significant finding has been that, although the entire muscle contained some glycogen after work periods of 20 to 30 minutes, certain fibers, particularly fast twitch fibers, were completely depleted (Saltin 1975, Gollnick et al. 1975). In this case, the swimmer would have to rely on the slower-acting slow twitch fibers for energy, and speed would be reduced accordingly. Thus, there is some evidence that partial muscle glycogen depletion could cause fatigue.

Another approach to this question is to measure blood lactate at the time of exhaustion when exercise periods of different durations were used to cause the fatigue. If lactic acid were the cause, we would expect to find blood lactate at maximal levels. If other factors, such as muscle glycogen depletion, were causing fatigue, those figures would not be maximal. In one such study, the concentration of blood lactate was lower after 10 to 20 minutes of all-out effort than following shorter maximal work periods of 2 to 3 minutes (Karlsson and Saltin 1970). Hermansen's work (1971) also gives some support to this position. He found a trend toward lower blood lactate concentrations when subjects worked for 10 minutes as compared to 1 minute. The subjects worked to exhaustion in both cases.

Although the data are too meager to state that partial depletion of muscle glycogen causes fatigue, the possibility exists that performances in races of 800 to 1,500 meters could be hindered when significant amounts of this substance are depleted. It is doubtful that muscle glycogen depletion could cause fatigue in shorter events. Taylor (1975) found only slight decreases in muscle glycogen content after 3 to 5 minutes of work to exhaustion.

Until research has identified, beyond a doubt, the effect of partial muscle glycogen depletion on performance, athletes are well-advised to eat high carbohydrate meals for two to three days before competition to insure that their muscles are full of glycogen when they enter competition.

Delaying Fatigue During Swimming Races

Fatigue has been defined as a loss of speed. In short sprints of 25 and 50 yards/meters the cause of fatigue is probably a reduction in the muscle's supply of CP and/or a reduction in the speed with which the ATP-CP reaction can release energy for muscular contraction. Both the quantity of CP (and possibly ATP) and the efficiency of the ATP-CP reaction can be increased by the proper type of training so that swimmers can maintain top speed for a longer period of time in sprint races.

In longer races, the rate of lactic acid accumulation in working muscle fibers is believed to cause fatigue. Several researchers have demonstrated that lactate accumulates at a slower rate in the muscles of trained athletes when they are working submaximally (Bang 1936, Cresticelli and Taylor 1944, Robinson and Harmon 1941).[1] The mechanisms for this reduction are believed to be a greater reduction in the rate of lactate production and an increased rate of lactate removal from working muscles.

Another approach to delaying fatigue that is caused by lactate accumulation, one which is particularly applicable to 100 and 200 events, is to increase tolerance to lactate accumulation. In so doing, swimmers may become capable of sustaining for a longer time the near-maximal speeds that are fueled by anaerobic glycolysis, in spite of the lactate buildup that accompanies them. Buffering is one of the ways the body can increase its tolerance to lactate accumulation. Buffers "dilute" the strong lactic acid to a weaker acid so that the pH of muscle tissues is not driven downward at a rapid rate. This makes it

---

1. Any pace that is less than an all-out sprint is considered submaximal. The effect of training on lactate accumulation at submaximal speeds is important because swimmers spend most of their time swimming at less than maximal speed in races. Thus, training that reduces lactate accumulation at submaximal speeds will reduce fatigue, making it possible to maintain a faster average pace throughout the race.

possible to continue the energy releasing processes of glycolysis at a rapid rate so that fast and powerful strokes can be maintained for a longer time. Another approach to increasing lactate tolerance is to improve pain tolerance. Athletes who are motivated to endure pain should find they can maintain near maximum speeds when other swimmers are giving in to pain.

Improving Efficiency of the ATP-CP Reaction

As indicated previously, the ATP-CP reaction is responsible for supplying the energy necessary to contract muscles at maximum speed. It is this reaction that provides the energy for sprints. Efficiency of the ATP-CP reaction is dependent upon:

1. The concentrations of these two chemical substances in muscles.
2. The activity of enzymes regulating this reaction. These enzymes and their functions in the reaction are listed in Table 7.2.

Muscles can contract at maximal speed until the supply of CP is partially depleted (diPrampero 1971), and at near maximum speed until the muscles are nearly devoid of CP (Saltin et al. 1976, Danforth 1965). Increases in the muscle stores of ATP and CP should extend a swimmer's ability to maintain near maximal speed for longer than the usual 5 to 10 seconds.

Regarding the possibilities of such increases with training, Eriksson, Gollnick, and Saltin (1973) reported increases of 39 percent in muscle CP after training, while Karlsson et al. (1972) reported increases of 25 percent in the ATP content of trained muscles. Both research studies used endurance training programs. MacDougall et al. (1977) reported increases of 18 percent and 22 percent in ATP and CP content of muscles with heavy resistance training. Increases in CP, but not ATP, were reported in other studies (Karlsson, Diamant, and Saltin 1971; Yakolev 1965). Thus, it seems certain that training will increase the CP supply of muscles. The effect of training on the ATP content is unresolved at this time.

Of even greater importance may be the effects of training on the enzymes that regulate the breakdown of ATP and CP. The rate of energy release by ATP is controlled by the enzyme ATPase while the replacement of ATP is influenced by myokinase (MK) and creatine phosphokinase (CPK). The activities of these enzymes have been found to increase with training (Wilkerson and Evonuk 1971; Kendrick-Jones and Perry 1967; Thorstensson, Sjödin, and Karlsson 1975; Costill 1978; Eriksson, Gollnick, and Saltin 1973). The results of some of these

Table 7.2 *Enzymes That Regulate the ATP-CP Reaction*

Enzyme	Function
ATPase	Regulates the breakdown of ATP to ADP and releases energy for muscular contraction
Myokinase (MK)	Regulates the breakdown of ADP to AMP. ATP is replaced in the process.
Creatine phosphokinase (CPK)	Regulates the replacement of ATP from CP

Table 7.3 *Effects of Training on the Enzymes Involved in the ATP-CP Reaction*

Study	Enzyme		
	ATPase	Myokinase	CPK
Thorstensson, Sjodin, and Karlsson 1975			
5-second treadmill runs	30% increase	20% increase	36% increase
Costill 1978			
6-second maximal effort		No change	No change
30-second maximal effort		13% increase	15% increase
Ericksson, Gollnick, and Saltin 1973			
Endurance training			40% increase

studies are listed in Table 7.3. The type of training that was used to produce these increases is also designated.

Increases in the activity of these enzymes may increase the rate of energy release from ATP and also the rate of replacement of that substance from ADP and CP. If that is the case, greater speed would be possible for a longer period of time in the sprints. At present, the activity of these enzymes is not believed to limit the rate of energy availability. The importance of an increase in their activity on sprint speed remains to be discovered.

Although both sprint and endurance drills produce muscular adaptations that could improve the efficiency of the ATP-CP reaction, sprint drills seem to be the superior way to train. Some repeat sets that may enhance ATP and CP storage and increase the activity of the enzymes ATPase, MK, and CPK are described in Chapter 9.

Table 7.4 *The Effect of Training on Certain Enzymes Involved in Anaerobic Metabolism*

Enzyme	Study		
	Costill et al., 1978[a]	Costill et al., 1976[b]	Ericksson et al., 1973[c]
Phosphorylase	8% increase (30-sec. max. efforts)	2.2% increase (power training)	
Phosphofructokinase	7% increase (6-sec. max. efforts) 22% increase (30-sec. max. efforts)		30% increase (endurance training)
LDH	No change with 6- or 30-sec. max. efforts	Increase with power training Decrease with endurance training	

[a]Costill, Coyle, Fink, Lesmes, and Witzman 1978.
[b]Costill, Daniels, Evans, Fink, Krahenbuhl, and Saltin 1976.
[c]Ericksson, Gollnick, and Saltin 1973.

Increasing Lactate Production

Several researchers have reported increases in blood lactate after training (Karlsson et al. 1972, Robinson and Harmon 1941, Cunningham and Faulkner 1969, Saltin et al. 1976). This indicated that the subjects had become capable of producing more lactic acid during exercise. The effect of an increase in lactic acid production should be that more energy can be supplied anaerobically, and faster speeds can be maintained for a longer time during races.

The production of lactic acid is regulated by enzymes that are known collectively as the anaerobic enzymes. These enzymes were listed in Figure 7.1.

Those enzymes that appear to be most prominent in regulating anaerobic glycolysis are hexokinase, phosphorylase, phosphofructokinase (PFK), aldolase, and the muscle form of lactate dehydrogenase (M-LDH). Several researchers have demonstrated increases in the activity of certain of these enzymes after training (Costill, Fink, and Pollock 1976; Costill et al. 1978; Eriksson, Gollnick, and Saltin 1973). Their results are summarized in Table 7.4. The most significant increases have been demonstrated with high intensity sprint training and resistance training. Endurance training generally causes little or no increase in the activity of these enzymes (Holloszy 1973). In fact, distance training has produced a decrease in the activity of some of them (Baldwin et al. 1973, Gollnick and Simmons 1967, Holloszy et al. 1973).

Any training swims that are of sufficient intensity to produce severe acidosis should increase the activity of the anaerobic enzymes. Since peak blood lactates can be achieved with 30 to 90 seconds of maximal effort (Keul 1975), it follows that high intensity repeats of 50 to 200 yards/meters should be excellent for this purpose. Longer swims may also increase the activity of these enzymes, provided those swims are performed at maximal or near maximal speeds.

Delaying Fatigue Caused by Lactate Accumulation

The lactic acid that was produced during exercise accumulates as excess lactate. When this amount reaches a certain level, acidosis occurs, the rate of anaerobic glycolysis is reduced, and movements become slower, less powerful, and more painful.

Athletes have three methods by which they can delay the fatigue caused by lactate accumulation. The first is by reducing the rate of lactate accumulation. The second is by increasing the rate of the removal of lactate from working muscles, and the third is by increasing the tolerance to lactate accumulation.

Reducing the rate of lactate accumulation. The rate of lactate accumulation during exercise can be reduced by decreasing the rate of lactate production in muscles and by increasing the rate of lactate removal from those same muscles.[2]

A reduction of lactate production is often accomplished during exercise through an increase in oxygen consumption. When the supply of oxygen to

---

2. Other methods by which lactate accumulation may be reduced are through increased stroke efficiency and proper pacing. Both will reduce the energy cost for races and therefore the need for anaerobic glycolysis.

muscle cells is increased, greater quantities of the pyruvate and hydrogen ions produced during glycolysis can enter the mitochondria where they are oxidized to CO_2 and H_2O. When the oxygen supply is insufficient to permit oxidation, the pyruvate and hydrogen ions will combine to form lactic acid.

A second mechanism for reducing lactate production has only recently been acknowledged. Apparently some pyruvate is removed from working muscles when it combines with ammonia to form alanine, an amino acid (Keul, Doll, and Keppler 1972). The alanine can then diffuse into the blood and be converted to glucose in the liver. The conversion of pyruvate to alanine is believed to be catalyzed by the enzyme alanine transaminase (Holloszy et al. 1975). Increases in alanine have been found in the muscles of animals (Baldwin et al. 1972) and in the blood of humans during exercise (Carlsten et al. 1962, Carlsten et al. 1965, Felig and Wahren 1971), indicating that some of the pyruvate is indeed diverted to alanine rather than being converted to lactate.

Increasing the rate at which pyruvate converts to alanine could be a major factor in reducing fatigue during exercise. Felig and Wahren (1971) estimate that this process could reduce lactate formation by 35 to 60 percent in trained subjects. They found that alanine production increased 500 percent in the leg muscles of men subjected to strenuous exercise. Because little is known so far about how training can produce the "alanine shift," suggestions for training are not made in this volume. The assumption can be made, however, that any training that increases oxygen consumption and reduces lactate production may also increase the pyruvate entering the "alanine pathway."

Increasing lactate removal from working muscles. Lactic acid is a small molecule that diffuses (or perhaps is transported) easily from muscle cells into the blood and other extracellular spaces. The importance of lactate removal from working muscle fibers has been largely overlooked in discussions of training. The usual concept has been that the energy cost of exercise is "paid" by oxygen consumption during work and the "extra" oxygen consumed during recovery (the oxygen debt). It is now evident that some of the lactate produced during exercise (1) diffuses into adjacent resting fibers within the same muscle where it is metabolized for energy and (2) is "poured" into the bloodstream where it can be transported to other resting muscles and the heart and liver where it is also metabolized (Knuttgen 1971, Minnaire and Forichon 1975, Saltin and Karlsson 1971b, Jorfeldt 1971, Essen et al. 1971, Hermansen et al. 1975).

An increase in the removal of lactate from muscles during exercise has the effect of delaying the reduction in muscle pH that causes fatigue. Swimmers should be able to swim at a faster pace for a longer distance because more energy can be supplied anaerobically without severe acidosis occurring. Training that increases the rate of lactate removal may be as important to distance races as training that reduces the rate of lactate production. It may be even more important in long sprints and middle-distance races. The time involved in shorter events is not sufficient to allow delivery of a significant amount of oxygen to the working muscles while the competition is going on. (It takes 2 to 3 minutes for athletes to reach maximal rates of oxygen consumption.) However, if it is possible for lactate removal mechanisms to reach peak capacity shortly after exercise begins, an improvement of these mechanisms could be important for reducing lactate accumulation in long sprints and middle-distance races. Therefore, the removal of lactate from working muscles may be the most effective method of delaying fatigue at distances of 500 yards and less. This would support the desirability of distance training for sprinters because the rate of lactate removal is probably increased most by distance training.

It is reasonable to expect that lactate removal mechanisms could respond within a few seconds after a race begins. They appear to be dependent on fast reacting physiological phenomena such as the enzyme activity within muscles and the diffusion rate of lactic acid out of the muscles and into the blood and other muscle fibers. It is probably also dependent on the speed of blood flow to working muscles which might require some time to become mobilized. However, the blood flow, which is to a great extent determined by cardiac output, should increase more rapidly than oxygen consumption.

Since the importance of lactate removal to exercise has only recently been discovered, there is no information available yet as to (1) whether the rate of lactate removal can be increased by training and (2) if it can, what methods would be most effective for doing so. However, it is not difficult to support an assumption that lactate removal can be improved by training. Circulatory phenomena should contribute to an increased removal rate and since some of these mechanisms are amenable to training, it is reasonable to assume that training would improve the rate of lactate removal as well. In addition, there are enzymes in the muscles and other organs that encourage the metabolism of lactate. The activity of some of these enzymes has been increased by training.

Circulatory mechanisms involved in lactate removal. Any improvement in circulatory function that increases the quantity of blood that reaches working muscles should improve the rate of lactate removal. Increases in *cardiac output, capillary density,* and the distribution of blood flow to working muscles will cause more blood to flow past the muscles in a given period of time. This in turn, should allow more lactic acid to diffuse out of the muscles and into the bloodstream where it can be transported to the liver, the heart, and other resting muscle fibers. However, since training decreases cardiac output and muscle blood flow during submaximal work, any increases in removal rate that are due to these factors should operate only during maximal efforts.

There is some feeling that athletes with larger hearts have an advantage where lactate removal is concerned (Keul, Doll, and Keppler 1972). Cardiac muscle fibers can metabolize lactate for energy, therefore, athletes with large hearts should be able to remove more lactic acid from the blood and metabolize it, allowing for additional lactate to diffuse into the blood. Keul et al. (1972)

have reported that persons with large hearts show smaller increases in blood lactate during exercise. Although heart size is to a great extent determined by heredity, it is possible to increase it by training (Mathews and Fox 1976). In this case, any form of training, including nonswimming activities, that causes the heart to beat forcefully should be beneficial. High-intensity long sprints and middle-distance efforts would seem to be best for this purpose because they increase the heart rate to maximum and keep it beating as fast as possible for an extended period of time.

Enzyme activity involved in lactate removal. The enzyme lactate dehydrogenase (LDH) is involved in the metabolism of lactic acid. Therefore, an increase in the activity of this enzyme should increase lactate removal. There are two principal forms of lactate dehydrogenase (LDH) in human muscles, a heart form and a muscle form.[3] The muscle form (M-LDH) regulates the formation of lactate *from* pyruvate, while the heart form (H-LDH) regulates the reverse reaction, that is, the conversion of lactate *to* pyruvate. The heart form is most prevalent in cardiac fibers, although slow twitch skeletal muscle fibers also contain H-LDH (Essen et al. 1971). The muscle form is found in skeletal muscle fibers.

The metabolism of lactate by LDH sets off a chain reaction that increases the rate of lactate removal from the working muscle fibers. When more lactate is metabolized in the heart, liver, and resting muscle fibers, additional blood lactate is able to diffuse into these organs. The increase in diffusion rate will reduce the lactate content of the blood, which should in turn increase the quantity of lactic acid that can diffuse from the working muscle fibers into the bloodstream. Any increase in H-LDH activity should increase the rate of lactate metabolism and in so doing increase the rate of lactate removal from working muscle fibers.

It should be mentioned that this observation is highly theoretical. There is a possibility that the activity of H-LDH is inhibited by acidosis. If that is true, this mechanism would be limited in its ability to increase lactate removal during exercise. Keul, Doll, and Keppler (1972) observed such an inhibition in muscle tissue that was removed from animals. However, they doubt that such inhibition occurs in humans during exercise.

There has been no definite determination concerning the effect of training on LDH activity. A decrease of LDH activity was reported in one study (Baldwin et al. 1972), while no change was reported in another (Holloszy et al. 1973). Unfortunately, most researchers have failed to differentiate between the two forms of LDH when studying the effects of training on this enzyme. Some information is provided by the research of Gollnick and Simmons (1967), however. They reported an increase of H-LDH activity in the cardiac muscle of rats who were trained for several weeks in endurance swimming. Interestingly, the researchers also found a corresponding decrease in M-LDH activity of skeletal muscle.

3. Actually, there are five forms of LDH in human muscles; however, three are derivations of the two principal forms (Keul, Doll, and Keppler 1972).

The significance of these findings is that while endurance training would be beneficial for increasing the rate of lactate metabolism in cardiac and possibly slow twitch muscle fibers, where H-LDH is also found in significant quantity, the corresponding decrease in M-LDH in muscles could be detrimental if it limits an athlete's ability to sustain near maximal speeds in long sprints and middle-distance races by reducing lactate production.

It is too soon to draw any conclusions concerning the significance of LDH to lactate removal during exercise. Future research will need to differentiate the two forms of this enzyme in skeletal muscle before we will know (1) whether an increase in H-LDH increases the rate of lactate removal, (2) if endurance training is the most effective method for encouraging such an increase, and (3) if increases in H-LDH activity cause a corresponding decrease in M-LDH activity.

Lactate permease activity. Although the prevalent belief is that the removal of lactic acid is largely dependent on its rate of diffusion from muscle fibers, some researchers have theorized the existence of a system that transports lactic acid from working muscle fibers (Achs and Garfinkel 1977). The enzyme that regulates this system has been named *lactate permease* (Kübler et al. 1965). If a system exists for transporting lactate out of muscle cells, the activity of the enzyme that regulates it may be amenable to training. An increase in this enzyme would increase the rate of lactate removal accordingly. There is at present too little evidence to speculate on the existence of this transport system. These suppositions concerning enzyme activity and lactate removal are presented as a reference in case of future revelations.

Increasing Lactate Tolerance: The Oxygen Debt

When lactic acid accumulates to high levels, acidosis occurs and athletes experience pain. Athletes who are willing to tolerate more pain should be able to produce more lactate. Thus, they will be able to use anaerobic glycolysis to a greater extent, which will allow them to swim near maximal speed for a greater distance.

Two mechanisms that may improve an athlete's tolerance to the pain of acidosis are improved buffering capacity and improved pain tolerance.

Improved buffering capacity. Improved buffering reduces the effect of lactic acid on pH. A buffer contains a weak acid and a salt of that same acid. Buffers are found in the blood and in other fluids inside the muscle cells. They can combine with lactic acid and weaken or buffer it. This buffering action prevents marked reductions in pH during exercise. For example, with efficient buffering, a 10-fold increase in lactic acid production would only cause a 40 percent decrease in pH (Keul, Doll, and Keppler 1972, p. 134).

There are three major buffer systems in body fluids. They are the bicarbonate buffers, the phosphate buffers, and the protein buffers. The protein buffers are by far the most important where exercise is concerned. It is estimated that approximately 75 percent of all buffering is accomplished by protein buffers (Guyton 1961, p. 115). They are found in greatest quantities in hemoglobin and in muscles. The amino acids that make up proteins contain weak acids which can dissociate and react with lactic acid to weaken it. The buffering capacity of hemoglobin has been well researched; however, the capacity of muscles to buffer lactic acid has received little attention and is not well understood at this time. It is believed that muscle buffers may be at least five times more effective for neutralizing lactic acid than blood buffers (Astrand and Rodahl 1977, p. 139).

An increase in the quantity of both muscle and blood buffers should permit tolerance for greater lactic acid production during exercise. Since more lactic acid would be neutralized, muscle pH would not decline as rapidly, fatigue would not occur as soon, and anaerobic glycolysis could proceed at a faster rate for a longer period of time. The net result would be that swimmers could maintain a faster pace for the entire race.

Buffer systems can react almost immediately with the onset of exercise to prevent drops in pH. Therefore, improved buffering may be very important to success in long sprints and middle-distance races where most of the energy is supplied by anaerobic metabolism.

Once again, research results are contradictory concerning the effects of training on the buffering systems of the body. Hollman and Liesen (1973) have reported increases in buffering capacity with training, while Doll et al. (1966) have presented evidence to the contrary.

Svarc and Novák (1975) reported a decrease in acidosis following training that they believed was caused by an increase in buffering capacity. This study is particularly significant since it involved swimmers. The subjects were trained with forty 30-meter sprints. The sprints were done in sets of 10 with rest periods of 30 seconds between swims and 10-minute rest periods between sets.

In spite of contradictory reports, it is reasonable to assume that training will increase buffering capacity. The fact that physiological mechanisms in the body adapt to specific demands is well documented. It would seem that when buffering systems are repeatedly utilized during training, the components of these systems should adapt so that they increase in quantity and/or efficiency. Coaches and athletes would be wise to train on the assumption that buffering systems can be increased. They have nothing to lose by such a procedure because the training will improve other lactate tolerance mechanisms in the process, and the gains in performance could be considerable.

If buffering capacity can be improved, 50-yard sprints or longer efforts at high intensity should be the most effective way to train. These swims produce acute acidosis, which is probably the required training stimulus. The most effective buffering activity takes place in the muscles, so specific training utilizing each swimmer's competitive stroke(s) is indicated. The next most effective chemical buffering system is located in the hemoglobin. It should be possible to increase the capacity of this system with both nonspecific and specific training.

Increased pain tolerance. Pain tolerance is another factor that can affect a swimmer's ability to maintain fast speeds. Athletes who can tolerate more pain can swim at maximal speed for greater distances. They can supply more energy anaerobically and thus maintain rapid rates of muscular contraction for a longer period of time. By subjecting themselves to pain in training, some athletes improve their tolerance for it. Through such training they find they can tolerate more pain than they believed possible.

The effects of training on an athlete's ability to tolerate the pain of lactate accumulation have not been given much consideration in the physiological literature. However, coaches and athletes consider improved tolerance to pain one of the most beneficial effects athletes can receive from training. Much of a swimmer's training is designed to push back the "pain barriers" whether they be psychological or physiological in origin. Motivation plays a role in increasing pain tolerance because athletes who are highly motivated will endure more pain without giving up.

The training procedures recommended for increasing anaerobic enzyme activity and buffering capacity are also recommended for increasing pain tolerance. This training must be used sparingly. Too much can cause an overtrained state where performance deteriorates. Overtraining seems to have both attitudinal and physiological aspects; it will be discussed in more detail in a later chapter.

REFERENCES

Achs, M. J., and Garfinkel, D. 1977. "Computer Simulation of Rat Heart Metabolism After Adding Glucose to the Perfusate." *Amer. J. Physiol.* 232:R175–R184.

Astrand, P. O., and Rodahl, K. 1977. *Textbook of Work Physiology.* New York: McGraw-Hill.

Baldwin, K. M., Campbell, P. J., and Cooke, D. A. 1977. "Glycogen, Lactate, and Alanine Changes in Muscle Fiber Types During Graded Exercise." *J. Appl. Physiol.* 43:288–291.

Baldwin, K. M., Winder, W. W., Terjung, R. L., and Holloszy, J. O. 1973. "Glycolytic Enzymes in Red, White and Intermediate Skeletal Muscle: Adaptations to Exercise." *Amer. J. Physiol.* 225:962–966.

Baldwin, K. M., Klinkerfuss, G. H., Terjung, R. L., Molé, P. A., and Holloszy, J. O. 1972. "Respiratory Capacity of White, Red and Intermediate Muscle: Adaptive Response to Exercise." *Amer. J. Physiol.* 222:373–378.

Bang, O. 1936. "The Lactate Content of the Blood During and After Muscular Exercise in Man." *Scand. Arch. Physiol.* 74:51–82.

Bergstrom, J. 1962. "Muscle Electrolytes in Man." *Scand. J. Clin. Lab. Inves.* 14: Supp. 68.

Carlson, L. A., Ekelund, L. C., and Fröberg, S. 1971. "Concentration of Triglycerides, Phospholipids, and Glycogen in Skeletal Muscle and of Free Fatty Acids and B-hydroxybutyric Acid in Blood in Man in Response to Exercise." *Europ. J. Clin. Invest.* 1:248–254.

Carlsten, A., Hallgren, R., Jagenborg, R., Svanborg, A., and Werko, L. 1962. "Arterial Concentrations of Free Fatty Acids and Free Amino Acids in Healthy Human Individuals at Rest and at Different Work Loads." *Scand. J. Clin. Lab. Invest.* 14:185–191.

Carlsten, A., Häggendal, J., Hallgren, R., Jagenborg, R., Svanborg, A., and Werko, L.

1965. "Effect of Ganglionic Blocking Drugs on Blood Glucose, Amino Acids, Free Fatty Acids and Catecholamines at Exercise in Man." *Acta Phys. Scand.* 64:439–447.

Costill, D. L. 1978a. "Adaptations in Skeletal Muscle During Training for Sprint and Endurance Swimming." *Swimming Medicine IV*, ed. B. Eriksson and B. Furberg, pp. 233–248. Baltimore: University Park Press.

Costill, D. L., Coyle, E. F., Fink, W. J., Lesmes, G. R., and Witzman, F. A. 1978. "Adaptations in Skeletal Muscle Following Strength Training." Unpublished research study, Ball State University, Muncie, Indiana.

Costill, D. L., Daniels, J., Evans, W., Fink, W. J., Krahenbuhl, G., and Saltin, B. 1976. "Skeletal Muscle Enzymes and Fiber Composition of Male and Female Track Athletes." *J. of Appl. Physiol.* 40:149–153.

Costill, D. L., Fink, W. J., and Pollock, M. L. 1976. "Muscle Fiber Composition and Enzyme Activities of Elite Distance Runners." *Med. Sci. Sports.* 8:96–100.

Cresticelli, F., and Taylor, C. 1944. "The Lactate Response to Exercise and Its Relationship to Physical Factors." *Amer. J. Physiol.* 141:630–640.

Cunningham, D., and Faulkner, J. 1969. "The Effect of Training on Aerobic and Anaerobic Metabolism During a Short Exhaustive Run." *Med. Sci. Sports* 1:65–69.

Danforth, W. H. 1965. "Activation of Glycolytic Pathway in Muscle." *Control of Energy Metabolism*, ed. B. Chance, R. W. Estabrook, and J. R. Williamson, pp. 287–297. New York: Academic Press.

diPrampero, P. E. 1971. "The Alactic Oxygen Debt: Its Power, Capacity and Efficiency." *Muscle Metabolism During Exercise*, ed. B. Pernow and B. Saltin, pp. 371–382. New York: Plenum Press.

Doll, E., Keul, J., Maiwald, C. H., and Reindell, H. 1966. "Das Verhalten von Sauerstoffdruck, Kohlensäuredruck, pH. Standardbikarbonat und base excess in arteriellen Blut bei verschieden Belastungsformen." *Int. Z. Angew. Physiol.* 22:327. Cited in *Energy Metabolism of Human Muscle*, ed. J. Keul, E. Doll, and D. Keppler. Baltimore: University Park Press, 1972.

Edgerton, V. R., Essen, B., Saltin, B., and Simpson, D. R. 1975. "Glycogen Depletion in Specific Types of Human Skeletal Muscle Fibers in Intermittent and Continuous Exercise." *Metabolic Adaptations to Prolonged Physical Exercise*, ed. H. Howald and J. R. Poortmans, pp. 402–415. Basel: Birkäuser Verlag.

Edington, D. W., and Edgerton, V. R. 1976. *The Biology of Physical Activity*. Boston: Houghton Mifflin.

Eriksson, B. O., Gollnick, P. D., and Saltin, B. 1973. "Muscle Metabolism and Enzyme Activities After Training in Boys 11–13 Years Old." *Acta Physiol. Scand.* 87:485–497.

Essen, B., Pernow, B., Gollnick, P. D., and Saltin, B. 1971. "Muscle Glycogen Content and Lactate Uptake in Exercising Muscles." *Muscle Metabolism During Exercise*, ed. B. Pernow and B. Saltin, pp. 130–134. New York: Plenum Press.

Felig, P., and Wahren, J. 1971. "Interrelationship Between Amino Acid and Carbohydrate Metabolism During Exercise: The Glucose-Alanine Cycle." *Muscle Metabolism During Exercise*, ed. B. Pernow and B. Saltin, pp. 205–214. New York: Plenum Press.

Gollnick, P. D., Armstrong, R. B., Saubert IV, C. W., Sembrowich, W. L., Shepard, R. E., and Saltin, B. 1973. "Glycogen Depletion Patterns in Human Skeletal Muscle During Prolonged Work." *Pflugers Arch. ges. Physiol.* 344:1–12.

Gollnick, P. D., and Hermansen, L. 1973. "Biochemical Adaptations to Exercise: Anaerobic Metabolism." *Exercise and Sport Sciences Review*, Vol. 1, ed. J. Wilmore, pp. 1–43. New York: Academic Press.

Gollnick, P. D., Piehl, K., Karlsson, J., and Saltin, B. 1975. "Glycogen Depletion Patterns in Human Skeletal Muscle Fibers After Varying Types and Intensities of Exercise." *Metabolic Adaptations to Prolonged Physical Exercise*, ed. H. Howald and J. R. Poortmans, pp. 416–421. Basel: Birkäuser Verlag.

Gollnick, P. D., and Simmons, S. W. 1967. "Physical Activity and Liver Cholesterol." *Int. Z. Angew. Physiol.* 23:322–330.

Guyton, A. C. 1961. *Textbook of Medical Physiology.* Philadelphia: Saunders.

Hermansen, L. 1969. "Anaerobic Energy Release." *Med. Sci. Sports* 1:32.

———. 1971. "Lactate Production During Exercise." *Muscle Metabolism During Exercise*, ed. B. Pernow and B. Saltin, pp. 401–407. New York: Plenum Press.

Hermansen, L., Machlum, S., Pruell, E. D. R., Vaage, O., Waldrum, H., and Wessel-Aas, T. 1975. "Lactate Removal at Rest and During Exercise." *Metabolic Adaptations to Prolonged Physical Exercise*, ed. H. Howald and J. R. Poortmans, pp. 101–105. Basel: Birkäuser Verlag.

Hermansen, L., and Osnes, J. B. 1972. "Blood and Muscle pH After Maximal Exercise in Man." *J. Appl. Physiol.* 32:304–308.

Hill, D. K. 1940. "Anaerobic Recovery of Heat." *J. Physiol., London* 98:460–467.

Hollman, W., and Liesen, H. 1973. "The Influence of Hypoxia and Hyperoxia Training in a Laboratory on the Cardiopulmonal Capacity." *Limiting Factors of Physical Performance*, ed. J. Keul, pp. 212–218. Stuttgart: Georg Thieme Verlag.

Holloszy, J. O. 1973. "Biochemical Adaptations to Exercise: Aerobic Metabolism." *Exercise and Sport Sciences Review*, Vol. 1, ed. J. Wilmore, pp. 45–71. New York: Academic Press.

Holloszy, J. O., Booth, F. W., Winder, W. W., and Fitts, R. H. 1975. "Biochemical Adaptations of Skeletal Muscle to Prolonged Physical Exercise." *Metabolic Adaptations to Prolonged Physical Exercise*, ed. H. Howald and J. R. Poortmans, pp. 438–447. Basel: Birkäuser Verlag.

Holloszy, J. O., Molé, P. A., Baldwin, K. M., and Terjung, R. L. 1973. "Exercise Induced Enzymatic Adaptations in Muscle." *Limiting Factors of Physical Performance*, ed. J. Keul, pp. 63–77. Stuttgart: Georg Thieme Verlag.

Holloszy, J. O., Oscai, L. B., Molé, P. A., and Don, I. J. 1971. "Biochemical Adaptations to Endurance Exercise in Skeletal Muscle." *Muscle Metabolism During Exercise*, ed. B. Pernow and B. Saltin, pp. 51–61. New York: Plenum Press.

Hultman, E. 1967a. "Studies on Muscle Metabolism of Glycogen and Active Phosphate in Man with Special Reference to Exercise and Diet." *J. Clin. Lab. Invest.* 19, Suppl. 94:39–40.

———. 1967b. "Physiological Role of Muscle Glycogen in Man with Special Reference to Exercise." *Circulation Res.* 20/21, Suppl. 1:99–114.

Hultman, E., and Bergström, J. 1973. "Local Energy Supplying Substrates As Limiting Factors in Different Types of Leg Muscle Work in Normal Man." *Limiting Factors of Physical Performance*, ed. J. Keul, pp. 113–124. Stuttgart: Georg Thieme Verlag.

Hultman, E., Bergström, J., and Roch-Norlund, A. E. 1971. "Glycogen Storage in Human Skeletal Muscle." *Muscle Metabolism During Exercise*, ed. B. Pernow and B. Saltin, pp. 273–287. New York: Plenum Press.

Hultman, E., and Nilsson, N. 1971. "Liver Glycogen As a Glucose Supplying Source During Exercise." *Muscle Metabolism During Exercise*, ed. B. Pernow and B. Saltin, pp. 179–188. New York: Plenum Press.

Jorfeldt, L. 1971. "Turnover of ^{14}C-L(+)-Lactate in Human Skeletal Muscle During Exercise." *Muscle Metabolism During Exercise*, ed. B. Pernow and B. Saltin. New York: Plenum Press.

Karlsson, J., Diamant, B., and Saltin, B. 1971. "Muscle Metabolites During Submaximal and Maximal Exercise in Man." *Scand. J. Clin. Lab. Invest.* 26:385–394.

Karlsson, J., Nordesjö, L-O, Jorfeldt, L., and Saltin, B. 1972. "Muscle Lactate, ATP and CP Levels During Exercise After Physical Training in Man." *J. Appl. Physiol.* 33:199–203.

Karlsson, J., and Saltin, B. 1970. "Lactate, ATP and CP in Working Muscle During Exhaustive Exercise in Man." *J. Appl. Physiol.* 29:598–602.

Kendrick-Jones, J., and Perry, S. V. 1967. "Protein Synthesis and Enzyme Response to Contractile Activity in Skeletal Muscle." *Nature* (London) 213:406–408.

Kerly, M., and Ronzoni, E. 1933. "The Effect of pH on Carbohydrate Changes in Isolated Anaerobic Frog's Muscle." *J. Biol. Chem.* 103:161–173.

Keul, J. 1975. "Muscle Metabolism During Long Lasting Exercise," *Metabolic Adaptations to Prolonged Physical Exercise*, ed. H. Howald and J. R. Poortmans, pp. 31–42. Basel: Birkäuser Verlag.

Keul, J., Doll, E., and Keppler, D. 1972. *Energy Metabolism of Human Muscle.* Baltimore: University Park Press.

Kiessling, K. H., Piehl, K., and Lundquist, C.-G. 1971. "Effect of Physical Training on Ultrastructural Features in Human Skeletal Muscle." *Muscle Metabolism During Exercise*, ed. B. Pernow and B. Saltin, pp. 97–101. New York: Plenum Press.

Klaussen, K., Piehl, K., and Saltin, R. 1975. "Muscle Glycogen Stores and Capacity for Anaerobic Work." *Metabolic Adaptations to Prolonged Physical Exercise*, ed. H. Howald and J. R. Poortmans, pp. 127–130. Basel: Birkäuser Verlag.

Knuttgen, H. G. 1971. "Lactate and Oxygen Debt: An Introduction." *Muscle Metabolism During Exercise*, ed. B. Pernow and B. Saltin. New York: Plenum Press.

Kübler, W., Bretschneider, H. J., Voss, W., Gehl, W., Wenthe, F., and Colas, J. L. 1965. "Über die Milchsäure und Brentztraugensäurepermeation aus dem hypotherman Myvkard." *Pflugers Arch. ges. Physiol.* 287:203–223. Cited in *Energy Metabolism of Human Muscle*, ed. J. Keul, E. Doll, and D. Keppler. Baltimore: University Park Press, 1972.

Lamb, D. R. 1978. *Physiology of Exercise: Responses and Adaptations.* New York: Macmillan.

McArdle, W. D., Katch, F. I., and Katch, V. L. 1981. *Exercise Physiology: Energy, Nutrition, and Human Performance.* Philadelphia: Lea and Febiger.

MacDougall, J. D., Ward, G. R., Sale, D. C., and Sutton, J. R. 1975. "Muscle Glycogen Repletion After High Intensity Intermittent Exercise." *J. Appl. Physiol.* 42:129–132.

MacDougall, J. D., Ward, G. R., Sale, D. C., and Sutton, J. R. 1977. "Biochemical Adaptations of Human Skeletal Muscle to Heavy Resistance Training and Immobilization." *J. Appl. Physiol.: Respirat. Environ. Exercise Physiol.* 43:700–703.

Mathews, D. K., and Fox, E. L. 1976. *The Physiological Basis of Physical Education and Athletics.* Philadelphia: W. B. Saunders Company.

Minnaire, Y., and Forichon, J. 1975. "Lactate Metabolism and Glucose Lactate Conversion in Prolonged Physical Exercise." *Metabolic Adaptations to Prolonged Physical Exercise*, ed. H. Howald and J. R. Poortmans, pp. 106–112. Basel: Birkäuser Verlag.

Robinson, S., and Harmon, P. M. 1941. "The Lactic Acid Mechanism and Certain Properties of the Blood in Relation to Training." *Amer. J. Physiol.* 132:757–769.

Saltin, B. 1975. "Adaptative Changes in Carbohydrate Metabolism with Exercise." *Metabolic Adaptations to Prolonged Physical Exercise*, ed. H. Howald and J. R. Poortmans, pp. 94–100. Basel: Birkäuser Verlag.

Saltin, B., and Essen, B. 1971. "Muscle Glycogen, Lactate, ATP and CP in Intermittent Exercise." *Muscle Metabolism During Exercise*, ed. B. Pernow and B. Saltin, pp. 419–424. New York: Plenum Press.

Saltin, B., and Karlsson, J. 1971a. "Muscle Glycogen Utilization During Work of Different Intensities." *Muscle Metabolism During Exercise*, ed. B. Pernow and B. Saltin, pp. 289–299. New York: Plenum Press.

Saltin, B., and Karlsson, J. 1971b. "Muscle ATP, CP, and Lactate During Exercise After Physical Conditioning." *Muscle Metabolism During Exercise*, ed. B. Pernow and B. Saltin, pp. 395–399. New York: Plenum Press.

Saltin, B., Nazar, K., Costill, D. L., Stein, E., Jansson, E., Essen, B., and Gollnick, P. D. 1976. "The Nature of the Training Response: Peripheral and Central Adaptations to One-legged Exercise." *Acta Physiol. Scand.* 96:289–305.

Svarc, V., and J. Novák. 1975. "The Changes of Acid Base Balance During Interval Swimming Training in Trained and Untrained Men," *Metabolic Adaptations to Prolonged Physical Exercise*, ed. H. Howald and J. R. Poortmans, pp. 73–77. Basel: Birkäuser Verlag.

Taylor, A. W. 1975. "The Effect of Exercise and Training on the Activities of Human Skeletal Muscle Glycogen Cycle Enzymes." *Metabolic Adaptations to Prolonged Physical Exercise*, ed. H. Howald and J. R. Poortmans, pp. 451–462. Basel: Birkäuser Verlag.

Thorstensson, A., Sjödin, B., and Karlsson, J. 1975. "Enzyme Activity and Muscle Strength After 'Sprint Training' in Man." *Acta Physiol. Scand.* 94:313–318.

Torma, Z. D., and Székely, G. 1978. "Parameters of Acid-Base Equilibrium at Various Swimming Intensities and Distances." *Swimming Medicine IV*, ed. B. Eriksson and B. Furberg, pp. 274–281. Baltimore: University Park Press.

Wilkerson, J., and Evonuk, E. 1971. "Changes in Cardiac and Skeletal Muscle Myosin ATPase Activities After Exercise." *J. Appl. Physiol.* 30:328–330.

Yakolev, N. N. 1950. "The Order of Biochemical Changes in Muscle Training and Breaking of Training." [Russ.] *Fziol. J.* 36:744. Cited in *Energy Metabolism of Human Muscle*, ed. J. Keul, E. Doll, and D. Keppler. Baltimore: University Park Press, 1972.

———. 1965. "Comparative Biochemical Estimation of the Energetic Metabolism of the Striated Muscles Depending on Their Functional Profile." [Russ.] *Ukr. Biokem. Zh.* 37:137. Cited in *Energy Metabolism of Human Muscle*, ed. J. Keul, E. Doll, and D. Keppler. Baltimore: University Park Press, 1972.

CHAPTER *8*

The Importance of Oxygen Consumption, the Anaerobic Threshold, and Muscle Structure to Swimming Performance

For many years an athlete's ability to consume oxygen during exercise has been considered one of the most, if not the most, important determinants of endurance performance. That is because an increase in the muscle's oxygen supply allows more energy to be metabolized aerobically so that the rate of lactate accumulation is slowed and fatigue is delayed. The circulatory system, because it transports oxygen to the muscles, has received considerable attention in the physiological literature with volumes of research aimed at identifying training methods that could improve the transport of oxygen.

Recently, another physiological concept that may be a more reliable indicator of endurance performance has been identified. That concept is termed the **anaerobic threshold.** The anaerobic threshold is a measure of a person's ability to do work without accumulating significant amounts of excess lactate in the blood. It is now evident that an increase in oxygen consumption is only one method of reducing lactate accumulation. Physiological mechanisms that remove lactic acid from muscles may be equally important to endurance performance. In addition there may also be ways other than the delivery of oxygen that reduce the rate of lactate production. The anaerobic threshold may be the most reliable indicator of endurance performance because it reflects the efficiency of these and other, as yet undiscovered, physiological mechanisms. Both of these training concepts, oxygen consumption and the anaerobic threshold, will be described in this chapter.

The effect of the fast twitch and slow twitch muscle fibers on athletic performance is another area of exercise physiology that has gotten much attention recently. Large volumes of sometimes confusing technical information (and misinformation) have found their way into the literature. There is speculation that the properties of fast twitch and slow twitch muscle fibers determine the events an athlete should swim, that fibers can be changed from one type to another by training, and that distance training will cause fast twitch fibers to lose their capacity for speed and power, while sprint training will cause them to lose endurance.

Oxygen Consumption

Oxygen consumption is the term used to designate the amount of oxygen supplied to your muscles and other tissues. It is measured in the laboratory by calculating the amount of oxygen exhaled in one minute and subtracting that amount from the amount inhaled during the same period of time. The difference between the two is the amount that was consumed by the muscles. Each of us possesses a finite capacity to consume oxygen. This capacity is designated the maximal oxygen consumption capacity, (abbreviated $\dot{V}O_2$ max) or maximal oxygen uptake. As you might expect, research indicates that people with large oxygen consumption capacities generally perform better in endurance events (Costill 1970).

$\dot{V}O_2$ max is typically 2 liters per minute for adult females and 3 liters per minute for adult males. Gifted female athletes have been measured beyond 4 liters per minute, while their male counterparts have maximal oxygen consumption capacities in excess of 5 liters per minute.

$\dot{V}O_2$ max (and $\dot{V}O_2$) can also be expressed in relative terms according to the number of milliliters of oxygen consumed per kilogram of body weight per minute (ml/kg/min). This measurement eliminates biases resulting from differences in size. For example, a large person who consumes 4 liters of oxygen per minute because he has greater muscle mass will have less oxygen available for each kilogram of muscle than a smaller person with a similar capacity. Expressing $\dot{V}O_2$ max in relation to size gives a more accurate representation of a person's endurance capabilities.[1]

Oxygen capacity in ml/kg/min is calculated by dividing oxygen consumption in liters/min by the subject's body weight in kilograms. The procedure for converting an absolute oxygen consumption capacity to a relative capacity is shown here:

Subject has $\dot{V}O_2$ of 4.2 liters/min (or 4,200 ml/min).
His weight is 70 kg (154 lb)
4,200 ml ÷ 70 kg = 60 ml/kg/min

Average values for relative $\dot{V}O_2$ max are 35 and 45 ml/kg/min for women and

---

1. Eriksson, Berg, and Taranger (1978) have suggested that a relative $\dot{V}O_2$ max expressed in ml/kg/min may cause inaccurate assessments of the aerobic capacity of swimmers. They feel absolute values for aerobic capacity (liters/min) or oxygen consumption relative to height (ml/height^2/min) should be used. This is because swimmers do not support their entire body weight as do athletes in most other sports.

men respectively. Outstanding endurance athletes have been tested beyond 60 and 80 ml/kg/min.[2]

$\dot{V}O_2$ can be improved by training. However, research has indicated that heredity sets limits to the amount of improvement possible for a given person. This, in turn, means that heredity influences performance in endurance events. A season of training has been shown to increase absolute $\dot{V}O_2$ max by 10 to 20 percent. Relative $\dot{V}O_2$ max can be increased 20 to 40 percent if excess body fat is lost during the training process. Thus, athletes who are fortunate enough to inherit tendencies toward large maximal oxygen consumption capacities have a natural advantage.

Regarding hereditary influences on $\dot{V}O_2$ max, Klissouras (1971) measured the aerobic capacities of 25 pairs of male twins, ages 7 to 13. He found remarkable similarities in their ability to consume oxygen during exercise. That similarity was greater among identical (monozygous) twins than among fraternal (dizygous) twins.[3] The greatest difference in $\dot{V}O_2$ max between pairs of identical twins was found to be 3.5 ml/kg/min. This is less than the average difference between the 10 pairs of fraternal twins. It is also interesting that among identical twins the anaerobic capacity and maximal heart rates were concluded to be 86 percent genetically determined. This means that other physiological mechanisms may be also limited by heredity.

The Effects of Training on $\dot{V}O_2$ Max

Oxygen enters the body via the respiratory system, is transported by the circulatory system to the muscles, and diffuses into the muscles. Thus, there are three physiological systems directly involved in transporting oxygen to the muscles: the respiratory system, the circulatory system, and the muscular system. Each of these systems involves several mechanisms that must be considered in determining how best to train for improvements in $\dot{V}O_2$ max. The respiratory system does not seem to limit oxygen consumption. Since humans exhale nearly half of the oxygen they inhale during strenuous exercise, increases in $\dot{V}O_2$ max most probably result from an improved transportation of oxygen by the circulatory system and increased extraction and utilization of oxygen by the muscular system.

Circulatory Adaptations That Increase $\dot{V}O_2$ Max

The transportation of oxygen from lungs to muscles has many phases, each of which is amenable to change with training. The diffusion of oxygen from the alveoli of the lungs into the blood stream is dependent upon the number of

2. It should be mentioned that the absolute and relative figures quoted were derived from measures of persons doing work on land. Holmer et al. (1974) calculated the $\dot{V}O_2$ max values for a group of elite swimmers both on land and when swimming in a flume, a type of water treadmill. They found $\dot{V}O_2$ max was 6 to 7 percent lower when swimming than when running. Astrand et al. (1963) reported similar results with a group of twenty-two female swimmers. Five of these subjects attained higher values in the water than on land, however. The researchers were of the opinion that trained swimmers may learn to better utilize their complete oxygen consumption capacity when in the water so that the difference between land and water values is eliminated.

3. Monozygous twins come from one egg which splits, whereas dizygous twins are fertilized in two separate eggs. Monozygous twins, therefore, inherit exactly the same set of genes, whereas dizygous twins have some differences in genealogy.

capillaries around the alveoli and the number of red blood cells available to carry that oxygen. Once the oxygen enters the blood stream, the speed of transportation is dependent upon the speed of blood flow through the body (cardiac output) and the volume of blood that reaches the working muscles (the distribution of blood flow). When the oxygen-saturated blood reaches the working muscle fibers, the amount of oxygen that diffuses into these muscle cells depends, once again, on the number of capillaries around each muscle fiber (capillary density) as well as the ability of the muscle fibers to extract oxygen from the blood. Thus the mechanisms for improving transportation of oxygen to working muscle fibers involve increasing cardiac output, capillary density, the distribution of blood flow and blood volume, and the number of red blood cells. Another possible factor is increased oxygen extraction by working muscle fibers.

Cardiac output. Cardiac output is a measure of the quantity of blood supplied by the heart and circulatory system to the tissues of the body. The heart is essentially the pump for a recirculating system of blood. The right side of the heart pumps blood to the lungs where it picks up oxygen and gives up carbon dioxide. This blood then travels to the left side where it is pumped to the skeletal muscles and other tissues of the body. During its path through the tissues, the blood gives up some of its oxygen (and glucose and free fatty acids) and takes up carbon dioxide (and lactic acid).

The cardiac output is calculated by multiplying the heart rate, in beats per minute, by the stroke volume (the amount of blood pumped from the left ventricle with each beat). Only the amount of blood ejected from the left side of the heart is measured because that blood carries oxygen to the skeletal muscles. (A nearly equal quantity of blood is simultaneously being pumped from the right side of the heart to the lungs.)

The cardiac output varies from a normal of 5 liters/min at rest to over 30 liters/min during strenuous exercise. A typical exercise cardiac output is computed as follows:

Heart Rate = 180 beats per min.
Stroke Volume = 160 ml of blood per beat.
180 × 160 = 28,800 ml of blood per min or 28.8 liters/min.

It is well documented that cardiac output during all-out effort is increased by training. The increase was 18 percent in one study (Clausen 1973). The available evidence indicates that training does not cause a similar increase at submaximal workloads (Hartley et al. 1969, Saltin et al. 1968). In fact, a decrease has been reported by some researchers (Clausen 1969, Ekblom et al. 1968, Hanson et al. 1968).

The major adaptation resulting in increased maximal cardiac output is an increase in the stroke volume. This increase is seen at both maximal and submaximal workloads. However, at submaximal levels it is coupled with a decrease in heart rate that causes the cardiac output to remain essentially the same.

	Submaximal Effort	*Maximal Effort*
Before Training	Event: 400-meter swim Time: 4:25 Heart rate: 170 Stroke volume: 140 170 × 140 = 23,800 ml/min or 23.8 liters/min	Event: 400-meter swim Time: 4:05 Heart rate: 190 Stroke volume: 140 190 × 140 = 26,600 ml/min or 26.6 liters/min
After Training	Event: same Time: same Heart rate: 147 Stroke volume: 160 147 × 160 = 23,520 ml/min or 23.52 liters/min	Event: same Time: 3:59.0 Heart rate: 190 Stroke volume: 160 190 × 160 = 30,400 ml/min or 30.4 liters/min

Figure 8.1. The effect of training on stroke volume and cardiac output.

The effect of training on the stroke volume and cardiac output at both submaximal and maximal workloads is illustrated in Figure 8.1.

Reductions in exercise heart rate that typically occur with training are excellent indicators that your stroke volume has increased and also that your potential for performance has been enhanced. This is one reason for monitoring heart rates frequently in practice.

Since the maximum stroke volume is reached when oxygen consumption exceeds 40 percent of maximal (Astrand and Rodahl 1977), some experts have suggested that training the stroke volume and the maximal cardiac output is best accomplished with long swims and short rest repeats at moderate speeds. They reason that a greater volume of work can be performed with less strain. Although this approach has not been completely verified by research, it seems a reasonable way to train.

Capillary density. Each muscle fiber is surrounded by capillaries, which are extensions of the arteries. Oxygen, carried in the blood, diffuses from these capillaries into the muscle fibers and waste products diffuse out of the muscle fibers into the capillaries. Capillaries are quite small. They will admit only one molecule of oxygen at a time. Therefore, an increase in the number of capillaries that surround a particular muscle fiber should make more oxygen available to that fiber. The location of muscle capillaries is shown in the illustration in Figure 8.2.

Training probably increases the total number of capillaries surrounding muscle fibers. Some people have argued against such an increase, claiming that

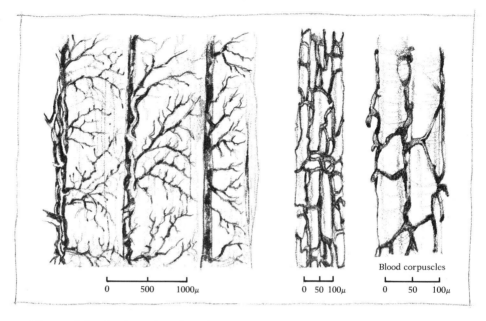

Figure 8.2. Blood supply in muscle tissue.

what seems to be an increase in capillarization is nothing more than an "opening up" of previously nonfunctional capillaries.

The fact that some researchers have not found increases in the total number of capillaries is probably due to their methods of counting. When the number of capillaries *per area of muscle* is counted, hypertrophy may hide true increases. When fibers become larger they occupy more area so that an increase in the number of capillaries around each fiber may go unnoticed. There may even appear to be fewer capillaries. However, when the number of capillaries per fiber is counted, an increase is usually found after training (Tittel et al. 1966; Carrow, Brown, and Van Huss 1967; Hermansen and Wachlova 1971).

Whether the total number of capillaries increases with training or nonfunctional capillaries become functional is really an academic matter where performance is concerned. Regardless of the mechanism, training will increase the number of capillaries that function in diffusion, and more oxygen will be available to the muscles.

Blood flow to working muscles. The human body contains approximately 5 liters of blood. When the body is at rest, the total blood volume is equally distributed to all tissues. During exercise, a greater amount of blood is sent to the working muscles and the supply to nonworking muscles and certain other tissues is reduced. For example, at rest, 15 to 20 percent of the total blood volume may go to the skeletal muscles. During exercise, 85 to 90 percent of the total blood volume will go to muscles, with most of it going to the muscle fibers that are contracting (Mathews and Fox 1976). This redistribution of blood occurs because arteries that supply the working muscles dilate (get larger), while those serving inactive areas of the body constrict (get smaller). Greater quantities of blood then flow through the larger arteries where the pressure and thus the resistance to flow is less.

Research indicates that training increases the amount of blood flowing to working muscles during maximal work (Clausen 1973; Keul, Doll, and Keppler 1972; Saltin 1973b; Simmons and Shepard 1972). Information about the effect of training on muscle blood flow during submaximal exercise is contradictory, however. Some experts have shown a decrease while others have found an increase during submaximal work. In one study, after training, the amount of blood flowing to working muscles decreased 15 percent during submaximal work and increased 8.6 percent during maximal efforts (Clausen et al. 1971). In another study, blood flow increased by 56 percent during maximal work and by 25 percent during submaximal work (Simmons and Shepard 1972). Other studies have also presented evidence of increased muscle blood flow during submaximal work (Saltin et al. 1976).

Increases in cardiac output, capillary density, and perhaps blood vessel elasticity probably account for the increase in blood flow observed during maximal work. A decrease in blood flow at submaximal efforts is more difficult to interpret. It could mean that fewer muscle fibers are required to perform the same amount of work after training. It could also represent increased oxygen extraction by the muscles. With more oxygen being extracted, the demand for blood would be reduced. An increase of blood flow at submaximal efforts is easier to interpret. Such an adaptation would increase oxygen transport to the muscles without increasing the work of the heart.

Blood volume and red blood cells. Trained athletes generally have more total blood volume and a greater number of red blood cells than untrained persons (Astrand and Rodahl 1977). Red blood cells contain hemoglobin. Most of the oxygen transported by the blood is carried in combination with hemoglobin; therefore, it has been assumed that an increase in hemoglobin would increase the quantity of oxygen carried in the blood.

While research has shown that reductions in the normal hemoglobin content of blood will decrease oxygen consumption (Ekblom, Goldbarg, and Gullbring 1972), there is still debate over whether an increase in hemoglobin beyond normal amounts will augment the oxygen supply.

Some experts feel that, at sea level, a normal amount of hemoglobin is sufficient to completely saturate the blood with oxygen (Doll 1973, Stainsby 1973, Kaijser 1973). They reason, therefore, that an increase in hemoglobin could not increase the oxygen supply. They also point out that, during exercise, reductions in the oxygen saturation of the blood can be compensated for by an increase in oxygen extraction by the working muscles.

While these arguments may be valid, there is a possibility that an increase in oxygen extraction would not compensate for reductions in oxygen saturation, particularly during maximal efforts. Certainly at altitudes where the oxygen saturation is severely reduced, a condition known as *hypoxia*, better performances have been associated with an increase in red blood cells (Keul, Doll, and Keppler 1972). Whether hypoxia occurs during maximal exercise at sea level remains to be seen. If it does, increasing hemoglobin content would improve performance. Under no circumstances should athletes allow their hemoglobin levels to fall below normal (a condition known as *anemia*), or their performances will surely suffer. Anemia can be prevented by including adequate amounts of iron in the diet. More will be said about this subject in a later chapter on nutrition.

The significance of an increase in blood volume after training is that an increase in plasma accompanies the increase in red blood cells (Kjellberg, Rudhe, and Sjöstrand 1949; Oscai, Williams, and Hertig 1968) so that the blood does not become too thick (viscous). Greater viscosity would have the effect of reducing the rate of blood flow.

In some cases the increase in plasma volume is proportionally greater than the increase in red blood cells, which is a desired training effect because it should improve the flow rate (Wilmore 1977). There is one problem associated with a training-induced increase in plasma volume. The dilution of red blood cells may cause athletes to appear anemic, a condition known as *false anemia*. This is because an increase in plasma volume will cause the relative concentration of red blood cells in the plasma to decrease even though training has actually increased the total number of red blood cells. This may account for the relatively frequent reports of anemia among athletes.

Little evidence is available concerning the best training procedures for producing increases in blood volume and red blood cells. However, moderate to high-intensity middle-distance swims with short rest periods should be an effective method for producing these adaptations. These swims create a great demand for oxygen and may also produce the hypoxia that precipitates training increases in blood volume and red blood cells.

Adaptations in Muscle Cells That Improve Oxygen Consumption

Oxygen diffuses from the blood across the cell membrane and into the muscle cells. It is transported across the sarcoplasm of the cells to the mitochondria by myoglobin. Once in the mitochondria, the oxygen is utilized to metabolize pyruvate in the citric acid cycle and electron transport chain. Therefore, increases in the myoglobin content of muscles and increases in the mitochondria could be expected to augment oxygen extraction.

Endurance training has repeatedly been reported to increase both the size and number of mitochondria (Morgan et al. 1971; Kiessling, Piehl, and Lundquist 1971). Myoglobin content has also been shown to increase with endurance training (Pattengale and Holloszy 1967). Endurance training also increases the activity of certain of the enzymes located in the mitochondria that are involved in aerobic metabolism. These enzymes regulate the oxidation of pyruvate and hydrogen ions to CO_2 and H_2O. Some of these enzymes and their functions are listed in Table 8.1. An increase in the activity of these enzymes should have the same effect as an increase in the number and size of mitochondria. That is, aerobic glycolysis could proceed at a faster rate so that there is less need for anaerobic glycolysis and fatigue will be delayed.

Table 8.1   *Enzymes of the Citric Acid Cycle Electron Transport Chain and Lipid Metabolism*

Enzyme	Function
Citric acid cycle	
Pyruvate dehydrogenase (PDN)	Regulates conversion of pyruvate to acetyl Co-A for entry into the citric acid cycle
Citrate synthase	Regulates conversion of acetyl Co-A and oxaloacetate to citric acid
Aconitase	Regulates conversion of citric acid to isocitrate
Isocitrate dehydrogenase (IDN)	Regulates conversion of isocitrate to α-keto-glutarate
α-ketoglutarate dehydrogenase	Regulates conversion of α-ketoglutarate to succinyl Co-A
Succinic thiokinase	Regulates conversion of succinyl Co-A to succinic acid
Succinate dehydrogenase (SDH)	Regulates conversion of succinic acid to fumaric acid
Fumarase	Regulates conversion of fumaric acid to malic acid
Malate dehydrogenase (MDA)	Regulates conversion of malic acid to oxaloacetate
Electron transport chain	
Cytochromes a, b, c	Transport electrons through chain for resynthesis of ATP and formation of H_2O
Lipid metabolism	
Lipoprotein lipase (LPL)	Regulates release of free fatty acids from triglycerides
Carnitine palmytil transferase	Regulates transport of fatty acids into the mitochondria where they can be metabolized in the citric acid cycle to provide energy for ATP resynthesis

The activity of one of the most prominent of the mitochondrial enzymes, succinate dehydrogenase, was found to increase between 38 and 95 percent in humans after training (Eriksson, Gollnick, and Saltin 1973; Costill 1978a; Gollnick, Armstrong, Saltin, Saubert, Sembrowich, and Shepard 1973).

Although these adaptations are associated with improvements in oxygen consumption, the mechanisms by which they increase the rate of oxygen extraction by muscles are unknown. One possible explanation is that an increase in the rate of aerobic glycolysis (that results from having more and larger mitochondria and greater activity of the mitochondrial enzymes) causes more oxygen to be used. This probably reduces the partial pressure of oxygen in the muscle cells so that a greater pressure differential between blood and muscles causes more oxygen to diffuse into the cell and be transported to the mitochondria in combination with myoglobin.

Increases in the size and number of mitochondria, increases in the activity of the mitochondrial enzymes, and increases in oxygen consumption seem to be encouraged most by endurance training programs and least by sprint training (Costill 1978; Holloszy 1967; Gollnick and King 1968; Barnard, Edgerton, and Peter 1970; Eriksson, Gollnick, and Saltin 1973; Gollnick, Armstrong, Saltin,

Saubert, Sembrowich, and Shepard 1973; Saltin et al. 1976). This is not surprising because sprint work would cause lactate to accumulate and in so doing reduce rather than increase the rate of aerobic glycolysis.

It should be mentioned that these increases in mitochondrial density and enzyme activity will occur only in muscle fibers that were used in the training process, a fact which has been verified by research (Costill et al. 1978, Gollnick and King 1968, Holloszy 1967). Therefore, if an improvement in oxygen extraction by muscles is desired, it is imperative that swimming be the form of training used by swimmers and that the competitive strokes be swum frequently in practice so they will be sure to train the same muscle fibers that are used in competition.

The Importance of Myoglobin to Oxygen Consumption

Myoglobin is a reddish pigment found in the cytoplasm of muscle cells. The red color comes from an iron-containing heme that is part of the structure of myoglobin. Oxygen is carried by myoglobin in combination with heme in a manner similar to that in which oxygen is carried in combination with blood hemoglobin. Myoglobin is found in greater quantity in slow twitch muscle fibers. It gives them their dark red appearance as compared to the pale pink color of fast twitch muscle fibers, which have a lower myoglobin content.

Myoglobin serves two important functions in the metabolic process: (1) it carries oxygen from the cytoplasm of the muscle cell to the mitochondria and (2) it serves as a storage system for small amounts of oxygen.

An increase in the rate with which myoglobin transports oxygen to the mitochondria may have considerable significance in middle-distance and distance races. The rate of aerobic metabolism could be increased and more pyruvate and hydrogen ions would be oxidized with less lactate being produced. Endurance training may increase the rate of oxygen transport by increasing the quantity of the "carrier" myoglobin. Pattengale and Holloszy (1967) found an increase of 80 percent in the myoglobin content of the hind legs of rats trained on a treadmill for twelve weeks. This was accompanied by a 600 percent improvement in running time to exhaustion. If similar increases occur in humans, the rate of oxygen extraction and transport by the muscles would be augmented considerably.

The storage function of myoglobin is thought to be insignificant where exercise is concerned because only a small amount, approximately 240 ml, of oxygen can be "stored" in the muscles. This oxygen can be transported to the mitochondria during the first few seconds of exercise, before oxygen from the atmosphere can be delivered to the muscles. However, such a small amount could only reduce lactate production for a few seconds at most and should have little bearing on the outcome of a middle-distance or distance race. Myoglobin-bound oxygen may play a significant role in the success of sprinters, however. An increase in myoglobin content could improve the oxygen supply enough in the early stages of a sprint race to reduce lactate production for the all-important few tenths of a second that can make the difference between winning and losing these races. More will be said about this in the next chapter in a discussion of the importance of distance training for sprinters.

Very few researchers have investigated the effects of training on the myoglobin content of muscles, therefore the best forms of training are not known. Submaximal distance swims and short rest repeats should be most effective for this purpose. This type of work should cause the myoglobin transport system to work at maximal or near maximal capacity to supply oxygen to the mitochondria. On the other hand, high-intensity sprints should be less effective because they cause lactate to accumulate before the demands for aerobic metabolism can stress the myoglobin-transport function sufficiently to produce an optimum training effect. Sprinting can supply a training stimulus by emptying myoglobin of oxygen during the first few seconds of effort. However, it should not create the sustained demand for oxygen transport that occurs with longer submaximal efforts and therefore should be less effective for producing an increase in myoglobin content.

The rest interval during short-rest repeat swimming should probably not be greater than 10 to 20 seconds if your goal is to increase the quantity of myoglobin in muscles. This is particularly true of short distance repeats (25 to 50 yards). At these distances, a longer rest period will allow the muscles' CP supply to be replaced. When this happens, CP, rather than the oxygen delivered to the mitochondria by myoglobin, becomes the primary source of energy for ATP replacement and the training stimulus for an increase in myoglobin should be considerably reduced (Saltin and Essen 1971).

Since myoglobin increases occur only in muscles that have been exercised (Holloszy 1973), it goes without saying that swimming your major stroke(s) in training is the safest way to insure maximum improvement.

The Concept of Limiting Factors in $\dot{V}O_2$ Max

All of the mechanisms listed in the previous sections can improve with training; however, they are not all equally important in the training process. Certain of these mechanisms are "weak links" in the oxygen transportation chain and therefore assume a position of greater concern. That is, they represent the phase of the process where the transportation system first becomes insufficient to supply all of the oxygen needed during exercise. These mechanisms are known as **limiting factors** because they are the first to reduce performance. The significance of a limiting factor is that since it is a "weak link" more of your training efforts must be focused on improving that mechanism rather than others in the metabolic chain. As mentioned earlier, there are three major physiological systems involved in transporting oxygen, the respiratory system, the circulatory system, and the muscular system. The respiratory system has not been found to be a limiting factor in oxygen consumption. It delivers more oxygen to the circulatory system than can be transported in the blood. During even the most strenuous exercise, you exhale more than half of the oxygen you inhale. Thus such respiratory mechanisms as the vital capacity and the number of functional alveoli are not considered limiting factors, and are not of particular concern in the training process. This leaves the circulatory and muscular systems to consider.

Until recently it was believed that the circulatory system was the weak link in the oxygen transportation chain. Experts felt the heart could not transport oxygen to the muscles as fast as it was needed during exercise. Therefore extensive research was conducted to determine the most effective training methods for increasing the transport of oxygen by the blood. The concern was so great that endurance training was equated with training the circulatory system, with the muscular system given little or no consideration except in sprint training.

The concept that the circulatory system is the major limiting factor in endurance performance is now being challenged. Some researchers believe the ability of the muscle cells to extract oxygen from the blood is the actual "weak link" in the chain. This belief is based on the discovery that, even during the most strenuous exercise, muscles do not extract all of the oxygen that is delivered to them by the circulatory system (Doll, Keul, and Maiwald 1968). Because more oxygen is transported to the muscles than they can absorb, it is reasoned that the extraction of oxygen by the muscles is the factor that limits performance—not the transportation of oxygen to the muscles. In fairness, it should be mentioned that some experts remain convinced that transportation of oxygen by the circulatory system is the major limiting factor in endurance exercise (Clausen et al. 1971, Balke 1973). Balke believes that contracting muscle fibers extract all of the oxygen from the blood that passes by and could take more if it was available. He further believes that the oxygen remaining in the blood after it leaves the muscles is carried by red blood cells that passed by fibers that were not contracting. He reasons, therefore, that the rate of transportation by the blood and not extraction by the muscles is still the limiting factor.

At the present time the experts take three positions on this issue. Some insist the circulatory system is the major limiting factor in endurance exercise. Others cautiously state that 50 percent of the increase in $\dot{V}O_2$ seen with training results from circulatory phenomena, while the remaining portion results from increased extraction of oxygen by the muscles (Holloszy 1973, p. 66). Still others, including this writer, are convinced that improved extraction by muscle cells is responsible for most of that increase. This controversy has important implications for training.

Since we have only one heart that functions during any type of exercise, any number of activities would be adequate for training the transport of oxygen by the circulatory system. If this is the case, activities such as running, circuit weight training, water polo, racquetball, and others should have a beneficial effect on swimming performance and could be used in conjunction with or in place of swimming without fear of a reduced training effect.

On the other hand, if the major limiting factor is the extraction of oxygen by muscle cells, substituting other forms of exercise for swimming could prevent swimmers from attaining the maximum possible improvement in performance. It is known that training effects in the muscular system occur only in those fibers that have been exercised. We cannot be certain that the same muscle fibers are used in swimming as are used in other activities, i.e., running. Training with other forms of exercise than swimming is a questionable procedure. In addition, although kinesiological analysis reveals that many of the same muscles are used when swimming the four competitive strokes, we have no evidence that the work is being performed by the same muscle fibers within those muscles. Therefore, it is also advisable to swim your major stroke(s) frequently in training.

Does this mean we should dispense with the notion that nonspecific training will improve endurance and concentrate only on swimming the strokes used in competition at competition speed? It is too early to say. Information about the relative contributions of the central circulatory and muscular systems to oxygen consumption is at present too controversial to support any judgment. The variety afforded by nonspecific training is also an important factor to consider. Nevertheless, swimmers would be well advised to swim rather than train with other activities when facilities and motivation permit and to swim their major strokes frequently in practice.

The Anaerobic Threshold: A New Training Concept

Anaerobic threshold (AT) is a term that designates the exercise intensity at which the rate of lactic acid diffusion into the bloodstream exceeds its rate of removal from the blood. Actually, this term is a misnomer because anaerobic metabolism is occurring before the anaerobic threshold is reached. However, the lactate produced in the muscles is kept from raising the lactate concentration in the blood significantly above normal by the following mechanisms:

1. The aerobic metabolism of muscles becomes more efficient, reducing the need for anaerobic metabolism.
2. Lactate is metabolized in the working muscles.
3. It diffuses into adjacent resting muscle fibers.
4. It is removed from the blood by the heart, liver, and other muscles as rapidly as it accumulates.

When lactate production exceeds the ability of these mechanisms to dispose of it, the body has reached the anaerobic threshold.

The anaerobic threshold is expressed as the percentage of maximal oxygen consumption where excess lactate appears in the blood. Well-trained endurance athletes appear to reach their AT when working at efforts requiring them to consume oxygen at 85 to 90 percent of their maximal capacity (Costill 1970, MacDougall 1977, Londeree 1977). Excess lactate appears in the blood of untrained persons at efforts requiring only 50 to 60 percent of their $\dot{V}O_2$ max (Ekblom et al. 1968, Karlsson 1971, Londeree 1977). Londeree (1977) reported one untrained subject with an AT of 38 percent of $\dot{V}O_2$ max. The AT of well-trained athletes in nonendurance events has been reported at between 70 and 75 percent of $\dot{V}O_2$ max (Nagle et al. 1970). The difference in AT between well-trained endurance athletes and nonendurance athletes could be accounted for by differences in their forms of training or by differences in hereditary factors such as the proportions of fast twitch and slow twitch muscle fibers. Because slow twitch fibers have a greater capacity for aerobic metabolism than their fast twitch counterparts, athletes with a greater percentage of slow twitch fibers should produce less lactate during work. Unfortunately the relative contributions of training and heredity to the anaerobic threshold are not known at this time.

An explanation of the significance of a higher AT has been given by Mac-Dougall (1977), and adapted here to apply to competitive swimming. If two athletes who have $\dot{V}O_2$ max values of 5.0 liters/min were swimming at a pace that requires them to consume oxygen at 85 percent of $\dot{V}O_2$ max, the athlete with an AT that comes closest to or exceeds that percentage should be able to maintain that pace for a longer time because less lactate is accumulating in the muscles. Acidosis will be steadily increasing in the muscles of the athlete with the lower AT because that person will be producing more lactic acid and will not be able to remove it as rapidly. When acidosis becomes severe this swimmer will be forced to reduce swimming speed.

There is increasing agreement among exercise physiologists that improving the anaerobic threshold may be the most important training adaptation for improving performances in distance races—more important, perhaps, than improving $\dot{V}O_2$ max. This is because an improvement in the anaerobic threshold reflects not only increases in $\dot{V}O_2$ max, but also indicates a reduction in lactate production in working muscles and an increase in lactate removal. The anaerobic threshold involves all three physiological mechanisms.

The relationship between an improvement in the anaerobic threshold and $\dot{V}O_2$ max is obvious. If an athlete becomes capable of consuming more oxygen at maximum workloads, the amount consumed at any intensity below maximum should also be increased, which in turn will reduce the rate of lactate production at all percentages below $\dot{V}O_2$ max.

Those mechanisms that increase the rate of lactate removal are equally important to the anaerobic threshold. It has been shown that athletes with smaller VO_2 max have been able to work at higher rates of oxygen consumption than athletes with a larger VO_2 max without accumulating excess lactate (Costill 1970). Presumedly, more effective lactate removal allowed them to maintain a faster pace in spite of an inferior maximal oxygen consumption capacity.

This fact has been demonstrated most notably with the great marathon runner Derek Clayton (Costill 1970). Clayton had a lower VO_2 max than other distance runners of his time but he was able to run at 90 percent of that maximum value without accumulating excess lactate. Many runners with larger maximal oxygen consumption capacities could not match his pace because they could only work at 80 percent of VO_2 max or less without incurring acidosis. An example of how a high anaerobic threshold can compensate for a lower VO_2 is shown in Figure 8.3.

Athlete *A* has a VO_2 max of 70 ml/kg/min and an AT of 90 percent while athlete *B* has a VO_2 max of 80 ml/kg/min and an AT of 70 percent. When both are competing at a speed that requires an oxygen consumption of 60 ml/kg/min, athlete *A* would not be accumulating excess lactate in his blood because that speed would be below his anaerobic threshold (90 percent of 70/ml/kg/min equals 63 ml/kg/min). On the other hand, athlete *B* would be approaching acidosis.

Athlete A	Athlete B
$\dot{V}O_2$ max = 70 ml/kg/min	$\dot{V}O_2$ max = 80 ml/kg/min
AT = 90% of $\dot{V}O_2$ max	AT = 70% of $\dot{V}O_2$ max

At a speed requiring an oxygen consumption of 60 ml/kg/min, the two will be working at the following percentages of $\dot{V}O_2$ max:

$60 \div 70 = 86\%$	$60 \div 80 = 75\%$
Athlete A is working at approximately 86% of $\dot{V}O_2$ max, well below his anaerobic threshold.	Athlete B is working at approximately 75% of $\dot{V}O_2$ max, which is above his anaerobic threshold.

Figure 8.3. The relationship between anaerobic threshold and endurance capacity.

Since the anaerobic threshold is a recent training concept, there is little information available about training this mechanism. Fox (1975) has demonstrated that interval training efforts of 2 minutes duration, 7 in number, with approximately 90 seconds rest between efforts, were effective in reducing the accumulation of excess lactate in the blood. The fact that distance performers have higher AT's suggests that the aerobic type of training they engage in may be even more effective.

It is probable that any workload which causes excess lactate to accumulate will provide a stimulus for improving the anaerobic threshold. The advantage of distance swims and short-rest repeats at submaximal paces may be that more training can be done with less strain.

The Significance for Swimmers of Slow Twitch and Fast Twitch Muscle Fibers

A muscle biopsy technique pioneered in Sweden has permitted exercise physiologists to remove and study samples of muscle tissue. The significance of this

Figure 8.4. A sample of tissue from a muscle biopsy. This small piece of tissue was removed from a muscle and placed in a freezing tray. It will be frozen and mounted for microscopic examination.

development is that it is now possible to study directly the effects of exercise and training on muscles rather than inferring these effects from blood samples and gas analysis.

Large muscles such as the vastus lateralis, gastrocnemius, latissimus dorsi, and deltoid are biopsied because muscle samples can be removed with little danger of damaging nerves or blood vessels. A small incision is made through previously anesthetized skin, fascia, and muscle tissue. A small sample of muscle is removed with a biopsy needle. The sample is mounted and frozen. The photograph in Figure 8.4 shows a sample of muscle tissue that has just been removed being mounted and prepared for freezing. Later that sample will be sectioned, stained, and viewed under an electron microscope. These procedures make it possible to determine the proportion of the various types of fibers within the muscle, the size of the fibers, their glycogen, ATP, and CP content, and the activity of a wide assortment of enzymes. Muscle biopsies have revealed that human muscles contain two distinct types of fibers; slow twitch fibers, which are red in appearance, and fast twitch fibers, which are pale pink in appearance. In addition, several subtypes of fast twitch muscle fibers have been identified.

The Properties of Fast Twitch and Slow Twitch Muscle Fibers

Fast twitch (FT) muscle fibers are so named because they contract rapidly (30 to 50 times per second). Slow twitch muscle fibers contract at a slower rate (10 to 15 times per second). Another important difference between the two fiber types concerns their capacities for work of either an endurance or power nature. Slow twitch muscle fibers have more endurance because of their greater capacity for aerobic metabolism. They do not have a great capacity for anaerobic metabolism, however. Fast twitch muscle fibers possess a greater ability to metabolize energy anaerobically but fatigue more rapidly because of their limited capacity for aerobic metabolism.

The greater capacity of slow twitch fibers for aerobic metabolism results from several factors:

1. A myoglobin content that is 2 to 5 times greater than that of fast twitch fibers (Keul, Doll, and Keppler 1972). The myoglobin gives ST fibers their red color.
2. ST fibers have more and larger mitochondria and greater activity of the aerobic enzymes located within the mitochondria (Costill, Fink, and Pollock 1976; Howald 1975; Keul, Doll, and Keppler 1972; Pette and Staudte 1973). This makes it possible to prevent lactate accumulation by oxidizing more pyruvate.
3. ST fibers also have more capillaries around each fiber (Baldwin et al. 1972, Prins 1978). This should increase the rate of oxygen diffusion into and the rate of waste product diffusion out of these fibers.
4. ST fibers have greater lipid content and an increased activity of those enzymes involved in lipid metabolism (Pette and Staudte 1973; Howald 1975; Keul, Doll, and Keppler 1972). This allows them to rely less on glycolysis and in so doing to save muscle glycogen.

The fast twitch fibers have greater anaerobic capacity for the following reasons:

1. While the ATP and glycogen content of the two types of muscle fibers appear to be similar (Gollnick and Hermansen 1973, Pette and Staudte 1973), fast twitch fibers contain more creatine phosphate and the activity of the enzymes involved in the release of energy from the ATP-CP reaction is greater. This explains why FT fibers can contract rapidly for the first 10 to 20 seconds of exercise.

2. The enzymes involved in anaerobic glycolysis are more active than in ST muscle fibers (Lamb 1978; Keul, Doll, and Keppler 1972; Pette and Staudte 1973). This makes it possible for FT fibers to contract at nearly maximum speed for longer periods of time.

3. FT fibers also appear to have about 12 percent more total protein and greater quantities of sarcoplasmic Ca^{++} than ST fibers (Keul, Doll, and Keppler 1972). Ca^{++} "triggers" the contractile process; therefore, an increased quantity should allow rapid contractions to occur over a longer time.

Most muscles contain both fast twitch and slow twitch muscles fibers. The percentage of each varies according to the type of work performed by a given muscle. For example, postural muscles tend to contain a greater percentage of ST fibers and, consequently, are redder in color. Flexor muscles contain more FT fibers and are more pink.

In addition to different proportions of fast and slow twitch fibers occurring in the different muscles of the same person, there is evidence that the percentages of each fiber type within a given muscle will differ from one person to another. Variations have been found to be quite large (Houston 1978a). In one person certain muscles may contain more than 80 percent ST fibers while in another person, the same muscles may have 80 percent FT fibers. Experts have theorized that athletes with a preponderance of FT fibers should have an advantage in the events that require speed of movement. On the other hand, they would be at a disadvantage in endurance events. Athletes with more ST fibers are thought to possess the potential to excel in endurance events, but are at a disadvantage when sprinting. People with approximately equal distributions of the two fiber types—and that includes most of the human population—have greater potential in middle distance events, where some speed and some endurance are needed, but they may not have the potential to excel at either end of the spectrum. Research has partially confirmed these theories in some sports.

While there have been exceptions, muscle biopsies have revealed that the majority of successful endurance athletes possess more slow twitch fibers in the muscles that they use in performance while the reverse was true of athletes who excelled in sprint events. That is, sprinters' muscles have had a greater percentage of FT fibers (Costill, Fink, and Pollock 1976; Costill, Daniels et al. 1976; Prince, Hikida, and Hagerman 1976; Saltin et al. 1977; Gollnick et al. 1972; Forsberg et al. 1976).

Table 8.2   *Properties of Fast Twitch and Slow Twitch Muscle Fibers*

Property	FTa	FTb	ST
Contractile speed	fast	fast	slower
Capacity for anaerobic metabolism	greater	greater	lesser
Capacity for aerobic metabolism	lesser	least	greatest
Endurance	lesser	least	greatest
Power	greater	greater	lesser
Mitochondria	less	least	most
Capillaries	less	least	most
Anaerobic enzyme activity	greater	greater	lesser
Aerobic enzyme activity	lesser	least	greatest
ATPase activity	more	more	less
CPK activity	more	more	less
Glycogen content		no difference	
ATP content		no difference	
CP content	more	more	less
Fat content	less	less	more
Protein content	more	more	less
Size[a]	larger	larger	smaller
Myoglobin content	less	least	most
Calcium content	more	more	least

[a]FT fibers are larger in the average person. This relationship can easily be changed with training. Well-trained endurance athletes usually have ST fibers that are larger than their FT counterparts while athletes trained for sprint and power events have even larger FT fibers than found in the average population.

A New Classification of Muscle Fiber Types

Recently it has been discovered that humans possess three subtypes of fast twitch muscle fibers. One subtype appears to have greater aerobic capacity and thus more endurance than the other subtypes. Saltin et al. (1977) have identified these muscle fibers as Fast Twitch *a* (FTa), Fast Twitch *b* (FTb), and Fast Twitch *c* (FTc). Brooke and Kaiser (1970) have proposed a different classification scheme: they have labeled slow twitch fibers Type I and fast twitch, Type II. Within the fast twitch classification, the three subgroups are labeled types IIa, IIb, and IIc. You may run across this classification scheme in the literature. The classification method proposed by Saltin and associates will be used here.

The FTa fibers have greater aerobic capacity than either of the other two subtypes (although they do not equal ST fibers in this respect). Their increased capacity with respect to the other two subgroups is probably due to more and larger mitochondria, increased capillary density, greater myoglobin content, and greater activity of aerobic enzymes. The known differences among the various types of muscle fibers are summarized in Table 8.2.

Most people possess approximately 50 percent ST fibers and 50 percent FT fibers, with FTa and FTb fibers at approximately 25 percent each. The number of FTc fibers is usually quite small and is therefore discounted. A sample of muscle tissue is shown in Figure 8.5. The various fiber types are designated.

Figure 8.5. A magnified sample of biopsied rectus femoris muscle. This sample shows that the subject's muscle tissue contains 43 percent slow-twitch fibers (ST) and 57 percent fast-twitch fibers. Of the fast-twitch fibers, 35 percent are FT*a* fibers, and 25 percent are FT*b* fibers.

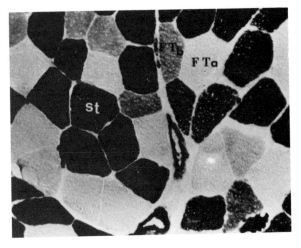

Can Sprint or Distance Ability Be Predicted from Muscle Biopsies?

As indicated previously, research has shown that athletes with a high percentage of FT muscle fibers excel at sprinting while those with a high percentage of ST fibers do better in the distance races. (Although there have been exceptions to these observations, they are true in the majority of cases.) It should be noted that the research referred to has focused on athletes in track. Does this mean that we can select a swimmer's best event by determining the percentages of the various fiber types in his or her swimming muscles? The answer to this question is probably no. The time and distance differences in swimming events are not as great as those in track. A 100-meter swim is not a sprint in the sense that a 100-meter dash is a sprint. Nor is the 1,650 in the same category as a marathon, where distance races are concerned.

In swimming, sprinters require more anaerobic and aerobic glycolytic capacity than runners because their events last long enough to reach high levels of lactate accumulation (The 50 is an exception to this statement.) Distance swimmers, although supplying much of their energy by aerobic glycolysis, compete in events requiring speeds that also make considerable demand on their anaerobic processes. We would expect sprint swimmers, because their events are longer, to have more slow twitch muscle fibers than sprint runners, while distance swimmers, because their events are shorter should probably have a greater percentage of fast twitch muscle fibers than the majority of distance runners. Thus, it is no surprise when Costill reports, "the majority of swimmers we have studied have fiber compositions in the deltoid muscle that range from 30 to 68 percent ST" (Costill and Maglischo 1979). A range of 10 to 90 percent ST fibers has been observed among sprint and distance runners respectively.

Since the difference between the percentage of FT and ST muscle fibers is usually less among sprint and distance swimmers, it seems reasonable to assume that sprint swimmers with less than the ideal percentage of FT muscle fibers could compensate through training, stroke efficiency, pace, and strategy, while distance swimmers with less than the ideal percentage of ST muscle fibers could do likewise. Of course, there may be limits to an athlete's ability to compensate. For example, a swimmer with 80 percent FT fibers may never swim a national-class 1,500 meters while an athlete with 80 percent ST fibers may never swim a national-class 50 or 100 race.

Swimmers who possess 40 to 70 percent FT fibers should be able to excel in events ranging from sprints to middle distance. A greater proportion of FT fibers might prove an advantage in the 50 but a disadvantage in longer events. (So-called "drop-dead" sprinters may have in excess of 80 percent FT fibers, although this has not been verified by research.) Swimmers with 40 percent or more ST fibers can probably achieve success in any event of 400 meters or longer. With proper training they may also swim an excellent 200. Of course, all of these observations concerning fiber type and event selection are based on supposition, not research, and may be proven inaccurate in time.

Fiber typing is probably of limited value where predicting success in certain swimming events is concerned. Muscle biopsies may only be useful for identifying people whose fiber type suits them for the very longest and shortest events. That is, swimmers with 80 percent or more FT fibers might be most successful in the 50 while those with 80 percent or more ST fibers are better suited for the 1,650. However, swimmers must compete at several distances, and the possibility is great that training can compensate for less than ideal fiber distribution. Consequently, the information that can be gained from actual fiber typing of individual athletes is probably not necessary. However, swimmers and coaches can apply general knowledge about muscle fibers to formulate effective training programs.

How Are Slow Twitch and Fast Twitch Fibers Used During Work?

According to Henneman and Olson (1965), the FT and ST muscle fiber groups are innervated by neurons with differing thresholds for excitability. Fast twitch fibers are innervated by large neurons that can only be stimulated when the demand for force is great. Hence, large numbers of FT fibers contract only when the demand for force is great, as in sprinting, or when fatigue increases the force required to maintain a certain pace during distance swims. ST fibers are connected to smaller neurons that are easily excited. At low levels of effort (distance swimming), ST fibers tend to be used in preference to FT fibers, whereas at high levels of effort they are used in addition to the FT fibers (Costill 1978a).

It was once thought that only FT muscle fibers were used when sprinting and that only ST fibers contracted at slow speeds. We now know that while ST fibers do most of the work at slow speeds, both ST and FT fibers are used when sprinting. This is because when sprinting the demand for force is great enough to stimulate both fiber types, while at slow paces the stimulation is not great enough to activate a large number of FT fibers and most of the work is done by the ST group. The so-called "ramp effect" of muscular contraction is illustrated in Figure 8.6. It shows that swimming speeds must be near maximal before a significant number of FT fibers are recruited to the effort.

Although both fiber types are activated when swimming at near maximal speeds, the FT fibers will do most of the work because of their ability to metab-

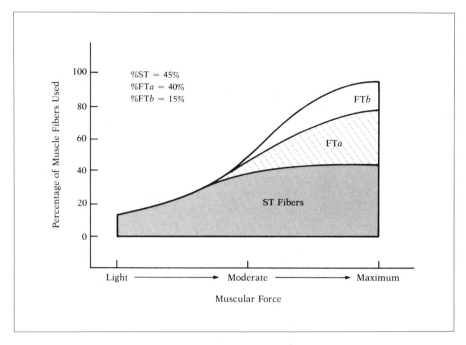

Figure 8.6. The ramp effect of muscular contraction. (Adapted from Costill, Sharp, and Troup, "Muscle Strength Combinations to Sprint Swimming," *Swimming World*, 21 [1980], p. 30, fig. 2, by permission of the publisher.)

olize glycogen anaerobically and thus release energy at a rate that will meet the demands of the swimmer's speed. However, they will also produce more lactic acid and the swimmer will fatigue more quickly.

The energy supplied by each fiber type can be determined from biopsies taken before and after swims of varying distances and speeds. If the glycogen content of one fiber type is considerably reduced compared to that of others, then that fiber supplied most of the energy during the swim.

Costill (1978a) found that FT fibers were the first to become depleted when swimmers completed a set of sixty 100-yard repeats with 1 minute rest intervals between repeats. However, the ST fibers were also empty at the completion of the set. During repeated 400 swims, the ST fibers were depleted first, although the FT fibers were also depleted by the end of the set.

Results of laboratory research using ergometers can add to our knowledge concerning the probable patterns of fiber recruitment if we match the time of the laboratory work periods to the time for certain swimming events. Energy metabolism is dependent on time and effort more than distance and activity. Therefore, where the recruitment of certain fiber types is concerned, a 45-second all-out effort on a bicycle ergometer would be similar to a 100-yard swim.

Although the muscle groups doing the work differ in the two activities (legs for bicycle riding and arms for swimming), the patterns of fiber recruitment should be similar.

The graph in Figure 8.7 shows the glycogen depletion pattern for a sprint workout consisting of six 1-minute all-out rides on a bicycle ergometer and a distance race of 30 kilometers. Notice that the FT fibers were depleted of glycogen to a greater extent during the rides (Costill et al. 1971). On the other

Figure 8.7. Glycogen depletion patterns during sprint and endurance exercise. The graphs illustrate the glycogen depletion patterns during (**A**) six 1-minute bicycle rides at maximum effort and (**B**) one 30-kilometer run. Samples of muscle tissue were taken before the run and at 20 and 30 kilometers. Notice that the FT muscle fibers are depleted more completely than the ST fibers during the rides. The reverse occurred during the run: The ST muscle fibers were depleted of glycogen more completely than the FT muscle fibers.

(Adapted from Gollnick, Armstrong, Sembrowich, Shepherd, and Saltin, "Glycogen Depletion Pattern in Human Skeletal Muscle Fibers After Heavy Exercise," *J. Appl. Physiol.*, 34 [1973], p. 617, fig. 3; and Costill, Gollnick, Saltin, Jannson, Saltin, and Stein, "Glycogen Depletion Patterns in Human Muscle Fibers During Distance Running," *Acta Physiol. Scand.*, 89 [1973], p. 378, fig. 3, by permission of the authors and publishers.)

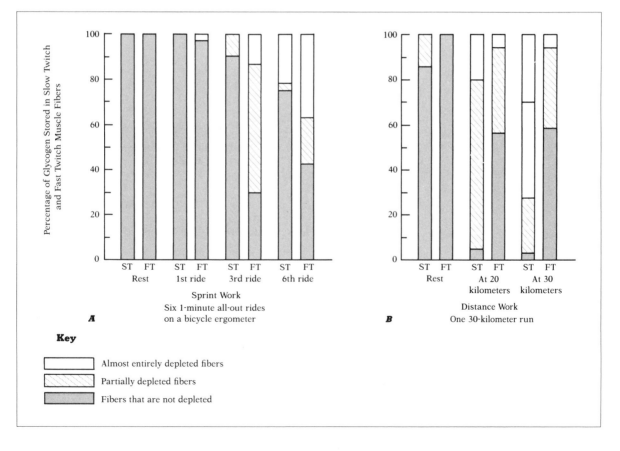

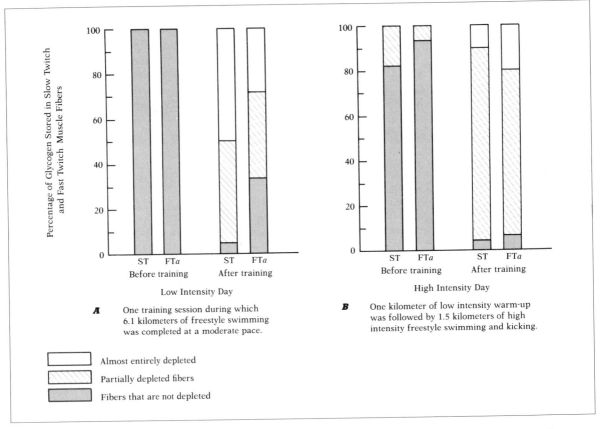

Figure 8.8. Glycogen depletion patterns during two successive days of swim training. (Adapted from M.E. Houston, "Metabolic Responses to Exercise with Special Reference to Training and Competition in Swimming," *Swimming Medicine IV*, ed. B. Eriksson and B. Furberg [Baltimore: University Park Press, 1978], p. 222, fig. 4, by permission of the author and publisher.)

hand the ST muscle fibers were depleted more completely during the run (Costill et al. 1973). The rectus femoris was the muscle from which the samples were taken.

Houston (1978b) showed a similar pattern of glycogen depletion during alternating days of high-and low-intensity swimming training. The results are shown in Figure 8.8. On the low-intensity day, the swimmers completed 6.1 km of freestyle swimming at a moderate pace. The repeat distances varied from 50 to 400 meters with short rests. On the high-intensity day, the swimmers warmed up with five 200-meter swims at low intensity and then swam and kicked 1.15 kilometers of long rest repeats at distances of 25 to 100 meters. These repeats were completed at near maximum speed. While the test for glycogen depletion showed that both ST and FT fibers were used on both training days, more ST than FT fibers were depleted or partially depleted on the low-intensity day, while the ST and FTa fibers were nearly equally depleted during the high-intensity day.

What can this information teach us about training? We can see that FT fibers supply most of the energy in sprints (observe the glycogen depletion pattern during the first 1-minute ride in fig. 8.7) while they are not used nearly so much during distance swims (see the low-intensity graph in fig. 8.8). Therefore, if sprinters expect to improve the anaerobic capacity of FT fibers, they will have to sprint frequently in practice. In addition, they will need to swim the strokes they use in competition. The training adaptations that will take place occur only in muscle fibers that are exercised. The only way to be absolutely certain the muscle fibers being used in training are those that will be used in competition is to swim the same stroke that will be used in races. While sprinters must sprint to train the anaerobic capacity of FT muscle fibers, distance swimmers will need to swim long repeats or short repeats with short rests in order to train the aerobic capacity of both the ST and FT fibers. Middle-distance swimmers face the problem of training the aerobic and anaerobic capacities of both fiber types.

These observations are simplistic and may be easily misinterpreted to mean that sprinters should only sprint in practice and that distance swimmers should swim only distance. This is not the case. Every swimmer requires a combination of all types of training to achieve a peak performance. The difference is in the proportions of each type of training they complete. Sprinters should spend more time sprinting in practice, while distance swimmers should spend more time on long swims and short rest repeats. Middle-distance swimmers should do less sprinting but more distance than sprinters and less distance and more sprinting than distance swimmers. Suggested proportions of each type of training will be discussed, by event, in a later chapter.

Other implications are that swimmers may need to engage in some form of cycle training that permits partial recovery of certain fiber types from day to day and that they should pay careful attention to the carbohydrate intake in their diets so that the greatest possible repletion of muscle glycogen occurs between training sessions.

Figure 8.8 shows, in graphic form, that one 2-½ hour practice session per day can cause over half of the muscle fibers used in training to be almost entirely depleted of glycogen. Therefore, it is quite likely that most muscle fibers would be completely depleted of glycogen when training is increased to two sessions per day. Judging from the results of this study, swimmers should eat at least three meals per day. Each meal should be high in carbohydrate content. It has been shown that muscle glycogen repletion is faster when high-carbohydrate meals are eaten within a few hours after exercise (Costill 1978b). It might also be wise to intersperse low-intensity and higher-intensity training days so that each fiber type has additional time for repletion. It requires 24 to 48 hours for complete repletion of muscle glycogen (Hultman, Bergström, and Roch-Norlund 1971; MacDougall et al. 1975).

Can Fiber Types Be Changed by Training?

A few years ago the answer to the question of whether fiber types can be changed by training would have been no. Today it is maybe. When four athletes were trained aerobically for 18 weeks, muscle biopsies revealed an increase in the percentage of ST muscle fibers and a decrease in the percentage of FTc fibers. When the same group of athletes were subjected to 11 weeks of anaerobic training a reverse effect was noted. That is, there was an increase in the percentage of FTc muscle fibers and a decrease in the percentage of ST fibers.

These findings suggest that training may cause an actual conversion of ST fibers to FT fibers and vice versa with the FTc fibers being the medium for transformation (Jansson, Sjödin, and Tisch 1978). The direction of change was apparently specific to the type of training which indicates the intriguing possibility that sprint training could increase the number of FT muscle fibers and that distance training could increase the number of ST muscle fibers.

Since these results are based on data from only four subjects, more research is needed before a definite statement can be made concerning the effect of training on athletes' inherited proportions of FT and ST muscle fibers. In the meantime, a growing volume of research indicates that training of a specific nature can produce two very significant changes within each of the two groups of muscle fibers that will improve performance.

There is evidence that specific training can cause ST muscle fibers to become faster contracting and FT fibers more enduring. Secondly, recent research indicates that training may stimulate cell division (fiber splitting) that would increase the total number of fibers of a particular type within a muscle.

Regarding the metabolic adaptations of muscle fibers, Gollnick, Armstrong, Saltin, Saubert, Sembrowich, and Shepard (1973) found the contractile speed of ST fibers was increased by six months of sprint training on a bicycle ergometer. The contractile speed of the ST muscle fibers never equaled that of the FT fibers, however. They also observed the ST fibers lost some of their aerobic capacity, a fact that could have important implications for training.

While the mechanism for increasing the contractile speed of ST fibers is not known, several researchers are of the opinion that training increases the endurance of FT fibers by increasing the FTa population. Nygaard and Nielsen (1978) found a large number of FTa but no FTb fibers in the upper body muscles (middle deltoid and latissimus dorsi) of a group of swimmers who had been in training for three to eight years. They expected these muscles would contain 15 to 20 percent FTb fibers, which was the range found in a control population of males and females from the same age group. The researchers' belief that training, rather than heredity, was responsible for the absence of FTb fibers in the upper body musculature of the swimmers was substantiated by the presence of a small number of FTb fibers in the quadriceps muscles of their legs. It was assumed that the presence of FTb fibers in the legs indicated that the upper body muscles had also contained FTb fibers before training.

Additional evidence of increases in the FTa fiber population has been presented by Costill, Daniels et al. (1976) and Houston (1978a). Costill and his associates found only 2.2 percent FTb fibers in the gastrocnemius muscles of distance runners. A group of trained kayakers observed by Houston had only

8.5 percent FTb fibers in their biceps, but 13 percent FTb fibers in the vastus lateralis muscles of their legs.

One possible explanation for the reduction or complete absence of FTb fibers in the FT population is that training causes FT fibers to become more oxidative so that, when stained, they are classified as FTa subtypes rather than FTb. Thus, the FTa fibers may be "trained" FT muscle fibers and FTb fibers may be untrained or partially trained.

Another possible explanation for larger percentage of FTa fibers may be that training causes an actual increase in the total number of these fibers. Regarding this possibility, evidence is accumulating that training can cause muscle fibers to undergo cell division. The idea that training increased the number of muscle fibers was abandoned years ago but is being reconsidered today. Gonyea, Ericson, and Bonde-Peterson (1977) have demonstrated cell division in cats that were trained by lifting heavy weights. Fiber splitting occurred in both the ST and FT fibers although the increase in the number of FT fibers was greater. (FT fibers would be expected to divide more rapidly because of the intense nature of the exercise.) Ho et al. (1980) reported similar results with rats.

Along this same line, studies by Nygaard and Nielsen (1978) and Costill, Coyle et al. (1978) have provided indirect evidence of fiber splitting in humans. Whereas Gonyea and his associates and Ho and his co-workers actually observed the splitting of fibers, these researchers have based their theories of cell division in humans on changes in the percentages of the various fiber types that are produced by training.

The research of Nygaard and Nielsen (1978) is particularly significant because it involved competitive swimmers. They performed muscle biopsies on a group of 25 male and female swimmers, ages 15 to 17. The swimmers had been training for 3 to 8 years. The researchers based their contention of fiber splitting on the following observations:

1. The swimmers possessed more muscle mass than an age- and sex-matched control group, yet their fibers were smaller.
2. Some extremely small fibers were found between fibers of normal size.
3. There were incisions in the cell membranes that almost split some fibers in two.

Nygaard and Nielsen believed these observations were indicative that the total number of muscle fibers had increased through fiber splitting.

Costill, Fink, Foster, and Ivy (1978) reported that FTa fibers increased 4 percent (from 29.2 percent to 33 percent) in the leg muscles of men trained with high-speed isokinetic exercises. This in itself is not evidence of fiber splitting. However, the percentage of FTb fibers decreased by only 0.8 percent and the ST fiber population decreased by 7.7 percent. If FTb fibers were taking on the properties of FTa fibers or even if ST fibers were becoming like FT fibers, the percentage increase in FTa fibers should have been in proportion to the decrease in the other two fiber types. On the other hand, if an increase in the absolute number of FTa fibers had occurred, the percentage increase of those

Table 8.3 *Changes in the Percentages of Slow Twitch and Fast Twitch Muscle Fibers with Sprint Training*

Fiber type	Pretraining percentages	Posttraining percentages
ST	46.5 ($\pm$ 3)	38.8 ($\pm$ 5)
FTa	29.2 ($\pm$ 3)	33.0 ($\pm$ 2)
FTb	24.3 ($\pm$ 2)	23.5 ($\pm$ 2)

Source: Data from Costill, Fink, Foster, and Ivy, "Adaptations in Skeletal Muscle of Juvenile Diabetics During Physical Training" (Unpublished research study, 1978), used by permission of the authors.

fibers would be out of proportion to decreases of the other fiber types. That is exactly what happened, so the researchers were led to believe that training could cause FTa fibers to increase in number. The data from this study are summarized in Table 8.3.

Judging from these two studies, it seems probable that in human muscle tissue, fiber splitting occurs in the FTa fiber subgroups. Nygaard and Nielsen's (1978) finding of no FTb fibers in the upper body muscles of swimmers seems to indicate that FTb fibers are also taking on the aerobic properties associated with FTa fibers. If fiber splitting in the FTa subgroup had been the only training adaptation taking place, there should have been a small percentage of FTb fibers in these muscles as well, especially since a small percentage of FTb fibers were found in the leg muscles of those same swimmers.

It is not known whether fiber splitting also takes place in the ST fibers of humans. Gonyea, Ericson, and Bonde-Peterson (1977) and Ho, et al. (1980) demonstrated cell division in the ST fibers of cats and rats respectively; however, to date, no evidence has been presented of this occurring in humans.

If fiber splitting does take place in humans, whether in the FTa population only or in the ST population as well, it could be the most important adaptation to training where improved performances are concerned. An increase in the total number of fibers would be advantageous to athletic performance, particularly if that increase occurred in the fiber type that provided most of the energy for a particular athlete's best event(s). An increase in FT (and ST) fibers would aid middle-distance and distance swimmers. Middle-distance swimmers would find that such increases permit faster paces with less fatigue because of the greater oxidative capacity of the fibers involved. Sprinters would find an increase in FTa fibers advantageous for the same reason. There would be a greater number of fibers available to increase power and more of those fibers would be able to supply energy without producing lactate in large quantities. Fiber splitting would also improve the potential for performance because the smaller fibers resulting from cell division have greater potential for growth than those that have already hypertrophied.

Can Distance Training Reduce Sprint Speed?

The observation of Gollnick, Armstrong, Saltin, Saubert, Sembrowich, and Shepard (1973) that sprint training increased the contractile speed of ST fibers while also reducing their aerobic capacity poses a serious dilemma. If distance training should produce the opposite effect, that is, if gains in endurance were accompanied by decreases in speed, the performances of sprinters could be hampered by too much distance swimming. The possibility of such an effect occurring is particularly crucial in light of the preponderance of high-mileage programs in the U.S.

There is also the possibility that the shift of FTb to FTa fibers in swimmers reported by Nygaard and Nielsen (1978) could be speed limiting. This would be true only if the FTa fibers were the slower reacting of the two subtypes, however. In this respect, Secher and Nygaard (1976) have presented evidence that FTb fibers provide more energy than FTa and ST fibers during maximum resistance training. This preferential use could be indicative that FTb fibers are faster contracting, or capable of releasing energy at a faster rate anaerobically.

Although it is possible, based on these observations, that speed could be reduced by increases in the number of FTa fibers that result from endurance training, the possibility of this occurring is, in this writer's opinion, remote. This opinion is based on a study by Costill, Coyle et al. (1978) in which subjects were trained with 6- and 30-second maximum leg extension exercises. They found an increase in the FTa fiber population that was accompanied by increases in peak force and work output for 60 seconds. Thus, the shift of FTb to FTa fibers (and perhaps the fiber splitting in the FTa subgroup) did not limit speed. Of course, the subjects were sprint trained; nevertheless, the changes in the FT population were similar to those reported for subjects who had been endurance trained (Nygaard and Nielsen 1978).

The resolution of this apparent contradiction in the results of Secher and Nygaard and those of Costill and associates may be that the former studied the effects of a few bouts of exercise, whereas the latter observed the effects of several weeks of training. It is possible, as indicated by Secher and Nygaard, that FTb fibers are utilized preferentially during the first few days of training. Perhaps, then, over a period of weeks these fibers become more oxidative, and when stained they are identified as FTa fibers. This would account for the results of Costill and his associates.

REFERENCES

Andersen, P., and Sjøgaard, G. 1975. "Selective Glycogen Depletion in the Subgroup of Type II Muscle Fibers During Intense Submaximal Exercise in Man." *Acta Physiol. Scand.* 96:26A–27A.

Astrand, P. O., Engstrom, L., Eriksson, B. O., Karlberg, P., Nylander, I., Saltin, B., and Thoren, C. 1963. "Girl Swimmers." *Acta Paediat* (Suppl. 147):43–63.

Astrand, P. O., and Rodahl, K. 1977. *Textbook of Work Physiology.* New York: McGraw-Hill.

Baldwin, K. M., Klinkerfuss, G. H., Terjung, R. L., Molé, P. A., and Holloszy, J. O. 1972. "Respiratory Capacity of White, Red and Intermediate Muscle: Adaptive Response to Exercise." *Amer. J. Physiol.* 222:373–378.

Balke, B. 1973. "The Development of Higher Oxygen Intake Through Training." *Limiting Factors of Physical Performance*, ed. J. Keul, pp. 267–280. Stuttgart: Georg Thieme Verlag.

Barnard, R. J., Edgerton, V. R., and Peter, J. B. 1970. "Effect of Exercise on Skeletal Muscles: I. Biochemical and Histological Properties." *J. Appl. Physiol.* 28:762–766.

Bloom, W., and Fawcett, D. W. 1975. *A Textbook of Histology.* Philadelphia: W. B. Saunders Co.

Brodel, M. 1937. *Johns Hopkins Hospital Bulletin.* 61:295.

Brooke, M. H., and Kaiser, K. K. 1970. "Muscle Fiber Types: How Many and What Kinds." *Arch. of Neurol.* 23:369–379.

Carrow, R., Brown, R., and Van Huss, W. 1967. "Fiber Sizes and Capillary to Fiber Ratios in Skeletal Muscles of Exercised Rats." *Anat. Rec.* 159:33–38.

Clausen, J. P. 1969. "Effect of Physical Condition: A Hypothesis Concerning Circulatory Adjustments to Exercise." *Scand. J. Clin. Lab. Invest.* 24:305–313.

———. 1973. "Muscle Blood Flow During Exercise and Its Significance for Maximal Performance." *Limiting Factors of Physical Performance*, ed. J. Keul, pp. 253–265. Stuttgart: Georg Thieme Verlag 1973.

Clausen, J. P., Klausen, K., Rasmussen, B., Trap-Jensen, J. 1971. "Effect of Selective Arm and Leg Training on Cardiac Output and Regional Blood Flow." *Acta Physiol. Scand.* 82:35–36a.

Costill, D. L. 1970. "Metabolic Resources During Distance Running." *J. Appl. Physiol.* 28:251–255.

———. 1978a. "Adaptations in Skeletal Muscle During Training for Sprint and Endurance Swimming." *Swimming Medicine IV*, ed. B. Eriksson and B. Furberg, pp. 233–248. Baltimore: University Park Press.

———. 1978b. "Sports Nutrition: The Role of Carbohydrates." *Nutrition News* 41:1, 4.

Costill, D. L., Bowers, R., Branum, G., and Sparks, K. 1971. "Muscle Glycogen Utilization During Prolonged Exercise on Successive Days." *J. Appl. Physiol.* 31:834–838.

Costill, D. L., Coyle, E. F., Fink, W. J., Lesmes, G. R., and Witzman, F. A. 1978. "Adaptations in Skeletal Muscle Following Strength Training." Unpublished research study, Ball State University, Muncie, Indiana.

Costill, D. L., Daniels, J., Evans, W., Fink, W. J., Krahenbuhl, G., and Saltin, B. 1976. "Skeletal Muscle Enzymes and Fiber Composition of Male and Female Track Athletes." *J. of Appl. Physiol.* 40:149–153.

Costill, D. L., Fink, W. J., Foster, C., and Ivy, J. 1978. "Adaptations in Skeletal Muscle of Juvenile Diabetics During Physical Training." Unpublished research study, Ball State University, Muncie, Indiana.

Costill, D. L., Fink, W. J., and Pollock, M. L. 1976. "Muscle Fiber Composition and Enzyme Activities of Elite Distance Runners." *Med. Sci. Sports* 8:96–100.

Costill, D. L., Gollnick, P. D., Jansson, E., Saltin, B., and Stein, E. 1973. "Glycogen Depletion Patterns in Human Muscle Fibers During Distance Running." *Acta Physiol. Scand.* 89:374–383.

Costill, D. L., and Maglischo, E. W. 1979. "Muscle Biopsy Research: Application of Fiber Composition to Swimming." *1978 World Clinic Year Book*, ed. R. M. Ousley, pp. 47–54. Ft. Lauderdale, Fla.: American Swimming Coaches Association.

Costill, D. L., Sharp, R., and Troup, J. 1980. "Muscle Strength Contributions to Sprint Swimming." *Swimming World* 21:29–34.

Davis, J. A., Vodok, P., Wilmore, J., Vodok, J. and Kurtz, P. 1976. "Anaerobic Threshold and Maximal Aerobic Power for Three Modes of Exercise." *J. Appl. Physiol.* 41:544–550.

Doll, E. 1973. "Oxygen Pressure and Content in the Blood During Physical Exercise and Hypoxia." *Limiting Factors of Physical Performance*, ed. J. Keul, pp. 201–211. Stuttgart: Georg Thieme Verlag.

Doll, E., Keul, J., and Maiwald, C. 1968. "Oxygen Tension and Acid-base Equilibria in Venous Blood of Working Muscles." *Amer. J. Physiol.* 215:23–29.

Ekblom, B., Astrand, P. O., Saltin, B., Stenberg, J., and Wallström, B. 1968. "Effect of Training on Circulatory Responses to Exercise." *J. Appl. Physiol.* 24:518–528.

Ekblom, B., Goldbarg, A. N., and Gullbring, B. 1969. "Effect of Physical Training on the Oxygen Transport System in Man." *Acta Physiol. Scand.*, Supp. 328:1–45.

Ekblom, B., Goldbarg, A. N., and Gullbring, B. 1972. "Response to Exercise After Blood Loss and Reinfusion." *J. Appl. Physiol.* 33:175–180.

Eriksson, B. O., Berg, K., and Taranger, J. 1978. "Physiological Analysis of Young Boys Starting Intensive Training in Swimming." *Swimming Medicine IV*, ed. B. O. Eriksson and B. Furberg, pp. 143–160. Baltimore: University Park Press.

Eriksson, B. O., Gollnick, P. D., and Saltin, B. 1973. "Muscle Metabolism and Enzyme Activities After Training in Boys 11–13 Years Old." *Acta Physiol. Scand.* 87:485–497.

Forsberg, A., Tesch, P., Sjödin, B., Thorstensson, A., and Karlsson, J. 1976. "Skeletal Muscle Fibers and Athletic Performance." *Biomechanics V-A*, ed. P. V. Komi, pp. 112–117. Baltimore: University Park Press.

Fox, E. L. 1975. "Differences in Metabolic Alterations with Sprint versus Endurance Interval Training Programs." *Metabolic Adaptations to Prolonged Physical Exercise*, ed. H. Howald and J. R. Poortmans, pp. 119–126. Basel: Birkäuser Verlag.

Gollnick, P. D., Armstrong, R. B., Saltin, B., Saubert IV, C. W., Sembrowich, W. L., and Shepard, R. E. 1973. "Effect of Training on Enzyme Activity and Fiber Composition of Human Skeletal Muscle." *J. Appl. Physiol.* 34:107–111.

Gollnick, P. D., Armstrong, R. B., Saubert IV, C. W., Piehl, K., and Saltin, B. 1972. "Enzyme Activity and Fiber Composition in Skeletal Muscle of Untrained and Trained Men." *J. Appl. Physiol.* 33:312–319.

Gollnick, P. D., Armstrong, R. B., Sembrowich, W. L., Shepard, R. E., and Saltin, B. 1973. "Glycogen Depletion Patterns in Human Skeletal Muscle Fibers After Heavy Exercise." *J. Appl. Physiol.* 34:615–618.

Gollnick, P. D., and Hermansen, L. 1973. "Biochemical Adaptations to Exercise: Anaerobic Metabolism." *Exercise and Sport Sciences Review*, Vol. 1, ed. J. Wilmore, pp. 1–43. New York: Academic Press.

Gollnick, P. D., and King, D. W. 1968. "The Immediate and Chronic Effect of Exercise on the Number and Structure of Skeletal Muscle Mitochondria." *Biochemistry of Exercise*, Vol. 3, ed. J. R. Poortmans, pp. 239–244. Baltimore: University Park Press.

Gollnick, P. D., Piehl, K., and Saltin, B. 1974. "Selective Glycogen Depletion Patterns in Human Muscle Fibers After Exercise of Varying Intensity and at Varying Pedalling Rates." *J. Physiol.* 241:45–57.

Gonyea, W., Ericson, G. E., and Bonde-Peterson, F. 1977. "Skeletal Muscle Fiber Splitting Induced by Weight Lifting Exercise in Cats." *Acta Physiol. Scand.* 99(1):105–109.

Hanson, J., Tabakin, B., Levy, A., and Neede, W. 1968. "Long Term Physical Training and Cardiovascular Dynamics in Middle Aged Men." *Circulation* 38:783–799.

Hartley, L., Grimby, C., Kilblom, A., Nilsson, N., Astrand, P., Ekblom, B., and Saltin, B. 1969. "Physical Training in Sedentary Middle Aged and Older Men: III. Cardiac Output and Gas Exchange at Submaximal and Maximal Exercise." *Scand. J. Clin. Lab. Invest.* 24:335–344.

Henneman, E., and Olson, C. B. 1965. "Relation Between Structure and Function in the Design of Skeletal Muscle." *J. Neurophysiology* 28:581–598.

Hermansen, L., and Wachlova, M. 1971. "Capillary Density of Skeletal Muscle in Well-trained and Untrained Men." *J. Appl. Physiol.* 30:860–863.

Ho, K. E., Roy, R. R., Tweedle, C. D., Heusner, W. W., Van Huss, W. D., and Carrow, R. E. 1980. "Skeletal Muscle Fiber Splitting with Weight Lifting Exercise in Rats." *Amer. J. of Anat.*, 157:433–440.

Holloszy, J. O. 1967. "Biochemical Adaptations in Muscle: Effect of Exercise on Mitochondrial Oxygen Uptake and Respiratory Enzyme Activity in Skeletal Muscle." *J. Biol. Chem.* 242:2278–2282.

———. 1973 "Biochemical Adaptations to Exercise: Aerobic Metabolism." *Exercise and Sport Sciences Review*, Vol. 1, ed. J. Wilmore, pp. 45–71. New York: Academic Press.

Holmer, I., Stein, E. M., Saltin, B., Ekblom, B., and Astrand, P. O. 1974. "Hemodynamic and Respiratory Responses in Swimming and Running." *J. Appl. Physiol.* 37:49–54.

Houston, M. E. 1978a. "The Use of Histochemistry in Muscle Adaptation: A Critical Assessment." *Canadian J. Appl. Sport Sci.* 3:109–118.

———. 1978b. "Metabolic Responses to Exercise with Special Reference to Training and Competition in Swimming. *Swimming Medicine IV*, pp. 207–232. Baltimore: University Park Press.

Howald, H. 1975. "Ultrastructural Adaptation of Skeletal Muscles to Prolonged Physical Exercise." *Metabolic Adaptations to Prolonged Physical Exercise*, ed. H. Howald and J. R. Poortmans, pp. 372–383. Basel: Birkäuser Verlag.

Hultman, E., Bergström, J., and Roch-Norland, A. E. 1971. "Glycogen Storage in Human Skeletal Muscle." *Muscle Metabolism During Exercise*, ed. B. Pernow and B. Saltin, pp. 273–287. New York: Plenum Press.

Jansson, E., Sjödin, B., and Tisch, P. 1978. "Changes in Muscle Fiber Type Distribution in Man After Physical Training." *Acta Phys. Scand.* 104:235–237.

Kaijser, L. 1973. "Oxygen Supply as a Limiting Factor in Physical Performance." *Limiting Factors of Physical Performance*, ed. J. Keul, pp. 145–155. Stuttgart: Georg Thieme Verlag.

Karlsson, J. 1971. "Muscle ATP-CP and Lactate in Submaximal and Maximal Exercise." *Muscle Metabolism During Exercise*, ed. B. Pernow and B. Saltin, pp. 383–393. New York: Plenum Press.

Keul, J., Doll, E., and Keppler, D. 1972. *Energy Metabolism of Human Muscle.* Baltimore: University Park Press.

Kiessling, K. H., Piehl, K., and Lundquist, C-G. 1971. "Effect of Physical Training on Ultrastructural Features in Human Skeletal Muscle." *Muscle Metabolism During Exercise*, ed. B. Pernow and B. Saltin, pp. 97–101. New York: Plenum Press.

Kjellberg, S. R., Rudhe, V., and Sjöstrand, T. 1949. "Increase of the Amount of Hemoglobin and Blood Volume in Connection with Physical Training." *Acta Phys. Scand.* 19:146–151.

Klissouras, V. 1971. "Inherited Ability of Adaptive Variation." *J. Appl. Physiol.* 31:338–344.

Lamb, D. R. 1978. *Physiology of Exercise: Responses and Adaptations.* New York: Macmillan.

Londeree, B. R. 1977. "Anaerobic Threshold Training." *Toward an Understanding of Human Performance*, ed. E. J. Burke, pp. 15–16. Ithaca, N.Y.: Mouvement Publications.

MacDougall, J. D. 1977. "The Anaerobic Threshold: Its Significance for the Endurance Athlete." *Canadian J. Appl. Sports Sci.* 2:137–140.

MacDougall, J. D., Ward, G. R., Sale, D. C., and Sutton, J. R. 1975. "Muscle Glycogen Repletion After High Intensity Intermittent Exercise." *J. Appl. Physiol.* 42:129–132.

Mathews, D. K., and Fox, E. L. 1976. *The Physiological Basis of Physical Education and Athletics.* Philadelphia: W. B. Saunders Company.

Morgan, T. E., Cobb, L., Short, F. A., Ross, R., and Gunn, D. 1971. "Effects of Long-term Exercise on Human Muscle Mitochondria." *Muscle Metabolism During Exercise*, ed. B. Pernow and B. Saltin, pp. 87–95. New York: Plenum Press.

Nagle, F. D., Robinhold, E., Howley, J., Daniels, G., Baptista, C., and Stoedefalke, K. 1970. "Lactic Acid Accumulation During Running at Submaximal Aerobic Demands." *Med. Sci. Sports* 2:182–186.

Nygaard, E., and Nielsen, E. 1978. "Skeletal Muscle Fiber Capillarization with Extreme Endurance Training in Man." *Swimming Medicine IV*, ed. B. Eriksson and B. Furberg, pp. 282–296. Baltimore: University Park Press.

Oscai, L., Williams, B., and Hertig, B. 1968. "Effects of Exercise on Blood Volume." *J. Appl. Physiol.* 24(5):622–624.

Pattengale, P. K., and Holloszy, J. O. 1967. "Augmentation of Skeletal Muscle Myoglobin by a Program of Treadmill Running." *Amer. J. Physiol.* 213:783–785.

Pette, D., and Staudte, H. W. 1973. "Differences Between Red and White Muscles." *Limiting Factors of Physical Performance*, ed. J. Keul, pp. 23–33. Stuttgart: Georg Thieme Verlag.

Prince, F. P., Hikida, R. S., and Hagerman, F. C. 1976. "Human Muscle Fiber Types in Power Lifters, Distance Runners and Untrained Subjects." *Pflugers Arch. ges. Physiol.* 363:19–26.

Prins, J. H. 1978. "Histological Changes in Human Skeletal Muscle with Isokinetic Strength Training at Two Distinct Limb Speeds." Doctoral dissertation, Indiana University.

Saltin, B. 1973a. "Metabolic Fundamentals in Exercise." *Med. Sci. Sports* 5:137–146.
———. 1973b. "Oxygen Transport by the Circulatory System During Exercise in Man." *Limiting Factors of Physical Performance*, ed. J. Keul, pp. 235–251. Stuttgart: Georg Thieme Verlag.

Saltin, B., Blomquist, G., Mitchell, J. H., Johnson, R. L. Jr., Wildenthal, K., and Chapman, C. B. 1968. "Response to Exercise After Bed Rest and Training." *Circulation* 38, Suppl. 7:1–78.

Saltin, B., Henriksson, J., Nygaard, E., and Andersen, P. 1977. "Fiber Types and Metabolic Potentials of Skeletal Muscle in Sedentary Men and Endurance Runners." *Ann. N.Y. Acad. Sci.* (In press.)

Saltin, B., Nazar, K., Costill, D. L., Stein, E., Jansson, E., Essen, B., and Gollnick, P. D. 1976. "The Nature of the Training Response: Peripheral and Central Adaptations to One-legged Exercise." *Acta Physiol. Scand.* 96:289–305.

Secher, W. H., and Nygaard, E. 1976. "Glycogen Depletion Pattern in Type I, IIa, and IIb Muscle Fibers During Maximal Voluntary, Static and Dynamic Exercise." *Acta Physiol. Scand.*, Suppl. 440:100.

Simmons, R., and Shepard, R. J. 1972. "The Influence of Training Over the Distribution of Cardiac Output." *Training: Scientific Basis and Application*, ed. A. W. Taylor, pp. 131–138. Springfield, Ill.: Thomas.

Stainsby, W. N. 1973. "Oxygen Tensions in Muscle." *Limiting Factors of Physical Performance*, ed. J. Keul, pp. 137–155. Stuttgart: Georg Thieme Verlag.

Tittel, K., Knacke, W., Brauer, B., and Otto, H. 1966. "Der Einfluss Körperlicher Belastungen unterschiedlicher Dauer und Intensität auf die Kapillarisier und der Herz- und Skelettmuskulatur bei Albinoratten," 16 Weltkongr. Sportmed., Hanover, 1966. Cited in *Energy Metabolism of Human Muscle*, ed. J. Keul, E. Doll, and D. Keppler. Baltimore: University Park Press. 1972.

Wasserman, K., Whipp, B. J., Koyal, S., and Beaver, W. 1973. "Anaerobic Threshold and Respiratory Gas Exchange During Exercise." *J. Appl. Physiol.* 35:236–243.

Wilmore, J. H. 1977. *Athletic Training and Physical Fitness*. Boston: Allyn and Bacon.

CHAPTER 9

Applying Physiological Principles to the Conditioning Program

An effective conditioning program depends first on a knowledge of the physiological processes involved in improving swimming performance, and second on the ability to apply that knowledge. An attempt will be made in this chapter to apply information on muscular physiology and metabolism to the conditioning process. Although there are many ways to condition the body for maximum performance, they all depend on three basic principles of training.

The Principles of Training

The three overriding principles that are involved in the training of all athletes, including swimmers, are specificity, overload, and progression.

Specificity of Training: A Different Interpretation

The principle of **specificity** maintains that for training to be most effective, athletes must make the same demands on their bodies in practice that are made on them in competition. Although it is agreed that the principle of training specifically is a valid one, many exercise physiologists have misinterpreted it to mean that swimmers should swim most of their training yardage at competition speeds. Coaches who have trained swimmers according to this interpretation have not had good results. "Burning out" is a common problem in such programs.

Swimming at race speed in practice is only one way the principle of training specifically can be applied. There are many other ways to train specifically. Truly specific training involves all of the metabolic processes that supply energy during the race. Each of these should be isolated and stressed in practice in ways that will result in their maximum improvement. Although it is probably true that swimming at race pace in practice will cause all of the various aerobic and anaerobic metabolic processes to supply energy in a manner that is similar to the way it is supplied in races, no one process may be overloaded for maximum improvement. If, on the other hand, each of the major metabolic processes that supply energy was trained in a somewhat isolated manner and overloaded maximally without interference from other processes, each might improve separately to a greater extent and then contribute more to performance when integrated with the other processes during a race.

Perhaps an analogy will clarify this point. Swimmers commonly perform kicking and pulling drills in order to isolate and overload their arms or their legs so that each will make a greater contribution when the whole stroke is swum in competition. In the same way, each phase of the metabolic process should be isolated and trained for maximum improvement after which it should be combined with the others in order to improve the interaction between the processes so that the energy for races is supplied in the most efficient manner.

Thus, when we speak of training specifically, we should consider more than race-pace swimming. The concept of training specifically must be broadened to include any paces and any exercises that can be used to isolate and train the various energy-storing and energy-releasing metabolic functions that contribute to a swimmer's success at a particular race distance. This means that swimmers in every event should include a variety of distances and speeds in their training. Some of these repeats should, of course, be swum at race speed for integration purposes. However, there are certain muscular adaptations that are best obtained by swimming repeats at speeds that are faster than race pace while still other muscular and circulatory adaptations are achieved by swimming repeats that are slower than race speed.

In keeping with this interpretation, there are five forms of training that should be included in the programs of all competitive swimmers; speed training, maximum oxygen consumption training, anaerobic threshold training, lactate tolerance (oxygen debt) training,[1] and race-pace training. Speed training will improve the efficiency of the ATP-CP reaction and increase muscular power providing swimmers with the ability to "get races out faster." The primary result of maximum oxygen consumption and anaerobic threshold training should be that athletes reduce the rate of lactate production, thereby delaying fatigue and allowing them to swim faster through the middle of races. Lactate tolerance training should increase their anaerobic energy supply and their pain tolerance enabling them to "bring races home" faster. Race-pace swimming is an integrating form of training. Once each of the various metabolic processes have been improved by training that was specifically designed

---

1. The term *oxygen debt*, although popularly used to refer to anaerobic metabolism, does not accurately reflect all of the metabolic activities involved in withstanding the fatiguing effect of acidosis. The term *lactate tolerance* is preferred because it refers to all of the mechanisms that improve an athlete's tolerance to the accumulation of lactic acid.

for that purpose, race-pace training should improve the interaction of these processes so that the energy needed for each race distance will be supplied in the most economical manner.

Overload The most effective training occurs when you make truly challenging demands on your various energy-restoring metabolic processes. Creating these demands is called **overloading**. For example, if exercise creates a demand for greater than normal quantities of oxygen in the mitochondria of working muscle cells, certain adaptations take place in the circulatory and muscular systems so that more oxygen can be delivered to the mitochondria. The demands must be of sufficient intensity to stimulate adaptation; however, they must not be greater than your present ability to meet them or decrements in performance and possibly illness or injury will occur.

Training must be paced correctly if peak performances are to occur. Swimming as fast as you can all of the time is a crude and usually detrimental approach to training. The most effective training occurs when swimmers swim at speeds that are appropriate for improving each metabolic process. As you will see later in this chapter, the appropriate speeds are frequently submaximal, while there are other times when the appropriate speeds are faster than race speed, for example, sprint-assisted training.

Progression When you overload specific metabolic processes for several days, a sensation of reduced effort occurs. This sensation indicates that certain physiological adaptations have occurred which have enhanced your ability to replace energy and

Figure 9.1. The effect of training progression on blood lactate. (Adapted from Astrand and Rodahl 1977, p. 432.)

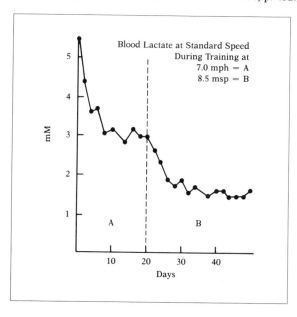

remove waste products. It also indicates that your training is no longer in the overload zone. If you continue to train at that same intensity, you will only maintain, not improve, your present state of conditioning. In order to improve, you need to increase your training until you have, once again, overloaded the appropriate metabolic process. This continual increase in training intensity is an example of the principle of **progression**. The graph in Figure 9.1 illustrates the importance of this principle to the training process. It shows the reductions in blood lactate content that typically take place with training. Notice that when the training speed was 7 mph the blood lactate content decreased rapidly for the first 10 days of training. It then leveled off and a further decrease did not occur until the training speed was increased to 8.5 mph.

Many programs do not include deliberate plans for progression, yet swimmers improve because those who are highly motivated employ this principle by increasing the speed of their repeats as the season progresses. Nevertheless, most swimmers—particularly swimmers with marginal motivation—will benefit more from training programs in which the intensity is regulated to encourage progression. Some swimmers, even motivated swimmers, do not progress at their optimum rate because they are not aggressive in their training. They wait until they feel faster before increasing the intensity of training, rather than forcing that improvement by systematic attempts to increase training speeds.

The sport of weight training exemplifies the importance of progression in training, perhaps more than any other. Weight trainers do not continue at one pace until they feel stronger before increasing the weight they are using in a particular exercise. Instead, they increase the number of repetitions systematically (or at least attempt to increase them) with each training session until they reach a predetermined goal, at which time they increase the weight and begin again at the original number of repetitions. Swimmers are well advised to use a similar method of progression in their training. Systematic attempts to increase training intensity may encourage certain metabolic adaptations to take place more rapidly and to a greater extent than would occur by simply waiting for them to happen. The most effective method for systematically increasing the intensity of training is interval training.

Interval Training

Interval training involves completing a specified number of repeats at a prescribed speed with a specified rest period between swims. There are four variables to deal with in an interval training series:

1. The *number* of swims,
2. The *distance* of each swim,
3. The average *speed* of the swims,
4. The length of the *rest interval* between swims.

A typical interval training series is written as follows:[2]

20	×	100 yds.	/	30 sec.	—	59.0
number	times	distance	on	rest interval	at	average speed

The three principles of training can be applied rather easily with interval training simply by manipulating one or more of the four variables. Specificity and overload are achieved by swimming your competitive stroke or strokes in practice and by regulating the distance, the number of repeats, and the rest interval to supply enough stress to produce adaptations in the metabolic process you wish to improve. The training of each of the metabolic processes will be discussed later in this chapter with special reference to the distance, number of repeats, and rest intervals that are most appropriate for improving that particular process.

Progression can be achieved by systematically increasing intensity by manipulating one or more of the variables so that the workload is increased while the other variables remain unchanged. For example, the number of repeats in a particular interval training series could be increased gradually over the course of several weeks. This method of progression, the manipulation of the number of repeats, seems to be particularly effective for improving a swimmer's ability to maintain a certain pace over a longer distance. However, these interval systems are seldom used in swim training because they are not practical. Most coaches have limited pool time and must use every available minute from the beginning to the end of the season. Therefore, there is usually no time available for increasing the number of repeats as the season progresses.

Another method of progression, manipulating the intensity of repeat sets, can be easily accomplished by gradually decreasing the rest interval during the course of the season. Early in the season, swimmers can be asked to complete a set of 20 × 100 repeats with a rest interval of 30 seconds. As the season progresses, the rest interval should first be reduced to 25 seconds, later to 20 seconds, then to 15 seconds, and finally to 10 seconds. Distance swimmers should find this a very effective way to train. A gradual reduction of the rest interval should condition them to swim a particular pace longer without fatigue.

A third method of progression involves decreasing the average time for a set of repeats over the course of a season. Manipulating this variable, known as the **speed interval**, is probably the most common form of progression used by competitive swimmers. It may be the most effective way for sprinters and middle-distance swimmers to train. Swimmers in these events are trying to train themselves to maintain a faster average pace over the entire race distance.

2. This same series would more commonly be written as: 20 × 100/1:30 sec. − 59.0. because most series are written according to send-off time rather than indicating the rest interval. This is because it is easier to organize a workout with send-off times. A send-off time of 1:30 seconds will provide most high school and college-age swimmers with approximately 30 seconds of rest between swims. The length of rest intervals, rather than send-off times will be designated in the repeat series listed in this chapter. This is done so that the repeat series can be adjusted to provide the appropriate rest intervals for swimmers of other ages and swimmers of differing ability.

Systematically increasing the average speed for a set of repeats is probably the most direct means of achieving this goal.

These three methods of progression can also be used in combinations that will provide very effective improvements in condition. For example, the rest interval could be decreased progressively over the course of a few weeks, followed by a return to the previous rest interval and an increase in the average speed of the repeats. Here is an example of a progression plan that is a combination of these methods:

> Start in November with a set of 8 × 200/2 min. at an average speed of 2:10. Gradually decrease the rest interval each time the set is completed until in December the rest interval is approximately 1 minute. At that time return to the original rest interval and increase the speed so that the swimmer is now repeating a set of 8 × 200/2 min. at an average speed of 2:08.

A combination of various interval systems could supply progression by increasing the number of repeats, followed by a return to the previous number and an increase in repeat speed. Other interval training systems could be combined by increasing the number and then decreasing the rest.

The number of possible progression plans is limited only by the inventiveness of coaches and swimmers. The combinations you select are probably not as important as incorporating some form of progression into your interval training program. Any method that is motivating and that fits comfortably into your training environment is suitable. This is providing, of course, that the interval training series are constructed properly. Research that can aid in constructing interval training series for each of the metabolic processes that are important to race performance is discussed in the sections that follow.

Training the Metabolic Processes That Contribute to Improved Race Performances

It was mentioned earlier that five forms of training should be included in the programs of all competitive swimmers:

1. Speed training.
2. Maximum oxygen consumption training.
3. Anaerobic threshold training.
4. Lactate tolerance training.
5. Race-pace training.

The following questions need to be answered before we can understand how to construct interval training series that will improve each of these metabolic processes:

1. What are the best repeat distances for each form of training?
2. What is the optimum speed?
3. What is the optimum number of repeats?
4. What is the optimum length of the rest intervals?

The answers to these questions may be different for each individual swimmer and will most certainly be different for each metabolic process.

The second question, concerning the optimum speed will be the most difficult to answer because speed is relative to each swimmer's ability. For example, a swimmer with a best time of 52.0 seconds for 100 yards and a swimmer with a best time of 46.0 seconds should not swim their repeats at the same speed. The speed would be too slow for one or too fast for the other. For this reason, percent efforts will be used to indicate the appropriate speeds for certain forms of training so that each individual swimmer can train at a pace that is suited to his or her present level of ability. The procedure for determining percent efforts is as follows: If a particular swimmer's best time is 48.0 seconds, the speed corresponding to a 70 percent level of effort can be determined by taking 30 percent of race speed and adding it to 48.0 seconds. The procedure for performing these calculations is as follows:

$$100\% \quad - \ 70\% \quad = \ 30\%$$
$$0.30 \quad \times \ 48.0 \text{ secs.} \ = \ 14.4 \text{ secs.}$$
$$48.0 \text{ secs.} \ + \ 14.4 \text{ secs.} \ = \ 62.4 \text{ secs.}$$

Thus, a 70 percent effort is equal to a repeat speed of 62.4 seconds.

Because of individual differences in body physiology and skill, percent efforts are not always reliable indicators of the proper training speed. Another method that can be used is counting the heart rate. Some knowledge of the heart rate response to exercise is required, however, before it can be used as an indicator of the appropriate training intensity.

There is a maximum number of times each person's heart will beat during each minute of exercise. This maximum heart rate is relatively stable throughout various stages of training and also during various periods of our lives (although it does decrease after middle age). It will not be the same for every athlete, however. Most athletes have a maximum heart rate that is between 180 and 220 beats per minute.

A maximum heart rate indicates near maximum to maximum effort and therefore approximates a training intensity of 100 percent. Swimmers should be expected to attain maximal heart rates during interval training series that are designed to increase lactate tolerance. The heart rates should be less than maximal (submaximal) in interval training series that are designed to improve the anaerobic threshold and maximal oxygen consumption.

There are obvious problems in determining an accurate exercise heart rate when you are swimming. Therefore, it needs to be estimated from a count that is taken immediately upon completion of a repeat. Swimmers usually gauge training intensity by counting their heart rates for 6, 10, or 15 seconds immediately after repeats. You may simply add a zero to a 6-second count to estimate your heart rate per minute during exercise. This estimate may be in error by nearly 10 beats because you are multiplying the heart rate by a factor of 10. This amount of error is well within the range for estimating the proper intensity for most forms of training. Therefore 6-second counts are an excellent way to estimate the exercise heart rate. They are quickly taken, simple to convert to

Table 9.1   *Estimating the Exercise Heart Rate*

Seconds of count	Obtain minute rate by	Possible margin of error
6	Adding zero	10 beats/minute
10	Multiplying by 6	6 beats/minute
15	Multiplying by 4	4 beats/minute

a minute rate, and are not greatly affected by the recovery rate. One minute, or even 30-second counts would not accurately reflect the exercise heart rate because the heart rates of well-trained swimmers begin to decline within 15 seconds after they finish a repeat.

If you prefer greater accuracy than is afforded by 6-second counts, you can count your heart rate for 10 or 15 seconds after finishing a repeat. Multiply the results of a 10-second count by 6 to get the minute rate; with this method the error should be no greater than 6 beats per minute. Multiply the 15-second count by 4 to obtain the minute rate; the possible error is 4 beats (see Table 9.1).

The heart rate should be counted at the neck or chest as shown in Figure 9.2. It is difficult to get an accurate count at the wrist during exercise.

The research of experts can often be instructive in deciding on the best repeat distance, the optimum repeat speed, the optimum number of repeats, and the appropriate rest interval for each form of training. However, in many cases, research is so meager that the best that can be done is to include it in the making of educated guesses that result from deductive reasoning, personal experience, and examinations of the training programs of highly successful swimmers.

Figure 9.2. Procedures for taking an exercise heart rate. Swimmer **A** is counting her heart rate at the carotid artery immediately after finishing a repeat. Swimmer **B** is counting his heart rate at the left breast.

A

B

Improving Sprint Speed

An increase in sprint speed can be achieved by:

1. Increasing the total amount of propulsive force that can be applied by improving stroke mechanics and by recruiting a greater number of muscle fibers, particularly fast twitch muscle fibers, into the effort.
2. Increasing the quantity of ATP-CP that is stored in muscles.
3. Increasing the activity of enzymes that release energy through the ATP-CP reaction, ATPase and Creatinephosphokinase (CPK).

The little research that is available indicates that these metabolic adaptations are best produced by short repeats at maximal speeds. Since all of the training adaptations that increase the rate of energy release during sprints occur in the muscle cells, it is important to swim these sprints with the stroke(s) you will swim in competition.

Repeats of 12½, 25, and 50 yards/meters should be ideal for improving sprint speed. Research by Mathews and Fox (1976) and Costill (1978) support this observation. It is very important that each repeat be swum as fast as possible in order to overload and thus provide the stimulus for improvements in muscle fiber recruitment and the ATP-CP reaction. Repeat speeds should be in excess of 95 percent of race speed, although, as you will see later, it may be even more effective to swim faster than race speed. Heart rates are not a good guide to training intensity since the duration of each repeat is too short to elicit maximum heart rates. Swimmers should be given rest periods that allow nearly

Table 9.2 *Drills for Improving Sprint Speed*

Distance	Optimum number	Rest interval	Speed
½ length sprints	40–60 in sets of 10	20–30 sec.	Faster than your best 25-yd. time ÷ 2
25s	20–40 in sets of 10	20–30 sec.	Within 1 sec. of best 25 time
50s	6–20 in sets of 5	2–3 min.	Within 2 sec. of best 50 time
Broken 50s (2 × 25)	6–10	10 sec. between 25s; 1–2 min. between 50s	Present or predicted 50 speed
Broken 100s	4–8	10 sec. between 25s; 2–3 min. between 100s	Present or predicted 100 speed
Resistance Training	10–30 repetitions in 10–20 sec.	30 secs. to 1 min.	Maximum effort
Swim Belts	20–40	30 secs. to 1 min.	Faster than race speed
Tethered Swimming	20–40 swims of 10–20 sec. duration	30 secs. to 1 min.	Maximum effort
Fins (25 and 50 repeats)	6–40	30 secs. to 2 min.	Faster than race speed

complete replacement of the muscles' CP supply so that subsequent repeats can be completed at sprint speed. If the CP supply is not restored between swims, anaerobic glycolysis will become the major source of energy replacement and lactate will accumulate. When lactate accumulates speed will be reduced, the ATP-CP reaction will not be overloaded, and the purpose of speed drills will be defeated. Rest periods of 20 to 30 seconds are recommended for 25-yard/meter repeats, and rest periods of 2 to 3 minutes are suggested for 50-yard/meter swims (Fox 1979).

Sprint training should not hurt. Pain is a sign that anaerobic glycolysis rather than the ATP-CP reaction is providing most of the energy. While swimming in pain will improve the ability to "bring races home," speed drills are designed to improve your "going out" speed. Therefore, pain should be avoided in these drills so that acidosis does not interfere with the rate of energy release. Some interval training sets that should improve sprint speed are listed in Table 9.2.

Sprint-assisted Versus Sprint-resisted Training

Since muscular power is a valuable component of sprint speed, many training methods have been developed to improve strength by artificially increasing the resistance a swimmer works against. This form of training has been termed sprint-resisted. The small amount of research that is available concerning the effect of sprint-resisted training on swimming speed has not been favorable. In most cases speed was not improved (Good 1973, Hutinger 1970, Murray 1962, Ross, 1973).

This may surprise you because it seems logical that swimming against added resistance would be an ideal method for increasing stroking power. However, there is evidence that sprint-resisted training can be detrimental to speed. For one thing, working against added resistance may slow rather than increase speed of movement. Recent research with isokinetic training indicates increases in power are specific to the speed of motion used in training (Moffroid and Whipple 1970, Costill et al. 1978, Pipes and Wilmore 1975). That is, strength that is developed at slower speeds may only increase the force that can be applied at those speeds. If this is true, any land drills or sprint-resisted swimming that cause athletes to move their limbs at rates that are slower than the stroking rate they use in competition may not improve the propulsive force that can be applied in races. (This interesting possibility is discussed more fully in Chapter 12.)

Sprint-resisted training may also have a detrimental effect on stroke mechanics. There is cinematographical evidence that this occurred with runners who were trained with sprint-resisted methods (Dintiman 1974). They shortened their stride and changed their body lean and foot placement in ways that reduced their efficiency.

Because of the possibility that sprint-resisted training had a detrimental effect on speed, track coaches developed an alternative method, sprint-assisted training. They had runners run downhill at speeds exceeding those they could achieve on a level surface. Although the research is limited, this method has shown promise (Dintiman 1974). Cinematographic analysis indicated increases in stride length with no decrease in stride rate, a change that is believed to improve running speed. This would be akin to a swimmer applying force over a greater distance with no decrease in turnover rate. Treadmill running has also been used as a form of sprint-assisted training. The speed of the belt is increased to simulate sub-8.0 second 100-yard dashes (26.5 mph). The athletes train by running several 3- to 5-second repeats at this speed.

Another successful form of sprint-assisted training that has been used by runners is towing. They have been reported to run for 50 yards at speeds that were in excess of an 8.0-second 100-yard pace. Some runners have improved their unassisted 100-yard dash times from 10.5 to 9.9 seconds after using this form of training for only five weeks (Sandwick 1967).

Although it may not seem obvious at first, sprint-assisted training should apply the principles of specificity, overload, and progression more effectively than sprint-resisted methods. Sprint-assisted training allows runners to run faster than they can run unassisted, which may produce an overload effect in a way that no other form of training can. Being assisted to run faster than they can actually run may increase the force they can apply because the additional speed may cause more muscle fibers (particularly FTb fibers) to be recruited for the effort. Sprint-assisted training may also increase the speed of energy conversion through the ATP-CP reaction beyond a rate that can be achieved by regular sprint training. Both of these adaptations, if they occur, should allow athletes to apply more force at a faster rate.

Since sprint-assisted training had been shown to increase the speed of sprint runners, Eleanor Rowe, Don Lytle, and the author decided to study the effects of a sprint-assisted method of training on the sprint speed of swimmers (Rowe, Maglischo, and Lytle 1977). Swim fins were used as the assisting device because swimmers could exceed their best race times when using them. The authors were aware of the deleterious effects swim fins might have on stroke mechanics. That is, swimmers might change their armstrokes or their timing or might develop leg-dominated rather than arm-dominated strokes. Nevertheless, this is one of the few methods that allow swimmers to swim faster than race speed.

Two groups of 7- and 8-year-old competitive swimmers were matched according to their best competitive times for the 25-yard freestyle and sprint trained for an 8-week period. The training programs for both groups were identical in all respects but one. Three times each week, the experimental group wore fins for a set of 15 × 25-yard freestyle sprints. The experimental group was encouraged to swim each 25 sprint faster than their best unassisted time. The control group also swam these sprints, but without fins. They were encouraged to swim each repeat within 90 percent of their best competitive time. All subjects were trained in the same pool at the same time and by the same coach. Members of the experimental and control groups were interspersed among the lanes in a random manner to reduce the probability of competing against one another in training. The subjects were cooperative throughout the training program.

Following completion of the training period, the swimmers were again timed for 25 yards of freestyle in competition. Both groups had improved significantly. This result was not unexpected since both groups were sprint trained. However, the important finding was that the average 25-yard freestyle speed of the experimental group improved significantly more than that of the control group. They were 0.41 seconds faster on the average. The initial and final times of each swimmer, the before and after training group averages, and levels of significance are listed in Table 9.3. This method of sprint-assisted training seems to have been successful and its use is recommended. Future research is planned with older swimmers and at longer distances.

Another form of sprint-assisted training that shows promise has been developed by Randy Reese at the University of Florida and has also been used successfully by others, including Nort Thornton at the University of California, Berkeley campus. This method allows athletes to swim 25 yards at speeds that are faster than their best unassisted 25-yard time. It involves the use of a device called a swim belt, pictured in Figure 9.3. The swim belt is constructed of 20 to

Table 9.3 *The Use of Swim Fins for Development of Swimming Speed*

	Comparison of control group pretraining and posttraining times			Comparison of experimental group pretraining and posttraining times	
Pair number	Pretraining time	Posttraining time	Pair number	Pretraining time	Posttraining time
1	16.9	17.0	1	17.0	16.7
2	21.6	21.4	2	21.6	21.9
3	17.9	17.8	3	18.0	17.4
4	17.6	17.1	4	17.6	15.9
5	22.9	22.7	5	22.8	22.8
6	17.9	17.8	6	17.8	17.5
7	17.7	17.5	7	17.7	17.0
8	17.2	17.1	8	17.1	16.8
9	20.2	19.9	9	20.1	19.0
10	27.1	27.0	10	27.3	26.5
11	17.9	17.8	11	17.9	17.2
12	16.9	16.8	12	16.8	16.3
13	17.7	17.9	13	17.8	17.2
14	17.8	17.8	14	17.9	17.8
Mean Time	19.09	18.97	Mean Time	19.10	18.57
Standard Deviation	2.92	2.90	Standard Deviation	2.95	3.04
t		2.71	t		4.01
Level of Significance		.01	Level of Significance		.005

Source: Adapted from E. L. Rowe, E. W. Maglischo, and D. E. Lytle, "The Use of Swim Fins for Development of Sprint Swimming Speed," *Swimming Technique,* 14 (1977), p. 75, tables 2 and 3, by permission of the publishers.

Figure 9.3. The swim belt, a device for sprint-assisted training. The swim belt is constructed of 20 to 25 feet of thin-walled surgical tubing that is connected to one end of the pool, under water. The adjustable belt is made of webbing.

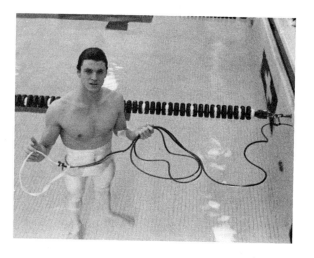

25 feet of thin-walled surgical tubing and an adjustable belt made of webbing. The tubing is tied to the end of the pool, below water level, and the swimmer swims down the pool stretching the tubing as he goes. He then swims back as fast as possible allowing the "snap-back" of the surgical tubing to assist him in swimming faster than he can swim unassisted.

A third form of sprint-assisted training has been suggested by Rushall and Thomson (1974). They believe ultrashort repeats of 10 and 12½ yards/meters are useful for improving sprint speed because swimmers can swim them faster than their present speed for 25 yards/meters. Some suggestions for using this and other forms of sprint-assisted training are listed in Table 9.2.

Improving Maximal Oxygen Consumption

There is a considerable amount of research available that concerns methods for improving $\dot{V}O_2$ max. Although most of the research has been conducted on bicycle ergometers and treadmills, the results can be applied to competitive swimming if we remember that energy metabolism is dependent upon time rather than activity. That is, any procedures that increase $\dot{V}O_2$ max on land should produce similar results in the water if the exercise is performed at the same intensity for the same length of time.

Apparently a variety of repeat distances can be used to improve $\dot{V}O_2$ max, provided close attention is paid to the rest interval. If there is one range of distances that would be best for increasing maximum oxygen consumption it would be between 300 and 600 yards/meters. This recommendation is based on the work of Astrand and Rodahl (1977). They recommend 3- to 5-minute work periods performed at 80 to 90 percent effort for improving $\dot{V}O_2$ max. The graph in Figure 9.4 illustrates the rationale behind this recommendation. Referring to that graph, you can see that it requires approximately 2 to 3 minutes for the body to adjust to the demand for additional oxygen and to begin providing it at a maximum rate. This is because the need for oxygen must be created before

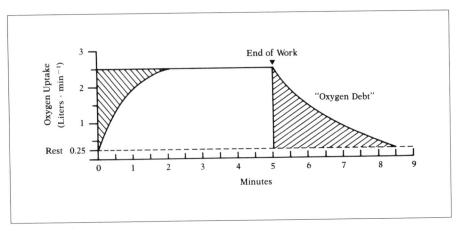

Figure 9.4. The typical pattern of oxygen consumption during exercise. (Data from *Textbook of Work Physiology* by P. O. Astrand and K. Rodahl. Copyright © 1977 by McGraw-Hill Book Company. Used with the permission of McGraw-Hill Book Company.)

the mechanisms that deliver it from the atmosphere to the muscles can be stimulated to maximum performance. All of these increases require 2 to 3 minutes to take place. Thus, working for 3 to 5 minutes should be an effective training procedure because it provides sufficient time to reach your present maximal rate of oxygen consumption and then remain there long enough (1 to 3 minutes) to produce a training stimulus.

It is no wonder distances of 300 to 600 yards/meters are used so frequently in the training of middle-distance and distance swimmers. These distances require 3 to 7 minutes to complete, therefore they are in the time range that is recommended for increasing $\dot{V}O_2$ max. The proper intensity for these swims is within 80 to 90 percent of race speed. Swimming with heart rates that are within 10 beats of maximum is also recommended as a guide to the proper intensity.

The length of the rest interval is not critical when repeats of 300 yards/meters and greater are used for improving $\dot{V}O_2$ max. The training effect occurs within each repeat swim because it will be sufficiently long (3 minutes or more) to overload the processes that result in maximal rates of oxygen consumption. Nevertheless, most coaches prefer rest intervals of 1 to 3 minutes so that practice time is not wasted. These rest intervals probably allow sufficient recovery time to swim each succeeding repeat at the proper intensity.

Although middle-distance repeats may be the most effective means to improve $\dot{V}O_2$ max, a season could become quite boring if these distances were repeated every day in training. Therefore, it is good to know that both shorter and longer distances can also be used for this purpose. Actually, any distance can be used if the intensity of the swims and rest intervals are appropriate for the distance in question. In the case of shorter distances (less than 300 yards), the rest periods must be shorter than the work periods. This is because the training effect results from the accumulative effect of several swims. A short rest period does not allow complete recovery between repeats so that each succeeding repeat in a set begins with oxygen consumption elevated more than it was in the previous swim. After 4 to 8 minutes of such repeats, swimmers should reach $\dot{V}O_2$ max and remain there throughout the remainder of the set.

Perhaps Figure 9.5 will demonstrate this point. It represents the rate of oxygen consumption for a swimmer who is swimming a set of 100-yard repeats on 1:15 seconds and one who is swimming a set of 100-yard repeats on 2 minutes. With a send-off time of 1:15, the rest interval is too short for complete recovery (10 to 15 seconds) and each swim begins at a higher oxygen consumption rate than the previous repeat until $\dot{V}O_2$ max is reached during the fifth repeat. After that, the swimmer attains maximal oxygen consumption levels during each swim and this should provide the overload to produce an increase in $\dot{V}O_2$ max.

When the rest interval is too long, such as occurs when this same set is swum on 2 minutes, the rate of oxygen consumption recovers to near resting levels after each swim. Since each repeat is not, in itself, long enough to stimulate oxygen consumption mechanisms to maximum, these mechanisms will not be fully overloaded and the training effect should be reduced. Astrand and Rodahl (1977) have indicated that the rest interval for short distance repeats should be between one fourth and one half the time it takes to swim the repeat. Research on which this recommendation is based is shown in Table 9.4. Notice that maximum oxygen consumption is not reached until the work–rest ratio is 2:1. Research by Mathews and Fox (1976) supports these data.

Applying these data to swim training, the optimum rest intervals for 25- and 50-yard repeats would be 5 to 10 seconds. Thirty seconds or less would be

Figure 9.5. Improving maximum oxygen consumption with 100-yard repeats.

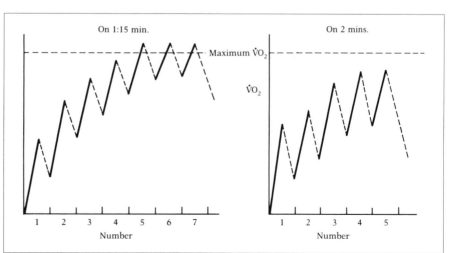

Table 9.4   *The Relationship of Work and Rest to Maximal Oxygen Consumption During Training*

| Work-rest in seconds | Oxygen consumption in liters/min. | | |
W R	Highest	Average	Rest
5–5		4.3	4.5
5–10		3.4	3.0
10–5	5.6	5.1	4.9
10–10	4.7	4.4	3.8
15–10	5.3	5.0	4.5
15–15	5.3	4.6	3.8
15–30	3.9	3.6	2.8

Source: Christensen, Hedman, and Saltin 1960. (Adapted from Astrand and Rodahl 1977, p. 401.)

Note: Maximum oxygen consumption (5.6 liters/min) is not reached until the work-rest ratio is 2:1. This is an indication that, where $\dot{V}O_2$ max is concerned, the length of the work period must be at least twice as great as the rest period for training to be effective.

appropriate for 100-yard repeats and 1 minute or less is probably optimal for 200-yard swims. The pace of these swims should continue to be within 80 to 90 percent of maximum speed for that repeat distance.

Regarding training intensity, Mathews and Fox (1976) have made the most extensive study to date of the physiological reactions to various interval training programs. They suggest that repeats that are designed to train $\dot{V}O_2$ max should be done in sets. This seems a reasonable procedure. The rate of work required to reach $\dot{V}O_2$ max is so intense that some lactate will be accumulating during the swims causing fatigue to occur after a short number of repeats. This will, in turn, cause a reduction in repeat speed and oxygen consumption will drop below maximal so that the repeat set is no longer effective for improving $\dot{V}O_2$ max. If, instead, the set was terminated before the pace declined and a short rest period was taken, several additional sets could be completed. With more yardage covered at maximal rates of oxygen consumption, the training effect should be enhanced.

The effect on $\dot{V}O_2$ max of a straight set of repeats is compared to the effect of several shorter sets in Figure 9.6. The graph on the left depicts the oxygen consumption response of a swimmer who is completing a set of twelve 200-yard repeats in a straight set. The graph on the right illustrates the oxygen consumption response of another swimmer to the same workout when it is constructed as three sets of four 200s. Assuming both swimmers are equal in ability and that they are swimming at the same intensity, the effort required to reach $\dot{V}O_2$ max would cause the swimmer on the left to become fatigued after 4 or 5 swims, after which he would have to reduce the pace in order to recover. This would reduce oxygen consumption to below maximum and the training effect will be reduced. The swimmer represented by the graph on the right spends more time swimming at $\dot{V}O_2$ max and does not experience the fatigue

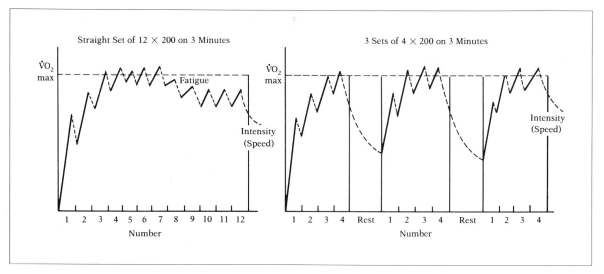

Figure 9.6. A comparison of the effect on $\dot{V}O_2$ max of swimming repeats in one straight set and of swimming several short sets with rests. These graphs show that swimming several short sets of repeats is probably more effective for improving $\dot{V}O_2$ max than swimming the same number of repeats in a long straight set. This is because the pace required to attain $\dot{V}O_2$ max, although it is not all-out, is too intense to be maintained for a long set. As a result, fatigue probably causes swimmers to reduce their speed midway through the set. Therefore, the intensity of the swims may not be sufficient to maintain oxygen consumption at maximum levels and the purpose of the exercise will be defeated. If, on the other hand, periodic rest periods are taken, swimmers should be able to maintain the proper speed for a greater number of repeats. This faster pace should enhance the training effect of increasing $\dot{V}O_2$ max because oxygen can be consumed at maximal rates for a greater number of yards.

incurred by the other because the rest between sets allows him to recover sufficiently to swim the remaining sets at an intensity that stimulates oxygen consumption to maximum. The rest periods between sets should probably be between 3 and 5 minutes. Most of the lactate produced in the muscle cells can diffuse into the blood stream in that length of time and the pH of the muscles can be restored near normal so that more work can be done (Keul, Doll, and Keppler 1972).[3]

Some examples of repeat sets that can be used for improving $\dot{V}O_2$ max are given in Table 9.5. The speeds indicated are guides to the proper intensity for each repeat distance. Remember also, that heart rates within 10 beats of maximum are indicative of the proper intensity regardless of the repeat distance.

Training the Anaerobic Threshold

The anaerobic threshold plays a significant role in distances of 400 yards and longer. As indicated in the previous chapter, it may also play a role in 200 and

3. Although excess lactate can be found in the blood for 15 to 30 minutes after exercise (Keul, Doll, and Keppler 1972), the removal of lactate from the working muscles determines when work can recommence.

Table 9.5 *Training Maximum Oxygen Consumption ($\dot{V}O_2$ max)*

Distance	Optimum number of repeats	Rest intervals	Speed
50	40–60 in sets of 10	10 sec. rest between 50s; 2–3 min. between sets	From 80% to 85% of 50 speed
75–100	20–30 in sets of 5–10	10–20 sec. rest between repeats; 2–3 min. between sets	From 80% to 85% of 100 speed
150–200	10–20 in sets of 3–5	30 sec. rest between repeats; 3–5 min. rest between sets	85% to 90% of 200 pace
300, 400, 500	4–8	2–3 min.	80% to 90% of race speed
600, 700, 800	3–4	3–5 min.	80% to 90% of race speed

100 races. Applying the principles of specificity, overload, and progression to training the anaerobic threshold, it would seem that the rate of lactate removal from working muscles could be improved by training at speeds that are slightly in excess of the present AT. This should provide the overload to stimulate faster removal rates without interference from severe acidosis. The principle of progression is applied by gradually increasing the training pace as the rate of lactate accumulation decreases. The problem often posed by coaches is how to determine the exact training speeds that correspond to each swimmer's anaerobic threshold.

Some insight into this question was provided by Dr. Max Mader, one of the architects of the East German training program until he defected to the West. He, in conjunction with H. Heck and W. Hollman, described the blood testing procedures used with East German swimmers in a 1976 publication (Mader, Heck, and Hollman 1976). These procedures involved collecting samples of blood from earlobe pricks and analyzing them for lactic acid content after each of two time trials. The first time trial was swum at approximately a 70 percent effort and the second was in excess of 90 percent of race speed. The times for the two swims were graphed with the blood lactate concentrations they produced. A line of best fit was then established by connecting the two points. This line made it possible to predict the blood lactate concentration of any swim that fell between the two points. This graphing procedure is illustrated in Figure 9.7. The data are taken from an actual analysis performed on an Oakland University swimmer. The blood lactic acid concentration is expressed in millimoles per 100 milliliters of blood (mM).

The information on such a graph can be used, among other things, to determine the optimal pace for training. The East Germans believe swimmers should train at speeds that will produce blood lactate concentrations slightly in excess of 4 mM. This is because a concentration of 4 mM represents a small but significant increase of blood lactate above the normal resting concentration of lactic acid in the blood. (The resting level of lactate in the blood is usually be-

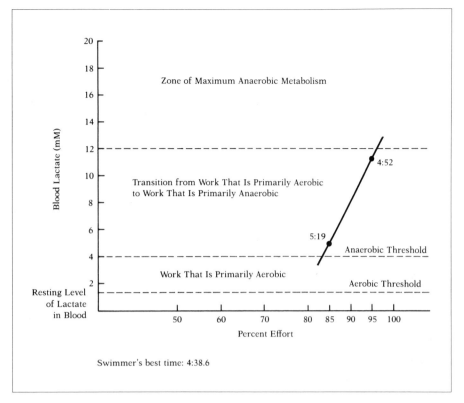

Figure 9.7. The procedure for establishing a line of best fit from analyses of blood lactic acid concentration following two 500-yard time trials.

tween 1 and 2 mM.) The fact that the lactic acid content of the blood has increased slightly indicates that it is being produced in the muscles at a faster rate than it can be metabolized, with some of the excess being poured into the blood stream. The slight increase of blood lactic acid signifies that aerobic metabolism is operating at near-maximal to maximal capacity. In other words, the aerobic metabolic processes are overloaded and should improve as rapidly as it is possible for them to improve.

Since the maximum concentration of blood lactate that can be tolerated by most swimmers is somewhere between 12 and 20 mM, they do not need to swim at maximum speeds to produce concentrations of 4 mM. The East Germans reason, therefore, that the submaximal speeds that produce concentrations of 4 mM are optimal for improving aerobic endurance because they overload the aerobic metabolic processes and because more yards can be swum without interference from acidosis and the danger of overtraining.

Some experts use 4 mM concentration of blood lactate as a determinant of the anaerobic threshold. There is, however, some disagreement over the definition of this term. Other experts prefer to define AT in terms of exercise intensities that will produce blood lactate concentrations slightly in excess of 2 mM.

Skinner and McLellan (1980) have presented a useful model for interpreting the training effects associated with various blood lactate concentrations. They refer to the 2 mM level as the **aerobic threshold** and the 4 mM level is designated the **anaerobic threshold**. The aerobic threshold is the minimum training intensity that will improve aerobic endurance while the anaerobic threshold is the intensity where aerobic metabolism is overloaded. This model has excellent applicability to the training process and will be used later to summarize the concepts presented in this chapter.

Training should produce improvements in the anaerobic threshold. That is, as swimmers become better conditioned they should find that the concentrations of lactic acid in their blood are reduced at certain speeds. This is undoubtedly the result of both a reduction in the rate of lactate production and an increase in the rate of removal. Actual improvements in the anaerobic threshold that occurred for one swimmer over the course of a season are shown in Figure 9.8. Notice that the line of best fit shifted to the right from the first to last test periods. This indicated that he could swim faster with less lactic acid accumulating in his blood. The improvement in swimming speed required to reach a blood lactate concentration of 4 mM was 6 percent (82 percent to 86

Figure 9.8. Changes in blood lactate concentrations during training at submaximal swimming speeds. This graph shows the actual changes that took place in one swimmer's anaerobic threshold during six weeks of training. The swimmer was tested on January 27, February 24, and March 9, 1980.

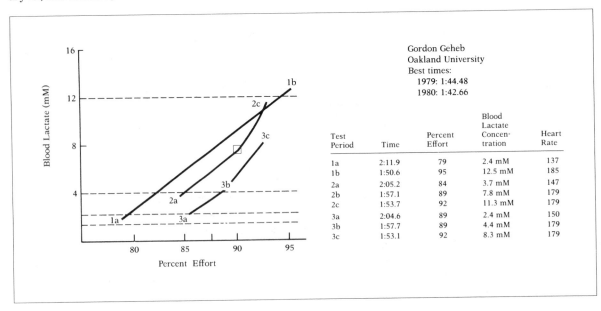

Gordon Geheb
Oakland University
Best times:
  1979: 1:44.48
  1980: 1:42.66

Test Period	Time	Percent Effort	Blood Lactate Concentration	Heart Rate
1a	2:11.9	79	2.4 mM	137
1b	1:50.6	95	12.5 mM	185
2a	2:05.2	84	3.7 mM	147
2b	1:57.1	89	7.8 mM	179
2c	1:53.7	92	11.3 mM	179
3a	2:04.6	89	2.4 mM	150
3b	1:57.7	89	4.4 mM	179
3c	1:53.1	92	8.3 mM	179

	January 27, 1981	March 8, 1980	Difference
Percent effort estimated to produce a blood lactate concentration of 4 mM	82%	88%	6%
Conversion to time	2:07.00	1:59.0	8.00 secs.

Figure 9.9. Possible improvements in performance as indicated by increases in the speed estimated to produce a blood lactate concentration of 4 mM. The swimmer in this example had a best time of 1:44.5 for 200 yards at the time these calculations were made.

percent efforts) from the first to the last test period. This means that by March 7, 1980, he could swim approximately 8 seconds faster for each 200-yard segment of a race without becoming any more fatigued than he had been on January 27, 1980. The calculations supporting this observation are shown in Figure 9.9.

These data were gathered as part of a study to find methods other than blood testing to determine the proper intensities for training the anaerobic threshold. Since repeat speeds and heart rates are the two measures of training intensity that are most available to the coach, a study was designed to determine if blood lactate concentrations could be predicted from these two measures of effort.

Blood samples were taken, by means of fingertip pricks, from members of the 1980 Oakland University swim team after each of two 200-yard time trials. These samples were later analyzed for lactate content. Trial times and heart rates were also recorded. Reduction in blood lactate accumulation at certain speeds was observed among all swimmers tested. The graphs in Figure 9.10 show the average increases in percent effort and heart rate required to reach a blood lactate concentration of 4 mM from the beginning to the end of the season. Efforts are expressed as a percent of each swimmer's lifetime best 200-yard swim prior to completion of the 1980 season.

Efforts of 65 percent to 83 percent (mean 74 percent) were required to produce a blood lactate concentration of 4 mM in November. This increased to between 82 and 88 percent (mean 85 percent) by mid-season and then increased even further to between 84 and 90 percent (mean 87 percent) during the first week of the taper. This means that swimmers had to increase repeat speed an average of 13 percent over the course of the season in order to continue training above their anaerobic threshold.

A surprising result was that progressively higher heart rates were also required to produce a blood lactate concentration of 4 mM as the season went on. Heart rates of 135 to 152 bpm (mean 143) were sufficient for this purpose in November; however, by mid-season swimmers had to swim repeats at speeds eliciting heart rates of 152 to 172 bpm (mean 161) to produce blood lactate

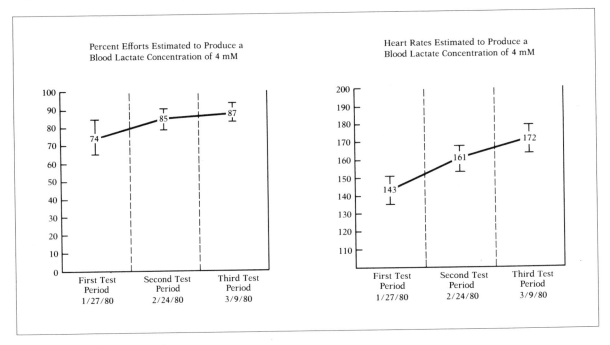

Figure 9.10. The effect of six weeks of swim training on the percent efforts and heart rates estimated to produce a blood lactate concentration of 4 mM.

concentrations of 4 mM. The rates had further increased to between 160 and 182 bpm (mean 172) by the end of the season.

We expected that the heart rates that corresponded to a particular training intensity (i.e., the anaerobic threshold), would remain relatively stable throughout the season. It is generally accepted that training reduces the heart rate for specific workloads as athletes become better conditioned. This was obviously not the case, however. One possible explanation for this phenomenon may be that the early adaptations to training occur in the central circulatory system resulting in a reduced heart rate at certain submaximal work levels. Adaptations that take place later in the season may be predominantly muscular in nature and will not be accompanied by reduced heart rates.

We tested the accuracy of our determinations by taking blood samples after six swimmers completed some sets of repeats at speeds that we had estimated from our blood testing results, to be equivalent to their anaerobic thresholds. Three of the swimmers swam a set of 8 × 200-yard swims on 2:30 at an average speed that was estimated to produce a blood lactate concentration of 4 mM. Three additional swimmers completed a set of 4 × 500-yard swims on 6 minutes at speeds that approximated anaerobic threshold intensity. The 500 swimmers' speeds were calculated by converting their anaerobic threshold speeds for 200-yard swims into yards/second and dividing that number into 500 yards. The results of the blood analyses are listed in Table 9.6.

Table 9.6 *Blood Lactate Concentration for Six Swimmers Doing Sets of 200-Yard and 500-Yard Repeats at Their Estimated Anaerobic Thresholds*

Swimmer	Repeat set	Estimated speed that will produce a blood lactate concentration of 4 mM	Average speed for the repeat set	Actual blood lactate concentration in mM	Heart rate estimated to produce a blood lactate concentration of 4 mM	Immediate postset heart rate
1	6 × 200 on 2:30	2:09	2:08	3.72	175	192
2	6 × 200 on 2:30	2:07	2:06	2.10	189	180
3	6 × 200 on 2:30	2:05	2:02	5.22	185	192
4	4 × 500 on 6:00	5:05	5:04	6.72	165	180
5	4 × 500 on 6:00	5:07	5:05	4.11	186	180
6	4 × 500 on 5:30	5:19	5:30	2.49	175	170

Source: E. W. Maglischo and C. W. Maglischo, unpublished research report.

Our estimates approximated the anaerobic threshold for four of the six swimmers. Subject #2 had a blood lactate concentration of 2.10 mM despite the fact that he swam the set of 200-yard repeats 1 second faster than his target time. Subject #6 also had a blood lactate concentration that was less than 4 mM (2.49 mM). This was expected, however, since he swam the set of 500-yard repeats eleven seconds slower than his target time. The immediate postexercise heart rates were also very close to the heart rates that were estimated to produce blood lactate concentrations of 4 mM. These results indicate that blood testing is indeed a reliable method for estimating the training speeds and heart rates for anaerobic threshold training.

Based on these data we suggest that repeat speeds of 75 to 85 percent of maximum and heart rates of 140 to 150 are indicative of the optimal training speeds for most athletes early in the season. Later in the season efforts of 85 to 90 percent and heart rates of 150 to 170 bpm will be required for the same purpose.

Treffene's Anaerobic Triangle Theory

In 1971 Treffene presented some equations for predicting a swimmer's optimal training speed. He termed this speed the "critical maximum velocity" (CMV). The CMV is believed to approximate the anaerobic threshold.

We tested Treffene's hypothesis by calculating the critical maximum velocities of our subjects for 200-yard repeats. We then compared these with the speeds our blood testing data indicated would produce blood lactate concentrations of 4 mM. These were termed the optimal training speed. The comparisons are shown in Table 9.7. The critical maximum velocities were consistently faster than our optimal training speeds and according to our estimates, would have produced blood lactate concentrations between 5 mM and 8 mM for our group of subjects.

Although the critical maximum velocities computed by Treffene's method are faster than the training speeds recommended for improving the anaerobic threshold by Mader and associates, they are not excessive and should produce improvements in the anaerobic threshold without risk of overtraining.

Table 9.7 *Comparisons of Optimal Training Speeds Predicted from Blood Lactate Concentrations and Critical Maximum Velocities Calculated According to Treffene's Anaerobic Triangle Theory*

Subject	Stroke	Optimal training speed estimated from blood testing	Critical maximum velocity calculated by Treffene's method	The estimated blood lactate concentrations of the subjects when swimming at Treffene's critical maximum velocities
M.D.	Backstroke	2:08.5	2:07.4	5 mM
G.H.	Backstroke	2:17.4	2:10.8	6 mM
B.B.	Butterfly	2:11.8	2:07.7	6.5 mM
G.G.	Freestyle	1:59.5	1:55.6	7 mM
T.M.	Freestyle	2:03.0	1:55.4	7 mM
M.O.	Freestyle	2:00.0	1:53.1	7.8 mM

Source: E. W. Maglischo et al., unpublished research report; R. J. Treffene, 1979.

In addition to percent efforts and immediate postexercise heart rates, there is a third indicator of intensity for AT training. That is by monitoring your subjective feelings of fatigue. AT repeats should be sufficiently intense to cause mild distress, however there should not be a great deal of pain from lactate accumulation. As you improve you will find yourself swimming faster in practice with no noticeable increase in distress. Always train at speeds that are just a few seconds faster than those that feel comfortable. Try to force increases in the anaerobic threshold by increasing your speed slightly each week as the season progresses.

Since the highest AT's are found among athletes who engage in considerable amounts of continuous distance running it would seem that long straight sets of repeats at the prescribed rate of speed are the best method to improve this particular physiological mechanism. However, as with $\dot{V}O_2$ max training, any repeat distance can be used for AT training, provided that the swims are completed at an adequate speed and that the proper rest period is used. High-speed repeats should not be used for anaerobic threshold training. They will only increase lactate accumulation and perhaps cause fatigue before the mechanisms involved in lactate removal have received a sufficient training stimulus.

The repeat speeds that will improve the anaerobic threshold are slower than those that are recommended for training $\dot{V}O_2$ max. It follows, therefore, that the rest periods between repeats can be shorter. The rest periods should be no longer than is necessary to maintain the proper repeat speed. When swimmers are permitted only minimal recovery time between repeats, the swimmers do not recover between repeats and the lactate removal mechanisms should operate at peak efficiency for nearly the entire set. Many coaches use rest periods as short as 5 seconds for repeats of 25, 50, and 100 yards/meters. The rest periods seldom exceed 1 to 2 minutes for longer repeat distances. Some suggested interval training sets for training the anaerobic threshold are presented in Table 9.8.

Table 9.8 *Anaerobic Threshold Training*

Distance (in yards)	Optimum number	Rest interval	Speed
25 50–75 100	20–40	5–10 sec. between repeats	65% to 80% of race speed in early season 75% to 90% of race speed later
150–200 300–400 500–600	10–20 6–10	10 sec. rest between repeats 10–30 sec.	65% to 80% of race speed in early season 75% to 90% of race speed later 85% to 90% of race speed in early season 90% to 95% of race speed later
700–800 900–1,000	3–5 or more	30 sec.–1 min.	90% to 95% of race speed in early season 95% of race speed later
1,650	1–3 or more	1–2 min.	90% to 95% of race speed in early season 95% of race speed later
3,000–5,000	1–2 or more	1–2 min.	90% to 95% of best practice time early in the season 95% of best practice time later

Note: Heart rates should be between 140 and 170 beats per minute.

The Danger of Excessive Speeds

Astrand and Rodahl (1977) have shown that it is possible to reach maximum oxygen consumption levels without working at maximum speed. The same statement is, of course, also true where the anaerobic threshold is concerned. In one of their studies, maximum oxygen consumption was reached on a bicycle ergometer at a work rate of 250 watts. Further increases in the workload did not increase oxygen consumption, but instead increased the accumulation of lactate. When this occurs the training effect on $\dot{V}O_2$ max and the anaerobic threshold is probably reduced. Kipke (1978) demonstrated just such an effect in a swimming flume. The results are shown in Figure 9.11. At simulated speeds that were in excess of a time of 2:13 for a 200-meter freestyle, the swimmer's oxygen consumption was reduced while his blood lactate concentration increased dramatically. These points are marked by the arrows in Figure 9.11.

Based on these data, it is possible that a swimmer could work so hard that attempts to improve the anaerobic threshold and $\dot{V}O_2$ max are interfered with by excess lactate accumulation. For this reason, it is important to swim $\dot{V}O_2$ max and anaerobic threshold repeats at submaximal speeds. For these forms of training, a large number of repeats, provided they are completed at an appropriate speed, is probably more effective than swimming fewer repeats at a faster pace.

Increasing Lactate Tolerance

Swimmers who train to increase their ability to tolerate (or perhaps buffer) the lactic acid that accumulates during races should be able to "bring races home" faster. As swimmers increase their tolerance to lactate accumulation, they can produce more and more lactic acid during exercise and not be inhibited by it. This permits energy to be supplied anaerobically and thus at a faster rate during races so that near maximum speeds can be maintained for a longer time.

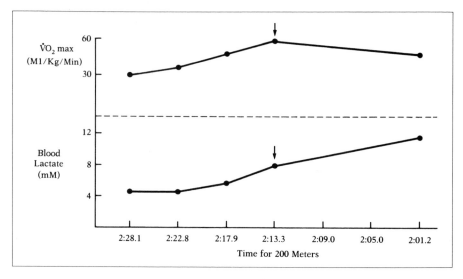

Figure 9.11. The effect of swimming speeds on V̇O$_2$ max and blood lactate concentrations. (Adapted from L. Kipke, "Dynamics of Oxygen Intake During Step-by-Step Loading in a Swimming Flume," *Swimming Medicine IV*, ed. B. Eriksson and B. Furberg [Baltimore: University Park Press, 1978], p. 139, fig. 1, by permission of the publisher and author.)

Two ways that lactate tolerance can probably be improved are through improved buffering and through an increased activity of the muscle form of LDH. Another way swimmers can improve lactate tolerance is by increasing their tolerance to the pain of acidosis. Improvements in pain tolerance should aid swimmers in maintaining a fast pace in spite of a progressively declining pH in the muscles.

Improvements in lactate tolerance are particularly important to success in 100 and 200 events. The short time required to complete these races does not allow oxygen to be consumed in sufficient quantity to cause significant reductions in lactate production. Because of this fact and because fast speeds are required for success in these events, lactate accumulates rapidly in the working muscles. The graph in Figure 9.12 indicates the relationship between improvements in lactate tolerance in 100- and 200-yard events.[4] Increases in the swimmer's oxygen debt capacity correspond to improvements of 2.1 seconds in the 100-meter and 5 seconds for the 200-meter freestyles.

The ability to tolerate lactic acid is also important in longer races, particularly during the final one-half to one-third of those races. However, improvements in oxygen consumption capacity and lactate removal play more important roles in these races. When these physiological processes are not im-

4. The ability to go into debt for oxygen represents the amount of lactate accumulating in muscles.

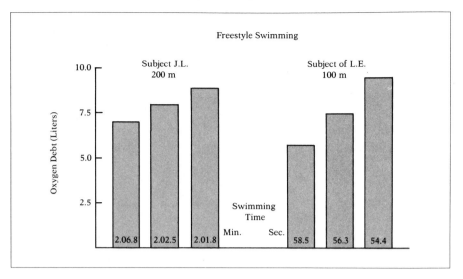

Figure 9.12. The effect of improvements in oxygen debt on race times. (Adapted from L. Hermansen, *Medicine and Science in Sport*, 1 [1969], p. 37, fig. 12, by permission of the American College of Sports Medicine and the author.)

proved the limits of lactate tolerance will be reached early in a race. Even a 100 percent improvement in lactate tolerance would improve an athlete's time by only 3 to 6 seconds, whereas improvements in $\dot{V}O_2$ max and the anaerobic threshold could lead to improvements of 8 or more seconds, depending on the length of the race.

Applying the principles of specificity and overload to increasing lactate tolerance would indicate that swimmers should swim their major stroke or strokes at speeds that will produce blood lactate concentrations somewhere between 12 mM and the maximum concentration of lactic acid that they can tolerate. Astrand and Rodahl (1977) believe 1-minute maximum efforts followed by rest periods of 4 to 5 minutes are most effective for this purpose. This is because you can reach your maximum limit for lactate tolerance in 40 to 50 seconds of all-out effort. Thus, a 1-minute effort should permit the overload required for improvement. After this occurs, 4 to 5 minutes of rest is required to allow removal of lactate from the working muscles so that additional all-out efforts can be completed. If subsequent efforts were performed without sufficient rest, the lactate accumulating in your muscles would force reductions in speed as acidosis becomes severe. This mistake is illustrated by the graph in Figure 9.13. The graph on the left illustrates the probable effect on blood lactate when swimmers attempt to swim their repeats too fast on short rest. There is not sufficient recovery time between repeats and after two or three 100s acidosis becomes so severe that the reduction in energy metabolism causes a reduction in speed that drops them below the appropriate intensity for increasing lactate production and the purpose of the set is defeated. With longer rest the

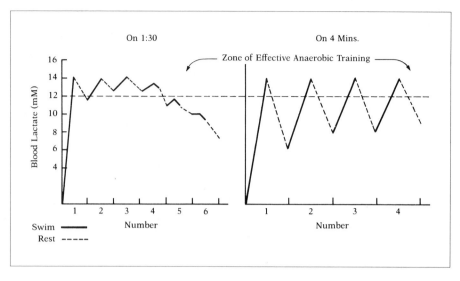

Figure 9.13. The probable effect on speed of inadequate and adequate rest periods.

swimmers should be able to remove some lactate from their muscles so that they can swim several repeats at the proper speed. This is illustrated in the graph on the right.

Many other repeat distances can be used to train lactate tolerance provided repeat sets are constructed so that the appropriate combinations of work, rest, and speed are used. When the repeat distances are less than 100 yards, several repeats are required to reach the limits of lactate tolerance. For example, a series of 20 × 50-yard swims at a very fast rate of speed will cause lactate to accumulate to near maximum levels after several repeats are completed if the rest interval does not provide enough time for complete removal between swims. This is indicated by the graph in Figure 9.14. It shows the blood lactate concentrations of three competitive swimmers during a set of 20 × 50-yard freestyles on 1½ minutes. Two blood samples were taken from each swimmer, the first one after the tenth repeat, and the second after the twentieth repeat. Blood lactate accumulations were still below the maximum range at the end of the tenth 50. However, when the twentieth 50 was completed, two of the three swimmers had blood lactate concentrations in excess of 12 mM.

For improving lactate tolerance, the appropriate number of 50-yard repeats is probably between 16 and 30, performed as a straight set or perhaps in sets of 6 to 10. Rest periods of 10 to 30 seconds are recommended between repeats with 3 to 5 minutes rest between sets. The shorter rest intervals can be used when the sets are short (between 4 and 8 repeats per set). If the repeats are done as a straight set, a rest interval of 30 to 60 seconds is recommended.

Distances that are longer than 100 yards can be used to train lactate tolerance if the repeats are completed at a speed that causes excess lactate to accumulate. Occasional high-intensity 200-yard/meter repeats are excellent for training the lactate tolerance of 100-yard swimmers. When swimmers tolerate pain for more than twice the length of time required to swim 100 races the pain of the shorter swims seems easier to bear. Three to four 200s should be sufficient for this purpose. Once again, the rest interval should be sufficiently long, 3 to 5 minutes, to allow for removal of most of the excess lactate from the working muscles so that subsequent repeats can be completed near maximum speed.

Middle-distance swims of 300 to 800 yards should also produce training adaptations that improve lactate tolerance, provided the speed is sufficient to bring a swimmer to his or her present limit of lactate tolerance. Middle-distance and distance swimmers should swim such repeats on a weekly basis. Sprinters would be better advised to train this process with shorter repeats in which the pace, muscle fiber recruitment patterns, stroke mechanics, and turning techniques are more like those they will use in their races.

Distance swims may not be very effective for improving lactate tolerance.

Figure 9.14. Blood lactate concentrations during a set of 20 × 50 yard swims on 1½ minutes.

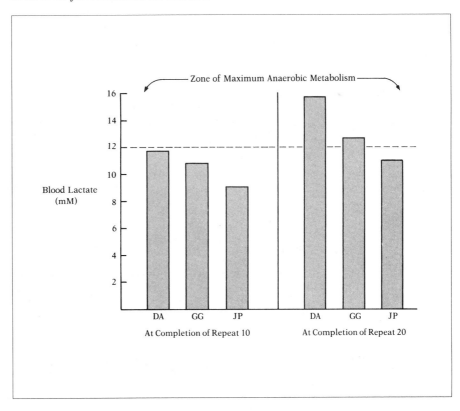

Research indicates the possibility that maximum levels of lactate accumulation are not reached in long distance efforts (Karlsson and Saltin 1970, Hermansen 1971).

Our blood analysis work indicates that, early in the season, speeds in excess of 85 percent of race speed are required to reach maximum rates of anaerobic metabolism when the repeats are 100 yards or less in length. Repeat speeds should approach 90 percent for these distances near the end of the season. Middle-distance repeats should be in excess of a 90 percent effort early in the season and beyond 95 percent of race speed later.

Your working heart rate and subjective feelings of effort are also good indicators of the proper intensity for lactate tolerance drills, perhaps better than percent efforts. Your heart rate should be maximum or near maximum at the end of each repeat. You should feel that you swim each repeat or set of repeats at or near maximum effort. The purpose of lactate tolerance drills should be to push yourself beyond your present pain level. In this way you can be sure you have overloaded the mechanisms that increase lactate production and pain tolerance.

Obviously, swimmers cannot be expected to swim such stressful repeats on a daily basis. They would come to dread practice and the physiological strain might cause illness or injury. Most experts recommend 2 to 4 high-intensity anaerobic training sessions per week. This may seem too few. However, you must remember that there is always some overlap of training effects among the various metabolic processes. Thus, swimmers will be receiving some lactate tolerance training on other days when the repeat sets are designed primarily to improve other functions. Some repeat sets that should improve lactate tolerance are listed in Table 9.9.

Race-Pace Training

Race-pace training simulates race conditions and, in so doing, may encourage some integrating forms of metabolic adaptations that are not produced by other training methods. Race-pace training probably improves the interaction of the various metabolic processes so that energy is supplied in the most eco-

Table 9.9 *Lactate Tolerance Training for Swimmers*

Distance (in yards)	Optimum number	Rest interval	Speed
50	16–20 in sets of 4–10 or as a straight set	10–15 sec. rest between repeats when performed in multiple sets; 30 to 60 sec. when done as a straight set	85% to 90% of best time
75	4–20 in sets of 4 or 5	10–15 sec. rest between repeats in multiple sets; 3–5 min. between repeats in straight sets	85% to 90% of best time
100	8–12 in sets of 3 or 5	30 sec. to 5 min. rest between repeats; 3–5 min. between sets	85% to 95% of best time
150 to 200	3–6	30 sec. to 5 min. rest between repeats	90% to 95% of race speed
300–400–500– 600–700–800	3–5	3–5 min. rest between repeats	95% to 99% of race speed

nomical manner for each race distance. Other improvements that should result from this form of training are an improvement in pacing ability and an improvement in stroke efficiency at race speed. Pacing races in the most economical manner reduces the energy used during the first half to three-quarters of the race so that some energy is available for bringing the race home. Improvements in stroke efficiency make it possible to swim a particular pace with less effort which, in turn, reduces the energy requirement and delays fatigue.

Certainly duplicating race speed increases the probability of FTa, FTb, and ST muscle fibers being used in patterns that are identical to those of competition. In this way the recruitment process may be improved so that fewer muscle fibers, particularly FTb fibers, are used at that pace, with most of the energy supplied by the more enduring FTa and ST fibers. Therefore, race-pace swimming may provide a means of reducing the contributions of anaerobic energy sources during races in favor of the more economical aerobic sources.

Swimming at or near race pace is the most important aspect of race-pace training. Repeat sets should be constructed with this in mind. It goes without saying that swimmers should swim the strokes they will use in competition when they swim race-pace sets. They must be sure to use the same muscle fibers in training that they will use in competition.

One word of caution: this form of training, like lactate tolerance training, is very stressful both physiologically and psychologically and overtraining may occur if it is used too frequently. Race-pace sets should be administered judiciously throughout the season at the rate of 2 to 4 sessions per week. Some race-pace sets are recommended for each competitive distance in Table 9.10.

Table 9.10 *Race-Pace Training*

Distance	Optimum number	Rest interval	Speed
Race-Pace Training for 50-Yard Freestylers			
25	10–20 in sets of 4	5–10 sec. rest between repeats; 2–3 min. rest between sets	Present or predicted 50 speed
50	4–10	2–3 min. rest between repeats	90% to 95% of race speed
Broken 50	4–10	10 sec. rest between 25s; 2–3 min. rest between 50s	Present or predicted race speed
Race-Pace Training for 100-Yard Swimmers			
25	15–40 in sets of 8–12	10–15 sec. rest between repeats; 2–3 min. rest between sets	Present or predicted 100 pace
50	20–30 in sets of 4–6	15–30 sec. rest between repeats; 3–5 min. rest between sets	Present or predicted 100 speed
75	10–20 in sets of 3–5	30 sec.–1 min. rest between repeats; 3–5 min. rest between sets	85% to 90% of present or predicted 100 speed
100	4–6	4–5 min. rest between repeats	90% to 95% of race speed
Broken 100 (4 × 25)	4–10	5 sec. rest between 25s; 2–3 min. rest between 100s	Present or predicted race speed
Broken 100 (2 × 50)	3–5	10–20 sec. rest between 50s; 3–4 min. rest between 100s	Present or predicted race speed

continued overleaf

Table 9.10. *continued*

Distance	Optimum number	Rest interval	Speed
Race-Pace Training for 200-Yard Swimmers			
25	30–60 in sets of 8–16	5–10 sec. rest between repeats; 2–3 min. rest between sets	Present or predicted race speed
50	20–40 in sets of 6–8	10–15 sec. rest between repeats; 2–7 min. rest between sets	Present or predicted race speed
75	12–20 in sets of 4–8	20–30 sec. rest between repeats; 2–4 min. rest between sets	Present or predicted race speed
100	10–15 in sets of 3–4	1 min. rest between repeats; 3–5 min. rest between sets	Present or predicted race speed
150–200	3–5	5–6 min. rest between repeats	90% to 95% of 200 pace
Broken 200 (4 × 50)	4–8	10 sec. rest between 50s; 2–4 min. rest between 200s	Present or predicted race speed
Broken 200 (2 × 100) or (2 × 75) + (1 × 50)	3–5	20–30 sec. rest between parts; 3–5 min. rest between 200s	Present or predicted race speed
Race-Pace Training for 500 Freestylers and 400 I.M.ers			
50	30–60 in sets of 10–15	10–15 sec. rest between repeats; 2–4 min. rest between sets	Present or predicted race speed
75–100	15–30 in sets of 8–12	20–30 sec. rest between repeats; 3–5 min. rest between sets	At present or predicted race speed
150–200	5–10	2–3 min. rest between repeats	Present or predicted race speed
300–400–500	3–4	3–5 min. rest between repeats	90% to 95% of 500 pace
Broken 500/400	3–5	10 sec. rest between 50s or 100s; 3–5 min. rest between swims	Present or predicted race speed
Race-Pace Training for 1650-Yard Freestylers			
50	60–80 in sets of 30–40	5–10 sec. rest between repeats; 3–5 min. rest between sets	Present or predicted race speed
100	30–50 in sets of 15–16	10–20 sec. rest between repeats; 3–5 min. rest between sets	Present or predicted race speed
150–200–300	10–20 in sets of 8–10	30–60 sec. rest between repeats; 3–5 min. rest between sets	95% of 1650 pace
400–500–600	6–12 in sets of 3–4	1–3 min. rest between repeats; 4–8 min. rest between sets	90% of 1650 pace
700–800–1,000	3–4	3–5 min. rest between repeats	90% of 1650 pace
1,650	2–3	5–10 min. rest between repeats	90% to 95% of race speed
Broken 1,650	2–3	10 sec. rest between 50s or 100s; 4–8 min. rest between 1650s	Present or predicted race speed

Blood Lactate Studies

In the process of writing this chapter it became apparent that there were no physiological data regarding the anaerobic and aerobic nature of certain repeat sets. For this reason, blood samples were collected from swimmers as they completed several of the most frequently used repeat sets. These samples were then analyzed for lactate concentrations in order to estimate the relative effectiveness of each set for improving either the aerobic or anaerobic metabolic processes that operate during races. Sets that produced near maximum concentrations of blood lactate (in excess of 12 mM for most people) are probably most useful for improving lactate tolerance. Sets that produced concentrations of between 4 and 12 mM are probably very effective for improving the anaerobic threshold and maximum oxygen consumption, while those that produced concentrations of between 2 mM and 4 mM are probably only marginally effective for this purpose.

Samples were taken from a minimum of three male swimmers for each repeat set. Each swimmer's average speed for each set was expressed in two ways: as a percentage of the swimmer's lifetime best performance for that distance and as a percent of his season best for that distance. The repeat times

Table 9.11 *Blood Lactate Concentrations Produced by Some of the More Frequently Used Repeat Sets*

Repeat sets	Range of average times for the set	The range of percent efforts based on the swimmers' lifetime-best performance	The range of percent efforts based on the swimmers' season-best performance prior to testing	Range of blood lactate concentrations in mM	Range of heart rate	Probable training effect
Aerobic Sets						
4 × 500/6 min.	5:05–5:30	89–94	91–89	2.49–6.72	170–180	Anaerobic Threshold
8 × 200/2:30	2:02–2:08	80–87	86–92	2.10–5.22	180–192	Anaerobic Threshold
20 × 100/1:15	58.5–61.5	78–83	81–83	5.30–8.90	180–204	Anaerobic Threshold & VO₂ max.
3 × 500/6 Descending set	5:10–5:16 (last repeat of set 5:03–5:04)	94–95	96–97	3.60–4.59	180–185	Anaerobic Threshold
3 × 200/2:45 Descending set	2:04–2:07 (last repeat of set 1:53–2:03	83–85	87–89	5.42–6.00	190–192	Anaerobic Threshold
20 × 25/30	12–17 (butterfly)	87–96	91–98	1.70–11.75		Speed
Anaerobic Sets						
6 × 200/5	1:53–2:08	86–89	91–93	12.58–13.57	180–190	Lactate Tolerance
10 × 100/2½	54–1:13	86–89	89–92	11.94–14.36	180–198	Lactate Tolerance
20 × 50/1¼	25.2–27.3	84–89	89–91	9.22–15.23	187–200	Lactate Tolerance
1 broken 200	1:44.2–1:48.3	96–98	101–103	6.40–13.68	168–180	Anaerobic Threshold and Lactate Tolerance if the Elapsed Time is near 100% of the Swimmers' Lifetime-Best
1 broken 100	46.9–54.4	101–108	105–110	9.33–12.74		

were expressed as percent efforts so that readers could adapt this information for swimmers of different ages, sex, and ability levels. Postset heart rates were also recorded for the same reason. The results are shown in Table 9.11.

As expected, long-distance, middle-distance and short-distance repeat sets that are completed on short rest intervals were aerobic in nature. Blood lactate concentrations seldom exceeded 6 mM. Nevertheless, the heart rates were quite high in the range of 170 to 200 bpm. Efforts were between 78 and 94 percent of the swimmers' lifetime best performances and between 81 and 98 percent of their season best swims for the same distances.

Repeat distances of 50 to 200 yards that were completed on medium and long rest intervals were most effective for producing near maximum rates of anaerobic metabolism. Efforts between 84 and 89 percent of the swimmers' best times or between 87 and 92 percent of their season best performances were required for this purpose. Heart rates were generally between 180 and 200 bpm. Twenty-five-yard repeats were not anaerobic regardless of the intensities and the length of rest intervals. Such repeats, as indicated, can be used to train aerobic endurance if the rest is short and, of course, are excellent for improving speed.

Training for Other Circulatory and Muscular Adaptations

Circulatory and muscular adaptations that are amenable to training were discussed in the previous chapter. The circulatory adaptations that take place with training include increases in cardiac output, muscle blood flow, capillary density, blood volume, hemoglobin content, and heart size. Muscular adaptations to training include increases in myoglobin content, buffering capacity, enzyme activity, and muscle glycogen content, as well as shifts in the FT fiber population from the fast but nonenduring FTb fibers to the more oxidative FTa fibers, and the possibility of fiber splitting in both the FT and ST fiber groups. Certain types of repeat sets can be identified as most effective for producing each of these adaptations.

Circulatory Adaptations   Anaerobic threshold and maximum oxygen consumption drills are probably the best forms of training for producing adaptations in the circulatory system. $\dot{V}O_2$ max drills are probably most effective for increasing heart size, capillary density, muscle blood flow, blood volume, and hemoglobin content. These drills make the greatest demands on oxygen consumption and are therefore most likely to provide the stimulation needed for improvement. Training can be nonspecific where increases in heart size, blood volume, and hemoglobin are concerned, since any form of work that is performed at the proper speed and intensity for the necessary length of time will make appropriate demands on the central circulatory mechanisms. However, increases in muscle blood flow and capillary density will occur only around muscle fibers that have been exercised. Therefore, swimmers must swim their competitive strokes or engage in activities that utilize the same muscle fibers if they want these adaptations to take place.

Cardiac output can also be increased by anaerobic threshold or $\dot{V}O_2$ max training of a nonspecific nature. This is because the dominant adaptation that improves cardiac output is an increase in stroke volume. Increases in stroke volume can be effectively produced by a variety of activities, including but not restricted to, swimming.

Muscular Adaptations Some of the most important adaptations to training that take place in muscle cells, increases in myoglobin content, enzyme activity, glycogen content and perhaps buffering capacity, will increase the energy available for races while at the same time providing more of that energy through aerobic metabolism so that fatigue is delayed.

Myoglobin is the pigment that transports oxygen across the cell to the mitochondria. The quantity of myoglobin has been found to increase markedly with training (Holloszy 1973). When the activity of the aerobic enzymes in muscle cells is increased, the muscles can, of course, metabolize more energy aerobically and reduce the rate of lactic acid accumulation during races. Training that increases the activity of the anaerobic enzymes will increase swimmers' abilities to produce lactic acid so that more energy can be made available at fast speeds. Since glycogen is the source of most of the energy for races, an increase in the quantity of this substance will, of course, increase the muscle's potential supply of energy. These and other changes cause muscle fibers to become more enduring. When this occurs in the fast twitch muscle fibers, the primarily low-endurance FTb fibers within the group will take on some of the aerobic properties of the more enduring FTa fibers. When this occurs a shift of FTb to FTa fibers is said to take place. There is also evidence that training causes fast twitch and perhaps slow twitch fibers to split so that the total number of fibers that are available for work is increased. Buffers prevent lactic acid from driving the pH of muscle cells so low that the rate of energy metabolism is curtailed. Although increases in buffering capacity have not been consistently demonstrated by research, it is reasonable to assume that training could improve the supply of buffers in muscle cells. Therefore, it is wise to include repeats that might improve buffering capacity. If buffering capacity can be increased it would surely be one of the more beneficial adaptations, particularly for sprint and middle-distance swimmers.

Myoglobin content. Anaerobic threshold training should be the best method for stimulating significant increases in the myoglobin content of swimmers' muscles. Since most of the myoglobin is found in ST fibers, the moderate speeds of AT repeats should be ideal for this purpose. Swimmers, particularly sprinters, will want to increase the myoglobin content of their FT fibers as well. $\dot{V}O_2$ max drills, because they require faster speeds, may be best for this purpose. Since increased myoglobin will occur only in fibers that are exercised (Holloszy 1973), swimmers who desire this adaptation must be certain to swim their competitive stroke(s) often in training.

Enzyme activity. The activity of aerobic enzymes should be increased most rapidly by anaerobic threshold training because it stimulates aerobic metabolism to maximum capacity for long periods of time without interference from acidosis. The aerobic enzymes should be quite active under those circumstances, which will, in turn, provide the training overload required to increase their activity. Since anaerobic threshold training probably involves the ST muscle fibers to a greater extent than the FT fibers, you may want to include some $\dot{V}O_2$ max drills in your training program so that the aerobic enzymes of FT fibers are overloaded to a greater extent. The activity of the anaerobic enzymes should be increased most by lactate tolerance and long intense sets of race-pace training because repeats of both types stimulate anaerobic metabolism to near maximum rates.

Since increases in both aerobic and anaerobic enzyme activity will take place only in fibers that are exercised, the muscle fibers that will be used in competition must be used in practice. Therefore, the safest procedure is to swim your major stroke or strokes in practice.

Special mention should be made of the enzyme H-LDH because this enzyme increases the rate of lactate removal from working muscles. Since the largest quantities are found in the ST muscle fibers and the cardiac muscle fibers, combinations of specific and nonspecific anaerobic threshold training can be used for increasing the activity of this enzyme.

The rate of removal of lactate from the muscle fibers that were used in the competitive stroke to other resting ST muscle fibers that are lying adjacent (another important training adaptation that may be regulated by enzyme activity) should be improved most by swimming your competitive strokes in practice. The H-LDH content of cardiac fibers can probably be increased by any form of training that stimulates the heartbeat.

Muscle glycogen content. It is well documented that the muscle glycogen content of muscles is increased by training. The increases have ranged from 40 to 100 percent in the various studies that were surveyed (Hultman, Bergström, and Roch-Norlund 1971; Morgan et al. 1971; Short, Cobb, and Morgan 1969; Taylor 1975; MacDougall et al. 1975). Increases in muscle glycogen content are probably best produced by anaerobic threshold training. This is because long sets of repeats cause large amounts of glycogen to be metabolized, which should, in turn, stimulate the muscles to store this substance in greater quantity.

Only middle-distance and distance swimmers need be concerned about increasing muscle glycogen content because depletion is not a cause of fatigue in sprint events. Since increases in glycogen content are found only in those fibers that are used in training, it is best to swim your major stroke or strokes in repeats that are designated for this purpose.

Shifts and splitting within the FT muscle fibers. $\dot{V}O_2$ max, race-pace, and anaerobic and speed repeats are recommended for these purposes. $\dot{V}O_2$ max repeats, because they are more intense than AT drills, should make greater demands on the aerobic capacity of FT fibers, which will provide the stimulus for the increases in the aerobic capacity of these fiber groups that have been reported to result from training.

High-speed swims at maximum effort are required to cause the recruitment of FTb fibers. Therefore, if fiber splitting occurs in the FTb muscle fibers, and perhaps the FTa fibers as well, it should be stimulated best by speed training, lactate tolerance repeats, and resistance training. The research of Costill and associates (Costill et al. 1978), indicates resistance training involving 6- and 30-second maximal efforts is effective for increasing the total number of FT muscle fibers.

If, at a later date, fiber splitting is found to occur in the ST muscle fibers of humans, it is probable that anaerobic threshold training would be the ideal method for producing this effect. At the risk of being repetitious, it should once again be emphasized that if you want to be certain that fiber shifts and fiber splitting occur in the muscle fibers you use in competition, you must swim the same stroke or strokes in training that you will swim in competition.

Buffering capacity. If it is possible to increase the buffering capacity of muscles, lactate tolerance and race-pace repeats should be the most effective method for accomplishing this purpose. Both types of repeats stimulate anaerobic metabolism and, in the process, should make demands on the buffer systems. Once again, swimmers are well advised to swim their major competitive strokes during these repeats to make certain that any increases that occur will be in the muscle fibers they use in competition.

The Importance of Distance Training for Sprinters

The experiences of coaches and swimmers have repeatedly verified the benefits of distance training for sprinters. On the other hand, some researchers have suggested that distance training is not essential to success in sprinting because distance swimmers rely on aerobic metabolism, while sprinting is supported primarily by anaerobic metabolism. While this statement is true, it is a generalization that overlooks certain physiological adaptations, best produced by distance training, that will improve performances in sprint events.

Such adaptations as increased lactate removal from working muscles, increased myoglobin content, and possibly an increase in the pyruvate to alanine shift may all play an important role in improving the endurance of 100 and 200 swimmers. These mechanisms, unlike oxygen consumption, which requires 2 to 3 minutes to reach maximum capacity, should be able to operate at full capacity during the first 40 seconds to 2 minutes of work and, therefore, make a substantial contribution toward reducing the rate of lactate accumulation in working muscle fibers. $\dot{V}O_2$ max repeats, lactate tolerance, and race-pace drills of 200 yards and longer are recommended for this purpose. Anaerobic threshold training may not be effective because the speed of these repeats may not be sufficient to stimulate the use of large numbers of the FT muscle fibers that are used to swim sprint races.

The role that myoglobin may play in sprint events deserves special clarification because this substance has been shown to increase with endurance training (Pattengale and Holloszy 1967), whereas the quantity of pyruvate that is converted to alanine is speculative.

Myoglobin serves both a storage and transportation function for oxygen in the muscles. While the transportation function has received some attention with regard to endurance events, the storage function has been dismissed as inconsequential because the amount of oxygen stored in the myoglobin of muscle fibers is quite small. It has been estimated at 240 ml (Keul, Doll, and Keppler 1972), an amount that could delay lactate production for 2 to 4 seconds at the beginning of exercise. Consider also that an 80 percent increase in myoglobin, such as has been reported in endurance trained rats (Pattengale and Holloszy 1967), should it also occur in humans, could delay lactate production an additional 1 to 2 seconds. While these delays would be insignificant in endurance events, they might reduce the rate of lactate production enough to enable a 100 or 200 swimmer to complete the second half of a race an all-important fraction of a second faster. Most sprint swimmers would surely agree that overdistance repeats are worth swimming if they increase the myoglobin content of their muscles and improve their times by a few tenths of a second.

Observations about the benefits of overdistance training should not be interpreted to mean that distance swimming is the most important form of training for sprinters. It must be emphasized that improvements in sprint speed and lactate tolerance yield the most significant reductions of time in these events. Therefore, these forms of training should never be neglected for the sake of distance training. However, it is difficult to visualize a situation in which such a conflict would exist. The total distance covered in speed, lactate tolerance, and race-pace drills must of necessity be short because of the intensity required. Two to four training sessions per week involving 500 to 1,500 yards/meters of such training is usually all that most swimmers can tolerate. Thus, there should be plenty of time remaining for $\dot{V}O_2$ max training and quality sets of middle-distance repeats.

The Importance of Sprint Training for Distance Swimmers

Obviously, the best form of training for distance swimmers consists primarily of long swims and short-rest underdistance repeats because they improve aerobic capacity. However, distance swimmers also need to improve the anaerobic capacity of their muscle fibers so they can swim faster in the final portions of their races. Rested sprints of 50 and 100 yards/meters have traditionally been utilized for this purpose. Although this method may have some value, it is probably not the best way to train for "bringing it home" in distance races. Rested sprints improve your speed for "getting races out."

Distance swimmers must be able to sprint when fatigued. They do not need to improve their sprint speed, but, instead, their ability to maintain or increase a particular submaximal pace (which could be swum easily when rested) when they are rapidly approaching acidosis in the last part of a race.

The ability to sprint when fatigued should be improved most by sets of high-speed 50s, 100s, and 200s that are performed late in a practice session, after the swimmers are fatigued. Some of the lactate tolerance and race-pace repeats listed in Tables 9.9 and 9.10 are ideal for this purpose. If the repeats are to be specific to the race situation, the speed of these repeats should be at least as fast as a particular swimmer expects to "bring it home" in the actual race.

Swimming repeats in descending sets should be an excellent way to increase the ability to sprint when fatigued. The first half to three-quarters of the set will provide the fatigue while the last few repeats will provide the training effect. Many successful swimmers intuitively swim their repeats in descending sets. Perhaps this is one reason they have been successful.

Training Middle-Distance Swimmers

Middle-distance swimmers must have the sprint speed to get their races out, the aerobic capacity to maintain a fast pace in the middle, and the anaerobic capacity to bring the race home when they are fatigued. They should, therefore, include all forms of training in their programs.

Rested sprints will improve their ability to get the race out with less effort. Anaerobic threshold and $\dot{V}O_2$ max repeats will reduce lactate production and increase lactate removal from working muscles making it possible to maintain a faster average speed through the middle of the race. High-quality fatigued sprints, such as lactate tolerance and underdistance race-pace drills, will improve their ability to bring the race home.

Special Forms of Training

Interval training, although it is the most popular form of training, is only one of several methods swimmers can use to improve their speed and their anaerobic and aerobic endurance. There are several other forms of training in popular use today. Some of these are worthwhile and deserve a place in the training program of all swimmers while others have limited usefulness. The special forms of training that will be discussed are broken swimming, marathon and fartlek training, hypoxic training, and running.

Broken Swimming   Broken swimming is a form of interval training in which a particular race distance is separated or broken into parts. These parts are repeated in sequence with minimal rest between them and the total time (minus rest periods) is compared to a swimmer's best time for that distance. For example, a 200-yard race could be broken into four 50-yard swims. Each of these 50s would be swum at present or predicted race pace with perhaps 5 to 10 seconds rest between swims. The sum of the four 50 swims would be expected to approach or exceed present race speed.

Broken swimming is a very motivating and effective form of training. Swimmers enjoy completing a broken 200 in 1:45, whereas a time of 2:03 for an unbroken 200-yard swim is not nearly so exciting. There is, however, a question as to whether the stress of broken swims is identical to that of an unbroken swim over the same distance. The rest period between parts, although short, does provide some restoration of creatine phosphate and perhaps myoglobin and for this reason they probably do not duplicate the metabolic environment of a straight swim in competition. Nevertheless, near maximum concentrations of blood lactate were found after swimmers completed broken swims with elapsed times (minus the rest intervals) that were as fast or faster than their race times (see Table 9.11).

In addition, the pacing training that is provided by broken swims should play a very important role in the training process. This is one of the few ways a swimmer can practice swimming at race speed. Therefore, they may be one of the more effective methods for simulating competitive conditions. Some forms of broken swimming are recommended in the tables concerning the five forms of training presented in this chapter.

Marathon and Fartlek Training

Both marathon and fartlek training involve swimming long distances continuously. The major difference between the two is that the pace of the swim is constant in marathon training, while in fartlek training it can be varied in any manner the swimmer or coach desires. Any combination of strokes, and various combinations of pulling, kicking, and swimming can be used in fartlek training and the speeds may vary from moderate to sprinting.

Both training methods are very effective for improving your anaerobic threshold, provided the average intensity of the swim is slightly above your present AT. Maximum oxygen consumption capacity can also be improved by marathon and fartlek training. Fartlek training may also aid in the development of lactate tolerance if the sprint portions of the swims are sufficient in intensity and duration to create near maximum rates of anaerobic metabolism.

There has been considerable controversy concerning the merits of interval as opposed to marathon and fartlek styles of training. Interval training would seem to be the superior method because it affords greater control over the intensity of training, and the principles of overload and progression can be applied in a more systematic manner. Nevertheless, research with distance runners has not demonstrated a superiority of interval training over marathon and fartlek methods where improvements of aerobic capacity are concerned (Costill 1968). For this reason, coaches and swimmers should feel free to include marathon and fartlek training in their conditioning programs.

Hypoxic Training

Hypoxic training has enjoyed considerable popularity in recent years. It is based on the premise that a reduction in the breathing rate will reduce the oxygen supply and in so doing, will enhance both the aerobic and anaerobic training effects of a particular repeat set.

The rationale for hypoxic training has been drawn from research conducted at altitudes and at simulated altitudes where improvements in aerobic capacity were reported that were superior to increases that resulted from training at sea level (Hollmann and Leisen 1973). The major adaptations that are believed to result from training at high altitudes are an increase in pulmonary diffusing capacity and an increase in the extraction of oxygen by working muscles. Improvements in lactate tolerance are also thought to occur because lactate production should be increased when the oxygen supply is restricted.

Although these data seem to support the practice of hypoxic training, it should be recognized that training which involves restricted breathing at sea level (hypoxic training) and altitude training that involves the unrestricted breathing of air with lower than normal concentrations of oxygen (hypoxia training) may not produce the same physiological effects in an athlete's body. In fact, research by Craig (1978) and others (Dicker et al. 1980) indicate that hypoxic training and hypoxia training do not produce the same effects.

Craig (1978) measured the composition of alveolar air of subjects who were running on a treadmill while using restricted breathing patterns similar to those used in hypoxic swim training. Although there was a slight reduction in the oxygen content of the subjects' alveolar air, it was not sufficient to produce hypoxia. It is doubtful, therefore, that hypoxic training could produce improvements in oxygen consumption like those that result from training at high altitudes.

The major effect of hypoxic breathing was an increase in the CO_2 content of the subjects' alveolar air, a condition known as *hypercapnea* which produces no known training effect except an improved ability to hold your breath. Dicker and associates (1980) reported similar findings in a study in which the pulmonary response of competitive swimmers was tested when they used some of the more popular forms of hypoxic breathing while performing tethered swimming.

The major response to hypoxic training is probably an improved ability to swim races with fewer breaths. Freestyle sprinters and butterflyers may want to do some hypoxic training for this reason. Swimmers in other events may be subjecting themselves to needless discomfort and are better advised to use the same breathing patterns in training that they will use in competition.

Running Versus Swimming

Many coaches now include running in their training programs. The rationale behind this practice is that running will improve aerobic capacity more than swimming. This rationale was originally based on research in which subjects attained higher heart rates and higher rates of oxygen consumption when they were running than when they were swimming (Holmer 1974). However, proponents of running apparently failed to notice that these same researchers also reported that subjects who had been trained in the water achieved higher heart rates and oxygen consumption values when swimming than when running.

Running might be a valid form of training for swimmers if the major training adaptations that improve aerobic capacity occurred in the circulatory system. However, many, if not most, of the adaptations that improve aerobic capacity occur in the muscles. Swimming, because it makes demands on the

Table 9.12 *A Hypothetical Model for Training the Energy Systems Used in Competitive Swimming*

	Rest	Phase I	The aerobic threshold	Phase II	The anaerobic threshold	Phase III	$\dot{V}O_2$ max.	Phase IV	Maximum anaerobic metabolism
Predominant type of metabolism		Aerobic		Aerobic		Aerobic		Anaerobic	
Predominant muscle fiber types used		Slow twitch		Slow twitch		Slow twitch Fast twitch A		Slow twitch, Fast twitch A, Fast twitch B	
Heart rate	35–80		130		150		170		185
Percent effort									
50–150 repeats			60% to 70%		65% to 75%		70% to 80%		80% to 90%
200–400 repeats			65% to 75%		75% to 85%		80% to 90%		90% to 99%
Longer swims			70% to 75%		85% to 95%		90% to 95%		95%
Blood lactate	1.2		2		4		8*		12–20
Training effect		Little or no improvement of aerobic or anaerobic endurance		Some improvement of aerobic endurance		Considerable improvement of aerobic endurance		Considerable improvement of anaerobic endurance	

Source: Adapted from J. S. Skinner and T. H. McLellan, "The Transition from Aerobic to Anaerobic Metabolism," *Research Quarterly for Exercise and Sport,* 51, 1980, pp. 234–248, by permission of the American Alliance for Health, Physical Education, Recreation and Dance, 1900 Association Drive, Reston, Va. 22091, and the authors.
*Not verified.

proper muscle groups, should be a much more effective form of training for swimmers. It is doubtful that the improvements in aerobic capacity that swimmers attain from running are worth the time and effort involved.

Holmer and Astrand (1972) have presented some research that is interesting in this regard. They tested identical twins who had both been age group competitive swimmers. One twin had continued training and, as a senior swimmer, attained national prominence, while the other left the sport and became active in track and field hockey. Both girls were tested for maximal oxygen consumption while swimming, while bicycling, and while running. The swimming test was conducted in a specially constructed flume which acts as a water treadmill. The bicycle test was performed on a bicycle ergometer, and the running test was performed on a treadmill.

Results of the bicycle ergometer test indicated that both girls were nearly identical in oxygen consumption capacity. This was to be expected since they inherited the same capacities and neither girl had trained on a bicycle. The interesting result was that the twin who was a competitive swimmer consumed more oxygen than her running sister when they were tested in the swimming flume, while the twin who was active in track and field hockey achieved a higher rate of oxygen consumption when they were tested on a treadmill. This experiment demonstrates, quite convincingly, that a significant number of physiological adaptations that improve oxygen consumption are specific to the activity that is used in training.

While it is true that circulatory adaptations such as an increased cardiac output, increased heart size, increases in red blood cells, and increases in blood volume can be produced by several forms of training, swimmers who run when they could be swimming are losing the opportunity to produce additional and perhaps more important improvements in the aerobic capacity of those muscle cells that are only used when swimming. For this reason, running can only be recommended for training those swimmers who lack the motivation to train in the water for a sufficient length of time. Swimmers who prefer training in the water would be ill-advised to reduce their time in the water in order to make time for running.

A Model for Monitoring Swim Training

A model for determining the proper intensities for aerobic and anaerobic training has been suggested by Skinner and McLellan (1980). This model has been adapted to competitive swimming. The results of our blood lactate research, that were presented earlier in Figures 9.10 and 9.14 and in tables 9.6 and 9.11 were used to develop guidelines for determining the proper intensities for anaerobic threshold, $\dot{V}O_2$ max, and lactate tolerance training. The model is presented in Table 9.12. It includes four phases of training.

Phase I   There is probably little benefit from training at intensities that fall within phase I. Heart rates below 130 bpm and efforts below 60 percent are probably not sufficiently intense to produce a significant training effect in well-conditioned competitive swimmers. This is indicated by blood lactate concentrations that do not increase above the aerobic threshold. Swimmers who train at intensities falling within this phase should be given a bar of soap to use for bathing so their time is not completely wasted.

Phase II   Training intensities that fall within this phase, although not sufficient to increase blood lactate concentrations above the anaerobic threshold (4 mM), may be beneficial for improving aerobic endurance. Many athletes who achieve good times in competition spend a considerable amount of their time training at intensities that fall between the aerobic and anaerobic thresholds. The value of training in this phase may be that the aerobic endurance of ST and FTa muscle fibers can be improved without excessive effort. Therefore, although it is probably not intense enough to overload aerobic metabolism, there may be more value in this form of training than is generally believed. Nevertheless, much of the energy for the majority of swimming races is provided through anaerobic metabolism. Therefore, swimmers, particularly middle-distance and sprint swimmers, should spend a considerable portion of their time training at intensities that fall within phases III and IV.

Phase III   Training at intensities that fall within this phase is probably the most effective means for improving anaerobic threshold and maximum oxygen consumption. Repeat speeds are sufficiently intense to overload aerobic metabolism and to cause the recruitment of some fast twitch muscle fibers so that their aerobic capacity will be improved.

It is probably advisable to train at heart rates and percent efforts that are near the anaerobic threshold boundary of this phase during the early part of swimming seasons. Later, the intensity should be increased until training is near the $\dot{V}O_2$ max border.

Phase IV   Training at intensities that are near the $\dot{V}O_2$ max border of this phase should improve that physiological mechanism, while also providing some anaerobic training effects. Training speeds and heart rates that fall near the maximum anaerobic metabolism (max. an. met.) border should improve lactate tolerance. Swimmers, regardless of the events they are training for, should not train in phase IV on a daily basis, at least not at intensities that fall near the maximum anaerobic metabolism border, or overtraining may result. They must allow sufficient recovery time between these intense sessions. Sprinters should spend more time training in this phase than swimmers in longer events. Middle-distance swimmers should train in phases II and III most of the time. However, they should spend a sizable portion of their time training in phase IV. Distance swimmers should spend most of their time training in phases II and III and should train in phase IV only occasionally.

REFERENCES

Astrand, P. O., and Rodahl, K. 1977. *Textbook of Work Physiology*. New York: McGraw-Hill.

Christensen, E. H., Hedman, R., and Saltin, B. 1960. "Intermittent and Continuous Running." *Acta Physiol. Scand.* 50:269. Cited by P. O. Astrand and K. Rodahl, *Textbook of Work Physiology*. New York: McGraw-Hill, 1977.

Costill, D. L. 1968. *What Research Tells the Coach About Distance Running*. Washington: American Association for Health, Physical Education, and Recreation.

———. 1978. "Adaptations in Skeletal Muscle During Training for Sprint and Endurance Swimming." *Swimming Medicine IV*, ed. B. Eriksson and B. Furberg, pp. 233–248. Baltimore: University Park Press.

Costill, D. L., Coyle, E. F., Fink, W. J., Lesmes, G. R., and Witzman, F. A. 1978. "Adaptations in Skeletal Muscle Following Training." Unpublished research study, Ball State University, Muncie, Indiana.

Craig, A. B. Jr. 1978. "Fallacies of Hypoxic Training in Swimming." *Abstracts of the International Congress of Sports Sciences, July 25–29, 1978*. University of Alberta, Edmonton, Alberta, Canada.

Davis, J. A., Vodak, P., Wilmore, H. J., Vodak, J., and Kurtz, P. 1976. "Anaerobic Threshold and Maximal Aerobic Power for Three Modes of Exercise." *J. Appl. Physiol.* 41:544–549.

deVries, H. A. 1974. *Physiology of Exercise*. Iowa: Wm. C. Brown Co., Publishers.

Dicker, S. G., Lofthus, G. K., Thornton, N. W., and Brooks, G. A. 1980. "Respiratory and Heart Rate Responses to Tethered Controlled Frequency Swimming." *Medicine and Science in Sports*, 12: 20–23.

Dintiman, G. 1974. *What Research Tells the Coach About Sprinting*. Washington: American Association for Health, Physical Education, and Recreation.

Edwards, H. T., Brouha, L., and Johnson, R. T. "Effect de l'entraînement sur le taux de l'acide lactique au cours du travail musculaire." *Le Travail Human.* 8:1.

Fox, E. L. 1979. *Sports Physiology*. Philadelphia: W. B. Saunders Co.

Good, V. 1973. "Effects of Isokinetic Exercise Program on Sprint Swimming Performance of College Women." Master's thesis, California State University, Chico.

Hermansen, L. 1971. "Lactate Production During Exercise." *Muscle Metabolism During Exercise*, ed. B. Pernow and B. Saltin, pp. 401–407. New York: Plenum Press.

Hollmann, W., and Leisen, H. 1973. "The Influence of Hypoxia and Hyperoxia Training in a Laboratory on Cardiopulmonal Capacity." *Limiting Factors in Physical Performance*, ed. J. Keul, pp. 213–218. Stuttgart: Georg Thieme Verlag.

Holloszy, J. O. 1973. "Biochemical Adaptations to Exercise: Aerobic Metabolism." *Exercise and Sports Sciences Review*, vol. 1, ed. J. Wilmore, pp. 45–71. New York: Academic Press.

Holmer, J. 1974. "Physiology of Swimming in Man." *Acta Physiol. Scan.* (Suppl. 407).

Holmer, I., and Astrand, P. O. 1972. "Swimming Training and Maximal Oxygen Uptake." *J. Appl. Physiol.* 33:510–513.

Hultman, E., Bergström, J., and Roch-Norlund, A. E. 1971. "Glycogen Storage in Human Skeletal Muscle." *Muscle Metabolism During Exercise*, ed. B. Pernow and B. Saltin, pp. 273–287. New York: Plenum Press.

Hutinger, P. W. 1970. "Comparisons of Isokinetic, Isotonic, and Isometric Developed

Strength to Speed in Swimming the Crawl Stroke." Doctoral dissertation, Indiana University.

Karlsson, J., and Saltin, B. 1970. "Lactate, ATP and CP in Working Muscle During Exhaustive Exercise in Man." *J. Appl. Physiol.* 29:598–602.

Keul, J., Doll, E., and Keppler, D. 1972. *Energy Metabolism of Human Muscle.* Baltimore: University Park Press.

Kipke, L. 1978. "Dynamics of Oxygen Intake During Step-by-step Loading in a Swimming Flume." *Swimming Medicine IV*, pp. 137–142. Baltimore: University Park Press.

Londeree, B. R. 1977. "Anaerobic Threshold Training." *Toward an Understanding of Human Performance*, ed. E. J. Burke, pp. 15–16. New York: Mouvement Publications.

MacDougall, J. D. 1977. "The Anaerobic Threshold: Its Significance for the Endurance Athlete." *Canadian J. Appl. Sport Sciences* 2:137–140.

MacDougall, J. D., Ward, G. R., Sale, D. C., and Sutton, J. R. 1975. "Muscle Glycogen Repletion After High Intensity Intermittent Exercise." *J. Appl. Physiol.* 4:129–132.

Mader, A., Heck, H., and Hollmann, W. 1976. "Evaluation of Lactic Acid Anaerobic Energy Contribution by Determination of Post-Exercise Lactic Acid Concentration of Ear Capillary Blood in Middle Distance Runners and Swimmers." *Exercise Physiology*, eds. F. Landing and W. Orban, pp. 187–199. Florida: Symposia Specialists, Inc.

Maglischo, E. W., Maglischo, C. W., Bishop, R. A., Smith, R. E., and Hovland, P. N. "Prescribing Training Through Blood Analysis." Unpublished report.

Mathews, D. K., and Fox, E. L. 1976. *The Physiological Basis of Physical Education and Athletics.* Philadelphia: Saunders.

Moffroid, M. T., and Whipple, R. H. 1970. "Specificity of Speed of Exercise." *Phys. Ther.* 50:1692–1700.

Morgan, T. E., Cobb, L., Short, F. A., Ross, R., and Gunn, D. 1971. "Effects of Long Term Exercise on Human Muscle Mitochondria." *Muscle Metabolism During Exercise*, ed. B. Pernow and B. Saltin, pp. 87–95. New York: Plenum Press.

Murray, J. L. 1962. "Effects of Precisely Prescribed Progressive Resistance Exercises with Pulley Weights on Speed and Endurance in Swimming." Master's thesis, Pennsylvania State University.

Pattengale, P. K., and Holloszy, J. O. 1967. "Augmentation of Skeletal Muscle Myoglobin by a Program of Treadmill Running." *Amer. J. Physiol.* 213:783–785.

Pipes, T., and Wilmore, J. H. 1975. "Isokinetic vs. Isotonic Strength Training in Adult Men." *Med. Sci. Sports* 7:262–274.

Ross, D. T. 1973. "Selected Training Procedures for the Development of Arm Extensor Strength and Swimming Speed of the Sprint Crawl Stroke." Master's thesis, University of Oregon.

Rowe, E., Maglischo, E. W., and Lytle, D. E. 1977. "The Use of Swim Fins for the Development of Sprint Swimming Speed." *Swimming Technique* 14:73–76.

Rushall, B., and Thomson, J. M. 1974. "A Component of Sprint Training." *Swimming Technique* 10:107–108, 112.

Sandwick, D. M. 1967. "Pacing Machine." *Athletic J.* 47:36–38.

Short, F. A., Cobb, L. D., and Morgan, T. E. 1969. "Influence of Exercise Training on *in vitro* Metabolism of Glucose and Fatty Acid by Human Skeletal Muscle." *Biochemistry of Exercise*, ed. J. R. Poortmans. Basel: Karger.

Skinner, J. S. and McLellan, T. H. 1980. "The Transition from Aerobic to Anaerobic Metabolism." *Research Quarterly* 51:234–248.

Taylor, A. W. 1975. "The Effect of Exercise and Training on the Activities of Human Skeletal Muscle Glycogen Enzymes." *Metabolic Adaptations to Prolonged Physical Exercise*, ed. H. Howald and J. R. Poortmans, pp. 451–462. Basel: Birkhäuser Verlag.

Treffene, R. J. 1979. "Swimming Performance Test: A Method of Training and Performance Time Selection." *Swimming Technique*, vol. 15, no. 4, pp. 120–124.

Wasserman, K., Whipp, B. J., Kuyal, S., and Beaver, W. 1973. "Anaerobic Threshold and Respiratory Gas Exchange During Exercise." *J. Appl. Physiol.* 35:236–243.

CHAPTER 10

Planning the Swimming Season

A successful swimming season requires weeks of careful planning. The first step is to divide the season into phases with differing emphases so swimmers can be brought to peak performance at the proper time of the season. The next questions to be considered are those of daily and weekly yardages. Once the framework for the season has been established, specialized training programs should be designed for each competitive stroke and for each event. These programs should include all five forms of training in proportions similar to the relative contributions of speed, anaerobic metabolism, aerobic metabolism, and pace to success in that particular event. Programs should be further individualized to correct deficiencies of individual swimmers. Swimmers in the same event may require somewhat different programs if, for example, some lack speed but have reasonable aerobic endurance while others have no problem getting their races out but lack the ability to bring them home. After all of this planning has been completed, the season can be filled in with carefully constructed weekly and daily workouts that include the five forms of training in the proper proportions and the proper order. A final consideration is the prevention and treatment of overtraining.

The Yearly Plan

Most world-class and national level swimmers train for ten or eleven months of every year. The year is usually divided into two seasons, each culminating with a championship meet. The winter season lasts from October to April. It is generally called the **short-course season** because the competition takes place in 25-

Table 10.1 *The Short-Course and Long-Course Seasons*

Phase	Short-course season	Long-course season
Early season	October to January	April to July
Competition period	January to March	July to August
Taper period	2 to 4 weeks before the most important championship meet	2 to 4 weeks before the most important championship meet

yard pools. The summer season begins in late April and continues into August. Since competition is frequently held in 50-meter pools during this time it is referred to as the **long-course season**.

Each of the seasons is divided into various phases. Different aspects of training are emphasized in each phase, all leading toward a peak performance near the end of each particular season. A typical yearly plan is shown in Table 10.1.

Each season should be structured so there is a gradual increase in training intensity from the early season through the competition period, with training reaching its greatest intensity just before the taper.

The Early Season Period

Emphasis during the early season should be on the following:

- Improving stroke mechanics and starting and turning techniques. This should be done early in the year before swimmers become concerned about swimming fast in meets. Many swimmers are not willing to suffer through the temporary decrements in performance that usually accompany changes in techniques when important meets are imminent.
- Improving the anaerobic threshold and increasing $\dot{V}O_2$ max. Swimmers should spend a considerable portion of each session swimming repeats that are designed to improve these processes. They should swim the greater portion of that yardage with the stroke or strokes they will swim in competition.
- Improving muscular power, muscular endurance, and joint flexibility with land and water drills that are designed for these purposes. Some of these drills are described in Chapter 12.
- Establishing season goals. Goals serve a motivational function. They give the season direction and determine what swimmers should work toward in terms of speed, lactate tolerance, and race-pace drills.
- Improving maximal swimming speed. This aspect of training is frequently saved for late in the season in many programs. This is a mistake. Just as with adaptations of the other metabolic processes, it probably requires considerable time to produce changes in the ATP-CP system. Therefore, speed drills should be used throughout the entire season to provide time for the proper training adaptations to take place. There is no danger of overtraining with speed drills because they are not particularly stressful. There is also no danger that speed training will cause an early peak.

Lactate tolerance and race-pace repeats should be used sparingly during the early season period. These repeats are both mentally and physically stressful and overtraining may occur later, during the competition period, if they are used too frequently early in the season.

Although all swimmers should stress anaerobic threshold and $\dot{V}O_2$ max swimming during this period, the amount of emphasis will differ according to the event or events each particular swimmer plans to compete in. Of course, distance and middle-distance swimmers should spend most of their time swimming AT and $\dot{V}O_2$ max repeats. Sprinters and short middle-distance swimmers should swim these repeats less frequently. Sprint and power drills should occupy a greater portion of their training day. Suggestions for training sprint, middle-distance, and distance swimmers follow.

Sprinters. Swimmers in the 50, 100, and 200 events should train at least 5 days per week, although 6 days per week are recommended. They must concentrate on increasing speed and improving the anaerobic threshold.

Speed work should consist primarily of sprints at 25 yards/meters or less. Perhaps 800 to 1,200 yards/meters should be devoted to this type of training at maximum speed during 4 training sessions of each week.

Some high-intensity short rest repeats should be performed for the purpose of increasing the aerobic capacity of fast twitch fibers. These swims should be done 3 to 4 sessions per week with repeat sets totaling perhaps 800 to 1,200 yards/meters per session.

Although sprinters will spend more time on lactate tolerance drills than middle-distance and distance swimmers, the bulk of this training occurs in the competition period. There should be no more than 1 or 2 race-pace or lactate tolerance training sessions per week. The distance devoted to these drills should be approximately 800 to 1,200 yards/meters per session. Anaerobic threshold drills should comprise the remainder of the daily training yardage. These will increase lactate removal and the aerobic capacity of both fiber types. Land drills for improving muscular power should be used 3 to 5 days of each week. These will be described in a later chapter.

Middle-distance swimmers. Athletes in middle-distance events should place considerable emphasis on repeats that improve $\dot{V}O_2$ max and improve the anaerobic threshold. They should train twice a day for at least 5 days of each week. Lactate tolerance and race-pace drills should be used sparingly, perhaps 1 or 2 sessions per week, 800 to 1,200 yards/meters per session. Some speed work is desirable. Three to four sessions per week, 800 to 1,200 yards/meters per session should suffice. Land drills for increasing muscular power and muscular endurance should be used at least 3 days per week. Swimmers who compete in the 200 and who have the 500 as a second event should train with the distance swimmers during 2 days of each week.

Distance swimmers. Distance swimmers should emphasize improving the anaerobic threshold and increasing $\dot{V}O_2$ max, in that order. A serious distance swimmer should train twice a day 6 days a week.

Forty to fifty percent of distance swimmers' daily yardage should be devoted to moderate-intensity overdistance repeats. An additional 10 to 20 percent of the yardage should be in the form of moderate-intensity underdistance repeats on short rest. Twenty to thirty percent of the training yardage should be in the form of middle-distance $\dot{V}O_2$ max repeats. Rested sprints should comprise 500 to 800 yards/meters per session for 3 sessions of each week. Fatigued sprints should be completed during 1 or 2 sessions per week, totaling 800 to 1,000 yards/meters per session. One or two sessions per week should be devoted to race-pace and lactate tolerance training. These forms of training can be combined with fatigued sprints. Land drills for improving muscular endurance can be used during 2 or 3 days of each week.

Swimmers in the 400-meter and the 500-yard events should be included with the distance swimmers during the early season if their second event is the 1,500 or 1,650. If their second event is the 200, they would be better advised to swim in the distance group 2 days per week and spend the remaining sessions with the middle-distance swimmers.

The Competitive Season

During the competitive phase of the season the emphasis should be on:

- Maintaining the anaerobic threshold and $\dot{V}O_2$ max adaptations developed in the early season.
- Developing the anaerobic components of races.
- Swimming more repeats at predicted race speed or faster (race-pace training) in order to adapt the body for maintaining the fastest possible pace.
- Learning the pace and strategy of competitive events.
- Improving the ability to maintain correct stroke mechanics and turning techniques when fatigued.
- Continuing the progressive increase in training intensity that is necessary to maintain overload and progression in the training program.

The competitive season corresponds to the period of time when the most important dual meets are scheduled. There should be an increase in lactate tolerance and race-pace training for swimmers in all events. It is best to delay until the competitive period before increasing the quantities of lactate tolerance and race-pace swimming because experience has shown that few swimmers can tolerate such intense training for longer than 6 to 8 weeks without becoming overtrained.

The daily yardage should decrease slightly during the competitive period to allow for longer rest periods during the high-quality repeats. Weekly training yardage will decrease significantly because weekend practice times will now be devoted to meets.

Sprinters. Sprinters should markedly increase the number and intensity of lactate tolerance and race-pace repeats. The length of the repeat sets will vary from 400 to 1,500 yards/meters. Three to five sessions per week should be devoted to this form of training.

Sprinters should continue to complete 800 to 1,200 yards/meters of speed training on certain days with the frequency of this training increasing to 4 to 6 sessions per week. It is recommended that sprint-assisted training be used at least 3 days weekly.

The remainder of the daily training yardage should be devoted to anaerobic threshold and $\dot{V}O_2$ max drills. There should be at least 4 training sessions weekly in which no lactate tolerance or race-pace drills are performed. These serve as recovery days from the stress of high-intensity swimming. Recovery days should be interspersed with days of high-intensity swimming. Anaerobic threshold, sprint, and sprint-assisted drills are ideal for recovery days because they will maintain and even improve aerobic endurance. Swimmers competing in the 100- and 200-yard/meter events should complete a short set of double distance repeats once every week or week and a half.

Land drills for muscular power should continue to be performed 3 days per week. Land drills for increasing muscular endurance should also be used.

Middle-distance swimmers. Lactate tolerance and race-pace drills should gradually increase for middle-distance swimmers from 1 to 2 sessions per week during the early period to 4 to 6 training sessions weekly midway through the competitive period. These repeat sets should be 400 to 2,400 yards/meters in length.

Most of the repeats should be underdistance at speeds that equal present or predicted race pace. A short, high-quality set of double-distance repeats should be done at least once each week.

Four to six sessions weekly should be devoted to anaerobic threshold training and sprinting. These days should be interspersed with high-intensity sessions. One day each week should be set aside for complete rest or easy swimming.

Middle-distance swimmers who specialize at the 400-meter and 500-yard distances should train with the distance swimmers for 3 to 4 sessions each week. If their best event is the 200 and their second event is the 500, distance training can be reduced to 2 sessions per week.

Middle-distance swimmers should engage in 800 to 1,000 yards/meters of rested sprint training during at least 2 sessions per week. Sets of fatigued sprints should also be completed a minimum of 2 days per week. Underdistance, lactate tolerance, and race-pace drills will serve this purpose nicely.

Middle-distance swimmers with the 200 as their best event and the 100 as a second event should engage in more sprint training and some form of sprint-assisted training. These swimmers would be well advised to train with the sprinters during 5 sessions of each week.

All middle-distance swimmers should perform land drills for muscular power and muscular endurance.

Distance swimmers. Anaerobic threshold and $\dot{V}O_2$ max training should continue to comprise most of the training yardage for distance swimmers. More underdistance and fewer overdistance repeats should be used to allow swimmers to progressively increase the intensity of their training. Six to eight sessions per week should be devoted to anaerobic threshold and $\dot{V}O_2$ max repeats. Race-pace training should increase from 2 to 4 sessions per week. Lactate tolerance training is not necessary since race-pace training will also increase lactate tolerance.

Swimmers in the 1,500 and 1,650 events should complete an over-distance distance time trial for the event at least once every 2 weeks. Swimmers in the 400 and 500 events should swim over-distance time trials once every week or week and a half.

Distance swimmers need to spend some time training with rested and fatigued sprints, particularly the latter. Fatigued sprints, as indicated earlier, train distance swimmers to "bring a race home." Repeats such as 3 to 5 × 100 with 20 to 30 seconds rest, 3 to 4 × 200 with 30 to 60 seconds rest, and 8 to 12 × 50 with 10 to 30 seconds rest are excellent for this purpose. They should be done at the end of practice and swimmers should attempt to swim each repeat near the speed they hope to achieve for the same distance at the end of their races. Two to four sessions weekly are optimal for this purpose.

Rested sprints are valuable if the third event is a 200 or 100 swim. Three to four sprint sessions per week involving 800 to 1,200 yards/meters of sprinting should suffice for this purpose.

There should be one complete day of rest each week. Athletes who dislike being out of the water may want to do some easy swimming on these days. Distance swimmers with the 200 as a second event may find it beneficial to reduce their yardage somewhat and train with the sprinters for 1 or 2 sessions each week. They will also want to do some land drills for muscular endurance.

The Taper Period   The taper period comprises the final 2 to 4 weeks of the season and culminates in the most important meet, usually a championship. The resting process for such a meet is called a major taper. The usual practice is to plan for one major taper per season. Swimmers may also take minor (shorter) tapers and retapers during the season. A minor taper is used when a good performance is needed at a particular meet prior to the championship. The process of retapering refers to a second taper following closely after a major taper.

Coaches seem split over the advisability of minor tapers. Some feel they interfere with training and prevent swimmers from achieving peak performances. Coaches who favor several tapers point out that many swimmers have been able to equal or improve their times in subsequent tapers. They feel, therefore, that swimmers can use several minor tapers with no detrimental effect at season's end. The process of retapering is becoming more important as an increasing number of swimmers must go through a major taper prior to a championship in order to make the cutoff times for entry into the meet. There are also an increasing number of international competitions following national meets that require retapers.

Logic favors one major taper per season with perhaps one or two minor tapers. Tapering too frequently can cause swimmers to lose valuable training time and their conditioning may deteriorate as a result. A typical winter swim season is 20 to 24 weeks in length. The summer season may be 10 to 14 weeks long, depending upon whether training begins in April or June. Since each major taper reduces training time by 2 to 4 weeks, with minor tapers interrupting training for 3 to 7 days, a considerable amount of training time would be lost by swimmers who had gone through 2 or more major tapers and several minor tapers during a season. The time spent in training could be reduced by 50 percent as a result. No more than one major taper per season is recommended. Minor tapers are recommended only when absolutely necessary.

Physiological factors in the taper. The improvements of tapered swimmers are well documented. It is not unusual to improve 1 to 2 seconds in 100 races and 2 to 4 seconds at the 200 distances. Improvements of 4 to 8 seconds are commonplace at distances of 400 meters and 500 yards, while improvements of 20 seconds are not uncommon in the 1,500-meter and 1,650-yard freestyles.

The reasons for these improvements have not been identified at the present time. Some people have theorized that carbohydrate loading may be involved. This is a possibility in races of 400 meters and longer. However, it does not explain the tapered performances of swimmers in shorter events, nor does it explain why 2 to 4 weeks are required to produce a taper effect. Carbohydrate loading can be accomplished in 2 to 3 days.

Although we cannot identify the physiological factors involved in producing a taper effect, we can theorize as to the training stimulus that produces it. Training has repeatedly been shown to produce temporary overcompensating (super adaptation) effects on body physiology. It is reasonable, therefore, to assume that the process of tapering involves some as yet unidentified physiological overcompensation effects. It is conceivable that future research will demonstrate that a long period of training followed by a short period of rest will produce a super adaptation effect where such mechanisms as enzyme activity, lactate removal, and buffering capacity are concerned.

The stimulus for a super adaptation effect in these and other physiological mechanisms may be a training program that does not permit complete recovery from day to day. That is, some components of the training program could be depleting certain metabolic reserves faster than they can be replaced. After 10 to 20 weeks in which these metabolic processes are operating near peak capacity in their attempt to replace the resources that are being depleted, they become so conditioned that they continue supplying energy at high rates during the 2 to 4 weeks that follow. Since the resources are no longer being depleted the quantity of energy available for work will be considerably increased and swimmers will become capable of far better performances than they were able to achieve earlier in the season.

The timing of the taper is critical. If it is too short, the complete overcompensation effect may not be realized. If it is too long, the super adaptation effect will recede as lack of exercise causes a reversal of the training process and the body's homeostatic mechanisms restore the normal untrained internal environment.

The important questions to be answered concerning the taper are: How long should it last? and How much should the workload be reduced? There are no definitive answers to these questions. They differ according to the race distance, the volume of training that was completed prior to the taper, and the unique physiology of each swimmer. Obviously, the most effective tapers are individualized. However, since most coaches must taper large groups of swimmers, a general framework should be established for the team, with individual variations occurring within that framework. Following are some suggestions for establishing a general framework together with recommendations for individualizing it to meet the requirements of certain swimmers.

General guidelines for the taper. The taper should begin 3 weeks before the most important meet of the season, although it may be preceded by a pretaper of 1 to 2 weeks for swimmers who appear excessively fatigued. A pretaper is a period of reduced work that affords excessively fatigued swimmers some additional rest with no loss of conditioning. Daily yardage should be reduced by 1,000 to 2,000 yards/meters during the pretaper. More important, there should be a reduction in training intensity.

The first week. Each swimmer's state of fatigue should be assessed at the beginning of the first week. Those who do not appear overly fatigued may continue hard training until the next week. Swimmers who, based on previous experience, recover quickly from training, may also wait an extra week before beginning the taper. Those who show signs of excessive fatigue should begin resting during this week. The best sign of excessive fatigue is unusually slow times in meets and practice sessions.

Daily training yardage should be reduced to 3,000 to 5,000 yards/meters for those swimmers who are beginning to taper in this week (3,000 for sprinters and middle-distance swimmers and 5,000 for distance swimmers). The intensity of training is reduced even more drastically. Some anaerobic threshold and $\dot{V}O_2$ max training is used to maintain aerobic endurance, and sprint training is used to maintain the adaptations of the ATP-CP phase of energy metabolism. These forms of training are not stressful and will maintain training adaptations gained earlier in the season without causing further fatigue.

Stressful drills such as lactate tolerance and race-pace repeats are also reduced to maintenance levels. Two high-intensity training sessions per week should be sufficient to maintain anaerobic training adaptations (Chaplouka and Fox 1975). The distance of each high-intensity set should be reduced from those that were used during the competitive season. Continue with 3 to 5 sessions of sprint training per week but reduce the yardage in these sets to between 400 and 800 yards/meters per session. Swimmers may get tired in their training during this week but they should not be overly fatigued at the end of each practice session. Muscular endurance and power training on land should also be reduced to maintenance levels. Flexibility exercises should be continued throughout the taper period.

Considerable time should be spent practicing starts, turns, relay starts, race-pace, and race strategy. Race-pace is extremely important. Swimmers should be aware not only of the time they hope to swim at the meet but also the splits they must swim to achieve that time. They should enter the competition able to swim repeats within 0.2 to 0.5 of a second of the splits they hope to attain over the first three-quarters of their races.

Stroke drills should be done daily and swimmers should be encouraged to use perfect mechanics. Fatigue may have introduced some faulty mechanics during the competitive season that need to be corrected when the swimmers are resting.

Swimmers should continue to train twice daily if the meet will be swum in preliminary and final heats. By doing so, they can keep their physiological "time clocks" adjusted to competing twice daily. It is also advisable to train during the same hours the meet will be held. This helps to adjust the physiological "time clock" for maximum effort at the correct time of day. Training twice per day is not necessary if the meet is swum as timed finals or if the taper is for a dual meet.

The second week. All swimmers begin tapering at this time even if they are swimming well in meets and practices. However, distance swimmers who are swimming well may taper more gradually. They may begin the week at normal training yardage and decrease that distance by 1,000 to 1,500 yards/meters per day throughout the week. The training pattern should be similar to that described for the first week of the taper.

Those swimmers who have been resting for one week should be evaluated once again. If they appear to be recovering faster than anticipated, add 2,000 to 3,000 yards/meters to their daily training during three days of the week. A small amount of that yardage should be in the form of high-intensity race-pace repeats. Sprinters and middle-distance swimmers who continue to show signs of fatigue should reduce their daily distances by an additional 1,500 to 3,000 yards/meters. These swimmers should reduce the number of high-intensity training sessions to 1 or 2 for the week.

The final week. Training yardage should be reduced to 2,000 to 3,000 yards/meters per day for sprinters and middle-distance swimmers, and 4,000 to 5,000 yards per day for distance swimmers. Most of this yardage should be in the form of warm-up swimming and low-intensity anaerobic threshold swimming. Intense training, race-pace swimming, and sprinting should comprise no more than 400 to 1,200 yards/meters during 2 or 3 sessions during the week. All-out sprints should be limited to the 25 and 50 distances since they are not stressful physiologically and recovery is rapid.

The last three days prior to the beginning of the meet are, perhaps, the most crucial of the taper. Swimmers should rest as much as possible during these days so training will not interfere with the super adaptation effects that may be occurring. If the taper has been correct swimmers will not lose conditioning in 3 days of easy swimming. If it has been too long, there is nothing that will remedy the situation during the last 3 days. Therefore, rest is the logical option if you are uncertain about what to do.

Daily yardage is inconsequential during these days, provided, of course, that it is minimal. Begin each session by warming up as you will at the meet. Then, practice stroke drills, starts, turns, and relay starts. Next, practice race pace by swimming a few underdistance repeats. Finish by loosening down for 400 to 500 yards/meters.

Many swimmers make the mistake of sprinting too much during the taper. If sprint training was used throughout the season, rest, rather than additional speed work, will be required during the taper if you expect to produce super adaptations in the energy systems of the muscles that make fast speeds possible. Too much sprinting at this time may delay recovery of the fast twitch muscle fibers, causing sprinters to enter competition with a reduced metabolic capacity in the fibers they must rely on for energy during their races.

There will be a tendency for body weight to increase during the taper because reduced training requires fewer calories. Swimmers should be advised to reduce their food intake so unnecessary fat is not deposited during these final weeks.

Psychological factors in the taper. The success of tapers may stem as much from psychological factors as from those which are physiological in nature. Swimmers must believe they will swim well in order for a taper to have its full effect. Psychological preparation should begin at the first team meeting of the season. The season should be put in perspective by identifying the most important meet or meets and explaining the relative importance of each of the other meets. This will help swimmers maintain their perspective during the season so that their most intense motivation occurs during the taper. This will lead to a psychological as well as a physical peak.

The uncertainties of the taper, particularly whether a swimmer feels he or she is getting too much or too little rest, can create anxieties that may erode confidence. Leading coaches around the world are unanimous in their advice to remain positive during the taper. Athletes need the reassurance that a calm, positive coach can give. This does not mean that a coach should lie to swimmers if the taper is not going as expected. If setbacks make it impossible to honestly indicate that the taper is on schedule, the swimmers should be told so. The environment can then be kept positive by instituting procedures to remedy the situation.

Swimmers should be prepared for any meet conditions that could upset their confidence. Such problems as crowded warm ups, unusually cold or warm water, inadequate wave control, flat turning walls, poor visibility, and unusual starting blocks should be discussed and practice drills instituted to prepare for these conditions. If possible, arrive at the meet site a few days in advance of the competition so swimmers will have time to adjust to these conditions.

The minor taper. A minor taper is used to produce fast times in a mid-season meet. It is generally 2 to 3 days in length. Performances are expected to improve during a minor taper although not to the extent that they will improve following a major taper.

There seem to be two methods to achieve a minor taper that are commonly used. In the first method, swimmers reduce their daily yardage drastically for 2 to 3 days before the meet and train as they would during the final 3 days of a major taper. In the second, the daily yardage is reduced only slightly but the intensity of training is decreased until nearly all swimming is at a moderate pace. Both methods have been effective for improving performances and they have the advantage of causing only minimal loss of training time and little or no loss in conditioning.

The retaper. The first procedure in retapering after a major taper, is to resume training near pretaper training levels. The workout should be sufficiently intense to maintain your present state of condition without causing the fatigue you experienced during the competitive season. This pattern is followed until you are within 3 to 7 days of the next important competition.

It will not be necessary to retaper for the same number of days that were required for a major taper because once swimmers have been fully tapered it will not take so much time to recover during the retaper. If the next meet follows closely, within 1 or 2 weeks, the retaper should be 3 days in length. If the time between meets is greater, the taper period can increase accordingly.

In cases where the performances during the major taper were not as fast as expected, more rest should be given during the retaper. If the next meet is only 1 week away it would be wise to continue resting without returning to hard work. The additional recovery time may correct the situation and produce the desired performances. If the poor performance was caused by too much rest, there is little you can do to correct the situation in 1 week.

When important meets are separated by more than a week it becomes necessary for the coach to make a judgment regarding whether the previous taper has been too long or too short. If you suspect that swimmers have had too much rest and have lost conditioning, work near mid-season levels of distance and intensity until you are within 3 to 4 days of the next meet. If you suspect that they have not had enough rest, maintain a reduced schedule of yardage and intensity similar to that followed in the first and second weeks of a major taper until you are within 5 to 7 days of the next meet. At that time the workload should be reduced and the training should be similar to that followed during the final week of a major taper.

Yardage

There is considerable controversy concerning the number of yards swimmers should swim each day and each week. During the past 10 years we have seen the average daily training distances increase from 5,000 yards/meters to between 12,000 and 20,000 yards/meters. Some teams are reported to train 30,000 yards/meters per day for short periods during the season, and during the same period weekly yardages have escalated from 25,000 to in excess of 100,000 yards.

It is extremely difficult to separate cause and effect where training yardage is concerned. Excellent swimmers have come from high-yardage programs and they have also come from low-yardage programs. The most talented and most motivated swimmers frequently join clubs with high-mileage programs because for the last decade success has been equated with yardage. When they improve we can never be certain whether the additional yardage or simply their desire to excel was responsible for their performances.

As with most controversies, the debate over quality (high-intensity low-yardage) and quantity (moderate-intensity high-yardage) training has obscured the real nature of effective training. Training must include both quality and quantity swimming with the amount of each determined by the metabolic demands of the events swimmers are training for and the strengths and weaknesses of individual swimmers.

Moderately intense high-yardage swimming seems to be the most effective method for accomplishing anaerobic threshold training. If there is an optimum daily yardage for such training it is not known at this time. For now, the more yardage the better at the proper intensity is the maxim for effective training. As mentioned earlier, athletes with the highest anaerobic thresholds are found in endurance events that require large volumes of submaximal training. Perhaps 20,000 or more yards per day is defensible where such training is concerned.

Intensity, not yardage, is the most important factor in training other metabolic processes, however. The effective conduct of $\dot{V}O_2$ max, lactate tolerance, race-pace, and sprint training requires faster speeds and more rest, which necessarily reduces the number of yards that can be covered in a training session.

An effective training program will include some high-yardage days for anaerobic threshold training and other days where the yardage is reduced to allow time to sprint and swim $\dot{V}O_2$ max, lactate tolerance, and race-pace repeats at the proper speed. Further, the amount of time swimmers spend with each form of training will depend on the events they are training for. Obviously distance swimmers will swim many more yards per day and per week because moderate-intensity short-rest anaerobic threshold training is the most important form for them to use. On the other hand, sprinters should cover less yardage per day and per week because their training should include more high-intensity low-rest sprints and lactate tolerance swims. Middle-distance swimmers must, of course, include both quantity and quality swims in their training in equal proportions. Therefore, they will swim fewer yards per day than the distance swimmers and more yards per day than the sprinters.

With this in mind, some daily and weekly training yardages are suggested in Table 10.2. These suggestions are listed according to three categories: sprinters, middle-distance, and distance swimmers. They are further arranged according to the 3 seasonal phases. Recommendations are made for both experienced swimmers (several years of training) and novice swimmers who are in their first or second year of competitive swimming.

The lesser daily yardages are ideal for days when a great number of high-intensity repeats are swum. The larger figures are the recommended optimums for days when most of the yardage consists of submaximal anaerobic threshold swimming.

Table 10.2 *Suggested Daily and Weekly Training Yardage for Senior Swimmers*

	Experienced		Novice	
Season/category	Daily yardage	Weekly yardage	Daily yardage	Weekly yardage
Early season				
Sprinters	8,000–12,000	50,000–60,000	3,000–5,000	30,000
Middle-distance	10,000–15,000	60,000–80,000	4,000–6,000	40,000
Distance	12,000–18,000	80,000–100,000	6,000–8,000	50,000
Competitive season				
Sprinters	7,000–11,000	55,000	5,000–6,000	30,000
Middle-distance	8,000–12,000	65,000	7,000–9,000	45,000
Distance	12,000–18,000	70,000–75,000	8,000–10,000	55,000
Taper (week 2)				
Sprinters	3,000–6,000	25,000	3,000–4,000	20,000
Middle-distance	5,000–6,000	30,000	4,000–5,000	25,000
Distance	6,000–9,000	35,000–40,000	5,000–7,000	35,000

Planning Weekly Training Programs

Once the season framework has been formed, training sessions must be constructed on a weekly and daily basis. Weekly planning increases the probability of maintaining the proper proportions of stroke work, speed drills, race-pace, anaerobic threshold, $\dot{V}O_2$ max, and lactate tolerance repeats throughout the season.

The first things to consider in planning the weekly program are the number of high-intensity (lactate tolerance and race-pace repeats) and medium-intensity (anaerobic threshold, $\dot{V}O_2$ max, and sprint repeats) sessions you wish to hold each week, and the spacing of these sessions throughout the week.

Regarding the number of training sessions devoted to each metabolic process, physiological literature is replete with studies indicating that 2 to 4 training sessions per week will produce significant improvements in speed, strength, and endurance. Therefore, each of the 5 forms of training should be included in the workouts for 2 to 4 sessions of each week. Since there are indications that overtraining can occur when high-intensity training is used too often, race-pace, lactate tolerance, and the longer distance and more intense $\dot{V}O_2$ max drills (300s and beyond) should probably be limited to 2 to 4 sessions weekly. If this seems too few sessions, remember that there is some overlap in all training, thus these processes will be receiving some training on other days as well. Anaerobic threshold repeats and the shorter distance $\dot{V}O_2$ max drills can be swum 4 to 6 days weekly. They are not particularly stressful and there are indications that more frequent training of an aerobic nature improves recovery ability (Mathews and Fox 1976).

The effect of frequent sprint swimming is not known. Fatigue does not re-

Monday	AT and speed drills at both morning and afternoon sessions. $\dot{V}O_2$ max repeats during one session.
Tuesday	Race-pace or lactate tolerance and AT drills during both sessions.
Wednesday	AT, $\dot{V}O_2$ max, and speed drills during both sessions.
Thursday	Race-pace or lactate tolerance drills during both sessions. AT repeats during both sessions.
Friday	AT repeats and speed drills during both sessions, $\dot{V}O_2$ max drills at one session.
Saturday	AT repeats during both sessions. Speed and race-pace or lactate tolerance drills at one session.

Figure 10.1. A weekly training program for sprinters.

sult from lactate accumulation in sprint repeats. However, there may be certain other metabolic processes that require rest and restoration. Nevertheless, short sets of sprint repeats (200 to 400 yards/meters) can probably be completed daily with no ill effects.

Weekly programs for sprinters, middle-distance swimmers, and distance swimmers could be structured during the competition period as outlined in Figures 10.1, 10.2, and 10.3.

Preparation for multiple-day championship meets must also be considered in planning a weekly training program. Since these meets require 2 to 4 maximum efforts per day over a 3 to 5 day period, it is advisable to set aside some weeks when 6 to 10 consecutive race-pace training sessions are held. This need not be done every week, but should definitely be included in the weekly plan during the competition period.

Figure 10.2. A weekly training program for middle-distance swimmers.

Monday	AT and $\dot{V}O_2$ max and speed drills at both sessions.
Tuesday	Race-pace or lactate tolerance drills at both sessions. AT repeats during both sessions.
Wednesday	AT, $\dot{V}O_2$max, and speed drills at both sessions.
Thursday	AT and lactate tolerance or race-pace repeats at both sessions.
Friday	AT and speed drills at both sessions. $\dot{V}O_2$ max drills at one session.
Saturday	Race-pace or lactate tolerance repeats at one session. AT drills at both sessions.

Monday	At and $\dot{V}O_2$ max drills at both sessions.
Tuesday	Speed and AT drills at both sessions. Race-pace drills at one session.
Wednesday	AT and $\dot{V}O_2$ max drills at both sessions.
Thursday	Speed and AT drills at both sessions. $\dot{V}O_2$ max drills at one session.
Friday	AT drills at both sessions. Fatigued sprinting at one session.
Saturday	AT drills at both sessions. Race-pace drills at one session.

Figure 10.3. A weekly training program for distance swimmers.

Planning Daily Training Sessions

For maximum effectiveness, each daily training session must be constructed to encourage swimmers to complete their practice lengths at the proper intensity for the training adaptations that are desired. This will not occur if the five forms of training are mixed indiscriminately. For example, the placement of speed drills determines their effectiveness. If swimmers are fatigued by other repeats before swimming sprints, the sprints will not be sufficiently fast to be effective. Lactate tolerance and race-pace repeats should generally be saved for the end of the session or followed by a set of moderate-intensity repeats that permit partial recovery before going on to the rest of the workout. If they are placed early in the workout, acidosis may cause later repeat sets to be completed at such a slow speed that little or no training effects take place.

Following is a suggested arrangement of the five forms of training within one training session:

1. Begin the practice with a set of moderate-intensity anaerobic threshold repeats that serve the dual purpose of providing a warm up and an aerobic training effect. Stroke drills are excellent for this purpose.
2. Next, swim some rested sprints for improving "getting-out" ability.
3. Some additional anaerobic threshold repeats can then be included for continued aerobic improvement and partial recovery from the sprints. Pulling, kicking, and stroke drills are excellent for this purpose.
4. Swimmers will then be ready for a high-intensity set of race-pace, lactate tolerance, or $\dot{V}O_2$ max repeats.
5. The high-intensity efforts should be followed by some more anaerobic threshold repeats for recovery and aerobic training.
6. After recovery, the swimmers could complete another short set of race-pace or lactate tolerance drills to improve their ability to bring races home.

Middle-distance and distance swimmers should use this time for some additional $\dot{V}O_2$ max drills on certain days.

7. Finish with more anaerobic threshold repeats to continue aerobic training while encouraging some removal of lactic acid so the swimmers will recover faster.

As with all general plans, there are occasions when you should deviate from the suggested pattern:

1. Occasionally it is good to produce acidosis early in a practice session and then force yourself to complete the workout with reasonable quality. This is good training for pain tolerance and mental toughness. It can be advantageous when, for reasons of strategy, a swimmer must take a race out faster than usual and "hang on." This pattern should be used infrequently. Some swimmers will lose their motivation for such intense efforts if they are asked to produce them too frequently.

2. Occasional placing of two major race-pace or lactate tolerance drills in a single practice session may help improve swimmers' abilities to compete in several events during a dual meet or single session of a championship meet. These drills should be separated by moderate-intensity anaerobic threshold drills of 15 to 30 minutes duration to simulate meet conditions. Too frequent use of this regimen can also cause loss of motivation.

3. A surprise time trial at the end of practice can also have a beneficial effect on pain tolerance and mental toughness. Swimmers discover they are capable of faster swims than they believed possible. This increases their pride and confidence in their ability to swim well in several events during the meet.

Special Training Considerations for Events Other Than Freestyle

It has been repeatedly stressed that athletes must swim their competitive strokes frequently in training. The trend, however, is to train all swimmers with a large volume of freestyle in order to squeeze the most yards into the available time. Becoming slaves to yardage may cause swimmers in events other than freestyle to lose the opportunity to produce some important training adaptations in the muscle fibers that are used only when they swim their competitive stroke or strokes. Therefore, they should swim their strokes in practice and in addition, spend some time kicking and pulling even though doing so means sacrificing yardage. Some considerations for training in the nonfreestyle events are discussed in the following sections.

Training Butterfly Swimmers

The butterfly stroke is so rigorous that it is difficult to maintain correct mechanics during long sets of repeats. As a result, bad habits can develop, such as gliding after the arm entry, using only 1 kick, and early breathing. For this reason, it is advisable to train with the crawl stroke in the longer repeats and during some of the shorter distance AT and $\dot{V}O_2$ max drills. These will condition the circulatory and respiratory systems and will probably also produce training effects in some of the muscle fibers used when swimming butterfly.[1]

While most of the long-distance and short-rest aerobic repeats can be swum with the crawl stroke, most of the speed, lactate tolerance, and race-pace repeats should be swum butterfly to be certain that all of the correct muscle fibers receive a training stimulus. In addition, it is advisable to swim butterfly during a certain percentage of the AT and $\dot{V}O_2$ max drills for this same reason. Most such repeats should probably be at distances of 25 to 100 yards/meters so that correct stroke mechanics can be maintained.

Although mechanics may deteriorate when swimming overdistance, it is wise to occasionally swim some high-intensity butterfly repeats at race distance and distances 1½ to 2 times race distance. Swimming butterfly incorrectly on occasion should not produce any lasting damage to stroke mechanics if sufficient attention is given to proper mechanics during stroke drills and underdistance repeats. The aerobic and anaerobic training adaptations and the mental toughness encouraged by such repeats are well worth the time and effort required. One or two 400-yard/meter butterfly swims or 3 to 5 high-intensity 200 butterfly swims are ideal for this purpose.

Butterfly swimmers should spend a considerable amount of time working on their kicks. Although most kicking drills should be of the anaerobic threshold type, some sprint and lactate tolerance kicking should be included during 2 or 3 sessions each week in order to train the metabolic processes of the leg muscles.

Training Backstroke Swimmers

Crowded pool conditions have forced many United States backstrokers to swim freestyle during most of their training sessions. This situation should be remedied so backstrokers are given more opportunity to swim their stroke in practice. They should swim backstroke on a daily basis during some of the repeats included in each of the five forms of training. Backstrokers should also include a considerable amount of kicking in their training since the kick seems to play a prominent role in backstrokers' success. As with butterfly swimmers, these kicking drills should include, in addition to anaerobic threshold training, some speed and lactate tolerance drills. Backstrokers should be encouraged to swim some moderate-intensity long-distance backstroke repeats because overdistance training may produce certain muscular adaptations more effectively than they can be produced by underdistance repeats. They should also swim short sets of high-intensity double-distance backstroke repeats occasionally to improve lactate tolerance and mental toughness.

Training Breaststroke Swimmers

Breaststrokers must complete far more yardage in the form of kicking and pulling drills than swimmers in other strokes. There is a tendency for breaststrokers with weak armstrokes to rely on their legs and vice versa when they swim the full stroke. As a result, the weak phase of the stroke will remain weak

---

1. The similarity between the butterfly and crawl stroke is great enough that although muscle fiber involvement may not be identical, there should be some overlap.

until it is strengthened by isolating and overloading it. Both moderate- and high-intensity kicking and pulling drills should be used in training so that the ATP-CP reaction, and both the aerobic and anaerobic metabolic processes of the arms and legs are overloaded.

Long-distance breaststroke swimming may not be advisable because of the tendency to glide and rely on the kick at slow speeds. However, high-intensity breaststroke repeats that are double the race distance or more are advisable for improving mental toughness and for training both the aerobic and anaerobic capacity of the muscle fibers involved in breaststroke swimming.

Breaststroke swimmers with knee problems will be forced to swim more freestyle in practice. However, they should be sure to swim breaststroke in most of their race-pace, lactate tolerance, and speed repeats since these repeats encourage the most important muscular adaptations for 100 and 200 events.

Training Individual Medley Swimmers

Swimmers in the individual medley events must, of course, train for all four competitive strokes and the repeats for each stroke must include all 5 forms of training to be maximally effective. Since there will be much to do and little time to do it, individual medley swimmers should give preference to breaststroke, butterfly and backstroke kicking over freestyle kicking because of the greater importance of the kicks in these strokes. The breaststroke armstroke should be practiced frequently to correct any imbalance between the arms and legs in this stroke.

The changeover from one stroke to another is an aspect unique to individual medley swimming and should also be practiced. After changing strokes, many swimmers find the first half-length to be somewhat difficult because they require time to establish a new rhythm. Some drills should be used to practice the changeover so new stroke rhythms can be established with minimal effort and loss of speed.

Sets of repeats in which the four strokes are swum in IM order are excellent for this purpose. For example, a set of 12 × 100 repeats could be completed as follows: repeats 1 through 4, butterfly for the first 50 yards, swimming backstroke for the final 50; repeats 5 through 8, 50 yards of backstroke and 50 yards of breaststroke; repeats 9 through 12, 50 yards of breaststroke and 50 yards of freestyle. Four hundred IM swimmers could swim a set of 9 × 200 in a similar manner; that is, in repeats 1 through 3, swim the first 100 yards butterfly and the second 100 yards backstroke; in repeats 4 through 6, swim the first 100 yards backstroke and the second 100 yards breaststroke; in repeats 7 through 9, swim the first 100 yards breaststroke and the second 100 yards freestyle.

Training Age-Group Swimmers

An attempt has been made throughout this book to present information in such a way that it could be applied to swimmers of any age and sex. There are, however, some specific recommendations that should be made concerning age-group swimming.

Table 10.3 *Recommended Daily and Weekly Yardage*
for Age Group Swimmers

	Novice		Experienced	
Age group	Daily	Weekly	Daily	Weekly
8 & under	400–800	1,200–2,400	1,000–1,500	3,000–4,500
10 & under	600–1,200	2,400–4,800	1,500–3,000	6,000–12,000
11–12	1,000–2,000	5,000–10,000	4,000–5,000	20,000–25,000
13–14[a]	2,000–4,000	10,000–20,000	6,000–12,000	30,000–50,000

aRecommendations are for nonnationally oriented swimmers. Those making national cut-offs should train as senior swimmers.

The first concerns training yardage. Obviously, age-group swimmers should not cover the same distances as senior swimmers. Some daily and weekly training yardages are recommended for each age group in Table 10.3. Experience and ability are also considered in these recommendations.

The principles of specificity, overload, and progression that were previously presented should also be adhered to when training age-group swimmers. However, in this case we must question whether the training should be specific to the short events they are presently swimming in competition or to the longer events they will swim later in their careers.

When answering this question most coaches recommend that training should be aimed at attaining peak performances in longer events as senior swimmers. This should not be taken to mean that all age-group swimmers should be trained as potential distance swimmers. Only those who show potential in the distance events should be trained in this manner. If certain age-group swimmers show potential for sprinting or middle-distance swimming, their training should include a sizable percentage of speed and lactate tolerance drills from an early age. This may encourage, during the formative years, muscular adaptations such as increased anaerobic enzyme activity and fiber splitting in the fast twitch muscle fibers that will help them perform better as seniors.

This suggestion notwithstanding, the training of all age-group swimmers should include a sizable number of repeats for improving the anaerobic threshold as should the training of any competitive swimmer regardless of age or ability.

The rest intervals between repeats should not be appreciably different for age-group and senior swimmers, although you may prefer to give the former slightly more rest in order to provide for progression later in their careers. The rest periods should never be so long that they defeat the purpose of the repeats, however. It may also be advisable, when training age-group swimmers, to keep the length of a particular repeat set shorter than the number recommended for senior swimmers in order to provide for progression at a later age.

Regarding repeat distances, coaches should remember that age-group swimmers will swim their repeats at a slower rate. Since energy metabolism is dependent on time rather than distance, this may cause the training effects from these repeats to be different from those attained by senior swimmers. For example, a 9-year-old who swims a set of 20 × 50 repeats with a 30-second rest interval at an average speed of 60.0 seconds is training the anaerobic threshold and $\dot{V}O_2$ max processes more than he or she is improving speed and lactate tolerance. The work-rest ratio is 2:1 and the swimmer will need to rely primarily on aerobic metabolism to complete the set. The primary training effect for a senior swimmer who completes the same set of repeats at an average speed of 24.0 seconds will be an improvement in lactate tolerance because the speed of the repeats and the work-rest ratio dictate that most of the energy will be supplied anaerobically.

Keep in mind, when constructing workouts for age-group swimmers, that repeats for improving speed should be 5 to 30 seconds in duration, while the most effective repeats for increasing lactate tolerance are 1 to 3 minutes in length. Remember also that rest periods of 15 to 60 seconds provide adequate recovery for sprint repeats while 3 to 5 minutes of rest are required to remove lactic acid from muscles so that lactate tolerance drills can be swum at the proper speed.

Any repeat distance can be used for aerobic training; however, the rest periods between repeats should be shorter than the work periods so that complete recovery does not occur. Work-rest ratios of 2:1 or less are recommended.

Another matter that should be discussed is the high attrition rate of age-group swimmers. The usual explanation for the high drop-out rate between the ages of 13 and 18 is that excessive training yardages at an early age cause swimmers to burn out. Although excessive yardage may play a role in the high attrition rate, there is another more plausible explanation. That is that lack of improvement causes swimmers to become disappointed or disillusioned as they grow older. For example, when young swimmers fail to improve or when rivals pass them as they get older, their expectations and the expectations of others generally cause them to endure intense emotional pressure. It is probably this pressure and not overwork that causes them to retreat from the sport. This observation notwithstanding, too much training at an early age, while not the root of the problem, may still be a related factor.

Eight- to ten-year-old swimmers who train 5 or more times per week, 6,000 to 8,000 yards/meters per day during 10 months of the year, may experience success in the form of national rankings as age-group swimmers. This success may be transitory, however, because it results from the extra training (or early motivation), rather than from superior physical ability relative to others in the same age group.

Perhaps the drop-out rate could be reduced by maintaining the training loads of age-group swimmers within reasonable limits so they have a better chance to improve relative to their competitors when they reach adolescence and adulthood. If these swimmers feel they are catching up or even holding their own, rather than falling behind, more of them may remain motivated to continue in the sport. Of course, coaches, parents, and teammates can help reduce the emotional pressure that results when swimmers fail to maintain their positions relative to their competition by accepting them unconditionally so that they can enjoy being members of the team regardless of their win-loss record.

Overtraining

Overtraining is a condition in which an athlete's adaptive mechanisms are stressed to the point of failure. When the adaptive mechanisms fail, further training of a similar nature will cause athletes to lose rather than gain conditioning. For this reason, overtraining can have devastating effects on performance. Unfortunately, it occurs most frequently among those swimmers who work hardest.

Excessive stress is the cause of overtraining. Stress has been defined as "wear and tear" on the body (Selye 1956). It can be both psychological and physiological in origin. Boredom, anxiety, fear, and loss of self-esteem are among the psychological stressors that may cause an overtrained state. Excessive physical exercise, lack of sleep, poor nutrition, illness, and injury are some of the more prominent physiological stressors.

It is difficult, if not impossible, to determine whether overtraining is psychological or physiological in origin. Physiological stress is always accompanied by psychological stress and vice versa, so that regardless of the origin of the problem, both types of stressors will be contributing to the deterioration in performance once an athlete becomes overtrained.

It is important to understand that overtraining can have a physiological as well as a psychological basis, that many athletes can become overtrained because they try too hard and care too much, rather than because they are lazy and lack motivation. Swimmers, coaches, and parents are prone to explain poor performances from a purely psychological perspective. "I wasn't motivated," "he was psyched out," or "she quit trying," are common statements that are heard after subpar races. This tendency to regard overtraining (usually referred to as staleness) as attitudinal can have devastating effects on some athletes. They may come to doubt their dedication, their ability to compete, or worse, their adequacy as human beings.

An understanding of the physiological and psychological bases of overtraining is needed for prevention and treatment of this condition. Hans Selye, a noted Canadian endocrinologist, has presented a theory of stress that helps explain the relationship of the physiological and psychological aspects of overtraining. It has become known as the **stress syndrome.**

The Stress Syndrome   Selye (1956) defines stress as "the nonspecific responses of the body to demands made upon it." A nonspecific response is one that may result from excessive exposure to any stressing agent or agents, whereas a specific response would be a reaction that can only be caused by a certain stressing agent. Every activity stresses the body in a specific manner and also in a nonspecific manner. We can usually manage the specific stresses because they are different for each situation and usually will not interfere with the body's metabolic and homeostatic mechanism to the point that failing adaptation occurs. However, when a number of stresses are acting on the body at once, their cumulative effect can cause failing adaptation although no single stressor is, by itself, severe enough to cause such a reaction.

Selye has theorized that the resources for dealing with stress come from a store of general adaptation energy used for all forms of stress and from several stores of specific adaptation energy that are each used to support the energy requirement of certain stressors. A diagram of these theoretical relationships appears in Figure 10.4. A failure of the body's adaptive mechanisms can be caused by too much stress of any one type (for example, excessive physical exercise) or the accumulation of stresses that are emanating from many sources. Thus, when swimmers are staying up late, eating poorly, worrying and dealing with personal conflicts that involve family and friends, and worrying about their performance in school, the cumulative effects of these stressors, together with the stress of the large volume of physical training they are engaged in, is to deplete the body's store of general adaptation energy and cause a failure of its adaptive mechanisms.

The need to avoid depleting the body's general adaptation energy does not mean that swimmers should avoid stress altogether. It is only through the application of a *particular* stress that the body's store of specific adaptation energy can be increased. Where swimmers are concerned, the periodic and judicial application of physical exercise increases the ability to train longer and with greater intensity so that they become better conditioned. Other stressors should be reduced during this time to prevent the occurrence of overtraining. When it is not possible to reduce other stressors, swimmers and coaches have no choice but to reduce the amount of physical exercise or failing adaptation will occur and the swimmers' performances will deteriorate.

There is a fine line between adequate doses of stress and overdoses. Adequate amounts will cause adaptations, while overdoses will cause failing adaptation. This was demonstrated by Arcos and his associates (Arcos et al. 1968) in a study concerning the effects of continuous swimming on the mitochondria of rats. The rats swam continuously for 6 hours a day, 6 days a week. After 161 hours of this regimen they showed positive adaptations in the form of increases in mitochondrial mass. After 610 hours, the mitochondrial mass had receded to the point that it was no greater than that of an untrained control group. Since aerobic metabolism takes place in the mitochondria, the aerobic endurance of exercised rats had deteriorated some time after the first 161 hours of swimming until it was no greater than the endurance of an untrained control group.

The point made by this study is that swimmers and coaches should be aware of the signs of overtraining and not push on in spite of them in the mistaken notion that swimmers' poor performances are "all in their heads." To do so may cause athletes to lose all of the training adaptations they worked so

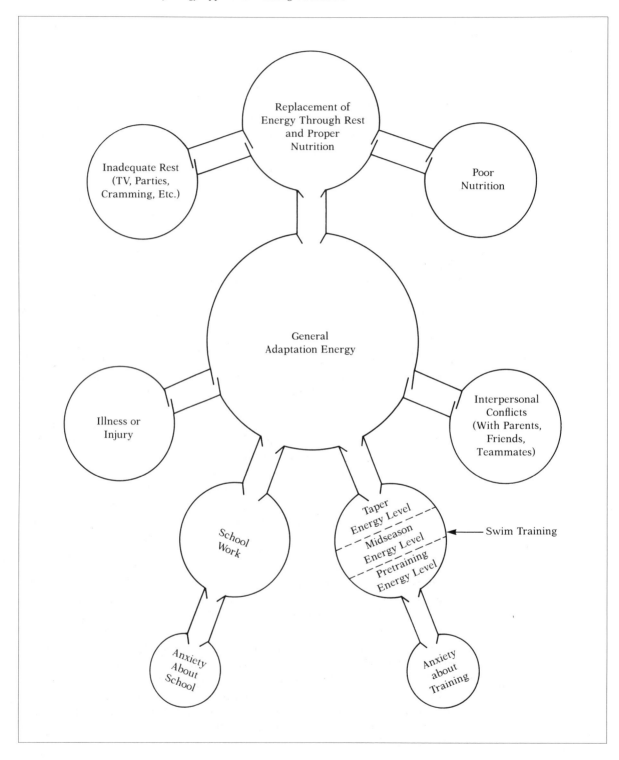

hard to gain. Stress should not be avoided in training; however, it must be "dosed" properly for best results. The effect of adequate, inadequate, and over- doses of training stress are illustrated by the graph in Figure 10.5.

There are three zones of stress indicated in Figure 10.5. In one zone, that of nonadaptive stress, the amount of stress is too slight to produce the desired training effects. Adequate doses are indicated by the zone of adaptive stress. Swimmers should train in this zone as often as possible. The final zone, the zone of excessive stress, is indicative of an overdose. Swimmers may occasion- ally train into this zone; however, such sessions must be followed by adequate rest or overtraining will occur.

Proper training is illustrated by swimmer *A*. Most of her training is in the zone of adaptive stress. She rarely trains in the zone of nonadaptive stress, and periods of very hard training that send her into the zone of excessive stress are always followed by periods of moderate-intensity training that permit recovery. If she never trained into the zone of excessive stress, the stimulus for improve- ments in anaerobic capacity would not be present. If she trained only in the zone of nonadaptive stress, her performances would not improve. The upward inclination of the zones indicates that if she is to stay in the zone of adaptive stress her training swims should increase in speed or decrease in rest as her condition improves so that she will achieve a peak performance at the end of the year.

The graph of swimmer *B* is descriptive of a person who does not train conscientiously. He remains in the zone of nonadaptive stress for most of each training session, entering the zone of adaptive stress infrequently and only oc- casionally training into the zone of excessive stress. As a result, he improves slightly at the beginning of the season and then has no further improvement for the remainder of the year.

The graph of swimmer *C* describes the typical pattern of an overtrained swimmer. She trains in the zone of excessive stress too frequently and without adequate recovery periods. She reaches a state of exhaustion midway through the season, becoming so fatigued that she has only enough energy and moti- vation to train in the zone of nonadaptive stress. As a result, she loses condition- ing while recovering from the exhaustive work and, with so little time remaining in the season, is unable to regain the lost training adaptations in time to achieve a peak performance.

Figure 10.4. The Selye Stress Syndrome. Selye has the- orized that we have a store of general adaptation energy for dealing with all stresses and several stores of specific adapation energy for dealing with certain stresses. Some of the more common stresses that swimmers deal with are indicated in the diagram. The stores of specific adap- tation energy can, apparently, be increased by the periodic and judicial application of a particular stress. When swimmers are being stressed from too many sources at one time, the store of general adaptation en- ergy may become depleted and the body's adaptive mechanisms will fail. The body's stores of general and specific adaptation energy can be replaced through rest and proper nutrition. When swimmers do not get enough rest and they do not eat properly, energy is not replaced as rapidly as it is being used. This will contrib- ute to failing adaptation.

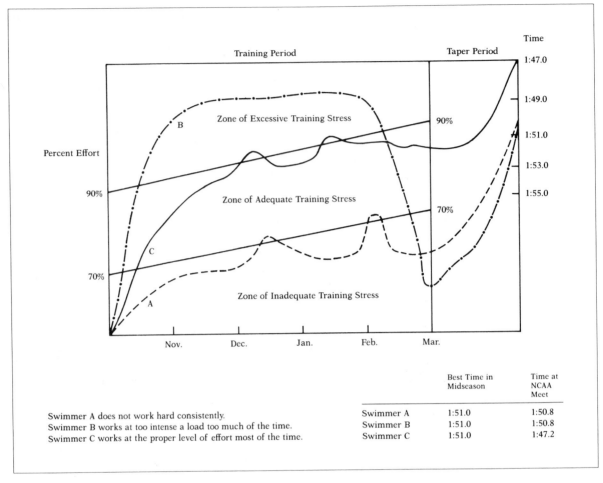

Figure 10.5. Adequate, inadequate, and excessive stress in the training period.

Diagnosing Overtraining

There have been repeated attempts to find accurate methods for determining excessive stress. None has proven 100 percent effective, however. One method that has been used is to measure the quantity of 17-ketosteroids in the urine. There is an increase in this substance when the activity of the adrenal glands is high.[2] Unfortunately, these tests were not conclusive because urination is only one way ketosteroids can be removed from the body.

Schubert (1977) has reported increases in white blood cells (eosinophils)

2. Selye (1956) has shown an increased secretion of pro-inflammatory hormones from the adrenal glands during periods of excessive stress. These hormones in large quantity irritate the tissues of the body.

during the stress of exhaustive exercise. It is not clear whether this is a sign of stress or simply a normal reaction to hard exercise, however. The white blood cell count usually increases after exercise (Lamb 1978). Carlile (1966) has presented data based on research with members of the 1960 Australian Olympic swimming team which indicated that overtraining was accompanied by distorted T-waves in electrocardiographic tracings. Normal and abnormal electrocardiographic tracings are shown in Figure 10.6. In the abnormal tracing, the T-wave is inverted, one of the conditions that was reported among swimmers who showed signs of overtraining (Carlile and Carlile 1978). A change in the T-wave is one of the most important indicators of mild abnormalities of cardiac muscle fibers that can result from several causes including infection, overstimulation of cellular metabolism, glandular dysfunction, and changes in the acid-base balance in the body (Guyton 1964). Unfortunately, Carlile and Carlile (1978) also reported that several swimmers who were clearly overtrained had normal electrocardiographic tracings.

Carlile and Carlile (1978) have also reported considerable increases in the activity of the enzymes creatine phosphokinase (CPK) and glutamic oxalic transaminase (SGOT) when swimmers appeared overtrained. Both of these enzymes are associated with muscle metabolism: CPK with skeletal muscle metabolism and SGOT with smooth muscle metabolism. These increases were, in some cases, 10 times the normal level. The activity of both enzymes returned to normal when the training loads were reduced.

An unusually high resting blood lactate concentration has also been rumored to be a sign of failing adaptation. The author's personal experience with blood lactate measurements has tended to verify this possibility. Many of the swimmers we tested during the blood lactate studies discussed in Chapter 9 had high resting concentrations of lactic acid when they were swimming

Figure 10.6. Normal (**A**) and abnormal (**B**) electrocardiographic tracings. Note the distorted T-wave in **B**.

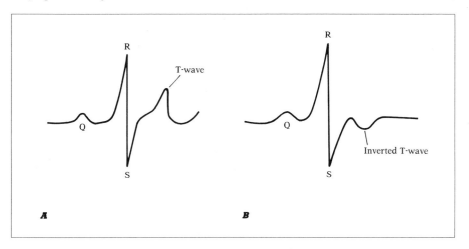

Table 10.4 *Symptoms of Overtraining*

General	Physical	Psychological
Poor performances in meets and practices	Loss of weight Joint and muscle pains with no apparent injury Hives and rashes Nausea Head colds and stuffy nose	Depression Irritability Insomnia Anxiety

poorly in meets and practice, and they showed normal concentrations when they were swimming well. This finding was not universal, however. Some swimmers had normal concentrations when they were swimming poorly.

Disregarding the inconsistencies in some of the research studies, none of them are useful to the coach and athlete because of the time, equipment, and specialized training required to administer and interpret them accurately, to say nothing of the expense involved. There are certain readily observable physical symptoms that consistently accompany overtrained states and these can be used as diagnostic aids by coaches and swimmers. Some of the more common ones are listed in Table 10.4.

Through the years, the symptoms listed in Table 10.4 have proven to be the most reliable indicators of overtraining. It should be understood, however, that each of these symptoms could indicate conditions other than overtraining. Therefore, do not be too hasty in your diagnosis. Investigate the other possibilities first. If the symptoms persist and there is no apparent reason for them, overtraining should be suspected and procedures instituted to relieve the condition.

Relieving Overtraining

The stressor with which coaches and swimmers should be most concerned is excessive physical exercise. In this respect, the intensity of the training seems to be a more potent stressor than total yardage (Miller and Mason 1964). The best procedure when overtraining is suspected is 1 to 3 days of low-intensity anaerobic threshold training. Swimming off-strokes may be beneficial during this time so that exhausted muscle fibers can rest while circulatory and respiratory training adaptations are maintained. If this procedure does not cause the symptoms to disappear, it may be necessary to allow 2 to 5 days of complete rest.

If you suspect that factors other than physical exercise are contributing to the condition, steps should be taken to relieve these stressors. In some cases counseling may be required to help swimmers budget time, resolve personal conflicts, and establish priorities so that they can expend more effort in training without becoming overtrained. In other cases swimmers may need to eat more nutritious foods and get more sleep. A visit to the doctor may be indicated when signs of illness are present.

Preventing Overtraining

Prevention is always preferable to curing an overtrained state. The use of cycle training is an excellent way to prevent overtraining. There are several ways to cycle train so that certain of the metabolic processes in muscle fibers can periodically recover and adapt from training. The most common form of cycle training is to follow each day or two of high-intensity training with a day or two of moderate-intensity anaerobic threshold swimming. Another, possibly superior, method is to alternate the 5 forms of training every day or two. For example, 1 or 2 days of lactate tolerance and race-pace training can be followed by a day or two of anaerobic threshold, $\dot{V}O_2$ max, and sprint training. Lactate tolerance and race-pace training tend to deplete both the fast twitch and slow twitch muscle fibers. The slower repeat speeds of anaerobic threshold and $\dot{V}O_2$ max training do not require as much muscular force and therefore probably allow partial recovery of some of the fast twitch muscle fibers, most likely the FTb fibers. Although considerable force is required in sprint training, the primary source of energy is creatine phosphate; therefore, this type of training should also provide an opportunity for partial restoration of the muscles' glycogen supply.

Experience indicates that the number of high-intensity sessions should not exceed 3 to 4 per week and that this schedule should only be maintained for 6 to 8 weeks of each season.[3] This does not mean that short sets of high-intensity swimming cannot comprise a portion of your training sessions on a more frequent basis. These recommendations refer to sessions where a considerable amount of yardage is swum at intensities that bring on a state of near-exhaustion.

Preventing overtraining is also a matter of anticipating other stressors and reducing them before they accumulate to dangerous levels. Swimmers frequently take on more responsibilities than are permitted by their training schedule. Part-time jobs, organizational membership, examinations, papers, and socializing may make it impossible to maintain the present training schedule without becoming overtrained. If these problems are anticipated and relief is given in the form of days off and a reduction in other responsibilities, overtraining can be prevented. Occasionally allowing swimmers a few days off to catch up on school work and to put their other affairs in order can do wonders toward preventing overtraining.

Breaks in Training

Breaks in training are essential to the conditioning process. They allow swimmers time to pursue other interests, to rest, and to regain enthusiasm for the coming season. Senior USS swimmers seldom lay off more than 4 weeks at a time, while some high school, college, and age-group swimmers discontinue training for 6 to 9 months of the year. Such long lay-offs are detrimental to performance and cannot be recommended. The training adaptations that are gained during the season are lost during long lay-offs and much of the time in the next season is spent regaining them rather than building on them.

3. Overtraining is a gradual process that results from several weeks of excessive stress. Athletes may enter a stage of failing adaptation within 8 to 16 weeks after training begins. Hence, the reason for this recommendation.

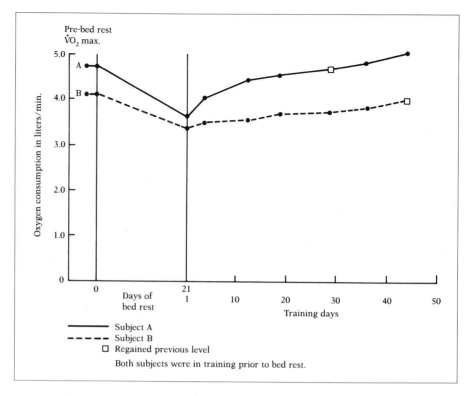

Figure 10.7. The effect of bed rest on $\dot{V}O_2$ max. Two moderately trained subjects were put in bed for 21 days. During this time they did no physical exercise. Both showed a marked reduction in $\dot{V}O_2$ max. The subjects were then retrained. The loss of conditioning was so drastic that it required 30 to 45 days to recover to pre-bed-rest levels. (Adapted from Saltin, Blomquist, Mitchell, Johnson, and Chapman, "Responses to Submaximal and Maximal Exercise After Bed Rest and Training," *Circulation*, 38, Suppl. 7 [1968], p. 11, by permission of the American Heart Association, Inc., and the authors.)

The graph in Figure 10.7 indicates the losses in aerobic capacity among a group of well-trained subjects who were kept in bed for 21 days. As would be expected, the losses in $\dot{V}O_2$ max were quite large. However, the most important aspect of this study concerns the length of time required to retrain these subjects to their previous maximal oxygen consumption capacities. It required between 30 and 45 days of training to regain the capacities they had lost during just 21 days of bed rest.

Of course, no swimmer is going to sleep for 21 days when they are not training. Therefore, their losses in physical condition will not be so dramatic. Nevertheless, most, if not all of the training adaptations they produced during the season will be lost during a long lay-off. This study demonstrates that when these adaptations are lost, a considerable portion of the next season will be spent regaining, not improving upon them.

Swimmers who lay off for no more than a few weeks between seasons need not be concerned about significant losses in conditioning. Those who prefer longer breaks would be well advised to engage in some form of physical activity for the purpose of maintaining their physical conditioning. Swimming is the preferred form of activity. It will not be necessary to train as long or as hard as you trained during the regular season because less work is required to maintain certain training adaptations than is needed to attain them.

Swimming three days per week, once a day, should be sufficient to maintain some adaptations near competitive season levels. The training periods should be structured like those of the competitive period. All 5 forms of training should be used at least 2 to 3 times per week with those forms of training that are most important to races receiving the most attention. It goes without saying that most of the yardage should be completed with each swimmer's competitive stroke or strokes so that adaptations will be maintained in the muscle fibers used in competition.

Swimmers who, for whatever reason, feel they need to stay out of the water for several weeks should use some form of land training for maintenance purposes. Circuit training, running, cycling, calisthenics, and vigorous games will maintain certain circulatory and respiratory adaptations. However, swimmers who choose this form of maintenance should realize that some or possibly all of their specific muscular adaptations may be lost during the off-season.

If you use land training be sure to work a minimum of 45 minutes per day for 3 days of every week. It would be even better to train for 1½ hours per day for 3 to 5 days of each week. When possible, select activities that utilize the same muscle groups that are used in swimming.

REFERENCES

Arcos, J. C., Sohal, R. S., Sun, S., Argus, M. F., and Burch, G. E. 1968. "Changes in Ultra-structure and Respiratory Control in Mitochondria of Rat Muscle Hypertrophied by Exercise." *Experimental Molecular Pathology* 8:49–65.

Carlile, F. 1966. *Forbes Carlile on Swimming.* London: Pelham.

Carlile, F., and Carlile, U. 1978. *New Directions in Scientific Training.* Sydney, Australia: published by the authors.

Chaplouka, E. C., and Fox, E. L. 1975. "Physiological Effects of Two Maintenance Programs Following Eight Weeks of Interval Training." *Fed. Proc.* 34:443.

Guyton, A. C. 1964. *Textbook of Medical Physiology.* Philadelphia: W. B. Saunders.

Lamb, D. R. 1978. *Physiology of Exercise.* New York: MacMillan.

Mathews, D. K., and Fox, E. L. 1976. *The Physiological Basis of Physical Education and Athletics.* Philadelphia: W. B. Saunders.

Miller, R. E., and Mason, J. W. 1964. "Changes in 17-hydroxycorticosteroid Excretion Related to Increased Muscular Work." *Medical Aspects of Stress in the Military Climate*, pp. 137–151. Washington: Walter Reed Army Institute of Research.

Saltin, B., Blomquist, B., Mitchell, J. H., Johnson, R. L. Jr., Wildenthal, K., and Chapman, C. B. 1968. "Response to Submaximal and Maximal Exercise After Bed Rest and Training." *Circulation* 38, Suppl. 7:1–78.

Schubert, M. 1977. "Blood Testing and Training of Distance Swimmers." *1976 American Swimming Coaches Association Clinic Yearbook*, ed. B. M. Ousley, pp. 71–86. Ft. Lauderdale, Fla.: American Swimming Coaches Association.

Selye, Hans. 1956. *The Stress of Life*. New York: McGraw-Hill.

PART Three

Other Aspects of Training

CHAPTER 11

Preparing for Swimming Races

This chapter is devoted to those aspects of competitive swimming that are often overlooked: pace, strategy, warming up, massage, hyperventilation, and cooling down.

Pacing

Until the early 1960s the usual strategy in races was to get out front and stay there. Today we see evidence that swimmers are holding back or pacing in the early stages of their races. Attempts at pacing are particularly noticeable in races of 400 meters and longer. Although some people continue to think of 100 and 200 events as sprints, they also should be paced. Evidence will be presented later in this chapter showing that the faster swimmers are pacing these races. The purpose of pacing is to prevent the early accumulation of lactate and the subsequent acidosis that reduce the rate of energy metabolism and therefore the swimmer's speed. Even a well-trained athlete will find anaerobic metabolism nearly shut down after 40 to 45 seconds of an all-out effort. With this in mind, it may not seem necessary for a national-class male swimmer to pace a 100-yard race because he could complete 100 yards in 43 to 45 seconds. However, it is not necessary for anaerobic metabolism to be shut down before the effects of lactate accumulation cause a reduction in speed. Actually, the effects of lactate accumulation can probably reduce the glycolytic rate within 20 to 30 seconds after the race begins if it is an all-out effort. That is because it requires 10 to 15 seconds for the creatine phosphate supply of muscles to become depleted and perhaps another 10 to 15 seconds for anaerobic glycolysis to result in the accumulation of a significant amount of lactic acid.

Holding back in the early stages of a race delays the accumulation of lactate so that anaerobic metabolism is not curtailed so severely and faster rates of speed can be maintained through the middle and during the final sprint. Most swimmers find that swimming faster later in the race more than compensates for their slower pace in the beginning and that the total race time is faster.

A word of caution: Although pacing generally produces faster times, swimmers may sometimes make the mistake of swimming the first half of the race so slowly that they cannot catch their competitors in the second half no matter how fast they bring it home. It is important, therefore, to have a race plan that will prevent such mistakes from occurring. Researchers have studied various methods of pacing to determine the best pattern.

Race Plans   There are three general race plans that have been studied: even pacing, fast-slow pacing, and slow-fast pacing (more commonly known as negative splitting). When you even-pace a race, each portion of the distance is swum at a constant speed. With a fast-slow race plan, the pattern most commonly used by inexperienced swimmers, the early portions of the race are swum faster than the later portions. This procedure is reversed with negative splitting; the early portions of the race are swum at a slower speed than the later portions.

In one of the few studies that has been conducted concerning race plans, Robinson and his colleagues (Robinson et al. 1958) concluded that negative splitting was the most efficient way to pace. When the subjects used a slow-fast pace during treadmill runs to exhaustion, their oxygen requirements were significantly less than when they used an even pace or fast-slow race plan.

Contrary to these results, Mathews and associates (Mathews et al. 1963) concluded that an even pace was a more efficient race plan than negative splitting. The subjects in their study were tested while pedaling a bicycle ergometer at 60 rpm. Their riding time was 6 minutes.

It is interesting that both groups of researchers concluded that a fast-slow plan was the least efficient method. This is undoubtedly because the relatively faster speed in the first half of the race causes a rapid accumulation of lactate which, in turn, forces a reduction in speed early in the race that becomes progressively more pronounced the longer the race continues. Even pacing and slow-fast race plans delay lactate accumulation until later in the race so the swimmer can hold a faster average pace through the middle and can then sprint faster at the end. The major difference between even pacing and negative splitting is in the extent of the delay. Even pacers begin the race at a pace they can maintain for the total distance, while negative splitters begin at a speed that can be increased later in the race.

Although it is evident that pacing slower in the beginning of races will improve performance, and since the available research has been inconclusive, the author has relied on an empirical approach to determine the most effective race plans for the various competitive events. The paces that swimmers have used when establishing world records, American records, and U.S. Open records over a 20-year period have been analyzed for similarities. This approach has revealed definite similarities in the ways swimmers have paced certain race distances when they produced national or world records. An even pace was used most frequently at all competitive distances of 100 yards and more, indicating that it is probably the most efficient race plan. That conclusion is inescapable when swimmers of different sexes and different ages, from different parts of the world, and even from different eras have split their most outstanding races in an even or nearly even manner. It should be mentioned, however, that some excellent distance swims have been achieved by negative splitting. Only rarely have national or world records been set by swimmers who used a fast-slow race plan.

There is a unique aspect of swim pacing that must be explained in order for the reader to understand how these conclusions were reached. Unlike track races, split times for swimming races do not need to be identical or nearly identical to indicate that the swimmers are swimming at a constant speed. Although track athletes must accelerate to race speed after the start of their race, a swimmer decelerates after entering the water. Thus, because swimming races begin with a dive, the first split will usually be faster than later splits. This is true even if the swimmer is holding back. In addition, later portions of a swimming race begin with a turn which adds to the split time causing us to underestimate the swimmer's actual speed.

Due to the advantage gained with a dive and the time added by the turn, the first split of butterfly, backstroke, and breaststroke races will generally be 2 to 3 seconds faster than later splits, even though the swimmers are swimming at a constant speed. The first split will usually be 1.5 to 2.0 seconds faster than later splits in freestyle events because later splits are taken from a foot touch, so that a portion of the turn is included in the first split. Thus, any swimmer who completes the first portions of butterfly, backstroke, or breaststroke races 2 to 3 seconds faster than the later portions is really even-pacing, while a drop-off of 1.5 to 2.0 seconds from the first to later splits indicates even-pacing in freestyle events. By the same token breaststroke, butterfly, and backstroke swimmers who have drop-offs that are less than 2 or 3 seconds are actually negative splitting. When the first split of a race is more than 2 to 3 seconds faster than later splits, a fast-slow plan is being used. In freestyle events, a drop-off that is less than 1.5 seconds is indicative of negative splitting, while drop-offs that exceed 2.0 seconds indicate a fast-slow race plan.

Some examples may clarify this point. Suppose a female swimmer with a best time of 1:58.0 seconds for a 200-yard freestyle completed the first half of the race in 58.0 seconds and the second half in 60.0 seconds. Her drop-off was 2.0 seconds; therefore, she has probably even-paced the race.

Suppose also that her race plan was compared to that of a male swimmer who swims the same event in 1:48.0 seconds by swimming the first half in 53.0 seconds and the second half in 55.0 seconds. These two swimmers, although their times are dissimilar, have used the same race plan.

At this point it might be best to consider the relationships of splits that have consistently produced great swims. In this way we can then counsel swimmers concerning the pace pattern for each race and can help them set realistic goals. For example, a swimmer with a best time of 54.0 seconds for the 100-yard freestyle could not be expected to swim 1:50.0 for 200 yards. If the splits were 54.0 for the first 100 yards of the race and 56.0 for the second 100 yards, the swimmer would be required to swim the first half of the race at maximum speed and could not then be expected to maintain that speed for another 100 yards. More than likely, the second half of the race would be swum at a speed of 1:02.0 or slower.

In order to counsel swimmers intelligently concerning the splits they should swim, we must know how fast they can complete the first portion of a race relative to their best time for that distance, and still be able to swim the remainder of the race with an appropriate drop-off. The appropriate going out speed can also be determined by examining the splits of national and world record swims. For example, outstanding swims for the 200-yard freestyle have usually been taken out in times that are approximately 2 seconds slower than the swimmer's best time for 100 yards and they have been able to swim the second half of the race with no more than a 2-second drop-off.

We can conclude, therefore, that 200 freestyle swimmers, regardless of age or sex, should attempt to swim the first half of the race 2 seconds slower than their best time for the 100 and that their drop-off during the second 100 should approximate 2 seconds.

With this in mind the swimmer with a best time of 54.0 seconds for 100 yards of freestyle should be counseled to try for a time of 1:54.0 for 200 yards by swimming the first 100 yards in 56.0 seconds and the second 100 yards in 58.0 seconds.

This same procedure can be used for determining the appropriate going out speeds and the expected drop-off times for all of the competitive events. Following are descriptions of the race plans for each event that have been used most frequently in outstanding swims.

1,500 and 1,650 Freestyle

Most distance swimmers use an even pace until the final 100 meters or 150 yards, at which time they increase their speed and sprint to the finish. The splits for two representative American record swims in the 1,650 and two world record swims in the 1,500 are shown in Table 11.1.

In the 1,650, the first 500 yards is generally 8 to 12 seconds slower than a swimmer's best time for that distance. The next two 500s are held within 2 to 3 seconds of the first, and the final 150 yards is sprinted as fast as possible. Usually the final 150 yards is 1 to 2 seconds faster than the average 100 pace for the previous 500 yards.

An even more useful method for describing the pace pattern for the 1,650 is in terms of 100 splits. However, in this case it is not possible to determine how much swimmers are holding back because 100 freestyle times are seldom available for distance swimmers. The hold-back times recommended therefore, are based on the author's personal experience with distance swimmers.

The first 100 yards is usually 6 to 7 seconds slower than the swimmer's best time for 100 yards. The next fourteen 100s are swum at a relatively constant

Table 11.1 *Splits for Representative American Record and World Record 1650-Yard and 1500-Meter Freestyles*

Distance	1650 Mike Bruner—15:15.33 Time for 500 yards = approximately 4:21.+		1650 Brian Goodell—14:47.27 American and U.S. Open Record 1979 National AAU Championships. Time for 500 yards = 4:16.40	
	Cumulative time	Split time	Cumulative time	Split time
By 500s				
500 yards	4:36.8	4:36.8	4:26.78	4:26.78
1,000	9:15.6	4:38.8	8:56.25	4:29.47
1,500	13:53.5	4:37.9	13:28.18	4:31.93
1,650	15:15.33	1:21.83	14:27.27	1:19.09
By 100s				
100	53.3	53.3	51.32	51.32
200	1:49.0	55.7	1:45.00	53.68
300	2:45.0	56.0	2:39.12	54.12
400	3:41.0	56.0	3:32.94	53.82
500	4:36.8	55.8	4:26.78	53.84
600	5:32.0	55.2	5:20.54	53.76
700	6:27.4	55.4	6:14.41	53.87
800	7:23.3	55.9	7:08.32	53.91
900	8:19.3	56.0	8:02.21	53.89
1,000	9:15.6	56.3	8:56.25	54.04
1,100	10:11.6	56.0	9:50.72	54.47
1,200	11:07.1	55.5	10:45.07	54.35
1,300	12:03.3	56.2	11:39.35	54.28
1,400	12:58.8	55.5	12:33.98	54.63
1,500	13:53.5	54.7	13:28.12	54.14
1,600	14:47.9	54.4	14:21.56	53.44
1,650	15:15.33	27.43	14:47.27	25.71

speed which is approximately 2 to 3 seconds slower than the first 100. The final 150 yards are swum at a pace approximately 1 to 2 seconds faster than the pace for the previous splits.

The pace pattern for 1,500 meters is similar to the 1,650. When splits for 1,500 meters are taken for each 100 meters, the pace is nearly identical to that of the 1,650. The first 100 is 6 to 7 seconds slower than the swimmer's best time for 100 meters. The next thirteen 100s are approximately 2 to 3 seconds slower than the first, and the final 100 meters is approximately equal to the first.

800 Meters A relatively even pace throughout with a fast finish also seems to be preferred by swimmers in the 800-meter event. Examples of the typical race plans used by world-class swimmers are shown in Table 11.2.

The first 400 meters is approximately 6 to 8 seconds slower than the swim-

Table 11.2 *Splits for Representative American Record and World Record 800-Meter Swims*

Distance	Tracey Wickham—8:24.62 World Record 1978 World Swimming Championships Time for 400 meters = 4:06.28		Kim Linehan—8:31.99 American Record 1978 National AAU Championships Time for 400 meters = 4:07.66	
	Cumulative time	Split time	Cumulative time	Split time
By 400s				
400 meters	4:14.00	4:14.00	4:15.27	4:15.27
800	8:24.62	4:10.62	8:31.99	4:16.72
		(Drop-off = −3.38)		(Drop-off = 1.45)
By 100s				
100	1:02.55	1:02.55	1:02.65	1:02.65
200	2:06.35	1:03.80	2:07.34	1:04.69
300	3:10.12	1:03.77	3:11.35	1:04.01
400	4:14.00	1:03.88	4:15.27	1:03.92
500	5:18.22	1:04.22	5:19.58	1:04.31
600	6:20.92	1:02.70	6:23.89	1:04.31
700	7:22.67	1:01.75	7:28.20	1:04.31
800	8:24.62	1:01.95	8:31.99	1:03.79

mer's best time for 400 meters. The second 400 meters is 1 to 2 seconds slower than the first (see Linehan's splits).

Considering the pace by 100 splits, the first 100 meters is approximately 4 to 5 seconds slower than an all-out 100 swim. The next six 100s are approximately 1 to 2 seconds slower than the first, and the final 100 meters is nearly equal in speed to the first 100 meters.

Wickham's splits do not follow this pattern exactly. Her race is an example of a typical negative splitting race plan. She swam an even pace for the first ⅔ to ¾ of the race and then increased the pace. This race plan has been used successfully, although not as frequently as even-paced plans, in several outstanding distance swims. It may be an excellent plan for certain swimmers.

400-Meter and 500-Yard Freestyle

Both even-pace and negative-split race plans have been used successfully in the 400-meter and 500-yard freestyles. Examples of even pacing for two American record 500-yard freestyles are presented in Table 11.3. Two world record 400-meter swims where negative-split race plans were used are shown in Table 11.4.

Most swimmers in the 500-yard freestyle swim the first 100 yards 4 to 5 seconds slower than their best time for 100 yards (their 200-yard split is generally 5 to 6 seconds slower than their best 200-yard time). The next three 100s are swum at a relatively constant speed that is approximately 2 seconds slower than the first, and the final 100 is somewhere between 0.5 and 1.0 second faster than the previous three 100s.

Table 11.3 *Splits for Representative American Record 500-Yard Freestyle Swims*

Distance	Tracy Caulkins—4:36.25 American Record 1979 National AAU Championships Time for 200 yards = 1:45.38		Brian Goodell—4:16.40 American Record 1978 National AAU Championships Time for 200 yards = 1:35.93	
	Cumulative time	Split time	Cumulative time	Split time
By 200s				
200 yards	1:49.74	1:49.74	1:41.7	1:41.7
400	3:41.49	1:52.25	3:25.0	1:43.3
500	4:36.25	54.26	4:16.40	51.4
By 100s				
100	53.55	53.55	50.1	50.1
200	1:49.74	56.19	1:41.7	51.6
300	2:45.63	55.89	2:33.1	51.4
400	3:41.99	56.36	3:25.0	51.9
500	4:36.25	54.26	4:16.40	51.4

Table 11.4 *Splits for Representative World Record 400-Meter Swims*

Distance	Tracey Wickham—4:06.28 World Record 1978 World Championships Time for 200 meters unknown		Peter Szmidt—3:50.49 World Record 1980 Canadian Olympic Trials Time for 200 meters = 1:50.27	
	Cumulative time	Split time	Cumulative time	Split time
By 200s				
200 meters	2:04.11	2:04.11	1:55.57	1:55.57
400	4:06.28	2:02.17	3:50.49	1:54.92
		(Drop-off = −1.94)		(Drop-off = −.65)
By 100s				
100	1:01.16	1:01.16	56.88	56.88
200	2:04.11	1:02.95	1:55.57	58.69
300	3:05.58	1:01.47	2:53.10	57.53
400	4:06.28	1:00.70	3:50.49	57.39

The race plan for even pacing 400 meters is nearly identical to that of the 500. The splits of Wickham and Szmidt (see Table 11.4) are examples of negative splitting. Swimmers who use this race plan generally swim the first 200 meters at an even pace that is 5 to 6 seconds slower than their best time for 200 meters and then swim the final 200 at an even pace that is approximately 1 to 2 seconds faster than the first.

200-Meter and
200-Yard Freestyle

Most 200 swimmers use an even pace. Splits for two American record 200-yard freestyle swims and two world record 200-meter swims are shown in Tables 11.5 and 11.6.

Swimmers in the 200 events swim the first 100 approximately 2.0 to 3.0 seconds slower than their best 100 time and their drop-off is generally 2.0 to 3.0 seconds during the next 100 yards. The pace by 50s is as follows. The first 50 is approximately 2.0 to 2.5 seconds slower than their best 50 time. The second and

Table 11.5 *Splits for Representative American Record 200-Yard Freestyle Swims*

Distance	Cynthia Woodhead— 1:44.10 American and U.S. Open Record 1979 National AAU Championships Time for 100 yards = 49.39		Rowdy Gaines—1:34.57 American and U.S. Open Record 1980 National AAU Championships Time for 100 yards = 44.22	
	Cumulative time	Split time	Cumulative time	Split time
By 100s				
100 yards	50.58	50.58	45.9	45.9
200	1:44.10	53.52	1:34.57	48.6
	(Drop-off = 2.94)		(Drop-off = 2.74)	
By 50s				
50	24.61	24.61	22.1	22.1
100	50.58	25.97	45.9	23.8
150	1:17.39	26.81	1:10.4	24.5
200	1:44.10	26.71	1:34.57	24.1+

Table 11.6 *Splits for Representative World Record 200-Meter Freestyle Swims*

Distance	Cynthia Woodhead—1:58.23 World Record 1978 World Championships Time for 100 meters = 56.73		Rowdy Gaines—1:49.16 World Record 1980 National AAU Championships Time for 100 meters = 49.61	
	Cumulative time	Split time	Cumulative time	Split time
By 100s				
100 meters	58.31	58.31	52.52	52.52
200	1:58.23	59.92	1:49.16	56.64
	(Drop-off = 1.61)		(Drop-off = 4.12)	
By 50s				
50	28.13	28.13	25.03	25.03
100	58.31	30.18	52.52	27.49
150	1:28.38	30.07	1:20.92	28.40
200	1:58.23	29.85	1:49.16	28.24

Table 11.7 *Splits for Representative U.S. Open Record 200-Yard Butterfly Swim and World Record 200-Meter Butterfly Swim*

Distance	Craig Beardsley—1:58.21 World Record 1980 U.S. Olympic Trials Time for 100 meters unknown		Per Arvidsson—1:44.43 U.S. Open Record 1980 NCAA Championships Time for 100 yards = 47.36	
	Cumulative time	Split time	Cumulative time	Split time
By 100s				
100	58.00	58.00	50.2	50.2
200	1:58.21	1:00.21	1:44.43	54.2
		(Drop-off = 2.21)		(Drop-off = 4.00)
By 50s				
50	27.35	27.35	23.9	23.9
100	58.00	30.65	50.2	26.3
150	1:27.87	29.87	1:16.9	26.7
200	1:58.21	30.34	1:44.43	27.5+

third 50s are evenly paced and are approximately 1.5 to 2.0 seconds slower than the first. The final 50 is equal to, or sometimes slightly faster than, the middle two.

There is a tendency for some 200-meter swimmers to swim the first 100 meters at a slower relative speed than they might swim it in a 200-yard race. This is probably because they fatigue more quickly when they have fewer turns. Therefore, they save a small amount of additional energy for the last half of the race.

200-Meter and 200-Yard Butterfly

The 200 butterfly is also an even-paced race, although butterflyers usually hold back more than freestylers when they go out and their drop-off is slightly greater from the first to the second half of the race. The splits for a representative U.S. Open record 200-yard and a world record 200-meter butterfly are shown in Table 11.7.

Butterfly swimmers characteristically swim the first 100 approximately 3.0 to 4.0 seconds slower than their best 100 time. Their drop-off is between 2.5 to 4.0 seconds during the next 100. Considering the splits by 50s, the first 50 is usually 2.0 seconds slower than their all-out 50 times and their next three 50s are approximately 2.0 to 3.0 seconds slower than the first.

200-Meter and 200-Yard Backstroke and Breaststroke

Most successful swimmers in the 200 backstroke and breaststroke events also even pace their races. They go out approximately 2 to 3 seconds slower than their best 100 and come back with 2- to 4-second drop-offs. When viewing their pace by 50s, they tend to swim the race in the same manner indicated for butterflyers. Splits for American, U.S. Open, and world record 200-meter and 200-yard backstroke and breaststroke swims are shown in Tables 11.8 and 11.9.

Table 11.8 *Splits for Representative American Record and World Record 200-Yard and 200-Meter Backstroke Swims*

	Linda Jezek—1:57.79 American Record 1978 National AAU Championships Time for 100 yards = 54.94		John Naber—1:46.09 1977 NCAA Championships American Record Time for 100 yards = 49.31	
Distance	Cumulative time	Split time	Cumulative time	Split time
By 100s				
100 yards	57.4	57.4	51.16	51.16
200	1:57.79	1:00.3	1:46.09	54.93
		(Drop-off = 2.9 +)		(Drop-off = 3.77)
By 50s				
50	27.6	27.6	24.58	24.58
100	57.4	29.8	51.16	26.58
150	1:27.3	29.9	1:18.36	27.20
200	1:57.79	30.4+	1:46.09	27.73
	Rina Reinisch—2:11.77 World Record 1980 Olympic Games Time for 100 meters = 1:00.86			
By 100s				
100 meters	1:04.55	1:04.55		
200	2:11.77	1:07.22		
		(Drop-off = 2.67)		
By 50s				
50	31.18	31.18		
100	1:04.55	33.37		
150	1:38.49	33.94		
200	2:11.77	33.28		

100-Meter and 100-Yard Freestyle

Analysis of the pace for 100 meter events indicates that swimmers use even pacing. They do not go out as fast as possible but instead hold back slightly during the first 50. Most record-breaking 100 freestylers have completed the first 50 approximately one second slower than their best time for that distance. (The amount swimmers hold back is actually between 0.5 and 1 second because the split is taken from a foot touch, whereas the 50 time that was used for comparison did not include a turn.) Their drop-off is usually 1.5 to 2.0 seconds during the second 50. Splits from some American, U.S. Open, and world record swims are shown in Table 11.10.

100-Meter and 100-Yard Butterfly

The 100-meter and 100-yard butterfly races are probably even paced also. However, since 50 times are not always available for record holders in the 100 butterfly (or for the backstroke and breaststroke events discussed next) suggestions regarding the amount swimmers should hold back are based on the

Table 11.9 *Splits for Representative American Record and World Record 200-Yard and 200-Meter Breaststroke Swims*

Tracy Caulkins—2:14.07
American Record 1978
National AAU Championships
Time for 100 yards = 1:02.20

Distance	Cumulative time	Split time
By 100s		
100 yards	1:05.6	1:05.6
200	2:14.07	1:08.4 +
		(Drop-off = 2.8 +)
By 50s		
50	30.9	30.9
100	1:05.6	34.7
150	1:40.0	34.4
200	2:14.07	34.0 +

David Wilkie—2:15.11
World Record 1976 Olympic Games
Time for 100 meters = 1:03.43

Distance	Cumulative time	Split time
By 100s		
100 meters	1:06.49	1:06.49
200	2:15.11	1:08.62
		(Drop-off = 2.13)
By 50s		
50	31.24	31.24
100	1:06.49	35.25
150	1:40.84	34.35
200	2:15.11	34.27

author's personal experience. Butterfly swimmers, like freestylers, swim the first 50 from half a second to a second slower than their best 50 time. Their drop-off is approximately 2 to 3 seconds. The splits for representative U.S. Open and world record swims are shown in Table 11.11.

100-Meter and 100-Yard Breaststroke

The 100 breaststroke races should be split in the same manner butterfly swims are split. Examples of American, U.S. Open, and world record 100 breaststroke swims are given in Table 11.12.

100-Meter and 100-Yard Backstroke

Backstrokers also swim the first 50 of the 100 race approximately 0.5 to 1 second slower than their best time for that distance. They seem to drop-off less in the second half, however. Their drop-off is usually 1.5 to 2.5 seconds in both meters and yards races. Splits for some representative American and world record swims are shown in Table 11.13.

Table 11.10 *Splits for Representative American Record and World Record 100-Yard and 100-Meter Freestyle Swims*

	Jill Sterkel—48.76 American Record 1979 National AAU Championships Time for 50 yards = 22.83		Rowdy Gaines—43.16 American and U.S. Open Record 1980 NCAA Championships Time for 50 yards = 19.80	
Distance	Cumulative time	Split time	Cumulative time	Split time
50 yards	23.41	23.41	20.5	20.5
100	48.76	25.35	43.16	22.6
		(Drop-off = 1.94)		(Drop-off = 2.1)
	Barbara Krause—54.79 World Record 1980 Olympic Games		Jonty Skinner—49.44 World Record 1976 National AAU Championships	
50 meters	26.81	26.81	23.83	23.83
100	54.79	27.98	49.44	25.61
		(Drop-off = 1.17)		(Drop-off = 1.78)

Table 11.11 *Splits for Representative U.S. Open and World Record 100-Yard and 100-Meter Butterfly Swims*

	Per Arvidsson—47.36 U.S. Open Record 1980 NCAA Championships			
Distance	Cumulative time	Split time		
50 yards	22.6	22.6		
100	47.36	24.7		
		(Drop-off = 2.10)		
	Mary Meagher—59.26 World Record		Per Arvidsson—54.14 World Record	
50 meters	28.24	28.24	25.90	25.90
100	59.26	31.02	54.15	28.25
		(Drop-off = 2.78)		(Drop-off = 2.35)

Individual Medleys   Determining the best pace patterns for individual medleys presents a special problem. Drop-off times are inconclusive when strokes are changed during each quarter of the race. The approach that has been used is to compare each leg of the individual medley to a particular swimmer's best time for the same stroke and distance.

Table 11.12　*Splits for Representative American Record and World Record 100-Yard and 100-Meter Breaststroke Swims*

Distance	Tracy Caulkins—1:01.82 American Record, American and U.S. Open Record 1979 National AAU Championships		Steve Lundquist—53.59 American and U.S. Open Record 1980 NCAA Championships	
	Cumulative time	Split time	Cumulative time	Split time
50 yards	29.01	29.01	25.3	25.3
100	1:01.82	32.81	53.59	28.3
		(Drop-off = 3.80)		(Drop-off = 3.00)
	Uwe Gewinger—1:10.11 World Record		Gerald Moerken—1:02.86 World Record	
	Cumulative time	Split time	Cumulative time	Split time
50 meters	33.69	33.69	29.60	29.60
100	1:10.11	36.42	1:02.86	33.26
		(Drop-off = 2.73)		(Drop-off = 3.66)

Table 11.13　*Splits for Representative American Record and World Record 100-Yard and 100-Meter Backstroke Swims*

Distance	Linda Jezek—54.94 American Record		John Naber—49.31 American Record 1977 NCAA Championships	
	Cumulative time	Split time	Cumulative time	Split time
50 yards	26.54	26.54	23.46	23.46
100	54.94	28.40	49.31	25.85
		(Drop-off = 1.86)		(Drop-off = 2.39)
	Rina Reinisch—1:00.86 World Record 1980 Olympic Games		John Naber—55.49 World Record	
	Cumulative time	Split time	Cumulative time	Split time
50 meters	29.69	29.69	26.55	26.55
100	1:00.86	31.17	55.49	28.94
		(Drop-off = 1.48)		(Drop-off = 2.39)

200-meter and 200-yard individual medley. Swimmers in the 200 individual medley complete the first 50-yard butterfly about 1 second slower than an all-out sprint for the same distance. The backstroke split is approximately 3 seconds slower than their best time for 50 yards of that stroke. The breaststroke is 5 to 6 seconds slower, and the freestyle is approximately 4 seconds

Table 11.14   *Splits for Representative American, U.S. Open, and World Record 200-Yard and 200-Meter Individual Medley Swims*

Distance	Tracy Caulkins—1:57.86 American Record 1978 National AAU Championships		Bill Barrett—1:46.25 American and U.S. Open Record 1980 NCAA Championships	
	Cumulative time	Split time	Cumulative time	Split time
50 yards	25.16	25.16	22.8	22.8
100	55.49	30.33	50.6	27.8
150	1:29.95	34.46	1:21.0	30.4
200	1:57.86	27.91	1:46.25	25.25

Distance	Tracy Caulkins—2:13.69 American and U.S. Open Record		Bill Barrett—2:03.24 World Record 1980 U.S. Olympic Trials	
50 meters	28.76	28.76	25.98	25.98
100	1:03.05	34.29	58.97	32.99
150	1:42.38	39.33	1:33.19	34.22
200	2:13.69	31.31	2:03.24	30.05

slower. This same pace pattern is used in both short-course and long-course events. Splits for some American, U.S. Open, and world record swims are shown in Table 11.14.

400-meter and 400-yard individual medley. In both long-course and short-course 400 individual medley events swimmers complete the first 100 butterfly 2 to 3 seconds slower than their best time for the same distance. The backstroke and freestyle legs are 6 to 7 seconds slower than a particular swimmer's best times for those strokes and distances. The breaststroke leg is generally 8 to 10 seconds slower. The splits for some representative American, U.S. Open, and world record swims are listed in Table 11.15.

Exceptions to the Recommended Pace Patterns

Occasionally swimmers have set records by going out faster than was recommended in the previous discussion of race plans. One explanation for these exceptions is, of course, that the swimmers in question compete best with a fast-slow race plan. However, because of the preponderance of records that have been set with even-pace and negative-split race plans, there is another and perhaps more plausible explanation. That is that they might have gone faster by using an even pace. Following are two examples of swimmers going faster by swimming the first half of the race somewhat slower. Several more could be cited.

1. Brigette Treiber set a world record of 2:15.46 in the 200-meter backstroke, which broke her previous record of 2:16.10. Her splits were 1:05.45–1:10.65

Table 11.15 *Splits for Representative American, U.S. Open, and World Record 400-Yard and 400-Meter Individual Medley Swims*

Distance	Tracy Caulkins—4:08.09 American Record 1979 National AAU Championships		Jesse Vassallo—3:48.24 U.S. Open Record 1979 National AAU Championships	
	Cumulative time	Split time	Cumulative time	Split time
100 yards	55.22	55.22	52.19	52.19
200	1:58.52	1:03.30	1:48.74	56.55
300	3:11.10	1:12.58	2:54.46	1:05.72
400	4:08.09	56.99	3:48.24	53.78
	Petra Schneider—4:36.29 World Record 1980 Olympic Games		Jesse Vassallo—4:20.05 World Record 1978 World Championships	
100 meters	1:01.72	1:01.72	59.99	59.99
200	2:12.12	1:10.40	2:03.53	1:03.54
300	3:32.19	1:20.07	3:19.15	1:15.62
400	4:36.29	1:04.10	4:20.05	1:00.90

for the previous swim. In the later swim, she went out slower, 1:06.95, and came back faster, 1:08.51.

2. John Hencken set an American record of 2:01.78 in the 200-yard breaststroke. His splits were 59.90–1:01.88. In a later race he swam 2:02.25, even though his first 100 split was more than one second faster. His splits were 58.74–1:03.49 for the slower swim.

Teaching Swimmers to Pace

The best method for teaching pace is with underdistance repeats and broken swims. Swimmers should be able to repeat swims of one quarter the race distance or less within 0.2 to 0.5 seconds of their ideal pace by the time their most important meets are scheduled.

Going out paces should be practiced with a block start for greater accuracy. Middle paces should begin from a turn so the time accurately reflects the true pace for the race in question. The time should be taken from a hand or foot touch depending upon the event for which the pace is being practiced.

Swimmers must also learn how to fluctuate their pace. If a particular race develops in such a way that they must deviate from their planned pace, they should be able to do so without losing control of the race. Swimming repeats at a variety of speeds that are both faster and slower than race pace is ideal for this purpose. Swimmers become capable of judging just how much they can deviate from an ideal pace without seriously reducing the possibility of swimming a fast time.

Strategy

Pacing will usually result in the fastest possible time. That time will not always win the race, however. Races between swimmers with similar times are often won when one swimmer's race plan is upset by a competitor making an unexpected move sometime during the race. Following are descriptions of some of the more common tactics that swimmers have used successfully.

1. *Going out faster than expected.* This tactic works well against opponents who are inexperienced and opponents who have a strong finishing sprint. Inexperienced swimmers may become demoralized when you take an early lead. Fast finishers may not be able to bring it home when they are forced to go out faster than they had planned.

2. *Going out slower than expected.* This tactic is useful against opponents who are not fast finishers. Where normally they might have gone out at a pace that would be too fast for you to keep up, your slower early pace may fool them into swimming slower than they planned. As a result, both of you will reach the final portion of the race less fatigued than usual, in which case your superior speed may permit you to out-sprint them to the finish.

3. *A fast breakaway sprint in the middle of the race.* This is a good tactic to use against opponents who tend to give up when they are behind. Your sprint may demoralize them, after which you can slow down to your previous pace while maintaining the lead you have gained to the finish of the race.

Swimmers should also be aware that there are defensive strategies that can be used to counter each of the offensive tactics that were just described. The more common of these are described as follows:

1. If a competitor starts the race at a faster pace than expected, you should stay close enough that you can overtake him or her even if it means swimming faster than you had planned. Your opponent will have to work harder to stay ahead than you will be working to stay close. Therefore, if your opponent tires first, you will be able to take the lead.

2. When a competitor tries to set a slow early pace, don't be afraid to take the lead and swim your own race. Some swimmers are so devoted to negative splitting that they expect to be behind in the early stages of a race. These swimmers refuse to take the lead in a race even when the pace is too slow for them. These swimmers may find themselves outsprinted at the end of the race by a faster and less-enduring opponent if they do not build an early lead.

3. Don't let an opponent sprint away from you in the middle of the race even if the pace seems to be too fast. Your opponent may become demoralized if the sprint doesn't cause you to fall behind. In addition, your opponent will probably tire from this burst of speed and you may be able to take the lead.

4. There is an advantage to taking the lead when swimming in pools that have considerable turbulence. This is particularly true in butterfly races.

Swimming in the wake of competitors increases the energy that must be expended to combat wave drag. In such cases it is advisable to disregard pace and strategy and try to maintain a lead throughout the race. If the pace is too fast for you to take the lead, you should remain as close as possible.

The previous suggestions notwithstanding, you should be aware that seldom will any offensive or defensive strategy allow you to win against an experienced competitor who has superior speed. Tactics work best when two competitors of equal or nearly equal ability are racing.

Warm Up

The precompetition ritual of warming up is firmly entrenched in our culture. Research regarding the value of this procedure is surprisingly contradictory, however. One source indicates: "During an extensive review of the research on warmup the authors found eight reports which support the idea that warmup is beneficial and seven reports that claim that warmup has no effect on performance" (Jensen and Fisher 1972, p. 161).

Why is a practice that is deemed so essential to athletic performance not supported by research? The answer probably lies in the standardization of such research. Scientists have used different warm-up procedures with regard to skill, intensity, and duration in their studies, making it impossible to determine whether the outcome of their studies reflected the value of warming up in general or the effectiveness of the specific procedures that were used in a particular study.

Due to this lack of consistent data, we must base our decisions about warm up on indirect evidence and empirical judgments. The indirect evidence comes from research that demonstrates the effect of increased muscle temperature on the physiological processes involved in athletic performance. According to some sources, there must be an increase in muscle temperature before many of the values of warming up can be realized (deVries 1974).

The Effect of Increased Muscle Temperature on Body Physiology

It has been well documented that muscles contract more rapidly when their temperature is increased. Astrand and Rodahl (1977) have reported that nerve impulses travel faster at higher internal temperatures. There is also less resistance to movement because increases in muscle temperature lower internal viscosity (deVries 1974). These alterations in function provide an internal environment that is conducive to faster reaction times, and more powerful movements.

It is reported that pulmonary ventilation and cardiac output are also elevated with increased muscle temperature, suggesting the possibility that warming up improves oxygen transport (deVries 1974). This observation is supported by a study in which postexercise blood lactate concentration was reduced when strenuous exercise was preceded by a warm up (Keul, Doll, and Keppler 1972).

It is interesting that the decreases in blood lactate accumulation that were reported in this study followed a warm up consisting of mild exercise.

Since increases in muscle temperature are proportional to work intensity we would expect that a warm up that includes vigorous exercise should be more effective than one in which only mild activities are used. However, vigorous warm ups, while they will increase muscle temperature, also deplete muscle glycogen and cause excess lactate to accumulate in the muscles. If the warm up is too vigorous, athletes could enter competition with elevated muscle lactic acid levels and partially depleted muscle glycogen stores, which would in turn cause them to fatigue earlier in the race. Therefore, in order to plan a warm up that will aid rather than hinder performance, we need to know the minimum intensity and duration of vigorous work that will produce the desired increase in muscle temperature without causing undue fatigue.

Concerning warm-up intensity, Hermiston and O'Brien (1972) reported a decreased oxygen cost for a treadmill-simulated 220-yard run following a 10-minute warm up at 30 percent of $\dot{V}O_2$ max. A warm-up intensity of 60 percent of $\dot{V}O_2$ max, although it was superior to no warm up at all, increased the oxygen debt more than the less intense warm up. This indicates that efforts of 60 percent of $\dot{V}O_2$ max are probably unnecessarily intense and could possibly cause early fatigue. Therefore, the ideal work intensity for warming up is probably between 30 to 50 percent of $\dot{V}O_2$ max. It should be mentioned, in fairness, that only 1-minute rest periods were permitted between the warm ups and the runs. Longer rest periods may have permitted more intense efforts to be included in the warm up with no increase in oxygen cost during the runs.

Where duration is concerned, deVries (1974) has reported that warm ups of moderate intensity that are 15 to 30 minutes in length will increase muscle temperature. Try to finish your warm up within 20 to 30 minutes of the start of your race. It has been reported that the warm-up effect will last 35 to 85 minutes (deVries 1974). The rest period could be considerably shorter if only low-intensity swimming is used. In fact, it probably should be reduced in such cases. Muscle temperature will probably not be elevated to the same extent by low-intensity swimming as it would be with a warm up that includes some moderate-intensity efforts and some sprinting.

How can swimmers tell if their warm up has been sufficiently vigorous to increase muscle temperature? The warm up should produce feelings of warmth and some reddening of the skin, both of which are signs of increased muscle temperature.

To summarize, warm ups of 15 to 30 minutes duration at 30 to 50 percent effort should increase muscle temperature and therefore improve performance. Some short sprints should also be included in the warm up because they help increase muscle temperature without causing fatigue.

Other Aspects of Warming Up

Other important benefits of warming up that should not be overlooked are that stretching the muscles, loosening connective tissue, and increasing flexibility should improve stroking efficiency and reduce the possibility of joint injuries. Warm ups also provide a rehearsal effect. During this time stroke mechanics, starts, and turns can be refined for the coming competition. Race strategy can be planned and race pace can be practiced. The final purposes for warming up should be to get acquainted with strange pools and to establish a good attitude toward the competition.

Moderate-intensity swimming, in addition to its effect on muscle temperature, is also an excellent method for stretching muscles, loosening connective tissue, and practicing stroking and turning techniques. It is also advisable to include some shoulder- and ankle-flexibility exercises as part of the warm up to aid in stretching muscles and loosening connective tissue.

Strategy and race pace can be practiced by swimming some underdistance repeats. One-hundred-yard swimmers should swim some 25s or 50s. Some of these should be off the block at going-out pace and some of them should be from a turn at the desired pace for the middle two lengths of the race. Fifty-yard swimmers should limit their sprints to 25s off the block. Astrand and Rodahl (1977) report that the use of intense sprints during warm up have tended to be beneficial in sprint events.

Two-hundred-yard/meter swimmers should swim some 50s off the block and some 50s from a turn at the appropriate paces for the first half of their race. Four-hundred-meter and five-hundred-yard swimmers can use either 50 or 100 swims to rehearse race pace, while swimmers in longer races will most certainly want to practice pace by swimming 100s during their warm up.

Each pool has a different feel and distinctive problems with visibility. Each has starting and turning peculiarities that may require adjustments in your techniques. Therefore, you should get acquainted with the pool during your warm up. Be particularly careful to practice starts and turns until you are confident of your ability to execute them at race speed.

Finally, the warm up should be a time when you establish a positive mental set toward your races. You should picture yourself swimming your goal times and placing as high as you believe it is possible for you to place. Make every attempt to dismiss negative thoughts from your mind. Plan your offensive strategy and consider the defensive tactics you will use if you are forced to change that strategy after the race begins.

Warm-up Procedures On the basis of the available information regarding the effects of warming up, the following procedures are recommended:

1. Engage in 5 to 10 minutes of ankle- and shoulder-flexibility exercises prior to entering the water. This will stretch the connective tissue around muscles and joints and permit more relaxed and efficient stroking movements.
2. Then spend 15 to 30 minutes swimming, pulling, and kicking at 30 to 50 percent effort. Muscle temperature, cardiac output, and oxygen consumption should be elevated by this procedure. The intensity of the swimming should be sufficient to create a feeling of warmth and some reddening of the skin. This is an excellent time to rehearse your offensive and defensive strategies. See yourself swimming well and succeeding. Eliminate negative thoughts from your mind. Concentrate on using the most perfect stroke mechanics possible. Make your stroke feel efficient and powerful.
3. Spend some time practicing starts and turns. Practice these until you feel

confident that you can perform them successfully in the race. Practice relay starts if you are swimming on a relay.

4. Swim some repeats at race pace. Swim repeats for both the going out and middle portions of your race until the proper pace is firmly established in your mind.

5. You may want to finish your warm up with some 25 or 50 sprints to insure that your muscle temperature is elevated.

6. Complete your warm up 15 to 30 minutes before your first event. This will give you time to metabolize any lactic acid that may have accumulated.

7. You may want to re-enter the water within 5 or 10 minutes of race time in order to maintain your flexibility and "feel" for the race. You may also want to do some additional flexibility exercises if you feel tight. Finish this final portion of the warm up within 2 to 5 minutes of race time.

Other Competition Procedures

Massage and hyperventilation are two precompetition rituals that are believed to improve performance. Cooling down after races is a procedure that aids recovery so that swimmers can swim subsequent races in faster times.

Massage The prerace massage or rubdown has become increasingly popular among swimmers. However, research concerning the benefits of this procedure has been contradictory.

Asmussen and Boje (1945) found massage had no effect on 1-mile rides on a bicycle ergometer. Several studies by Karpovich (1965) utilizing the treadmill and bicycle ergometer also failed to show any beneficial effect from massage. In opposition to these results, Schmid (1947) found massage had a beneficial effect on swimming 50 meters, running 100 meters, and riding a bicycle ergometer.

Once again, the conflicting reports force us to resort to empirical judgments in order to conjecture concerning the effects of massage on swimming performance. In theory, massage should be beneficial for several reasons:

- Muscle temperature can be increased through the heat generated from the balm and the friction from the hands of the person giving the massage.
- Flexibility should be increased by manipulation of the limbs. Muscle tension and prerace anxiety may be reduced by the relaxing combinations of increased body heat and joint manipulation.

The possibility that massage may produce these benefits makes it advisable to include this procedure in your precompetition ritual until its value has been disproven.

Hyperventilation Many swimmers and coaches believe that hyperventilating before races aids performance. There seems to be some physiological support for this practice, although not for the reasons that are usually stated.

Hyperventilation does not improve performances because deep breathing

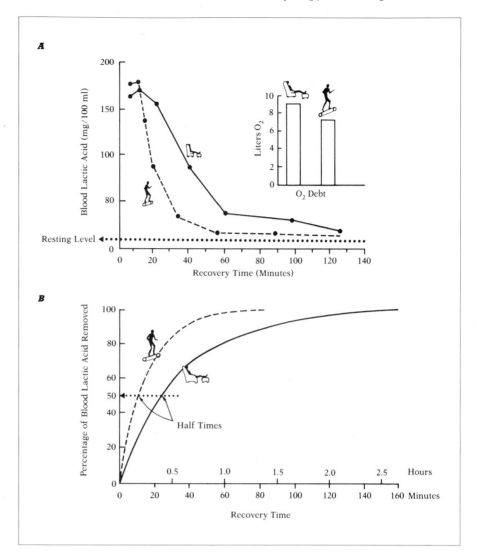

Figure 11.1. Removal of lactic acid from the blood during exhaustive exercise. The removal of blood lactic acid is more rapid if the recovery period is used for light exercise rather than for resting. In **A**, the actual decrease in blood lactic acid during rest-recovery and exercise is shown. In **B**, the rate of lactic acid removal is shown. Notice that the time it takes for one-half of the total accumulated lactic acid to be removed during rest-recovery is twice as long as that during exercise-recovery. [Data in **A** from Gisolli and coworkers, 1966; data in **B** from Hermansen and coworkers, 1975. Adapted from E. L. Fox, *Sports Physiology*, copyright © 1979 by W. B. Saunders Company, by permission of Holt, Rinehart and Winston and the author.]

increases your oxygen supply before the race. The oxygen that was inhaled while standing on the block cannot be stored in your body.

Although a breath of air prior to diving into the water may help you swim more of a 25 or 50 race without breathing, the real value of hyperventilation lies in reducing the carbon dioxide content of your blood. It is carbon dioxide accumulation and not oxygen deprivation that precipitates the feelings of breathlessness and the need for air that swimmers experience during races. Forceful and complete exhalations that lower the CO_2 content of your blood prior to the beginning of the race can delay these sensations. Therefore, the emphasis during hyperventilation should be on exhaling CO_2 rather than inhaling oxygen.

The most effective procedure for hyperventilating is to take three or four normal inhalations followed by complete exhalations as you wait for the race to begin. This will reduce the CO_2 content of your blood. Taking one deep inhalation as you dive into the water will be sufficient to completely fill your alveoli with oxygen. While hyperventilating should be most helpful in 25, 50, and 100 races where breathing is restricted, it has questionable value as a precompetition procedure for middle-distance and distance races.

Cooling Down After Races

Swimmers should always swim 600 to 1,000 yards/meters after a race in order to increase their rate of recovery. Lactate is more rapidly removed from the muscles when they remain active at low intensity (Keul, Doll, and Keppler 1972). The graph in Figure 11.1 illustrates this effect. The rate of lactic acid removal is almost twice as fast when some mild exercise is used during the recovery period, compared to simply resting (Fox 1979). The removal of lactate is accomplished through a mechanism called the "muscle pump." The contraction of muscles exerts a squeezing effect on the veins that pushes blood back to the heart at an accelerated rate where the excess lactate can be removed and metabolized by cardiac muscle fibers. In addition, the elevated cardiac output will cause more blood to reach the lungs where it will give up its carbon dioxide and take on oxygen, which can then be transported to the muscles to increase the rate of lactate removal by metabolizing it to glucose.

The cooling-down swim should be sufficient to increase circulation but not so intense as to cause further increase in lactate accumulation. Efforts of 50 percent or less should not be fatiguing for well-trained athletes. Since most of the lactate can be removed from the muscles and blood within 10 to 15 minutes after exercise, it is recommended that athletes swim for at least that long.

REFERENCES

Asmussen, E., and Boje, O. 1945. "Body Temperature and Capacity for Work." *Acta Physiol. Scand.* 10:1–22.

Astrand, P. O., and Rodah, K. 1977. *Textbook of Work Physiology.* New York: McGraw-Hill.

deVries, H. A. 1974. "Warm-up: Its Values and Efficient Utilization." *Proceedings:*

International Symposium on the Art and Science of Coaching, Vol. 2, ed. L. Percival, pp. 207–213. Ontario, Canada: F. I. Productions.

Fox, E. L. 1979. *Sports Physiology.* Philadelphia: W. B. Saunders.

Hermiston, R. T., and O'Brien, M. E. 1972. "The Effects of Three Types of Warm-up on the Total Oxygen Cost of a Short Treadmill Run." *Training: Scientific Basis and Application*, ed. A. W. Taylor, pp. 70–75. Springfield, Illinois: Charles C. Thomas.

Jensen, C. R., and Fisher, A. G. 1972. *Scientific Basis of Athletic Training.* Philadelphia: Lea and Febiger.

Karpovich, P. V. 1965. *Physiology of Muscular Activity.* Philadelphia: W. B. Saunders.

Keul, J., Doll, E., and Keppler, D. 1972. *Energy Metabolism of Human Muscle.* Baltimore: University Park Press.

Mathews, D. K., Bowers, R., Fox, E., and Wilgus, W. 1963. "Aerobic and Anaerobic Work Efficiency." *Research Quarterly* 34:356–360.

Robinson, S., Robinson, D. L., Montjoy, R. I. J., and Bullard, R. W. 1958. "Fatigue and Efficiency of Men During Exhausting Runs." *J. Appl. Physiol.* 12:197–201.

Schmid, L. 1947. "Increase in Bodily Output by Warming-up." *Casop. Lek. Cesk.* 86:950.

CHAPTER 12

Muscular Strength and Joint Flexibility

Strength and flexibility have for some time been considered important elements of swim training programs. The belief is that improvements in muscular strength will provide greater power which, in turn, will increase swimming speed. "Strength is power is speed" is an oft-quoted maxim. Where flexibility is concerned, increasing the range of motion in several joints, particularly the shoulders and ankles, is believed to permit more efficient stroke mechanics. The purpose of this chapter will be to examine the physiological bases for muscular strength and joint flexibility and to recommend programs for improving them.

Muscular Strength

Although the relationship between muscular strength and fast swimming seems justifiable on an empirical basis, there is little scientific evidence to substantiate that relationship. No significant differences in swimming speed were reported in seven of nine studies where resistance training was used to improve muscular strength and muscular endurance (Clark 1965, Cooper 1966, Davis 1955, Good 1973; Hutchinson 1959, Hutinger 1970, Murray 1962, Nunney 1960, Ross 1973). A variety of supplemental resistance training methods and equipment were used in these studies including weight training, isometrics, isokinetic exercises, Exergenies, surgical tubing, and pulley weights. Some programs were restricted to land while others also included resistance pulling in the water. Swimming speeds were measured at distances of 25, 50, and 100 yards.

Why has research failed to substantiate a relationship between improvements in strength and improvements in swimming speed? Is it because muscular strength is not necessary to good performances? Or is it that most programs do not increase strength in ways that permit it to be used to improve swimming speed? The latter explanation is probably correct.

The basis for traditional forms of resistance training is that increasing the strength of muscles will permit any movements involving contractions of those muscles to be completed with greater force. However, recent research indicates that improvements in strength are specific to the type of resistance training used, to the speed of the movements performed, and to the similarity of these movements to the test procedure that was used to measure strength. That means that even though the same musculature may be involved, training that improves the force generated at a slow speed in a nonswimming movement may have a minimal effect on the force that can be produced when swimming in competition.

Moffroid and Whipple (1970), Costill and his associates (Costill et al. 1978) and Pipes and Wilmore (1975) have presented quite conclusive evidence concerning the specificity of speed and motion to strength improvements. They have shown that strength developed at slow speeds does not improve power at faster speeds and that strength developed with one type of movement does not necessarily transfer to other dissimilar movements.

Moffroid and Whipple tested subjects on an isokinetic leg extension apparatus at 0, 3, 6, 9, 12, 15, and 18 revolutions per minute. Group I trained at 6 rpm, Group II at 18 rpm, and Group III acted as a control. The data in Table 12.1 show the results of the study.

Although both experimental groups improved, they improved most when tested at the speed at which they trained. They also improved at speeds that were slower than their training speed. Notice, however, that the group that trained at 6 rpm did not improve significantly at speeds that were faster than their training rate. This indicates that resistance training for swimmers should

Table 12.1 *Mean Increases for Peak Torque of the Quadriceps Muscles After Training at 6 rpm and 18 rpm on a Cybex Apparatus*

Test velocity	Group I (6 rpm)	Group II (18 rpm)	Group III (control)
0 rpm	28.6	21.8	14.1
3 rpm	35.4	16.8	3.0
6 rpm[1]	47.1	24.8	8.3
9 rpm	14.5	14.5	8.4
12 rpm	14.1	17.5	6.9
15 rpm	10.8	12.3	4.8
18 rpm[2]	8.4	15.6	2.0

Source: Data from Moffroid and Whipple, "Specificity of Speed of Exercise," *Physical Therapy*, 50 (December 1970), p. 1695; used with permission of the American Physical Therapy Association.
[1]Training speed for Group I
[2]Training speed for Group II

be performed at the same or a faster turnover rate than will be used in races if increases in power are to be usable in competition. It is particularly significant, since most swimming motions are executed at a rapid speed, that the improvement of the fast speed group (18 rpm) was almost double that of the slow speed group (6 rpm) at the fastest training speed.

Similar results were reported by Costill and his associates (1978) in a study in which subjects trained with 6- and 30-second leg extensions against a Cybex leg extension apparatus. All subjects trained at 3.14 radians per second. They were tested for knee-extension strength at velocities ranging from 1.05 to 5.23 radians per second.

Significant improvements in knee-extension strength (peak torque) were found at the training velocity (3.14 radians per second) and all velocities below that speed. Increases were not found at velocities exceeding the training velocity.

In a different approach to the topic of specificity and strength training, Pipes and Wilmore (1975) compared traditional weight training, slow-speed isokinetic exercises, and fast-speed isokinetic exercises for improvements in muscular strength.

Where strength was concerned, they found improvements were specific to the form and the speed of training that was used for its development. That is, fast-speed isokinetic training improved strength most on fast-speed isokinetic tests. The group trained with slow-speed isokinetic exercises improved most on the slow-speed isokinetic tests, while the weight training group improved most when the tests of strength involved lifting weights.

These findings have been verified in some research conducted with male swimmers at Oakland University. A nonsignificant relationship of 0.22 was found between their scores for a maximum bench press (a test of muscular power) and their speed for a 25-yard freestyle. However, when power was tested with one maximum pull on a Biokinetic Swim Bench, a very high positive relationship (0.87) was found (Maglischo and Maglischo 1980). Costill and his associates (1980) were the first researchers to demonstrate a relationship between power and sprint speed. They reported a high positive relationship of 0.93. These results indicate that muscular power is not a general quality but is, instead, specific to the manner in which it has been developed.

It is quite possible that the major adaptations that are involved in improving strength occur in the nervous system rather than in the muscles. It is known that we never use all of the strength available in our muscles because the nervous system exerts inhibitory effects that prevent contraction of all of the fibers in a muscle. Strength training may be a process of progressively removing these inhibitory effects, allowing more muscle fibers to be recruited for the activity.

In this respect, it has been theorized that we train movements rather than muscles (Davis, Logan, and McKinney 1965). Since the central nervous system is organized according to movements rather than muscles, it does send messages that call for individual muscles to contract but the messages stimulate contractions of certain muscle fibers within these muscles in a sequence that is unique to a particular movement. Other movements utilizing those same muscles may employ different muscle fibers and sequences of contraction within that same muscle group. It is possible, therefore, that we learn to be strong by performing movements against resistance. If this is true, the transfer of training principle would indicate the most significant improvements will occur when the resistance exercises are similar in direction and speed to the mechanics of competition. Therefore, the power for swimming will probably be developed best by exercises that simulate the stroke mechanics as well as the turnover rates used in competition.

With the preceding information in mind, three assumptions about resistance training seem justified where swimmers are concerned:

1. The exercises should duplicate the stroke mechanics the swimmers will use in competition as closely as possible.
2. The exercises should be performed at competition speeds.
3. As in all training, the principles of overload and progression should be applied. That is, the resistance must be greater than encountered in competition and there must be provision for increasing resistance as power improves.

Although swimming against resistance that is supplied by surgical tubing, Exergenies, hand paddles, and resistance belts simulates stroke mechanics and adds resistance, these methods are largely ineffective because they retard turnover rate or encourage swimmers to slip their hands through the water. Mini-Gyms and Biokinetic Swim Benches are more effective since stroke mechanics can be simulated against resistance at turnover rates comparable to or exceeding those of competition.

Establishing Training Programs for Improving Stroking Power

Since power improvements seem to be specific to the speed of training, this is the first factor to consider in establishing training programs for improving stroking power. Inasmuch as it requires 0.6 to 0.8 seconds to complete one underwater stroke, each repetition should be completed at that rate of speed or faster.

The duration of work is the second factor to consider. Some research is available to guide us in determining the most effective length of work periods. Apparently power can be improved with work periods of 5 to 30 seconds (Thorstensson, Sjödin, and Karlsson 1975; Costill et al. 1978; Astrand and Rodahl 1977; Mathews and Fox 1976; Lamb 1978). Mathews and Fox (1976) recommend work periods of 10 to 25 seconds. They further recommend 32 to 50 such work periods with rest periods of 30 to 75 seconds between them.

Regarding the type of resistance training that should be performed, isokinetic forms of exercise are recommended. They have been shown to be more effective than other forms of training (Pipes and Wilmore 1975). Certain forms of isokinetic exercise such as Mini-Gyms, and Biokinetic Swim Benches permit you to duplicate stroke mechanics at competitive turnover rates, something

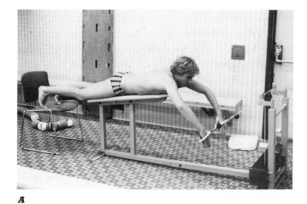

A

B

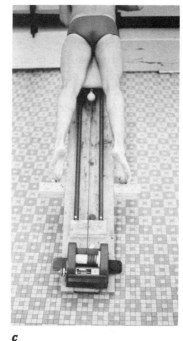

C

Figure 12.1. Isokinetic training equipment for swimmers: the isokinetic swim bench (**A**), a swim trolley (**B**), and a mini-gym leg exerciser (**C**).

which cannot be done with traditional forms of weight training, Universal Gyms and Nautilus equipment. Swimmers are shown working on a swim bench that is mounted for push-off simulated leg extension in Figure 12.1.

Other forms of resistance training such as barbells, pulley weights, and Universal Gyms, can be used in the absence of isokinetic exercisers if the exercises involve the swimming muscles in movements that are as similar to swimming as possible, and if the rate of exercise approximates the race turnover rate. The work periods should be similar to those recommended. If you prefer working on a repetition rather than time basis, the approximate turnover rate for most would be one stroke per second at sprint speed.

Training Procedures for Improving Muscular Endurance

Thus far the emphasis has been on improving muscular power for improvement of sprinting speed. Swimmers should also use resistance training to improve muscular endurance. Perhaps the following example will illustrate this point.

Suppose a male freestyle swimmer has best times of 20.2 for 50 yards and 45.5 for 100 yards. Based on his time for 50 yards, this swimmer obviously has the sprint speed to swim the 100 in a faster time. Allowing for fatigue and turns, a conservative estimate of this swimmer's potential time for 100 yards would be 44.2 seconds. His present 50 speed should permit splits of 21.2 for the first half of the race and 23.0 for the second half, for a total time of 44.2. It is obvious that this swimmer's most glaring weakness is that he lacks the anaerobic muscular endurance to maintain his speed near maximum during the final half of his race. Anaerobic endurance should, of course, be improved by lactate tolerance and race-pace repeats. Nevertheless, certain land resistance exercises that are specifically designed to increase the anaerobic endurance of the swimming muscles may have some advantages over water training. With a solid object to push against, swimmers may be motivated to maintain their power output above what they could maintain in the water. When swimming, attempts to apply more force when fatigued sometimes result in slipping the hands through the water rather than a systematic progression in intensity. Land resistance training may produce a systematic progression in specific muscular endurance that supplements that which is developed in the water.

When you are training to improve your muscular endurance for a particular event, your exercise rate should approximate the turnover rate for the event. The number of repetitions should be at least the same as the number of strokes you will take in the race. The work time should be identical to your goal time for the event. For example, if you are a freestyle swimmer who takes 60 strokes in a 100-yard race and you would like to swim that race in 48.0 seconds you should perform 60 repetitions of a particular resistance exercise in 48.0 seconds.

Two or three sets of 60 repetitions should be sufficient to increase anaerobic muscular endurance. Rest periods of 3 to 5 minutes should be allowed between sets. Three days per week of muscular endurance training should be satisfactory. The remaining three days can be used for muscular power training.

Power Training and Muscular Endurance Training for the Legs

A complete resistance program should also include exercises for improving push-off power for starts and turns and exercises for improving the anaerobic capacity of the leg muscles that are used in the various kicks. Leg presses and calf raises on a Universal Gym or a leaper are excellent for this purpose. Another very effective device can be constructed for this purpose. It was shown in Figure 12.1. It utilizes a Mini-Gym mounted on a swimming trolley.

The swimming trolley is a bench on wheels that moves on two channel irons. The channel irons are mounted on a plank with a "T" support for the swimmer's feet. A Mini-Gym can be mounted at the rear of the plank and connected to the rear of the trolley by means of a strap. Swimmers can lie on the bench with their feet on the "T" support and exercise the quadriceps and gastrocnemius muscles by extending their legs. The swimming trolley can also be used to improve the power and muscular endurance of the arms and upper body muscles. Swimmers lie on the bench, grasp the handles, and pull their

Figure 12.2. A swimmer using the swim trolley to improve the power of her armstroke.

bodies forward using whatever stroke they prefer. Two handles can be suspended from the front supports by ropes that are measured to allow a complete armstroke.

The advantage of this form of land resistance training over other forms is that swimmers can pull or push their bodies forward as they do when swimming. Although the true stroking and kicking movements cannot be duplicated, swimmers can come closer to duplicating them with this device than with most others. A swimmer is shown using the swimming trolley to improve the power of her armstroke in Figure 12.2.

Mini-Gyms can be used in combination with an electronic pacer (which can be purchased) that gives a readout of the power generated with each repetition and a cumulative record of the total power produced during a given work period. The pacer provides an excellent way to measure progress and is quite motivating. Surgical tubing, elastic cords, or pulley weights can be used to supply resistance for the trolley if the cost of an isokinetic exerciser is prohibitive. Gravity can also be used. The trolley can be angled upward, making swimmers overcome more resistance to lift their body weight. Progression can be achieved by increasing the inclination. The repetitions should be performed as rapidly as possible when increasing power is your goal. For muscular endurance, the number of repetitions should equal the number of strokes you will take in the race.

Joint Flexibility

Although joint flexibility is believed to be important to efficient swimming, there is, once again, little scientific evidence to substantiate that belief. Hypothetically, however, the rationale for a positive relationship between flexibility and performance warrants including stretching exercises in training programs despite the lack of evidence supporting their benefits. Some of the reasons increased joint flexibility should contribute to faster times follow:

- An increased range of motion in certain joints may allow more propulsive stroke mechanics.
- With increased range of motion in certain joints, there should be fewer disruptions in horizontal and lateral alignment and drag should be reduced.
- An increased range of motion should reduce the energy cost of swimming because internal resistance to motion should be reduced.

Programs of flexibility training for swimmers have traditionally focused on joints of the lower back, hips, shoulders, and ankles. Exercises for the shoulders and ankles seem justified. However, what seem to be restrictions in lower back and hip movements are usually due to incorrect stroke mechanics rather than lack of flexibility in these joints. The hip flexion and back hyperextension that take place when swimming the butterfly and breaststroke are reactions to an effective kick and armstroke and are not in themselves propulsive. For example, when the dolphin kick is weak the hips may not rise. This is not because swimmers lack the hip flexibility. It is, instead, due to a weak downbeat that does not push the hips upward. It is doubtful that an improvement in hip or lower back flexibility will improve the kick. When the downbeat of the kick is improved the swimmer's hips will rise.

There are several reasons why greater than average shoulder flexibility and ankle flexibility are advantageous in all strokes. Backstrokers need shoulder flexibility in a hyperflexing direction in order to downsweep effectively at the beginning of their underwater stroke. Butterflyers and freestylers need shoulder flexibility in extension and abduction directions in order to recover their arms without "dragging" them through the water or, in the case of freestylers, swinging them laterally and disturbing lateral alignment.

Swimmers in all strokes should find greater than average ankle flexibility an asset for producing more propulsive force with their kicks. Butterflyers and backstrokers need plantar flexing and inverting flexibility (toes pointed and turned inward) because it allows them to maintain an effective pitch for a longer time during the downbeat of the former and upkick of the latter stroke.

Improving dorsiflexing and everting flexibility (feet flat and turned outward) are major concerns of breaststroke swimmers. They also need inverting ability during the insweep of the kick. They do not need plantar flexing ability because plantar flexion will reduce, rather than increase, propulsive force. Dorsiflexion and eversion flexibility of the ankles and feet are not required in the butterfly, backstroke, or freestyle. Swimmers in these events need only relax their feet on the upbeat (downbeat in backstroke) and water pressure will push them into a natural position.

Measuring Flexibility Swimmers should measure their ankle and shoulder flexibility periodically to evaluate their progress in developing an increased range of motion in these joints. Cureton (1941) developed some tests of shoulder flexibility that are ideal for this purpose. Some ankle flexibility tests have been developed by the author. No expensive equipment or lengthy training is required to administer these tests. They are described in detail in the sections that follow.

Shoulder flexion. The test procedure for shoulder flexion is illustrated in Figure 12.3. Lie in a prone position with your chin touching the floor or mat. Stretch your arms forward with your palms in contact with the floor and your fingers locked together. At a signal, lift your arms as high as possible without unlocking your fingers or lifting your chin from the floor. Have someone measure the distance from the floor to your fingertips with a ruler or yardstick. You may also mount a yardstick as shown in Figure 12.3. Backstroke swimmers should be particularly flexible in this direction.

Shoulder extension. The procedure for this test is illustrated in Figure 12.4. Sit on the floor or stand and swing your arms back as far as possible. Keep your hands level with your shoulders and your palms facing forward. After a few swings, stretch your arms backward as far as you can. Have someone measure the distance between your fingertips.

Butterflyers should be flexible in this direction so they can recover their arms without dragging them through the water and with a minimum of internal resistance. Freestylers need shoulder extension flexibility so they can use a high-elbow recovery that will not cause disruptions in lateral alignment.

Ankle plantar flexion and dorsiflexion. The usual procedure for evaluating ankle flexibility is to measure the total range of motion in the ankle joint. However, swimmers should not measure ankle flexibility in this manner. Measuring

Figure 12.3. The procedure for measuring shoulder flexion.

Figure 12.4. The procedure for measuring shoulder extension.

A

B

Figure 12.5. Measuring ankle plantar flexion and dorsiflexion.

A. This homemade protractor can be used to measure ankle flexibility. It is made with plexiglass, but it could just as well be marked off on plywood or masonite.

B. This swimmer is measuring her ankle plantar flexing ability.

C. This swimmer is measuring her ankle dorsiflexing ability.

C

the total range of motion may obscure the fact that a particular athlete has poor flexibility in a dorsiflexion direction and has compensated for it by superior plantar-flexing ability or vice versa. Procedures for measuring both the plantar flexing and dorsiflexing flexibility at the ankle joints are illustrated in Figure 12.5.

A piece of plexiglass, plywood, or cardboard can be marked off in degrees like a protractor and mounted in some convenient way. Sit with your legs extended and your feet together. Your feet should be beside the measuring device with your heels at zero and your feet in a natural position with ankles neither plantar flexed or dorsiflexed. To measure plantar flexion, point your toes as much as possible. Have someone measure the number of degrees your big toe travels. Keep both feet together during the test. Both ankles can be measured at once for convenience or each can be measured separately for greater accuracy.

Procedures for measuring dorsiflexion are also illustrated in Figure 12.5.

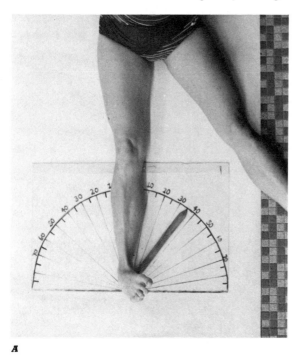 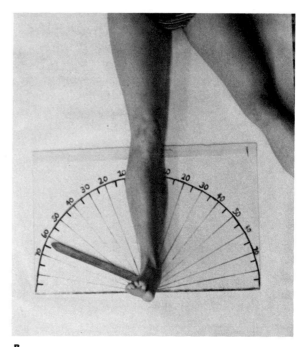

A *B*

Figure 12.6. Measuring the inversion and eversion flexibility of the feet. The procedure for measuring inversion is shown in **A**, and the procedure for measuring eversion is shown in **B**.

Start with your heels at point zero and pull your toes backward as far as possible without removing your heels or your knees from the floor. Have someone measure the distance traveled by your big toe or toes if you are measuring both ankles at the same time.

Foot eversion and inversion. The importance of inverting and everting motions of the feet has been ignored in swimming literature. Lack of flexibility in these directions will reduce kicking efficiency just as will inadequate plantar flexing and dorsiflexing abilities. The procedures for measuring inversion and eversion flexibility are shown in Figure 12.6. You can use a large homemade protractor like the one shown in Figure 12.6 or a smaller, commercially produced protractor.

Sit with your legs straight and your heel on the zero point of the protractor. To measure inversion, turn the sole of your foot inward as much as possible without bending your knee or removing your heel from the zero point. Have someone measure the distance in degrees that your big toe moves from the baseline. To measure eversion, turn your foot outward as much as possible and have someone measure the distance in degrees that your little toe travels from the baseline.

Exercises for Increasing Flexibility

Little is known about increasing the range of motion in joints. There are three principle methods in common use; ballistic stretching, static stretching, and proprioceptive neuromuscular facilitation (PNF). Ballistic stretching includes quick swinging, bending, and twisting motions that exceed the normal range of motion in certain joints. Static stretching involves slowly forcing a joint beyond its normal range of motion and holding it there. With some exercises, the swimmer can supply the force that holds the joints in a stretched position, while in others, the exercise is best performed by having a partner hold the joint in a stretched position. The PNF method is a combination of static stretching and isometric contractions. Subjects place the joint in a stretched position by themselves or with the help of a partner. They then execute a 6-second isometric contraction in which they try to move the joint opposite the direction it is to be stretched. This contraction can be resisted by a partner or some immovable object. After the isometric contraction is completed, they stretch the joint in the opposite direction.

Research has not indicated any clear superiority of one method over the other. However, most people have accepted the fact that static stretching and the PNF methods are superior, mainly on the basis of the strong theoretical argument offered by deVries (1974) to the effect that they permit joints to be stretched further with less injury. When ballistic stretching is used, the momentum of moving body parts may cause the extensibility of joints to be exceeded resulting in injuries to tendons and ligaments. Holt (n.d.) believes the combination of isometric contractions and static stretching used in PNF stretching permits even greater ranges of motion than static stretching alone. The isometric contraction supposedly causes the muscles to relax more completely around the joint that is being stretched so that a greater range of motion is possible. This contention was supported by a study in which 21 female gymnasts compared PNF stretching to two other methods of static stretching (Moore and Hutton 1980). The PNF method produced the largest gains in hip flexion.

Although the arguments supporting static stretching are impressive, a point in favor of ballistic stretching that has been overlooked is that improvements in joint flexibility, like improvements in muscular strength, may be specific to the training methods used. That is, while static stretching and PNF methods may be effective for increasing the total range of motion when a joint is held in a stretched position, they may not significantly improve flexibility when joints are being moved through a range of motion during exercise. When we assume that increases in static flexibility result in similar increases in ballistic flexibility, we may be guilty of the same oversight that was made when it was assumed that increases in strength can improve athletic performance, regardless of the type and speed of resistance exercises that are used.

A

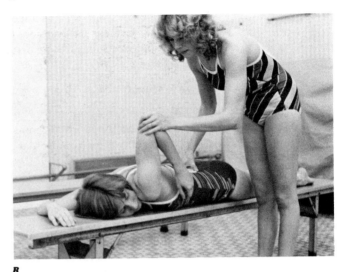

B

C

D

Figure 12.7. Some ballistic stretching exercises for improving shoulder flexibility.

A. With arms in front, grip a towel and swing it overhead and down behind your back. As your flexibility improves, place your hands closer together when you grip the towel.

B. Lie on a bench and have a partner move your arms through an exaggerated high-elbow recovery.

C. Stand and swing your arms backward at shoulder level. Backstrokers should swing their arms overhead.

D. Lock your hands behind your back. Bend over and swing your arms up and forward.

Ballistic stretching may be a superior method for improving flexibility for ballistic movement. This is particularly true where the shoulder joint is concerned. The armstroke recoveries of the various strokes are ballistic motions that require only adequate flexibility and minimal internal resistance to motion. It is possible that ballistic stretching may reduce internal resistance more than either static or PNF stretching.

Static stretching and PNF stretching may be the superior methods for improving plantar flexing, dorsiflexing, everting, and inverting flexibility of the feet and ankle joints. An effective kick requires that swimmers allow water pressure to push their relaxed ankles into plantar flexed or dorsiflexed positions. The action of the water is not unlike static stretching. Therefore, it is

Figure 12.8. Some static stretching exercises for developing ankle flexibility. Additional exercises are shown on the following page.

A

B

C

D

continued overleaf

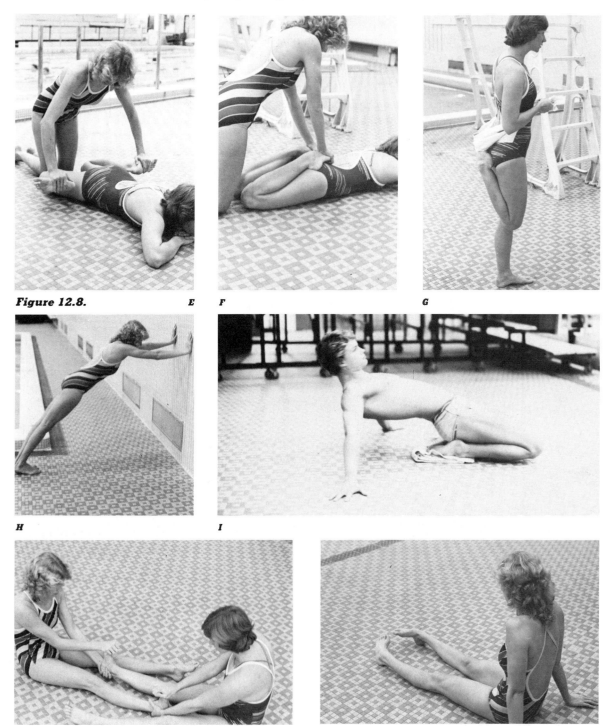

Figure 12.8.

E   F   G

H   I

J   K

reasonable to assume that static stretching methods may be superior for increasing the range of motion in the ankles and feet so the feet can be pitched properly for the longest possible time during the kick.

Some ballistic exercises for improving shoulder extension and flexion are shown in Figure 12.7 and some static exercises for improving ankle flexibility are shown in Figure 12.8. Some exercises are also included for improving the extensibility of the quadriceps muscles so that breaststrokers can bring their feet closer to their buttocks when they begin the propulsive phase of their kick. This will allow them to apply force for a longer distance. These exercises can be executed with static or PNF methods, depending on your preference.

It should be mentioned that static stretching and PNF stretching can be just as dangerous as ballistic methods. If partners helping administer these exercises are not careful they may push your joints beyond the present limit of their extensibility and cause injury. Do not allow partners to stretch your joints too far beyond your point of pain. Week by week you should find that you are able to achieve a greater range of motion before pain is felt.

The optimum number of repetitions for flexibility exercises has not been determined by research. Some experts have made recommendations on an empirical basis, however. Jensen and Fisher (1972) recommend holding each static stretch for 8 to 10 seconds and performing 6 repetitions daily. Holt (n.d) recommends 6 to 8 repetitions when using PNF stretching. There are no recommendations available for ballistic stretching. Until research indicates the optimum number of repetitions, swimmers are limited only by time and motivation. An educated guess would be that 10 to 20 repetitions daily should be the minimum number performed.

REFERENCES

Astrand, P. O., and Rodahl, K. 1977. *Textbook of Work Physiology.* New York: McGraw-Hill.

Clark, David F. 1965. "The Effect of Prescribed Isometric Exercise on Strength, Speed, and Endurance in Swimming the Crawl Stroke." Master's thesis, Central Michigan University.

Cooper, Carol. 1966. "A Study of the Relationship of Increased Isometric Strength in Sprint Crawl Performance." Master's thesis, Smith College.

Costill, D. L., Coyle, E. F., Fink, W. J., Lesmes, G. R., and Witzman, F. A. 1978. "Adaptations in Skeletal Muscle Following Strength Training." Unpublished research report, Ball State University, Muncie, Indiana.

Costill, D. L., Sharp, R., and Troup, J. 1980. "Muscle Strength: Contributions to Sprint Swimming." *Swimming World* 21:29–34.

Cureton, T. K. 1941. "Flexibility As an Aspect of Physical Fitness." *Research Quarterly* 12:381–390.

Davis, E. C., Logan, G. A., and McKinney, W. C. 1965. *Biophysical Values of Muscular Activity.* Dubuque, Iowa: Brown.

Davis, J. F. 1955. "Effect of Training and Conditioning for Middle Distance Swimming upon Measures of Cardiovascular Condition, General Physical Fitness, Gross Strength, Motor Fitness and Strength of Involved Muscles." Master's thesis, University of Oregon.

deVries, H. A. 1974. *Physiology of Exercise for Physical Education and Athletics.* Dubuque, Iowa: Brown.

Good, Vickie. 1973. "Effects of Isokinetic Exercise Program on Sprint Swimming Performance of College Women." Master's thesis, California State University, Chico.

Holt, L. E. (n.d.) *Scientific Stretching for Sport (3-S).* Published by the author (n.p.).

Hutchinson, Bruce. 1959. "Effect of Systematic Weight Training upon Muscular Efficiency as Indicated by 100 Yards Swim Performance." Master's thesis, University of Maryland.

Hutinger, P. W. 1970. "Comparisons of Isokinetic, Isotonic and Isometric Developed Strength to Speed in Swimming the Crawl Stroke." Doctoral dissertation, Indiana University.

Jensen, C. R., and Fisher, G. A. 1972. *Scientific Basis of Athletic Conditioning.* Philadelphia: Lea and Febiger.

Lamb, D. R. 1978. *Physiology of Exercise: Responses and Adaptations.* New York: Macmillan.

Maglischo, E. W., and Maglischo, C. W. 1980. "The Relationship of Stroke Simulated and Non-simulated Tests of Power to Swimming Speed." Unpublished research.

Mathews, D. K., and Fox, E. L. 1976. *The Physiological Basis of Physical Education and Athletics.* Philadelphia: W. B. Saunders.

Moffroid, M. T., and Whipple, R. H. 1970. "Specificity of Speed of Exercise." *Phys. Ther.* 50:1692–1700.

Moore, M. A., and Hutton, R. S. 1980. "Electromyographic Investigation of Muscle Stretching Techniques." *Med. Sci. Sports* 12:322–329.

Murray, J. L. 1962. "Effects of Precisely Prescribed Progressive Resistance Exercises with Pulley Weights on Speed and Endurance in Swimming." Master's thesis, Pennsylvania State University.

Nunney, D. M. 1960. "A Relation of Circuit Training to Swimming." *Research Quarterly* 31:188–198.

Pipes, T., and Wilmore, J. H. 1975. "Isokinetic vs. Isotonic Strength Training in Adult Men." *Med. Sci. Sports* 7:262–274.

Ross, D. T. 1973. "Selected Training Procedures for the Development of Arm Extensor Strength and Swimming Speed of the Sprint Crawl Stroke." Master's thesis, University of Oregon.

Thorstensson, A., Sjödin, B., and Karlsson, J. 1975. "Enzyme Activity and Muscle Strength After Sprint Training in Man." *Acta Physiol. Scand.* 94:313–318.

CHAPTER **13**

Nutrition

Swimmers' diets must contain the essential nutrients in sufficient quantities to support their energy expenditure during training and competition. The essential elements are carbohydrates, fats, proteins, fluids, vitamins, and minerals. If the diet should be deficient in any of these, performances will suffer. On the other hand, consuming greater quantities than needed will not produce a superior performance. The purposes of this chapter will be to describe the essential nutrients, to recommend the quantities of each that are needed by swimmers in hard training, and to describe some methods for evaluating the nutritional status of athletes.

Carbohydrates, Fats, and Proteins

Every day you must consume enough carbohydrates, fats, and proteins to provide your body with energy for muscular contraction and with constituents for tissue growth and repair. Carbohydrates and fats provide most of the energy for training and competition, while proteins serve a growth and repair function.

Carbohydrates are stored in the form of glycogen in muscle cells and the liver. In all swimming races, with the possible exception of the 1,650 and the 1,500, the demand for energy is so rapid that it must be met by the breakdown of glycogen in muscular cells. Thus, glycogen supplies nearly 100 percent of the energy for muscular contraction during competition. Liver glycogen and fats contribute insignificantly small amounts. During training, particularly distance training, stored fat becomes an increasingly greater contributor, providing perhaps 30 to 40 percent of the total energy. This has the effect of reducing muscle glycogen depletion and making it possible to train at greater intensities from day to day.

The fact that large amounts of fats are burned for energy in training should not be taken to mean that athletes' diets must have a high fat content. Fats are essential in the diet, but only in small amounts. There will usually be enough stored fat (adipose tissue) to meet energy needs; therefore, it is not necessary to ingest large amounts on a daily basis.

Proteins are the substances from which muscle tissue is formed. They contain amino acids which are essential to muscular hypertrophy and tissue repair. There are 23 known amino acids of which 8 are essential. While the nonessential amino acids can be manufactured in the body, the 8 essential amino acids must be supplied through the diet (Krause and Hunscher 1972). Your body can also metabolize protein for energy when sufficient amounts of carbohydrate and fat are not available.

Carbohydrates   Carbohydrates comprise 40 to 50 percent of the calories consumed in the average American diet. There is recent evidence that athletes in hard training may accomplish more work on diets that contain 70 to 75 percent carbohydrates because a high-carbohydrate intake will allow them to replace the energy supply in their muscles more rapidly from day to day.

Muscle glycogen stores are systematically depleted during exercise. The rate of depletion depends upon the exercise intensity and the amount of glycogen in the muscles when exercise began. Sixty to seventy percent of the glycogen stored in muscles can be depleted within 15 minutes of severe exercise (Taylor 1975). Complete depletion can occur within 2 hours of hard training (Costill et al. 1971). It requires no stretch of the imagination, therefore, to conclude that there is nearly complete depletion of muscle glycogen after intense practice sessions. Once it is depleted, forty-eight hours will be required to replace the muscle glycogen stores under normal dietary conditions; that is, when the diet contains the usual 40 to 50 percent of carbohydrates. (Five days are required for repletion when the diet is low in carbohydrates [Costill et al. 1971].)

Failure to replace muscle glycogen from day to day can lead to a state of chronic fatigue where performances and motivation for training deteriorate. If this condition persists for several days, conditioning will suffer because athletes will not be able to train at sufficient intensity to maintain the adaptations they gained earlier in the season. Thus it is extremely important to replace the muscles' glycogen supply as completely as possible from day to day.

Several researchers have shown that a diet that is rich in carbohydrates (70 to 80 percent) can reduce repletion time from 48 to 24 hours (Hultman, Bergström, and Roch-Norlund 1971; MacDougall, Ward, Sale, and Sutton 1975). This is why a high-carbohydrate diet is recommended for swimmers in training. Foods that contain sugars (monosaccharides) and starches (polysaccharides) are our best sources of carbohydrates. Some of these are listed in Table 13.1.

Table 13.1 *Foods Rich in Carbohydrates*

Sugar forms	Starch forms
Cake	Beans: green, lima, red kidney
Candy	Bread and rolls
Chocolate syrup	Cereal
Cookies	Chick peas
Honey	Chili
Milkshakes	Chop suey
Pies	Corn
Pudding	Fruits
	Leafy vegetables
	Lentils
	Macaroni
	Milk
	Noodles
	Pancakes
	Peas
	Potatoes and sweet potatoes
	Poultry
	Rhubarb
	Rice
	Spaghetti
	Waffles

Athletes should be advised to reduce their sugar intake and to ingest most of their carbohydrates in the form of starches, which are far better for them from a health and training standpoint. Your body can use starch or sugar for glycogen repletion with equal ease (Costill 1978c). However, sugar forms provide almost no nutrients except carbohydrates, whereas you receive an additional bonus of several vitamins and minerals when you ingest starches. Starches also appear to produce a longer-lasting insulin stimulation and blood glucose elevation (Costill 1978c). Thus, they prevent the compensatory drop in blood sugar and the sensations of lethargy that normally occur 2 to 3 hours after eating sugary foods. With starch as your primary energy source, a higher work rate can be maintained for a longer period, symptoms of hunger are reduced, and replacement of liver and muscle glycogen proceeds at a faster rate.

Most Americans have come to rely on foods with high sugar content for their carbohydrate supply. This is unfortunate because a high sugar intake has been linked to cholesterol formation which, in turn, can lead to cardiovascular disease. In addition, a high sugar intake can precipitate other health problems such as dental caries and diabetes. Approximately 70 percent of the carbohydrates consumed by the average American are in the form of sugars. This represents a dramatic and alarming shift from dietary patterns during the first half of the twentieth century. Starches were then our major carbohydrate source, with sugar representing only 30 percent of our intake of this foodstuff.

Another possible problem that may result from a high sugar intake is a vitamin deficiency. There are indications that sugar metabolism requires large amounts of vitamin B_1 (thiamine) (Krause and Hunscher 1972). Therefore, swimmers who eat large quantities of sweets and other junk foods may find themselves deficient in one of the vitamins that plays an important role in energy metabolism during exercise.

Fats Fats are essential in the diet, but only in small amounts. As indicated previously, they can be used for energy during low-intensity training and in this way they reduce the rate of muscle glycogen depletion. Fats are also essential to vitamin metabolism. The fat soluble vitamins A, D, E, and K are transported in combination with triglycerides. Although essential in the body, most fats can be synthesized from foods that contain carbohydrates. Therefore, a high fat intake is not required.

There is, however, one essential fatty acid that must be ingested on a daily basis.[1] That is linoleic acid. Linoleic acid is required for normal growth and metabolism and is not manufactured in the body (Krause and Hunscher 1972). The daily dietary requirement for linoleic acid has been set at 1 to 2 percent of the daily caloric intake. It will be necessary to ingest more than 1 to 2 percent of your daily calories in the form of fats in order to get this amount since it is only available in small quantities from several sources. For this reason, the recommended daily consumption of fat should be equal to 10 to 15 percent of the total caloric intake. Most Americans eat much larger percentages of fats than that, however. The typical American diet contains 40 percent fats and in many diets fats make up 50 to 60 percent of the total caloric intake.

Since your body can synthesize all of the other fatty acids from carbohydrate sources, you need not worry about having sufficient fat for long training sessions. A high-carbohydrate diet will also supply the fatty acids needed for energy. Providing most of the fat in this way is not only more nutritious but also decreases the likelihood of developing poor eating habits that could lead to cardiovascular disease at a later time.

Fats are available in three forms: saturated, unsaturated, and polyunsaturated. The ingestion of large quantities of fats, particularly saturated fats, has been linked to cardiovascular disease. Saturated fats come from animal sources and dairy foods. They contain only single bonds along their carbon chain and therefore bind many hydrogen atoms. They harden and adhere to the interior of blood vessels obstructing circulation. Unsaturated and polyunsaturated fats come from vegetable oils. The difference between the two is that polyunsaturated fats have fewer hydrogen binding sites along their carbon chain than do simple unsaturated fats. They remain liquid at room temperature and do not appear to be as dangerous to health. Therefore, those fats that are ingested should be primarily of the unsaturated and polyunsaturated variety. They should easily supply more than the needed amounts of linoleic acid. A list of foods with high fat content is contained in Table 13.2. Saturated and polyunsaturated sources are listed as well as sources that contain linoleic acid.

1. There are actually three essential fatty acids; however, two of them can be synthesized in the body if linoleic acid is available through the diet.

Table 13.2 *Foods High in Fat Content*

Unsaturated and polyunsaturated	Saturated	
Corn oil*	Bacon	Gravy
Margarine*	Beef	Ham
Nuts	Butter	Hot dogs
Olive oil	Cake	Ice cream
Peanut oil	Cheese	Lamb
Soybean oil*	Cheese sauces	Pie
	Chop suey	Pork
	Doughnuts	Potato chips
	Eggs	Whipped cream
	French fries	Whole milk
	French toast	

*High in linoleic acid.

Proteins Because protein is needed to build and repair muscle tissue, many athletes and coaches have mistakenly assumed that they should consume excessive quantities of beef, pork, and ham, and other foods that have a high protein content so that their muscles will grow larger and stronger. Some have even taken to supplementing their diets with special high protein tablets and powders. Millions of dollars are wasted annually by athletes in search of "quick" power because the typical American diet contains more than enough protein to build and repair the muscle tissue of athletes who are engaged in even the most intense training. Most authorities recommend that 15 to 20 percent of the daily caloric intake should consist of foods that are high in protein. Since the typical American diet has a 20 to 30 percent protein content, most athletes could reduce their consumption of meat and other high protein foods with no ill effects.

The recommended daily protein requirement is less than 1 gram per kilogram of body weight for the general population while some nutritionists recommend 2 grams of protein per kilogram of body weight for athletes who are in hard training (Jensen and Fisher 1975). They have not made this recommendation because of evidence that shows that additional protein is needed by athletes, but rather as a precautionary measure against the possibility of a greater protein requirement. Assuming a 2 gram per kilogram of body weight requirement, swimmers weighing between 45 and 90 kilograms (99 to 198 pounds) would need no more than 180 grams of protein per day. It is estimated that most Americans consume well in excess of 200 grams of protein daily; therefore it is doubtful that a protein deficiency exists among athletes. Four to eight ounces of meat will supply 40 to 80 grams of protein. In addition, there are many other sources of protein in the typical American diet. An egg has 6 grams, a glass of milk contains 9 grams, and a slice of bread has 2 grams of protein.

A word of caution should be extended to those athletes who prefer vegetarian diets. While a reduction in meat consumption would have no ill effects, the absence of meat may prevent a person from receiving sufficient protein and particularly sufficient quantities of the essential amino acids. Very few vegeta-

Table 13.3 *Foods High in Protein Content*

Complete		Incomplete
Bacon	Lamb	Cornmeal
Beef	Liver	Dried beans
Cheese	Milk	Peanut butter
Chili	Pork	Peas
Egg	Poultry	Wheat bread
Fish	Veal	
Ham		

bles contain all of the essential amino acids, while most meats are complete sources of them. Vegetarians may develop a protein deficiency if they do not educate themselves as to the amino acid content of the foods they eat. Therefore, the wisest procedure is probably to add meat to the diet of all athletes as a precaution against a protein deficiency. If beef is not to your liking, poultry and fish will provide all of the essential amino acids. Reports that vegetarians are healthier and possess more endurance are unsubstantiated by research. Foods that are high in protein content are listed in Table 13.3. Those that are complete sources of protein, containing all of the essential amino acids, are indicated.

Applying Nutritional Guidelines

Based on modern nutritional data, the diets of swimmers should contain the following percentages of the three basic foodstuffs:

Carbohydrates	70 to 75 percent of the daily caloric intake
Fats	10 to 15 percent of the daily caloric intake
Protein	15 to 20 percent of the daily caloric intake

While these figures are recommended for the typical athlete, some experts have suggested slightly different proportions for sprinters because of the possibility that they may need more protein for tissue building. They have suggested dietary proportions of 44 to 67 percent carbohydrate, 22 to 33 percent protein, with 10 to 15 percent fat (Jensen and Fisher 1975). It is doubtful that such variations are necessary, since as indicated previously, most athletes are probably taking in far more protein than they need for tissue growth and repair. It is probably wiser to keep the protein content of sprinters at 15 to 20 percent of the daily caloric intake since this will more than meet their needs. This will permit them to maintain a higher carbohydrate intake for replacing energy.

Daily Caloric Intake   Once a swimmer has reached competition weight, the daily caloric intake should balance the caloric output so neither a gain nor loss in weight occurs. (This statement does not apply to children and adolescents during growth spurts. In this case a gain in weight is to be expected.) There is no cause for alarm when weight loss occurs early in the season because most athletes will

Table 13.4 *Estimated Daily Caloric Requirements for Children, Adolescents, and Adults*

Sex and age range	Pretraining caloric requirement	Estimated training requirement
Men		
10 & Under	2,400	2,800–3,000 (1 hr.)
11–12	2,800	3,600–4,200 (2 hr.)
13–14	2,800	4,800–5,500 (4 hr.)
15–18	3,000	5,000–6,000 (4 hr.)
18–25	3,000	5,000–6,000 (4 hr.)
Women		
10 & Under	2,400	2,800–3,000 (1 hr.)
11–12	2,400	3,200–3,800 (2 hr.)
13–14	2,400	4,000–5,000 (4 hr.)
15–18	2,100	4,100–4,800 (4 hr.)
18–25	2,100	4,100–4,800 (4 hr.)

have gained some additional adipose tissue during a lay-off and it should be removed. Once this fat has been removed they should maintain a daily balance between caloric intake (eating) and caloric output (exercise) so that they do not deposit any additional fat while obtaining enough energy for training.

When a weight loss occurs later in the season, after ideal competition weight has been reached, more calories need to be taken in. On the other hand, a weight gain during the season (assuming no growth spurt) indicates that the caloric intake is too high and it should be reduced accordingly.

The number of calories needed to achieve a balance between intake and output varies according to size, training volume (both distance and intensity), and to some extent the inherited metabolic rate of each swimmer. Unfortunately, the daily caloric requirement of the average athlete cannot be stated because there is insufficient research available to indicate those needs. Estimates can be made, however, based on the average daily caloric requirements of the general population. The chart in Table 13.4 shows the average daily caloric output of children, adolescents, and adults of both sexes. These figures provide an estimate of the pretraining needs of athletes. Swimming training will increase these requirements by 500 to 1000 calories per hour of training depending upon the size and skill of the athlete and the effort she or he expends in training. Bigger bodies and hard work require more calories while efficient swimmers expend fewer calories than inefficient swimmers when they swim the same distance at the same speed.

Fluids   The importance of liquids in the diet can be seen from the fact that fluids make up 60 percent of your body weight. In addition to cooling your body, the liquid content of the intracellular and extracellular fluids allows rapid transportation of nutrients and elimination of waste products (Costill 1978a). Some fluid is lost when you exercise and must be replaced in sufficient quantity to maintain the

Table 13.5 *Water Balance in Humans*

Fluid Intake

Fluids	1,250 ml
Water in foods	900 ml
Water from oxidation of foods in the body	350 ml
	2,500 ml

Fluid Output

Urine	1,400 ml
Water in feces	100 ml
Evaporation	700 ml
Lungs	300 ml
	2,500 ml

Source: Adapted from M. V. Krause and M. A. Hunscher, *Food, Nutrition and Diet Therapy* (Philadelphia: W. B. Saunders, 1972), p. 152, table 10-3, by permission of the publisher.

correct percentage. Work increases body heat, which accelerates the sweat rate. This in turn causes dehydration, which can result in heat cramps, heat exhaustion, or possibly heat stroke.

Dehydration is not as serious a problem among swimmers as it is with athletes in land sports because the cool water reduces the sweat rate by absorbing heat from the skin more quickly than it could be absorbed by the air. Nevertheless, swimmers do sweat when they train, and because of this they lose more fluid than the average person. This fluid must be replaced on a daily basis or work ability will be decreased and illness may occur. The usual way people maintain a balance between fluid intake and output is shown in Table 13.5.

The average daily intake of fluids is 1.5 to 2.0 liters. Athletes may require 2 to 3 times this amount because they can lose 1 to 4 liters of fluid an hour in sweat (Morehouse and Rasch 1958). Although swimmers undoubtedly lose less fluid than this, the difference has not been determined, and the following recommendations for fluid intake are not precise. Swimmers should probably ingest 4 to 8 liters of fluids daily. Because most foods contain considerable amounts of fluids, much of this amount can be obtained from eating solid foods. Perhaps half the needed fluids can be consumed in this way. The remaining quantity can be provided by drinking 6 to 10 glasses of liquids such as water, juices, and milk, every day.

Vitamin and Mineral Supplements

Vitamins are organic compounds that, while they do not furnish energy or build tissue, serve as catalysts for these processes through their actions on metabolic enzymes. Vitamins cannot be manufactured in the cells of the body; therefore, they must be ingested on a regular basis. Minerals are inorganic elements that are important to the regulation of ionic concentrations of extracellular and intracellular fluids. Certain of these elements participate in the transmission of nervous impulses and the contractile processes of muscles. Minerals also form a portion of the hard tissues of the body.

It is well established that performances suffer when an athlete's diet is deficient in certain vitamins and minerals. However, it has not been proven that ingesting more than the needed amounts will improve performances. The American Medical Association has been firm in its stance that it is not necessary to supplement an adequate diet. Yet many coaches recommend supplementation and athletes have been known to take megadoses of certain vitamins and minerals in an effort to improve their performances.

This controversy concerning whether to supplement and, if so, how much to supplement, may be resolved by considering two questions:

1. What are the vitamin and mineral requirements of swimmers in hard training?
2. How many athletes are liable to have diets that are adequate in meeting these requirements?

Regarding the first question, we have only the recommended daily allowances (RDA) to guide us. These amounts are probably not sufficient to meet the requirements of swimmers in training. We know that swim training increases the caloric requirement and since vitamins and minerals play an important role in energy metabolism, it seems logical that swimmers would use more of these substances than the average person when they are burning more calories daily. It is reasonable to assume that swimmers may need one and a half to two times the recommended daily allowance of some vitamins and minerals. The amount could be even greater for vitamins and minerals that are closely linked to energy metabolism.

Considering the second question, it is true that an increased caloric intake could supply the additional vitamins and minerals, but only if the extra food contains them in the needed amounts. However, there is evidence that athletes are not likely to meet their need for additional vitamins and minerals through food consumption. The late Lloyd Percival (1972) studied the dietary habits of 2,500 Canadians from all age groups and from a wide variety of occupations and economic levels. Over 70 percent of those surveyed had diets that were lacking in one or more of the essential nutrients. The probability of athletes having inadequate diets is, therefore, quite high if such a large portion of the general population exhibits dietary deficiencies. Although the population that was studied was Canadian rather than American, there is no reason to believe Americans have more adequate diets where the intake of vitamins and minerals are concerned. The increase in the number of meals that are eaten at fast food restaurants where nonnutritious fillers comprise a good portion of the bulk and where certain vitamins and minerals may have been cooked out of the food increases the probability for the diets of American athletes to be lacking in certain essential nutrients. Consequently, supplementation seems a valid precautionary procedure.

Megadoses of vitamins and minerals are not recommended. Supplements should be viewed as a safeguard against deficiency, not as ergogenic aids. There is no evidence that ingesting more of these substances than are required to prevent deficiencies will improve performance and megadoses of certain vitamins can be dangerous over a period of time. Vitamins A, D, E, and K are fat soluble and can be stored in the body. It is possible for these vitamins to accumulate to toxic levels if megadoses are continued over a long period. Therefore, these vitamins should probably not be supplemented. On the other hand, supplementing the water soluble vitamins that are washed out of the body on a daily basis is not dangerous and may be a wise precaution against the possibility of exercise induced deficiencies. Water soluble vitamins are easily washed out of food by improper cooking and destroyed by pasteurization and treatments that result in oxidation (Morehouse and Rasch 1958).

What are the vitamin and mineral requirements of athletes? We can use the RDA as a starting point and then investigate research on vitamin and mineral use during training to determine the additional amounts that might be required.

Vitamins   The known vitamins, their RDAs, their functions in humans, and the food sources that contain them are listed in Table 13.6.

The B-complex group and vitamin C seem to play very important roles in the diets of athletes. These vitamins are water soluble; therefore, a fresh supply must be ingested each day.

The B-complex vitamins. The B-complex vitamins are important to carbohydrate metabolism. A deficiency of thiamine results in the accumulation of lactic acid and pyruvate with a subsequent depression of muscular activity. Morehouse and Miller (1971) have reported a noticeable reduction in work output when subjects were fed diets that were deficient in the vitamin B-complex groups. Thiamine (B_1) is lost in the refining of sugar and the milling of flour and rice, which increases the possibility of deficiencies occurring, even when diets contain these foods.

The thiamine requirement may be increased 15 times during hard physical training. This would indicate 22.5 milligrams per day would be necessary to support hard training. It is not known whether the requirements of other members of the B-complex group are increased by training. However, the B-complex vitamins should always be supplemented as a group. Supplements of single members of the group may precipitate deficiencies of other members (Krause and Hunscher 1972). Therefore, it is advisable for athletes to supplement their diets with 20 to 25 milligrams of the B-complex vitamins. This is assuming some of the increased requirement is met through additional caloric intake. Cereal, rice, wheat, milk, eggs, potatoes, vegetables, and meat contain the B-complex vitamins.

Vitamin C. Vitamin C is known as the stress vitamin because it is important to the proper maintenance of homeostasis under conditions of excessive physical or emotional stress (Bourne 1968). Vitamin C is also in some unknown way involved with the elimination of lactic acid that accumulates during exercise. In addition, there are claims that vitamin C is important to maintenance of normal

Table 13.6 *Essential Vitamins*

Vitamin	RDA	Activity	Sources
Vitamin A (carotene)	1 mg	Essential for good vision, normal growth of bones and teeth, healthy skin. Deficiencies seldom exist.	Fish, milk, green leafy and yellow vegetables, fruits
Vitamin B$_1$ (thiamine)	1.5 mg	Important for combating fatigue and repairing injured tissues.	Cereals, egg yolk, milk, beef, potatoes, legumes
Vitamin B$_2$ (riboflavin)	1.8 mg	Aids in metabolism of fats, carbohydrates, and protein. Also needed for proper function of nerve tissue.	Milk, egg yolk, cereals, grains, legumes
Niacin	20 mg	Important for proper digestion of foods. Deficiency may lead to depression.	Milk, lean meats, fish, eggs, potatoes, green peas
Vitamin B$_6$	2 mg recommended	Aids in protein and fat metabolism.	Rice, wheat, corn, milk, lettuce, fish, tomatoes, spinach, green beans, peas
Pantothenic Acid	Unknown 10 mg recommended	May be important in the metabolism of cardiac and skeletal muscle tissue.	Liver, eggs, broccoli, cauliflower, lean beef, skim milk, tomatoes
Vitamin B$_{12}$	Unknown 0.003 mg recommended	Important to proper bone growth and production of red blood cells.	Liver, meat
Vitamin C (ascorbic acid)	70 mg	Important in metabolism of muscle tissue and bone growth; considered to be a stress vitamin in that, in adequate quantities, it aids in proper functioning of the adrenal gland. Also believed to aid in the utilization of oxygen, the production of red blood cells, and prevention of respiratory infections; improves recovery time and prevents fatigue.	Citrus fruits, melons, tomatoes, cabbage, leafy green vegetables, potatoes. Cooking may destroy some of the Vitamin C in vegetables, so it is important to eat these foods in their natural state or to ingest the juices in which they were cooked.
Vitamin D	0.01 mg	Important in the formation of bones and teeth.	Liver, butter, eggs, fish, sunlight
Vitamin E	Unknown 25–30 mg recommended	Received considerable publicity because of possibility of its role in improving endurance among athletes, prevention of cardiovascular disease, production of red blood cells, and as an aid in recovery.	Wheat germ oil, corn, lettuce, whole grain cereals, eggs, rice, leafy vegetables, and milk
Vitamin K	Unknown 0.03 mg recommended	Appears to be necessary in the clotting of blood. A deficiency hardly ever exists.	Green leafy vegetables, egg yolk
Vitamin M (folic acid)	Unknown 0.1 to 0.2 mg recommended	Important in production of red blood cells, oxygen consumption, carbohydrate and protein metabolism.	Liver, fresh green vegetables, lean beef, whole wheat cereals
Vitamin H (biotin)	Unknown 0.15 to 0.3 mg recommended	Important in the activity of many enzyme systems involved in energy metabolism.	Liver, chicken, fish, corn, spinach, peas

hemoglobin levels, the elasticity of capillaries, and the development of red blood cells. Buffering capacity may also be improved by adequate supplies of vitamin C because most foods that are high in this vitamin form an alkaline ash when they are metabolized.

Carlile (1963) reported that members of the 1951 Australian Olympic

Swimming Team required 100 milligrams of vitamin C per day during training that was described as not particularly strenuous. The RDA is 75 milligrams. Propkoff has demonstrated improved athletic performance when the diets of Russian athletes were supplemented with 100 milligrams of vitamin C per day. Tests in Holland indicated similar improvements on supplements of 300 milligrams daily (Percival 1973).

Considering the volume of training engaged in by competitive swimmers, the addition of 200 to 300 milligrams of vitamin C to their diets seems advisable. This quantity, in addition to the amount that is ingested through increased food intake, should safely meet the needs of training. This amount is considerably below the megadoses of 1,500 to 2,000 milligrams that have sometimes been recommended.

Megadosing should be avoided because of the possible deleterious response. An increased incidence of kidney stones can occur with megadoses. Previously it was believed that excess vitamin C was excreted in the urine. However, we now know the kidneys act to reclaim vitamin C, which in turn, alters the pH of the urine. In addition, megadoses of vitamin C can raise serum uric acid levels and precipitate gout. Although megadoses may aid in preventing colds and other respiratory infections, supplementation beyond the 200 to 300 milligrams needed to support the increased demands of training cannot be recommended until the possibility of toxicity has been disproven.

Vitamin E. Vitamin E has, for several years, been considered the most potent vitamin for improving endurance performance. Research has not been uniformly supportive of this contention, however. There is even recent evidence that megadoses may reduce endurance.

Increases in endurance are believed to occur because vitamin E is thought to improve oxygen transport by increasing circulation and capillarization. Cureton (1955) has reported improved endurance among humans and animals whose diets were supplemented with wheat germ oil, a good source of vitamin E.[2] Contrary to these findings, Talbot (1974) has reported decrements in performance when the diets of swimmers were supplemented with wheat germ oil. Supporting this contention, Mayer (1975) reported that megadoses produced symptoms of weakness and fatigue in some subjects. In addition, megadoses of vitamin E have been reported to cause headaches, blurred vision, gastrointestinal disturbances and low blood sugar (Herbert 1977).

Vitamin E is usually found in foods that also contain unsaturated fats. The diets of humans are rarely if ever deficient in this vitamin. The question of whether to supplement the intake of vitamin E is complex. With most vitamins, supplementation does not hurt and might help, but with vitamin E there is the possibility that supplementation might be detrimental. Because this possibility exists and since Mayer (1975) has reported that vitamin E deficiencies are rare in humans, supplementation cannot be recommended at this time.

2. It should be mentioned that some experts believe another substance in wheat germ oil, octocosanol, rather than vitamin E was responsible for the improvement.

Vitamins A and D. There should be no need for supplementation of vitamins A and D. These vitamins are fat soluble and can be stored in the body; therefore, deficiencies are very rare.

Vitamin K. Vitamin K seems to be important in the clotting of blood. The RDA has not been determined. Vitamin K occurs in abundant amounts in the normal diet of Americans. Being a fat-soluble vitamin, it can be stored in the body and supplementation is probably not necessary.

Pantothenic Acid. Pantothenic acid is a water soluble vitamin that is important in the aerobic metabolism of carbohydrates, fats, and proteins. It also seems to play a role in the relief of stress symptoms. It is quite likely that the demands of training could increase the requirement of this vitamin from the recommended 10 milligrams daily to well in excess of 20 milligrams. Therefore, a supplementation of 10 to 20 milligrams daily is recommended.

Vitamin M (Folic Acid). Vitamin M, which is also water soluble, is important in the formation of red blood cells and as such may be involved in providing an adequate supply of oxygen. It also has a role in carbohydrate metabolism. In addition, the need for folacin is increased during stress. It is available in most foods so deficiencies are rare. However, you may wish to supplement your dietary intake with 0.5 to 1.0 milligram per day as a precaution against exercise-induced deficiency.

Vitamin H (Biotin). Biotin is essential for the proper activity of many enzyme systems that provide energy for exercise. It is a water soluble vitamin. The usual diet contains 0.15 to 0.3 milligrams per day. Deficiencies have rarely been reported when the diet is adequate. The additional demands of exercise have not been determined, however. Therefore, you may wish to supplement your diet with 0.5 to 1.0 milligram daily.

Minerals   The minerals that are known to be needed in the diets of humans are iron, calcium, phosphorus, sulfur, potassium, sodium, chlorine, magnesium, and the trace elements manganese, copper, zinc, cobalt, and fluorine. These minerals, their functions in humans, their RDAs, and the foods that contain them are listed in Table 13.7.

Iron. An iron deficiency can lead to anemia, which is a reduction in the hemoglobin content of red blood cells. Since hemoglobin carries oxygen to the muscles, such a deficiency could be detrimental to endurance. Buskirk and Haymes (1972) and Schubert (1977) have reported iron deficiencies in female athletes during hard training. It is estimated that 30 percent of the female athletes in the United States may be suffering from iron deficiencies (McArdle et al. 1980). To the contrary, Wilmore (1977) and Costill (1978b) feel the incidence of anemia among athletes may be exaggerated. According to them, plasma volume tends to increase with training, which dilutes the hemoglobin concentration produc-

Table 13.7 *Mineral Requirements*

Mineral	RDA	Function	Foods containing
Iron	10–18 mg	Essential for formation of myoglobin and hemoglobin and for the transportation of oxygen.	Liver, shellfish and lean meats. Green leafy vegetables, dried beans and peas. Fruits. Whole grain and enriched breads and cereals.
Calcium	800 mg	Builds and maintains bones and teeth. Essential to the breakdown of ATP and release of energy for muscular contraction. Also involved in nerve impulse transmission.	Milk and milk products. Green leafy vegetables.
Phosphorus	800 mg	Builds and maintains bones and teeth. Needed in formation of cell membranes. Essential to metabolism of glucose. Many B-complex vitamins function only in combination with phosphorus.	Meat, poultry, fish and eggs. Milk and milk products. Nuts and legumes.
Sulfur	Not known; satisfied by sulfur containing amino acids and vitamins	Important to carbohydrate metabolism. A constituent of many amino acids. If diet is inadequate, protein deficiencies will occur.	Meat, fish, poultry, eggs, milk, cheese, legumes, and nuts.
Magnesium	0.350 mg	Functions similar to calcium.	Nuts. legumes, cereals, green leafy vegetables.
Sodium and Chlorine	4.5 grams (Average daily intake is 6–19 grams)	Maintenance of normal water balance and acid-base balance. Essential to neuromuscular function.	Table salt, seafoods, meats, milk, eggs.
Potassium	Unknown (Average diet contains 2–4 grams daily)	Maintenance of normal water balance and acid-base balance. Important in regulation of neuromuscular activity.	Fruits, milk, meat, cereals, vegetables, and legumes.
Zinc	Unknown (Average diet contains 10–15 mg daily)	Needed for normal growth. Found in most body tissues. Participates with insulin in carbohydrate metabolism.	Milk, liver, wheat, and bran.
Iodine	.15 mg	Needed for normal thyroid function.	Table salt, seafood, water, and vegetables.
Cooper	2 mg.	Important to formation of red blood cells and nerve cell membranes.	Liver, shellfish, whole grains, legumes, nuts.
Manganese	3–9 mg	Needed for strong bones. Essential to function of most enzyme systems.	Beets, whole grains, nuts, legumes, fruit.
Fluorine	Unknown (Average diet contains 1.5–2.0 mg daily)	Needed for growth and maintenance of bones and teeth.	Water, rice, soybeans and green leafy vegetables.
Cobalt	.3 to .5 mg as vitamin B_{12}	Found in Vitamin B_{12}. Important to formation of red blood cells.	Liver, poultry, milk.

Source: Katch and McArdle (1977); Krause and Hunscher (1972); McArdle, Katch, and Katch (1981).

ing a condition of false anemia. Iron is also a structural component of myoglobin and is present in the cytochrome, making it important to the transfer of oxygen within muscle cells as well as the transport of this substance to the cells.

The recommended daily allowance of iron is 12 milligrams for men and 18 milligrams for women. An adequate diet will contain approximately 6 milligrams of iron per 1,000 calories. Since the diets of swimmers usually contain 3,000 to 5,000 calories there should be no need for supplementation. If, because of contradictory opinions, you prefer supplementing your diet with iron, the addition of 6 to 12 milligrams should prevent any deficiency that might result from training. If you prefer your supplement in natural form, dietary sources of iron are eggs, liver, green leafy vegetables, dried peas, and dried fruits.

Calcium. Calcium is essential to the transmission of nerve impulses and to the contractile process of muscles; it activates ATPase, causing the breakdown of ATP. Calcium also combines with phosphates to form strong bones and teeth as well as encouraging the clotting of blood and the transport of fluids across cell membranes.

The RDA is 800 milligrams. Eight ounces of milk contains 300 milligrams. Thus, dietary deficiencies should be rare. Costill (1978b) has reported that repeated days of long-distance running did not reduce the body's supply of this element. Therefore, supplementation of this mineral should not be necessary. However, if you wish to supplement as a precautionary measure, 200 to 400 milligrams of additional calcium should eliminate any possibility of a deficiency occurring. In addition to milk, other good dietary sources of calcium are dark green leafy vegetables.

Potassium, magnesium, sodium, and chlorine. Potassium, magnesium, sodium, and chlorine are available in most of the foods we eat. Consequently, there is little possibility of incurring a deficiency in any of these elements. The usual intake of potassium is 200 to 400 milligrams daily. For magnesium it is 300 to 350 milligrams daily. The daily need for these elements has not been established. Knochel and his colleagues (Knochel, Dotin, and Hamburger 1972) have reported potassium deficiencies during training; however subsequent research did not verify these results (Costill 1978b). Therefore, supplementation is probably not required. A deficiency of potassium could interfere with the transfer of nutrients across cell membranes and upset the normal acid-base balance of the body. Therefore, those athletes who wish to supplement as a precaution should add 200 to 400 milligrams of potassium to their daily diet.

The usual intake of sodium chloride is 6 to 18 grams per day, which is above the RDA. In addition, the increased caloric intake of athletes increases their daily intake of sodium chloride to more than 24 grams. As a result, the possibility of a sodium deficiency occurring is so remote that supplementation is not necessary.

Phosphorus. Phosphorus is found in foods containing protein. It is needed for the resynthesis of ATP and CP since phosphorylation is the first step in the metabolism of glucose. Phosphorus also plays a role in the buffering of lactic acid. Many of the vitamins in the B-complex group function only in combination with phosphorus (Krause and Hunscher 1972); therefore, a deficiency could have a devastating effect on performance. Unfortunately, the possibility of deficiencies during hard training has not been investigated thoroughly. Until it has been, it is probably wise to supplement the diet with 400 to 800 milligrams daily as a precautionary measure.

Sulfur. Sulfur is a constituent of several amino acids. It is also present in insulin, the hormone that regulates carbohydrate metabolism. It is, in addition, a constituent of the B-complex vitamins thiamin and biotin. Since the protein intake of athletes is more than sufficient to meet their needs and since many supplement their diets with B-complex vitamins, there should be no need to supplement the diet with sulfur.

Cobalt. Although cobalt passes through the intestinal tract largely unabsorbed, the amount needed each day is quite low, less than 1 milligram. Therefore, deficiencies are rare except among strict vegetarians. For this reason, and because high intakes of cobalt have been shown to cause polycythemia (overproduction of red blood cells) and hyperplasia of bone marrow (Krause and Hunscher 1972), supplementation is not advised.

Iodine. A deficiency of iodine will affect thyroid function and interfere with growth. However, the RDA for this mineral is quite low, 0.15 milligram daily. Therefore, an additional supplement of 0.10 milligram daily is all that should be required as a precaution against deficiency. Iodized salt is the best source of dietary iodine and should be used in cooking and seasoning. Supplementation should be doubled if iodized salt is not used.

Zinc. Zinc is associated with the function of insulin and thus with carbohydrate metabolism. Therefore, the amount required by athletes in training is probably greater than for nonathletes. The daily need for zinc has not been determined; however, the average daily intake is thought to be between 10 and 15 milligrams. A supplement of 10 to 15 additional milligrams might be advisable because deficiencies of zinc impair growth.

Fluorine, copper, and manganese. The average daily intake of copper and manganese are in excess of the RDA; therefore, deficiencies are rare and supplementation is not recommended. There is an insignificant quantity of fluorine in the foods we eat, 0.25 to 0.35 milligram. Adequate amounts of this element are gained from drinking fluoridated water. If the water in your area is adequately fluoridated and you drink the recommended number of glasses per day, supplementation will not be necessary.

General Guidelines for Using Food Supplements

Vitamin and mineral supplements are recommended for athletes in hard training as a safeguard against deficiencies that might occur due to the increased use of these elements in metabolism. Deficiencies can be quite detrimental to performance. They develop over a period of time. Once they occur, it requires several weeks to correct the situation, so prevention rather than cure is the best approach to deficiencies. Megadosing is not recommended, however, because certain fat soluble vitamins can accumulate to toxic levels if ingested in very large amounts over a long period of time.

A vitamin-mineral supplement should be high in all of the B-complex vi-

Table 13.8 *Recommended Vitamin and Mineral Supplements*

B-complex vitamins	20–25 mg
Vitamin C	200–300 mg
Pantothenic acid	10–20 mg
Vitamin M (folic acid)	0.5–1.0 mg
Vitamin H (biotin)	200–300 mg
Iron	6–12 mg
Calcium	200–400 mg
Potassium	200–400 mg
Phosphorus	400–800 mg
Iodine	100 mg
Zinc	10–15 mg

tamins and vitamin C. It should also contain iron, calcium, potassium, phosphorus, iodine, and zinc in the amounts shown in Table 13.8.

While vitamin supplements are an advisable precaution, adequate amounts of food are an absolute necessity. The following quantities of food are recommended for athletes in hard training:

- Milk (and milk products): three to four glasses daily. Skim or low fat milk should be used since they contain fewer saturated fats.
- Lean meat: six to ten ounces daily. This will provide more than enough protein (170 to 283 grams) for even the largest athlete in the most intense training. Poultry, fish, liver, and veal are recommended over meats with high saturated fat content such as beef, pork, and ham.
- Fruit and fruit juice: six servings daily. Fruits should be fresh and juice should be in natural form rather than sweetened with sugar.
- Green and yellow vegetables: three servings daily.
- Grains: twelve servings daily. These can be in the form of breads, cereals, and starchy vegetables such as potatoes.
- Water: four to six glasses daily.

This diet will provide more than the optimum amounts of all of the essential foodstuffs and liquids in the amounts needed by athletes in hard training. Notice that nonnutritious foods that are high in calories such as desserts, sweets, and creamy dairy drinks have not been recommended.

The importance of potatoes. Potatoes are nutritionally one of the most perfect foods. They are high in starchy forms of carbohydrates (polysaccharides) and contain a better mixture of B-complex vitamins and protein than you will find in meats and milk. They contain no saturated fats. Unfortunately, the belief that potatoes are high in caloric content has led many Americans to eat less of this nutritious food than they should. Actually, the caloric content of potatoes is quite low. One baked potato, including the skin, contains approximately 100 calories. It is the butter, sour cream, and cheese sauces we put on potatoes and the oils in which we fry them that add the calories. If you eat baked or broiled potatoes with no condiments, many nutritional needs can be met without excessive caloric intake.

Carbohydrate Loading

For a long time we have known that athletes' performances in endurance events can be improved through a procedure known as **carbohydrate loading.** Carbohydrate loading is based on the research of Bergström and his associates (1967). They showed that a sequence of dietary manipulation and exercise could cause muscles to store twice the normal amount of glycogen. This increase in muscle glycogen content was associated with improvements of 33 percent in work time to exhaustion. Since these results were published, many swimmers and other athletes have employed carbohydrate loading to improve their performances. Although it has become quite popular, there have been some concerns expressed about this procedure in recent years.

The original loading procedure required three weeks, however later research indicated a one-week cycle produced similar results. The step-by-step loading procedures for 1 week are as follows:

1. Starting 7 days before the competition begins, eat a low-carbohydrate diet during the first 3 days of the week. The number of calories ingested in the form of fats and protein is not important provided it is not excessive. A strenuous two-hour training session should be completed on the first day of that week in order to deplete the muscles of glycogen. The low-carbohydrate diet prevents adequate replacement during the next 2 days causing the activity of enzymes involved in glycogen storage to increase far above normal. This increase of enzyme activity will cause your muscles to store more than the usual amount of glycogen when carbohydrates are once again introduced into the diet.

2. On the fourth day of the week, switch to a high-carbohydrate diet, in which carbohydrates are 70 to 80 percent of your total calories. Maintain this diet for three days. The availability of carbohydrates, plus the increased enzyme activity, will cause your muscles to store 2 to 3 times the normal amount of muscle glycogen. Your practices should include only easy swimming during these days. This will prevent your depleting any of the additional glycogen before the competition begins.

Although carbohydrate loading will allow swimmers to enter races with 2 to 3 times their usual supply of muscle glycogen, the question is whether they need this extra energy. The longest swimming event requires only from 14 to 20 minutes—not enough time to deplete muscles that already contain normal amounts of glycogen. In such cases, would an increase provide any additional benefit? This will depend on whether partial depletion can affect performance. Although the consensus seems to be that it will not, there are dissenters who feel that depletions of 60 to 100 percent of the glycogen supply of certain muscles can occur in the time required to swim a 1,500 or 1,650 race (Taylor 1975). This will cause those fibers to reduce their rate of anaerobic glycolysis in order to prevent further depletion. Any reduction in anaerobic glycolysis will, of course, be accompanied by a reduction in speed. Therefore, carbohydrate loading could conceivably be valuable for improving performances in distance swims.

It is also conceivable that partial muscle glycogen depletion could hinder performances in shorter events if several are swum in a championship meet over a period of 2 to 4 days. Since muscle glycogen cannot be completely replaced overnight, you can see that swimmers might enter the later days of competition with a partially depleted energy supply. In such cases the muscle glycogen supply may not be sufficient to support the anaerobic energy demands of the race. If, however, the muscles have stored 2 to 3 times their normal amount of glycogen, the depletion might not be so severe as to limit performance.

The fact that greater than normal amounts of muscle glycogen may improve performance should not be taken to mean that the procedure of carbohydrate loading is recommended. Athletes should be aware of certain drawbacks before they decide to use this procedure. One of these drawbacks is a weight increase that could create additional form drag. Approximately 3 grams of water are stored with each gram of glycogen. Therefore, if the muscle glycogen supply is doubled, we should expect water storage to cause a sizable weight gain. Increases of 4 to 8 pounds are not uncommon.

A second danger associated with carbohydrate loading is the emotional upset that some swimmers experience when they are deprived of a normal carbohydrate supply. Because carbohydrates are usually quite abundant in the diet, we become somewhat addicted to them. When athletes are placed on low-carbohydrate diets, some of them exhibit symptoms that are similar to mild withdrawal. Nervousness, irritability, and even depression occur. These conditions, coupled with poor performances in practice brought on by the depletion of muscle glycogen during the 3 days that they are on low-carbohydrate feedings can cause some swimmers to lose confidence in their ability to perform well in the approaching meet. Further research is indeed needed to determine whether carbohydrate loading has value. The arguments against its use are as compelling as those favoring it.

Luckily there is a solution to this dilemma. The three-day, low-carbohydrate portion of the process can probably be eliminated without a considerable reduction in muscle glycogen storage occurring. Indications are that athletes in hard training have maintained their muscles in a partially depleted condition for a good portion of the season. Therefore, the activity of glycogen storing enzymes is probably quite high so that when they simply rest for 2 to 3 days and eat a high-carbohydrate diet their muscles should increase glycogen stores considerably above normal pretraining values without the necessity of 3 days of low-carbohydrate feedings. The storage of muscle glycogen, even though it is not 2 to 3 times the normal amount, should be sufficient to support the energy demands of 3 or more days of swimming competition.

Body Fat and Swimming Performance

Many swimmers have found that they compete best at a particular body weight. This is probably because they have a maximum amount of working muscle tissue and the minimum amount of excess body fat at that weight. Large amounts of muscle tissue are desired because they provide greater potential for force production. It should be emphasized, however, that these increases are only useful in muscles that provide propulsive force. Excess hypertrophy of the nonpropulsive muscles, like excess fat, will increase form drag. An athlete's ideal competitive weight will be attained when the body has enough muscle tissue to produce the force required for success in the swimmer's particular events and a minimum amount of body fat to pull through the water.

While excess muscle tissue hinders performance by increasing form drag, excess fat tissue will hinder performance in this and several other ways. Fat also competes with the muscles for the blood supply, which could reduce the muscles' oxygen supply. It may also cause friction in contracting muscles that will increase heat production and cause fatigue to occur earlier in races.

The Scales Will Mislead You If You Don't Watch Out

Athletes who use the traditional method of consulting height-weight charts to select their best competitive weight will be in error more than two-thirds of the time. The inaccuracies of height-weight charts were first reported by Welham and Behnke in 1942. They measured the height and weight of 25 professional football players while also determining the percentage of their weight that was fat. According to the charts, seventeen of these athletes were classified as overweight to the point of being unfit for military service while, in reality 11 of the 17 had very small percentages of body fat.

The reason for such discrepancies is that the standard height-weight charts tell us only the average weight of persons of a particular sex, height and body build. They do not tell us what those persons should weigh. Athletes in many sports are falsely classified as overweight by the charts because exercise increases the size of their muscles while reducing body fat. Thus, they weigh more than the average person while at the same time possessing less adipose tissue.

It is also possible for athletes in certain sports to be misclassified as underweight by the charts. The large volume of training required for endurance events, such as distance running, reduces body fat to a minimum. Since great force is not required in these sports, athletes will usually have no more than average amounts of muscle tissue and therefore, may be classified as underweight by the charts when in reality they are at their proper competitive weight.

A swimmer's ideal competitive weight should not be determined from averages appearing in standard height and weight charts, but from assessments of **body composition.** Body composition refers to the proportions of body weight that are fat and muscle.

Experts generally separate body composition into two components; **fat**

weight and **lean body weight.** Fat weight includes **essential fat** stored in bone marrow, muscles, organs and nervous tissue, and the **storage fat** deposited beneath the skin (subcutaneously) as adipose tissue. The most useful methods of assessing body composition estimate total body fat (essential and storage) from indirect measurements of storage fat. These indirect methods can be used with confidence because they have been validated against more precise but also more technical procedures. (See the Appendix for a detailed discussion of methods, equipment, and procedures for determining body composition.)

Lean body weight includes muscle, bone, and other nonfat body tissues. It is computed by subtracting total body fat (fat weight) from total body weight. Increases in this figure indicate the addition of muscle tissue, since that is the element of lean body weight most amenable to growth.

The importance of body composition to athletic performance may become clearer by taking the hypothetical example of two swimmers, each weighing 130 pounds (59.1 kilograms) who are swimming in the same race. The first swimmer has a body fat content that is 25 percent of her total body weight, while the second is carrying only 18 percent of her weight in the form of fat. The first swimmer has 35.5 pounds (16.14 kilograms) of body fat and 97.5 pounds (44.32 kilograms) of lean body weight. The second swimmer has 23.4 pounds (10.64 kilograms) of body fat and 106.6 pounds (48.46 kilograms) of lean body weight. It is obvious that the first swimmer has less muscle and should have less power available and that her larger percentage of body fat may increase the drag she must overcome.

The optimum proportions of fat and lean body weight are not known. Some stored fat is essential for energy in training and for the growth and repair of tissues. Fat makes up 26 percent of the body weight of the average adult female. For males, the average body fat percentage is 15 percent. Serious swimmers should be well below these averages. Unfortunately, there have been few reported measurements of the body composition of competitive swimmers. However, body fat percentages of successful athletes can serve as a basis for estimating the ideal percentages for swimmers. Some of those figures are presented in Table 13.9. The athletes were college age and older.

These figures are not meant to represent the ideal body fat percentages for male and female athletes. They merely summarize the findings from several studies. While the average college-age female is 26 percent body fat, most female athletes are between 12 and 20 percent with some distance runners measured below 10 percent. Most male athletes are between 8 and 12 percent body fat as compared to an average of 15 percent for college-age males, while some male distance runners have been assessed as low as 4 percent. The information presented in Table 13.9 suggests that the ideal body fat percentages for females are somewhere between 6 and 16 percent, while the range for males appears to be between 4 and 12 percent.

Do not reduce below the suggested minimums. The complete absence of body fat is not desirable. Some fat, known as essential fat, is needed for energy, insulation, and protection, among other things. The amount of essential fat is between 3 and 6 percent for males and is probably between 6 and 12 percent

Table 13.9   *The Range of Body Fat Percentages for College-Age Athletes*

	Female athletes	Male athletes
Sport	*Percentage*	*Percentage*
Distance Running	6–14	4–8
Wrestling		4–8
Gymnastics	8–14	6–10
Swimming	8–11	6–12
Basketball	12–20	8–12
Baseball-Softball	12–16	8–14
Football		
Backs and Receivers		5–10
Linebackers		10–16
Linemen		12–20
Tennis	12–16	
Field Hockey	9–21	
Volleyball	13–23	

Source: Data from Fox (1979), Hall (1977), Forsyth and Sinning (1973), and Wilmore (1977).

for females. The minimum percent body fat that a particular swimmer can achieve is probably established by heredity. Athletes will lose speed and power and they may also become ill if they attempt to reduce below this essential amount. Their bodies will actually metabolize muscle tissue for energy rather than give up essential fat.

It should be mentioned that there is concern in some circles that females can suffer menstrual disorders, principally secondary amenorrhea (the abnormal cessation of menstruation), when their body fat drops below 15 percent. It has been suggested that the normal homeostatic mechanisms of a woman's body can be upset when reduction in total fat approaches the minimum of 12 percent that represents the quantity of essential fat that is stored in the body of the average female (Harris 1977).

Selecting Your Ideal Competition Weight

Repeated assessments of body composition can become time consuming when athletes attempt to reduce body fat to some desired minimum. After the initial evaluation has been made, there is a simple procedure for determining ideal weight that can save time by allowing athletes to monitor their progress with the scale. The process is described in Figure 13.1. Lean body weight is determined and then multiplied by the percentage body fat considered optimal for the athlete in question. Ideal body weight is then calculated by adding this amount to the lean body weight figure. (Procedures for determining the percentage of body fat and lean body weight are described in the Appendix.) Once the ideal body weight has been calculated, the athletes can monitor their progress toward that goal by daily or weekly weighings. The sample calculations in Figure 13.1 are for a 190-pound (86.4-kilogram) male athlete with 15 percent body fat who wishes to reduce that amount to 10 percent. In order to do so, he must reduce his weight to approximately 177.5 pounds (80.8 kilograms).

Step 1. Calculate fat weight by multiplying your body weight by your present percentage of body fat.

Fat weight = Body weight × % body fat

Step 2. Determine lean body weight by subtracting your fat weight from your body weight.

Lean body weight = Body weight − Fat weight

Step 3. Determine the desired minimum amount of fat you wish to have on your body by multiplying your lean body weight by the percentage of body fat you have selected as optimum.

Desired fat weight = Lean body weight × Optimal % body fat

Step 4. Calculate your ideal body weight by adding your desired fat weight to your lean body weight.

Ideal body weight = Lean body weight + Desired fat weight

Sample calculation for a 190-pound man (86.4 kgs) with 15 percent body fat who wishes to have 10 percent body fat.

Fat weight = 190 lbs. (86.4 kgs) × .15 = 28.5 lbs. (13 kgs)
Lean body weight = 190 − 28.5 = 161.5 lbs. (73.4 kgs)
Desired fat weight = 161.5 × .10 = 16.15 lbs. (7.3 kgs)
Ideal body weight = 161.5 + 16.15 = 177.65 lbs. (80.8 kgs)

Figure 13.1. Procedure for estimating ideal competitive weight.

Although the convenience of this procedure warrants its inclusion, you should know that when ideal body weight is calculated in this manner it will not be entirely accurate in its representation of body composition. This is because training will be stimulating muscle growth at the same time that the body fat is being reduced. For example, suppose the athlete in Figure 13.1 gained 3 pounds (1.4 kilograms) of muscle tissue in the process of reducing his weight to 177.5 pounds. His true body fat percentage would then be approximately 7 percent rather than the 10 percent he desired. Therefore, when using this procedure, it is best to allow for increases in muscle tissue by selecting a body fat percentage that is 1 to 3 percent above your desired minimum. Your goal each season should be to lose the extra pounds of body fat that accumulated during a lay-off while increasing, or at least not reducing your lean body weight.

Changing Body Composition: Bulking Up and Slimming Down

Some swimmers become overly concerned with gaining large amounts of weight. They mistakenly believe that such increases reflect muscle growth that will provide them with greater power. It is common for these athletes to consume large quantities of calories in the form of meat and high-protein supplements in their attempts to encourage muscle growth. Some athletes also use anabolic steroids, a practice which can produce dangerous side effects.

Unfortunately, such attempts at rapid weight gain, even when accompanied by heavy resistance training, cause only modest increases in muscle tissue. Most of the weight gained is due to large deposits of storage fat. Thus, the athletes get the opposite effect from that desired. They find themselves slowing down and tiring more easily because of their increased form drag.

You cannot increase muscle size simply by consuming large amounts of calories. The stimulation of training, particularly heavy resistance training, is also required. Such growth proceeds more slowly than the deposition of fat and requires several days to take place. One pound of muscle tissue can be gained by increasing caloric intake 2,500 kilocalories beyond the amount needed for maintenance of present body weight (Smith 1977). This additional caloric intake should be spread over a two- or three-day period to provide sufficient time for growth of new muscle tissue. Athletes should plan for a maximum gain of 1 to 2 pounds of muscle tissue per week.

Skinfolds should be measured at 1 or 2 week intervals to insure that weight gains are indeed muscle, rather than unwanted fat tissue. (See the discussion of skinfold measurements in the Appendix.) Weight gains accompanied by increases in skinfold measurements indicate a gain in fat weight, while you can be confident that such gains are primarily due to growth of new muscle tissue when skinfolds do not increase.

A program of weight loss should be instituted when swimmers have body fat percentages in excess of the minimums that were recommended. The most effective way for athletes to lose weight is by reducing caloric intake. They will lose one pound every time their caloric output exceeds their intake by 3,500 kilocalories. The recommended rate of weight loss is 1 to 2 pounds per week, which calls for a reduction in caloric intake of 500 to 1,000 kilocalories per day.

The Danger of Dieting During Hard Training

Serious swimmers should make certain they start the season within 2 to 4 percent of their ideal body fat percentage. This amount is generally within 4 to 6 pounds of the weight they have determined to be ideal for competition. The onset of training will normally cause them to lose 4 to 6 pounds with no need for dieting. This is preferable to dieting during training.

If you gain so much weight that you are forced to diet while training, your energy level will be low and you will not be able to maintain the appropriate training intensities that will result in maximum improvements in your physical condition. In addition, there is the danger that the absence of sufficient muscle glycogen may cause you to utilize greater amounts of protein for energy with a subsequent loss of muscle tissue. In this case, both power and endurance will be lost. Nitrogen is an indicator of protein metabolism. Pizzo (1961) tested the urine of college swimmers for nitrogen content after morning practice sessions when they had not eaten for the previous 12 hours. High levels of nitrogen were found in their urine, indicating that they were, perhaps, metabolizing their own muscle tissue for energy during training. Obviously swimmers on diets who are training twice a day may be in even greater danger of metabolizing proteins for energy.

It is strongly advised that all swimmers watch their weight during the off-season. When weight gains do occur, you should diet before the season begins so that when you report for training you are within 4 to 6 pounds of your ideal body weight.

When swimmers do not train during the off-season, body composition measurements, not scale weight, should be used to determine how much weight you should lose at the beginning of each season. It is conceivable that, even though there was no apparent weight gain, inactivity could have caused your muscles to atrophy so that there has been a change of body composition. In such a case, a greater percentage of your body weight will be fat rather than muscle. Engaging in some maintenance activity during breaks in training is recommended in order to prevent muscle atrophy and the resulting loss of power.

Maintaining Weight During the Off-Season and After Retirement

Why do athletes seem particularly susceptible to large increases in weight during the off-season and after retirement? The reason is probably because they have developed an appetite for a large number of calories during their years (or season) of training. When they stop training, caloric output is reduced dramatically; however, the appetite center of the brain continues to demand the same caloric intake. As a result, the unneeded calories are converted to fat and stored as adipose tissue.

These demands of the appetite center become even more difficult to control when large amounts of sugar are eaten on a regular basis. Sugar is one of the most addictive of foods. High sugar intake increases the appetite because of its effect on blood glucose. Sugar stimulates an immediate increase in blood glucose, which is followed by a compensatory drop after 2 to 3 hours. When blood sugar drops, the appetite center is stimulated, encouraging the intake of additional, unnecessary sweets, and the cycle begins again.

The dilemma facing the coach is that swimmers need encouragement to increase their carbohydrate intake during training so they can replace muscle glycogen from day to day. Yet this intake must be curtailed during off-season and, of course, after they retire. Curtailing carbohydrate intake will be no easy task after months and years of conditioning the appetite center to demand these substances. The solution is to recommend that swimmers in training ingest their additional carbohydrates in the form of starches rather than sugars. It is far easier to control the intake of starches after training is reduced, and weight gains will be less likely to occur.

The Precompetition Meal

Until recent years, steak or roast beef were considered indispensable to the precompetition meal. A baked potato, a vegetable, and tea with sugar or honey usually completed the menu. This meal had no particular ergogenic effect on performance, although some athletes and coaches claimed that it did. In actuality, eating meat just before competition is based on a tradition that has its roots in the ancient practice of eating the meat of animals in order to gain their qualities of speed, power, and endurance. It was common for gladiators and competitors in the ancient Greek Olympiads to eat the meat of lions in their attempts to improve their own strength, speed, and courage.

The practice of including meat in the precompetition meal is now dying out and rightly so. Protein does not make a good precompetition meal. It does not supply energy for competition. It is hard to digest and it may cause nausea both before and during races. Fats are an equally poor choice for a pregame meal. Fats, as well as proteins, may interfere with respiration and place excessive stress on the circulation when they are eaten within two hours of heavy exercise (Costill 1978c).

A sensible precompetition meal is one in which the protein and fat content are low and the carbohydrate content is high. Contrary to what you might think, the carbohydrates in the precompetition meal do not supply energy for the race. That energy should already be stored in your muscles and liver from the high-carbohydrate meals that were eaten during the 2 to 3 days prior to the contest. The major purpose of the high-carbohydrate precompetition meal should be to prevent hunger without causing nausea. In addition, the carbohydrates that were eaten in the precompetition meal will be digested and available as glucose after the meet so that they can be used to replace the muscle and liver glycogen that were metabolized during races.

The precompetition meal should be eaten 3 to 4 hours before the meet in order to allow sufficient time for digestion. It should be mentioned that, although 3 to 4 hours is the recommended interval, liquid sources of carbohydrates have been consumed within 30 minutes of competition with no ill effects reported (Mathews and Fox 1976).

The meal should be light, containing only 500 to 800 calories. The food should not be highly seasoned, especially if highly-seasoned foods have produced nausea in the past. The carbohydrates should be in a starch rather than sugar form. Eating candy bars, dextrose pills, honey, and other sugary forms of carbohydrates is not recommended. These foods, although they cause a sudden increase in blood glucose, will within a short time cause a compensatory drop in blood glucose that will leave you fatigued. Sugar stimulates the beta cells in the Islets of Langerhans to release insulin. The heavy flow of insulin increases deposition of glucose in the liver, causing a drop in blood glucose at a time when the muscles need it to supplement their energy supply. Costill (1978c) has reported a 19 percent decrease in work time to exhaustion when sugar was taken 30 to 40 minutes before exercise.

The Postcompetition Meal

The postcompetition meal has not received the attention it deserves in literature on athletic nutrition. The attitude has been that what an athlete eats is not important once the race is over. This attitude should change. A high-carbohydrate meal is needed after competition to encourage rapid replacement of the muscle and liver glycogen that was depleted during the races. Where depletion has been significant, as in distance races, this replacement may make the difference between a good performance and a poor one during races that are held 1 or 2 days later.

Costill (1978c) indicates the greatest replacement of muscle glycogen occurs during the first 10 hours following exercise. It is important, therefore, to be certain that swimmers encourage the rapid replacement of muscle glycogen by eating a high-carbohydrate meal soon after competition. They should eat a meal similar in content to the precompetition meal. The food should be taken as soon after competition as possible to allow the greatest amount of time for glycogen replacement.

Food Intake During Hard Training

Swimmers in hard training should eat frequently during the day so they can replace the glycogen, fat, and other nutrients that were consumed for energy during training. A minimum of 3 meals per day is essential for this purpose. Four to six meals per day may be preferable. Since blood sugar tends to fall within 2 to 3 hours after a meal, eating more frequently than 3 times per day may prevent a drop in blood sugar and swimmers will go through the day feeling more energetic. Liver and muscle glycogen replacement may proceed at a more rapid rate as well.

Of course, the practice of eating 4 to 6 times daily should not lead to a corresponding caloric increase or unwanted fat will accumulate. Rather, the usual number of calories that are needed to meet the demands of training should be spread over the day by eating 4 to 6 small meals rather than 2 to 3 large ones.

When training twice per day, it would be wise to consume 300 to 500 calories of a liquid or semiliquid carbohydrate substance if there is no time for breakfast before the morning workout. This can be followed by a normal breakfast after training, or a snack if you were able to eat breakfast before training. The noontime meal should contain fewer calories than usual, with the missing calories consumed at a midafternoon snack. A somewhat smaller than normal supper and an evening snack should complete the day.

REFERENCES

Bergström, J., Hermansen, L., Hultman, D., and Saltin, B. 1967. "Diet Muscle Glycogen and Physical Performance." *Acta Physiol. Scand.* 71:140–150.

Bourne, Geoffrey H. 1968. "Nutrition and Exercise." *Exercise Physiology*, ed. H. B. Falls, pp. 155–171. New York: Academic Press.

Buskirk, E. R., and Haymes, E. M. 1972. "Nutritional Requirements for Women in Sport." Proceedings of National Research Conference Sponsored by the College of Health, Physical Education and Recreation, Pennsylvania State University. University Park, Pennsylvania: Pennsylvania State University.

Carlile, F. 1963. *Forber Carlile on Swimming.* London: Pelham Books.

Costill, D. L. 1978a. "Fluids for Athletic Performance: Why and What Should You Drink During Prolonged Exercise?" *Toward an Understanding of Human Performance*, ed. E. J. Burke, pp. 63–67. Ithaca, New York: Mouvement Publications.

———. 1978b. "Nutritional Requirements for Endurance Athletes." *Toward an Understanding of Human Performance*, ed. E. J. Burke, pp. 45–47. New York: Mouvement Publications.

———. 1978c. "Sports Nutrition: The Role of Carbohydrates." *Nutrition News* 41:1, 4.

Costill, D. L., Bowers, R., Branum, G., and Sparks, K. 1971. "Muscle Glycogen Utilization During Prolonged Exercise on Successive Days." *J. Appl. Physiol.* 31:834–838.

Cureton, T. K. 1955. "Wheat Germ Oil, the 'Wonder' Fuel." *Scholastic Coach* 24:36–37, 67–68.

Forsyth, H. F., and Sinning, W. E. 1973. "The Anthropometric Estimation of Body Density and Lean Body Weight of Male Athletes." *Medicine and Science in Sports* 5:174–180.

Fox, E. L. 1979. *Sports Physiology.* Philadelphia: W. B. Saunders.

Hall, Linda K. 1977. *Anthropometric Estimation of Body Density of Women Athletes in Selected Athletic Activities.* Unpublished doctoral presentation. Columbus, Ohio: Ohio State University.

Harris, Dorothy V. 1977. "The Female Athlete: Strength, Endurance and Performance." *Toward an Understanding of Human Performance*, ed. E. J. Burke, pp. 41–44. Ithaca, New York: Mouvement Publications.

Herbert, V. 1977. "Toxicity of Vitamin E." *Nutritional Review* 35:158.

Hultman, E., Bergström, J., and Roch-Norlund, A. E. 1971. "Glycogen Storage in Human Skeletal Muscle." *Muscle Metabolism During Exercise*, ed. B. Pernow and B. Saltin, pp. 273–287. New York: Plenum Press.

Jensen, C. R., and Fisher, A. G. 1975. *Scientific Basis of Athletic Conditioning.* Philadelphia: Lea and Febiger.

Katch, F. I., and McArdle, W. D. 1977. *Nutrition, Weight Control and Exercise.* Boston: Houghton Mifflin Co.

Knochel, J. P., Dotin, L. N., and Hamburger, R. J. 1972. "Pathophysiology of Intense Physical Conditioning in a Hot Climate: I. Mechanisms of Potassium Depletion." *J. Clin. Invest.* 51:242–255.

Krause, M. V., and Hunscher, M. A. 1972. *Food Nutrition and Diet Therapy.* Philadelphia: W. B. Saunders.

McArdle, W. D., Katch, F. I., and Katch, V. L. 1981. *Exercise Physiology.* Philadelphia: Lea and Febiger.

MacDougall, J. D., Ward, G. R., Sale, D. C., and Sutton, J. R. 1975. "Muscle Glycogen Repletion After High Intensity Intermittent Exercise." *J. Appl. Physiol.* 42:129–132.

Mathews, D. K., and Fox, E. L. 1976. *The Physiological Basis of Physical Education and Athletics.* Philadelphia: W. B. Saunders.

Mayer, J. 1975. "Study of Vitamin E Dosage Inconclusive." *Sun-Sentinel* [Pompano Beach, Florida], February 10.

Morehouse, L. E., and Miller, A. T. 1971. *Physiology of Exercise.* St. Louis: Mosby.

Morehouse, L. E., and Rasch, P. J. 1958. *Scientific Basis of Athletic Training.* Philadelphia: W. B. Saunders.

Parizkova, J. 1961. "Total Body Fat and Skinfold Thickness in Children." *Metabolism* 10:794–807.

Percival, L. 1973. "Vitamin C: Looking Good in the Labs." *Sports and Fitness Instructor*, September (n.p.).

———. 1972. "Vitamin Supplements: Are They Really Necessary?" *Sports and Fitness Instructor*, November.

Pizzo, A. 1961. Unpublished research on the influence different preworkout breakfasts have on blood sugar levels of competitive swimmers. Indiana University, Bloomington, Indiana. Cited in Jensen, C. R., and A. G. Fisher, 1975. *Scientific Basis of Athletic Conditioning.* Philadelphia: Lea and Febiger.

Pollock, M. L., Wilmore, J. H., and Fox, S. M. III. 1978. *Health and Fitness Through Physical Activity.* New York: Wiley.

Schubert, Mark. 1977. "Blood Testing and Training of Distance Swimmers." *1976 American Swimming Coaches Association World Clinic Yearbook*, ed. B. M. Ousley, pp. 71–86. Fort Lauderdale, Florida: American Swimming Coaches Association.

Smith, N. J. 1977. "Gaining and Losing Weight in Athletics." *Toward an Understanding of Human Performance*, ed. E. J. Burke, pp. 48–50. Ithaca, New York: Mouvement Publications.

Talbot, D. 1974. "Training Distance Swimmers." Talk presented at 1974 World Swimming Coaches Clinic, Chicago, Illinois.

Taylor, A. W. 1975. "The Effect of Exercise and Training on the Activities of Human Skeletal Muscle Glycogen Cycle Enzymes." *Metabolic Adaptations to Prolonged Physical Exercise*, ed. H. Howald and J. R. Poortmans, pp. 451–462. Basel: Birkäuser Verlag.

Welham, W. C., and Behnke, A. R. 1942. "The Specific Gravity of Healthy Men." *Journal of the American Medical Association* 118:498–501.

Wilmore, J. H. 1977. *Athletic Training and Physical Fitness.* Boston: Allyn and Bacon.

Appendix:
Evaluating Body Composition

There are several methods of assessing body composition that can be used by coaches and athletes. They involve techniques that are quickly learned and require relatively inexpensive equipment. Although not without error, they all provide more accurate assessments of body composition than can be furnished by using the standard height-weight charts. The first group of procedures involves the simple method of measuring the circumference of certain body parts with a tape. In the second group, the thickness of skinfolds are measured at various sites on the body. These procedures require special calipers whose use is easily mastered with practice. The methods of assessing body composition that are presented in the following sections were selected for their simplicity. These procedures are based on the premise that areas of the body where adipose tissue tends to be deposited will be larger than average in persons with greater amounts of body fat.

The easiest method—with limitations. The simplest method for assessing the body composition of male swimmers is illustrated in Figure A.1. Unfortunately a similar method has not been developed for females. The athlete's waist size is measured with a tape held horizontal at the level of the belly button (umbilicus). The subject's body weight is also taken and the two values are converted to percent of body fat by means of the nomogram in Figure A.2. The example in that figure shows that a man weighing 170 pounds with a waist circumference of 34 inches is 18 percent body fat.

Skinfolds—the best method for coaches and athletes. Percent body fat can also be assessed by measuring the thickness of skinfolds at various sites on the body. The measurement includes two folds of skin and the storage fat that is deposited beneath the skin. Of course, larger values indicate more body fat. The amount of body

Figure A.1. A simple method for assessing the body composition of male swimmers. The waist measurement can be correlated with body weight to provide a reasonably accurate estimate of relative body fat.

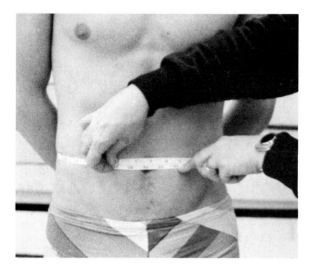

Figure A.2. Prediction of relative body fat in men from waist girth and body weight. (Courtesy of Dr. Brian J. Sharkey, University of Montana. Adapted from M. L. Pollock, J. H. Wilmore, and S. M. Fox, *Health and Fitness Through Physical Activity* [New York: Wiley, 1978], p. 104, by permission of John Wiley and Sons.)

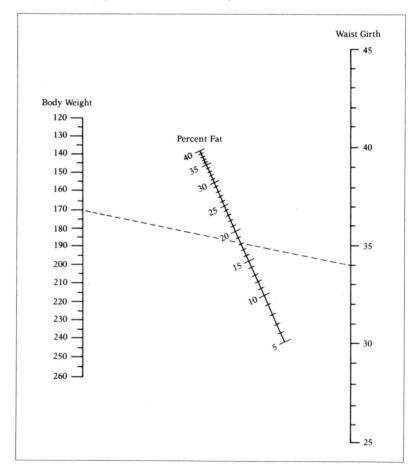

fat is calculated by substituting these measurements in equations that have been developed for this purpose. Skinfolds need only be measured at a few representative areas of the body since, through a process of statistical selection (multiple regression analysis), these sites have been found to estimate total body fat as accurately as those methods in which a greater number of measurements were taken.

The two most popular brands of skinfold calipers are the Harpenden and Lange models. They are accurate enough for research purposes but also expensive. Lange calipers are shown in Figure A.3. Several companies are now marketing less expensive calipers that, while not acceptable for research purposes, are quite adequate for use with athletic teams. They will give satisfactory results at one-tenth the cost of Harpenden and Lange models. Information about these can be gained from the American Alliance for Health, Physical Education, Recreation, and Dance, 1900 Association Drive, Reston, Virginia 22091.

The procedure for measuring skinfolds is illustrated at the triceps in Figure A.4. The skin and subcutaneous fat are grasped between the thumb and forefinger just above the measurement site. The skinfold should be pulled away from the underlying muscle so that no muscle tissue is included in the fold. The calipers are then applied to the fold about one-half inch below the thumb and forefinger. The handle is released and the reading taken.

All measurements should be taken on the right side of the body. Take several

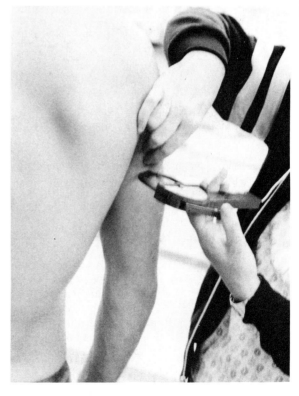

Figure A.3. Skinfold calipers. This is one of two brands in common use, Lange skinfold calipers. They can be purchased from Cambridge Scientific Industries, 101 Virginia Avenue, Cambridge, Maryland 21613. Harpenden calipers can be purchased from Quinton Instruments, 2121 Terry Avenue, Seattle, Washington 98121.

Figure A.4. Taking a skinfold measurement at the triceps.

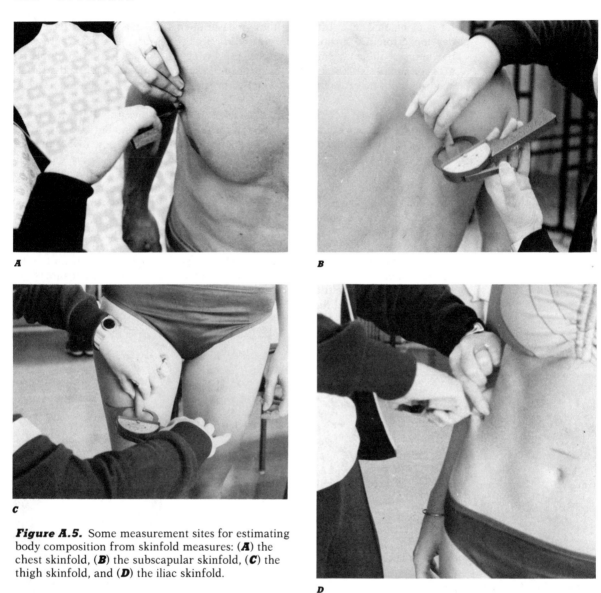

Figure A.5. Some measurement sites for estimating body composition from skinfold measures: (**A**) the chest skinfold, (**B**) the subscapular skinfold, (**C**) the thigh skinfold, and (**D**) the iliac skinfold.

readings at each site. When you get general agreement among them, select the average of two or three as the official measurement.

The measurement sites used for the various methods of assessing body composition that are presented later in this section are pictured in Figure A.5. Readings are taken at the chest, subscapular, thigh, iliac, and triceps sites. Following are some instructions for taking readings at each of these points.

- *Chest skinfold*: This site is midway between the right armpit and nipple. It is measured on a diagonal with the natural fold of the skin.

Sex	Age	Skinfold Site
Females	9–12	Subscapular
Females	13–16	Subscapular
Males	9–12	Subscapular
Males	13–16	Triceps

Figure A.6. The skinfold sites for estimating percentage of body fat for children and teenagers. (Adapted from Parizkova 1961.)

Figure A.7. The skinfold sites used for estimating the percentage of body fat for young adults. These procedures were developed by Pollock and associates (1978).

Sex	Skinfold Sites
Females	Iliac Thigh (Consult Table A.2 to determine the appropriate conversion factors for each measurement.)
Males	Chest Subscapular Thigh (Consult Table A.3 to determine the appropriate conversion factors for each measurement.)

- *Subscapular skinfold*: The reading is also taken on a diagonal, just below the tip of the scapula and slightly to the left of it.
- *Thigh skinfold*: This reading is taken vertically on the front of the right thigh, midway between the hip and knee.
- *Iliac skinfold*: This site is measured on a diagonal at the right hip, just above the hip bone (ilium).
- *Triceps skinfold* (pictured in fig. A.4): The reading is taken vertically on the back of the right upperarm (over the triceps), midway between the shoulder and elbow.

Using skinfold measurements to estimate the percent body fat of children and teenagers. One of the few procedures available for use with boys and girls is also one of the simplest to administer.[1] It requires only one measurement, at either the subscapular or triceps skinfold, depending on the age and sex of the athletes who are being assessed.

The measurement sites are listed in Figure A.6. The subscapular skinfold is used for estimating the body fat of females in the 9 to 12 and 13 to 16 age ranges. The same site is used for males in the 9 to 12 age group. The triceps skinfold is employed for males in the 13 to 16 age category. Once the thickness of the appropriate skinfold has been determined, it can be converted to percent body fat by consulting Table A.1.

Using skinfold measurements to estimate the percent body fat of young adults. Procedures developed by Pollock and associates[2] are appropriate for males and females between the ages of 18 and 22. The measurement sites for females are the iliac and thigh. For males they are the chest, subscapular, and thigh skinfolds (see fig. A.7).

1. Parizkova, J. "Total Body Fat and Skinfold Thickness in Children." *Metabolism* 10:794–807, 1961.
2. Pollock, M. L., Wilmore, J. H., and Fox, S. M. III. 1978. *Health and Fitness Through Physical Activity.* New York: Wiley.

Table A.1 *Conversion of Skinfold Measurements to Percentages of Body Fat for Children and Teenagers*

Skinfold thickness (mm) (Subscapular or Triceps)	Percent body fat			
	Females 9–12	Females 13–16	Males 9–12	Males 13–16
1.0	9		2.0	
1.2	10		4	
1.4	11		6	
1.6	12		7	
1.8	13		8	
2.0	14	6	9	
2.2	15	7	10	
2.4	16	8	11	
2.6	16.5	9	12	
2.8	17	10	13	
3.0	18	11	13.5	4
3.2	18.5	11.5	14	4.5
3.4	19	12.	14.5	5
3.6	19	12.5	15	6
3.8	19.5	13	15.5	7
4.0	20	14	16	8
4.2	20.5	14	17	8.5
4.4	21	14.5	17.5	9
4.6	21	15	18	10
4.8	21.5	15.5	18.5	10.5
5.0	22	16	18.75	11
5.2	22.5	16.5	19	12.0
5.4	22.5	17	19	12.5
5.6	23	17.5	19.5	13
5.8	23	18	20.0	13.5
6.0	23	18.5	20.5	14
6.2	23.5	19	21	14.5
6.4	24	19	21	15
6.6	24	19	21.5	15.5
6.8	24.5	19.5	22	16
7.0	25	20	22.5	16.5
7.2	25	20.5	22.5	17
7.4	25.5	20.5	22.75	17.5
7.6	25.5	21	23	17.75
7.8	26	21.5	23	18.0
8.0	26	21.5	23.5	19.0
8.2	26	22	23.5	19.0
8.4	26.5	22	24	19.5
8.6	26.5	22	24	20
8.8	27	23	24.5	20
9.0	27	23	24.5	20.5
9.2	27	23	24.5	21
9.4	27.5	23.5	25	21.5
9.6	27.5	23.5	25	21.5
9.8	28	24	25.5	22
10.0	28	24	26	22.5
10.5	28.5	24.5	26.5	23
11.0	29	25	27	23.5
11.5		25.5	27.5	24
12.0	29	26	28	25
12.5		26.5	28.5	26
13.0	30	27	28.75	26.5
13.5		27.5	29	27
14.0	31	28	29.5	28

Table A.1. *continued*

Skinfold thickness (mm) (Subscapular or Triceps)	Percent body fat			
	Females 9–12	Females 13–16	Males 9–12	Males 13–16
15.0	31.5	29	30	29
16.0	32	29.5	31	30
17.0	32.5	30	31.5	31
18.0	33	31	32	32
19.0	33.5	31.5	33	33
20.0	34	32	33.5	34
21.0	34	33	34	35
22.0	34.5	33.5	34.5	35.5
23.0	35	34	35	36
24.0	35.5	34.5	35.25	37
25.0	35.5	35	35.75	37.5
26.0	36	35.5	36	38
27.0	36.5	36	36.75	39
28.0	36.5	36.25	37	39.5
29.0	37	36.75	37.5	40
30.0	37.5	37	38	41
31.0	37.5	37.25	38	41.5
32.0	38	37.5	38.5	42
33.0	38	38	39	42.5
34.0	38.5	38.5	39.5	43
35.0	38.5	39	39.5	43.5
36.0	39	39	40	44
37.0	39	39.5	40	44.5
38.0	39.5	40	40.5	
39.0	39.5	40	41	
40.0	40.0	40.5	41	
41.0	40.0	40.5	41.5	
42.0	40.5	41	42	
43.0	40.5	41	42	
44.0	41	41.5	42.5	
45.0	41	42	42.5	
46.0	41	42	43	
47.0	41.5	42.5	43	
48.0	41.5	42.5	43.5	
49.0	42	43	43.5	
50.0	42	43	44.0	

Procedures for both sexes require that body density (body mass per unit of volume) must be calculated before percent body fat can be determined. To compute body density, the skinfold measurements are changed to conversion factors by consulting Table A.2 for females, and Table A.3 for males. The conversion factors are then inserted into the following formulas.

Formula for females:

Body Density = Conversion factor for the iliac skinfold − Conversion factor for the thigh skinfold

Formula for males:

Body Density = Conversion factor for the chest skinfold − Conversion factor for the subscapular skinfold − Conversion factor for the thigh skinfold

Table A.2 *Conversion Table for Determining the Percentage of Body Fat for Women Aged 19 to 21[a,b]*

Suprailiac skinfold (mm)	Conversion factor	Thigh skinfold (mm)	Conversion factor
1	1.0844	1	0.0011
2	1.0836	2	0.0022
3	1.0828	3	0.0033
4	1.0820	4	0.0044
5	1.0812	5	0.0055
6	1.0804	6	0.0066
7	1.0796	7	0.0077
8	1.0788	8	0.0088
9	1.0780	9	0.0099
10	1.0772	10	0.0110
11	1.0764	11	0.0121
12	1.0756	12	0.0132
13	1.0748	13	0.0143
14	1.0740	14	0.0154
15	1.0732	15	0.0165
16	1.0724	16	0.0176
17	1.0716	17	0.0187
18	1.0708	18	0.0198
19	1.0700	19	0.0209
20	1.0692	20	0.0220
21	1.0684	21	0.0231
22	1.0676	22	0.0242
23	1.0668	23	0.0253
24	1.0660	24	0.0264
25	1.0652	25	0.0275
26	1.0644	26	0.0286
27	1.0636	27	0.0297
28	1.0628	28	0.0308
29	1.0620	29	0.0319
30	1.0612	30	0.0330
31	1.0604	31	0.0341
32	1.0596	32	0.0352
33	1.0588	33	0.0363
34	1.0580	34	0.0374
35	1.0572	35	0.0385
36	1.0564	36	0.0396
37	1.0556	37	0.0407
38	1.0548	38	0.0418
39	1.0540	39	0.0429
40	1.0532	40	0.0440
41	1.0524	41	0.0451
42	1.0516	42	0.0462
43	1.0508	43	0.0473
44	1.0500	44	0.0484
45	1.0492	45	0.0495
46	1.0484	46	0.0506
47	1.0476	47	0.0517
48	1.0468	48	0.0528
49	1.0460	49	0.0539
50	1.0452	50	0.0550

Source: M. L. Pollock, J. H. Wilmore, and S. M. Fox, *Health and Fitness Through Physical Activity* (New York: Wiley, 1978), p. 97. Used by permission of John Wiley and Sons, Inc.

[a] Table developed by M. L. Pollock (Institute for Aerobics Research) and A. J. Jackson (University of Houston).

[b] Pollock, Laughridge, Coleman, Linnerud, and Jackson. "Prediction of body density in young and middle-aged women." *J. Appl. Physiol. 38:* 745–749 (1975).
Density = $1.0852 - 0.0008 \times$ suprailiac $- 0.0011 \times$ thigh
$R = 0.775$ Standard error $= 0.0091$

Table A.3 *Conversion Table for Determining the Percentage of Body Fat for Men Aged 18 to 22[a,b]*

Chest skinfold (mm)	Conversion factor	Subscapular skinfold (mm)	Conversion factor	Thigh skinfold (mm)	Conversion factor
1	1.90651	1	0.00055	1	0.0008
2	1.09586	2	0.00110	2	0.0016
3	1.09521	3	0.00165	3	0.0024
4	1.09456	4	0.00220	4	0.0032
5	1.09391	5	0.00275	5	0.0040
6	1.09326	6	0.00330	6	0.0048
7	1.09261	7	0.00385	7	0.0056
8	1.09196	8	0.00440	8	0.0064
9	1.09131	9	0.00495	9	0.0072
10	1.09066	10	0.00550	10	0.0080
11	1.09001	11	0.00605	11	0.0088
12	1.08936	12	0.00660	12	0.0096
13	1.08871	13	0.00715	13	0.0104
14	1.08806	14	0.00770	14	0.0112
15	1.08741	15	0.00825	15	0.0120
16	1.08676	16	0.00880	16	0.0128
17	1.08611	17	0.00935	17	0.0136
18	1.08546	18	0.00990	18	0.0144
19	1.08481	19	0.01045	19	0.0152
20	1.08416	20	0.01100	20	0.0160
21	1.08351	21	0.01155	21	0.0168
22	1.08286	22	0.01210	22	0.0176
23	1.08221	23	0.01265	23	0.0184
24	1.08156	24	0.01320	24	0.0192
25	1.08091	25	0.01375	25	0.0200
26	1.08026	26	0.01430	26	0.0208
27	1.07961	27	0.01485	27	0.0216
28	1.07896	28	0.01540	28	0.0224
29	1.07831	29	0.01595	29	0.0232
30	1.07766	30	0.01650	30	0.0240
31	1.07701	31	0.01705	31	0.0248
32	1.07636	32	0.01760	32	0.0256
33	1.07571	33	0.01815	33	0.0265
34	1.07506	34	0.01870	34	0.0272
35	1.07441	35	0.01925	35	0.0280
36	1.07376	36	0.01980	36	0.0288
37	1.07311	37	0.02035	37	0.0296
38	1.07246	38	0.02090	38	0.0304
39	1.07181	39	0.02145	39	0.0312
40	1.07116	40	0.02200	40	0.0320
41	1.07051	41	0.02255	41	0.0328
42	1.06986	42	0.02310	42	0.0336
43	1.06921	43	0.02365	43	0.0344
44	1.06856	44	0.02420	44	0.0352
45	1.06791	45	0.02475	45	0.0360
46	1.06726	46	0.02530	46	0.0368
47	1.06661	47	0.02585	47	0.0376
48	1.06596	48	0.02640	48	0.0384
49	1.06531	49	0.02695	49	0.0392
50	1.06466	50	0.02750	50	0.0400

Source: M. L. Pollock, J. H. Wilmore, and S. M. Fox, *Health and Fitness Through Physical Activity* (New York: Wiley, 1978), p. 95. Used by permission of John Wiley and Sons, Inc.

[a]Table developed by M. L. Pollock (Institute for Aerobics Research) and A. J. Jackson (University of Houston).

[b]Pollock, Hickman, Kendrick, Jackson, Linnerud, and Dawson, "Prediction of body density in young and middle-aged men." *J. Appl. Physiol.*, *40:*300–304 (1976).

Density $= 1.09716 - 0.00065 \times$ chest $- 0.00055 \times$ subscapular $- 0.0008 \times$ thigh

$R = 0.82$ Standard error $= 0.0080$

Female

Skinfold Measurements	Conversion Factors (According to Table A.2)
Iliac: 15 mm.	1.0732
Thigh: 12 mm.	0.0132

Body density $= 1.0732 - 0.0132$
$= 1.060$

% body fat $= 16.98$ (according to Table 6)

Male

Skinfold Measurements	Conversion Factors (According to Table A.3)
Chest: 5 mm.	1.09391
Subscapula: 10 mm.	0.00550
Thigh: 10 mm.	0.0080

Body density $= 1.09391 - 0.00550 - 0.0080$
$= 1.080$

% body fat $= 8.33$ (according to Table A.4)

Figure A.8. Computing body density from skinfold measurements.

Sample calculations for a young woman with skinfold measurements of 15 millimeters at the iliac site and 12 millimeters at the thigh are shown in Figure A.8. Calculations for a male with skinfolds of 5 millimeters at the chest, 10 millimeters at the subscapular site, and 10 millimeters at the thigh are also presented. Once the body density of either sex has been computed this figure can be converted to percent body fat by consulting Table A.4.

Table A.4 *Conversion of Body Density to Percentage of Body Fat*

Density	Percent fat	Density	Percent fat	Density	Percent fat
1.000	45.00	1.033	29.19	1.066	14.35
1.001	44.51	1.034	28.72	1.067	13.92
1.002	44.01	1.035	28.26	1.068	13.48
1.003	43.52	1.036	27.80	1.069	13.05
1.004	43.03	1.037	27.34	1.070	12.62
1.005	42.54	1.038	26.88	1.071	12.18
1.006	42.05	1.039	26.42	1.072	11.75
1.007	41.56	1.040	25.96	1.073	11.32
1.008	41.07	1.041	25.50	1.074	10.89
1.009	40.58	1.042	25.05	1.075	10.47
1.010	40.10	1.043	24.59	1.076	10.04
1.011	39.61	1.044	24.14	1.077	9.61
1.012	39.13	1.045	23.68	1.078	9.18
1.013	38.65	1.046	23.23	1.079	8.76
1.014	38.17	1.047	22.78	1.080	8.33
1.015	37.68	1.048	22.33	1.081	7.91
1.016	37.20	1.049	21.88	1.082	7.49
1.017	36.73	1.050	21.43	1.083	7.06
1.018	36.25	1.051	20.98	1.084	6.64
1.019	35.77	1.052	20.53	1.085	6.22
1.020	35.29	1.053	20.09	1.086	5.80
1.021	34.82	1.054	19.64	1.087	5.38
1.022	34.34	1.055	19.19	1.088	4.96
1.023	33.87	1.056	18.75	1.089	4.55
1.024	33.40	1.057	18.31	1.090	4.13
1.025	32.93	1.058	17.86	1.091	3.71
1.026	32.46	1.059	17.42	1.092	3.30
1.027	31.99	1.060	16.98	1.093	2.88
1.028	31.52	1.061	16.54	1.094	2.47
1.029	31.05	1.062	16.10	1.095	2.05
1.030	30.58	1.063	15.66	1.096	1.64
1.031	30.12	1.064	15.23	1.097	1.23
1.032	29.65	1.065	14.79	1.098	0.82

Source: M. L. Pollock, J. H. Wilmore, and S. M. Fox, *Health and Fitness Through Physical Activity* (New York: Wiley, 1978), p. 103. Used by permission of John Wiley and Sons, Inc.

Index